LEADERSHIP CLASSICS

LEADERSHIP CLASSICS

J. Timothy McMahon
Bauer College of Business
University of Houston

WAVELAND
PRESS, INC.
Long Grove, Illinois

For Ibu

For information about this book, contact:
Waveland Press, Inc.
4180 IL Route 83, Suite 101
Long Grove, IL 60047-9580
(847) 634-0081
info@waveland.com
www.waveland.com

I made every effort to insure the accuracy of Internet addresses. Neither the publisher nor I assumes any responsibility for changes after publication. We have no control over or responsibility for third-party Web sites or their content.
—J. Timothy McMahon

Contents

Section III
Leadership Behavior Concepts   163

Section VI
Enhancing Leadership Effectiveness   439

Preface

Interest in leadership has exploded in the past three decades. The number of articles on this topic, according to Stogdill's *Handbook of Leadership*, was 3500 in 1974, doubling to 7500 in 1990, doubling again to 15,000 in 2007. Adding popular press books and articles that generally are not included in these estimates would surely produce a total of 30,000 or higher.

This dramatic increase is clearly warranted given the enhanced complexity, interdependence, globalization, and accelerated pace of change in today's organizational environment. Gone is the predictability of the past; many of the methods, concepts, and techniques previously used for managing—and in many cases still used—are no longer effective. It is clear that coping with change is now the central element of organizational effectiveness and this requires inspired leadership throughout the organization. This pressure to cope and lead in times of uncertainty and rapid change has fueled the leadership information explosion.

The primary focus of this book is on leaders and their followers in formal organizations: business, government, and nonprofit. The material is relevant for those in or aspiring to leadership positions, which require both "leader" and "manager" behaviors. Gardner's suggestion in the first selection to adopt the term "leader/manager" makes a great deal of sense. Doing so embraces the broad responsibilities of the role, yet does not negate the very real differences between leader and manager behaviors—distinctions that are covered in detail in several of the selections.

So one might ask, "What is the role of the classics in this current change-driven environment?" Two cogent points provide the answer. The first is simply that these classics are as relevant today as when they were written. A recent issue of *Fortune* noted that, with few exceptions, we haven't done a very good job of implementing the ideas that Douglas McGregor offered over fifty years ago. It seems that much knowledge about leadership has been set aside in a rush to simple, easy-to-implement solutions. Thus, we might logically conclude that leadership effectiveness today has been constrained not so much by a lack of knowledge but by not applying what has been learned.

The second point is the paradox that to effectively employ the new, we must build upon the old. These classic readings provide a solid foundation from which thoughtful assessment and application of new and creative approaches can be undertaken. As in so many areas of human endeavor, a strong background is a prerequisite for moving forward.

Selecting fifty classic works covering the evolution of leadership concepts, research, and practice is a formidable and humbling task. The primary goal was to include works that constituted major breakthroughs on a topic and were judged to be enduring. Some are deemed classics because they stimulated important research and interest. The "younger" selections were viewed as likely to withstand the test of time.

A second criterion related to practical applications—all selections, even those that could be called theoretical, offer guidelines for leadership practice. A third criterion considered the supporting evidence. While most of the supporting evidence is research-based, some is based upon extensive practical experience and observation, while other support is based upon solid investigation in other fields that has been modified and usefully applied to the concept of leadership.

Books or articles on leadership in the popular media have been consciously avoided—they often lack the validity and depth of works based on research or extensive practical experience. There is much to know and consider about leadership, but one-size-fits-all panaceas, however enticing, do not add much to the conceptual understanding of leadership or its effective practice.

The fifty selections are grouped into six categories:

Section I   The Process and Roles of Leadership
Section II   Leadership Traits
Section III   Leadership Behavior Concepts
Section IV   Situational Approaches to Leadership
Section V   Leadership Power and Influence
Section VI   Enhancing Leadership Effectiveness

Given the subject matter, these categories are obviously not discreet or independent of each other. The placement of some selections in a specific category is somewhat arbitrary. In fact, several could have been placed in two or more categories. Such is the nature of leadership concepts. It is hoped that the organization of the selections provides some coherence and a useful framework for readers.

For some concepts and models it was readily apparent that providing the original source material would not be the most effective or efficient manner of presenting the information. Therefore, a few models and concepts are covered in secondary selections containing updated and expanded treatment of original works. In a few cases, an author has supplied a readable and useful summary of another writer's body of work. Several selections present the key points or findings of an entire book or a body of work composed of many articles. In all cases, the reader is encouraged to refer to the original work for details too extensive to include here.

Discussion questions and learning activities designed to stimulate interest, promote critical thinking, and reinforce learning are presented at the conclusion of each section. These features give instructors a powerful tool for helping students extend these seminal concepts into present-day contexts. Additionally, recognizing that self-awareness is the sine qua non of leadership development, I provide access to self-awareness exercises related to leadership concepts and keyed to specific readings at: www.waveland.com/McMahon/. These exercises recognize the more recent "inside-out" approaches to leadership development.

Seasoned managers and executives as well as new students of leadership often find that certain models, concepts, articles, or books are particularly insightful and useful. Given the size of the leadership literature, it would not be surprising if one or more such favorites are not included here. Please let the publisher know your thoughts and suggestions: info@waveland.com

Finally, I would like to thank my wife Susanna for her patience, support, and always-insightful suggestions, and my daughter Jennifer for her editorial inputs. I would also like to thank Walt Natemeyer for his suggestions during the planning phase of the book and Laurie Prossnitz of Waveland Press for her incomparable editing job.

Originators and Chronology

Originator (s)	Concept(s)/Date
Confucius	Values-based leadership (500 BC)
Machiavelli	Power and control (1532)
Lewin, White, & Lippitt	Autocratic vs. democratic leadership (1939)
Univ. of Michigan Group[1]	Employee-centered/production-centered leadership; goal achievement and group maintenance functions; peer leadership; principle of supportive relationships (1940 on)
McGregor	Conditions for effective leadership (1944)
Ohio State Group[2]	Membership maintenance, interaction facilitation; leadership style measurement—consideration and initiating structure; correlates of style (1945 on)
Stogdill	Personal factors associated with leadership (1948)
McClelland	Achievement motivation (1953)
Katz	Leadership skills (1955)
McGregor	Leadership and the nature of man (1957)
Argyris	Personality and organization conflict (1957)
Tannenbaum & Schmidt	Contingencies in choosing a leadership style (1958)
French & Raven	Leadership power bases (1959)
Blake & Mouton	The Managerial Grid (1964)
Bowers & Seashore	Four-factor theory of leadership (1966)
Fiedler	Contingency theory of leadership (1967)
Hersey & Blanchard	Life cycle theory of leadership (1969)
Reddin	3-D theory of managerial effectiveness (1970)

*Editor's Note: Please note that this list contains originators of the concepts. In a few readings within this collection, the original work is actually summarized and/or updated by an author other than the originator. Also, the dates listed represent when the concept first appeared, not necessarily the publication date of the corresponding article.

[1] Bowers, Cartwright, Kahn, Katz, Likert, Maccoby, Mann, Morse, Seashore, Zander et al.

[2] Coons, Fleishman, Halpin, Harris, Hempill, Stogdill, Winer et al.

Originator (s)	Concept(s)/Date
House	Path-goal theory of leadership (1971)
Mintzberg	Managerial roles (1973)
Vroom & Yetton	Decision-making contingency model (1973)
Graen & Cashman	Role-making and leader-member exchange (1975)
McClelland	Need for power (1975)
Calder	Attribution theory of leadership (1977)
House	Charismatic theory of leadership (1977)
Zaleznik	Leader-manager differences (1977)
Salancik & Pfeffer	Power contingencies (1977)
Greenleaf	Servant leadership (1977)
Burns	Transformational leadership (1978)
Hofstede	Role of culture in leadership (1980)
Bolman & Deal	Leadership frames (1984)
Schein	Leadership and organizational culture (1985)
Bandura	Self-efficacy, empowerment (1986)
Deming	Deming leadership method (1986)
Kouzes & Posner	Five practices of exemplary leadership (1987)
Conger & Kanungo	Empowerment contextual factors (1988)
Gardner	Nature and tasks of leadership (1990)
Senge	Personal mastery (1990)
Stayer	Employee leadership (1990)
Kotter	Leader vs. manager behaviors (1990)
Covey	Principle-centered leadership (1991)
Kirkpatrick & Locke	Key leadership traits (1991)
Wheatley	Leadership and self-organizing systems (1992)
Kets de Vries	Leadership mystique (1994)
Goleman	Emotional intelligence and leadership (1998)
Buckingham & Coffman	Leader behaviors and organization performance (1999)
Drucker	Self-management (1999)
Maccoby	Narcissism and leadership (2000)
Collins	Level 5 leadership (2001)
Bennis & Thomas	Crucibles of leadership (2002)
Bossidy & Charan	Leadership and execution (2002)
Goldsmith	Feedforward and leadership development (2002)
George	Authentic leadership (2003)

SECTION I

THE PROCESS AND ROLES OF LEADERSHIP

A thorough knowledge of the topic at hand is important for all leader/ managers because understanding is a primary driver of behavior. Any leader who unintentionally restricts his or her conception of leadership is very likely to behave in ways that detract from effectiveness. For example, defining leadership simply as "a process of influence" fails to account for much of the leadership role. The goal of this section is to provide a solid grounding in what leadership in formal organizations actually is and what it entails.

The Nature and Tasks of Leadership by John W. Gardner provides an excellent framework for thinking about the concept of leadership and for the contents of this volume. His insights about the relationship between power and leadership are especially useful and his position on the leader versus manager debate warrants careful consideration. The discussion of leadership tasks provides a lucid description of what all leaders must do to be effective.

In *Skills of an Effective Administrator,* Robert L. Katz promotes the position that effectiveness depends upon fundamental skills rather than personality traits. His discussion of human, conceptual, and technical skills has as much relevance today as when he wrote the article more than 50 years ago. His insights regarding the relative importance of these skills at different organization levels hold meaningful implications for leadership development.

Henry Mintzberg's *Managerial Roles* identifies and examines ten roles that leaders must play. It illuminates the complexity of the demands on a leader in a managerial role and underscores the various components of overall effectiveness. The observation that the roles form a *gestalt,* an integrated whole, certainly has implications for the practice of leadership and helps one understand that success requires more than influencing and inspiring followers.

Reframing Leadership by Lee G. Bolman and Terrence E. Deal provides new thinking on leadership effectiveness. The authors describe four traditions or frames of leadership: human resource, structural, political, and symbolic. They employ both qualitative and quantitative investigations to discern how many frames leaders use, the contexts in which different frames are used, and the impact on leadership effectiveness.

1

John P. Kotter's *What Leaders Really Do* was considered a major contribution to the leadership literature when it was published some twenty years ago. The article is rich in its comparison of leader and manager behaviors and emphasizes that effective organizations need to cultivate both strong leaders and strong managers. The author notes that while not all people have the capacity to be good leaders *and* good managers, the most forward-thinking organizations establish a "culture of leadership" that enhances their ability to develop leader-managers.

1

The Nature and Tasks of Leadership

John W. Gardner

The Nature of Leadership

Leadership is a word that has risen above normal workaday usage as a conveyor of meaning. There seems to be a feeling that if we invoke it often enough with sufficient ardor we can ease our sense of having lost our way, our sense of things unaccomplished, of duties unfulfilled.

All of that simply clouds our thinking. The aura with which we tend to surround the words *leader* and *leadership* makes it hard to think clearly. Good sense calls for demystification.

Leadership is the process of persuasion or example by which an individual (or leadership team) induces a group to pursue objectives held by the leader or shared by the leader and his or her followers.

In any established group, individuals fill different roles, and one of the roles is that of leader. Leaders cannot be thought of apart from the historic context in which they arise, the setting in which they function (e.g., elective political office), and the system over which they preside (e.g., a particular city or state). They are integral parts of the system, subject to the forces that affect the system. They perform (or cause to be performed) certain tasks or functions that are essential if the group is to accomplish its purposes. All that we know about the interaction between leaders and constituents or followers tells us that communication and influence flow in both directions; and in that two-way communication, non-rational, nonverbal, and unconscious elements play their part. In the process leaders shape and are shaped. This is true even in systems that appear to be led in quite autocratic fashion. In a state governed by coercion, followers cannot prevent the leader from violating their

1. They think longer term—beyond the day's crises, beyond the quarterly report, beyond the horizon.

2. In thinking about the unit they are heading, they grasp its relationship to larger realities—the larger organization of which they are a part, conditions external to the organization, global trends.

3. They reach and influence constituents beyond their jurisdictions, beyond boundaries. Thomas Jefferson influenced people all over Europe. Gandhi influenced people all over the world. In an organization, leaders extend their reach across bureaucratic boundaries—often a distinct advantage in a world too complex and tumultuous to be handled "through channels." Leaders' capacity to rise above jurisdictions may enable them to bind together the fragmented constituencies that must work together to solve a problem.

4. They put heavy emphasis on the intangibles of vision, values, and motivation and understand intuitively the non-rational and unconscious elements in leader-constituent interaction.

5. They have the political skill to cope with the conflicting requirements of multiple constituencies.

6. They think in terms of renewal. The routine manager tends to accept organizational structure and process as it exists. The leader or leader/manager seeks the revisions of process and structure required by ever-changing reality.

The manager is more tightly linked to an organization than is the leader. Indeed, the leader may have no organization at all. Florence Nightingale, after leaving the Crimea, exercised extraordinary leadership in health care for decades with no organization under her command. Gandhi was a leader before he had an organization. Some of our most memorable leaders have headed movements so amorphous that management would be an inappropriate word.

The Many Kinds of Leaders

One hears and reads a surprising number of sentences that describe leaders in general as having such and such attributes and behaving in such and such a fashion—as though one could distill out of the spectacular diversity of leaders an idealized picture of The Leader.

Leaders come in many forms, with many styles and diverse qualities. There are quiet leaders and leaders one can hear in the next county. Some find their strength in eloquence, some in judgment, and some in courage. I had a friend who was a superior leader in outdoor activities and sports but quite incapable of leading in a bureaucratic setting.

The diversity is almost without limit: Churchill, the splendidly eloquent old warrior; Gandhi, the visionary and the shrewd mobilizer of his people; Lenin, the coldly purposeful revolutionary. Consider just the limited category of military leadership. George Marshall was a self-effacing, low-keyed man with superb judgment and a limitless capacity to inspire trust. MacArthur was a brilliant strategist, a farsighted administrator, and flamboyant to his fingertips. (Eisenhower, who had served under MacArthur, once said, "I studied dramatics under a master.") Eisenhower in his wartime assignment was an outstanding leader/administrator and coalition builder. General Patton was a slashing, intense combat commander. Field Marshal Montgomery was a gifted, temperamental leader of whom Churchill said, "In defeat, indomitable; in victory, insufferable." All were great leaders yet extraordinarily diverse in personal attributes.

The fact that there are many kinds of leaders has implications for leadership education. Most of those seeking to develop young potential leaders have in mind one ideal model that is inevitably constricting. We should give young people a sense of the many kinds of leaders and styles of leadership, and encourage them to move toward those models that are right for them.

Leaders and History

All too often when we think of our historic leaders, we eliminate all the contradictions that make individuals distinctive. And we further violate reality by lifting them out of their historical contexts. No wonder we are left with pasteboard portraits. As first steps toward a mature view of leaders we must accept complexity and context.

Thomas Jefferson was first of all a gifted and many-sided human, an enigmatic man who loved—among other things—abstract ideas, agriculture, architecture and statecraft. He was a man of natural aloofness who lived most of his life in public; a man of action with a gift for words and a bent for research; an idealist who proved himself a shrewd, even wily, operator on the political scene. Different sides of his nature came into play in different situations.

Place him now in the context of the exhilarating events and themes of his time: a new nation coming into being, with a new consciousness; the brilliant rays of the Enlightenment reaching into every phase of life; the inner contradictions of American society (e.g., slavery) already rumbling beneath the surface.

Finally, add the overpowering impulse of succeeding generations to serve their own needs by mythologizing, idolizing, or debunking him. It turns out to be an intricately textured story and not one that diminishes Jefferson.

It was once believed that if leadership traits were truly present in an individual, they would manifest themselves almost without regard to the situation in which the person was functioning. No one believes that any more. Acts of leadership take place in an unimaginable variety of settings, and the setting does much to determine the kinds of leaders that emerge and how they play their roles.

We cannot avoid the bewhiskered question, "Does the leader make history or does the historical moment make the leader?" It sounds like a seminar question but it is of interest to most leaders sooner or later. Corporate chief executive officers fighting a deteriorating trend in an industry feel like people trying to run up the down escalator. Looking across town at less able leaders riding an upward trend in another industry, they are ripe for the theory that history makes the leader.

Thomas Carlyle placed excessive emphasis on the great person, as did Sidney Hook ("all factors in history, save great men, are inconsequential").[2] Karl Marx, Georg Hegel, and Herbert Spencer placed excessive emphasis on historical forces. For Marx, economic forces shaped history; for Spencer, societies had their evolutionary course just as species did, and the leader was a product of the process; for Hegel, leaders were a part of the dialectic of history and could not help what they did.

The balanced view, of course, is that historical forces create the circumstances in which leaders emerge, but the characteristics of the particular leader in turn have their impact on history.

It is not possible to understand Queen Isabella without understanding fifteenth-century Europe (when she was born, Spain as we know it did not exist), or without understanding the impact of the Reformation on the Catholic world and the gnawing fear stirred by the Muslim conquests. But many monarchs flourished on the Iberian Peninsula in that historical context; only Isabella left an indelible mark. Similarly, by the time Martin Luther emerged, the seeds of the Reformation had already sprouted in many places, but no one would argue that the passionate, charismatic priest who nailed his ninety-five theses to the church door was a puppet of history. Historical forces set the stage for him, but once there, he was himself a historical force.

Churchill is an even more interesting case because he tried out for leadership many times before history was ready for him. After Dunkirk, England needed a leader who could rally the British people to heroic exertions in an uncompromising war, and the eloquent, combative Churchill delivered one of the great performances of the century. Subsequently the clock of history ticked on, and with the war over, the voters dropped him unceremoniously. When a friend told him it was a blessing in disguise, he growled "If it is, the disguise is perfect."

Forces of history determined his rise and fall, but in his time on the world stage he left a uniquely Churchillian mark on the course of events.

Settings

The historical moment is the broadest context affecting the emergence and functioning of leaders; but immensely diverse settings of a more modest nature clearly affect leadership.

The makeup of the group to be led is, of course, a crucial feature of the context. According to research findings, the approach to leadership or style of leadership that will be effective depends on, among other things, the age level of the individuals to be led; their educational background and competence; the size, homogeneity and cohesiveness of the group; its motivation and morale; its rate of turnover; and so on.

Other relevant contextual features are too numerous and diverse to list. Leading a corporation is one thing, leading a street gang is something else.

Thomas Cronin has pointed out that it may take one kind of leadership to start a new enterprise and quite another kind to keep it going through its various phases.[3] Religious bodies, political parties, government agencies, the academic world—all offer distinctive contexts for leadership.

Judgments of Leaders

In curious ways, people tend to aggrandize the role of leaders. They tend to exaggerate the capacity of leaders to influence events. Jeffrey Pfeffer says that people want to achieve a feeling of control over their environment, and that this inclines them to attribute the outcomes of group performance to leaders rather than to context.[4] If we were to face the fact—so the argument goes—that outcomes are the result of a complex set of interactions among group members plus environmental and historical forces, we would feel helpless. By attributing outcomes to an identifiable leader we feel, rightly or not, more in control. There is at least a chance that one can fire the leader; one cannot "fire" historical forces.

Leaders act in the stream of history. As they labor to bring about a result, multiple forces beyond their control, even beyond their knowledge, are moving to hasten or hinder the result. So there is rarely a demonstrable causal link between a leader's specific decisions and consequent events. Consequences are not a reliable measure of leadership. Franklin Roosevelt's efforts to bolster the economy in the middle-to-late-1930s were powerfully aided by a force that did not originate with his economic brain trust, the winds of war. Leaders of a farm workers' union fighting for better wages may find their efforts set at naught by a crop failure.

Frank Lloyd Wright said, "A doctor can bury his mistakes. An architect can only advise his client to plant vines." Unlike either doctor or architect, leaders suffer from the mistakes of predecessors and leave some of their own misjudgments as time bombs for successors.

Many of the changes sought by leaders take time: lots of years, long public debate, and slow shifts in attitude. In their lifetimes, leaders may see little result from heroic efforts yet may be setting the stage for victories that will come after them. Reflect on the long, slow unfolding of the battles for racial equality or for women's rights. Leaders who did vitally important early work died without knowing what they had wrought.

Leaders may appear to have succeeded (or failed) only to have historians a generation later reverse the verdict. The "verdict of history" has a wonderfully magisterial sound, but in reality it is subject to endless appeals to later generations of historians with no court of last resort to render a final judgment.

In the real world, the judgments one makes of a leader must be multidimensional, taking into consideration great strengths, streaks of mediocrity, and perhaps great flaws. If the great strengths correspond to the needs of a critical moment in history, the flaws are forgiven and simply provide texture to the biographies. Each leader has his or her own unique pattern of attributes, sometimes conflicting in curious ways. Ronald Reagan was notably passive with respect to many important issues, but vigorously tenacious on other issues.

Leaders change over the course of their active careers as do other human beings. In looking back, it is natural for us to freeze them in that moment when they served history's needs most spectacularly, but leaders evolve. The passionately antislavery Lincoln of the Douglas debates was not the see-both-sides Lincoln of fifteen years earlier. The "national unity" Churchill of 1942 was not the fiercely partisan, adversarial Churchill of the 1930s.

Devolving Initiative and Responsibility

I have already commented on our dispersed leadership and on its importance to the vitality of a large, intricately organized system. Our most forward-looking business concerns are working in quite imaginative ways to devolve initiative downward and outward through their organizations to develop their lower levels of leadership.

There is no comparable movement in government agencies. But in the nation as a whole, dispersed leadership is a reality. In Santa Barbara County, California, Superintendent of Schools William Cirone is a leader in every sense of the word. A healthy school system requires a vital and involved citizenry. How does one achieve that? Given the aging population, fewer and fewer citizens have children in the schools. How do we keep them interested? Education is a lifelong process. How do we provide for that? These are questions to which Cirone has addressed himself with uncommon energy and imagination.[5]

The leaders of the Soviet Union did not launch the reforms of 1987 because they had developed a sudden taste for grass-roots democracy. They launched them because their system was grinding to a halt. Leader/managers at the lower levels and at the periphery of the system had neither the motivation nor the authority to solve problems that they understood better than the Moscow bureaucrats.

We have only half learned the lesson ourselves. In many of our large corporate, governmental, and nonprofit organizations we still make it all too difficult for potential leaders down the line to exercise initiative. We are still in the process of discovering how much vitality and motivation are buried at those levels awaiting release.

To emphasize the need for dispersed leadership does not deny the need for highly qualified top leadership. But our high-level leaders will be more effective in every way if the systems over which they preside are made vital by dispersed leadership. As I argued in *Excellence*, we must demand high performance at every level of society.[6]

Friends of mine have argued that in view of my convictions concerning the importance of middle and lower-level leaders, I lean too heavily on examples of high-level leaders. My response is that we know a great deal about the more famous figures, statements about them can be documented, and they are comfortably familiar to readers. No one who reads this work with care could believe that I consider such exalted figures the only ones worth considering.

Institutionalizing Leadership

To exercise leadership today, leaders must institutionalize their leadership. The issues are too technical and the pace of change too swift to expect that a leader, no matter how gifted, will be able to solve personally the major problems facing the system over which he or she presides. So we design an institutional system—a government agency, a corporation—to solve the problems, and then we select a leader who has the capacity to preside over and strengthen the system. Some leaders may be quite gifted in solving problems personally, but if they fail to institutionalize the process, their departure leaves the system crippled. They must create or strengthen systems that will survive them.

The institutional arrangements generally include a leadership team. Often when I use the word *leader,* I am in fact referring to the leadership team. No individual has all the skills, and certainly not the time, to carry out all the complex tasks of contemporary leadership. And the team must be chosen for excellence in performance. Loyalty and being on the boss's wavelength are necessary but not sufficient qualifications. I emphasize the point because more than one recent president of the United States has had aides who possessed no other qualifications.

I am attempting to say what leadership is and no such description would be complete without a careful examination of what leaders do. So next we look at the tasks of leadership.

The Tasks of Leadership

Examination of the tasks performed by leaders takes us to the heart of some of the most interesting questions concerning leadership. It also helps to distinguish among the many kinds of leaders. Leaders differ strikingly in how well they perform various functions.

The following eleven tasks seem to me to be the most significant functions of leadership, but I encourage readers to add to the list or to describe the tasks in other ways. Leadership activities implicit in all of the tasks (e.g., communicating, relating effectively with people) are not dealt with separately.

Envisioning Goals

The two tasks at the heart of the popular notion of leadership are goal setting and motivating. As a high school senior put it, "Leaders point us in the right direction and tell us to get moving." Although we take a more complicated view of the tasks of leadership, it is appropriate that we begin with the envisioning of goals. Albert Einstein said, "Perfection of means and confusion of ends seems to characterize our age."

Leaders perform the function of goal setting in diverse ways. Some assert a vision of what the group (organization, community, nation) can be at its best. Others point us toward solutions to our problems. Still others, presiding over internally divided groups, are able to define overarching goals that unify constituencies and focus energies. In today's complex world, the setting of goals may have to be preceded by extensive research and problem solving.

Obviously, a constituency is not a blank slate for the leader to write on. Any collection of people sufficiently related to be called a community has many shared goals, some explicit, some unexpressed (perhaps even unconscious), as tangible as better prices for their crops, as intangible as a better future for their children. In a democracy, the leader takes such shared goals into account.

The relative roles of leaders and followers in determining goals varies from group to group. The teacher of first-grade children and the sergeant training recruits do not do extensive consulting as to goals; congressional candidates do a great deal. In the case of many leaders, goals are handed to them by higher authority. The factory manager and the combat commander may be superb leaders, but many of their goals are set at higher levels.

In short, goals emerge from many sources. The culture itself specifies certain goals; constituents have their concerns; higher authority makes its wishes known. Out of the welter, leaders take some goals as given, and making their own contribution, select and formulate a set of objectives. It may sound as though leaders have only marginal freedom, but in fact there is usually considerable opportunity, even for lower-level leaders, to put their personal emphasis and interpretation on the setting of goals.

There is inevitable tension between long- and short-term goals. On the one hand, constituents are not entirely comfortable with the jerkiness of short-term goal seeking, and they value the sense of stability that comes with a vision of far horizons. On the other hand, long-term goals may require them to defer immediate gratification on at least some fronts. Leaders often fear that when citizens enter the voting booth, they will remember the deferral of gratification more vividly than they remember the reason for it.

Before the Civil War, Elizabeth Cady Stanton saw virtually the whole agenda for women's rights as it was to emerge over the succeeding century. Many of her contemporaries in the movement were not at all prepared for such an inclusive vision and urged her to play it down.

Another visionary far ahead of his time was the South American liberator, Simon Bolivar. He launched his fight in that part of Gran Colombia which is now Venezuela, but in his mind was a vision not only of independence for all of Spain's possessions in the New World, but also a peaceful alliance of the new states in some form of league or confederation. Although he was tragically ahead of his time, the dream never died and has influenced generations of Latin American leaders toward unity.

Affirming Values

A great civilization is a drama lived in the minds of a people. It is a shared vision; it is shared norms, expectations, and purposes. When one thinks of the world's great civilizations, the most vivid images that crowd in on us are apt to be of the physical monuments left behind—the Pyramids, the

Parthenon, the Mayan temples. But in truth, all the physical splendor was the merest by-product. The civilizations themselves, from beginning to end, existed in the minds of men and women.

If we look at ordinary human communities, we see the same reality: A community lives in the minds of its members—in shared assumptions, beliefs, customs, ideas that give meaning, ideas that motivate. And among the ideas are norms or values. In any healthy, reasonably coherent community, people come to have shared views concerning right and wrong, better and worse in terms of personal conduct, governing, art, whatever. They define for their time and place what things are legal or illegal, virtuous or vicious, good taste or bad. They have little or no impulse to be neutral about such matters. Every society is, as Philip Rieff puts it, "a system of moralizing demands."[7]

Values are embodied in the society's religious beliefs and its secular philosophy. Over the past century, many intellectuals have looked down on the celebration of our values as an unsophisticated and often hypocritical activity. But every healthy society celebrates its values. They are expressed in art, in song, in ritual. They are stated explicitly in historical documents, in ceremonial speeches, in textbooks. They are reflected in stories told around the campfire, in the legends kept alive by old folks, in the fables told to children.

In a pluralistic community there are, within the broad consensus that enables the community to function, many and vigorous conflicts over specific values.

The Regeneration of Values

One of the milder pleasures of maturity is bemoaning the decay of once strongly held values. Values always decay over time. Societies that keep their values alive do so not by escaping the processes of decay but by powerful processes of regeneration. There must be perpetual rebuilding. Each generation must rediscover the living elements in its own tradition and adapt them to present realities. To assist in that rediscovery is one of the tasks of leadership.

The leaders whom we admire the most help to revitalize our shared beliefs and values. They have always spent a portion of their time teaching the value framework.

Sometimes the leader's affirmation of values challenges entrenched hypocrisy or conflicts with the values held by a segment of the constituency. Elizabeth Cady Stanton, speaking for now-accepted values, was regarded as a thoroughgoing radical in her day.[8] Jesus not only comforted the afflicted but afflicted the comfortable.

Motivating

Leaders do not create motivation out of thin air. They unlock or channel existing motives. Any group has a great tangle of motives. Effective leaders tap those that serve the purposes of collective action in pursuit of shared goals. They accomplish the alignment of individual and group goals. They deal with the circumstances that often lead group members to withhold their best efforts. They call for the kind of effort and restraint, drive and discipline that make for great performance. They create a climate in which there is pride in making significant contributions to shared goals.

Note that in the tasks of leadership, the transactions between leaders and constituents go beyond the rational level to the non-rational and unconscious levels of human functioning. Young potential leaders who have been schooled to believe that all elements of a problem are rational and technical, reducible to words and numbers, are ill-equipped to move into an area where intuition and empathy are powerful aids to problem solving.

Managing

Most managers exhibit some leadership skills, and most leaders on occasion find themselves managing. Leadership and management are not the same thing, but they overlap. It makes sense to include managing in the list of tasks leaders perform.

In the paragraphs that follow I focus on those aspects of leadership that one might describe as managing without slipping into a conventional description of managing as such. And I try to find terminology and phrasing broad enough to cover the diverse contexts in which leadership occurs in corporations, unions, municipalities, political movements, and so on.

Planning and Priority Setting.   Assuming that broad goals have been set, someone has to plan, fix priorities, choose means, and formulate policy. These are functions often performed by leaders. When Lyndon B. Johnson said, early in his presidency, that education was the nation's number one priority, he galvanized the nation's educational leaders and released constructive energies far beyond any governmental action that had yet been taken. It was a major factor in leading me to accept a post in his Cabinet.

Organizing and Institution Building.   We have all seen leaders enjoy their brilliant moment and then disappear without a trace because they had no gift for building their purposes into institutions. In the ranks of leaders, Alfred Sloan was at the other extreme. Though he sold a lot of automobiles, he was not primarily a salesman; he was an institution builder. His understanding of organization was intuitive and profound.

Someone has to design the structures and processes through which substantial endeavors get accomplished over time. Ideally, leaders should not regard themselves as indispensable but should enable the group to carry on. Institutions are a means to that end. Jean Monnet said, "Nothing is possible without individuals; nothing is lasting without institutions."[9]

Keeping the System Functioning.   Presiding over the arrangements through which individual energies are coordinated to achieve shared goals sounds like a quintessential management task. But it is clear that most leaders find themselves occasionally performing one or another of the essential chores: mobilizing and allocating resources; staffing and ensuring the continuing vitality of the team; creating and maintaining appropriate procedures; directing, delegating and coordinating; providing a system of incentives; reporting, evaluating and holding accountable.

Agenda Setting and Decision Making. The goals may be clear and the organization well set up and smoothly operating, but there remain agenda-setting and decision-making functions that must be dealt with. The announcement of goals without a proposed program for meeting them is a familiar enough political phenomenon, but not one that builds credibility. There are leaders who can motivate and inspire but who cannot visualize a path to the goal in practical, feasible steps. Leaders who lack that skill must bring onto their team people who have it.

One of the purest examples of the leader as agenda setter was Florence Nightingale.[10] Her public image was and is that of the lady of mercy, but under her gentle manner, she was a rugged spirit, a fighter, a tough-minded system changer. She never made public appearances or speeches, and except for her two years in the Crimea, held no public position. Her strength was that she was a formidable authority on the evils to be remedied, she knew what to do about them, and she used public opinion to goad top officials to adopt her agenda.

Exercising Political Judgment. In our pluralistic society, persons directing substantial enterprises find that they are presiding over many constituencies within their organizations and contending with many outside. Each has its needs and claims. One of the tasks of the leader/manager is to make the political judgments necessary to prevent secondary conflicts of purpose from blocking progress toward primary goals. Sometimes the literature on administration and management treats politics as an alien and disruptive force. But Aaron Wildavsky, in his brilliant book, *The Nursing Father: Moses as a Political Leader,* makes the point that leaders are inevitably political.[11]

Achieving Workable Unity

A pluralistic society is, by definition, one that accepts many different elements, each with its own purposes. Collisions are inevitable and often healthy as in commercial competition, civil suits, and efforts to redress grievances through the political process. Conflict is necessary in the case of oppressed groups that must fight for the justice that is due them. All our elective officials know the intense conflict of the political campaign. Indeed, one could argue that willingness to engage in battle when necessary is a sine qua non of leadership.

But most leaders most of the time are striving to diminish conflict rather than increase it. Some measure of cohesion and mutual tolerance is an absolute requirement of social functioning.

Sometimes the problem is not outright conflict but an unwillingness to cooperate. One of the gravest problems George Washington faced as a general was that the former colonies, though they had no doubt they were all on the same side, were not always sure they wanted to cooperate. As late as 1818, John Randolph declared, "When I speak of my country, I mean the Commonwealth of Virginia."[12]

The unifying function of leaders is well illustrated in the actions of George Bush after winning the presidential election of 1988. He promptly met with his defeated opponent, Michael Dukakis; with his chief rival for the nomination, Senator Robert Dole; and with Jesse Jackson and Coretta Scott King, both of whom had opposed his election. He asked Jack Kemp, another of his rivals for the nomination, to be Secretary of Housing and Urban Development, and Senator Dole's wife, Elizabeth Hanford Dole, to be Secretary of Labor.

Leaders in this country today must cope with the fragmentation of the society into groups that have great difficulty in understanding one another or agreeing on common goals. It is a fragmentation rooted in the pluralism of our society, in the obsessive specialization of modern life, and in the skill with which groups organize to advance their concerns.

Under the circumstances, all our leaders must spend part of their time dealing with polarization and building community. There is a false notion that this is a more bland, less rigorous task than leadership of one of the combative segments. In fact, the leader willing to combat polarization is the braver person, and is generally under fire from both sides. I would suggest that Jean Monnet, the father of the European Common Market, is a useful model for future leaders. When there were conflicting purposes Monnet saw the possibility of shared goals, and he knew how to move his contemporaries toward those shared goals.

Trust

Much depends on the general level of trust in the organization or society. The infinitely varied and complex doings of the society, any society, would come to a halt if people did not trust other people most of the time—trust them to observe custom, follow the rules, and behave with some predictability. Countless circumstances operate to diminish that trust, but one may be sure that if the society is functioning at all, *some* degree of trust survives.

Leaders can do much to preserve the necessary level of trust. And the first requirement is that they have the capacity to inspire trust in themselves. In sixteenth-century Italy, where relations among the warring kingdoms were an unending alley fight, Machiavelli's chilling advice to the Prince, "It is necessary . . . to be a feigner and a dissembler," or, as another translator renders the same passage, "You must be a great liar and hypocrite"—may have been warranted.[13] And, under conditions of iron rule, Hitler and Stalin were able to live by betrayals. But in our society, leaders must work to raise the level of trust.

Explaining

Explaining sounds too pedestrian to be on a list of leadership tasks, but every leader recognizes it. People want to know what the problem is, why they are being asked to do certain things, why they face so many frustrations. Thurman Arnold said, "Unhappy is a people that has run out of words to describe what is happening to them."[14] Leaders find the words.

To be heard above the hubbub in the public forum today, explaining generally requires more than clarity and eloquence. It requires effective access to the media of communication or to those segments of the population that keep ideas in circulation such as editors, writers, intellectuals, association leaders, advocacy groups, chief executive officers, and the like.

The task of explaining is so important that some who do it exceptionally well play a leadership role even though they are not leaders in the conventional sense. When the American colonies were struggling for independence, Thomas Paine was a memorable explainer. In the powerful environmentalist surge of the 1960s and 70s, no activist leader had as pervasive an influence on the movement as did Rachel Carson, whose book *Silent Spring* burst on the scene in 1963.[15] Betty Friedan's *The Feminine Mystique* played a similar role for the women's movement.[16]

Leaders teach. Lincoln, in his second inaugural address, provided an extraordinary example of the leader as teacher. Teaching and leading are distinguishable occupations, but every great leader is clearly teaching and every great teacher is leading.

Serving as a Symbol

Leaders are inevitably symbols. Workers singled out to be supervisors discover that they are set apart from their old comrades in subtle ways. They try to keep the old camaraderie but things have changed. They are now symbols of management. Sergeants symbolize the chain of command. Parish religious leaders symbolize their churches.

In a group threatened with internal strife, the leader may be a crucial symbol of unity. In a minority group's struggle to find its place, combative leaders, troublesome to others, may be to their own people the perfect symbol of their anger and their struggle.

The top leader of a community or nation symbolizes the group's collective identity and continuity. For this reason, the death of a president produces a special reaction of grief and loss. Americans who were beyond childhood when John F. Kennedy was assassinated remember, despite the passage of decades, precisely where they were and what they were doing when the news reached them. Even for many who did not admire him, the news had the impact of a blow to the solar plexus. And those old enough to remember Franklin D. Roosevelt's death recognize the reaction.

For late eighteenth-century Americans, George Washington was the symbol of all that they had been through together. Thomas Jefferson became such a powerful symbol of our democratic aspirations that for generations politicians fought over his memory. Those who favored Hamiltonian views sought bitterly and unsuccessfully to shatter the Jefferson image. As Merrill Peterson has cogently argued, the man himself lost reality and the symbol took over.[17]

In the dark days of the Great Depression, the American impulse to face events in a positive spirit found its symbol in the ebullient Franklin D. Roosevelt.

Outside the political area, Albert Schweitzer, the gifted theologian and musician who in 1913 gave up a comfortable and respected life in his native Germany to spend the remainder of his years presiding over a medical mission in Equatorial Africa, stands as the pristine example of leader as symbol.

Some individuals newly risen to leadership have a hard time adjusting to the reality that they are symbols. I recall a visit with a young college president who had just come into the job fresh from a professorship, with no prior administrative experience. He confided that he was deeply irked by an incident the preceding day. In his first speech before faculty, students, trustees and alumni he had simply been himself, a man of independent mind full of lively personal opinions, and many of his listeners were nonplussed and irritated. They were not interested in a display of idiosyncratic views. They had expected him to speak as their new leader, their symbol of institutional continuity, their ceremonial collective voice. I told him gently that they had expected him to be their spokesman and symbol, and this simply angered him further. "I'll resign," he said, "*if I* can't be myself!" Over time, he learned that leaders can rarely afford the luxury of speaking for themselves alone.

Most leaders become quite aware of the symbolic aspects of their roles and make effective use of them. One of the twentieth-century leaders who did so most skillfully was Gandhi.[18] In the issues he chose to do battle on, in the way he conducted his campaigns, in the jail terms and the fasting, in his manner of dress, he symbolized his people, their desperate need, and their struggle against oppression.

Needless to say leaders do not always function as benign symbols. In the Iran-Contra affair of 1986–87 it became apparent that men bound by their oath of office were lying to the public, lying to the Congress of the United States, and lying to one another. To some Americans they became symbols of all the falsehoods and betrayals committed by a distant and distrusted government.

Representing the Group

In quieter times (we love to imagine that there were quieter times) leaders could perhaps concentrate on their own followers. Today representing the group in its dealings with others is a substantial leadership task.

It is a truism that all of the human systems (organizations, groups, communities) that make up the society and the world are increasingly interdependent. Virtually all leaders at every level must carry on dealings with systems external to the one in which they themselves are involved and engage in tasks of representing and negotiating, defending institutional integrity, public relations. As one moves higher in the ranks of leadership, such chores increase.

It goes without saying that people who have spent their careers in the world of the specialist or within the boundaries of a narrow community (their firm, their profession) are often ill-equipped for such leadership tasks. The young potential leader must learn early to cross boundaries and to know many worlds. The attributes that enable leaders to teach and lead their own constituencies may be wholly ineffective in external dealings. Military leaders who are revered by their troops may be clumsy with civilians. The business leader who is effective within the business culture may be lost in dealing with politicians. A distinctive characteristic of the ablest leaders is that they do not shrink from external representation. They see the long-term needs and goals of their constituency in the broadest context, and they act accordingly. The most capable mayors think not just of the city but of the metropolitan area and the region. Able business leaders are alert to the political climate and to world economic trends.

The most remarkable modern example of a leader carrying out the representative function is Charles DeGaulle. DeGaulle has his detractors, but none can fail to marvel at his performance in successfully representing the once and future France-as-a-great-power at a time when the nation itself was a defeated, demoralized, enemy-occupied land. By his own commanding presence, he kept France's place at the table through the dark days. Years later Jean Monnet wrote:

> It took great strength of character for him, a traditional soldier, to cross the great dividing line of disobedience to orders from above. He was the only man of his rank with the courage to do so; and in the painful isolation felt by those Frenchmen who had decided to continue the Allied struggle, DeGaulle's rare example was a source of great moral strength.[19]

Renewing

Leaders need not be renewers. They can lead people down old paths, using old slogans, toward old objectives. Sometimes that is appropriate. But the world changes with disconcerting swiftness. Too often the old paths are blocked and the old solutions no longer solve anything. DeGaulle, writing of France's appalling unpreparedness for World War II, said:

> The Army became stuck in a set of ideas which had had their heyday before the end of the First World War. It was all the more inclined that way because its leaders were growing old at their posts, wedded to errors that had once constituted their glory.[20]

Leaders must foster the process of renewal.

So much for the tasks of leadership. The individual with a gift for building a leadership team may successfully delegate one or another of those tasks to other members of the team. One function that cannot be delegated is that of serving as symbol. That the leader is a symbol is a fact, not a matter of choice. The task is to take appropriate account of that reality and to use it well in the service of the group's goals.

Another function that cannot be delegated entirely is the envisioning of goals. Unless the leader has a sense of where the whole enterprise is going and must go, it is not possible to delegate (or carry out personally) the other functions. To have "a sense of where the whole enterprise is going and must go" is, I am inclined to say, the very core and essence of the best leadership.

In a discussion of the tasks of leadership, a colleague of mine said, "I do not see 'enabling' or 'empowering' on the list. Aren't those the central tasks of leadership?"

For those unfamiliar with contemporary discussions of leadership, I should explain that reference to *enabling* or *empowering* has become the preferred method of condensing into a single word the widely held conviction that the purpose of leaders is not to dominate nor diminish followers but to strengthen and help them to develop. But enabling and empowering are not separable tasks. They require a variety of actions on the parts of leaders. For example:

- Sharing information and making it possible for followers to obtain appropriate kinds of education
- Sharing power by devolving initiative and responsibility
- Building the confidence of followers so that they can achieve their own goals through their own efforts
- Removing barriers to the release of individual energy and talent
- Seeking, finding, and husbanding the various kinds of resources that followers need
- Resolving the conflicts that paralyze group action
- Providing organizational arrangements appropriate to group effort

Any attempt to describe a social process as complex as leadership inevitably makes it seem more orderly than it is. Leadership is not tidy. Decisions are made and then revised or reversed. Misunderstandings are frequent, inconsistency inevitable. Achieving a goal may simply make the next goal more urgent: Inside every solution are the seeds of new problems. And as Donald Michael has pointed out, most of the time most things are out of hand.[21] No leader enjoys that reality, but every leader knows it.

It would be easy to imagine that the tasks described are items to be handled separately, like eleven items on a shopping list, each from a separate store. But the effective leader is always doing several tasks simultaneously. The best antidote to the shopping list conception is to look at the setting in which all the tasks are mingled, the complex interplay between leaders and those "led."

Notes

[1] Niccolo Machiavelli, *The Prince* (New York: New American Library, 1952).

[2] Sidney Hook, *The Hero in History* (Boston: Beacon Press, 1955).

[3] Thomas E. Cronin, *Chronicle of Higher Education* (February 1, 1989), pp. B1–B2.

[4] Jeffrey Pfeffer, "The Ambiguity of Leadership" in *Leadership: Where Else Can We Go?* Ed. Morgan W. McCall, Jr., and Michael Lombardo (Durham, NC: Duke University Press,1978).

[5] William J. Cirone and Barbara Margerum, "Models of Citizen Involvement and Community Education," *National Civic Review* 76, no. 3 (May–June 1987).

[6] John W. Gardner, *Excellence*, rev. ed. (New York: W. W. Norton, 1984).

[7] Philip Rieff, *The Triumph of the Therapeutic* (New York: Harper and Row, 1966).

[8] Elisabeth Griffith, *In Her Own Right: The Life of Elizabeth Cady Stanton* (New York: Oxford University Press, 1984).

[9] Jean Monnet, *Memoirs,* trans. Richard Mayne (New York: Doubleday Publishing, 1978).

[10] Elspeth Huxley, *Florence Nightingale* (New York: G. P. Putnam's Sons, 1975).

[11] Aaron Wildavsky, *The Nursing Father: Moses as a Political Leader* (Tuscaloosa: University of Alabama Press, 1984).

[12] William Cabell Bruce, *John Randolph of Roanoke* (New York: Putnam, 1922).

[13] Niccolo Machiavelli, *The Prince* (New York: New American Library, 1952), p. 93.

[14] Thurman Arnold, *The Folklore of Capitalism* (New Haven: Yale University Press, 1937).

[15] Rachel Carson, *Silent Spring* (New York: Houghton Mifflin, 1963).

[16] Betty Friedan, *The Feminine Mystique* (New York: Dell, 1963).

[17] Merrill D. Peterson, *The Jefferson Image in the American Mind* (New York: Oxford University Press, 1960).

[18] Erik Erikson, *Gandhi's Truth* (New York: W. W. Norton, 1969); Mohandas K. Gandhi, *An Autobiography* (Boston: Beacon Press, 1957).

[19] Monnet, *Memoirs,* p.147.

[20] Charles DeGaulle, *The War Memoirs, 1940–1946* (New York: Simon & Schuster, 1964).

[21] Donald M. Michael, "Competence and Compassion in an Age of Uncertainty," *World Future Society Bulletin,* January–February 1983.

2

Skills of an Effective Administrator

Robert L. Katz

Although the selection and training of good administrators is widely recognized as one of American industry's most pressing problems, there is surprisingly little agreement among executives or educators on what makes a good administrator. The executive development programs of some of the nation's leading corporations and colleges reflect a tremendous variation in objectives.

At the root of this difference is industry's search for the traits or attributes which will objectively identify the "ideal executive" who is equipped to cope effectively with any problem in any organization. As one observer of American industry recently noted:

> The assumption that there is an executive type is widely accepted, either openly or implicitly. Yet any executive presumably knows that a company needs all kinds of managers for different levels of jobs. The qualities most needed by a shop superintendent are likely to be quite opposed to those needed by a coordinating vice president of manufacturing. The literature of executive development is loaded with efforts to define the qualities needed by executives, and by themselves these sound quite rational. Few, for instance, would dispute the fact that a top manager needs good judgment, the ability to make decisions, the ability to win respect of others, and all the other well-worn phrases any management man could mention. But one has only to look at the successful managers in any company to see how enormously their particular qualities vary from any ideal list of executive virtues.[1]

Yet this quest for the executive stereotype has become so intense that many companies, in concentrating on certain specific traits or qualities, stand in danger of losing sight of their real concern: *what a man can accomplish.*

It is the purpose of this article to suggest what may be a more useful approach to the selection and development of administrators. This approach is based not on what good executives are (their innate traits and characteristics), but rather on what they do (the kinds of skills which they exhibit in carrying out their jobs effectively). As used here, a skill implies an ability which can be developed, not necessarily inborn, and which is manifested in performance, not merely in potential. So the principal criterion of skillfulness must be effective action under varying conditions.

This approach suggests that effective administration rests on *three basic developable skills* which obviate the need for identifying specific traits and which may provide a useful way of looking at and understanding the administrative process. This approach is the outgrowth of firsthand observation of executives at work coupled with study of current field research in administration.

In the sections which follow, an attempt will be made to define and demonstrate what these three skills are; to suggest that the relative importance of the three skills varies with the level of administrative responsibility; to present some of the implications of this variation for selection, training, and promotion of executives; and to propose ways of developing these skills.

Three-Skill Approach

It is assumed here that an administrator is one who (a) directs the activities of other persons and (b) undertakes the responsibility for achieving certain objectives through these efforts. Within this definition, successful administration appears to rest on three basic skills, which we will call *technical, human,* and *conceptual.* It would be unrealistic to assert that these skills are not interrelated, yet there may be real merit in examining each one separately, and in developing them independently.

Technical Skill

As used here, technical skill implies an understanding of, and proficiency in, a specific kind of activity, particularly one involving methods, processes, procedures, or techniques. It is relatively easy for us to visualize the technical skill of the surgeon, the musician, the accountant, or the engineer when each is performing his own special function. Technical skill involves specialized knowledge, analytical ability within that specialty, and facility in the use of the tools and techniques of the specific discipline.

Of the three skills described in this article, technical skill is perhaps the most familiar because it is the most concrete, and because, in our age of specialization, it is the skill required of the greatest number of people. Most of our vocational and on-the-job training programs are largely concerned with developing this specialized technical skill.

Human Skill

As used here, human skill is the executive's ability to work effectively as a group member and to build cooperative effort within the team he leads. As

Conceptual Skill

As used here, conceptual skill involves the ability to see the enterprise as a whole; it includes recognizing how the various functions of the organization depend on one another, and how changes in any one part affect all the others; and it extends to visualizing the relationship of the individual business to the industry, the community, and the political, social, and economic forces of the nation as a whole. Recognizing these relationships and perceiving the significant elements in any situation, the administrator should then be able to act in a way which advances the over-all welfare of the total organization.

Hence, the success of any decision depends on the conceptual skill of the people who make the decision and those who put it into action. When, for example, an important change in marketing policy is made, it is critical that the effects on production, control, finance, research, and the people involved be considered. And it remains critical right down to the last executive who must implement the new policy. If each executive recognizes the over-all relationships and significance of the change, he is almost certain to be more effective in administering it. Consequently the chances for succeeding are greatly increased.

Not only does the effective coordination of the various parts of the business depend on the conceptual skill of the administrators involved, but so also does the whole future direction and tone of the organization. The attitudes of a top executive color the whole character of the organization's response and determine the "corporate personality" which distinguishes one company's ways of doing business from another's. These attitudes are a reflection of the administrator's conceptual skill (referred to by some as his "creative ability")—the way he perceives and responds to the direction in which the business should grow, company objectives and policies, and stockholders' and employees' interests.

Conceptual skill, as defined above, is what Chester I. Barnard, former president of the New Jersey Bell Telephone Company, implies when he says: ". . . the essential aspect of the [executive] process is the sensing of the organization as a whole and the total situation relevant to it."[3] Examples of inadequate conceptual skill are all around us. Here is one instance:

> In a large manufacturing company which had a long tradition of job-shop type operations, primary responsibility for production control had been left to the foremen and other lower-level supervisors. "Village" type operations with small working groups and informal organizations were the rule. A heavy influx of orders following World War II tripled the normal production requirements and severely taxed the whole manufacturing organization. At this point, a new production manager was brought in from outside the company, and he established a wide range of controls and formalized the entire operating structure.
>
> As long as the boom demand lasted, the employees made every effort to conform with the new procedures and environment. But

when demand subsided to prewar levels, serious labor relations problems developed, friction was high among department heads, and the company found itself saddled with a heavy indirect labor cost. Management sought to reinstate its old procedures; it fired the production manager and attempted to give greater authority to the foremen once again. However, during the four years of formalized control, the foremen had grown away from their old practices, many had left the company, and adequate replacements had not been developed. Without strong foreman leadership, the traditional job-shop operations proved costly and inefficient.

In this instance, when the new production controls and formalized organizations were introduced, management did not foresee the consequences of this action in the event of a future contraction of business. Later, when conditions changed and it was necessary to pare down operations, management was again unable to recognize the implications of its action and reverted to the old procedures, which, under existing circumstances, were no longer appropriate. This compounded *conceptual* inadequacy left the company at a serious competitive disadvantage.

Because a company's over-all success is dependent on its executives' conceptual skill in establishing and carrying out policy decisions, this skill is the unifying, coordinating ingredient of the administrative process, and of undeniable over-all importance.

Relative Importance

We may notice that, in a very real sense, conceptual skill embodies consideration of both the technical and human aspects of the organization. Yet the concept of *skill,* as an ability to translate knowledge into action, should enable one to distinguish between the three skills of performing the technical activities (technical skill), understanding and motivating individuals and groups (human skill), and coordinating and integrating all the activities and interests of the organization toward a common objective (conceptual skill).

This separation of effective administration into three basic skills is useful primarily for purposes of analysis. In practice, these skills are so closely interrelated that it is difficult to determine where one ends and another begins. However, just because the skills are interrelated does not imply that we cannot get some value from looking at them separately, or by varying their emphasis. In playing golf the action of the hands, wrists, hips, shoulders, arms, and head are all interrelated; yet in improving one's swing it is often valuable to work on one of these elements separately. Also, under different playing conditions the relative importance of these elements varies. Similarly, although all three are of importance at every level of administration, the technical, human, and conceptual skills of the administrator vary in relative importance at different levels of responsibility.

At Lower Levels

Technical skill is responsible for many of the great advances of modern industry. It is indispensable to efficient operation. Yet it has greatest importance at the lower levels of administration. As the administrator moves further and further from the actual physical operation, this need for technical skill becomes less important, provided he has skilled subordinates and can help them solve their own problems. At the top, technical skill may be almost nonexistent, and the executive may still be able to perform effectively if his human and conceptual skills are highly developed. For example:

> In one large capital-goods producing company, the controller was called on to replace the manufacturing vice president who had been stricken suddenly with a severe illness. The controller had no previous production experience, but he had been with the company for more than 20 years and knew many of the key production personnel intimately. By setting up an advisory staff, and by delegating an unusual amount of authority to his department heads, he was able to devote himself to coordination of the various functions. By so doing, he produced a highly efficient team. The results were lower costs, greater productivity, and higher morale than the production division had ever before experienced. Management had gambled that this man's ability to work with people was more important than his lack of a technical production background, and the gamble paid off.

Other examples are evident all around us. We are all familiar with those "professional managers" who are becoming the prototypes of our modern executive world. These men shift with great ease, and with no apparent loss in effectiveness, from one industry to another. Their human and conceptual skills seem to make up for their unfamiliarity with the new job's technical aspects.

At Every Level

Human skill, the ability to work with others, is essential to effective administration at every level. One recent research study has shown that human skill is of paramount importance at the foreman level, pointing out that the chief function of the foreman as an administrator is to attain collaboration of people in the work group.[4] Another study reinforces this finding and extends it to the middle-management group, adding that the administrator should be primarily concerned with facilitating communication in the organization.[5] And still another study, concerned primarily with top management, underscores the need for self-awareness and sensitivity to human relationships by executives at that level.[6] These findings would tend to indicate that human skill is of great importance at every administrative level, but notice the difference in emphasis.

Human skill seems to be most important at lower levels, where the number of direct contacts between administrators and subordinates is greatest. As we go higher and higher in the administrative echelons, the number and frequency of these personal contacts decrease, and the need for human skill becomes proportionately, although probably not absolutely, less. At the same time, conceptual skill becomes increasingly more important with the need for policy decisions and broad-scale action. The human skill of dealing with individuals then becomes subordinate to the conceptual skill of integrating group interests and activities into a coordinated whole.

In fact, a recent research study by Professor Chris Argyris of Yale University has given us the example of an extremely effective plant manager who, although possessing little human skill as defined here, was nonetheless very successful:

> This manager, the head of a largely autonomous division, made his supervisors, through the effects of his strong personality and the "pressure" he applied, highly dependent on him for most of their "rewards, penalties, authority, perpetuation, communication, and identification."
>
> As a result, the supervisors spent much of their time competing with one another for the manager's favor. They told him only the things they thought he wanted to hear, and spent much time trying to find out his desires. They depended on him to set their objectives and to show them how to reach them. Because the manager was inconsistent and unpredictable in his behavior, the supervisors were insecure and continually engaged in interdepartmental squabbles which they tried to keep hidden from the manager.
>
> Clearly, human skill, as defined here, was lacking. Yet, by the evaluation of his superiors and by his results in increasing efficiency and raising profits and morale, this manager was exceedingly effective. Professor Argyris suggests that employees in modern industrial organizations tend to have a "built-in" sense of dependence on superiors which capable and alert men can turn to advantage.[7]

In the context of the three-skill approach, it seems that this manager was able to capitalize on this dependence because he recognized the interrelationships of all the activities under his control, identified himself with the organization, and sublimated the individual interests of his subordinates to *his* (the organization's) interest, set his goals realistically, and showed his subordinates how to reach these goals. This would seem to be an excellent example of a situation in which strong conceptual skill more than compensated for a lack of human skill.

At the Top Level

Conceptual skill, as indicated in the preceding sections, becomes increasingly critical in more responsible executive positions where its effects are maximized and most easily observed. In fact, recent research findings lead to the conclusion that at the top level of administration this conceptual skill becomes the most important ability of all. As Herman W. Steinkraus, president of Bridgeport Brass Company, said:

> One of the most important lessons which I learned on this job [the presidency] is the importance of coordinating the various departments into an effective team, and, secondly, to recognize the shifting emphasis from time to time of the relative importance of various departments to the business.[8]

It would appear, then, that at lower levels of administrative responsibility, the principal need is for technical and human skills. At higher levels, technical skill becomes relatively less important while the need for conceptual skill increases rapidly. At the top level of an organization, conceptual skill becomes the most important skill of all for successful administration. A chief executive may lack technical or human skills and still be effective if he has subordinates who have strong abilities in these directions. But if his conceptual skill is weak, the success of the whole organization may be jeopardized.

Implications for Action

This three-skill approach implies that significant benefits may result from redefining the objectives of executive development programs, from reconsidering the placement of executives in organizations, and from revising procedures for testing and selecting prospective executives.

Executive Development

Many executive development programs may be failing to achieve satisfactory results because of their inability to foster the growth of these administrative skills. Programs which concentrate on the mere imparting of information or the cultivation of a specific trait would seem to be largely unproductive in enhancing the administrative skills of candidates.

A strictly informative program was described to me recently by an officer and director of a large corporation who had been responsible for the executive development activities of his company, as follows:

> What we try to do is to get our promising young men together with some of our senior executives in regular meetings each month. Then we give the young fellows a chance to ask questions to let them find out about the company's history and how and why we've done things in the past.

It was not surprising that neither the senior executives nor the young men felt this program was improving their administrative abilities.

The futility of pursuing specific traits becomes apparent when we consider the responses of an administrator in a number of different situations. In coping with these varied conditions, he may appear to demonstrate one trait in one instance—e.g., dominance when dealing with subordinates—and the directly opposite trait under another set of circumstances—e.g., submissiveness when dealing with superiors. Yet in each instance he may be acting appropriately to achieve the best results. Which, then, can we identify as a desirable characteristic? Here is a further example of this dilemma:

A Pacific Coast sales manager had a reputation for decisiveness and positive action. Yet when he was required to name an assistant to understudy his job from among several well-qualified subordinates, he deliberately avoided making a decision. His associates were quick to observe what appeared to be obvious indecisiveness.

But after several months had passed, it became clear that the sales manager had very unobtrusively been giving the various salesmen opportunities to demonstrate their attitudes and feelings. As a result, he was able to identify strong sentiments for one man whose subsequent promotion was enthusiastically accepted by the entire group.

In this instance, the sales manager's skillful performance was improperly interpreted as "indecisiveness." Their concern with irrelevant traits led his associates to overlook the adequacy of his performance. Would it not have been more appropriate to conclude that his human skill in working with others enabled him to adapt effectively to the requirements of a new situation?

Cases such as these would indicate that it is more useful to judge an administrator on the results of his performance than on his apparent traits. Skills are easier to identify than are traits and are less likely to be misinterpreted. Furthermore, skills offer a more directly applicable frame of reference for executive development, since any improvement in an administrator's skills must necessarily result in more effective performance.

Still another danger in many existing executive development programs lies in the unqualified enthusiasm with which some companies and colleges have embraced courses in "human relations." There would seem to be two inherent pitfalls here: (1) Human relations courses might only be imparting information or specific techniques, rather than developing the individual's human skill. (2) Even if individual development does take place, some companies, by placing all of their emphasis on human skill, may be completely overlooking the training requirements for top positions. They may run the risk of producing men with highly developed human skill who lack the conceptual ability to be effective top-level administrators.

It would appear important, then, that the training of a candidate for an administrative position be directed at the development of those skills which are most needed at the level of responsibility for which he is being considered.

Executive Placement

This three-skill concept suggests immediate possibilities for the creating of management teams of individuals with complementary skills. For example, one medium-size midwestern distributing organization has as president a man of unusual conceptual ability but extremely limited human skill. However, he has two vice presidents with exceptional human skill. These three men make up an executive committee which has been outstandingly successful, the skills of each member making up for deficiencies of the others. Perhaps the plan of two-man complementary conference leadership proposed by

Robert F. Bales, in which the one leader maintains "task leadership" while the other provides "social leadership," might also be an example in point.[9]

Executive Selection

In trying to predetermine a prospective candidate's abilities on a job, much use is being made these days of various kinds of testing devices. Executives are being tested for everything from "decisiveness" to "conformity." These tests, as a recent article in *Fortune* points out, have achieved some highly questionable results when applied to performance on the job.[10] Would it not be much more productive to be concerned with skills of doing rather than with a number of traits which do not guarantee performance?

This three-skill approach makes trait testing unnecessary and substitutes for it procedures which examine a man's ability to cope with the actual problems and situations he will find on his job. These procedures, which indicate what a man can *do* in specific situations, are the same for selection and for measuring development. They will be described in the section on developing executive skills which follows.

This approach suggests that executives should *not* be chosen on the basis of their apparent possession of a number of behavior characteristics or traits, but on the basis of their possession of the requisite skills for the specific level of responsibility involved.

Developing the Skills

For years many people have contended that leadership ability is inherent in certain chosen individuals. We talk of "born leaders," "born executives," "born salesmen." It is undoubtedly true that certain people, naturally or innately, possess greater aptitude or ability in certain skills. But research in psychology and physiology would also indicate, first, that those having strong aptitudes and abilities can improve their skill through practice and training, and, secondly, that even those lacking the natural ability can improve their performance and effectiveness.

The *skill* conception of administration suggests that we may hope to improve our administrative effectiveness and to develop better administrators for the future. This skill conception implies *learning by doing*. Different people learn in different ways, but skills are developed through practice and through relating learning to one's own personal experience and background. If well done, training in these basic administrative skills should develop executive abilities more surely and more rapidly than through unorganized experience. What, then, are some of the ways in which this training can be conducted?

Technical Skill

Development of technical skill has received great attention for many years by industry and educational institutions alike, and much progress has been made. Sound grounding in the principles, structures, and processes of the individual specialty, coupled with actual practice and experience during which the individual is watched and helped by a superior, appear to be most effective. In view of the vast amount of work which has been done in training people in the technical skills, it would seem unnecessary in this article to suggest more.

Human Skill

Human skill, however, has been much less understood, and only recently has systematic progress been made in developing it. Many different approaches to the development of human skill are being pursued by various universities and professional men today. These are rooted in such disciplines as psychology, sociology, and anthropology.

Some of these approaches find their application in "applied psychology," "human engineering," and a host of other manifestations requiring technical specialists to help the businessman with his human problems. As a practical matter, however, the executive must develop his own human skill, rather than lean on the advice of others. To be effective, he must develop his own personal point of view toward human activity, so that he will (a) recognize the feelings and sentiments which he brings to a situation; (b) have an attitude about his own experiences which will enable him to re-evaluate and learn from them; (c) develop ability in understanding what others by their actions and words (explicit or implicit) are trying to communicate to him; and (d) develop ability in successfully communicating his ideas and attitudes to others.[11]

This human skill can be developed by some individuals without formalized training. Others can be individually aided by their immediate superiors as an integral part of the "coaching" process to be described later. This aid depends for effectiveness, obviously, on the extent to which the superior possesses the human skill.

For larger groups, the use of case problems coupled with impromptu role playing can be very effective. This training can be established on a formal or informal basis, but it requires a skilled instructor and organized sequence of activities.[12] It affords as good an approximation to reality as can be provided on a continuing classroom basis and offers an opportunity for critical reflection not often found in actual practice. An important part of the procedure is the self-examination of the trainee's own concepts and values, which may enable him to develop more useful attitudes about himself and about others. With the change in attitude, hopefully, there may also come some active skill in dealing with human problems.

Human skill has also been tested in the classroom, within reasonable limits, by a series of analyses of detailed accounts of actual situations involving administrative action, together with a number of role-playing opportunities in which the individual is required to carry out the details of the action he has proposed. In this way an individual's understanding of the total situation and his own personal ability to do something about it can be evaluated.

On the job, there should be frequent opportunities for a superior to observe an individual's ability to work effectively with others. These may appear to be highly subjective evaluations and to depend for validity on the human skill of the rater. But does not every promotion, in the last analysis, depend on someone's subjective judgment? And should this subjectivity be berated, or should we make a greater effort to develop people within our organizations with the human skill to make such judgments effectively?

Conceptual Skill

Conceptual skill, like human skill, has not been very widely understood. A number of methods have been tried to aid in developing this ability, with varying success. Some of the best results have always been achieved through the "coaching" of subordinates by superiors.[13] This is no new idea. It implies that one of the key responsibilities of the executive is to help his subordinates to develop their administrative potentials. One way a superior can help "coach" his subordinate is by assigning a particular responsibility, and then responding with searching questions or opinions, rather than giving answers, whenever the subordinate seeks help. When Benjamin F. Fairless, now chairman of the board of the United States Steel Corporation, was president of the corporation, he described his coaching activities as follows:

> When one of my vice presidents or the head of one of our operating companies comes to me for instructions, I generally counter by asking him questions. First thing I know, he has told me how to solve the problem himself.[14]

Obviously, this is an ideal and wholly natural procedure for administrative training, and applies to the development of technical and human skill, as well as to that of conceptual skill. However, its success must necessarily rest on the abilities and willingness of the superior to help the subordinate.

Another excellent way to develop conceptual skill is through trading jobs, that is, by moving promising young men through different functions of the business but at the same level of responsibility. This gives the man the chance literally to "be in the other fellow's shoes."

Other possibilities include: special assignments, particularly the kind which involve inter-departmental problems; and management boards, such as the McCormick Multiple Management plan, in which junior executives serve as advisers to top management on policy matters.

For larger groups, the kind of case-problems course described above, only using cases involving broad management policy and interdepartmental coordination, may be useful. Courses of this kind, often called "General Management" or "Business Policy," are becoming increasingly prevalent.

In the classroom, conceptual skill has also been evaluated with reasonable effectiveness by presenting a series of detailed descriptions of specific complex situations. In these the individual being tested is asked to set forth a course of action which responds to the underlying forces operating in each situation and which considers the implications of this action on the various functions and parts of the organization and its total environment.

On the job, the alert supervisor should find frequent opportunities to observe the extent to which the individual is able to relate himself and his job to the other functions and operations of the company.

Like human skill, conceptual skill, too, must become a natural part of the executive's makeup. Different methods may be indicated for developing different people, by virtue of their backgrounds, attitudes, and experience. But in every case that method should be chosen which will enable the executive to develop his own personal skill in visualizing the enterprise as a whole and in coordinating and integrating its various parts.

Conclusion

The purpose of this article has been to show that effective administration depends on three basic personal skills, which have been called *technical, human,* and *conceptual.* The administrator needs: (a) sufficient technical skill to accomplish the mechanics of the particular job for which he is responsible; (b) sufficient human skill in working with others to be an effective group member and to be able to build cooperative effort within the team he leads; (c) sufficient conceptual skill to recognize the interrelationships of the various factors involved in his situation, which will lead him to take that action which achieves the maximum good for the total organization.

The relative importance of these three skills seems to vary with the level of administrative responsibility. At lower levels, the major need is for technical and human skills. At higher levels, the administrator's effectiveness depends largely on human and conceptual skills. At the top, conceptual skill becomes the most important of all for successful administration.

This three-skill approach emphasizes that good administrators are not necessarily born; they may be developed. It transcends the need to identify specific traits in an effort to provide a more useful way of looking at the administrative process. By helping to identify the skills most needed at various levels of responsibility, it may prove useful in the selection, training, and promotion of executives.

Notes

[1] Perrin Stryker, "The Growing Pains of Executive Development," *Advanced Management,* August 1954, p. 15.

[2] From a mimeographed case in the files of the Harvard Business School; copyrighted by the President and Fellows of Harvard College.

[3] *Functions of the Executive* (Cambridge, Harvard University Press, 1948), p. 235.

[4] A. Zaleznik, *Foreman Training in a Growing Enterprise* (Boston, Division of Research, Harvard Business School, 1951).

[5] Harriet O. Ronken and Paul R. Lawrence, *Administering Changes* (Boston, Division of Research, Harvard Business School, 1952).

[6] Edmund P. Learned, David H. Ulrich, and Donald R. Booz, *Executive Action* (Boston, Division of Research, Harvard Business School, 1950).

[7] *Executive Leadership* (New York, Harper & Brothers, 1953); see also "Leadership Pattern in the Plant," HBR, January–February 1953, p. 63.

[8] "What Should a President Do?" *Dun's Review,* August 1951, p. 21.

[9] "In Conference," HBR, March–April 1954, p. 44.

[10] William H. Whyte, Jr., "The Fallacies of 'Personality' Testing," *Fortune,* September 1954, p. 117.

[11] For a further discussion of this point, see F. J. Roethlisberger, "Training Supervisors in Human Relations," HBR, September 1951, p. 47.

[12] See, for example, A. Winn, "Training in Administration and Human Relations," *Personnel,* September 1953, p. 139; see also, Kenneth R. Andrews, "Executive Training by the Case Method," HBR, September 1951, p. 58.

[13] For a more complete development of the concept of "coaching," see Myles L. Mace, *The Growth and Development of Executives* (Boston, Division of Research, Harvard Business School, 1950).

[14] "What Should a President Do?" *Dun's Review,* July 1951, p. 14.

3

Managerial Roles

Henry Mintzberg

In thinking about *what* managers do it is useful to consider the concept *role*, a term that has made its way from the theatre to management via the behavioral sciences. A role is defined as an organized set of behaviors belonging to an identifiable office or position. Individual personality may affect *how* a role is performed, but not *that* it is performed. Thus, actors, managers, and others play roles that are predetermined, although individuals may interpret them in different ways. . . .

A Set of Ten Roles

It should be made clear at the outset that the view of managerial roles presented here is one among many that are possible. The delineation of roles is essentially a categorizing process, a somewhat arbitrary partitioning of the manager's activities into affinity groups. The result must ultimately be judged in terms of its usefulness.

This statement of roles was derived initially from the observational study of the work of five chief executives. Each contact and piece of mail observed during this study was analyzed in terms of one basic question—why did the manager do this? The answers, gathered together in logical groupings, emerged as a statement of ten roles.

Despite the basis for these results, there is a logical argument as well as considerable empirical evidence to support the contention that these ten roles are common to the work of all managers. Each manager stands between his organizational unit and its environment. The president guides his firm and looks out to an environment consisting of competitors, suppliers, governments, and so on. The foreman guides his shop and looks out to other foremen and staff groups within the firm, and to suppliers (and others) outside

Excerpt reprinted with permission of Pearson Education, Inc., from *The Nature of Managerial Work* by Henry Mintzberg, © 1980, pp. 54–58, 92–93.

the firm. Each must manage an organization within a complex environment. To do so, the incumbent manager must perform a set of roles and the requirements of these roles lead to certain common work characteristics.

Various studies—of production foremen, field sales managers, and so on—provide support for this argument. Each makes reference to one or more of the roles presented here; between them the ten roles are mentioned in one form or another for managerial jobs ostensibly quite different from that of chief executives. Furthermore, there is evidence from three subsequent empirical studies using this role set to suggest that presidents of small firms and middle managers in business and government perform these ten roles.

Much of this anecdotal material is derived from my own study of chief executives, but the findings of other studies . . . enrich the theory and support the contention that these ten roles are performed by all managers. Again, the term *organization* refers to that unit directly under the manager's formal authority, whether it be a foreman's shop or a president's company.

Managerial activities may be divided into three groups—those that are concerned primarily with interpersonal relationships, those that deal primarily with the transfer of information, and those that essentially involve decision-making. It is for this reason that the ten roles are divided into three groups—three *interpersonal* roles, three *informational* roles and four *decisional* roles.

The manager's position provides the starting point for this analysis. Being in charge of an organizational unit presumes authority and this formal authority leads to a special position of status in the organization. And from formal authority and status come the three interpersonal roles. First and most simple is the role *of figurehead.* The manager has the duty of representing his organization in all matters of formality. Status enables him also to play the *liaison* role, in which interaction takes place with peers and other people outside the organization to gain favors and information. The third interpersonal role, that of *leader,* defines the manager's relationships with his subordinates—motivating, staffing, and so on.

The interpersonal roles place the manager in a unique position to get information. External contacts bring special outside information, and leadership activities serve to make him or her a focal point for organizational information. The result is that the manager emerges as the key nerve center of a special kind of organizational information. Of the three informational roles, the first—*monitor*—identifies the manager as receiver and collector of information, enabling him or her to develop a thorough understanding of the organization. The second role, termed *disseminator,* involves the transmission of special information into the organization. The third, the *spokesman* role, involves the dissemination of the organization's information into its environment.

The manager's unique access to information and special status and authority locates him or her at the central point in the system by which significant (strategic) organizational decisions are made. Here four roles may be delineated: In the *entrepreneur* role the manager's function is to initiate change; in the *disturbance handler* role the manager takes charge when his organization is threatened; in the *resource allocator* role the manager decides where the organization will expend its efforts; and in the *negotiator* role he deals with those situations in which negotiations on behalf of his organization are warranted.

In reading the following descriptions of these roles in Table 1, the reader should bear three points in mind:

First, each role is observable. For example, one can witness a manager handling disturbances or performing as *figurehead*. The description of each role will refer back to the set of observable activities from which it derives. It should, however, be noted that some activities may be accounted for by more than one role. . . .

Second, all of the observed contacts and mail in the study of the five executives are accounted for in the role set. There has been a tendency in the literature to exclude certain work that managers do as inherently non-managerial. . . .

If the president *must* negotiate the contract or preside at the dinner, how can one claim that this is not a part of his job? Omissions such as these are arbitrary—they suggest a preconceived notion of the job which may not be in accord with the facts. If a manager engages in an activity, we must begin with the assumption that this is part of his job and seek to understand why he does it in the broadest sense of his responsibilities. . . .

Third, the roles are described individually but they cannot be isolated and these ten roles form a *gestalt*—an integrated whole. In essence, the manager is an input-output system in which authority and status give rise to interpersonal relationships that lead to inputs (information), and these in turn lead to outputs (information and decisions). One cannot arbitrarily remove one role and expect the rest to remain intact. A manager that, for example, ceases to perform a *liaison* role loses access to external information, and so cannot disseminate good information or make effective strategic decisions. . . .

Table 1 Summary of the Ten Roles

Role	Description	Activities
Interpersonal		
Figurehead	Symbolic head; obliged to perform a number of routine duties of a legal or social nature	Ceremonies, status requests, solicitations
Liaison	Maintains self-developed network of outside contacts and informers who provide favors and information	Handling all mail and contacts categorized as concerned primarily with receiving information

(continued)

Role	Description	Activities
Leader	Responsible for the motivation and activation of subordinates; responsible for staffing, training, and associated duties	Virtually all managerial activities involving subordinates
Informational		
Monitor	Seeks and receives a wide variety of special information to develop a thorough understanding of organization and environ; emerges as nerve center of internal and external information	Forwarding mail into the organization for informational purposes, verbal contacts regarding information flow to subordinates (e.g. review sessions, instant contacts)
Disseminator	Transmits information to outsiders on organization's plans, policies, actions, results, etc.	Board meetings, handling mail and contacts involving transmission of information to outsiders
Spokesman	Represents the organization in the external environment	Acknowledgement of mail, external board work, other activities involving outsiders, serves as expert on organization's industry
Decisional		
Entrepreneur	Searches organization and its environment for opportunities and initiates "improvement projects" to bring about change; supervises design of projects as well	Strategy and review sessions regarding initiation or design of improvement
Disturbance Handler	Responsible for corrective action when organization faces important, unexpected disturbances	Strategy and review sessions regarding disturbances and crises
Resource Allocator	Responsible for the organizational resources	Scheduling; requests for authorization of all kinds—in effect the approval of all significant decisions
Negotiator	Responsible for representing the organization at major negotiations	Negotiation

4

Reframing Leadership

Lee G. Bolman and Terrence E. Deal

Several years ago, we distilled theories of organizations into four categories or traditions, which we labeled frames (Bolman & Deal, 1984, 1991). The structural frame emphasizes rationality, efficiency, structure, and policies. Structural leaders value analysis and data, keep their eye on the bottom line, set clear directions, hold people accountable for results, and try to solve organizational problems with new policies and rules—or through restructuring. The human resource frame focuses on the interaction between individual and organizational needs. Human resource leaders value relationships and feelings and seek to lead through facilitation and empowerment. The political frame emphasizes conflict among different groups and interests for scarce resources. Political leaders are advocates and negotiators who spend much of their time networking, creating coalitions, building a power base, and negotiating compromises. The symbolic frame sees a chaotic world in which meaning and predictability are socially constructed and facts are interpretative rather than objective. Symbolic leaders pay diligent attention to myth, ritual, ceremony, stories, and other symbolic forms.

Research on Leaders' Cognition

We have undertaken a series of studies to explore how leaders use frames: how many they use, which ones, and with what results. Our investigations combine qualitative and quantitative methods because both have advantages in studying leaders' worldviews. Qualitative methods uncover the subtleties of how leaders think and how they frame their experience. Quantitative methods are particularly useful in examining the relationship between the frames of leaders and their constituents in different settings. Regression

Excerpt reprinted with permission of Sage Publications Inc. Journals from *Educational Administration Quarterly*, Vol. 28, No. 3 (August 1992), pp. 314–329. Originally titled "Leading and Managing: Effects of Context, Culture and Gender." Copyright © 1992 Sage Publications Inc. Journals.

analysis, in particular, helps to determine the impact of different frames on leadership and managerial effectiveness.

Our research is guided by two general hypotheses. The first is that the capacity to reframe is a critical issue in success as both manager and leader. In a world of increasing ambiguity and complexity, we believe that the ability to use more than one frame increases an individual's ability to make clear judgments and to act effectively. The second hypothesis is that leadership is contextual: Different situations require different patterns of thinking. There are some organizations, for example, in which an inability to deal with political dynamics is only a modest handicap; in others, it is a fatal flaw.

Qualitative Investigations

Our qualitative work focuses on the implicit frames in administrators' accounts of their experience. We have used those accounts to answer two questions: How many frames do leaders use? Which frames do they use?

Indicators for coding narrative accounts are summarized in Table 1. Although the coding system is not fine-grained, it does allow us to make reliable judgments about the presence or absence of frames in administrators' descriptions of critical incidents.

This article reports the analyses of narratives from two different groups: a sample of principals from Broward County, Florida, and a sample of princi-

Table 1   Criteria for Coding Frame Responses

Frame	Frame-Related Issues	Frame-Related Actions
Structural	Coordination and control; clarity or lack of clarity about goals, roles, or expectations; references to planning, budgeting, and evaluation; discussion of analysis or its absence (e.g., feasibility studies, institutional analysis); issues around policies and procedures.	Reorganizing, implementing, or clarifying policies and procedures; developing new information, budgeting, or control systems; adding new structural units, planning processes.
Human Resource	Discussions of individuals' feelings, needs, preferences, or abilities (e.g., problems of individual performance or staff quality); references to the importance of participation, listening, open communications, involvement in decision making, morale; discussion of interpersonal relationships; emphasis on collaboration, win-win, and a sense of family or community.	Processes of participation and involvement (task forces, open meetings, etc.), training, recruiting new staff, workshops and retreats, empowerment, organization development, and quality-of-work-life programs.

| Political | Focus on conflict or tension among different constituencies, interest groups or organizations; competing interests and agenda disputes over allocation of scarce resources; games of power and self-interest. | Bargaining, negotiation, advocacy, building alliances and networking with other key players. |
| Symbolic | Discussions of institutional identity, culture, or symbols; the image that will be projected to different audiences; the symbolic importance of existing practices, rituals, or artifacts (e.g., symbolic attachment to an old building on campus); emphasis on influencing how different audiences will interpret or frame an activity or decision. | Creating or revitalizing ceremonies and rituals; working to develop or restate the institution's vision; working on influencing organizational culture, using self as symbol. |

pals from the Republic of Singapore. In both places, administrators were asked to write accounts of challenging leadership incidents in which they had been involved. The cases were typically one or two pages long (typed, double-spaced), although some were as short as a paragraph and others went on for several pages. Using the criteria in Table 1, each case was scored for the presence or absence of each of the frames. In both samples, the results (reported in Table 2) suggest that leaders rarely use more than two frames and almost never use all four. In each sample, less than a quarter of the administrators used more than two frames, and only 1 in 20 used all four.

Which Frames Do Leaders Use?

Table 3 reports the frames that were embedded in the cases. We would expect to find both similarities and differences between principals in Florida and Singapore. In both places, principals are expected to provide instructional leadership for staff, students, and community, often in multicultural and multilingual context. Both have made efforts in recent years to move toward school-based management and shared decision making. However, there are important institutional and cultural differences. Broward County is a large, rapidly growing, primarily urban and suburban district, with Fort

Table 2 How Many Frames Do Leaders Use? (in percentages)

How Many Frames	Florida Administrators	Singapore Administrators
1	16	26
2	58	55
3	19	13
4	6	5

Table 3   Which Frames Do Leaders Use? (in percentages)

Which Frames	Florida Administrators	Singapore Administrators
Structural	58	62
Human Resource	86	98
Political	50	21
Symbolic	11	17

Lauderdale as its hub. With about 150,000 students, it is the second largest school district in Florida and one of the 10 largest districts in the United States. Singapore is a city-state of about 3 million people living on 220 square miles (making it about the same size as Chicago in both population and area). It has a single national school system, with a unified curriculum and national examinations at various grade levels to assess how schools and students are doing. Overseas Chinese are about 75% of Singapore's population, with Malays and Tamils the primary minority groups. Chinese culture traditionally has considerable reverence both for authority and for education, and both characteristics are evident in Singapore's government and schools.

Our question was how contextual differences would affect the issues that principals saw as important. In both Florida and Singapore, the human resource frame was dominant in principals' critical incidents (appearing in 86% of the Florida cases and 98% of the cases from Singapore). Problems of underperforming teachers or students with specific needs were a regular agenda item for principals in both settings. Structural themes were the second most common, appearing in about 60% of the cases in both places. Political themes were the third most frequent in both places, but they were much more prominent for principals in Florida (about half the cases) than in Singapore (only one case in five). Florida principals often described incidents involving conflict with various groups or constituencies outside the school, such as parents, advocacy groups, or central office administrators. Singapore principals usually focused on events inside their school in which political battles were less prominent.

In both samples, symbolic issues were least often discussed, but they were noticeably more frequent in Singapore. Administrators were more likely to recognize and articulate structural than symbolic issues. Policies, procedures, legal requirements, committees, and control systems appeared to be recognized features of life in schools everywhere. Symbolic issues, on the other hand, often lurked in the background without being made explicit by the case writer.

Quantitative Investigations*

Measures of Leadership Orientations

Our quantitative investigations employed a survey instrument, Leadership Orientations. The instrument has two parallel forms: one for individuals

*See the original article for details on the research methodology and data interpretation.

to rate themselves and another in which their colleagues (superiors, peers, subordinates, and others) can rate them. In both versions, we employed two different approaches to measuring the Bolman and Deal frames. The first used 5-point rating scales, organized around eight separate dimensions of leadership, two for each frame:

1. Human resource dimensions

    Supportive—concerned about the feelings of others, supportive and responsive; *Participative*—fosters participation and involvement, listens and is open to new ideas

2. Structural dimensions

    Analytic—thinks clearly and logically, approaches problems with facts, attends to detail; *Organized*—develops clear goals and policies, holds people accountable for results

3. Political dimensions

    Powerful—persuasive, high level of ability to mobilize people and resources, effective at building alliances and support; *Adroit*—politically sensitive and skillful, a skillful negotiator in face of conflict

4. Symbolic dimensions

    Inspirational—inspires others to loyalty and enthusiasm, communicates a strong sense of vision; *Charismatic*—imaginative, creative, emphasizes culture and values, models organizational aspirations

The second section of the instrument contains a series of forced-choice items. Each item gives four options, and participants must rank them from 1 *(most like this individual)* to 4 *(least like this individual)*. The following is an example: The best way to describe this person is: technical expert, good listener, skilled negotiator, inspirational leader. . . .

Measures of Effectiveness

Both forms of the Leadership Orientations survey also contain two global ratings of perceived effectiveness: one for "overall effectiveness as a manager" and one for "overall effectiveness as a leader." We did not instruct respondents how to distinguish the terms "manager" and "leader." Instead, we wanted to learn how they gave meaning to the two terms. We expected that the two measures of perceived effectiveness would be highly correlated, and they were (typically in the range of .75 to .85). But we wanted to explore similarities and differences in the pattern of leaders' orientations that is associated with each. . . .

Our analyses explored three questions: How well do the frames capture administrators' thinking? How do cognitive orientations relate to effectiveness as a leader and a manager? How do context, culture, and gender influence "success patterns"?

The participating administrators rated themselves on the Leadership Orientations instrument and were rated by one or more groups of colleagues as well. Each administrator was promised a confidential feedback report summarizing both self and colleague ratings. Principals could choose to get separate feedback from different constituents, such as teachers, parents, and central office administrators. . . .

Where We Are: A Summary

The cognitive frames of school administrators can be measured using both qualitative and quantitative methods. Qualitative work suggests that most principals use only one or two of the frames, with context a significant determinant of which frames are salient. In both the United States and Singapore, for example, school administrators use the symbolic frame much less than any other, but administrators in Singapore appear to be significantly more attuned to symbols and less attuned to politics than are their American counterparts.

Both qualitative and quantitative results suggest that the ability to use multiple frames is critical to principals' effectiveness as both manager and leader. A survey measure of leadership orientations showed that leadership effectiveness is strongly associated with a symbolic orientation but only modestly related to the structural frame. Effectiveness as a manager is highly associated with a structural orientation, but the symbolic frame is more strongly associated with managerial effectiveness for principals than for administrators in other sectors.

The human resource and political frames are significant positive predictors of success as both leader and manager. Pre-service and in-service programs for school administrators rarely give much attention to symbolic and political skills, yet our results show that they are crucial components for effective leadership.

Comparisons of male and female administrators in both the United States and Singapore show that, on the whole, men and women in comparable jobs are not very different from each other, although women tend to be rated slightly higher than men on most variables. The findings are consistent with other research showing that women perform as well or better than men in comparable positions. Underrepresentation of women in school administration is not a function of their inability to do the job. Comparable performance may not yield comparable results because of subtle differences in what is expected of men and women. Among U.S. school administrators, women are judged more on their ability to be organized and rational, whereas men are judged more on their ability to be warm and participative.

References

Bowman, L. G., & Deal, T. E. (1984). *Modern approaches to understanding and managing organizations.* San Francisco: Jossey-Bass.

Bolman, L. G., & Deal, T. E. (1991). *Reframing organizations: Artistry, choice and leadership.* San Francisco: Jossey-Bass.

5

What Leaders Really Do

John P. Kotter

Leadership is different from management, but not for the reason most people think. Leadership isn't mystical and mysterious. It has nothing to do with having "charisma" or other exotic personality traits. It is not the province of a chosen few. Nor is leadership necessarily better than management or a replacement for it.

Rather, leadership and management are two distinctive and complementary terms of action. Each has its own function and characteristic activities. Both are necessary for success in an increasingly complex and volatile business environment.

Most U.S. corporations today are overmanaged and underled. They need to develop their capacity to exercise leadership. Successful corporations don't wait for leaders to come along. They actively seek out people with leadership potential and expose them to career experiences designed to develop that potential. Indeed, with careful selection, nurturing, and encouragement, dozens of people can play important leadership roles in a business organization.

But while improving their ability to lead, companies should remember that strong leadership with weak management is no better, and is sometimes actually worse, than the reverse. The real challenge is to combine strong leadership and strong management and use each to balance the other.

Of course, not everyone can be good at both leading and managing. Some people have the capacity to become excellent managers but not strong leaders. Others have great leadership potential but, for a variety of reasons, have great difficulty becoming strong managers. Smart companies value both kinds of people and work hard to make them a part of the team.

But when it comes to preparing people for executive jobs, such companies rightly ignore the recent literature that says people cannot manage *and* lead. They try to develop leader-managers. Once companies understand the fundamental difference between leadership and management, they can begin to groom their top people to provide both.

The Difference between Management and Leadership

Management is about coping with complexity. Its practices and procedures are largely a response to one of the most significant developments of the twentieth century: the emergence of large organizations. Without good management, complex enterprises tend to become chaotic in ways that threaten their very existence. Good management brings a degree of order and consistency to key dimensions like the quality and profitability of products.

Leadership, by contrast, is about coping with change. Part of the reason it has become so important in recent years is that the business world has become more competitive and more volatile. Faster technological change, greater international competition, the deregulation of markets, overcapacity in capital-intensive industries, an unstable oil cartel, raiders with junk bonds, and the changing demographics of the workforce are among the many factors that have contributed to this shift. The net result is that doing what was done yesterday, or doing it 5% better, is no longer a formula for success. Major changes are more and more necessary to survive and compete effectively in this new environment. More change always demands more leadership.

Consider a simple military analogy: A peacetime army can usually survive with good administration and management up and down the hierarchy, coupled with good leadership concentrated at the very top. A wartime army, however, needs competent leadership at all levels. No one yet has figured out how to manage people effectively into battle; they must be led.

These two different functions—coping with complexity and coping with change—shape the characteristic activities of management and leadership. Each system of action involves deciding what needs to be done, creating networks of people and relationships that can accomplish an agenda, and then trying to ensure that those people actually do the job. But each accomplishes these three tasks in different ways.

Companies manage complexity first by *planning and budgeting*—setting targets or goals for the future (typically for the next month or year), establishing detailed steps for achieving those targets, and then allocating resources to accomplish those plans. By contrast, leading an organization to constructive change begins by *setting a direction*—developing a vision of the future (often the distant future) along with strategies for producing the changes needed to achieve that vision.

Management develops the capacity to achieve its plan by *organizing and staffing*—creating an organizational structure and set of jobs for accomplishing plan requirements, staffing the jobs with qualified individuals, communicating the plan to those people, delegating responsibility for carrying out the plan, and devising systems to monitor implementation. The equivalent leadership activity, however, is *aligning people*. This means communicating the new direction to those who can create coalitions that understand the vision and are committed to its achievement.

Finally, management ensures plan accomplishment by *controlling and problem solving*—monitoring results versus the plan in some detail, both formally and informally, by means of reports, meetings, and other tools; identifying deviations; and then planning and organizing to solve the problems. But for leadership, achieving a vision requires *motivating and inspiring*—keeping people moving in the right direction, despite major obstacles to change, by appealing to basic but often untapped human needs, values, and emotions.

A closer examination of each of these activities will help clarify the skills leaders need.

Setting a Direction versus Planning and Budgeting

Since the function of leadership is to produce change, setting the direction of that change is fundamental to leadership. Setting direction is never the same as planning or even long-term planning, although people often confuse the two. Planning is a management process, deductive in nature and designed to produce orderly results, not change. Setting a direction is more inductive. Leaders gather a broad range of data and look for patterns, relationships, and linkages that help explain things. What's more, the direction-setting aspect of leadership does not produce plans; it creates vision and strategies. These describe a business, technology, or corporate culture in terms of what it should become over the long term and articulate a feasible way of achieving this goal.

Most discussions of vision have a tendency to degenerate into the mythical. The implication is that a vision is something mysterious that mere mortals, even talented ones, could never hope to have. But developing good business direction isn't magic. It is a tough, sometimes exhausting process of gathering and analyzing information. People who articulate such visions aren't magicians but broad-based strategic thinkers who are willing to take risks.

Nor do vision and strategies have to be brilliantly innovative; in fact, some of the best are not. Effective business visions regularly have an almost mundane quality, usually consisting of ideas that are already well known. The particular combination or patterning of the ideas may be new, but sometimes even that is not the case.

For example, when CEO Jan Carlzon articulated his vision to make Scandinavian Airlines System (SAS) the best airline in the world for the frequent business traveler, he was not saying anything that everyone in the airline industry didn't already know. Business travelers fly more consistently than other market segments and are generally willing to pay higher fares. Thus, focusing on business customers offers an airline the possibility of high margins, steady business, and considerable growth. But in an industry known more for bureaucracy than vision, no company had ever put these simple ideas together and dedicated itself to implementing them. SAS did, and it worked.

What's crucial about a vision is not its originality but how well it serves the interests of important constituencies—customers, stockholders, employees—and how easily it can be translated into a realistic competitive strategy. Bad visions tend to ignore the legitimate needs and rights of important constituencies—favoring, say, employees over customers or stockholders. Or they are strategically unsound. When a company that has never been better than a weak competitor in an industry suddenly starts talking about becoming number one, that is a pipe dream, not a vision.

One of the most frequent mistakes that overmanaged and underled corporations make is to embrace long-term planning as a panacea for their lack of direction and inability to adapt to an increasingly competitive and dynamic business environment. But such an approach misinterprets the nature of direction setting and can never work.

Long-term planning is always time consuming. Whenever something unexpected happens, plans have to be redone. In a dynamic business environment, the unexpected often becomes the norm, and long-term planning can become an extraordinarily burdensome activity. That is why most successful corporations limit the time frame of their planning activities. Indeed, some even consider "long-term planning" a contradiction in terms.

In a company without direction, even short-term planning can become a black hole capable of absorbing an infinite amount of time and energy. With no vision and strategy to provide constraints around the planning process or to guide it, every eventuality deserves a plan. Under these circumstances, contingency planning can go on forever, draining time and attention from far more essential activities yet without ever providing the clear sense of direction that a company desperately needs. After awhile, managers inevitably become cynical, and the planning process can degenerate into a highly politicized game.

Planning works best not as a substitute for direction setting but as a complement to it. A competent planning program serves as a useful reality check in direction-setting activities. Likewise, a competent direction-setting process provides a focus in which planning can then be realistically carried out. It helps clarify what kind of planning is essential and what kind is irrelevant.

Aligning People versus Organizing and Staffing

A central feature of modern organizations is interdependence, where no one has complete autonomy, where most employees are tied to many others by their work, technology, management systems, and hierarchy. These linkages present a special challenge when organizations attempt to change. Unless many individuals line up and move together in the same direction, people will tend to fall all over one another. To executives who are overeducated in management and undereducated in leadership, the idea of getting people moving in the same direction appears to be an organizational problem. What executives need to do, however, is not organize people but align them.

Managers "organize" to create a human system that can implement plans as precisely and efficiently as possible. Typically, this requires a number of potentially complex decisions. A company must choose a structure of jobs and reporting relationships, staff it with individuals suited to the job, provide training for those who need it, communicate plans to the workforce, and decide how much authority to delegate and to whom. Economic incentives also need to be constructed to accomplish the plan, as well as systems to monitor its implementation. These organizational judgments are much like architectural decisions. It's a question of fit within a particular context.

Aligning is different. It is more of a communications challenge than a design problem. Aligning invariably involves talking to many more individuals than organizing does. The target population can involve not only a manager's subordinates but also bosses, peers, staff in other parts of the organization, as well as suppliers, government officials, and even customers. Anyone who can help implement the vision and strategy or who can block implementation is relevant.

Trying to get people to comprehend a vision of an alternative future is also a communications challenge of a completely different magnitude from organizing them to fulfill a short-term plan. It's much like the difference between a football quarterback attempting to describe to his team the next two or three plays versus his trying to explain to them a totally new approach to the game to be used in the second half of the season.

Whether delivered with many words or a few carefully chosen symbols, such messages are not necessarily accepted just because they are understood. Another big challenge in leadership efforts is credibility—getting people to believe the message. Many things contribute to credibility: the track record of the person delivering the message, the content of the message itself, the communicator's reputation for integrity and trustworthiness, and the consistency between words and deeds.

Finally, aligning leads to empowerment in a way that organizing rarely does. One of the reasons some organizations have difficulty adjusting to rapid change in markets or technology is that many people in those companies feel relatively powerless. They have learned from experience that even if they correctly perceive important external changes and then initiate appropriate actions, they are vulnerable to someone higher up who does not like what they have done. Reprimand can take many different forms: "That's against policy," or "We can't afford it," or "Shut up and do as you're told."

Alignment helps overcome this problem by empowering people in at least two ways. First, when a clear sense of direction has been communicated throughout an organization, lower-level employees can initiate actions without the same degree of vulnerability. As long as their behavior is consistent with the vision, superiors will have more difficulty reprimanding them. Second, because everyone is aiming at the same target, the probability is less that one person's initiative will be stalled when it comes into conflict with someone else's.

Motivating People versus Controlling and Problem Solving

Since change is the function of leadership, being able to generate highly energized behavior is important for coping with the inevitable barriers to change. Just as direction setting identifies an appropriate path for movement and just as effective alignment gets people moving down that path, successful motivation ensures that they will have the energy to overcome obstacles.

According to the logic of management, control mechanisms compare system behavior with the plan and take action when a deviation is detected. In a well-managed factory, for example, this means the planning process establishes sensible quality targets, the organizing process builds an organization that can achieve those targets, and a control process makes sure that quality lapses are spotted immediately, not in 30 or 60 days, and corrected.

For some of the same reasons that control is so central to management, highly motivated or inspired behavior is almost irrelevant. Managerial processes must be as close as possible to fail-safe and risk free. That means they cannot be dependent on the unusual or hard to obtain. The whole purpose of systems and structures is to help normal people who behave in normal ways to complete routine jobs successfully, day after day. It's not exciting or glamorous. But that's management.

Leadership is different. Achieving grand visions always requires a burst of energy. Motivation and inspiration energize people, not by pushing them in the right direction as control mechanisms do but by satisfying basic human needs for achievement, a sense of belonging, recognition, self-esteem, a feeling of control over one's life, and the ability to live up to one's ideals. Such feelings touch us deeply and elicit a powerful response.

Good leaders motivate people in a variety of ways. First, they always articulate the organization's vision in a manner that stresses the values of the audience they are addressing. This makes the work important to those individuals. Leaders also regularly involve people in deciding how to achieve the organization's vision (or the part most relevant to a particular individual). This gives people a sense of control. Another important motivational technique is to support employee efforts to realize the vision by providing coaching, feedback, and role modeling, thereby helping people grow professionally and enhancing their self-esteem. Finally, good leaders recognize and reward success, which not only gives people a sense of accomplishment but also makes them feel like they belong to an organization that cares about them. When all this is done, the work itself becomes intrinsically motivating.

The more that change characterizes the business environment, the more that leaders must motivate people to provide leadership as well. When this works, it tends to reproduce leadership across the entire organization, with people occupying multiple leadership roles throughout the hierarchy. This is highly valuable, because coping with change in any complex business demands initiatives from a multitude of people. Nothing less will work.

Of course, leadership from many sources does not necessarily converge. To the contrary, it can easily conflict. For multiple leadership roles to work together, people's actions must be carefully coordinated by mechanisms that differ from those coordinating traditional management roles.

Strong networks of informal relationships—the kind found in companies with healthy cultures—help coordinate leadership activities in much the same way that formal structure coordinates managerial activities. The key difference is that informal networks can deal with the greater demands for coordination associated with nonroutine activities and change. The multitude of communication channels and the trust among the individuals connected by the channels allow for an ongoing process of accommodation and adaptation. When conflict arises among roles, those same relationships help resolve the conflicts. Perhaps most important, this process of dialogue and accommodation can produce visions that are linked and compatible instead of remote and competitive. All this requires a great deal more communication than is needed to coordinate managerial roles, but unlike formal structure, strong informal networks can handle it.

Informal relations of some sort exist in all corporations. But too often these networks are either very weak—some people are well connected but most are not—or they are highly fragmented—a strong network exists inside the marketing group and inside R&D but not across the two departments. Such networks do not support multiple leadership initiatives well. In fact, extensive informal networks are so important that if they do not exist, creating them has to be the focus of activity early in a major leadership initiative.

Creating a Culture of Leadership

Despite the increasing importance of leadership to business success, the on-the-job experiences of most people actually seem to undermine the development of the attributes needed for leadership. Nevertheless, some companies have consistently demonstrated an ability to develop people into outstanding leader-managers. Recruiting people with leadership potential is only the first step. Equally important is managing their career patterns. Individuals who are effective in large leadership roles often share a number of career experiences.

Perhaps the most typical and most important is significant challenge early in a career. Leaders almost always have had opportunities during their twenties and thirties to actually try to lead, to take a risk, and to learn from both triumphs and failures. Such learning seems essential in developing a wide range of leadership skills and perspectives. These opportunities also teach people something about both the difficulty of leadership and its potential for producing change.

Later in their careers, something equally important happens that has to do with broadening. People who provide effective leadership in important jobs always have a chance, before they get into those jobs, to grow beyond the narrow base that characterizes most managerial careers. This is usually the result of lateral career moves or of early promotions to unusually broad job assignments. Sometimes other vehicles help, like special task-force assignments or a lengthy general management course. Whatever the case, the breadth of knowledge developed in this way seems to be helpful in all aspects of leadership. So does the network of relationships that is often acquired both inside and outside the company. When enough people get opportunities like this, the relationships that are built also help create the strong informal networks needed to support multiple leadership initiatives.

Corporations that do a better-than-average job of developing leaders put an emphasis on creating challenging opportunities for relatively young employees. In many businesses, decentralization is the key. By definition, it pushes responsibility lower in an organization and in the process creates more challenging jobs at lower levels. Johnson & Johnson, 3M, Hewlett-Packard, General Electric, and many other well-known companies have used that approach quite successfully. Some of those same companies also create as many small units as possible so there are a lot of challenging lower-level general management jobs available.

Sometimes these businesses develop additional challenging opportunities by stressing growth through new products or services. Over the years, 3M has had a policy that at least 25% of its revenue should come from products introduced within the last five years. That encourages small new ventures, which in turn offer hundreds of opportunities to test and stretch young people with leadership potential.

Such practices can, almost by themselves, prepare people for small- and medium-sized leadership jobs. But developing people for important leadership positions requires more work on the part of senior executives, often over a long period of time. That work begins with efforts to spot people with great leadership potential early in their careers and to identify what will be needed to stretch and develop them.

Again, there is nothing magic about this process. The methods successful companies use are surprisingly straightforward. They go out of their way to make young employees and people at lower levels in their organizations visible to senior management. Senior managers then judge for themselves who has potential and what the development needs of those people are. Executives also discuss their tentative conclusions among themselves to draw more accurate judgments.

Armed with a clear sense of who has considerable leadership potential and what skills they need to develop, executives in these companies then spend time planning for that development. Sometimes that is done as part of a formal succession planning or high-potential development process; often it is more informal. In either case, the key ingredient appears to be an intelligent assessment of what feasible development opportunities fit each candidate's needs.

To encourage managers to participate in these activities, well-led businesses tend to recognize and reward people who successfully develop leaders. This is rarely done as part of a formal compensation or bonus formula, simply because it is so difficult to measure such achievements with precision. But it does become a factor in decisions about promotion, especially to the most senior levels, and that seems to make a big difference. When told that future promotions will depend to some degree on their ability to nurture leaders, even people who say that leadership cannot be developed somehow find ways to do it.

Such strategies help create a corporate culture where people value strong leadership and strive to create it. Just as we need more people to provide leadership in the complex organizations that dominate our world today, we also need more people to develop the cultures that will create that leadership. Institutionalizing a leadership-centered culture is the ultimate act of leadership.

Questions and Learning Activities

Section I

Questions:

1. Mintzberg (1980) and Katz (1955) articulated their views of the roles and skills of leaders decades ago. Have these roles and skills changed and, if so, how?

2. Gardner's opinion is that it is not useful to differentiate between managers and leaders. Do you agree? Why or why not?

3. Does Gardner's elaboration of the eleven tasks of leadership capture everything covered by Katz and Mintzberg? Does Gardner include any significant task that they do not? What are the practical implications of any differences you noted?

4. If we accept that the essential roles of leaders and managers are in conflict, how feasible is it for the activities of each to be carried out by the same person? If it is feasible, what skills are required?

5. What types of conflict would you expect to arise in an organization if leadership and management activities were carried out by completely separate groups of people?

6. Gardner asserts that studying well-known and visible leaders is useful for learning about leaders of all types and in a variety of leadership positions. Do you agree? Why or why not?

7. Who most often gets ahead in organizations, those who behave like leaders or those who behave like managers? Why? Give examples to support your position.

8. How does *Reframing Leadership* add to your understanding of leadership beyond what is provided by the other four readings in this section?

9. Describe what work life would be like for lower-level managers and workers in an organization with a great deal of management but not much leadership. Do the same for an organization with the opposite characteristics.

10. How does Kotter address leader/manager duties that are focused outside the organization? Which readings would you cite to support or contradict his treatment of these issues?

Activities:

1. Gardner believes that focusing on differences between leaders and managers is not particularly useful. Kotter, while also endorsing the leader/manager concept, would seem to disagree. Write a paper defending Kotter's position.

2. Describe an example you are familiar with, either as a participant or an observer, that illustrates the organizing activities of a manager according to Kotter. Next describe the aligning activities of a leader you have observed. Identify and highlight differences in the reactions of subordinates to being organized versus being aligned.

3. Choose a leader/manager or a manager with whom you are familiar, or one whose actions are well-documented, and explain how well he or she fulfills seven of the ten roles that Mintzberg describes.

4. Choose a leader/manager or a manager with whom you are familiar, or one whose actions are well-documented, and explain how he or she failed to fulfill five or more of the roles that Mintzberg describes.

5. Briefly survey at least thirty people who fall into either of the following groups:

   A. People who work full-time in a supervisory or management position.

   B. People who work full-time who are not in a supervisory or management position.

   Ask them the five following questions:

   a. What are the differences between managers and leaders?

   b. Do you think that people in nonmanagerial positions can exercise leadership in their organization?

   c. Are leaders born or made?

   d. What are the two most important things leaders do?

   e. Are the top-level managers in your organization effective leaders?

   Report your findings, and any implications you can draw from them, in a five-page paper.

6. Select a leader/manager who has received a considerable amount of press coverage. Choose two readings in this section and use their central points to evaluate this leader.

7. Write a paper comparing and contrasting the five articles in this section. Conclude your paper by proposing your own model of leadership, one that in your view integrates the most relevant portions of this section's readings as well as your own thoughts. Be creative!

SECTION II

LEADERSHIP TRAITS

Leadership traits have played a central role in attempts to explain leadership effectiveness. Early on, a number of writers and researchers endorsed the "Great Man Theory" explanation. Today, although there is near consensus that effectiveness is determined more by what leaders do rather than who they are, the role of leadership traits persists as an item of interest and investigation. Reframing traits into those inherited and those acquired has been helpful in appreciating their relative contributions to leadership effectiveness. The readings in this section will facilitate the quest to understand personal characteristics and traits as they relate to leadership.

In *Confucius's Values-Based Leadership,* Juan Antonio Fernandez explains the relevance of the Chinese philosopher's teachings for current and aspiring leader/managers. This timeless wisdom is possibly more critical today than when written some 2500 years ago. It is certainly easy to identify how the lack of values-based leadership in corporate America has contributed to the recent downfall of a number of organizations. On a more positive note, it is clear that values are a central element of the path to effective leadership. It is equally clear that the personal qualities described by Confucius can be cultivated by aspiring leaders who are willing to devote the time and energy to self-improvement.

In *Personal Factors Associated with Leadership,* Ralph M. Stogdill reviews and interprets studies investigating traits and characteristics of leaders through 1948, commenting on the relationship between these characteristics and effectiveness. The complexity of leadership as a relationship where traits play a role is an important insight. Stogdill's observations on the role of the situation in leadership effectiveness were more than 20 years ahead of the emergence of "situational" or "contingency" approaches to leadership.

One trait that plays an important role in performance is the achievement motive. The significant relationship between the desire to achieve and individual performance is well established. However, in *Leadership Run Amok,* the authors document the destructive potential of leaders who single-mindedly pursue individual achievement. The reading explores the interplay between the need for achievement, affiliation, and power, and concludes by offering would-be leaders advice on how to recognize, manage, and—in some cases—refocus an overactive drive to achieve.

In 1977 when Abraham Zaleznik wrote *Managers and Leaders: Are they Different?*, management development focused exclusively on building competence, control, and the appropriate balance of power. Zaleznik argued that this omitted essential leadership elements of inspiration, vision, and human passion. Today we know how right he was. This article stimulated serious debate and sits squarely in the middle of discussions of the role of individual traits and characteristics. In this reading Zaleznik introduces a new variable to the leadership mix—the role of, and reaction to, one's life situation as one is maturing. This, he asserts, is a major factor differentiating leaders and managers—their underlying conceptions of chaos and order.

The fourth reading in this section, *Leadership: Do Traits Matter?*, takes a nontraditional approach to the investigation of leader traits. Kirkpatrick and Locke view certain traits as critical not necessarily because they are directly related to leadership effectiveness, but because they are "preconditions" likely to lead to actions that will enhance leadership effectiveness. They go a long way in helping us understand the role of personal traits and characteristics as they relate to successful leadership.

Manfred Kets de Vries believes that much of the literature on leadership is too academic and thus in *The Leadership Mystique* he presents a view grounded in day-to-day life. This view includes the "inner theater" of the leader. His model of leadership captures the variables inherent in the charismatic and instrumental roles of the leader. A thorough discussion of the characteristic of narcissism and its role in leadership is particularly insightful.

As noted in several of the readings, some characteristics or personal traits of interest in the leadership arena are inherited while others are acquired. In *Emotional Intelligence and Leadership,* Daniel Goleman presents a workable definition of emotional intelligence and its components. He explains how such qualities as self-awareness, self-regulation, and empathy complement the more traditional characteristics associated with effective leaders. One of the encouraging elements of this presentation for any leader/manager is that emotional intelligence, unlike IQ, can be improved. It is, indeed, one of those personal characteristics that can be learned, although the process is not easy. However, those who expend the effort to develop their emotional intelligence will likely find the rewards well worth the effort.

The final selection in this section explores the bright and dark side of narcissistic leaders—those grandiose, self-promoting, larger-than-life individuals who emerged in the late 1990s and early 2000s. Michael Maccoby explains the difference between productive and unproductive narcissistic leaders, delineating the strengths and weaknesses of this personality type and providing suggestions on how productive narcissists can avoid the pitfalls of their own personality. The article also discusses narcissistic leaders from the perspective of followers, and presents options to those who happen to have a narcissist as their leader/manager.

6

Confucius's
Values-Based Leadership

Juan Antonio Fernandez

In a time when some of our corporate heroes have become villains, it is necessary to revisit our models of leadership. The problem resides in a wrong understanding of leadership as merely a series of behaviors that when properly applied will produce the desired results—namely, motivated followers who will happily strive to achieve the goals of the organization or, on some occasions, those of the leader. This concept of leadership contains a fundamental flaw: lack of internal consistency between behavior and values. One can adjust one's behavior to what is expected, but one's actions may not be the true reflection of one's convictions and preferences. The behavioral model of leadership can produce false or hypocritical leaders. A leader's actions may fit the situation, but his intentions do not. In today's business world, we need to search for a model in which behavior is a reflection of something deeper within the person. We need to search for a model not to substitute for, but to complement, views of leadership developed during recent decades. . . .

The Confucian Path to Leadership

In the Confucian system of thought, leadership is an emergent quality of the character that radiates and makes others want to follow, based on the respect and trust the leader generates. A critical condition for leadership is to have exemplary conduct, being a model to the people. Leadership originates from within the person, but this does not mean that one is born with those qualities; on the contrary, they can be acquired through a conscious effort of self-cultivation and constant learning. To be a true leader is therefore not reserved to a few, but to those willing to work hard and ceaselessly on their path to perfection. That is the Way of the Gentleman, gentleman being defined as the one who shows in superior behavior the true reflection of his or her character.

The challenge for anyone intending to cultivate his or her personal life is to start out on a hunt for the best in one's human nature and steadfastly to keep on it; in order to climb high, one has to begin from the low ground. The Confucian path to leadership has two aims—an internal aim of individual perfection through the practice of self-cultivation and an external aim of achieving social harmony through the exemplary conduct of the leader. Let's explore those two aims.

First Aim: Individual Perfection through Self-Cultivation

> Everything is here in me.
> —Mencius

The first and most important priority of a leader is to discover and cultivate his or her inherent qualities. This is a task that cannot be delegated, the same way one does not delegate eating or sleeping. Those good qualities cannot be obtained from external sources, just by learning a series of quick fixes. One has to look inside oneself to discover and work diligently to develop them. The attainment of knowledge in this context is not the accumulation of data about the external world, but the realization of our personal good qualities. Knowledge means the restoration of one's inherent virtues.

The path to perfection is therefore one of discovering what is already in us, and then, through persistent effort, being able to develop, perfect and apply it to our daily lives. What matters is the search for perfection—not so much the final destination, but the journey. The important thing is to be persistent in our efforts. Perfection is the goal to which we aspire, but as long as we try our best, we are not far from being perfect. Confucius said: "You must cultivate humility, simplicity of character, and loyalty in your conduct. You can still err, but you won't be far from the standard of true personhood." How do we achieve that final objective of perfection? By the attentive practice of three things: careful thinking, careful speaking, and careful acting.

Careful Thinking

The superior person thinks before acting and never preaches what he or she has not previously practiced. His or her actions and words are the product of clear thinking. In order to achieve a clear mind, the superior person must be open-minded, unselfish, and disciplined.

Open-mindedness.   A gentleman can see questions from all sides without bias. He is not partisan, but open to all. He does not take sides; he does not set his mind either absolutely for anything or absolutely against anything.

The small-minded person is biased and can see a question only from one angle, takes sides and holds fixed points of view.

Unselfishness. A gentleman is always considerate towards others, entirely unselfish. She seeks nothing from others; therefore she has no complaints to make. She does what is right without taking into account personal benefit. The small-minded person loves her property and always worries about her material possessions. What she does is for the benefits she can obtain from it.

Discipline. The superior person does not blame others for his faults; he looks at the cause of his mistakes in himself. He does not complain when people do not recognize his merits; he complains about his own incapacities. He does not follow the fashion of the day, always adheres to what's right, and never compromises his integrity. He never for a moment quits the correct way, and never is in a situation in which he is not master of himself. He is free from worries and fears. If he finds nothing wrong when he examines himself, what is there to worry about? The small-minded person blames others for his faults, and set demands on them. He is always thinking of devious means to obtain dubious ends and is always full of worries and fears.

Careful Speaking

The superior person values sincerity most. Sincerity is the combination of both clear thinking and clear action. She always says less than is necessary; as her words respect her actions and her actions respect her words. She is very slow to talk because it is important for her to do what she says. She only preaches what she practices, and is true and loyal to every word she says. She is ashamed when her words are better than her deeds.

Careful Acting

The superior person is always careful in his actions. He does not permit any act contrary to good taste and decency. Even when he is alone, he is prudent and afraid to do wrong, because though no one knows what he has done, he himself knows. He is dignified, but not proud. He is simple and frugal in his living. He blends simplicity and refinement, because those who show more simplicity than refinement are rude; those who show more refinement than simplicity are affected. Only proper blending of these two factors makes a gentleman. Whatever he does should always be practical and concrete. He always helps others to do good. When he repents of his mistakes, he makes amends by deeds. He is easy to serve but difficult to please, for he can only be pleased by what is right. He uses people according to their individual abilities. The small-minded person is difficult to serve but easy to please, for you can please her by catering to her weaknesses without necessarily being right. When she comes to using people, she demands perfection. The small-minded person is proud, but not dignified; she does wrong without any kind of self-restraint in her private life. When she repents of her mistakes, she makes amends by words only. She tries to cover up her bad deeds and pretend she has done good. But others will know what she has done as if her body was transparent. Sincerity and honesty show themselves outwardly.

Second Aim: Social Harmony through Exemplary Conduct

> In ancient times those who wished to bring harmony to the whole world would first bring order to their states. Those who wished to bring order to their states would first regulate their families. Those who wished to regulate their families would first cultivate their own moral character. When the moral character is cultivated, the family will be regulated; when the family is regulated, the state will be in order; when the state is in order, the whole world will be pacified.
>
> *—The Great Learning*

A Virtuous Leader

. . . The superior person never abandons the path of self-cultivation. He is constantly careful of his own conduct, believing that by example he has a great influence. He does not ask others to be kind if he himself is not kind. He only criticizes others if he himself makes no mistakes.

The effectiveness of the leader depends on the people carrying out her instructions, which requires that they trust her. When she does what is right, she will have influence over the people without giving commands, and when she does not do what is right all her commands will be of no use. How does the leader gain that trust? By showing respect and regard for everybody. First of all, she shows regard for herself. Then she shows regard for her family. When the leader carries out these things, her example will be imitated. She will be an example for others to follow. If she is modest, the people will be modest. If she is not tolerant and just, she cannot ask others to be tolerant and forgiving. If she preserves decorum in her public appearance, she will gain the people's respect. She is neither proud nor arrogant. She is courteous in her private life; diligent in her public life; and loyal in her relationships. By living a life of truth and earnestness, she herself serves as a worthy example; therefore the people take her for their model.

Who promotes talented and honest people to positions of responsibility? Duke Ai asked: "What must I do to make people believe in me?" Confucius answered: "Choose honest men and put them above the dishonest and the people will believe in you; choose dishonest men and put them above the honest and the people will not." If the leader does not appoint persons of virtue and talent to high position, he is guilty of negligence. If he does not dismiss a dishonest and incompetent person, he is guilty of making a grave mistake. He promotes those who are worthy, and trains those who lack competencies; that is the best form of encouragement.

The leader who wants to establish herself seeks also to establish others. If you are generous, you will win all. If you are sincere, people will trust you. If you are kind, you will be able to employ the services of others. She attracts good people to work with her by her own behavior and the quality of her character. She doesn't publicize others' faults, but their merits. She holds the principle of putting herself in the place of others. She does not treat her subordinates in a way that she would hate for her superiors to treat her. She will not serve her superior as she would hate her subordinates to serve her.

He despises those who like to criticize people or reveal their weaknesses. He avoids those who like to spread rumors. He rejects those who like to spy on others and think they are very clever. He ignores those who think they are brave when they are merely unruly. He avoids the cunning persons who pretend to be honest gentlemen. He despises the small-minded person. And he identifies himself with the interest and welfare of people.

A wise leader works for other people's interests, helps others to stand up and understand things. The ultimate purpose of her effort is to bring peace and happiness to society, because only those who fulfill their own nature can fulfill the nature of others (see Figure 1).

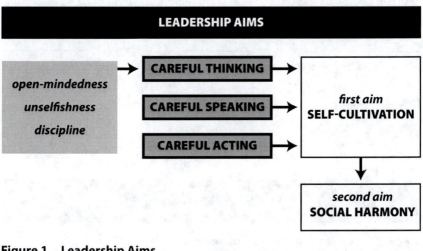

Figure 1   Leadership Aims

If you cannot improve yourself, how can you hope to succeed in improving others?

—Confucius

Values-Based Leadership

A sovereign who governs by virtue is like the North Polar Star, which remains in its place and the other stars revolve around it.

—Confucius

. . . The model of leadership presented in this article is the result of the leader's values. When his values are correct, correct actions will follow. Values are broad preferences concerning appropriate course of action or outcomes. They reflect a person's sense of right or wrong. "Equal rights for all" and "People should be treated with respect and dignity" are representative values. Values are deep-seated and difficult, though not impossible, to change. Many values have their roots in early childhood. Parents, friends, teachers, and external reference groups can all influence individual values. Values influence our attitudes and ultimately our behavior.

Whereas values have a general focus, attitudes are feelings of approval or disapproval of specific objects, actions, or people. An attitude is a predisposition to respond in a positive or negative way to someone or something in one's environment. "Employees should be allowed to participate" is a value; your positive or negative feeling about your job because it does or does not allow participation is an attitude. We cannot see values and attitudes; we can only infer them by what people say or do. There is a link between values, attitudes, and behaviors (see Figure 2). Values create our attitudes, which ultimately result in intended behaviors. There is always a problem of congruence between values and behaviors, a problem of personal integrity. Our intentions may or may not be carried out, depending on the circumstances.

Figure 2   Connecting Values and Behavior

Two values are fundamental in the Confucian system: kindness and justice. Kindness means loving people. Justice means treating things properly. Kindness comes from within, while justice is something external. Justice without kindness is inhumane, while kindness without justice is weakness.

Kindness means awakening all people to a realization of the fundamental goodness of human nature, of the right way to be a person. One who loves others will naturally do things that are beneficial to the people. There are always people who do not love others. Obviously, the way to deal with such people is to enforce the law, but a more enduring and effective solution lies in raising people's moral standards. Confucius upheld the principle of teaching everyone, without making distinctions. A benevolent person is not happy if he alone is successful or able to understand the truth, while others are not. He feels obliged to help others to succeed or comprehend themselves. Do not impose on others what you do not desire yourself. A humane person is always open, never doing anything he might regret, free from worries and fears, at peace with himself and the world. In living and working together, people should be helpful and cooperative, respectful and friendly to each other.

Justice means taking action for its own sake, because it is the right thing to do. From the idea of justice comes the idea of "doing for nothing." Justice and personal profit are opposed values. One does what one ought to do, simply because it is morally right to do it, and not for any consideration of personal gain. The value of doing what one ought to exists in the doing itself, and not in the external result. If we act in this way, we can never fail. We do our duty regardless of the external success or failure of our action. The gentleman knows what is right; the small-minded person knows what is profitable.

From the practice of kindness and justice we obtain trust and social harmony. Without trust, normal relationships between people would be impossible. Trustworthiness is what connects one person to another. The lack of sincerity and faithfulness in human relationships leads to the loss of all effective communication among people. Confucius put trust before prosperity. Strength is not measured in terms of material wealth but in the level of trust among people and to generate trust is the main responsibility of the leader. Confucius thought that people who are led by ones they trust will eventually overcome temporary difficulties. That will ultimately lead to the prosperity of the nation. However, if they do not trust their leaders, they will be disunited and disorderly, unable to do anything.

Harmony, the second result from the virtues of kindness and justice, means the observance of proper rules of behavior, which ensures social order and stability. When those above observe the correct rules of behavior, those below will be easy to command. The leader must aim at bringing harmony. But we should not confuse harmony with uniformity. The leader favors a world in which a multiplicity of diverse views and phenomena exist in harmony. Different ingredients make a tasty dish, and a variety of musical instruments produce beautiful music. Harmony presupposes difference. On the contrary, the small-minded person prefers uniformity, not harmony.

How do we develop kindness and justice? There are two conditions: family and study. The family is very important, because we typically spend our early years with our parents and form our character under their influence. The best predictor of our behavior in society is our behavior in the family. People's character and behavior are revealed first in their families. Having acquired habits of love and respect in the home, one cannot but extend this mental attitude of love and respect to other people's parents and brothers.

Finally, one must persistently study to understand the Way. We study extensively for the purpose of self-cultivation. This effort will certainly give us the wisdom to improve one's moral character (see Figure 3).

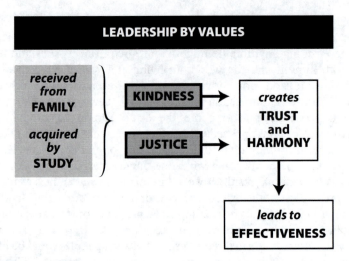

Figure 3   Leadership by Values

> Wealth and high position are desired by all men, but I would not have
> them if they were not won in the right way.
>
> —Confucius

Conclusion

The model of leadership put forward in this article is not a descriptive but a prescriptive one. It is not the result of empirical research to find the qualities of good leaders, but constructed from the ideas espoused by Confucius and his main disciples 2,500 years ago. The fundamental assumption underlying this article is that human nature has not changed much in all those years, despite our mobile phones and portable computers. Humans have needs, hopes and ideals and long for something more than simply daily gains. We have a need for meaning. What is required to achieve those transcendental goals?

And an even more important question: What type of person can create the conditions for others to achieve these goals? The answer was given by Confucius: a person with correct values, a person who practices kindness and justice toward all, without distinction. The Confucian leader is expected to have great aspirations, achieve great self-control, and be a model to others to follow. In this sense, leadership is an end in itself—not a means to obtain what we want from others. It is like health, happiness, or love. One does not ask: How do I apply health? How do I use happiness?

The model of leadership introduced here is a complement to other models. Some of those models are focused on applying the right behaviors given the situation; others are focused on the correct attitudes. Our model points at a deeper level, the values of the leader. The three approaches must consider one another, as they are complementary, not contradictory (see Figure 4).

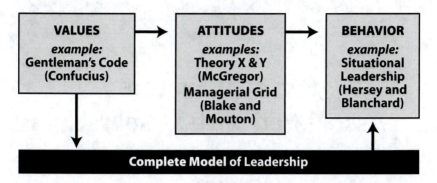

Figure 4   Three-Level Model of Leadership

Confucius sculpted a model of leadership that was the zenith of human relations—the perfect person in society, a person who is not divorced from daily activities, a leader who is both idealistic and realistic. For this leader, carrying on his task is the very essence of the development of the perfection of his responsibility. Through her actions, the leader improves the world and brings harmony. He or she is a leader who delivers results that go beyond short-term profit, a leader with a vision of a better society, a better life and a better place to work. This is a model of leadership in which the most perfect state is to be a sage on the inside and a king on the outside. . . .

> The great person knows that great effects are produced by small causes.
> —Confucius

Selected Bibliography

There are numerous editions of the four classic books. This article is based on the bilingual editions in the Library of Chinese Classics, published by the Foreign Language Press and Hunan People's Publishing House. An excellent translation and account of Confucian thought can be found in *The Wisdom of Confucius,* by Lin Yutang (Random House). Those interested in a deeper knowledge of the history of China can find an outstanding work by John Fairbank and Merle Goldman, *China: A New History,* published by The Belknap Press of Harvard University Press (1992). Lastly, those interested in an introduction to Chinese philosophy should consider *History of Chinese Philosophy,* by Fung Yu-lan, published by Princeton University Press (1983). It is a careful, comprehensive, and readable account of the main schools of thought in Chinese history and their evolution.

7

Personal Factors
Associated with Leadership

Ralph M. Stogdill

Smith and Krueger (1933) have surveyed the literature on leadership to 1933. Recent developments in leadership methodology, as related especially to military situations, were reviewed in 1947 by Jenkins. The present survey is concerned only with those studies in which some attempt has been made to determine the traits and characteristics of leaders. In many of the studies surveyed, leadership was not defined. In others the methods used in the investigation appeared to have little relationship to the problem as stated. An attempt has been made to include all studies bearing on the problem of traits and personal factors associated with leadership.

The present survey lists only those factors which were studied by three or more investigators. Evidence reported by fewer investigators has not been regarded as providing a satisfactory basis for evaluation. It is realized that the number of investigations in which a factor was studied is not necessarily indicative of the importance of the factor. However, the frequency with which a factor was found to be significant appears to be the most satisfactory single criterion for evaluating the data accumulated in this survey, but other criteria, such as the competency of the experimental methods employed and the adequacy of the statistical treatment of data have also been regarded in evaluating the results of a particular study.

In analyzing data obtained from various groups and by various methods the question arises as to the extent to which results may be influenced by differences in social composition of the groups and differences in methodology, and differences in leadership criteria. There is no assurance, for example, that the investigator who analyzes the biographies of great men is studying the

Excerpt reprinted with permission of the Helen Dwight Reid Educational Foundation from "Personal Factors Associated with Leadership: A Survey of the Literature," *Journal of Psychology* (January 1948), pp. 35–71. Published by Heldref Publications. Copyright © 1948.

same kind of leadership activities in group situations. It is of interest, however, that some of the studies employing the two different methods yield remarkably similar results. On the other hand, there are some factors that appear only when certain methods are employed. . . .

Summary of the Findings

The following conclusions are supported by uniformly positive evidence from 15 or more of the studies surveyed:

   a. The average person who occupies a position of leadership exceeds the average member of his group in the following respects: (1) intelligence, (2) scholarship, (3) dependability in exercising responsibilities, (4) activity and social participation, and (5) socioeconomic status.

   b. The qualities, characteristics, and skills required in a leader are determined to a large extent by the demands of the situation in which he is to function as a leader.

The following conclusions are supported by uniformly positive evidence from 10 or more of the studies surveyed:

   a. The average person who occupies a position of leadership exceeds the average member of his group to some degree in the following respects: (1) sociability, (2) initiative, (3) persistence, (4) knowing how to get things done, (5) self-confidence, (6) alertness to, and insight into, situations, (7) cooperativeness, (8) popularity, (9) adaptability, and (10) verbal facility.

In addition to the above, a number of factors have been found which are specific to well-defined groups. For example, athletic ability and physical prowess have been found to be characteristics of leaders in boys' gangs and play groups. Intellectual fortitude and integrity are traits found to be associated with eminent leadership in maturity.

The items with the highest overall correlation with leadership are originality, popularity, sociability, judgment, aggressiveness, desire to excel, humor, cooperativeness, liveliness, and athletic ability, in approximate order of magnitude of average correlation coefficient.

In spite of considerable negative evidence, the general trend of results suggests a low positive correlation between leadership and such variables as chronological age, height, weight, physique, energy, appearance, dominance, and mood control. The evidence is about evenly divided concerning the relation to leadership of such traits as introversion-extroversion, self-sufficiency, and emotional control.

The evidence available suggests that leadership exhibited in various school situations may persist into college and into later vocational and community life. However, knowledge of the facts relating to the transferability of leadership is very meager and obscure.

The most fruitful studies, from the point of view of understanding leadership, have been those in which leadership behavior was described and analyzed on the basis of direct observation or analysis of biographical and case history data.

Discussion

The factors which have been found to be associated with leadership could probably all be classified under the general headings of capacity, achievement, responsibility, participation, and status.

1. *Capacity* (intelligence, alertness, verbal facility, originality, judgment).

2. *Achievement* (scholarship, knowledge, athletic accomplishments).

3. *Responsibility* (dependability, initiative, persistence, aggressiveness, self-confidence, desire to excel).

4. *Participation* (activity, sociability, cooperation, adaptability, humor).

5. *Status* (socioeconomic position, popularity).

These findings are not surprising. It is primarily by virtue of participating in group activities and demonstrating his capacity for expediting the work of the group that a person becomes endowed with leadership status. A number of investigators have been careful to distinguish between the leader and the figurehead and to point out that leadership is always associated with the attainment of group objectives. Leadership implies activity, movement, getting work done. The leader is a person who occupies a position of responsibility in coordinating the activities of the members of the group in their task of attaining a common goal. This leads to consideration of another significant factor.

6. *Situation* (mental level, status, skills, needs and interests of followers, objectives to be achieved, etc.).

A person does not become a leader by virtue of the possession of some combination of traits, but the pattern of personal characteristics of the leader must bear some relevant relationship to the characteristics, activities, and goals of the followers. Thus, leadership must be conceived in terms of the interaction of variables which are in constant flux and change. The factor of change is especially characteristic of the situation, which may be radically altered by the addition or loss of members, changes in interpersonal relationships, changes in goals, competition of extra-group influences, and the like. The personal characteristics of leader and of the followers are, in comparison, highly stable.

The persistence of individual patterns of human behavior in the face of constant situational change appears to be a primary obstacle encountered not only in the practice of leadership, but in the selection and placement of leaders. It is not especially difficult to find persons who are leaders. It is quite another matter to place these persons in different situations where they will be able to function as leaders. It becomes clear that an adequate analysis of leadership involves not only a study of leaders, but also of situations.

The evidence suggests that leadership is a relationship that exists between persons in a social situation, and that persons who are leaders in one situation may not necessarily be leaders in other situations. Must it then be assumed that leadership is entirely incidental, haphazard, and unpredictable? Not at all.

The very studies which provide the strongest arguments for the situational nature of leadership also supply the strongest evidence indicating that leadership patterns as well as non-leadership patterns of behavior are persistent and relatively stable. Jennings (1943) observes that "the individual's choice behavior, in contrast to his social expansiveness, appears as an expression of needs which are, so to speak, so 'central' to his personality that he must strive to fulfill them whether or not the possibility of fulfilling them is at hand." A somewhat similar observation is made by Newstetter, Feldstein, and Newcomb (1938), who report that:

> Being accepted or rejected is not determined by the cordiality or antagonism of the individual's treatment of his fellows, nor evidently, is the individual's treatment of his fellows much affected by the degree to which he is already being accepted or rejected by them. Their treatment of him is related to their acceptance or rejection of him. Their treatment of him is, of course, a reaction to some or all of his behaviors, but we have been completely unsuccessful in attempting to measure what these behaviors are.

The authors conclude that these findings provide "devastating evidence" against the concept of the operation of measurable traits in determining social interactions. The findings of Newstetter and his associates do not appear to provide direct evidence either for or against a theory of traits, but they do indicate that the complex of factors that determines an individual's status in a group is most difficult to isolate and evaluate.

The findings of Jennings and Newstetter suggest that the problem of selecting leaders should be much less difficult than that of training non-leaders to become leaders. The clinician or group worker who has observed the fruitless efforts of socially isolated individuals to gain group acceptance or leadership status is aware of the real nature of the phenomena described by Jennings and Newstetter. Some individuals are isolates in almost any group in which they find themselves, while others are readily accepted in most of their social contacts.

A most pertinent observation on this point is made by Ackerson (1942), who reports that "the correlation for 'leaders' and 'follower' are not of opposite sign and similar magnitude as would be expected of traits supposed to be antithetical." These may not be the opposite poles of a single underlying trait. "It may be that the true antithesis of 'leader' is not 'follower,' but 'indifference,' i.e., the incapacity or unwillingness either to lead or to follow. Thus it may be that some individuals who under one situation are leaders may under other conditions take the role of follower, while the true 'opposite' is represented by the child who neither leads nor follows.

The findings suggest that leadership is not a matter of passive status, or of the mere possession of some combination of traits. It appears rather to be a working relationship among members of a group, in which the leader acquires status through active participation and demonstration of his capacity for carrying cooperative tasks through to completion. Significant aspects of this capacity for organizing and expediting cooperative effort appear to be intelligence, alertness to the needs and motives of others, and insight into situations, further reinforced by such habits as responsibility, initiative, persistence, and self-confidence. The studies surveyed offer little information as to the basic nature of these personal qualifications. Cattell's (1946) studies suggest that they may be founded to some degree on basic intelligence, but Cattell and others also suggest that they are socially conditioned to a high degree. Problems which appear to be in need of thorough investigation are those relating to factors which condition social participation, insight into situations, mood control, responsibility, and transferability of leadership from one situation to another. Answers to these questions seem basic not only to any adequate understanding of the personal qualifications of leaders, but also to any effective training for leadership. . . .

References

Ackerson, L. 1942. *Children's behavior problems: Relative importance and intercorrelations.* Chicago: University of Chicago Press.

Cattell, R. B. 1946. *Description and measurement of personality.* New York: World Book.

Jenkins, W. O. 1947. A review of leadership studies with particular reference to military problems. *Psychological Bulletin,* 44, 54–57.

Jennings, H. H. 1943. *Leadership and isolation.* New York: Longman and Green.

Newstetter, W. I., Feldstein, M. J., and T. M. Newcomb. 1938. *Group adjustment: A study in experimental sociology.* Cleveland: Western Reserve University.

Smith, H. L., and L. M. Krueger. 1933. A brief survey of literature on leadership. *Bull. Sch. Education,* Indiana University, 9, 4.

8

Leadership Run Amok

Scott W. Spreier, Mary H. Fontaine, and Ruth L. Malloy

The desire to achieve is a major source of strength in business, both for individual managers and for the organizations they lead. It generates passion and energy, which fuel growth and help companies sustain performance over the long term. And the achievement drive is on the rise. We've spent 35 years assessing executive motivation, and we've seen a steady increase during the past decade in the number of managers for whom achievement is the primary motive. Businesses have benefited from this trend: Productivity has risen, and innovation, as measured by the number of patents issued per year, has soared.

In the short term, through sheer drive and determination, overachieving leaders may be very successful, but there's a dark side to the achievement motive. By relentlessly focusing on tasks and goals—revenue or sales targets, say—an executive or company can, over time, damage performance. Overachievers tend to command and coerce, rather than coach and collaborate, thus stifling subordinates. They take frequent shortcuts and forget to communicate crucial information, and they may be oblivious to the concerns of others. Their teams' performance begins to suffer, and they risk missing the very goals that initially triggered the achievement-oriented behavior.

Too intense a focus on achievement can demolish trust and undermine morale, measurably reducing workplace productivity and eroding confidence in management, both inside and outside the corporation. While profits and innovation have risen during the past decade, public trust in big business has slid. In our executive coaching practice, we've seen very talented leaders crash and burn as they put ever more pressure on their employees and themselves to produce.

At the extreme are leaders like Enron's Jeffrey Skilling, a classic overachiever by most accounts, driven by results regardless of how they were achieved. He pitted manager against manager and once even praised an executive who went behind his back to create a service he had forbidden her to develop. For every Skilling, there are dozens of overachieving managers who don't make headlines but do cause significant harm. Consider Frank, a confident, results-oriented CEO of a large electronics manufacturer. He was so single-minded in his drive to achieve that he ran roughshod over the rest of the management team. He was arrogant, aloof, and demanding, and he never listened. In fewer than four years, with the company in disarray and members of his senior leadership team threatening to leave, he was fired.

Even if a narrow focus on achievement doesn't get an executive fired, it can stall a career. Jan, a brilliant lawyer, was a partner and the heir apparent in a large New York law firm. But she could be mean-spirited. She didn't tolerate colleagues who seemed less driven than she was, she treated subordinates in a demeaning manner, and she chewed up junior associates at a record pace. Opinions about her began to sour in the firm, and ultimately she was shuffled off to a small satellite office to work—usually alone—on special cases. Although she continued to woo clients and win cases, she never rose any further.

On the surface, controlling achievement overdrive sounds like Management 101: Be less coercive and more collaborative. Influence rather than direct. Focus more on people and less on numbers and results. Easy to say, difficult to master. Experienced, successful executives who should know better fall into overachievement mode again and again. In this article, we'll offer ways for managers to identify achievement overdrive in themselves and others and keep the destructive aspects in check. But first, let's look at the achievement motive and see how it affects the workplace.

The Growing Drive to Achieve

The drive to achieve is tough to resist. Most people in Western cultures are taught from early childhood to value achievement. For some people, the drive seems innate: They don't just *know* achievement is important, they *feel* it. Accomplishment is a natural high for them. Just ask admitted overachiever Karin Mayhew, who is senior vice president of organization effectiveness for Health Net, a large managed-care company. "I start to feel really good," she says of those moments when her achievement drive kicks into high gear and she feels a mounting sense of accomplishment. At such times, she says, she is excited and happy.

David McClelland, the late Harvard psychologist, spent much of his career studying motivation and how it affects leadership behavior. He identified achievement—meeting or exceeding a standard of excellence or improving personal performance—as one of three internal drivers (he called them "social motives") that explain how we behave. The other two are affiliation—maintaining close personal relationships—and power, which involves being strong and influencing or having an impact on others. He said the power motive comes in two forms: personalized—the leader draws strength from controlling others and making them feel weak; and socialized—the leader's strength comes from empowering people. Studies show that great charismatic leaders are highly motivated by socialized power; personalized power is often associated with the exploitation of subordinates. (See the exhibit "What's Your Motivation?")

McClelland's research showed that all three motives are present to some extent in everyone. Although we are not usually conscious of them, they give rise in us to needs and concerns that lead to certain behaviors. Meeting those needs gives us a sense of satisfaction and energizes us, so we keep repeating the behaviors, whether or not they result in the outcomes we desire.

McClelland initially believed that of the three motives, achievement was the most critical to organizational, even national, success. In *The Achieving Society,* his seminal study on the subject, first published in 1961, he reported that a high concern with achievement within a country was followed by rapid national growth, while a drop led to a decline in economic welfare. In another study, he reported a direct correlation between the number of patents generated in a country and the level of achievement as a motivation.

But McClelland also recognized the downside of achievement: the tendencies to cheat and cut corners and to leave people out of the loop. Some high achievers "are so fixated on finding a shortcut to the goal," he noted, "that they may not be too particular about the means they use to reach it." In later work, he argued that the most effective leaders were primarily motivated by socialized power: They channeled their efforts into helping others be successful.

We have continued McClelland's research and assessment of managers' and executives' motives (we have amassed data on more than 40,000 people). We show people a series of pictures and ask them to write a story about each. Experts score the stories for imagery that indicates the presence and strength of one or more of the motives. Beginning in the mid-1990s, achievement scores began rising dramatically, while the power drive declined and affiliation stayed more or less steady. (See the exhibit "Achievement Is on the Rise.")

We can't say definitively what triggered the increase in achievement scores, but we believe it was driven by the organizational, market, and economic forces that were in play. The quality movement of the 1980s, for example, with its emphasis on continuous improvement, no doubt enhanced the value of high achievers, who by nature want to continually improve. Then came recession and downsizing, which brought an increased emphasis on short-term performance and growth. Again, both goals were a perfect fit for high achievers, who revel in the need for personal heroics and the challenge of an ever-rising performance bar. Finally, the dot-com era transformed a large number of innovators and entrepreneurs—who tend to be highly motivated by achievement—into managers and executives.

Whatever the cause, the rise in scores coincided with increases in several of McClelland's other indicators of high achievement—in particular, economic growth, innovation, cheating, and cutting corners. Organizational per-

What's Your Motivation?

A small set of motives, present to some extent in all people, helps explain how leaders behave. The motives generate needs, which lead to aspirations, which in turn drive behavior.

	ACHIEVEMENT	AFFILIATION	POWER	
			Personalized Power	Socialized Power
When this motive is aroused in them, leaders experience a need to:	Improve their personal performance and meet or exceed standards of excellence	Maintain close, friendly relationships	Be strong and influence others, making them feel weak	Help people feel stronger and more capable
As a result, they wish to:	Meet or surpass a self-imposed standard Accomplish something new Plan the long-term advancement of their careers	Establish, restore, or maintain warm relationships Be liked and accepted Participate in group activities, primarily for social reasons	Perform powerful actions Control, influence, or persuade people Impress people inside or outside the company Generate strong positive or negative emotions in others Maintain their reputations, positions, or strength	Perform powerful actions Persuade people Impress people inside or outside the company Generate strong positive emotions in others Maintain their reputations, positions, or strength Give help, advice, or support
These aspirations lead them to:	Micromanage Try to do things or set the pace themselves Express impatience with poor performers Give little positive feedback Give few directions or instructions Cut corners Focus on goals and outcomes rather than people	Avoid confrontation Worry more about people than performance Look for ways to create harmony Avoid giving negative feedback	Be coercive and ruthless Control or manipulate others Manage up—that is, focus more on making a good impression than on managing their subordinates Look out for their own interests and reputations	Coach and teach Be democratic and involve others Be highly supportive Focus on the team or group rather than themselves Work through others; they enable others to do the work rather than doing it themselves

formance and innovation improved, as can be seen in the advance of the stock market and the number of U.S. patents. But there was also a lapse in business ethics, and, as a result, more high-profile scandals and reduced public trust in big corporations. (See the exhibit "So Is Creativity, But . . .")

The Six Styles of Leadership

Despite the advantages of an achievement mentality, executives who are overly motivated to achieve can weaken a company's or group's working climate and in turn its ability to perform well. That's because a leader's motives affect the way he or she leads. In our research over the years, we've identified six styles of leadership that managers and executives use to motivate, reward, direct, and develop others. These are *directive,* which entails strong, sometimes coercive behavior; *visionary,* which focuses on clarity and communication; *affiliative,* which emphasizes harmony and relationships; *participative,* which is collaborative and democratic; *pacesetting,* which is characterized by personal heroics; and *coaching,* which focuses on long-term development and mentoring. (See the sidebar "The Right Leadership Style . . . Creates a Strong Work Climate.")

There is no one best style of leadership. Each has its strengths and its limits. The directive approach, for instance, is useful in crises or when a leader must manage a poor performer, but overuse stifles initiative and innovation. The affiliative approach is appropriate in certain high-stress situations or when employees are beset by personal crises, but it is most effective when used in conjunction with the visionary, participative, or coaching styles. Pacesetting can get results in the short term, but it's demoralizing to employees and exhausting for everyone over the long haul.

The most effective leaders are adept at all six leadership styles and use each when appropriate. Typically, however, a manager defaults to the styles he or she is most comfortable using, a preference that reflects the person's dominant motive combined with the level of pressure in the workplace. People motivated mainly by achievement tend to favor pacesetting in low-pressure situations but to become directive when the pressure is on.

Jan, the achievement-driven lawyer, tried to involve herself in every detail of her client work. She was never satisfied with others on her team and continually second-guessed them. She rewrote perfectly good reports, claiming they didn't quite meet her standards. As the pressure and work mounted, she became even more demanding and controlling, confronting others and accusing them of incompetence.

It's not surprising that such pacesetting and coercion have been shown to suppress work-climate attributes that contribute to high performance, including flexibility, responsibility, team commitment, and the extent to which feedback and rewards are linked to performance. People high in socialized power, by contrast, naturally gravitate to coaching in low-stress situations and become visionary under pressure. Consider Luke, a senior executive we

Achievement Is on the Rise

We've seen a steady increase in the degree to which achievement is a motive for managers and executives, while power as a motivation has dropped. The affiliation motive has remained fairly level. (The lines show average motive scores.)

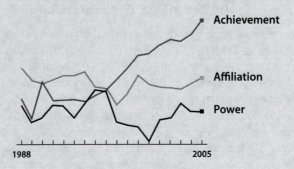

So Is Creativity, But . . .

As the achievement drive has risen among managers and executives, so has the level of innovation, as measured by the number of U.S. patents issued. But at the same time, public trust in big corporations has sunk as the relentless focus on results has led to unsavory behavior on the part of some executives.

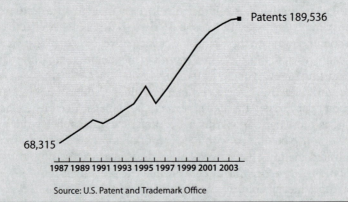

Source: U.S. Patent and Trademark Office

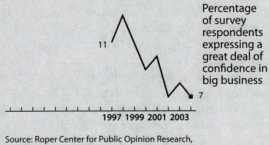

Source: Roper Center for Public Opinion Research, University of Connecticut

worked with who is known for his mentoring. When Luke learned that a subordinate who disagreed with him about a critical business decision had done an end run and was planning to speak to the chairman, Luke didn't react angrily, as most people would. Instead, he offered to coach the subordinate on how to effectively approach his meeting with the chairman. He was able to put aside the personal aspect of the situation and consider the big picture. As Luke told us: "I didn't want him to hurt himself any more than he had already. I wanted him to learn, to benefit, to grow. I don't know—maybe he can have my job some day."

To look at how motives and leadership style affect a group's climate and performance, we studied 21 senior managers at IBM. All led teams responsible for large global accounts with multimillion-dollar revenue targets. We assessed each manager using a set of six attributes of a high-performing climate, such as flexibility and clarity. Eleven of the managers created climates that were seen by their direct reports as strong or energizing. The other managers created climates that were perceived by their reports as neutral or demotivating. In just one year, the teams with strong or energizing climates generated $711 million more in profit than did those with neutral or poor climates. Achievement was the dominant driver for all 21 of these leaders. But the managers who created strong or energizing climates also had far higher scores in both power and affiliation than the other leaders. (See the exhibit "Profiles of Successful Leaders.")

Among the leaders who created neutral or demotivating climates, the dominant style was pacesetting, which can drive short-term growth, but at the expense of long-term profitability. In fact, the teams with weaker climates did produce more short-term revenue growth than the others. But most of it came about through personal heroics—leaders going out and doing deals themselves rather than building their organizations. The leaders who created high-performing and energizing climates got more lasting results by using a broad range of styles, choosing different styles for different circumstances. They were strong in the visionary, affiliative, participative, and coaching styles, relying least on the directive and pacesetting approaches. Rather than order people around or rely on personal heroics, they provided vision, sought buy-in and commitment, and coached their people. They were also more collaborative, building consensus among those they led.

Recognizing Your Motives

The good news about achievers is that when given a goal, they pull out all the stops to reach it—even if the goal is to manage their achievement drive. For an overachiever seeking to broaden his or her range, the first step is to become aware of how motives influence leadership style. Karin Mayhew, the Health Net executive, is a pacesetting manager by nature. She didn't understand the value of influencing others (rather than doing everything herself) until, as an internal consultant for a telecommunications firm, she was

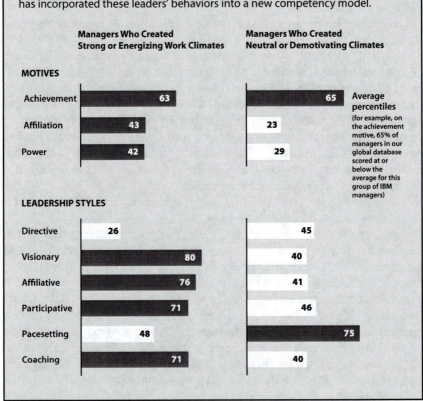

Profiles of Successful Leaders

When we studied 21 senior managers at IBM, we found that 11 of them created strong or energizing work climates. These leaders were driven primarily by the desire to achieve, but they were also driven more by the need for affiliation and power than the other executives, who created neutral or demotivating climates.

Moreover, the 11 managers employed at least four of the six leadership styles described in this article, using each when appropriate to the circumstances. IBM has incorporated these leaders' behaviors into a new competency model.

	Managers Who Created Strong or Energizing Work Climates	Managers Who Created Neutral or Demotivating Climates	
MOTIVES			
Achievement	63	65	Average percentiles (for example, on the achievement motive, 65% of managers in our global database scored at or below the average for this group of IBM managers)
Affiliation	43	23	
Power	42	29	
LEADERSHIP STYLES			
Directive	26	45	
Visionary	80	40	
Affiliative	76	41	
Participative	71	46	
Pacesetting	48	75	
Coaching	71	40	

asked to facilitate discussions between management and labor. For once, she had to be invisible. Forced to bite her tongue, she perceived that she could step out of the role of content expert and help other people understand the big picture and see how the pieces might fit together.

Often, it takes a nudge from someone to get the transformation moving. Consider Rooney Anand, CEO of Greene King, one of the UK's most successful brewing and pub companies. As a young marketing manager in an organization that put a premium on results, Anand found himself becoming increasingly aggressive and demanding. He saw the need to change when a fellow manager said to him, "I've met your type before. Normally they're not very nice people. But you're actually a great bloke when you're not working. So what is your problem?" Family and friends may also let you know; our motives, after all, don't shut down when we leave work.

If you're seeking to assess yourself as a manager, there are calibrated tools for measuring the three leadership motives, but you can get a good sense of which drive is dominant in you simply by examining the activities you like and why.

- People with high achievement drives tend to like challenging projects that allow them to accomplish something new. It may be as simple as stamp collecting or as difficult as getting a PhD in history. One executive we're working with is spending all of his spare time training for a spot on a Senior Olympics swim team. They also like to outperform people who represent a high standard of excellence. Achievers tend to be utilitarian in their communication—often brief and to the point.

- Those high in affiliation are energized by personal relationships. They like to spend time with family and friends and are attracted to group activities, largely for the opportunities to build relationships. They make heavy use of the phone and e-mail just to stay connected.

- People mainly motivated by personalized power need to feel strong and to be seen as important. They tend to be driven by status and image. They often seek status symbols (the right car, neighborhood, clothes) and engage in prestigious activities (dining at the right club with the right circle of friends).

- Individuals mainly driven by socialized power enjoy making a positive impact. They get satisfaction from helping people feel stronger and more capable; they're often energized by team activities. They like to advise and assist, whether or not the advice is wanted or needed. Such people are often attracted to teaching or politics and tend to be charismatic leaders.

Managing and Exercising Your Motives

Even trickier and more important than recognizing an overactive drive to achieve is figuring out how to channel that drive into new behaviors and continually practice them until they become almost second nature. Dean McAlister, a senior pharmaceuticals sales director with AstraZeneca, found himself promoted to a management position early in his career. Like Greene King's Anand, he was talented, sincere, and hardworking, and at times he drove people crazy. While he took pride in his high-achievement approach, others saw him as arrogant, impatient, and manipulative. "Dean was known for his 3 AM e-mails," said one colleague. "That was his normal pace—everything was a priority." Said another: "He outlined a problem, and before we could discuss it, he solved it himself."

McAlister's solutions were often well founded. He stayed ahead of the industry's information curve, regularly rising before dawn to study the latest market trends. But by always providing the answers, he stifled the input and creativity of his team members. He didn't realize this until his manager told him. In classic achievement mode, McAlister instantly turned his energy toward transforming his leadership. With the help of a coach, he began studying his own actions, trying to determine why he behaved as he did. He also monitored his behavior with his team, peers, and manager, asking them to give honest feedback. Much of what he learned was unexpected and, initially, difficult to swallow. At one point, he was describing his daily routine. A deeply spiritual man, McAlister spoke of taking time each day for prayer. When he was asked how much time he spent talking to God and how much time listening, he realized that even in his spiritual life he was focused on his own agenda. "Of course," he groaned, "I'm always talking."

Next, he adopted specific new behaviors. Rather than issue a set of directives on sales targets, for instance, he engaged his team in a discussion of how to achieve the goals. He consciously tried to listen and not jump to conclusions—a continuing struggle, though the behavior is becoming more natural with time and practice. He still slides into pacesetting from time to time. When a sales rep e-mailed him about closing on an important new contract, an excited McAlister fired back with a list of the next steps she should immediately take. It was only after he'd hit the "send" key that he realized his error. "I'd just laid out the plan instead of coaching her," he said. The new McAlister took steps to set things right: He quickly sent a second message, congratulating her and telling her to come up with her own plan. It's a testament to his shift in behavior that his team recently was honored for being the first region to attain market leadership with three of AstraZeneca's top drugs.

Like McAlister, Anand also still works to be aware of his achievement drive and to consciously change his behavior when it starts to overtake him. For example, he had a habit of challenging people during meetings. "My passion and desire to sort problems out, to rectify things, still kicks in," he says. "As a result of my behavior, the team becomes cranky or shuts down. It's taken me quite a long time to learn." So now he'll often refrain from saying what's on his mind, but he'll make a note to take up the matter after the meeting. With time and effort, he says, episodes of achievement overdrive have become less and less frequent for him.

Karin Mayhew has consciously chosen to limit her comments on an idea to a couple of minutes or less and tries to put them in the context of the organization and business. She has also trained herself to ask a lot of open-ended questions ("How can I help?") in an effort to draw people into the conversation. "I've learned to find my 'pause' button and drive the agenda by asking questions and having others take the lead," she says.

Another trick is to look to other areas of your life to satisfy your achievement drive. One executive, recognizing that his need to succeed was getting in the way of his effectiveness at work, refocused his drive on building violins at home on the weekends. Of course, he didn't just turn out run-of-the-mill instruments; his were exquisite pieces of art, one of which was played by a friend in the Boston Symphony. Another executive turned to restoring antique sports cars.

Mayhew now channels her achievement drive toward her home and family. She regularly prepares elaborate, multicourse Sunday night dinners. Although these events are a great deal of work, she finds the dinners exhilarating and energizing, and the effort gives her a sense of satisfaction in what she's achieved, a tonic for the coming workweek.

Changing the Culture

While behavior is the responsibility of the individual, organizations play a role, if sometimes unintentionally, in influencing executives' actions. Some companies unabashedly create cultures that foster and reward the achievement-at-all-costs mentality. Most organizations are less calculating; they simply select and promote high achievers for their obvious assets, let nature take its course, and then look the other way as long as the numbers are good.

But companies can redirect their focus and still achieve good numbers. In the early 1990s, when CEO Lou Gerstner set out to regain IBM's market dominance by transforming the company into a flatter, matrix-driven organization, he sought managers who would orchestrate and enable rather than command and control. He knew IBM needed to move away from its culture of personal heroics and individual achievement and begin valuing socialized power and managers who pay attention to the greater needs of the company.

As part of that transformation, we assessed the motives and leadership styles of 2,000 IBM managers, including the top 300 leaders. We found an achievement-oriented culture in which executives focused on their own departments or divisions, even if doing so had a negative impact on performance in other parts of the organization. Their client focus, too, was achievement driven: Managers often found themselves devoting more time and energy to making the sale than understanding the customer's needs. The dominant leadership style, which reflected this emphasis on individual achievement, was pacesetting, and the climate lacked a number of the attributes that contribute to high performance, especially in the areas of flexibility, rewards, clarity, and, most notably, team commitment.

Among the executives we interviewed, however, was a small but highly successful group that led very differently. They exhibited a drive to achieve, but they worked through others, created strong teams, provided coaching, and focused on increasing the capability of the whole organization, not just their departments. IBM incorporated these behaviors into a competency model that over the next eight years was used to select, develop, and promote leaders. The company also created a group to develop and coach managers and executives in the desired new behaviors. More important, Gerstner and his team used everything from public praise to stock options to reward the new behaviors.

Two years ago, when we returned to assist IBM in recalibrating the competency model, we found a very different leadership culture. Gone was the

The Right Leadership Style . . .

Each of the six leadership styles we've identified is appropriate to certain situations and settings; none is appropriate to all. The most effective leaders know how to use the right style for the circumstances.

Directive. This style entails command-and-control behavior that at times becomes coercive. When executives use this approach, they tell people what to do, when to do it, and what will happen if they fail. It is appropriate in crises and when poor performers must be managed, but it eventually stifles creativity and initiative. It is favored by high achievers under stress.

Visionary. This style is authoritative, but rather than simply telling people what to do, the leader gains employees' support by clearly expressing their challenges and responsibilities in the context of the organization's overall direction and strategy. This makes goals clear, increases employee commitment, and energizes a team. It is commonly used by people with a high personalized-power drive under low-stress situations and people with a high socialized-power drive when stress is high.

Affiliative. Leaders with this style emphasize the employee and his or her emotional needs over the job. They tend to avoid conflict. The approach is effective when a manager is dealing with employees who are in the midst of personal crises or in high-stress situations such as layoffs. It is most effective when used in combination with visionary, participative, or coaching styles. It is seldom effective alone.

Participative. This style of leadership is collaborative and democratic. Executives using this style engage others in the decision-making process. It's great for building trust and consensus, especially when the team consists of highly competent individuals and when the leader has limited knowledge or lacks formal power and authority, such as within highly matrixed organizations. It is favored under high-stress conditions by leaders with high affiliation drives.

Pacesetting. This style involves leading by example and personal heroics. Executives using this style typically have high standards and make sure those standards are met, even if they have to do the work themselves—which they frequently do. It can be effective in the short term, but it can demoralize employees over the long haul. It is a typical go-to style for high achievers, at least under relatively low-stress conditions.

Coaching. This style involves the executive in long-term professional development and mentoring of employees. It's a powerful but underused approach that should be part of any leader's regular repertoire. Leaders who score high on the socialized-power motive prefer it under low-stress conditions.

Creates a Strong Work Climate

We've also identified six factors that contribute to performance by affecting the workplace climate—how it feels to work in a particular area for a particular manager. A leader's behavior heavily influences the degree to which each of these factors is present and is a positive influence.

Flexibility reflects employees' perceptions about whether rules and procedures are really needed or are merely red tape. It also reflects the extent to which people believe they can get new ideas accepted. In high-performance climates, flexibility is high.

Responsibility means the degree to which people feel free to work without asking their managers for guidance at every turn. In high-performing climates, people feel they have a lot of responsibility. When high achievers overuse the directive and pacesetting styles, as they often do, they limit or destroy flexibility and responsibility within a group.

Standards represents the degree to which people perceive that the company emphasizes excellence—that the bar is set at a high but attainable mark, and managers hold people accountable for doing their best. When standards are strong, employees are confident they can meet the company's challenges.

Rewards is a reflection of whether people feel they are given regular, objective feedback and are rewarded accordingly. While compensation and formal recognition are important, the main component is feedback that is immediate, specific, and directly linked to performance.

Clarity refers to whether people know what is expected of them and understand how their efforts relate to organizational goals. In study after study, this dimension of climate has been shown to have the strongest link to productivity. Without clarity, the other elements of climate often suffer. Leaders who create high clarity often rely heavily on the visionary, participative, and coaching styles.

Team commitment is the extent to which people are proud to belong to a team or organization and believe that everyone is working toward the same objectives. The more widely shared the team's values are, and the greater its commitment to performance, the higher the team's pride.

A climate with high levels of standards, clarity, and team commitment and at most one gap in the other dimensions is very strong. A climate with no significant gaps in standards, clarity, or team commitment and two gaps in the other factors is still energizing to employees. Any more gaps, and the climate is neutral or demotivating. In such an environment, people tend to do only the minimum required, and performance suffers.

combative, turf protecting, isolationist attitude. In its place was an emerging culture of collaboration and team leadership—a culture that balanced influencing and helping others with the drive to achieve. Although the motives of the leaders had not changed (the executives were still very high achievers), their behavior had. The coaching style, measured through surveys of their direct reports, had increased by 17%, while pacesetting had decreased by 5%.

Of course, a high achievement drive is still a source of strength. But companies must learn when to draw on it and when to rein it in. The challenge for managers today, then, is to return some of the balance McClelland advised, seeking an approach to leadership that uses socialized power to keep achievement in check.

9

Managers and Leaders
Are They Different?

Abraham Zaleznik

What is the ideal way to develop leadership? Every society provides its own answer to this question, and each, in groping for answers, defines its deepest concerns about the purposes, distributions, and uses of power. Business has contributed its answer to the leadership question by evolving a new breed called the manager. Simultaneously, business has established a new power ethic that favors collective over individual leadership, the cult of the group over that of personality. While ensuring competence, control, and the balance of power among groups with the potential for rivalry, managerial leadership unfortunately does not necessarily ensure imagination, creativity, or ethical behavior in guiding the destinies of corporations.

Leadership inevitably requires using power to influence the thoughts and actions of other people. Power in the hands of an individual entails human risks: first, the risk of equating power with the ability to get immediate results; second, the risk of ignoring the many different ways people can legitimately accumulate power; and third, the risk of losing self-control in the desire for power. The need to hedge these risks accounts in part for the development of collective leadership and the managerial ethic. Consequently, an inherent conservatism dominates the culture of large organizations. In *The Second American Revolution*, John D. Rockefeller III describes the conservatism of organizations:

> An organization is a system, with a logic of its own, and all the weight of tradition and inertia. The deck is stacked in favor of the tried and proven way of doing things and against the taking of risks and striking out in new directions.[1]

Out of this conservatism and inertia, organizations provide succession to power through the development of managers rather than individual leaders.

Ironically, this ethic fosters a bureaucratic culture in business, supposedly the last bastion protecting us from the encroachments and controls of bureaucracy in government and education.

Manager versus Leader Personality

A managerial culture emphasizes rationality and control. Whether his or her energies are directed toward goals, resources, organization structures, or people, a manager is a problem solver. The manager asks: "What problems have to be solved, and what are the best ways to achieve results so that people will continue to contribute to this organization?" From this perspective, leadership is simply a practical effort to direct affairs, and to fulfill his or her task, a manager requires that many people operate efficiently at different levels of status and responsibility. It takes neither genius nor heroism to be a manager, but rather persistence, tough-mindedness, hard work, intelligence, analytical ability, and perhaps most important, tolerance and goodwill.

Another conception of leadership, however, attaches almost mystical beliefs to what a leader is and assumes that only great people are worthy of the drama of power and politics. Here leadership is a psychodrama in which a brilliant, lonely person must gain control of himself or herself as a precondition for controlling others. Such an expectation of leadership contrasts sharply with the mundane, practical, and yet important conception that leadership is really managing work that other people do.

Three questions come to mind. Is the leadership mystique merely a holdover from our childhood—from a sense of dependency and a longing for good and heroic parents? Or is it true that no matter how competent managers are, their leadership stagnates because of their limitations in visualizing purposes and generating value in work? Driven by narrow purposes, without an imaginative capacity and the ability to communicate, do managers then perpetuate group conflicts instead of reforming them into broader desires and goals?

If indeed problems demand greatness, then judging by past performance, the selection and development of leaders leave a great deal to chance. There are no known ways to train "great" leaders. Further, beyond what we leave to chance, there is a deeper issue in the relationship between the need for competent managers and the longing for great leaders.

What it takes to ensure a supply of people who will assume practical responsibility may inhibit the development of great leaders. On the other hand, the presence of great leaders may undermine the development of managers who typically become very anxious in the relative disorder that leaders seem to generate.

It is easy enough to dismiss the dilemma of training managers, though we may need new leaders, or leaders at the expense of managers, by saying that the need is for people who can be both. But just as a managerial culture differs from the entrepreneurial culture that develops when leaders appear in organizations, managers and leaders are very different kinds of people. They differ in motivation, in personal history, and in how they think and act.

Attitudes toward Goals

Managers tend to adopt impersonal, if not passive, attitudes toward goals. Managerial goals arise out of necessities rather than desires and, there-fore, are deeply embedded in their organization's history and culture.

Frederic G. Donner, chairman and chief executive officer of General Motors from 1958 to 1967, expressed this kind of attitude toward goals in defining GM's position on product development:

> To meet the challenge of the marketplace, we must recognize changes in customer needs and desires far enough ahead to have the right products in the right places at the right time and in the right quantity.
>
> We must balance trends in preference against the many compromises that are necessary to make a final product that is both reliable and good looking, that performs well and that sells at a competitive price in the necessary volume. We must design not just the cars *we* would like to build but, more important, the cars that our customers want to buy.[2]

Nowhere in this statement is there a notion that consumer tastes and pref-erences arise in part as a result of what manufacturers do. In reality, through product design, advertising, and promotion, consumers learn to like what they then say they need. Few would argue that people who enjoy taking snap-shots need a camera that also develops pictures. But in response to a need for novelty, convenience, and a shorter interval between acting (snapping the pic-ture) and gaining pleasure (seeing the shot), the Polaroid camera succeeded in the marketplace. It is inconceivable that Edwin Land responded to impres-sions of consumer need. Instead, he translated a technology (polarization of light) into a product, which proliferated and stimulated consumers' desires.

The example of Polaroid and Land suggests how leaders think about goals. They are active instead of reactive, shaping ideas instead of responding to them. Leaders adopt a personal and active attitude toward goals. The influence a leader exerts in altering moods, in evoking images and expecta-tions, and in establishing specific desires and objectives determines the direc-tion a business takes. The net result of this influence changes the way people think about what is desirable, possible, and necessary.

Conceptions of Work

Managers tend to view work as an enabling process involving some com-bination of people and ideas interacting to establish strategies and make deci-sions. They help the process along by calculating the interests in opposition, planning when controversial issues should surface, and reducing tensions. In this enabling process, managers' tactics appear flexible: On one hand, they negotiate and bargain; on the other, they use rewards, punishments, and other forms of coercion.

Alfred P. Sloan's actions at General Motors illustrate how this process works in situations of conflict. The time was the early 1920s when Ford

Motor Company still dominated the automobile industry using, as did General Motors, the conventional water-cooled engine. With the full backing of Pierre du Pont, Charles Kettering dedicated himself to the design of an air-cooled copper engine, which, if successful, would be a great technical and marketing coup for GM. Kettering believed in his product, but the manufacturing division heads opposed the new design on two grounds: First, it was technically unreliable, and second, the corporation was putting all its eggs in one basket by investing in a new product instead of attending to the current marketing situation.

In the summer of 1923, after a series of false starts and after its decision to recall the copper-engine Chevrolets from dealers and customers, GM management scrapped the project. When it dawned on Kettering that the company had rejected the engine, he was deeply discouraged and wrote to Sloan that, without the "organized resistance" against the project, it would have succeeded and that, unless the project were saved, he would leave the company.

Alfred Sloan was all too aware that Kettering was unhappy and indeed intended to leave General Motors. Sloan was also aware that, while the company's manufacturing divisions strongly opposed the new engine, Pierre du Pont supported Kettering. Further, Sloan had himself gone on record in a letter to Kettering less than two years earlier expressing full confidence in him. The problem Sloan had was how to make his decision stick, keep Kettering in the organization (he was much too valuable to lose), avoid alienating du Pont, and encourage the division heads to continue developing product lines using conventional water-cooled engines.

Sloan's actions in the face of this conflict reveal much about how managers work. First, he tried to reassure Kettering by presenting the problem in a very ambiguous fashion, suggesting that he and the executive committee sided with Kettering but that it would not be practical to force the divisions to do what they were opposed to. He presented the problem as being a question of the people, not the product. Second, he proposed to reorganize around the problem by consolidating all functions in a new division that would be responsible for the design, production, and marketing of the new engine. This solution appeared as ambiguous as his efforts to placate Kettering. Sloan wrote at the time:

> My plan was to create an independent pilot operation under the sole jurisdiction of Mr. Kettering, a kind of copper-cooled car division. Mr. Kettering would designate his own chief engineer and his production staff to solve the technical problems of manufacture.[3]

Sloan did not discuss the practical value of this solution, which included saddling an inventor with management responsibility, but in effect, he used this plan in order to limit his conflict with Pierre du Pont.

Essentially, the managerial solution that Sloan arranged limited the options available to others. The structural solution narrowed choices, even limiting emotional reactions to the point where the key people could do nothing but go along. It allowed Sloan to say in his memorandum to du Pont,

> We have discussed the matter with Mr. Kettering at some length this morning, and he agrees with us absolutely on every point we made. He appears to receive the suggestion enthusiastically and has every confidence that it can be put across along these lines.[4]

Sloan placated people who opposed his views by developing a structural solution that appeared to give something but in reality gave only limited options. He could then authorize the car division's general manager, with whom he basically agreed, to move quickly in designing water-cooled cars for the immediate market demand.

Years later, Sloan wrote, evidently with tongue in cheek, "The copper-cooled car never came up again in a big way. It just died out; I don't know why."[5]

To get people to accept solutions to problems, managers continually need to coordinate and balance opposing views. Interestingly enough, this type of work has much in common with what diplomats and mediators do, with Henry Kissinger apparently an outstanding practitioner. Managers aim to shift balances of power toward solutions acceptable as compromises among conflicting values.

Leaders work in the opposite direction. Where managers act to limit choices, leaders develop fresh approaches to long-standing problems and open issues to new options. To be effective, leaders must project their ideas onto images that excite people and only then develop choices that give those images substance.

John F. Kennedy's brief presidency shows both the strengths and weaknesses connected with the excitement leaders generate in their work. In his inaugural address he said, "Let every nation know, whether it wishes us well or ill, that we shall pay any price, bear any burden, meet any hardship, support any friend, oppose any foe, in order to assure the survival and the success of liberty."

This much-quoted statement forced people to react beyond immediate concerns and to identify with Kennedy and with important shared ideals. On closer scrutiny, however, the statement is absurd because it promises a position, which, if adopted, as in the Vietnam War, could produce disastrous results. Yet unless expectations are aroused and mobilized, with all the dangers of frustration inherent in heightened desire, new thinking and new choice can never come to light.

Leaders work from high-risk positions; indeed, they are often temperamentally disposed to seek out risk and danger, especially where the chance of opportunity and reward appears promising. From my observations, the reason one individual seeks risks while another approaches problems conservatively depends more on his or her personality and less on conscious choice. For those who become managers, a survival instinct dominates the need for risk, and with that instinct comes an ability to tolerate mundane, practical work. Leaders sometimes react to mundane work as to an affliction.

Relations with Others

Managers prefer to work with people; they avoid solitary activity because it makes them anxious. Several years ago, I directed studies on the psychological aspects of careers. The need to seek out others with whom to work and collaborate seemed to stand out as an important characteristic of managers. When asked, for example, to write imaginative stories in response to a picture showing a single figure (a boy contemplating a violin or a man silhouetted in a state of reflection), managers populated their stories with people. The following is an example of a manager's imaginative story about the young boy contemplating a violin:

> Mom and Dad insisted that their son take music lessons so that someday he can become a concert musician. His instrument was ordered and had just arrived. The boy is weighing the alternatives of playing football with the other kids or playing with the squeak box. He can't understand how his parents could think a violin is better than a touchdown.
>
> After four months of practicing the violin, the boy has had more than enough, Dad is going out of his mind, and Mom is willing to give in reluctantly to their wishes. Football season is now over, but a good third baseman will take the field next spring.

This story illustrates two themes that clarify managerial attitudes toward human relations. The first, as I have suggested, is to seek out activity with other people (that is, the football team), and the second is to maintain a low level of emotional involvement in those relationships. Low emotional involvement appears in the writer's use of conventional metaphors, even clichés, and in the depiction of the ready transformation of potential conflict into harmonious decisions. In this case, the boy, Mom, and Dad agree to give up the violin for sports.

These two themes may seem paradoxical, but their coexistence supports what a manager does, including reconciling differences, seeking compromises, and establishing a balance of power. The story further demonstrates that managers may lack empathy or the capacity to sense intuitively the thoughts and feelings of those around him. Consider another story written to the same stimulus picture by someone thought of as a leader by his peers:

> This little boy has the appearance of being a sincere artist, one who is deeply affected by the violin, and has an intense desire to master the instrument.
>
> He seems to have just completed his normal practice session and appears to be somewhat crestfallen at his inability to produce the sounds that he is sure lie within the violin.
>
> He appears to be in the process of making a vow to himself to expend the necessary time and effort to play this instrument until he satisfies himself that he is able to bring forth the qualities of music that he feels within himself.
>
> With this type of determination and carry-through, this boy became one of the great violinists of his day.

Empathy is not simply a matter of paying attention to other people. It is also the capacity to take in emotional signals and make them meaningful in a relationship. People who describe another person as "deeply affected," with "intense desire," "crestfallen," and as one who can "vow to himself" would seem to have an inner perceptiveness that they can use in their relationships with others.

Managers relate to people according to the role they play in a sequence of events or in a decision-making process, while leaders, who are concerned with ideas, relate in more intuitive and empathetic ways. The distinction is simply between a manager's attention to *how* things get done and a leader's to *what* the events and decisions mean to participants.

In recent years, managers have adopted from game theory the notion that decision-making events can be one of two types: the win-lose situation (or zero-sum game) or the win-win situation in which everybody in the action comes out ahead. Managers strive to convert win-lose into win-win situations as part of the process of reconciling differences among people and maintaining balances of power.

As an illustration, take the decision of how to allocate capital resources among operating divisions in a large, decentralized organization. On the surface, the dollars available for distribution are limited at any given time. Presumably, therefore, the more one division gets, the less is available for other divisions.

Managers tend to view this situation (as it affects human relations) as a conversion issue: how to make what seems like a win-lose problem into a win-win problem. From that perspective, several solutions come to mind. First, the manager focuses others' attention on procedure and not on substance. Here the players become engrossed in the bigger problem of *how* to make decisions, not *what* decisions to make. Once committed to the bigger problem, these people have to support the outcome since they were involved in formulating the decision-making rules. Because they believe in the rules they formulated, they will accept present losses, believing that next time they will win.

Second, the manager communicates to subordinates indirectly, using "signals" instead of "messages." A signal holds a number of implicit positions, while a message clearly states a position. Signals are inconclusive and subject to reinterpretation should people become upset and angry; messages involve the direct consequence that some people will indeed not like what they hear. The nature of messages heightens emotional response and makes managers anxious. With signals, the question of who wins and who loses often becomes obscured.

Third, the manager plays for time. Managers seem to recognize that with the passage of time and the delay of major decisions, compromises emerge that take the sting out of win-lose situations, and the original "game" will be superseded by additional situations. Compromises mean that one may win and lose simultaneously, depending on which of the games one evaluates.

There are undoubtedly many other tactical moves managers use to change human situations from win-lose to win-win. But the point is that such tactics focus on the decision-making process itself, and that process interests managers rather than leaders. Tactical interests involve costs as well as benefits; they make organizations fatter in bureaucratic and political intrigue and leaner in direct, hard activity and warm human relationships. Consequently, one often hears subordinates characterize managers as inscrutable, detached, and manipulative. These adjectives arise from the subordinates' perception that they are linked together in a process whose purpose is to maintain a controlled as well as rational and equitable structure.

In contrast, one often hears leaders referred to with adjectives rich in emotional content. Leaders attract strong feelings of identity and difference or of love and hate. Human relations in leader-dominated structures often appear turbulent, intense, and at times even disorganized. Such an atmosphere intensifies individual motivation and often produces unanticipated outcomes.

Senses of Self

In *The Varieties of Religious Experience,* William James describes two basic personality types, "once-born" and "twice-born." People of the former personality type are those for whom adjustments to life have been straightforward and whose lives have been more or less a peaceful flow since birth. Twice-borns, on the other hand, have not had an easy time of it. Their lives are marked by a continual struggle to attain some sense of order. Unlike once-borns, they cannot take things for granted. According to James, these personalities have equally different worldviews. For a once-born personality, the sense of self as a guide to conduct and attitude derives from a feeling of being at home and in harmony with one's environment. For a twice-born, the sense of self derives from a feeling of profound separateness.

A sense of belonging or of being separate has a practical significance for the kinds of investments managers and leaders make in their careers. Managers see themselves as conservators and regulators of an existing order of affairs with which they personally identify and from which they gain rewards. A manager's sense of self-worth is enhanced by perpetuating and strengthening existing institutions: He or she is performing in a role that is in harmony with the ideals of duty and responsibility. William James had this harmony in mind—this sense of self as flowing easily to and from the outer world—in defining a once-born personality.

Leaders tend to be twice-born personalities, people who feel separate from their environment. They may work in organizations, but they never belong to them. Their sense of who they are does not depend on memberships, work roles, or other social indicators of identity. And that perception of identity may form the theoretical basis for explaining why certain individuals seek opportunities for change. The methods to bring about change may be technological, political, or ideological, but the object is the same: to profoundly alter human, economic, and political relationships.

In considering the development of leadership, we have to examine two different courses of life history: (1) development through socialization, which prepares the individual to guide institutions and to maintain the existing balance of social relations; and (2) development through personal mastery, which impels an individual to struggle for psychological and social change. Society produces its managerial talent through the first line of development; leaders emerge through the second.

Development of Leadership

Every person's development begins with family. Each person experiences the traumas associated with separating from his or her parents, as well as the pain that follows such a wrench. In the same vein, all individuals face the difficulties of achieving self-regulation and self-control. But for some, perhaps a majority, the fortunes of childhood provide adequate gratification and sufficient opportunities to find substitutes for rewards no longer available. Such individuals, the "once-borns," make moderate identifications with parents and find a harmony between what they expect and what they are able to realize from life.

But suppose the pains of separation are amplified by a combination of parental demands and individual needs to the degree that a sense of isolation, of being special, or of wariness disrupts the bonds that attach children to parents and other authority figures? Given a special aptitude under such conditions, the person becomes deeply involved in his or her inner world at the expense of interest in the outer world. For such a person, self-esteem no longer depends solely on positive attachments and real rewards. A form of self-reliance takes hold along with expectations of performance and achievement, and perhaps even the desire to do great works.

Such self-perceptions can come to nothing if the individual's talents are negligible. Even with strong talents, there are no guarantees that achievement will follow, let alone that the end result will be for good rather than evil. Other factors enter into development as well. For one, leaders are like artists and other gifted people who often struggle with neuroses; their ability to function varies considerably even over the short run, and some potential leaders lose the struggle altogether. Also, beyond early childhood, the development patterns that affect managers and leaders involve the selective influence of particular people. Managerial personalities form moderate and widely distributed attachments. Leaders, on the other hand, establish, and also break off, intensive one-to-one relationships.

It is a common observation that people with great talents are often indifferent students. No one, for example, could have predicted Einstein's great achievements on the basis of his mediocre record in school. The reason for mediocrity is obviously not the absence of ability. It may result, instead, from self-absorption and the inability to pay attention to the ordinary tasks at hand. The only surefire way that an individual can interrupt reverie-like preoccupation and self-absorption is to form a deep attachment to a great teacher or other person who understands and has the ability to communicate with the gifted individual.

Whether gifted individuals find what they need in one-to-one relationships depends on the availability of teachers, possibly parental surrogates, whose strengths lie in cultivating talent. Fortunately, when generations meet and the self-selections occur, we learn more about how to develop leaders and how talented people of different generations influence each other.

While apparently destined for mediocre careers, people who form important one-to-one apprenticeship relationships often are able to accelerate and intensify their development. The psychological readiness of an individual to benefit from such a relationship depends on some experience in life that forces that person to turn inward.

Consider Dwight Eisenhower, whose early career in the army foreshadowed very little about his future development. During World War I, while some of his West Point classmates were already experiencing the war firsthand in France, Eisenhower felt "embedded in the monotony and unsought safety of the Zone of the Interior . . . that was intolerable punishment."[6]

Shortly after World War I, Eisenhower, then a young officer somewhat pessimistic about his career chances, asked for a transfer to Panama to work under General Fox Connor, a senior officer whom he admired. The army turned down his request. This setback was very much on Eisenhower's mind when Ikey, his firstborn son, succumbed to influenza. Through some sense of responsibility for its own, the army then transferred Eisenhower to Panama, where he took up his duties under General Connor with the shadow of his lost son very much upon him.

In a relationship with the kind of father he would have wanted to be, Eisenhower reverted to being the son he had lost. And in this highly charged situation, he began to learn from his teacher. General Connor offered, and Eisenhower gladly took, a magnificent tutorial on the military. The effects of this relationship on Eisenhower cannot be measured quantitatively, but in examining his career path from that point, one cannot overestimate its significance.

As Eisenhower wrote later about Connor,

> Life with General Connor was a sort of graduate school in military affairs and the humanities, leavened by a man who was experienced in his knowledge of men and their conduct. I can never adequately express my gratitude to this one gentleman. . . . In a lifetime of association with great and good men, he is the one more or less invisible figure to whom I owe an incalculable debt.[7]

Some time after his tour of duty with General Connor, Eisenhower's breakthrough occurred. He received orders to attend the Command and General Staff School at Fort Leavenworth, one of the most competitive schools in the army. It was a coveted appointment, and Eisenhower took advantage of the opportunity. Unlike his performance in high school and at West Point, his work at the Command School was excellent; he graduated first in his class.

Psychological biographies of gifted people repeatedly demonstrate the important part a teacher plays in developing an individual. Andrew Carnegie owed much to his senior, Thomas A. Scott. As head of the Western Division of the Pennsylvania Railroad, Scott recognized talent and the desire to learn in the young telegrapher assigned to him. By giving Carnegie increased responsibility and by providing him with the opportunity to learn through close personal observation, Scott added to Carnegie's self-confidence and sense of achievement. Because of his own personal strength and achievement, Scott did not fear Carnegie's aggressiveness. Instead, he gave it full play in encouraging Carnegie's initiative.

Great teachers take risks. They bet initially on talent they perceive in younger people. And they risk emotional involvement in working closely with their juniors. The risks do not always pay off, but the willingness to take them appears to be absolutely crucial in developing leaders.

Can Organizations Develop Leaders?

A myth about how people learn and develop that seems to have taken hold in American culture also dominates thinking in business. The myth is that people learn best from their peers. Supposedly, the threat of evaluation and even humiliation recedes in peer relations because of the tendency for mutual identification and the social restraints on authoritarian behavior among equals. Peer training in organizations occurs in various forms. The use, for example, of task forces made up of peers from several interested occupational groups (sales, production, research, and finance) supposedly removes the restraints of authority on the individual's willingness to assert and exchange ideas. As a result, so the theory goes, people interact more freely, listen more objectively to criticism and other points of view, and, finally, learn from this healthy interchange.

Another application of peer training exists in some large corporations, such as Philips N.V. in Holland, where organizational structure is built on the principle of joint responsibility of two peers, one representing the commercial end of the business and the other the technical. Formally, both hold equal responsibility for geographic operations or product groups, as the case may be. As a practical matter, it may turn out that one or the other of the peers dominates the management. Nevertheless, the main interaction is between two or more equals.

The principal question I raise about such arrangements is whether they perpetuate the managerial orientation and preclude the formation of one-to-one relationships between senior people and potential leaders.

Aware of the possible stifling effects of peer relationships on aggressiveness and individual initiative, another company, much smaller than Philips, utilizes joint responsibility of peers for operating units, with one important difference. The chief executive of this company encourages competition and rivalry among peers, ultimately rewarding the one who comes out on top with increased responsibility. These hybrid arrangements produce some unintended consequences that can be disastrous. There is no easy way to limit rivalry. Instead, it permeates all levels of the operation and opens the way for the formation of cliques in an atmosphere of intrigue.

One large, integrated oil company has accepted the importance of developing leaders through the direct influence of senior on junior executives. The chairman and chief executive officer regularly selects one talented university graduate whom he appoints as his special assistant and with whom he will work closely for a year. At the end of the year, the junior executive becomes available for assignment to one of the operating divisions, where he or she will be assigned to a responsible post rather than a training position. This apprenticeship acquaints the junior executive firsthand with the use of power and with the important antidotes to the power disease called *hubris*—performance and integrity.

Working in one-to-one relationships, where there is a formal and recognized difference in the power of the players, takes a great deal of tolerance for emotional interchange. This interchange, inevitable in close working arrangements, probably accounts for the reluctance of many executives to become involved in such relationships. *Fortune* carried an interesting story on the departure of a key executive, John W. Hanley, from the top management of Procter & Gamble to the chief executive officer position at Monsanto.[8] According to this account, the chief executive and chairman of P&G passed over Hanley for appointment to the presidency, instead naming another executive vice president to this post.

The chairman evidently felt he could not work well with Hanley who, by his own acknowledgment, was aggressive, eager to experiment and change practices, and constantly challenged his superior. A CEO naturally has the right to select people with whom he feels congenial. But I wonder whether a greater capacity on the part of senior officers to tolerate the competitive impulses and behavior of their subordinates might not be healthy for corporations. At least a greater tolerance for interchange would not favor the managerial team player at the expense of the individual who might become a leader.

I am constantly surprised at the frequency with which chief executives feel threatened by open challenges to their ideas, as though the source of their authority, rather than their specific ideas, was at issue. In one case, a chief executive officer, who was troubled by the aggressiveness and sometimes outright rudeness of one of his talented vice presidents, used various indirect methods such as group meetings and hints from outside directors to avoid dealing with his subordinate. I advised the executive to deal head-on with what irritated him. I suggested that by direct, face-to-face confrontation, both he and his subordinate would learn to validate the distinction between the authority to be preserved and the issues to be debated.

The ability to confront is also the ability to tolerate aggressive interchange. And that skill not only has the net effect of stripping away the veils of ambiguity and signaling so characteristic of managerial cultures but also encourages the emotional relationships leaders need if they are to survive.

Notes

1 (HarperCollins, 1973).

2 Alfred P. Sloan, Jr., *My Years with General Motors* (Doubleday, 1964).

3 Ibid.

4 Ibid.

5 Ibid.

6 Dwight D. Eisenhower, *At Ease: Stories I Tell to Friends* (Doubleday, 1967).

7 Ibid.

8 "Jack Hanley Got There by Selling Harder," *Fortune,* November 1976.

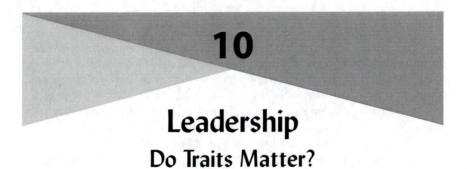

10

Leadership
Do Traits Matter?

Shelley A. Kirkpatrick and Edwin A. Locke

Few issues have a more controversial history than leadership traits and characteristics. In the 19th and early 20th centuries, "great man" leadership theories were highly popular. These theories asserted that leadership qualities were inherited, especially by people from the upper class. Great men were born, not made (in those days, virtually all business leaders were men). Today, great man theories are a popular foil for so-called superior models. To make the new models plausible, the "great men" are endowed with negative as well as positive traits. In a recent issue of the *Harvard Business Review,* for example, Slater and Bennis write,

> The passing years have . . . given the coup de grace to another force that has retarded democratization—the "great man" who with brilliance and farsightedness could preside with dictatorial powers as the head of a growing organization.[1]

Such great men, argue Slater and Bennis, become "outmoded" and dead hands on "the flexibility and growth of the organization." Under the new democratic model, they argue, "the individual *is* of relatively little significance."

Early in the 20th century, the great man theories evolved into trait theories. ("Trait" is used broadly here to refer to people's general characteristics, including capacities, motives, or patterns of behavior.) Trait theories did not make assumptions about whether leadership traits were inherited or acquired. They simply asserted that leaders' characteristics are different from non-leaders. Traits such as height, weight, and physique are heavily dependent on heredity, whereas others such as knowledge of the industry are dependent on experience and learning.

Reprinted with permission of Academy of Management (NY) from *Academy of Management Executive,* Vol. 5, No. 2 (June 1991), pp. 48–59. Copyright © 1991 Academy of Management (NY).

The trait view was brought into question during the mid-century when a prominent theorist, Ralph Stogdill, after a thorough review of the literature concluded that "A person does not become a leader by virtue of the possession of some combination of traits."[2] Stogdill believed this because the research showed that no traits were universally associated with effective leadership and that situational factors were also influential. For example, military leaders do not have traits identical to those of business leaders.

Since Stogdill's early review, trait theory has made a comeback, though in altered form. Recent research, using a variety of methods, has made it clear that successful leaders are not like other people. The evidence indicates that there are certain core traits which significantly contribute to business leaders' success.

Traits *alone,* however, are not sufficient for successful business leadership—they are only a precondition. Leaders who possess the requisite traits must take certain *actions* to be successful (e.g. formulating a vision, role modeling, setting goals). Possessing the appropriate traits only makes it more likely that such actions will be taken and be successful. After summarizing the core leadership traits, we will discuss these important actions and the managerial implications.

The Evidence: Traits Do Matter

The evidence shows that traits do matter. Six traits on which leaders differ from non-leaders include: drive, the desire to lead, honesty/integrity, self-confidence, cognitive ability, and knowledge of the business.[3] These traits are shown in Exhibit 1.

Drive

The first trait is labeled "drive," which is not to be confused with physical need deprivation. We use the term to refer to a constellation of traits and motives reflecting a high effort level. Five aspects of drive include achievement motivation, ambition, energy, tenacity, and initiative.

Achievement. Leaders have a relatively high desire for achievement. The need for achievement is an important motive among effective leaders and

---

Exhibit 1   Leadership Traits

Drive: achievement, ambition, energy, tenacity, initiative
Leadership Motivation (personalized vs. socialized)
Honesty and Integrity
Self-confidence (including emotional stability)
Cognitive Ability
Knowledge of the Business
Other Traits (weaker support): charisma, creative/originality, flexibility

even more important among successful entrepreneurs. High achievers obtain satisfaction from successfully completing challenging tasks, attaining standards of excellence, and developing better ways of doing things. To work their way up to the top of the organization, leaders must have a desire to complete challenging assignments and projects. This also allows the leader to gain technical expertise, both through education and work experience, and to initiate and follow through with organizational changes.

The constant striving for improvement is illustrated by the following manager who took charge of a $260 million industrial and office-products division:[4]

> After twenty-seven months on the job, Tom saw his efforts pay off: the division had its best first quarter ever. By his thirty-first month, Tom felt he had finally mastered the situation. . . . [Tom] finally felt he had the structure and management group in place to grow the division's revenues to $400 million and he now turned his attention to divesting a product group which no longer fit in with the growth objectives of the division.

Managers perform a large amount of work at an unrelenting pace. To perform well, a leader needs to constantly work toward success and improvement. Superior managers and executives are concerned with doing something better than they or others have ever done it. For example, at PepsiCo only "aggressive achievers" survive. Similarly, Thomas Watson of IBM has been described as "driven throughout by a personal determination to create a company larger than NCR."[5] This brings us to a second related motive: ambition.

Ambition. Leaders are very ambitious about their work and careers and have a desire to get ahead. To advance, leaders actively take steps to demonstrate their drive and determination. Ambition impels leaders to set hard, challenging goals for themselves and their organizations. Walt Disney, founder of Walt Disney Productions, had a "dogged determination to succeed" and C. E. Woolman of Delta Air Lines had "inexhaustible ambition."

Effective leaders are more ambitious than nonleaders. In their 20-year study, psychologists Ann Howard and Douglas Bray found that among a sample of managers at AT&T, ambition, specifically the desire for advancement, was the strongest predictor of success twenty years later. The following character sketches of two managers who successfully progressed illustrate the desire for advancement:[6]

> "I want to be able to demonstrate the things I learned in college and get to the top," said Al, "maybe even be president. I expect to work hard and be at the third level within 5 years, and to rise to much higher levels in the years beyond that. I am specifically working on my MBA to aid in my advancement. If I'm thwarted on advancement, or find the challenge is lacking, I'll leave the company."

> [He] had been promoted to the district level [after 8 years] and certainly expected to go further. Although he still wouldn't pinpoint wanting to be president (his wife's dream for him), he certainly had a

vice presidency (sixth level) in mind as early as year 2 in the study, after his first promotion.

The following sketches characterize two less ambitious individuals:

Even though Chet had the benefits of a college degree, his below-average scholastic performance did not fill him with confidence in his capabilities. He hedged a bit with his interviewer when asked about his specific aspirations, saying he wasn't sure what the management levels were. When pressed further, he replied, "I'd like to feel no job is out of my reach, but I'm not really possessed of a lot of ambition. There are times when I just want to say, 'To hell with everything.'"

After [his] promotion to the second level, he looked more favorably upon middle management, but he still indicated he would not be dissatisfied to stay at the second level. [He] just seemed to take each position as it came; if he ever looked ahead, he didn't appear to look up.

Energy. To sustain a high achievement drive and get ahead, leaders must have a lot of energy. Working long, intense work weeks (and many weekends) for many years requires an individual to have physical, mental, and emotional vitality.

Leaders are more likely than nonleaders to have a high level of energy and stamina and to be generally active, lively, and often restless. Leaders have been characterized as "electric, vigorous, active, full of life" as well as possessing the "physical vitality to maintain a steadily productive work pace."[7] Even at age 70, Sam Walton, founder of Wal-Mart discount stores, still attended Wal-Mart's Saturday morning meeting, a whoop-it-up 7:30 AM sales pep rally for 300 managers.

The need for energy is even greater today than in the past, because more companies are expecting all employees, including executives, to spend more time on the road visiting the organization's other locations, customers, and suppliers.

Tenacity. Leaders are better at overcoming obstacles than nonleaders. They have the "capacity to work with distant objects in view" and have a "degree of strength of will or perseverance."[8] Leaders must be tirelessly persistent in their activities and follow through with their programs. Most organizational change programs take several months to establish and can take many years before the benefits are seen. Leaders must have the drive to stick with these programs, and persistence is needed to ensure that changes are institutionalized.

An example of heroic perseverance in the face of obstacles from American history is the tale of John Paul Jones, a captain in the newly formed American Navy. On September 25, 1779, John Paul Jones, aboard the *Bonhomme Richard*, engaged in battle with the English ship *Serapis* off the coast of England. After being bombarded with cannon fire by the *Serapis*, having two old cannons explode causing a fire, and being fired at by their supposed ally, the *Alliance*, Jones appeared to have lost the battle. When asked to surrender in the face of almost certain defeat, Jones made his immortal reply: "I have not yet begun to fight."

Determined to sink the *Serapis*, Jones spotted an open hatch on the *Serapis'* deck and ordered a young sailor to climb into the rigging and toss grenades into the hatch, knowing the English had stored their ammunitions there. After missing with the first two grenades, the third grenade disappeared into the hatchway and was followed by a thunderous explosion aboard the *Serapis*. Engulfed in flames, the English captain surrendered to Jones. Even though the entire battle had gone against him, John Paul Jones was determined not to give up, and it was this persistence that caused him to finally emerge victorious.

It is not just the direction of action that counts, but sticking to the direction chosen. Effective leaders must keep pushing themselves and others toward the goal. David Glass, CEO of Wal-Mart, says that Sam Walton "has an overriding something in him that causes him to improve every day. . . . As long as I have known him, he has never gotten to the point where he's comfortable with who he is or how we're doing." Walt Disney was described as expecting the best and not relenting until he got it. Ray Kroc, of McDonald's Corporation, was described as a "dynamo who drove the company relentlessly."[9] Kroc posted this inspirational message on his wall:

> Nothing in the world can take the place of persistence.
> Talent will not; nothing is more common than unsuccessful men with great talent.
> Genius will not; unrewarded genius is almost a proverb.
> Education will not; the world is full of educated derelicts.
> Persistence, determination alone are omnipotent.

Persistence, of course, must be used intelligently. Dogged pursuit of an inappropriate strategy can ruin an organization. It is important to persist in the right things. But what are the right things? In today's business climate, they may include the following: satisfying the customer, growth, cost control, innovation, fast response time, and quality. Or, in Tom Peters' terms, a constant striving to improve just about everything.

Initiative.   Effective leaders are proactive. They make choices and take action that leads to change instead of just reacting to events or waiting for things to happen; that is, they show a high level of initiative. The following two examples from consultant Richard Boyatzis of McBer and Company illustrate proactivity:[10]

> I called the chief, and he said he couldn't commit the resources, so I called the budget and finance people, who gave me a negative response. But then I called a guy in another work group who said he was willing to make a trade for the parts I needed. I got the parts and my group was able to complete the repairs.

> One of our competitors was making a short, half-inch component and probably making $30,000–$40,000 a year on it. I looked at our line: we have the same product and can probably make it better and

cheaper. I told our marketing manager: "Let's go after that business." I made the decision that we would look at it as a marketplace rather than looking at it as individual customers wanting individual quantities. I said, here's a market that has 30,000 pieces of these things, and we don't give a damn where we get the orders. Let's just go out and get them. We decided we were going to charge a specific price and get the business. Right now we make $30,000–$40,000 on these things and our competitor makes zero.

Instead of sitting "idly by or [waiting] for fate to smile upon them," leaders need to "challenge the process."

Leaders are achievement-oriented, ambitious, energetic, tenacious, and proactive. These same qualities, however, may result in a manager who tries to accomplish everything alone, thereby failing to develop subordinate commitment and responsibility. Effective leaders must not only be full of drive and ambition, they must *want to lead others*.

Leadership Motivation

Studies show that leaders have a strong desire to lead. Leadership motivation involves the desire to influence and lead others and is often equated with the need for power. People with high leadership motivation think a lot about influencing other people, winning an argument, or being the greater authority. They prefer to be in a leadership rather than subordinate role. The willingness to assume responsibility, which seems to coincide with leadership motivation, is frequently found in leaders.

Sears psychologist Jon Bentz describes successful Sears executives as those who have a "powerful competitive drive for a position . . . authority. . . [and] the need to be recognized as men of influence."[11] Astronauts John Glenn and Frank Borman built political and business careers out of their early feats as space explorers, while other astronauts did not. Clearly, all astronauts possessed the same opportunities, but it was their personal makeup that caused Glenn and Borman to pursue their ambitions and take on leadership roles.

Psychologist Warren Bennis and colleague Burt Nanus state that power is a leader's currency, or the primary means through which the leader gets things done in the organization. A leader must want to gain the power to exercise influence over others. Also, power is an "expandable pie," not a fixed sum; effective leaders give power to others as a means of increasing their own power. Effective leaders do not see power as something that is competed for but rather as something that can be created and distributed to followers without detracting from their own power.

Successful managers at AT&T completed sentence fragments in the following manner:[12]

"When I am in charge of others I find my greatest satisfaction."
"The job I am best fit for is one which requires leadership ability."
"I depend on others to carry out my plans and directions."

A manager who was not as successful completed the sentence fragment "Taking orders . . ." with the ending "is easy for it removes the danger of a bad decision."

Successful leaders must be willing to exercise power over subordinates, tell them what to do, and make appropriate use of positive and negative sanctions. Previous studies have shown inconsistent results regarding dominance as a leadership trait. According to Harvard psychologist David McClelland, this may be because there are two different types of dominance: a personalized power motive, or power lust, and a socialized power motive, or the desire to lead.[13]

Personalized Power Motive.   Although a need for power is desirable, the leader's effectiveness depends on what is behind it. A leader with a personalized power motive seeks power as an end in itself. These individuals have little self-control, are often impulsive, and focus on collecting symbols of personal prestige. Acquiring power solely for the sake of dominating others may be based on profound self-doubt. The personalized power motive is concerned with domination of others and leads to dependent, submissive followers.

Socialized Power Motive.   In contrast, a leader with a socialized power motive uses power as a means to achieve desired goals, or a vision. Its use is expressed as the ability to develop networks and coalitions, gain cooperation from others, resolve conflicts in a constructive manner, and use role modeling to influence others.

Individuals with a socialized power motive are more emotionally mature than those with a personalized power motive. They exercise power more for the benefit of the whole organization and are less likely to use it for manipulation. These leaders are also less defensive, more willing to take advice from experts, and have a longer-range view. They use their power to build up their organization and make it successful. The socialized power motive takes account of followers' needs and results in empowered, independent followers.

Honesty and Integrity

Honesty and integrity are virtues in all individuals but have special significance for leaders. Without these qualities, leadership is undermined. Integrity is the correspondence between word and deed and honesty refers to being truthful or non-deceitful. The two form the foundation of a trusting relationship between leader and followers.

In his comprehensive review of leadership, psychologist Bernard Bass found that student leaders were rated as more trustworthy and reliable in carrying out responsibilities than followers. Similarly, British organizational psychologists Charles Cox and Cary Cooper's "high flying" (successful) managers preferred to have an open style of management, where they truthfully informed workers about happenings in the company. Morgan McCall and Michael Lombardo of the Center for Creative Leadership found that managers who reached the top were more likely to follow the following formula: "I will do exactly what I say I will do when I say I will do it. If I change my mind, I will tell you well in advance so you will not be harmed by my actions."[14]

Successful leaders are open with their followers, but also discreet and do not violate confidences or carelessly divulge potentially harmful information. One subordinate in a study by Harvard's John Gabarro made the following remark about his new president: "He was so consistent in what he said and did, it was easy to trust him." Another subordinate remarked about an unsuccessful leader, "How can I rely on him if I can't count on him consistently?"[15]

Professors James Kouzes, Barry Posner, and W. H. Schmidt asked 1500 managers "What values do you look for and admire in your superiors?" Integrity (being truthful and trustworthy, and having character and conviction) was the most frequently mentioned characteristic. Kouzes and Posner conclude:

> Honesty is absolutely essential to leadership. After all, if we are willing to follow someone, whether it be into battle or into the boardroom, we first want to assure ourselves that the person is worthy of our trust. We want to know that he or she is being truthful, ethical, and principled. We want to be fully confident in the integrity of our leaders.

Effective leaders are credible, with excellent reputations and high levels of integrity. The following description (from Gabarro's study) by one subordinate of his boss exemplifies the concept of integrity: "By integrity, I don't mean whether he'll rob a bank, or steal from the till. You don't work with people like that. It's whether you sense a person has some basic principles and is willing to stand by them."

Bennis and Nanus warn that today credibility is at a premium, especially since people are better informed, more cautious, and wary of authority and power. Leaders can gain trust by being predictable, consistent, and persistent and by making competent decisions. An honest leader may even be able to overcome lack of expertise, as a subordinate in Gabarro's study illustrates in the following description of his superior: "I don't like a lot of the things he does, but he's basically honest. He's a genuine article and you'll forgive a lot of things because of that. That goes a long way in how much I trust him."

Self-Confidence

There are many reasons why a leader needs self-confidence. Being a leader is a very difficult job. A great deal of information must be gathered and processed. A constant series of problems must be solved and decisions made. Followers have to be convinced to pursue specific courses of action. Setbacks have to be overcome. Competing interests have to be satisfied. Risks have to be taken in the face of uncertainty. A person riddled with self-doubt would never be able to take the necessary actions nor command the respect of others.

Self-confidence plays an important role in decision-making and in gaining others' trust. Obviously, if the leader is not sure of what decision to make, or expresses a high degree of doubt, then the followers are less likely to trust the leader and be committed to the vision.

Not only is the leader's self-confidence important, but so is others' perception of it. Often, leaders engage in impression management to bolster their image of competence; by projecting self-confidence they arouse followers' self-confidence. Self-confident leaders are also more likely to be assertive and decisive, which gains others' confidence in the decision. This is crucial for effective implementation of the decision. Even when the decision turns out to be a poor one, the self-confident leader admits the mistake and uses it as a learning opportunity, often building trust in the process. Manor Care, Inc., for example, lost over $21 million in 1988 when it was caught holding a large portion of Beverly Enterprise's stock. Chairman and CEO Stewart Bainum, Jr. stated, "I take full and complete responsibility for making the acquisition."[16] Considered to be the "best managed company in the [nursing home] industry," Manor Care's stock has rebounded, and it seems to be making a comeback. Less successful managers are more defensive about failure and try to cover up mistakes.

Emotional Stability.   Self-confidence helps effective leaders remain even-tempered. They do get excited, such as when delivering an emotionally-charged pep talk, but generally do not become angry or enraged. For the most part, as long as the employee did his/her homework leaders remain composed upon hearing that an employee made a costly mistake. For example, at PepsiCo, an employee who makes a mistake is "safe . . . as long as it's a calculated risk."

Emotional stability is especially important when resolving interpersonal conflicts and when representing the organization. A top executive who impulsively flies off the handle will not foster as much trust and teamwork as an executive who retains emotional control. Describing a superior, one employee in Gabarro's study stated, "he's impulsive and I'm never sure when he'll change signals on me."

Researchers at the Center for Creative Leadership found that leaders are more likely to "derail" if they lack emotional stability and composure. Leaders who derail are less able to handle pressure and more prone to moodiness, angry outbursts, and inconsistent behavior, which undermines their interpersonal relationships with subordinates, peers, and superiors. In contrast, they found the successful leaders to be calm, confident, and predictable during crisis.

Psychologically hardy, self-confident individuals consider stressful events interesting, as opportunities for development, and believe that they can influence the outcome. K. Labich in *Fortune* magazine argued that "by demonstrating grace under pressure, the best leaders inspire those around them to stay calm and act intelligently."[17]

Cognitive Ability

Leaders must gather, integrate, and interpret enormous amounts of information. These demands are greater than ever today because of rapid technological change. Thus, it is not surprising that leaders need to be intelligent enough to formulate suitable strategies, solve problems, and make correct decisions.

Leaders have often been characterized as being intelligent, but not necessarily brilliant and as being conceptually skilled. Kotter states that a "keen mind" (i.e., strong analytical ability, good judgment, and the capacity to think strategically and multidimensionally) is necessary for effective leadership, and that leadership effectiveness requires "above average intelligence," rather than genius.

An individual's intelligence and the perception of his or her intelligence are two highly related factors. Professors Lord, DeVader, and Alliger concluded that "intelligence is a key characteristic in predicting leadership perceptions."[18] Howard and Bray found that cognitive ability predicted managerial success twenty years later in their AT&T study. Effective managers have been shown to display greater ability to reason both inductively and deductively than ineffective managers.

Intelligence may be a trait that followers look for in a leader. If someone is going to lead, followers want that person to be more capable in some respects than they are. Therefore, the follower's perception of cognitive ability in a leader is a source of authority in the leadership relationship.

Knowledge of the Business

Effective leaders have a high degree of knowledge about the company, industry, and technical matters. For example, Jack Welch, president of GE, has a PhD in engineering; George Hatsopolous of Thermo Electron Corporation, in the years preceding the OPEC boycott, had both the business knowledge of the impending need for energy-efficient appliances and the technical knowledge of thermodynamics to create more efficient gas furnaces. Technical expertise enables the leader to understand the concerns of subordinates regarding technical issues. Harvard Professor John Kotter argues that expertise is more important than formal education.

Effective leaders gather extensive information about the company and the industry. Most of the successful general managers studied by Harvard's Kotter spent their careers in the same industry, while less successful managers lacked industry-specific experiences. Although cognitive ability is needed to gain a thorough understanding of the business, formal education is not a requirement. Only forty percent of the business leaders studied by Bennis and Nanus had business degrees. In-depth knowledge of the organization and industry allows effective leaders to make well-informed decisions and to understand the implications of those decisions.

Other Traits

Charisma, creativity/originality, and flexibility are three traits with less clear-cut evidence of their importance to leadership.[19] Effective leaders may have charisma; however, this trait may only be important for political leaders. Effective leaders also may be more creative than nonleaders, but there is no consistent research demonstrating this. Flexibility or adaptiveness may be important traits for a leader in today's turbulent environment. Leaders must be able to make decisions and solve problems quickly and initiate and foster change.

There may be other important traits needed for effective leadership; however, we believe that the first six that we discussed are the core traits.

The Rest of the Story

A complete theory of leadership involves more than specifying leader traits. Traits only endow people with the potential for leadership. To actualize this potential, additional factors are necessary which are discussed in our forthcoming book *The Essence of Leadership* (written with additional authors).

Three categories of factors are discussed here: skills, vision, and implementing the vision. *Skills* are narrower in meaning than traits and involve specific capacities for action such as decision making, problem solving, and performance appraisal.

The core job of a leader, however, is to create a *vision*—a concept of what the organization should be. To quote Bennis and Nanus, "A vision articulates a view of a realistic, credible, attractive future for the organization, a condition that is better in some important ways than what now exists. A vision is a target that beckons."[20] Next the leader must *communicate* this vision to followers through inspirational speeches, written messages, appeals to shared values and above all through acting as a role model and personally acting in a way that is consistent with the vision. Third, the leader must develop or at least help to develop a general *strategy* for achieving the vision (i.e. a strategic vision).

Implementing the vision requires at least six activities:

1. Structuring

Today's effective organizations have minimal bureaucracy: small corporate staffs, few layers of management and large spans of control. The leader must insure that the organization's structure facilitates the flow of information (downward, upward, and diagonally). Information from customers regarding product quality and services is especially crucial.

2. Selecting and Training

Leaders must make sure that people are hired who have the traits needed to accept and implement the vision. Maintaining and upgrading skills is assured by constant training, as is commitment to the organization's vision.

3. Motivating

Leaders cannot achieve the vision alone; they must stimulate others to work for it too. They must generate enthusiasm, commitment, and compliance. Besides communicating the vision, effective leaders use at least six procedures to motivate followers.

Formal Authority. The leader is the "boss" and must use his or her legitimate power constructively. The leader must start by asking directly for what he or she wants. *Thriving on Chaos* author Tom Peters said that if one wants something, then "just ask for it."

Role Models.   Leaders must behave the way they wish their followers would behave. For example, if they want subordinates to be customer-oriented, they should spend time themselves talking to customers. This has far more influence on employees than just telling them that customers are important.

Build Subordinate Self-Confidence.   If employees have been carefully selected and trained, such confidence will be justified. Jay Conger calls the process of strengthening subordinates' belief in their capabilities "empowerment."[21]

Delegation of Authority.   Giving autonomy and responsibility to employees also creates empowerment. In their book *Superleadership,* Charles Manz and Henry Sims[22] argue that delegating authority actually enhances the power of leaders by helping their subordinates become capable of attaining organizational goals. Effective delegation, of course, presupposes that subordinates are capable of holding the responsibilities they are given (as a result of extensive training and experience).

Specific and Challenging Goals.[23]   Ensuring that subordinates have specific and challenging goals leads to higher performance than ambiguous goals. Challenging goals are empowering because they demonstrate the leader has confidence in the follower. Goals must be accompanied by regular feedback indicating progress in relation to the goals. Feedback, in turn, requires adequate performance measurement.

For goals to be effective, employees must be committed to them. Inspiration, modeling, training, and delegation all facilitate commitment.

Rewards and Punishments.   Effective leaders are *not* tolerant of those who reject the vision or repeatedly fail to attain reasonable goals. Rewards (and punishments) send messages not only to the employee in question but also to others; followers often direct their own actions by looking at what happens to their peers. People may learn as much or more by observing models than from the consequences of their own actions.[24] Rewards may include pay raises, promotions and awards, as well as recognition and praise. Effective leaders do not just reward achievement, they celebrate it.

4. Managing Information

Leaders have a profound influence on how information is managed within the organization. Effective leaders are effective information gatherers because they are good listeners and encourage subordinates to express their opinions. They stay in contact with the rest of the organization by, in Tom Peters' terms, "wandering around." Leaders actively seek information from outside the organization. Good leaders also disseminate information widely so that followers will understand the reasons for decisions that are made and how their work fits into the organization's goals. At the same time, effective leaders try not to overwhelm subordinates with too much information.

5. Team Building

Achieving goals requires collaboration among many (in some cases, hundreds of thousands) individuals. Leaders need to help build effective teams, starting with the top management team.[25] While an effective leader cannot do everything, he or she can insure that everything gets done by hiring, training, and motivating skilled people who work together effectively. And they, in turn, can build effective teams of their own.

6. Promoting Change and Innovation

Finally, effective leaders must promote change and innovation. The vision, since it pertains to a desired future state, is the starting point of change. This must be reinforced by constant restructuring, continual retraining to develop new skills, setting specific goals for innovation and improvement, rewarding innovation, encouraging a constant information flow in all directions and emphasizing responsiveness to customer demands.

It is clear that leadership is a very demanding activity and that leaders who have the requisite traits—drive, desire to lead, self-confidence, honesty (and integrity), cognitive ability, and industry knowledge—have a considerable advantage over those who lack these traits. Without drive, for example, it is unlikely that an individual would be able to gain the expertise required to lead an organization effectively, let alone implement and work toward long-term goals. Without the desire to lead, individuals are not motivated to persuade others to work toward a common goal; such an individual would avoid or be indifferent to leadership tasks. Self-confidence is needed to withstand setbacks, persevere through hard times, and lead others in new directions. Confidence gives effective leaders the ability to make hard decisions and to stand by them. A leader's honesty and integrity form the foundation on which the leader gains followers' trust and confidence; without honesty and integrity, the leader would not be able to attract and retain followers. At least a moderate degree of cognitive ability is needed to gain and understand technical issues as well as the nature of the industry. Cognitive ability permits leaders to accurately analyze situations and make effective decisions. Finally, knowledge of the business is needed to develop suitable strategic visions and business plans.

Management Implications

Individuals can be selected either from outside the organization or from within non- or lower-managerial ranks based on their possession of traits that are less changeable or trainable. Cognitive ability (not to be confused with knowledge) is probably the least trainable of the six traits. Drive is fairly constant over time although it can change; it is observable in employees assuming they are given enough autonomy and responsibility to show what they can do. The desire to lead is more difficult to judge in new hires who may have had little opportunity for leadership early in life. It can be observed at lower levels of management and by observing people in assessment center exercises.

Two other traits can be developed through experience and *training*. Knowledge of the industry and technical knowledge come from formal training, job experience, and a mentally active approach toward new opportunities for learning. Planned job rotation can facilitate such growth. Self-confidence is both general and task specific. People differ in their general confidence in mastering life's challenges, but task-specific self-confidence comes from mastering the various skills that leadership requires as well as the technical and strategic challenges of the industry. Such confidence parallels the individual's growth in knowledge.

Honesty does not require skill building; it is a virtue one achieves or rejects by choice. Organizations should look with extreme skepticism at any employee who behaves dishonestly or lacks integrity, and should certainly not reward dishonesty in any form, especially not with a promotion. The key role models for honest behavior are those at the top. On this issue, organizations get what they model, not what they preach.

Conclusions

Regardless of whether leaders are born or made or some combination of both, it is unequivocally clear that *leaders are not like other people.* Leaders do not have to be great men or women by being intellectual geniuses or omniscient prophets to succeed, but they do need to have the "right stuff" and this stuff is not equally present in all people. Leadership is a demanding, unrelenting job with enormous pressures and grave responsibilities. It would be a profound disservice to leaders to suggest that they are ordinary people who happened to be in the right place at the right time. Maybe the place matters, but it takes a special kind of person to master the challenges of opportunity. Let us not only give credit, but also use the knowledge we have to select and train our future leaders effectively. We believe that in the realm of leadership (and in every other realm), the individual *does* matter.

Notes

[1] P. Slater and W. G. Bennis, "Democracy Is Inevitable," *Harvard Business Review,* Sept–Oct, 1990, 170, 171. For a summary of trait theories, see R. M. Stogdill's *Handbook of Leadership* (New York: Free Press, 1974). For reviews and studies of leadership traits, see R. E. Boyatzis, *The Competent Manager* (New York: Wiley & Sons, 1982); C. J. Cox and C. L. Cooper, *High Flyers: An Anatomy of Managerial Success* (Oxford: Basil Blackwell); G. A. Yukl, *Leadership in Organizations* (Englewood Cliffs, NJ: Prentice Hall, 1989), Chapter 9.

[2] R. M. Stogdill, "Personal Factors Associated with Leadership: A Survey of the Literature," *Journal of Psychology,* 1948, 25, 64.

[3] See the following sources for evidence and further information concerning each trait: 1) drive: B. M. Bass's *Handbook of Leadership* (New York: The Free Press, 1990); K. G. Smith and J. K. Harrison, "In Search of Excellent Leaders" (in W. D. Guth's *The Handbook of Strategy,* New York: War-

ren, Gorham, & Lamont, 1986). 2) desire to lead: V. J. Bentz, "The Sears Experience in the Investigation, Description, and Prediction of Executive Behavior" in F. R. Wickert and D. E. McFarland's *Measuring Executive Effectiveness* (New York: Appleton-Century-Crofts, 1967); J. B. Miner, "Twenty Years of Research on Role-Motivation Theory of Managerial Effectiveness," *Personnel Psychology,* 1978, 31, 739–760. 3) honesty/integrity: Bass, op. cit.; W. G. Bennis and B. Nanus, *Leaders: The Strategies for Taking Charge* (New York: Harper & Row, 1985); J. M. Kouzes and B. Z. Posner, *The Leadership Challenge: How to Get Things Done in Organizations* (San Francisco: Jossey-Bass); T. Peters, *Thriving on Chaos* (New York: Harper & Row, 1987); A. Rand, *For the New Intellectual* (New York: Signet, 1961). 4) self-confidence: Bass, op cit. and A. Bandura, *Social Foundations of Thought and Action: A Social Cognitive Theory* (Englewood Cliffs, NJ: Prentice-Hall). Psychological hardiness is discussed by S. R. Maddi and S. C. Kobasa, *The Hardy Executive: Health under Stress* (Chicago: Dorsey Professional Books, 1984); M. W. McCall Jr. and M. M. Lombardo, *Off the Track: Why and How Successful Executives get Derailed* (Technical Report No. 21, Greensboro, NC: Center for Creative Leadership, 1983). 5) cognitive ability: R. G. Lord, C. L. DeVader, and G. M. Alliger, "A Meta-analysis of the Relation Between Personality Traits and Leadership Perceptions: An Application of Validity Generalization Procedures," *Journal of Applied Psychology,* 1986; *61,* 402–410; A. Howard and D. W. Bray, *Managerial Lives in Transition: Advancing Age and Changing Times* (New York: Guilford Press, 1988). 6) Knowledge of the business: Bennis and Nanus, op. cit.; J. P. Kotter, *The General Managers* (New York: MacMillan); Smith and Harrison, op. cit.

4 From J. J. Gabarro, *The Dynamics of Taking Charge* (Boston: Harvard Business School Press, 1987).

5 All PepsiCo references are from B. Dumaine, "Those highflying managers at PepsiCo," *Fortune,* April 10, 1989, 78–86. The Watson quote is from Smith and Harrison, op. cit., as are the Disney and Woolman quotes in the following paragraph.

6 The four quotes are from Howard and Bray, op. cit.

7 From Kouzes and Posner, op. cit., pp. 122 and V. J. Bentz, op. cit. The Sam Walton quote is from J. Huey, "Wal-Mart: Will it take over the world?" *Fortune,* January 30, 1989, 52–59.

8 From Bass, op. cit.

9 The Walton quote is from Huey, op. cit., and the Kroc quote is from Smith and Harrison, op. cit. The quote on Kroc's wall is taken from Bennis and Nanus, op. cit.

10 From Boyatzis, op. cit. Also, Kouzes and Posner, op. cit. stress the importance of leader initiative.

11 From Bentz, op. cit.

12 From Howard and Bray, op. cit.

13 The distinction between personalized and socialized power motive is made by D. C. McClelland, "N-achievement and entrepreneurship: A longitudinal study," *Journal of Personality and Social Psychology,* 1965, 1, 389–392. These two power motives are discussed further by Kouzes and Posner, op. cit.

14 From McCall and Lombardo, op. cit.

15 From Gabarro, op. cit.

16 K. F. Girard examines Manor Care in "To the Manor Born," *Warfield's,* March, 1989, 68–75.

17 From K. Labich, "The Seven Keys to Business Leadership," *Fortune,* October 24, 1988, 58–66.

18 From Lord, DeVader, and Alliger, op cit.

19 For research on charisma, see Bass, op. cit. and R. J. House, W. D. Spangler, and J. Woycke, "Personality and charisma in the U.S. presidency: A psychological theory of leadership effectiveness" (Wharton School, University of Pennsylvania, 1989, unpublished manuscript); on creativity/originality, see Howard and Bray, op. cit. and A. Zaleznik, *The Managerial Mystique* (New York: Harper and Row, 1989); on flexibility, see Smith and Harrison, op. cit.

20 From Bennis and Nanus, op. cit.

21 From J. A. Conger, *Charismatic Leadership* (San Francisco: Jossey-Bass, 1988).

22 C. Manz and H. P. Sims, *Superleadership* (New York: Prentice Hall, 1989).

23 See E. A. Locke and G. P. Latham, *A Theory of Goal Setting & Task Performance* (Englewood Cliffs, NJ: Prentice Hall, 1990).

24 See Bandura, op. cit.

25 See D. C. Hambrick, "The top management team: Keys to strategic success," *California Management Review,* 1987, 30, 1–20.

11

The Leadership Mystique

Manfred F. R. Kets de Vries

Why Follow the Leader?

What do leaders really do? What makes people follow leaders? Why are certain types of leaders more effective than others? Do effective leaders have certain characteristics in common?

Although effective leadership strongly depends on a complex pattern of interaction among leader, follower, and situation, in general successful leaders fulfill two roles. One can be called the *charismatic* role, the other the more *instrumental* role. The first role encompasses the way in which leaders *envision, empower,* and *energize* in order to motivate their followers. At the same time, every effective leader has to fulfill the *instrumental* role and be an *organizational designer,* and *control* and *reward* behavior appropriately.

Coming back to the first dimension of the charismatic role, we all know that a primary part of the leadership role is to determine where a company needs to go and to build commitment to go in that direction. There can be no leadership without vision. Hopefully, everyone who comes within the leader's sphere of influence will align themselves behind this vision. It represents the leader's core values and beliefs, and enables him or her to define the guiding philosophy of the organization: the mission.

Furthermore, in order to arrive at some kind of vision, leaders need to have the knack of perceiving salient trends in the environment. They must be able to process many different kinds of information, and use their perceptions as a basis for judging the direction in which environmental forces are going. And in studying leaders closely, it becomes clear that they are much better than other people at *managing cognitive complexity.* They are good at searching out and structuring the kind of information they need; their strength lies in making sense of an increasingly complex environment and then in using the

Reprinted with permission of Academy of Management (NY) from *Academy of Management Executive*, Vol. 8, No. 3 (September 1994), pp. 73–88. Copyright ©1994 Academy of Management (NY).

data obtained in problem solving. This talent manifests itself in their knack for simplification, of making highly complex issues very palatable. Carlo De Benedetti of Olivetti, and Percy Barnevik of ABB, are examples of individuals who have used this talent to good effect.

Moreover, if people are to be motivated, if they are to commit themselves to the prevalent vision, the mission statement derived from the vision also needs to be inspirational. To talk merely about increasing the shareholders' wealth, or to stress the company's style ("We want to be fast followers"), is not good enough. It is much more effective to find a niche in the market where one can be the best and say so. The mission statement should be simple, yet it should stretch the minds of all the company's executives.

People in the political arena are particularly good at developing visions and they often excel at articulating them. Such people are inspirational because, when there is dissatisfaction with the existing status quo, they recognize it, are able to present an acceptable alternative, and rally others around them to make it happen. For example, Mahatma Gandhi had a vision of an independent India where Moslems and Hindus would live together in peace. Martin Luther King had a vision of harmony between blacks and whites. John F. Kennedy, when he was president, had a very specific vision of wanting a man on the moon by the end of the sixties. Gorbachev had a vision of a more open Soviet society. Then there were the darker visions of Adolf Hitler's thousand year Reich. In the domain of business, we find Ingmar Kamprad of IKEA who wanted to make affordable furniture for the common man, while Mads Øvlisen, the president of the Danish pharmaceutical company NovoNordisk, emphasizes his company's desire to improve human life by preventing and treating diseases.

It also helps to have an enemy to focus on while enacting a mission. Doing so gets the competitive juices flowing. Moreover, it provides a focus, concentrating the mind. "Enemies" help in shaping the organizational identity. And successful companies watch their competitors very closely. They want to know everything about a competitor so that they can build a base of attack. Think about the Pepsi- and Coca-Cola wars. Remember Nike, Adidas, and Reebok? Compaq and Dell seem to take pleasure out of destroying each other in their advertisements. And what about Honda, which once used the slogan: "We will crush, squash, and slaughter Yamaha." If something like that doesn't get you going, nothing will! Another factor that differentiates leaders from ordinary mortals is their ability to get people involved. They know how to take advantage of the Pygmalion effect in management. Effective leaders are very good at building alliances and creating commitment so that others will share their vision. They possess great *team building skills.* They know how to get the best out of their people.

The term *empowerment* is often used in this context. Leaders make the empowerment of followers seem deceptively simple. The trick is to express high performance expectations. This shows employees that their leader has confidence in their ability to reach certain predetermined goals. Given the needed resources and a facilitating structure (the instrumental part of the leadership role), in most instances empowered employees will do their utmost to oblige. This is the obvious way to build commitment. By empowering people one enhances their self-esteem and feelings of self-confidence, often motivating them to perform beyond expectations. Catherine the Great already seemed to be familiar with the Pygmalion effect in business. Wasn't it she who said, "Praise loudly, blame softly"? And Napoleon declared that every French soldier carried a marshal's baton in his knapsack. This process of empowering may also work the other way: if you tell a person regularly that he is an idiot he may start behaving like one. Unfortunately, however, empowerment is difficult for some leaders, given their addiction to power. It is hard for them to let go and push power down in the organization. They lack the perspective to realize that by empowering their followers in a positive way, they are in fact strengthening their organization and thus their own hold on power. In the domain of the psychology of power, the desire for short-term gains tends to dominate the consideration of long-term benefits.

Truly great leaders realize, however, that envisioning without empowerment leads to a poor enactment of the vision. They recognize that the art of leadership is to create the kind of environment where people have peak experiences, where in their excitement they become completely involved in what they are doing and lose their sense of time. Here, the empowerment process plays a major role, and this should be reflected in the design of the organization. Organizational structures have to be created in which people have a sense of control, a feeling of ownership in what they are doing. As General Patton used to say: "If you tell people where to go, but not how to get there, you will be amazed at the results."

Another key word in describing successful leaders is *energizing*. In every organization there is an enormous amount of free-floating aggressive and affectionate energy. Leaders know how to channel this energy in the right direction. Well-channeled energy will positively influence the *enactment* process. One should never forget that a vision without action is a form of hallucination.

Here it is important for aggressive energy to be directed externally. People in the organization should not fight each other but fight the competition. As Jack Welch of General Electric used to say, "I don't want you to fight your neighbor at the next desk. If you are in plastics, I want you to fight Du Pont; if in electronics, I want you to fight Westinghouse."

The other part of the energy management process is to use affectionate energy appropriately. Every leader, at whatever level, is to some extent a kind of psychiatric social worker, a container of the emotions of his or her subordinates. The way he or she goes about creating this kind of holding environment distinguishes effective from ineffective leaders. Remember, the derailment of the CEO is seldom caused by his or her being insufficiently informed about the latest techniques in marketing, finance, or production, but rather by a lack of interpersonal skills, a failure to get the best out of the people who may possess this information.

In managing energy in organizations, empathy becomes critical. Interpersonal and intrapersonal sensitivity is a *sine qua non* for leaders. Closely linked to these qualities are the willingness to *trust* others and the ability to convince them that one is trustworthy. In this context, it is also essential to possess a sense of *generativity,* which basically means obtaining pleasure from helping the next generation. When leaders lack this quality and are envious of others, organizational learning will be stifled and the future of the organization will be endangered.

The envisioning, empowering, and energizing facets of the charismatic role rest on the solid foundation of the instrumental role. The elements of the instrumental role—organizational design, control and reward—have been amply described in the leadership literature and so I will not expand on them here. I do want to emphasize, however, that the combination of the charismatic role with the instrumental role can be very powerful: The charismatic part of leadership becomes more concrete and focused, and the instrumental part becomes more flexible and human.

Obviously implicit in a number of the dimensions of the two main leadership roles are characterological issues.[1] Certain aspects of character make some leaders more suitable than others to taking on these roles. The singularities in a person's cognitive, affective, and behavioral functioning affect the way a person adapts to the external environment.

Looking at the current literature on leadership traits we find that, although the quantity of this literature is overwhelming and often confusing, there is a certain amount of commonality among the findings.[2] Among the traits that have been discerned regularly among effective leaders (confirmed by my own observations) are *conscientiousness* (which includes dependability, achievement orientation and perseverance), *extroversion, dominance, self-confidence, energy, agreeableness* (meaning flexibility and sense of trust), *intelligence, openness to experience* (including a lack of ethnocentricism), and *emotional stability.* A closer look at many of these traits, however, makes it clear that each of them can be the subject of a heated polemic about its true meaning and its applicability to specific character types.[3] In addition, particularly in the clinical literature, labels such as agreeableness and emotional stability may open an enormous can of worms. It can be argued that leaders will be more or less effective depending on the specific combination of these traits. To understand these building blocks of character, we have to go to the roots of leaders' developmental histories. (For an overview of the various aspects of effective leadership mentioned in the first section of this paper see Figure 1.)

Deciphering the Roots of Leadership

Describing some of the behavioral patterns and traits that make for effective leadership is one thing, but to explain how they evolve we have to go beyond the obvious and ask deeper questions. Where does this vision and sense of mission come from? What is the source of charisma? How do these various traits develop?

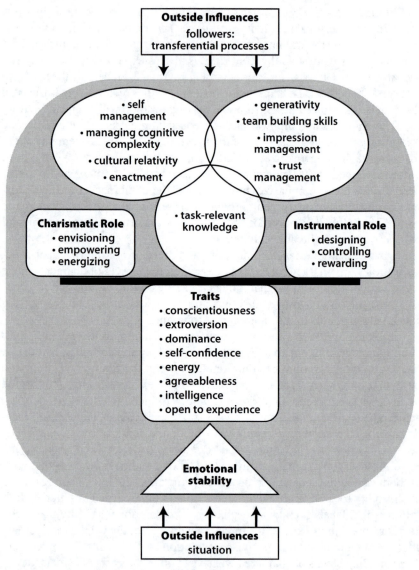

Figure 1   Leadership in a Global Context

And more pragmatically, what differentiates two powerful and visionary leaders like Jack Welch and Robert Maxwell? Why should one succeed while the other derails? How much of the credit or blame for their company's situation lies with them personally? My clinical work with executives has shown that the personality of a top executive influences the strategy, corporate culture and even structure of his or her organization to a much greater extent than most people, in particular executives themselves, are likely or willing to admit.

In organizations, people tend to seek the holy grail of the perfect business model managed by a logical, rational leader. There seems to be an obstinate survival of the myth of rationality. Many people cling to the reassuring notion that humans are logical decision makers, that irrational forces do not play a role in organizational life.

Of course there is a rational element to actions of senior executives. Leaders process large amounts of information; they look for strategic niches; they define the parameters of the corporate culture; they create the structures and set strategy. In spite of this preoccupation with rational data processing, however, even the best of leaders may be driven by motives that are less sensible and obvious than they seem. For example, was Henry Ford's introduction of the assembly line based on a rational analysis of the economic benefits of division of labor? Did he do an in-depth quantitative analysis of all the relevant economic factors? Or were there irrational elements that pushed him in that direction? Could one of his motivations for wanting to make cheap cars for farmers have been to redeem himself in the eyes of his own father, who was a farmer? Similar speculations can be made about the behavior of Walt Disney. How much had Disney's extraordinary vision to do with his own unhappiness as a child?

In the best of all worlds, a leader's vision is compatible with external forces in the environment. But in many instances that is not the case. As many of us have learned the hard way, a CEO can be completely derailed by his or her hidden motives, and not only make life miserable for his or her staff but disrupt the organization's equilibrium enough to contribute significantly to its decline. As clinical investigation shows, the reasons why leaders have a particular outlook tend to be deeply rooted. All of them are driven and influenced by a very strong, vivid inner theater—a specific script that determines a person's character. This inner theater is what drives them to externalize private motives and present them on a public stage. Consequently, transcending the model of the economic man and looking closely at the inner theater of the top executive will give us a unique perspective on the dynamics of an organization.

But how do we go about it? How do we arrive at insights about this inner theater? How do we decipher a person's character? What I have found is that putting executives on the couch (metaphorically speaking) proves to be a good way of analyzing the conflicts and motivations that occur within their organizations. It adds an additional dimension to understanding organizational dynamics.

I should explain here the basis of my clinical approach to management. The clinical paradigm, which takes concepts from psychoanalysis, dynamic psychiatry, family systems theory and cognition, rests on a number of premises. The first is that all behavior is somehow determined. What at first glance may seem completely irrational may on closer inspection have an explanation and a deeper rationale. Second, there is such a thing as the unconscious. We are not always aware of many of our wishes and fantasies; a considerable amount of our actions and behavior appears to be beyond conscious awareness. Furthermore, in order to understand behavior patterns it is important to realize that intrapsychic and interpersonal processes determine the way we act and make decisions. Patterns of behavior acquired in the past strongly influence present and future behavior.

All of us possess some kind of inner theater and are motivated by a specific inner script. Over time, through interactions with caretakers, teachers, and other influential people, this inner theater develops. The internalized core conflictual relationship themes which make up this inner theater form the core of an individual's personality and are the matrix on which behavior and actions are based.[4] Our internal theater, in which the patterns that underlie our character come into play, influences our behavior throughout our lives and plays an essential role in the molding of leaders.

Setting the Stage

Clinical observation confirms that even the most successful organizational leaders are not exactly rational, logical, sensible, and dependable human beings, but in fact are prone to irrational behavior. That being the case, the application of the clinical paradigm will be helpful in providing insight into the underlying reasons for their behavior and action. Organizations cannot perform successfully if the quirks and irrational processes that are part and parcel of the leader's inner theater are ignored. This dimension of human action needs attention if one wants to engage in preventive maintenance and successful intervention.

In my teaching and consulting work, I push executives to open the curtains of their inner theater, to find the deeper meaning behind their actions. I want them to understand that they, and sometimes their organization, get into trouble because of unconscious processes they neither see, understand nor accept. I have learned from bitter experience, however, that it is very difficult for most executives to delve into the dark corners of their own psyche. In many cases they cannot do it alone; they need help. And it can be even harder for them to understand how strongly something as personal as their inner theater can affect their company.

To facilitate the sometimes painful process of self-examination, in my MBA and executive classes I ask participants to become organizational detectives by studying well-known business leaders and their companies, to try to make sense out of their behavior and actions. Leaders such as Jack Welch, Percy Barnevik, Richard Branson, Carlo de Benedetti, and Ernest Saunders are the subjects of key case studies used in my classes. To set the investigative process in motion, I ask participants leading questions. For example, why did Henry Ford of the Ford Motor Company stick to the Model T for nineteen years in spite of changing market conditions and an enormous drop in market share? Why did he behave so strangely and erratically? When his engineers presented him with a slightly modified version of the Model T, he flew into a tantrum and kicked the car apart. Why? What made him so unwilling to change the car? What did the car symbolize to him? Why did he unleash a reign of terror in the company, employing henchmen like Harry Bennett, a person with close connections to the Detroit underworld? What lay behind his strange political activities, his isolationism and his anti-Semitism? Why did he consistently undermine his son Edsel's efforts to steer the company back on course? And what was it, despite all these quirks, that made him such a visionary? He was the first person to recognize the value of using the assembly line to make a mass-produced car at a time when consumer trends were pointing in the opposite direction. What were his anxieties, his defenses, his conflicts? What were his strengths and his weaknesses? What differentiated him from other people? What could be said about his character? What made him such an innovator?

Ford's personal history gives us insight into many of his seemingly bizarre actions. He was extremely close to his mother, whom he felt loved him unconditionally. Unfortunately, she died when Ford was thirteen. Ford's relationship with his father was very difficult. According to Ford, his father disapproved of Ford's mechanical bent, his wish to leave the farm, and his vision of the future of the automobile, although Ford's sister felt that their father was not nearly as opposed to his son's ideas as Ford led people to believe. In any case, Ford's relationships with other men were never intimate, and he had few real friends. A quotation from the man who Ford hired to run the personnel department is very revealing:

> A judge of national repute once said to me, "I have a great admiration for Henry Ford, but there is one thing about him that I regret and can't understand, and that is his inability to keep his executives and old time friends around him. The answer is that it is not a matter of inability, but disability. He can't help it. He is built that way."[5]

Observing that "he is built that way" is not enough, however. The challenge of organizational detective work is to find the underlying reasons for his peculiar leadership style; to understand better the critical dimensions that made up his inner script. To arrive at deeper insight in our discussions, theories are introduced, and inferences are made, shot down and replaced by others. And while struggling with their confusion, participants gradually arrive at a better idea of what kind of person Ford really was, the nature of his interpersonal relationships, his defensive patterns, and how his style affected the organization. They begin to realize the extent to which his behavior in the Ford Motor Company was colored by his personal history. They realize how much Ford was a prisoner of his past.[6]

Interestingly enough, class participants occasionally begin to see the symptoms of similar patterns of behavior and character traits in themselves. At times this may be frightening, but this process of recognition generally makes them think. My experience is that this process triggers self-reflection and growing insight. Fledgling and experienced consultants, entrepreneurs, investment bankers, or industrialists all profit from this new way of looking at organizational dynamics. It gives them a better idea of how to master processes like power, authority, influence, and control. It makes them realize how easily they themselves could get stuck in vicious circles and become prisoners of their own past. Furthermore, they may become aware of the kind of organizations they should avoid, realizing the extent to which certain types of organization may adversely affect them mentally or even physically.

A play like Arthur Miller's *Death of a Salesman* or films such as Orson Welles' *Citizen Kane* or Ingmar Bergman's *Wild Strawberries* can provide further insight into these elusive phenomena. The right side of the brain, the part responsible for more intuitive processes, is not exactly nurtured in the daily routine of an organization. But that is even more reason to become sensitized to what makes a person or an organization really tick.

During this process of mutual exploration, many questions come up in my classes which I cannot answer immediately and which lead to further investigation. Eventually, these deliberations lead to a kind of closure. My work with my patients has also been an important contributing factor to the understanding of executive behavior: Many of their initially puzzling remarks have helped me greatly with the process of discovery and self-discovery.

In addition, an executive seminar which I have been teaching for a number of years at INSEAD has also helped me in clarifying issues associated with leadership. This very unusual program, different from all the others I participate in, focuses on the *life* case study. Spending three intensive weeks (spread out over a period of six months) working with twenty senior executives, discussing their lives, their major concerns, their fears, and their efforts to change their lives, is an emotionally draining experience. This exercise of mutual problem solving, combined with a mirroring process in which participants are brought firmly up against the image others have of them, can be dramatically powerful. The discovery that people are not alone in facing a particular type of problem, that they are not that different from other people, can counteract frequently intense feelings of isolation and give a sense of reintegration with the human race.

Of course, helping executives understand how their behavior affects their companies is not the same as psychoanalyzing a company. What I try to do in my seminars, in consultation, and in therapy, is to bring out the underlying dynamics of an individual executive's problems—these core conflictual relationship themes or inner scripts that make up character—and look at how they affect his or her organization. I want executives to face those themes and become aware that certain problems are deeply rooted, and cannot be resolved by merely introducing a new planning system, changing appraisal and reward systems, writing up new job descriptions, or tinkering with the organization's design. I want executives to face their weaker points, obtain deeper insights about their ways of functioning, understand their defensive structure and character traits, and recognize how their behavior affects their organization. I want them to recognize the psychological pressures leaders are particularly subjected to. And I want executives to become self-confident enough to create a culture of trust and fair play in their organization, in which one doesn't kill the messenger of bad news and one allows people to engage in contrarian thinking.

Creating this kind of company culture is much more easily said than done. Neutralizing the darker side of leadership can be quite difficult. Many leaders are not up to the challenge. Many of them prefer to remain blind and deaf to what is happening around them. Executives have to look beyond the superficial, however, and realize that in organizational change and development there is no such thing as a quick fix. They need to understand the extent to which they, and ultimately their organizations, are influenced by their own inner theater; they need to realize the deeper meaning of their actions.

Psychological Pressures on Leadership

What are some of the psychological themes that emerge when talking to leaders? What preoccupies them? What are the pressures that trouble them? Dealing with their inner world, we quickly recognize that making it to a top position is not necessarily a bed of roses. Along with the perks comes a great deal of pressure. First, there is the problem of the loneliness of command. The moment one becomes top dog, old relationships are going to be disturbed. The original support network changes. Every move leaders make has a great deal of symbolism attached to it. If they have to make critical decisions about people's future, they cannot be as close to old colleagues as they once were. Whether the new leader likes it or not, some distance has to be kept. This is not always easy. After all, leaders still have their own dependency needs, and who is going to take care of them? This can cause a considerable amount of stress and frustration.

Then there is the troublesome problem of envy. Many people look at the power and trappings of leadership and become envious. To some senior executives, the envy of others can be extremely disturbing and may cause a great deal of anxiety.

There is the fear—not always unreasonable—that others will try to take away what has cost the leader so much to gain. The fear of losing the power of office, being the subject of envy, can put a debilitating strain on leaders. They become, ironically, afraid of success. Some may act accordingly and behave in a dysfunctional manner, snatching defeat out of the jaws of victory through self-destructive behavior. Others may become depressed, and seemingly paralyzed by the demands of decision making. In certain instances, clinical investigation demonstrates that this dysfunctional behavior is based on the irrational, originally unconscious, fear of surpassing parents' accomplishments. Unconsciously, the person may believe that such a victory could have terrible consequences. They fear (correctly, in some cases) that it will cause an envious parent to withdraw affection, or even provoke a hostile reaction.[7]

Another cause of depression for an executive who has finally made it to the top may be the sense of "what now?" The goals that the leader has worked for all his or her life have been accomplished; there is nothing else to strive for. One can call this sense of unease "the Faust Syndrome," the melancholia of having completed everything. Again, if these feelings are not dealt with, they may lead to irresponsible action as the individual tries to fight emerging depression.

A frequent problem is what Freud described as the phenomenon of a "false connection," meaning that followers may not perceive and respond to their leader according to the reality of the situation, but as if the leader is a significant figure from the past, such as a parent or other authoritative person.[8] This misplaced attachment, known as transference in clinical terminology, is an ubiquitous element of the human condition, a way in which we process information and organize experience. It is a strange but nevertheless a very real process: the emotional legacy of the past pushes followers into displacing many of their historic hopes and fantasies onto the present leader. A frequent result of this process of displacement of person and time is that followers will try to do anything they can to please their leader.

In many instances, this need to idealize authority figures (a universal need that is part and parcel of our early developmental processes) is likely to meet with a very receptive response, particularly from leaders with strong narcissistic dispositions. Leaders of this type welcome the outpouring of applause and admiration. Even worse, they may arrive at the stage where they cannot function without this kind of emotional fix. Of course, it is possible for this kind of mutual admiration society to create a lot of energy in the system. It can be useful in aligning and energizing subordinates in order to enact a common vision. The leader's ability to transform what were once only fantasies into reality adds to the heady experience of being on top.

However, the danger of this form of interaction is that some leaders may find themselves in a hall of mirrors, only hearing and seeing what they *want* to hear or see. And, even worse, if people do not oblige—if followers are unwilling to share these leaders' distorted view of the world—they may throw an adult version of a tantrum, re-enacting patterns of childhood behavior. Such leaders will perceive non-compliance as a direct attack on the very essence of their personality, given their fragile sense of self-esteem. Past feelings of helplessness and humiliation may be revived, leading to blind rage. However, this time, given the power they wield, their tantrums make a great difference. The impact of their rage on their immediate environment can be devastating.

Predictably, such outbursts of rage will intimidate people and can lead to regressive, childlike behavior and a climate of dependency among followers. The dynamics of such leaders' lives are very simple: People are either for them or against them in a world of black and white. There is no room for nuances. Independent thinkers cannot survive; those who do not collaborate immediately become the new villains; deviants from these leaders' ideals are assigned an inferior, sub-human status and are targets for their anger.

Most people quickly fall in line and collude, either passively or actively, with the leader's victimization of those who are not prepared to conform.

This is self-protective in two ways. First of all, it limits the possibility that one will become a victim of the leader oneself. Secondly, "identifying with the aggressor" is a way of resolving one's sense of helplessness and powerlessness in the face of totalitarianism. Feeling close to the leader—becoming part of the system—creates the illusion of being more powerful oneself.[9]

Thus the individual, in this special form of identification with the aggressor (which does not necessarily happen on a conscious level), assumes the latter's attributes and thus transforms himself or herself from threatened to threatening. It is basically a defensive maneuver, a way of controlling the severe anxiety caused by the perceived aggressor. The person in the one-down position hopes to acquire some of the power that the other person possesses. The wish to obtain some of the dominant person's power can explain why people hang in there, in spite of the abrasive behavior of the aggressor. For example, this process may explain to some extent the kind of group dynamics which prevailed in the companies run by the late Robert Maxwell.

This process of "identification with the aggressor," the inducement to participate in a form of group think, is accompanied by certain rites of passage, the least subtle of which is the pressure to participate in the violence directed towards the aggressor's designated enemies. Sharing the guilt in this way becomes a sign of commitment which the leader can feed with an endless supply of people to be made into villains. The majority of followers, torn between love and fear of their leader, will submit to the demands put upon them. They are presented with many handy scapegoats on which to enact group revenge when things do not go the way the leader wants—tangible entities on which to project everything of which they are afraid, everything that is perceived as evil and threatening to the system. This kind of development can have terrifying results. It can lead to the complete self-destruction of an organization or, in the case of a national leader, the end of an entire nation.

These negative personality traits are present to a lesser degree in many individuals, but as far as leaders are concerned, the pressure of their exposed position can encourage extreme manifestations of their emotional disability. The question is how do these traits develop, and why are some leaders more affected than others?

The Inner Theater of Leaders

The shaping of an individual's personality begins early in life. Child psychologists have pointed out that the first three years of life are particularly critical to development. These are the years during which the core patterns of personality are shaped; it is the period when we emerge as a person with a sense of our own body, gender identity, name, mind, and personal history. The foundations are laid for the kind of person we are going to be, and are likely to remain, for the rest of our life. Of course, this does not mean that later life experiences are of no importance, but these tend not to have the same impact as the ones we encounter early in life.

The clinical term for the changes that take place during these early years of life is narcissistic development. Narcissism is the engine that drives people. And narcissism and leadership are intricately connected.

A healthy dose of narcissism is essential for human functioning. It is the danger of excess, particularly in the case of leaders, which gives narcissism its often derogatory connotation. We may be amused by Oscar Wilde's statement that "to love oneself is the beginning of a life-long romance," but when we consider how the word is generally used, narcissism evokes associations of egotism, self-centeredness, and exaggerated self-love. After all, who wants to be compared to that unfortunate young man, the Narcissus of Greek myth, who fell in love with his own reflection and pined to death?

Narcissism is a strange thing, a double-edged sword. Having either too much or too little of it can throw a person off balance, and when that equilibrium is lost, instability may develop in the core of an individual's personality. We must remember that narcissistic elements help constitute the basis of self-esteem and identity.

Narcissism (when we go beyond the everyday usage of the word) refers to a stage of infantile development we all have to pass through, a stage during which the growing child derives pleasure from his own body and its functions. And this early stage is a very delicate time in the child's life. The kind of treatment received during this critical period of development will very much color his or her view of the world right through to adulthood.

The role of parents or caretakers in the development of narcissism is obviously very important. Have they been supportive or inconsistent? Have family circumstances meant that the child has experienced a series of deprivations? The key question is whether the child received a large enough narcissistic supply. Was a solid foundation laid for positive self-regard and initiative in establishing stable relationships? Did the child have the opportunity to acquire a healthy dose of self-esteem? Unfortunately, of course, no parent is perfect. Becoming a person is not at all like that comfortable period of intra-uterine existence when everything was automatically taken care of. In most instances, growing up implies a certain amount of inevitable frustration. For normal development, however, frustration should occur in tolerable doses.

In an attempt to deal with this sense of frustration, the child tries to retain the original impression of the perfection and bliss of her or his early years by creating both a grandiose, exhibitionistic image of his or her self and an all-powerful, idealized image of her or his parents (the latter taking on the roles of saviors and protectors). Psychoanalysts call these two narcissistic configurations the "grandiose self" and the "idealized parent image."[10] Over time, if the child receives what we call "good enough" care, these two configurations which make up the bipolar self will be tamed by the forces of reality. Parents, siblings and other important figures in the child's life will modify his or her exhibitionistic displays, channeling grandiose fantasies of power and glory in proper directions, thus laying the foundation for realistic ambitions, stable values, well-defined career interests, and a secure sense of self-esteem and identity.

But not everyone is lucky enough to have a special bond, or to receive age-appropriate frustration. Many things can go wrong in the process of growing up. In some situations, prolonged disappointment due to parental overstimulation, understimulation, or highly inconsistent, arbitrary behavior can lead to problems of a narcissistic nature. And if violence and abuse are part and parcel of the package, the stage is set for an inner theater complete with malevolent imagery.

The cartoonist Matt Groening once drew an illuminating but very disturbing cartoon. In the drawing is an extremely unhappy, monstrous-looking little child who has been tied up and locked in a cell. Two pairs of eyes are looking through the cell-door windows, and the caption reads, "I hope you realize you're breaking our hearts." This cartoon, which portrays the alarmingly mixed signals given by some parents, is a good illustration of the kind of childrearing which contributes to one's not becoming a healthy individual.

Children who have been exposed to these types of parenting may come to believe that they cannot reliably depend on anyone's love or loyalty. As adults, they will act according to these convictions. These are people who, despite their claims to self-sufficiency, are troubled in the depth of their being by a sense of deprivation, anger and emptiness. In order to cope with these feelings, and perhaps as a cover for their insecurity, their narcissistic needs will turn into obsessions. Such individuals become fixated on issues of power, beauty, status, prestige, and superiority. They try continually to maneuver others into strengthening their shaky sense of self-esteem. They are also preoccupied with thoughts of getting even for the hurts (real or imagined) they experienced during childhood. And in the case of public figures, these scenes may be acted out on a world stage later in life.

Reactive and Constructive Narcissism

From many in-depth studies of leaders I have concluded that a considerable percentage of them have become what they are for negative reasons. On many occasions I have found that, due to hardships encountered in childhood, they are driven to prove the world wrong. After having been belittled and maltreated when young, they are determined to show everyone that they amount to something as adults. Some may even suffer from what may be called (after Alexander Dumas's novel) the "Monte Cristo Complex": they have a very strong need to get even for the wrongs done to them at earlier periods in their lives.

Pierre Cardin, the French couturier, may be an example of the "Monte Cristo Complex." Growing up as an Italian youngster in France, Cardin was teased by other children and called names like "macaroni," all of which hurt. Second-class status is not easy to take. Cardin's family had lost most of their possessions during the war, and this had affected his father very badly.[11] As a result his father drifted from job to job, adding to the sense of upheaval in the family. The young Cardin was kept going, in spite of all the turmoil around him, by the strong support of his mother. (This brings to mind Freud's famous statement that the child who has been the "mother's undisputed darling [will] retain throughout life the triumphant feeling, the confidence in success, which not seldom brings actual success with it.") We can speculate, however, that this whole experience left Cardin with a sense of having to get back at his tormentors, to show them that he amounted to something, to become the redeemer of the family. And he certainly did. Perhaps because once people had looked down at him and his family, he became a specialist in leveling. He democratized fashion and brought *haute couture* to the common man. At present, sales under his name amount to over a billion dollars. Almost two hundred thousand people work for his label through more than 840 licensing arrangements in 125 countries. He has put his name on everything. He even thumbed his nose at the French upper classes by buying the famous restaurant Maxim, once their favorite watering hole. But no longer: Maxim has been democratized. You can now eat there with salesmen from Cleveland!

Pierre Cardin's example illustrates that it is entirely possible for a person with a narcissistic disposition to be very successful. In some of my earlier writings, I made a distinction between people guided by this kind of reactive narcissism driven by a need to get even and to somehow come to grips with their past, and a type of constructive narcissism (individuals who are well-balanced, have a positive self-regard, and a secure sense of self-esteem).[12] Thus, to summarize these two ways of dealing with the world, constructive narcissists have the capacity for introspection; they radiate a sense of positive vitality and are capable of empathic feelings. Narcissists of this type can become the kind of excellent leader that I described at the beginning of this article. This contrasts with the reactive narcissists, who are continually trying to boost a defective sense of self-esteem and are preoccupied with emotions such as envy, spite, revenge, or vindictive triumph over others. (Some reactive narcissists, however, eventually overcome their original feelings of bitterness and are motivated by reparation; that is, trying to prevent others from suffering as they have.)

True reactive narcissists tend to have a grandiose sense of self-importance. They habitually take advantage of others in order to achieve their own ends. They also live under the illusion that their problems are unique. Then there is a sense of entitlement, the feeling that they deserve especially favorable treatment and that the rules set for others do not apply to them. Furthermore, they are addicted to compliments—they can never get enough. They lack empathy, being unable to experience how others feel. Last, but certainly not least, their envy of others, and their rage when prevented from getting their own way, can be formidable.[13]

Reactive narcissism is probably the most salient indicator of defective leadership. It is at the center of a host of characterological problems such as paranoid, schizoid, passive-aggressive, histrionic, and compulsive behavior patterns or "neurotic styles."[14] What is already bad enough in an individual can, in an organizational context, lead to serious repercussions. The observation of senior executives shows that parallels can be drawn between individual pathology—excessive use of one neurotic style, such as reactive narcissism—and organizational pathology, the latter resulting in poorly functioning organizations, or what I have called elsewhere "neurotic" organizations.[15] In these earlier writings, I illustrate how the "irrational" personality characteristics of principal decision makers can seriously affect the overall management process. At the head of a "neurotic" organization (especially one in which power is highly centralized) one is likely to find a top executive whose rigid neurotic style is strongly mirrored in the nature of inappropriate strategies, structures, and organizational cultures of his or her firm. If this situation continues for too long, the organization may self-destruct. A comparison of the most recent *Fortune* 500 list with the same list of twenty years ago is very revealing. A large number of the firms listed in the early 1970s are no longer in existence.

In classifying these various neurotic types, I have made a distinction among the dramatic, suspicious, compulsive, detached, and depressive organization, each with its unique, salient features.[16] For a description of how—among these various neurotic types—inner scripts, personal styles, organizational types, culture, and strategy interrelate, see the summary in Exhibit 1.

Struggling with the Demon

For leaders who are caught up in a web of irrationality at the head of a neurotic organization, escape is not easy. In most cases, they cannot break out of their self-constructed prison alone. They are the captives of their character and they will need some kind of professional help to break the chains that restrict their behavior and lead to dysfunctional organizations. Leaders must recognize the potential destructiveness of their actions, and understand the extent to which past experiences can influence their present and future behavior. In talking to leaders, however, I am often struck by the number of them who fail to realize the continuity in their past, present and future. These people make the same mistakes over and over again because they are unable to recognize certain repetitive patterns in their behavior which have become dysfunctional. They are stuck in a vicious circle, and do not know how to get out. It makes one realize that mental health really comes down to having choices in life. The Danish philosopher Kierkegaard expressed the sadness and poignancy of this when he said that the tragedy of life is that we can only understand it backwards, but we have to live it forwards.

Freud once told the novelist Stefan Zweig that all his life he had been "struggling with the demon"—the demon of irrationality. Wise leaders do the same. They realize the extent to which unconscious, irrational processes affect their behavior. They recognize the limits of rationality and become more aware of their own character traits. Leaders who fail to take their irrational side into account, however, are like captains who blindly plow their ships into a field of icebergs; the greatest danger is hidden below the surface.

Exhibit 1   The Characteristics of "Neurotic" Organizations

Type	Organization	Executive	Culture	Strategy	Guiding Theme
Dramatic	Too primitive for its many products and broad market; overcentralization obstructs the development of effective information systems; second tier executives retain too little influence in policy making	Needs attention, excitement, activity, and stimulation; feels a sense of entitlement, has a tendency toward extremes	Dependency needs of subordinates complement "strong leader" tendencies of chief executive; leader is idealized by "mirroring" subordinates; leader is catalyst for subordinates' initiative and morale	Hyperactive, impulsive, venturesome, dangerously uninhibited; executive prerogative to initiate bold ventures; diversifications and growth rarely consistent or integrated; action for action's sake; nonparticipative decision making	Grandiosity: "I want to get attention from and impress the people who count in my life."
Suspicious	Elaborate information processing; abundant analysis of external trends; centralization of power	Vigilantly prepared to counter any and all attacks and personal threats; hypersensitive; cold and lacks emotional expression; suspicious, distrustful, and insists on loyalty; overinvolved in rules and details to secure complete control; craves information; sometimes vindictive	"Fight-or-flight" culture, including dependency, fear of attack, emphasis on the power of information, intimidation, uniformity, lack of trust	Reactive, conservative; overly analytical; diversified; secretive	"Some menacing force is out to get me; I had better be on my guard. I cannot really trust anybody."

Detached	Internal focus, insufficient scanning of external environment, self-imposed barriers to free flow of information	Withdrawn and not involved; lacks interest in present or future; sometimes indifferent to praise or criticism	Lack of warmth or emotions; conflicts, jockeying for power; insecurity	Vacillating, indecisive, inconsistent; the product of narrow, parochial perspectives	"Reality does not offer satisfaction; interactions with others will fail; it is safer to remain distant."
Depressive	Ritualistic; bureaucratic; inflexible; hierarchical; poor internal communications; resistant to change; impersonal	Lacks self-confidence, self-esteem, or initiative; fears success and tolerates mediocrity or failure; depends on messiahs	Lack of initiative; passivity; negativity; lack of motivation; ignorance of markets; leadership vacuum	"Decidiphobia;" attention focused inward; lack of vigilance over changing market conditions; drifting with no sense of direction; confinement to antiquated "mature" markets	"It is hopeless to change the course of events; I am just not good enough."
Compulsive	Rigid formal codes; elaborate information systems; ritualized evaluation procedures; thoroughness; exactness; a hierarchy in which individual managers' status derives directly from specific positions	Tends to dominate organization from top to bottom; insists that others conform to tightly prescribed procedures and rules; dogmatic or obstinate personality; perfectionist or is obsessed with detail, routine, rituals, efficiency, and lockstep organization	Rigid, inward directed, insular; subordinates are submissive, uncreative, insecure	Tightly calculated and focused, exhaustive evaluation; slow, unadaptive; reliance on a narrow established theme; obsession with a single aspect of strategy; e.g., cost-cutting or quality, the exclusion of other factors	"I don't want to be at the mercy of events; I have to master and control all the things affecting me."

Whatever happens to leaders, however enlightened they may be, it is important that they keep a check on their narcissism. The hubris of leaders is all too familiar, and narcissism and hubris go hand in hand. Glory is a great temptress and the pursuit of glory can be surprisingly self-destructive. All too often, insufficient heed is paid to its dangers. For leaders, the narcissistic pull is frequently too strong. As Napoleon (an expert on the topic) once said: "Glory is fleeting but obscurity lasts forever." In pursuing glory, many leaders end up as victims of hubris. Such an ending could be avoided, however, if they paid attention to their intrapsychic life, and found help in exploring their blind spots.

In their interpersonal relationships, leaders who are wary of the dangers of hubris should bear in mind what I term the three H's of leadership: humility, humanity, and a good sense of humor. Such qualities help to prevent excessive organizational neurosis, and may contribute to emotional stability. As someone who obviously had some knowledge of leadership once said to me, "Any time you think you possess power as a leader, try ordering around someone else's dog!"

Notes

[1] Manfred Kets de Vries and Sidney Perzow, *Handbook of Character Studies* (Madison, CT: International Universities Press, 1991).

[2] Bass, op. cit.; Murray R. Barrick and Michael K. Mount, "The Big Five Personality Dimensions and Job Performance: A Meta-Analysis," *Personnel Psychology* 44, 1991, 1–26.

[3] Theodore Millon, *Disorders of Personality* (New York: John Wiley and Sons, 1981).

[4] Lester Luborsky, Paul Crits-Christoph, Jim Minz, and Arthur Auerbach, *Who Will Benefit from Psychotherapy?* (New York: Basic Books, 1988).

[5] Samuel S. Marquis, *Henry Ford: An Interpretation* (Boston: Little, Brown, 1923).

[6] Anne Jardim, *Henry Ford and the Ford Motor Company* (Cambridge: MIT Press, 1969).

[7] Manfred F. R. Kets de Vries, *Leaders, Fools and Impostors* (San Francisco: Jossey-Bass, 1993).

[8] Josef Breuer and Sigmund Freud, "Studies on Hysteria," *The Standard Edition of the Complete Psychological Works of Sigmund Freud, Vol II,* transl. and ed. James Strachey (London: The Hogarth Press and The Institute of Psychoanalysis, 1955).

[9] Anna Freud, *The Ego and the Mechanisms of Defense* (New York: International Universities Press, 1936).

[10] "Heinz Kohut, *The Analysis of the Self* (Madison, CT: International Universities Press, 1971); Heinz Kohut and Ernest S. Wolf, "The Disorders of the Self and their Treatment: An Outline," *International Journal of Psychoanalysis*, 58, 1978, 413–426.

[11] Richard Morais, *Pierre Cardin: The Man Who Became a Label* (New York: Bantam Press, 1991).

[12] Manfred F. R. Kets de Vries and Danny Miller, "Narcissism and Leadership: An Object Relations Perspective," *Human Relations*, 38(6), 1985, 583–601; M. F. R. Kets de Vries, *Prisoners of Leadership* (New York: Wiley, 1989); Kets de Vries, 1993, op.cit.

[13] Otto Kernberg, *Borderline Conditions and Pathological Narcissism* (New York: Jason Aronson, 1975).

[14] Kets de Vries and Perzow, *op. cit.*

[15] Manfred F. R. Kets de Vries and Danny Miller, *The Neurotic Organization* (San Francisco: Jossey-Bass, 1984).

[16] Manfred F. R. Kets de Vries and Danny Miller, *Unstable at the Top* (New York: New American Library Penguin, 1987).

12

Emotional Intelligence and Leadership

Daniel Goleman

Every businessperson knows a story about a highly intelligent, highly skilled executive who was promoted into a leadership position only to fail at the job. And they also know a story about someone with solid—but not extraordinary—intellectual abilities and technical skills who was promoted into a similar position and then soared.

Such anecdotes support the widespread belief that identifying individuals with the "right stuff" to be leaders is more art than science. After all, the personal styles of superb leaders vary: Some leaders are subdued and analytical; others shout their manifestos from the mountaintops. And just as important, different situations call for different types of leadership. Most mergers need a sensitive negotiator at the helm, whereas many turnarounds require a more forceful authority.

I have found, however, that the most effective leaders are alike in one crucial way: They all have a high degree of what has come to be known as *emotional intelligence.* It's not that IQ and technical skills are irrelevant. They do matter, but mainly as "threshold capabilities"; that is, they are the entry-level requirements for executive positions. But my research, along with other recent studies, clearly shows that emotional intelligence is the sine qua non of leadership. Without it, a person can have the best training in the world, an incisive, analytical mind, and an endless supply of smart ideas, but he still won't make a great leader.

In the course of the past year, my colleagues and I have focused on how emotional intelligence operates at work. We have examined the relationship between emotional intelligence and effective performance, especially in leaders. And we have observed how emotional intelligence shows itself on the job.

How can you tell if someone has high emotional intelligence, for example, and how can you recognize it in yourself? In the following pages, we'll explore these questions, taking each of the components of emotional intelligence—self-awareness, self-regulation, motivation, empathy, and social skill—in turn.

Evaluating Emotional Intelligence

Most large companies today have employed trained psychologists to develop what are known as "competency models" to aid them in identifying, training, and promoting likely stars in the leadership firmament. The psychologists have also developed such models for lower-level positions. And in recent years, I have analyzed competency models from 188 companies, most of which were large and global and included the likes of Lucent Technologies, British Airways, and Credit Suisse.

In carrying out this work, my objective was to determine which personal capabilities drove outstanding performance within these organizations, and to what degree they did so. I grouped capabilities into three categories: purely technical skills like accounting and business planning; cognitive abilities like analytical reasoning; and competencies demonstrating emotional intelligence, such as the ability to work with others and effectiveness in leading change.

To create some of the competency models, psychologists asked senior managers at the companies to identify the capabilities that typified the organization's most outstanding leaders. To create other models, the psychologists used objective criteria, such as a division's profitability, to differentiate the star performers at senior levels within their organizations from the average ones. Those individuals were then extensively interviewed and tested, and their capabilities were compared. This process resulted in the creation of lists of ingredients for highly effective leaders. The lists ranged in length from seven to 15 items and included such ingredients as initiative and strategic vision.

When I analyzed all this data, I found dramatic results. To be sure, intellect was a driver of outstanding performance. Cognitive skills such as big-picture thinking and long-term vision were particularly important. But when I calculated the ratio of technical skills, IQ, and emotional intelligence as ingredients of excellent performance, emotional intelligence proved to be twice as important as the others for jobs at all levels.

Moreover, my analysis showed that emotional intelligence played an increasingly important role at the highest levels of the company, where differences in technical skills are of negligible importance. In other words, the higher the rank of a person considered to be a star performer, the more emotional intelligence capabilities showed up as the reason for his or her effectiveness. When I compared star performers with average ones in senior leadership positions, nearly 90% of the difference in their profiles was attributable to emotional intelligence factors rather than cognitive abilities.

Other researchers have confirmed that emotional intelligence not only distinguishes outstanding leaders but can also be linked to strong performance. The findings of the late David McClelland, the renowned researcher in human and organizational behavior, are a good example. In a 1996 study of a global food and beverage company, McClelland found that when senior managers had a critical mass of emotional intelligence capabilities, their divisions outperformed yearly earnings goals by 20%. Meanwhile, division leaders without that critical mass underperformed by almost the same amount. McClelland's findings, interestingly, held as true in the company's U.S. divisions as in its divisions in Asia and Europe.

In short, the numbers are beginning to tell us a persuasive story about the link between a company's success and the emotional intelligence of its leaders. And just as important, research is also demonstrating that people can, if they take the right approach, develop their emotional intelligence. (See the sidebar "Can Emotional Intelligence Be Learned?")

Self-Awareness

Self-awareness is the first component of emotional intelligence—which makes sense when one considers that the Delphic oracle gave the advice to "know thyself" thousands of years ago. Self-awareness means having a deep understanding of one's emotions, strengths, weaknesses, needs, and drives. People with strong self-awareness are neither overly critical nor unrealistically hopeful. Rather, they are honest—with themselves and with others.

People who have a high degree of self-awareness recognize how their feelings affect them, other people, and their job performance. Thus, a self-aware person who knows that tight deadlines bring out the worst in him plans his time carefully and gets his work done well in advance. Another person with high self-awareness will be able to work with a demanding client. She will understand the client's impact on her moods and the deeper reasons for her frustration. "Their trivial demands take us away from the real work that needs to be done," she might explain. And she will go one step further and turn her anger into something constructive.

Self-awareness extends to a person's understanding of his or her values and goals. Someone who is highly self-aware knows where he is headed and why; so, for example, he will be able to be firm in turning down a job offer that is tempting financially but does not fit with his principles or long-term goals. A person who lacks self-awareness is apt to make decisions that bring on inner turmoil by treading on buried values. "The money looked good so I signed on," someone might say two years into a job, "but the work means so little to me that I'm constantly bored." The decisions of self-aware people mesh with their values; consequently, they often find work to be energizing.

How can one recognize self-awareness? First and foremost, it shows itself as candor and an ability to assess oneself realistically. People with high self-awareness are able to speak accurately and openly—although not necessarily effusively or confessionally—about their emotions and the impact they have on their work. For instance, one manager I know of was skeptical about a new personal-shopper service that her company, a major department-store chain, was about to introduce. Without prompting from her team or her boss, she offered them an explanation: "It's hard for me to get behind the rollout of this service," she admitted, "because I really wanted to run the project, but I wasn't selected. Bear with me while I deal with that." The manager did indeed examine her feelings; a week later, she was supporting the project fully.

Such self-knowledge often shows itself in the hiring process. Ask a candidate to describe a time he got carried away by his feelings and did something he later regretted. Self-aware candidates will be frank in admitting to failure—and will often tell their tales with a smile. One of the hallmarks of self-awareness is a self-deprecating sense of humor.

Self-awareness can also be identified during performance reviews. Self-aware people know—and are comfortable talking about—their limitations and strengths, and they often demonstrate a thirst for constructive criticism. By contrast, people with low self-awareness interpret the message that they need to improve as a threat or a sign of failure.

Self-aware people can also be recognized by their self-confidence. They have a firm grasp of their capabilities and are less likely to set themselves up to fail by, for example, overstretching on assignments. They know, too, when to ask for help. And the risks they take on the job are calculated. They won't ask for a challenge that they know they can't handle alone. They'll play to their strengths.

Consider the actions of a midlevel employee who was invited to sit in on a strategy meeting with her company's top executives. Although she was the most junior person in the room, she did not sit there quietly, listening in awe-struck or fearful silence. She knew she had a head for clear logic and the skill to present ideas persuasively, and she offered cogent suggestions about the company's strategy. At the same time, her self-awareness stopped her from wandering into territory where she knew she was weak.

Despite the value of having self-aware people in the workplace, my research indicates that senior executives don't often give self-awareness the credit it deserves when they look for potential leaders. Many executives mistake candor about feelings for "wimpiness" and fail to give due respect to employees who openly acknowledge their shortcomings. Such people are too readily dismissed as "not tough enough" to lead others.

In fact, the opposite is true. In the first place, people generally admire and respect candor. Furthermore, leaders are constantly required to make judgment calls that require a candid assessment of capabilities—their own and those of others. Do we have the management expertise to acquire a competitor? Can we launch a new product within six months? People who assess themselves honestly—that is, self-aware people—are well suited to do the same for the organizations they run.

Self-Regulation

Biological impulses drive our emotions. We cannot do away with them—but we can do much to manage them. Self-regulation, which is like an ongoing inner conversation, is the component of emotional intelligence that frees us from being prisoners of our feelings. People engaged in such a conversation feel bad moods and emotional impulses just as everyone else does, but they find ways to control them and even to channel them in useful ways.

Imagine an executive who has just watched a team of his employees present a botched analysis to the company's board of directors. In the gloom that follows, the executive might find himself tempted to pound on the table in anger or kick over a chair. He could leap up and scream at the group. Or he might maintain a grim silence, glaring at everyone before stalking off.

But if he had a gift for self-regulation, he would choose a different approach. He would pick his words carefully, acknowledging the team's poor performance without rushing to any hasty judgment. He would then step back to consider the reasons for the failure. Are they personal—a lack of effort? Are there any mitigating factors? What was his role in the debacle? After considering these questions, he would call the team together, lay out the incident's consequences, and offer his feelings about it. He would then present his analysis of the problem and a well-considered solution.

Why does self-regulation matter so much for leaders? First of all, people who are in control of their feelings and impulses—that is, people who are reasonable—are able to create an environment of trust and fairness. In such an environment, politics and infighting are sharply reduced and productivity is high. Talented people flock to the organization and aren't tempted to leave. And self-regulation has a trickle-down effect. No one wants to be known as a hothead when the boss is known for her calm approach. Fewer bad moods at the top mean fewer throughout the organization.

Second, self-regulation is important for competitive reasons. Everyone knows that business today is rife with ambiguity and change. Companies merge and break apart regularly. Technology transforms work at a dizzying pace. People who have mastered their emotions are able to roll with the changes. When a new program is announced, they don't panic; instead, they are able to suspend judgment, seek out information, and listen to the executives as they explain the new program. As the initiative moves forward, these people are able to move with it.

Sometimes they even lead the way. Consider the case of a manager at a large manufacturing company. Like her colleagues, she had used a certain software program for five years. The program drove how she collected and reported data and how she thought about the company's strategy. One day, senior executives announced that a new program was to be installed that would radically change how information was gathered and assessed within the organization. While many people in the company complained bitterly about how disruptive the change would be, the manager mulled over the reasons for the new program and was convinced of its potential to improve performance. She eagerly attended training sessions—some of her colleagues refused to do so—and was eventually promoted to run several divisions, in part because she used the new technology so effectively.

I want to push the importance of self-regulation to leadership even further and make the case that it enhances integrity, which is not only a personal virtue but also an organizational strength. Many of the bad things that happen in companies are a function of impulsive behavior. People rarely plan to exaggerate profits, pad expense accounts, dip into the till, or abuse power for selfish ends. Instead, an opportunity presents itself, and people with low impulse control just say yes.

By contrast, consider the behavior of the senior executive at a large food company. The executive was scrupulously honest in his negotiations with local distributors. He would routinely lay out his cost structure in detail, thereby giving the distributors a realistic understanding of the company's pricing. This approach meant the executive couldn't always drive a hard bargain. Now, on occasion, he felt the urge to increase profits by withholding information about the company's costs. But he challenged that impulse—he saw that it made more sense in the long run to counteract it. His emotional self-regulation paid off in strong, lasting relationships with distributors that benefited the company more than any short-term financial gains would have.

The signs of emotional self-regulation, therefore, are easy to see: a propensity for reflection and thoughtfulness; comfort with ambiguity and change; and integrity—an ability to say no to impulsive urges.

Can Emotional Intelligence Be Learned?

For ages, people have debated if leaders are born or made. So too goes the debate about emotional intelligence. Are people born with certain levels of empathy, for example, or do they acquire empathy as a result of life's experiences? The answer is both. Scientific inquiry strongly suggests that there is a genetic component to emotional intelligence. Psychological and developmental research indicates that nurture plays a role as well. How much of each perhaps will never be known, but research and practice clearly demonstrate that emotional intelligence can be learned.

One thing is certain: Emotional intelligence increases with age. There is an old-fashioned word for the phenomenon: maturity. Yet even with maturity, some people still need training to enhance their emotional intelligence. Unfortunately, far too many training programs that intend to build leadership skills—including emotional intelligence—are a waste of time and money. The problem is simple: They focus on the wrong part of the brain.

Emotional intelligence is born largely in the neurotransmitters of the brain's limbic system, which governs feelings, impulses, and drives. Research indicates that the limbic system learns best through motivation, extended practice, and feedback. Compare this with the kind of learning that goes on in the neocortex, which governs analytical and technical ability. The neocortex grasps concepts and logic. It is the part of the brain that figures out how to use a computer or make a sales call by reading a book. Not surprisingly—but mistakenly—it is also the part of the brain targeted by most training programs aimed at enhancing emotional intelligence. When such programs take, in effect, a neocortical approach, my research with the Consortium for Research on Emotional Intelligence in Organizations has shown they can even have a *negative* impact on people's job performance.

To enhance emotional intelligence, organizations must refocus their training to include the limbic system. They must help people break old behavioral habits and establish new ones. That not only takes much more time than conventional training programs, it also requires an individualized approach.

Imagine an executive who is thought to be low on empathy by her colleagues. Part of that deficit shows itself as an inability to listen; she interrupts people and doesn't pay close attention to what they're saying. To fix the problem, the executive needs to be motivated to change, and then she needs practice and feedback from others in the company. A colleague or coach could be tapped to let the executive know when she has been observed failing to listen. She would then have to replay the incident and give a better response; that is, demonstrate her ability to absorb what others are saying. And the executive could be directed to observe certain executives who listen well and to mimic their behavior.

With persistence and practice, such a process can lead to lasting results. I know one Wall Street executive who sought to improve his empathy—specifically his ability to read people's reactions and see their perspectives. Before beginning his quest, the executive's subordinates were terrified of working with him. People even went so far as to hide bad news from him. Naturally, he was shocked when finally confronted with these facts. He went home and told his family—but they only confirmed what he had heard at work. When their opinions on any given subject did not mesh with his, they, too, were frightened of him.

Enlisting the help of a coach, the executive went to work to heighten his empathy through practice and feedback. His first step was to take a vacation to a foreign country where he did not speak the language. While there, he monitored his reactions to the unfamiliar and his openness to people who were different from him. When he returned home, humbled by his week abroad, the executive asked his coach to shadow him for parts of the day, several times a week, to critique how he treated people with new or different perspectives. At the same time, he consciously used on-the-job interactions as opportunities to practice "hearing" ideas that differed from his. Finally, the executive had himself videotaped in meetings and asked those who worked for and with him to critique his ability to acknowledge and understand the feelings of others. It took several months, but the executive's emotional intelligence did ultimately rise, and the improvement was reflected in his overall performance on the job.

It's important to emphasize that building one's emotional intelligence cannot—will not—happen without sincere desire and concerted effort. A brief seminar won't help; nor can one buy a how-to manual. It is much harder to learn to empathize—to internalize empathy as a natural response to people—than it is to become adept at regression analysis. But it can be done. "Nothing great was ever achieved without enthusiasm," wrote Ralph Waldo Emerson. If your goal is to become a real leader, these words can serve as a guidepost in your efforts to develop high emotional intelligence.

Like self-awareness, self-regulation often does not get its due. People who can master their emotions are sometimes seen as cold fish—their considered responses are taken as a lack of passion. People with fiery temperaments are frequently thought of as "classic" leaders—their outbursts are considered hallmarks of charisma and power. But when such people make it to the top, their impulsiveness often works against them. In my research, extreme displays of negative emotion have never emerged as a driver of good leadership.

Motivation

If there is one trait that virtually all effective leaders have, it is motivation. They are driven to achieve beyond expectations—their own and everyone else's. The key word here is *achieve*. Plenty of people are motivated by external factors, such as a big salary or the status that comes from having an impressive title or being part of a prestigious company. By contrast, those with leadership potential are motivated by a deeply embedded desire to achieve for the sake of achievement.

If you are looking for leaders, how can you identify people who are motivated by the drive to achieve rather than by external rewards? The first sign is a passion for the work itself—such people seek out creative challenges, love to learn, and take great pride in a job well done. They also display an unflagging energy to do things better. People with such energy often seem restless with the status quo. They are persistent with their questions about why things are done one way rather than another; they are eager to explore new approaches to their work.

A cosmetics company manager, for example, was frustrated that he had to wait two weeks to get sales results from people in the field. He finally tracked down an automated phone system that would beep each of his salespeople at 5 PM every day. An automated message then prompted them to punch in their numbers—how many calls and sales they had made that day. The system shortened the feedback time on sales results from weeks to hours.

That story illustrates two other common traits of people who are driven to achieve. They are forever raising the performance bar, and they like to keep score. Take the performance bar first. During performance reviews, people with high levels of motivation might ask to be "stretched" by their superiors. Of course, an employee who combines self-awareness with internal motivation will recognize her limits—but she won't settle for objectives that seem too easy to fulfill.

And it follows naturally that people who are driven to do better also want a way of tracking progress—their own, their team's, and their company's. Whereas people with low achievement motivation are often fuzzy about results, those with high achievement motivation often keep score by tracking such hard measures as profitability or market share. I know of a money manager who starts and ends his day on the Internet, gauging the performance of his stock fund against four industry-set benchmarks.

The Five Components of Emotional Intelligence at Work

	Definition	Hallmarks
Self-Awareness	• the ability to recognize and understand your moods, emotions, and drives, as well as their effect on others	• self-confidence • realistic self-assessment • self-deprecating sense of humor
Self-Regulation	• the ability to control or redirect disruptive impulses and moods • the propensity to suspend judgment—to think before acting	• trustworthiness and integrity • comfort with ambiguity • openness to change
Motivation	• a passion to work for reasons that go beyond money or status • a propensity to pursue goals with energy and persistence	• strong drive to achieve • optimism, even in the face of failure • organizational commitment
Empathy	• the ability to understand the emotional makeup of other people • skill in treating people according to their emotional reactions	• expertise in building and retaining talent • cross-cultural sensitivity • service to clients and customers
Social Skill	• proficiency in managing relationships and building networks • an ability to find common ground and build rapport	• effectiveness in leading change • persuasiveness • expertise in building and leading teams

Interestingly, people with high motivation remain optimistic even when the score is against them. In such cases, self-regulation combines with achievement motivation to overcome the frustration and depression that come after a setback or failure. Take the case of another portfolio manager at a large investment company. After several successful years, her fund tumbled for three consecutive quarters, leading three large institutional clients to shift their business elsewhere.

Some executives would have blamed the nosedive on circumstances outside their control; others might have seen the setback as evidence of personal failure. This portfolio manager, however, saw an opportunity to prove she could lead a turnaround. Two years later, when she was promoted to a very senior level in the company, she described the experience as "the best thing that ever happened to me; I learned so much from it."

Executives trying to recognize high levels of achievement motivation in their people can look for one last piece of evidence: commitment to the organization. When people love their jobs for the work itself, they often feel committed to the organizations that make that work possible. Committed employees are likely to stay with an organization even when they are pursued by headhunters waving money.

It's not difficult to understand how and why a motivation to achieve translates into strong leadership. If you set the performance bar high for yourself, you will do the same for the organization when you are in a position to do so. Likewise, a drive to surpass goals and an interest in keeping score can be contagious. Leaders with these traits can often build a team of managers around them with the same traits. And of course, optimism and organizational commitment are fundamental to leadership—just try to imagine running a company without them.

Empathy

Of all the dimensions of emotional intelligence, empathy is the most easily recognized. We have all felt the empathy of a sensitive teacher or friend; we have all been struck by its absence in an unfeeling coach or boss. But when it comes to business, we rarely hear people praised, let alone rewarded, for their empathy. The very word seems unbusinesslike, out of place amid the tough realities of the marketplace.

But empathy doesn't mean a kind of "I'm OK, you're OK" mushiness. For a leader, that is, it doesn't mean adopting other people's emotions as one's own and trying to please everybody. That would be a nightmare—it would make action impossible. Rather, empathy means thoughtfully considering employees' feelings—along with other factors—in the process of making intelligent decisions.

For an example of empathy in action, consider what happened when two giant brokerage companies merged, creating redundant jobs in all their divisions. One division manager called his people together and gave a gloomy speech that emphasized the number of people who would soon be fired. The manager of another division gave his people a different kind of speech. He was up-front about his own worry and confusion, and he promised to keep people informed and to treat everyone fairly.

The difference between these two managers was empathy. The first manager was too worried about his own fate to consider the feelings of his anxiety-stricken colleagues. The second knew intuitively what his people were feeling, and he acknowledged their fears with his words. Is it any surprise that the first manager saw his division sink as many demoralized people, especially the most talented, departed? By contrast, the second manager continued to be a strong leader, his best people stayed, and his division remained as productive as ever.

Empathy is particularly important today as a component of leadership for at least three reasons: the increasing use of teams; the rapid pace of globalization; and the growing need to retain talent.

Consider the challenge of leading a team. As anyone who has ever been a part of one can attest, teams are cauldrons of bubbling emotions. They are often charged with reaching a consensus—which is hard enough with two people and much more difficult as the numbers increase. Even in groups with as few as four or five members, alliances form and clashing agendas get set. A team's leader must be able to sense and understand the viewpoints of everyone around the table.

That's exactly what a marketing manager at a large information technology company was able to do when she was appointed to lead a troubled team. The group was in turmoil, overloaded by work and missing deadlines. Tensions were high among the members. Tinkering with procedures was not enough to bring the group together and make it an effective part of the company.

So the manager took several steps. In a series of one-on-one sessions, she took the time to listen to everyone in the group—what was frustrating them, how they rated their colleagues, whether they felt they had been ignored. And then she directed the team in a way that brought it together: She encouraged people to speak more openly about their frustrations, and she helped people raise constructive complaints during meetings. In short, her empathy allowed her to understand her team's emotional makeup. The result was not just heightened collaboration among members but also added business, as the team was called on for help by a wider range of internal clients.

Globalization is another reason for the rising importance of empathy for business leaders. Cross-cultural dialogue can easily lead to miscues and misunderstandings. Empathy is an antidote. People who have it are attuned to subtleties in body language; they can hear the message beneath the words being spoken. Beyond that, they have a deep understanding of both the existence and the importance of cultural and ethnic differences.

Consider the case of an American consultant whose team had just pitched a project to a potential Japanese client. In its dealings with Americans, the team was accustomed to being bombarded with questions after such a proposal, but this time it was greeted with a long silence. Other members of the team, taking the silence as disapproval, were ready to pack and leave. The lead consultant gestured them to stop. Although he was not particularly familiar with Japanese culture, he read the client's face and posture and sensed not rejection but interest—even deep consideration. He was right: When the client finally spoke, it was to give the consulting firm the job.

Finally, empathy plays a key role in the retention of talent, particularly in today's information economy. Leaders have always needed empathy to develop and keep good people, but today the stakes are higher. When good people leave, they take the company's knowledge with them.

That's where coaching and mentoring come in. It has repeatedly been shown that coaching and mentoring pay off not just in better performance but also in increased job satisfaction and decreased turnover. But what makes coaching and mentoring work best is the nature of the relationship. Outstanding coaches and mentors get inside the heads of the people they are helping.

They sense how to give effective feedback. They know when to push for better performance and when to hold back. In the way they motivate their protégés, they demonstrate empathy in action.

In what is probably sounding like a refrain, let me repeat that empathy doesn't get much respect in business. People wonder how leaders can make hard decisions if they are "feeling" for all the people who will be affected. But leaders with empathy do more than sympathize with people around them: They use their knowledge to improve their companies in subtle but important ways.

Social Skill

The first three components of emotional intelligence are self-management skills. The last two, empathy and social skill, concern a person's ability to manage relationships with others. As a component of emotional intelligence, social skill is not as simple as it sounds. It's not just a matter of friendliness, although people with high levels of social skill are rarely mean-spirited. Social skill, rather, is friendliness with a purpose: moving people in the direction you desire, whether that's agreement on a new marketing strategy or enthusiasm about a new product.

Socially skilled people tend to have a wide circle of acquaintances, and they have a knack for finding common ground with people of all kinds—a knack for building rapport. That doesn't mean they socialize continually; it means they work according to the assumption that nothing important gets done alone. Such people have a network in place when the time for action comes.

Social skill is the culmination of the other dimensions of emotional intelligence. People tend to be very effective at managing relationships when they can understand and control their own emotions and can empathize with the feelings of others. Even motivation contributes to social skill. Remember that people who are driven to achieve tend to be optimistic, even in the face of setbacks or failure. When people are upbeat, their "glow" is cast upon conversations and other social encounters. They are popular, and for good reason.

Because it is the outcome of the other dimensions of emotional intelligence, social skill is recognizable on the job in many ways that will by now sound familiar. Socially skilled people, for instance, are adept at managing teams—that's their empathy at work. Likewise, they are expert persuaders—a manifestation of self-awareness, self-regulation, and empathy combined. Given those skills, good persuaders know when to make an emotional plea, for instance, and when an appeal to reason will work better. And motivation, when publicly visible, makes such people excellent collaborators; their passion for the work spreads to others, and they are driven to find solutions.

But sometimes social skill shows itself in ways the other emotional intelligence components do not. For instance, socially skilled people may at times appear not to be working while at work. They seem to be idly schmoozing—chatting in the hallways with colleagues or joking around with people who are not even connected to their "real" jobs. Socially skilled people, however, don't think it makes sense to arbitrarily limit the scope of their relationships. They build bonds widely because they know that in these fluid times, they may need help someday from people they are just getting to know today.

For example, consider the case of an executive in the strategy department of a global computer manufacturer. By 1993, he was convinced that the company's future lay with the Internet. Over the course of the next year, he found kindred spirits and used his social skill to stitch together a virtual community that cut across levels, divisions, and nations. He then used this de facto team to put up a corporate Web site, among the first by a major company. And, on his own initiative, with no budget or formal status, he signed up the company to participate in an annual Internet industry convention. Calling on his allies and persuading various divisions to donate funds, he recruited more than 50 people from a dozen different units to represent the company at the convention.

Management took notice: Within a year of the conference, the executive's team formed the basis for the company's first Internet division, and he was formally put in charge of it. To get there, the executive had ignored conventional boundaries, forging and maintaining connections with people in every corner of the organization.

Is social skill considered a key leadership capability in most companies? The answer is yes, especially when compared with the other components of emotional intelligence. People seem to know intuitively that leaders need to manage relationships effectively; no leader is an island. After all, the leader's task is to get work done through other people, and social skill makes that possible. A leader who cannot express her empathy may as well not have it at all. And a leader's motivation will be useless if he cannot communicate his passion to the organization. Social skill allows leaders to put their emotional intelligence to work.

It would be foolish to assert that good-old-fashioned IQ and technical ability are not important ingredients in strong leadership. But the recipe would not be complete without emotional intelligence. It was once thought that the components of emotional intelligence were "nice to have" in business leaders. But now we know that, for the sake of performance, these are ingredients that leaders "need to have."

It is fortunate, then, that emotional intelligence can be learned. The process is not easy. It takes time and, most of all, commitment. But the benefits that come from having a well-developed emotional intelligence, both for the individual and for the organization, make it worth the effort.

13

Narcissistic Leaders
The Incredible Pros, the Inevitable Cons

Michael Maccoby

There's something new and daring about the CEOs who are transforming today's industries. Just compare them with the executives who ran large companies in the 1950s through the 1980s. Those executives shunned the press and had their comments carefully crafted by corporate PR departments. But today's CEOs—superstars such as Bill Gates, Andy Grove, Steve Jobs, Jeff Bezos, and Jack Welch—hire their own publicists, write books, grant spontaneous interviews, and actively promote their personal philosophies. Their faces adorn the covers of magazines like *Business Week, Time,* and the *Economist.* What's more, the world's business personalities are increasingly seen as the makers and shapers of our public and personal agendas. They advise schools on what kids should learn and lawmakers on how to invest the public's money. We look to them for thoughts on everything from the future of e-commerce to hot places to vacation.

There are many reasons today's business leaders have higher profiles than ever before. One is that business plays a much bigger role in our lives than it used to, and its leaders are more often in the limelight. Another is that the business world is experiencing enormous changes that call for visionary and charismatic leadership. But my 25 years of consulting both as a psychoanalyst in private practice and as an adviser to top managers suggest a third reason—namely, a pronounced change in the personality of the strategic leaders at the top. As an anthropologist, I try to understand people in the context in which they operate, and as a psychoanalyst, I tend to see them through a distinctly Freudian lens. Given what I know, I believe that the larger-than-life leaders we are seeing today closely resemble the personality type that Sigmund Freud dubbed narcissistic. "People of this type impress others as being 'personalities,'" he wrote, describing one of the psychological types that clearly fall within the range of normality. "They are especially suited to act as a support for others, to take on the role of leaders, and to give a fresh stimulus to cultural development or damage the established state of affairs."

Throughout history, narcissists have always emerged to inspire people and to shape the future. When military, religious, and political arenas dominated society, it was figures such as Mahatma Gandhi, Napoléon Bonaparte, and Franklin D. Roosevelt who determined the social agenda. But from time to time, when business became the engine of social change, it, too, generated its share of narcissistic leaders. That was true at the beginning of this century, when men like Andrew Carnegie, John D. Rockefeller, Thomas Edison, and Henry Ford exploited new technologies and restructured American industry. And I think it is true again today.

But Freud recognized that there is a dark side to narcissism. Narcissists, he pointed out, are emotionally isolated and highly distrustful. Perceived threats can trigger rage. Achievements can feed feelings of grandiosity. That's why Freud thought narcissists were the hardest personality types to analyze. Consider how an executive at Oracle describes his narcissistic CEO, Larry Ellison: "The difference between God and Larry is that God does not believe he is Larry." That observation is amusing, but it is also troubling. Not surprisingly, most people think of narcissists in a primarily negative way. After all, Freud named the type after the mythical figure Narcissus, who died because of his pathological preoccupation with himself.

Yet narcissism can be extraordinarily useful—even necessary. Freud shifted his views about narcissism over time and recognized that we are all somewhat narcissistic. More recently, psychoanalyst Heinz Kohut built on Freud's theories and developed methods of treating narcissists. Of course, only professional clinicians are trained to tell if narcissism is normal or pathological. In this article, I discuss the differences between productive and unproductive narcissism but do not explore the extreme pathology of borderline conditions and psychosis.

Leaders like Jack Welch and George Soros are examples of productive narcissists. They are gifted and creative strategists who see the big picture and find meaning in the risky challenge of changing the world and leaving behind a legacy. Indeed, one reason we look to productive narcissists in times of great transition is that they have the audacity to push through the massive transformations that society periodically undertakes. Productive narcissists are not only risk takers willing to get the job done but also charmers who can convert the masses with their rhetoric. The danger is that narcissism can turn unproductive when, lacking restraining anchors and self-knowledge, narcissists become unrealistic dreamers. They nurture grand schemes and harbor the illusion that only circumstances or enemies block their success. This tendency toward grandiosity and distrust is their Achilles' heel. Because of it, even brilliant narcissists can come under suspicion for self-involvement, unpredictability, and—in extreme cases—paranoia.

It's easy to see why narcissistic leadership doesn't always mean successful leadership. Consider the case of Volvo's Pehr Gyllenhammar. He had a dream that appealed to a broad international audience—a plan to revolutionize the industrial workplace by replacing the dehumanizing assembly line caricatured in Charlie Chaplin's *Modern Times*. His wildly popular vision called for team-based craftsmanship. Model factories were built and publicized to international acclaim. But his success in pushing through these dramatic changes also sowed the seeds for his downfall. Gyllenhammar started to feel that he could ignore the concerns of his operational managers. He pursued chancy and expensive business deals, which he publicized on television and in the press. On one level, you can ascribe Gyllenhammar's falling out of touch with his workforce simply to faulty strategy. But it is also possible to attribute it to his narcissistic personality. His overestimation of himself led him to believe that others would want him to be the czar of a multinational enterprise. In turn, these fantasies led him to pursue a merger with French carmaker Renault, which was tremendously unpopular with Swedish employees. Because Gyllenhammar was deaf to complaints about Renault, Swedish managers were forced to take their case public. In the end, shareholders aggressively rejected Gyllenhammar's plan, leaving him with no option but to resign.

Given the large number of narcissists at the helm of corporations today, the challenge facing organizations is to ensure that such leaders do not self-destruct or lead the company to disaster. That can take some doing because it is very hard for narcissists to work through their issues—and virtually impossible for them to do it alone. Narcissists need colleagues and even therapists if they hope to break free from their limitations. But because of their extreme independence and self-protectiveness, it is very difficult to get near them. Kohut maintained that a therapist would have to demonstrate an extraordinarily profound empathic understanding and sympathy for the narcissist's feelings in order to gain his trust. On top of that, narcissists must recognize that they can benefit from such help. For their part, employees must learn how to recognize—and work around—narcissistic bosses. To help them in this endeavor, let's first take a closer look at Freud's theory of personality types.

Three Main Personality Types

While Freud recognized that there are an almost infinite variety of personalities, he identified three main types: erotic, obsessive, and narcissistic. Most of us have elements of all three. We are all, for example, somewhat narcissistic. If that were not so, we would not be able to survive or assert our needs. The point is, one of the dynamic tendencies usually dominates the others, making each of us react differently to success and failure.

Freud's definitions of personality types changed over time. When talking about the erotic personality type, however, Freud generally did not mean a sexual personality but rather one for whom loving and, above all, being loved is most important. This type of individual is dependent on those people they fear will stop loving them. Many erotics are teachers, nurses, and social workers. At their most productive, they are developers of the young as well as enablers and helpers at work. As managers, they are caring and supportive, but they avoid conflict and make people dependent on them. They are, according to Freud, outer-directed people.

Obsessives, in contrast, are inner directed. They are self-reliant and conscientious. They create and maintain order and make the most effective operational managers. They look constantly for ways to help people listen better, resolve conflict, and find win-win opportunities. They buy self-improvement books such as Stephen Covey's *The 7 Habits of Highly Effective People.* Obsessives are also ruled by a strict conscience—they like to focus on continuous improvement at work because it fits in with their sense of moral improvement. As entrepreneurs, obsessives start businesses that express their values, but they lack the vision, daring, and charisma it takes to turn a good idea into a great one. The best obsessives set high standards and communicate very effectively. They make sure that instructions are followed and costs are kept within budget. The most productive are great mentors and team players. The unproductive and the uncooperative become narrow experts and rule-bound bureaucrats.

Narcissists, the third type, are independent and not easily impressed. They are innovators, driven in business to gain power and glory. Productive narcissists are experts in their industries, but they go beyond it. They also pose the critical questions. They want to learn everything about everything that affects the company and its products. Unlike erotics, they want to be admired, not loved. And unlike obsessives, they are not troubled by a punishing superego, so they are able to aggressively pursue their goals. Of all the personality types, narcissists run the greatest risk of isolating themselves at the moment of success. And because of their independence and aggressiveness, they are constantly looking out for enemies, sometimes degenerating into paranoia when they are under extreme stress. (For further discussion of personality types, see the sidebar "Fromm's Fourth Personality Type.")

Strengths of the Narcissistic Leader

When it comes to leadership, personality type can be instructive. Erotic personalities generally make poor managers—they need too much approval. Obsessives make better leaders—they are your operational managers: critical and cautious. But it is narcissists who come closest to our collective image of great leaders. There are two reasons for this: They have compelling, even gripping, visions for companies, and they have an ability to attract followers.

Great Vision

I once asked a group of managers to define a leader. "A person with vision" was a typical response. Productive narcissists understand the vision

---

Fromm's Fourth Personality Type

Not long after Freud described his three personality types, psychoanalyst Erich Fromm proposed a fourth personality type, which has become particularly prevalent in today's service economy. Fromm called this type the marketing personality, and it is exemplified by the lead character in Woody Allen's movie *Zelig*, a man so governed by his need to be valued that he becomes exactly like the people he happens to be around.

Marketing personalities are more detached than erotics and so are less likely to cement close ties. They are also less driven by conscience than obsessives. Instead, they are motivated by a radarlike anxiety that permeates everything they do. Because they are so eager to please and to alleviate this anxiety, marketing personalities excel at selling themselves to others.

Unproductive marketing types lack direction and the ability to commit themselves to people or projects. But when productive, marketing types are good at facilitating teams and keeping the focus on adding value as defined by customers and colleagues. Like obsessives, marketing personalities are avid consumers of self-help books. Like narcissists, they are not wedded to the past. But marketing types generally make poor leaders in times of crisis. They lack the daring needed to innovate and are too responsive to current, rather than future, customer demands.

---

thing particularly well, because they are by nature people who see the big picture. They are not analyzers who can break up big questions into manageable problems; they aren't number crunchers either (these are usually the obsessives). Nor do they try to extrapolate to understand the future—they attempt to create it. To paraphrase George Bernard Shaw, some people see things, and they say "why?"; narcissists dream things that never were and say, "Why not?"

Consider the difference between Bob Allen, a productive obsessive, and Mike Armstrong, a productive narcissist. In 1997, Allen tried to expand AT&T to reestablish the end-to-end service of the Bell System by reselling local service from the regional Bell operating companies (RBOCs). Although this was a worthwhile endeavor for shareholders and customers, it was hardly earth-shattering. By contrast, through a strategy of combining telecommunications and high-speed broadband Internet access over cable, Mike Armstrong has "created a new space with his name on it," as one of his colleagues puts it. Armstrong is betting that his costly strategy will beat out the RBOCs' less expensive solution of digital subscriber lines over copper wire. This example illustrates the different approaches of obsessives and narcissists. The risk Armstrong took is one that few obsessives would feel comfortable taking. His vision is galvanizing AT&T. Who but a narcissistic leader could achieve such a thing? As Napoléon—a classic narcissist—once remarked, "Revolutions are ideal times for soldiers with a lot of wit—and the courage to act."

As in the days of the French Revolution, the world is now changing in astounding ways; narcissists have opportunities they would never have in ordinary times. In short, today's narcissistic leaders have the chance to change the very rules of the game. Consider Robert B. Shapiro, CEO of Monsanto. Shapiro described his vision of genetically modifying crops as "the single most successful introduction of technology in the history of agriculture, including the plow" (*New York Times,* August 5, 1999). This is certainly a huge claim—there are still many questions about the safety and public acceptance of genetically engineered fruits and vegetables. But industries like agriculture are desperate for radical change. If Shapiro's gamble is successful, the industry will be transformed in the image of Monsanto. That's why he can get away with painting a picture of Monsanto as a highly profitable life sciences company—despite the fact that Monsanto's stock has fallen 12% from 1998 to the end of the third quarter of 1999. (During the same period, the S&P was up 41%.) Unlike Armstrong and Shapiro, Bob Allen was content to win against his competitors in a game measured primarily by the stock market. But narcissistic leaders are after something more. They want—and need—to leave behind a legacy.

Scores of Followers

Narcissists have vision—but that's not enough. People in mental hospitals also have visions. The simplest definition of a leader is someone whom other people follow. Indeed, narcissists are especially gifted in attracting followers, and, more often than not, they do so through language. Narcissists believe that words can move mountains and that inspiring speeches can change people. Narcissistic leaders are often skillful orators, and this is one of the talents that make them so *charismatic.* Indeed, anyone who has seen narcissists perform can attest to their personal magnetism and their ability to stir enthusiasm among audiences.

Yet this charismatic gift is more of a two-way affair than most people think. Although it is not always obvious, narcissistic leaders are quite dependent on their followers—they need affirmation and, preferably, adulation. Think of Winston Churchill's wartime broadcasts or J.F.K.'s "Ask not what your country can do for you" inaugural address. The adulation that follows from such speeches bolsters the self-confidence and conviction of the speakers. But if no one responds, the narcissist usually becomes insecure, overly shrill, and insistent—just as Ross Perot did.

Even when people respond positively to a narcissist, there are dangers. That's because charisma is a double-edged sword—it fosters both closeness and isolation. As he becomes increasingly self-assured, the narcissist becomes more spontaneous. He feels free of constraints. Ideas flow. He thinks he's invincible. This energy and confidence further inspire his followers. But the very adulation that the narcissist demands can have a corrosive effect. As he expands, he listens even less to words of caution and advice. After all, he has been right before when others had their doubts. Rather than try to persuade those who disagree with him, he feels justified in ignoring them—creating further isolation. The result is sometimes flagrant risk taking that can lead to catastrophe. In the political realm, there is no clearer example of this than Bill Clinton.

Weaknesses of the Narcissistic Leader

Despite the warm feelings their charisma can evoke, narcissists are typically not comfortable with their own emotions. They listen only for the kind of information they seek. They don't learn easily from others. They don't like to teach but prefer to indoctrinate and make speeches. They dominate meetings with subordinates. The result for the organization is greater internal competitiveness at a time when everyone is already under as much pressure as they can possibly stand. Perhaps the main problem is that the narcissist's faults tend to become even more pronounced as he becomes more successful.

The Rise and Fall of a Narcissist

The story of Jan Carlzon, the former CEO of the Scandinavian airline SAS, is an almost textbook example of how a narcissist's weaknesses can cut short a brilliant career. In the 1980s, Carlzon's vision of SAS as the businessperson's airline was widely acclaimed in the business press; management guru Tom Peters described him as a model leader. In 1989, when I first met Carlzon and his management team, he compared the ideal organization to the Brazilian soccer team—in principle, there would be no fixed roles, only innovative plays. I asked the members of the management team if they agreed with this vision of an empowered front line. One vice president, a former pilot, answered no. "I still believe that the best organization is the military," he said. I then asked Carlzon for his reaction to that remark. "Well," he replied, "that may be true, if your goal is to shoot your customers."

That rejoinder was both witty and dismissive; clearly, Carlzon was not engaging in a serious dialogue with his subordinates. Nor was he listening to other advisers. Carlzon ignored the issue of high costs, even when many observers pointed out that SAS could not compete without improving productivity. He threw money at expensive acquisitions of hotels and made an unnecessary investment in Continental Airlines just months before it declared bankruptcy.

Carlzon's story perfectly corroborates the often-recorded tendency of narcissists to become overly expansive—and hence isolated—at the very pinnacle of their success. Seduced by the flattery he received in the international press, Carlzon's self-image became so enormously inflated that his feet left the ground. And given his vulnerability to grandiosity, he was propelled by a need to expand his organization rather than develop it. In due course, as Carlzon led the company deeper and deeper into losses, he was fired. Now he is a venture capitalist helping budding companies. And SAS has lost its glitter.

Sensitive to Criticism

Because they are extraordinarily sensitive, narcissistic leaders shun emotions as a whole. Indeed, perhaps one of the greatest paradoxes in this age of teamwork and partnering is that the best corporate leader in the contemporary world is the type of person who is emotionally isolated. Narcissistic leaders typically keep others at arm's length. They can put up a wall of defense as thick as the Pentagon. And given their difficulty with knowing or acknowledging their own feelings, they are uncomfortable with other people expressing theirs—especially their negative feelings.

Indeed, even productive narcissists are extremely sensitive to criticism or slights, which feel to them like knives threatening their self-image and their confidence in their visions. Narcissists are almost unimaginably thin-skinned. Like the fairy-tale princess who slept on many mattresses and yet knew she was sleeping on a pea, narcissists—even powerful CEOs—bruise easily. This is one reason why narcissistic leaders do not want to know what people think of them unless it is causing a real problem. They cannot tolerate dissent. In fact, they can be extremely abrasive with employees who doubt them or with subordinates who are tough enough to fight back. Steve Jobs, for example, publicly humiliates subordinates. Thus, although narcissistic leaders often say that they want teamwork, what that means in practice is that they want a group of yes-men. As the more independent-minded players leave or are pushed out, succession becomes a particular problem.

Poor Listeners

One serious consequence of this oversensitivity to criticism is that narcissistic leaders often do not listen when they feel threatened or attacked. Consider the response of one narcissistic CEO I had worked with for three years, who asked me to interview his immediate team and report back to him on what they were thinking. He invited me to his summer home to discuss what I had found. "So what do they think of me?" he asked with seeming nonchalance. "They think you are very creative and courageous," I told him, "but they also feel that you don't listen." "Excuse me, what did you say?" he shot back at once, pretending not to hear. His response was humorous, but it was also tragic.

In a very real way, this CEO could not hear my criticism because it was too painful to tolerate. Some narcissists are so defensive that they go so far as to make a virtue of the fact that they don't listen. As another CEO bluntly put it, "I didn't get here by listening to people!" Indeed, on one occasion when this CEO proposed a daring strategy, none of his subordinates believed it would work. His subsequent success strengthened his conviction that he had nothing to learn about strategy from his lieutenants. But success is no excuse for narcissistic leaders not to listen.

Lack of Empathy

Best-selling business writers today have taken up the slogan of "emotional competencies"—the belief that successful leadership requires a strongly developed sense of empathy. But although they crave empathy from others, productive narcissists are not noted for being particularly empathetic themselves. Indeed, lack of empathy is a characteristic shortcoming of some of the most charismatic and successful narcissists, including Bill Gates and Andy Grove. Of course, leaders do need to communicate persuasively. But a lack of empathy did not prevent some of history's greatest narcissistic leaders from knowing how to communicate—and inspire. Neither Churchill, de Gaulle, Stalin, nor Mao Tse-tung were empathetic. And yet they inspired people because of their passion and their conviction at a time when people longed for certainty.

In fact, in times of radical change, lack of empathy can actually be a strength. A narcissist finds it easier than other personality types to buy and sell companies, to close and move facilities, and to lay off employees—decisions that inevitably make many people angry and sad. But narcissistic leaders typically have few regrets. As one CEO says, "If I listened to my employees' needs and demands, they would eat me alive."

Given this lack of empathy, it's hardly surprising that narcissistic leaders don't score particularly well on evaluations of their interpersonal style. What's more, neither 360-degree evaluations of their management style nor workshops in listening will make them more empathic. Narcissists don't want to change—and as long as they are successful, they don't think they have to. They may see the need for operational managers to get touchy-feely training, but that's not for them.

There is a kind of emotional intelligence associated with narcissists, but it's more street smarts than empathy. Narcissistic leaders are acutely aware of whether or not people are with them wholeheartedly. They know whom they can use. They can be brutally exploitative. That's why, even though narcissists undoubtedly have "star quality," they are often unlikable. They easily stir up people against them, and it is only in tumultuous times, when their gifts are desperately needed, that people are willing to tolerate narcissists as leaders.

Distaste for Mentoring

Lack of empathy and extreme independence make it difficult for narcissists to mentor and be mentored. Generally speaking, narcissistic leaders set very little store by mentoring. They seldom mentor others, and when they do they typically want their protégés to be pale reflections of themselves. Even those narcissists like Jack Welch who are held up as strong mentors are usually more interested in instructing than in coaching.

Narcissists certainly don't credit mentoring or educational programs for their own development as leaders. A few narcissistic leaders such as Bill Gates may find a friend or consultant—for instance, Warren Buffet, a super-productive obsessive—whom they can trust to be their guide and confidant. But most narcissists prefer "mentors" they can control. A 32-year-old marketing vice president, a narcissist with CEO potential, told me that she had rejected her boss as a mentor. As she put it, "First of all, I want to keep the relationship at a distance. I don't want to be influenced by emotions. Second, there are things I don't want him to know. I'd rather hire an outside consultant to be my coach." Although narcissistic leaders appear to be at ease with others, they find intimacy—which is a prerequisite for mentoring—to be difficult. Younger narcissists will establish peer relations with authority rather than seek a parentlike mentoring relationship. They want results and are willing to take chances arguing with authority.

An Intense Desire to Compete

Narcissistic leaders are relentless and ruthless in their pursuit of victory. Games are not games but tests of their survival skills. Of course, all successful managers want to win, but narcissists are not restrained by conscience. Organizations led by narcissists are generally characterized by intense internal competition. Their passion to win is marked by both the promise of glory and the primitive danger of extinction. It is a potent brew that energizes companies, creating a sense of urgency, but it can also be dangerous. These leaders see everything as a threat. As Andy Grove puts it, brilliantly articulating the narcissist's fear, distrust, and aggression, "Only the paranoid survive." The concern, of course, is that the narcissist finds enemies that actually aren't there—even among his colleagues.

Avoiding the Traps

There is very little business literature that tells narcissistic leaders how to avoid the pitfalls. There are two reasons for this. First, relatively few narcissistic leaders are interested in looking inward. And second, psychoanalysts don't usually get close enough to them, especially in the workplace, to write about them. (The noted psychoanalyst Harry Levinson is an exception.) As a result, advice on leadership focuses on obsessives, which explains why so much of it is about creating teamwork and being more receptive to subordinates. But as we've already seen, this literature is of little interest to narcissists, nor is it likely to help subordinates understand their narcissistic leaders. The absence of managerial literature on narcissistic leaders doesn't mean that it is impossible to devise strategies for dealing with narcissism. In the course of a long career counseling CEOs, I have identified three basic ways in which productive narcissists can avoid the traps of their own personality.

Find a Trusted Sidekick

Many narcissists can develop a close relationship with one person, a sidekick who acts as an anchor, keeping the narcissistic partner grounded. However, given that narcissistic leaders trust only their own insights and view of reality, the sidekick has to understand the narcissistic leader and what he is trying to achieve. The narcissist must feel that this person, or in some cases persons, is practically an extension of himself. The sidekick must also be sensitive enough to manage the relationship. Don Quixote is a classic example of a narcissist who was out of touch with reality but who was constantly saved from disaster by his squire Sancho Panza. Not surprisingly, many narcissistic leaders rely heavily on their spouses, the people they are closest to. But dependence on spouses can be risky, because they may further isolate the narcissistic leader from his company by supporting his grandiosity and feeding his paranoia. I once knew a CEO in this kind of relationship with his spouse. He took to accusing loyal subordinates of plotting against him just because they ventured a few criticisms of his ideas.

It is much better for a narcissistic leader to choose a colleague as his sidekick. Good sidekicks are able to point out the operational requirements of the narcissistic leader's vision and keep him rooted in reality. The best sidekicks are usually productive obsessives. Pehr Gyllenhammar, for instance, was most effective at Volvo when he had an obsessive COO, Hakan Frisinger, to focus on improving quality and cost, as well as an obsessive HR director, Berth Jönsson, to implement his vision. Similarly, Bill Gates can think about the future from the stratosphere because Steve Ballmer, a tough obsessive president, keeps the show on the road. At Oracle, CEO Larry Ellison can afford to miss key meetings and spend time on his boat contemplating a future without PCs because he has a productive obsessive COO in Ray Lane to run the company for him. But the job of sidekick entails more than just executing the leader's ideas. The sidekick also has to get his leader to accept new ideas. To do this, he must be able to show the leader how the new ideas fit with his views and serve his interests. (For more on dealing with narcissistic bosses, see the sidebar "Working for a Narcissist.")

Indoctrinate the Organization

The narcissistic CEO wants all of his subordinates to think the way he does about the business. Productive narcissists—people who often have a dash of the obsessive personality—are good at converting people to their point of view. One of the most successful at this is GE's Jack Welch. Welch uses toughness to build a corporate culture and to implement a daring business strategy, including the buying and selling of scores of companies. Unlike other narcissistic leaders such as Gates, Grove, and Ellison, who have transformed industries with new products, Welch was able to transform his industry by focusing on execution, pushing companies to the limits of quality and efficiency, bumping up revenues, and wringing out costs. In order to do so, Welch hammers out a huge corporate culture in his own image—a culture that provides impressive rewards for senior managers and shareholders.

Welch's approach to culture building is widely misunderstood. Many observers, notably Noel Tichy in *The Leadership Engine*, argue that Welch forms his company's leadership culture through teaching. But Welch's "teaching" involves a personal ideology that he indoctrinates into GE managers through speeches, memos, and confrontations. Rather than create a dialogue, Welch makes pronouncements (either be the number one or two company in your market or get out), and he institutes programs (such as Six

> ## Working for a Narcissist
>
> Dealing with a narcissistic boss isn't easy. You have to be prepared to look for another job if your boss becomes too narcissistic to let you disagree with him. But remember that the company is typically betting on *his* vision of the future—not yours. Here are a few tips on how to survive in the short term:
>
> **Always empathize with your boss's feelings, but don't expect any empathy back.** Look elsewhere for your own self-esteem. Understand that behind his display of infallibility, there hides a deep vulnerability. Praise his achievements and reinforce his best impulses, but don't be shamelessly sycophantic. An intelligent narcissist can see through flatterers and prefers independent people who truly appreciate him. Show that you will protect his image, inside and outside the company. But be careful if he asks for an honest evaluation. What he wants is information that will help him solve a problem about his image. He will resent any honesty that threatens his inflated self-image and will likely retaliate.
>
> **Give your boss ideas, but always let him take the credit for them.** Find out what he thinks before presenting your views. If you believe he is wrong, show how a different approach would be in his best interest. Take his paranoid views seriously; don't brush them aside—they often reveal sharp intuitions. Disagree only when you can demonstrate how he will benefit from a different point of view.
>
> **Hone your time-management skills.** Narcissistic leaders often give subordinates many more orders than they can possibly execute. Ignore the requests he makes that don't make sense. Forget about them. He will. But be careful: Carve out free time for yourself only when you know there's a lull in the boss's schedule. Narcissistic leaders feel free to call you at any hour of the day or night. Make yourself available, or be prepared to get out.

Sigma quality) that become the GE party line. Welch's strategy has been extremely effective. GE managers must either internalize his vision, or they must leave. Clearly, this is incentive learning with a vengeance. I would even go so far as to call Welch's teaching brainwashing. But Welch does have the rare insight and know-how to achieve what all narcissistic business leaders are trying to do—namely, get the organization to identify with them, to think the way they do, and to become the living embodiment of their companies.

Get into Analysis

Narcissists are often more interested in controlling others than in knowing and disciplining themselves. That's why, with very few exceptions, even productive narcissists do not want to explore their personalities with the help of insight therapies such as psychoanalysis. Yet since Heinz Kohut, there has been a radical shift in psychoanalytic thinking about what can be done to help narcissists work through their rage, alienation, and grandiosity. Indeed, if they can be persuaded to undergo therapy, narcissistic leaders can use tools such as psychoanalysis to overcome vital character flaws.

Consider the case of one exceptional narcissistic CEO who asked me to help him understand why he so often lost his temper with subordinates. He lived far from my home city, and so the therapy was sporadic and very unorthodox. Yet he kept a journal of his dreams, which we interpreted together either by phone or when we met. Our analysis uncovered painful feelings of being unappreciated that went back to his inability to impress a cold father. He came to realize that he demanded an unreasonable amount of praise and that when he felt unappreciated by his subordinates, he became furious. Once he understood that, he was able to recognize his narcissism and even laugh about it. In the middle of our work, he even announced to his top team that I was psychoanalyzing him and asked them what they thought of that. After a pregnant pause, one executive vice president piped up, "Whatever you're doing, you should keep doing it, because you don't get so angry anymore." This CEO, instead of being trapped by narcissistic rage, was learning how to express his concerns constructively.

Leaders who can work on themselves in that way tend to be the most productive narcissists. In addition to being self-reflective, they are also likely to be open, likable, and good-humored. Productive narcissists have perspective; they are able to detach themselves and laugh at their irrational needs. Although serious about achieving their goals, they are also playful. As leaders, they are aware of being performers. A sense of humor helps them maintain enough perspective and humility to keep on learning.

The Best and Worst of Times

As I have pointed out, narcissists thrive in chaotic times. In more tranquil times and places, however, even the most brilliant narcissist will seem out of place. In his short story "The Curfew Tolls," Stephen Vincent Benét speculates on what would have happened to Napoléon if he had been born some 30 years earlier. Retired in prerevolutionary France, Napoléon is depicted as a lonely artillery major boasting to a vacationing British general about how he could have beaten the English in India. The point, of course, is that a visionary born in the wrong time can seem like a pompous buffoon.

Historically, narcissists in large corporations have been confined to sales positions, where they use their persuasiveness and imagination to best effect. In settled times, the problematic side of the narcissistic personality usually conspires to keep narcissists in their place, and they can typically rise to top management positions only by starting their own companies or by leaving to lead upstarts. Consider Joe Nacchio, formerly in charge of both the business and consumer divisions of AT&T. Nacchio was a supersalesman and a popular leader in the mid-1990s. But his desire to create a new network for business customers was thwarted by colleagues who found him self-promoting, abrasive, and ruthlessly ambitious.

Two years ago, Nacchio left AT&T to become CEO of Qwest, a company that is creating a long-distance fiber-optic cable network. Nacchio had the credibility—and charisma—to sell Qwest's initial public offering to financial markets and gain a high valuation. Within a short space of time, he turned Qwest into an attractive target for the RBOCs, which were looking to move into long-distance telephone and Internet services. Such a sale would have given Qwest's owners a handsome profit on their investment. But Nacchio wanted more. He wanted to expand—to compete with AT&T—and for that he needed local service. Rather than sell Qwest, he chose to make a bid himself for local telephone operator U.S. West, using Qwest's highly valued stock to finance the deal. The market voted on this display of expansiveness with its feet—Qwest's stock price fell 40% between last June, when he made the deal, and the end of the third quarter of 1999. (The S&P index dropped 5.7% during the same period.)

Like other narcissists, Nacchio likes risk—and sometimes ignores the costs. But with the dramatic discontinuities going on in the world today, more and more large corporations are getting into bed with narcissists. They are finding that there is no substitute for narcissistic leaders in an age of innovation. Companies need leaders who do not try to anticipate the future so much as create it. But narcissistic leaders—even the most productive of them—can self-destruct and lead their organizations terribly astray. For companies whose narcissistic leaders recognize their limitations, these will be the best of times. For other companies, these could turn out to be the worst.

Questions and Learning Activities

Section II

Questions

1. Is what Confucius taught about leadership 2500 years ago relevant in today's environment? Support your opinion. Are any of his teachings not relevant? Why?

2. What are Stogdill's conclusions regarding the relationship between personal traits and leadership?

3. Zaleznik claims that "second-born" personality types are more likely to be effective leaders. Do you agree or disagree? Give examples.

4. What does Zaleznik mean when he speaks of the "conservatism" of organizations and what does this have to do with leadership and management?

5. What are the potential advantages and disadvantages of having a boss who is a "once-born" personality type? And one who is "twice-born"?

6. How might a strong need to achieve detract from effective leadership?

7. Is it possible for a person with a very low need for power to become an effective leader/manager?

8. How does the Kirkpatrick and Locke reading contribute to resolving the age-old argument of whether leaders are born or made?

9. Goleman claims that emotional intelligence can be learned. Do you think this is probable for most people? What is needed to facilitate improving emotional intelligence?

10. Which element of emotional intelligence is the prerequisite for all others? Why?

11. Many people with low emotional intelligence seem to get ahead in organizations. If you accept the notion that emotional intelligence is related to leadership effectiveness, then how do you reconcile this with the existence of so many with low emotional intelligence in high positions?

12. Why should all leaders be concerned about their "inner theater" and what can they realistically do in this area?

13. Why do so many people willingly follow narcissistic leaders? Are there any conditions or situations that might encourage one to follow a narcissistic leader?

14. What are the similarities and differences between the treatment of narcissistic leaders by Kets de Vries and Maccoby?

Activities

1. Choose two well-known leader/managers who obviously do not subscribe to the teachings of Confucius. Discuss how the negative outcomes they caused could have been prevented if they had followed his guidelines.

2. Assess your needs for achievement, affiliation, and power based upon the guidelines presented in *Leadership Run Amok*. What are the leadership implications for you?

3. Find out more about your personality type by taking the online Big Five Personality test and Myers Briggs test. See the editor's Web site (www.waveland.com/McMahon/) for more information.

4. Lead a discussion about a leader/manager you and your colleagues have observed who possessed a high achievement motive. What were some of the positive and negative outcomes?

5. Two additional personality variables related to leadership are Type A/B behavior patterns and Locus of Control. Gain additional self-awareness with the editor's suggestions on the Web site.

6. Discuss with classmates/colleagues instances where leader/managers demonstrated high and low self-control. For each example, briefly discuss what happened and the outcomes or consequences.

7. Discuss with classmates/colleagues instances where leader/managers demonstrated high and low empathy. For each example, briefly discuss what happened and the outcomes or consequences.

8. Discuss with classmates/colleagues instances where leader/managers demonstrated high and low self-awareness. For each example, briefly discuss what happed and the outcomes or consequences.

9. The Goleman article will become more personal after you complete the editor's suggested Emotional Intelligence assessment on the Web site.

10. The direct and indirect evidence supporting the contribution of emotional intelligence to leadership effectiveness appears to be solid. Yet, many with low emotional intelligence seem to get ahead in organizations. Lead a discussion on why this occurs.

11. Using a variety of news sources, write a paper about two narcissistic leaders who held great sway over their followers and ultimately harmed them in some way. Identify the reasons you believe these individuals can be classified as narcissists. What observations persuaded you? Why did people follow these leaders? What happened to their followers? Could the negative outcomes have been prevented?

12. You have learned about narcissism and leadership from the articles by Kets de Vries and Maccoby. Check your narcissistic tendencies using the editor's suggestion on the Web site.

13. Lead a discussion about personal experiences you and your colleagues had working for a leader/manager who exhibited narcissistic tendencies. Note what happened and the consequences.

14. Several articles have stressed the importance of the desire to lead as an important variable in the leadership equation. Gain insight into your motivation to lead using the editor's suggestion on the Web site.

15. Develop an action plan to improve your emotional intelligence. Your plan should include the actions that you will take as well as how you intend to track your improvement.

SECTION III

LEADERSHIP BEHAVIOR CONCEPTS

As the evolution of leadership theory and research moved from *who* the leader is to *what* the leader does, the variables of interest increased geometrically. This change of direction expanded the potential determinants of leader effectiveness considerably and launched many research investigations. This research continues today and has produced new theories and models. The selections in this section represent the most important contributions in the area of leadership behavior.

The first selection, drawn from *Autocracy and Democracy* by Ralph K. White and Ronald Lippitt, summarizes the findings of the famous 1938 studies of autocratic, democratic, and laissez-faire leadership. This research stimulated significant interest and resulted in many studies and articles focused on the outcomes of different leadership styles. The findings still resonate today even though the original subjects were eleven-year-old boys.

The Ohio State Leadership Studies represent a watershed in the history of leadership theory and research. The most widely used models in leadership development programs have their roots in the Ohio State definitions and measurement of leadership style—*consideration* and *initiating structure*. Valid measurement of leadership style is obviously the *sine qua non* of any effort to determine the relationship between style and such outcomes as performance and satisfaction. This body of work stimulated the development of a number of leadership theories and inspired hundreds of research studies with meaningful practical implications. The selection here, *Conceptual Contributions of the Ohio State Leadership Studies* by Chester Schriesheim and Barbara Bird, explicitly recognizes practical applications as well as important conceptual ones.

In 1957 Chris Argyris wrote about the inherent conflict between classical organization and the mature person, captured here in *Leadership Implications of Personality Development*. This selection provides a lucid explanation of one of the historical sources of discontent in many organizations. Unfortunately, what Argyris describes still exists today in many organizations. While his work did not focus exclusively on leadership—a number of elements of organization are included—the relevance for aspiring leaders is inescapable.

The contributions of Douglas McGregor are pivotal in the evolution of thought in both organizational behavior and leadership. *Leadership and the Nature of Man* dovetails nicely with the Argyris selection. McGregor observed that a leader/manager's beliefs about the nature of man determine that leader's actions. Further, if those beliefs are negative, the result is likely to be a self-fulfilling prophecy. McGregor's keen insight into why leaders' attempts to implement change often fail is right on the mark.

The Managerial Grid, published in 1964, was the most popular platform for leadership development for many years and still has adherents around the world today. This model, based upon the Ohio State conceptualization of leadership, contains significant detail regarding the categorization of leadership styles and the implications for practicing managers. The managerial grid model came under heavy criticism with the advent of contingency or situational theories of leadership, which are covered in the next section. However, it is important to note that this original work did not totally ignore elements of the leadership situation as so often claimed.

While the research on leadership was being undertaken at Ohio State, another series of milestone studies were underway at the University of Michigan. This work is nicely summarized in the selection by David G. Bowers and Stanley E. Seashore, *A Four-Factor Theory of Leadership*. The work done at the University of Michigan converges in several respects with the Ohio State studies but is also unique in a number of ways. One of the most important is the concept of peer leadership. Other important contributions include the principle of supportive relationships and importance of performance goals. The work at Michigan is an excellent example of how programmatic research on leadership supplied important practical implications for leaders as well as systemic recommendations for organizations.

In the mid-1970s, Robert Greenleaf's ideas about "servant leadership" marked a significant departure from the traditional notion of the "leader." The idea of the person who first puts other people's needs, desires, and interests above his or her own, and then transitions into the leadership role, stimulated a great deal of interest which continues today, more than 30 years later. While the research on servant leadership as a complete theory is nonexistent, elements of the theory are supported in the research literature. Interest outside of academia is robust and a number of organizations report significant success with elements of this model. The essentials of this concept are ably summarized in *Servant Leadership: Its Origin, Development and Application* by Sen Sendjaya and James Sarros.

At the heart of leadership lies the interaction between leader and follower. These interactions revolve around performance; leaders react to poor or outstanding performance by the followers who, in turn, react to leader behaviors. These reactions are driven to a large extent by beliefs and perceptions of the reasons or causes for variations in performance. *The Leader/Member Attribution Process*, by Mark Martinko and William Gardner, explains the process by which leaders and followers assign causes (i.e., *attribute*) for behavior and performance. It is critical that leaders understand the interplay between attributions, expectations, and responses because attribution errors can lead to ill-advised actions which, in turn, can lead to unintended consequences.

Robert House's seminal work on charisma has spawned many investigations and articles about this elusive quality. The concept of charisma, though central to understanding effective leadership, can be difficult to define and, in fact, is often approached in terms of its effect on followers. House's *A 1976 Theory of Charismatic Leadership* remains, more than 30 years later, one of the most cogent treatments of the subject.

Bernard M. Bass provides a clear and practical explanation of the differences between transactional and transformational leaders and highlights the implications of these differences for the performance of followers. The transactional leader essentially defines what is expected and then informs the subordinate of the consequences of meeting these expectations. It is easy to understand how this approach produces mediocre performance. The transformational leader, on the other hand, stimulates higher performance by generating awareness and acceptance of the organization's purpose and mission, thereby creating motivated followers. Bass asserts that through training, managers can develop the qualities they need to move beyond transactional to transformational leadership.

14

Autocratic vs. Democratic Leadership

Ralph K. White and Ronald Lippitt

This is the report of an inquiry into the psychological dynamics of demo-cratic, autocratic, and unorganized social situations. In collaboration with our senior partner, the late Kurt Lewin, we conducted these experiments in an attic at the University of Iowa in 1938. The focus here is on the second experiment which involved groups of eleven-year-old boys, with five mem-bers in each group meeting after school with an adult leader and carrying on interesting activities. . . .

The one factor deliberately varied was the type of leadership, while other factors were held as constant as possible. A bank of observers took continuous notes on the behavior of the children, and the types of leadership were evaluated primarily on the basis of a systematic analysis of those observers' notes. . . .

Definition of Leader Roles

The definition of the three leadership roles are:

Autocratic	Democratic	Laissez-Faire
All determination of policy by the leader.	All policies a matter of group discussion and decision, encouraged and assisted by the leader.	Complete freedom for group or individual decision, with a mini-mum of leader partici-pation.

Autocratic	Democratic	Laissez-Faire
Techniques and activity steps dictated by the authority, one at a time, so that future steps are always uncertain to a large degree.	Activity perspective gained during discussion period. General steps to group goal sketched and leader suggests two or more alternatives when technical advice needed.	Various materials supplied by the leader who makes it clear he will supply information when needed. He takes no other part in the work discussion.

. . .

Leader behaviors of the three styles:

Autocratic	Democratic	Laissez-Faire
The leader usually dictates the particular work task and work companion of each member.	The members are free to work with whomever they choose, and the division of tasks is left up to the group.	Complete non-participation of the leader in determining tasks and companions.
The leader tends to be "personal" in his praise and criticism of the work of each member, but remains aloof from active group participation except when demonstrating.	The leader is "objective" or "fact-minded" in his praise and criticism, and tries to be a regular group member in spirit without doing too much of the work.	Infrequent spontaneous comments on member activities unless questioned, and no attempt to appraise or regulate the course of events.

. . .

Summary of the Findings

A bird's-eye view of the more important results is given in Figures 1 and 2 which represent, respectively, the boys' behavior toward their leader and toward each other. The chief differences to be noted in Figure 1 are: (1) the large number of leader-dependent actions in both reactions to autocracy; (2) the large extent of critical discontent and of aggressive behavior in the aggressive reaction to autocracy; (3) the frequency of "friendly, confiding" conversation and of group-minded suggestions in democracy; and (4) the contrast between democracy and laissez-faire in work-minded conversation. . . .

The behavior of the boys toward each other is summarized in similar fashion in Figure 2. Here the following differences should be noticed: (1) the large difference between the two reactions to autocracy in amount of aggressive behavior, and the intermediate position of democracy and laissez-faire in this respect; (2) the generally subdued atmosphere in the submissive reaction to autocracy, as shown by the small absolute totals of aggressive behavior, attention demands, group-minded suggestions, out-of-club-field conversation, and play-minded remarks; (3) the small proportion of group-minded suggestions in both reactions to autocracy; and (4) the small amount of play-minded conversation in both reactions to laissez-faire. . . .

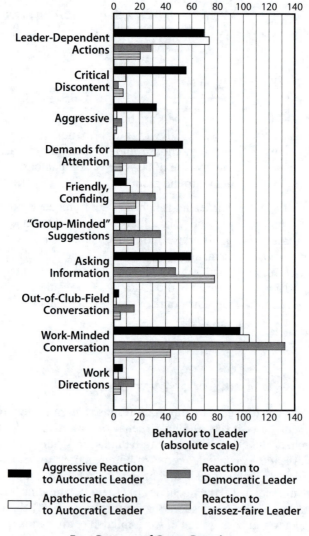

Four Patterns of Group Reaction
to the Three Different Types of Leadership

Figure 1   Boys' Behavior toward Their Leaders

Summarizing, then, we can say that the statistical results and other qualitative types of evidence tend to support the following descriptive generalizations:

A. Laissez-faire was not the same as democracy.

   1. There was less work done in it, and poorer work.

   2. It was more characterized by play.

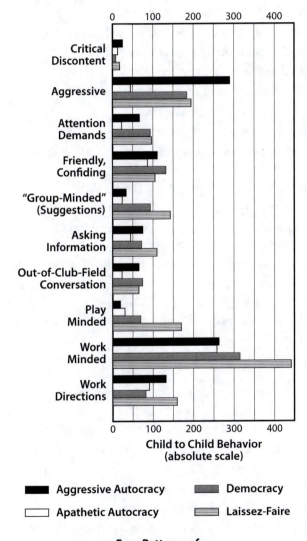

**Four Patterns of
Child to Child Relationship**

Figure 2   Boys' Behavior toward Each Other

    3. More discontent was expressed during the meetings.

    4. In interviews the boys expressed preference for their democratic leader.

B. Democracy can be efficient.

    1. The quantity of work done in autocracy was somewhat greater.

    2. On the other hand, work motivation was stronger in democracy.

    3. Originality was greater in democracy.

C. Autocracy can create much hostility and aggression.

    1. Much more hostility (in a ratio of 30 to 1).

    2. More demands for attention.

    3. More destruction of own property.

    4. More scapegoat behavior.

D. Autocracy can create discontent that does not appear on the surface.

    1. Four boys dropped out, and all of them did so during autocratic periods.

    2. Nineteen out of twenty boys preferred their democratic leader.

    3. There was more discontent expressed in autocracy.

    4. "Release" behavior on the day of transition to a freer atmosphere suggested the presence of previous frustration.

E. There was more dependence and less individuality in autocracy.

    1. There was more "submissive" or "dependent" behavior.

    2. In the submissive reaction to autocracy there was an absolute (though not a relative) reduction in statistical measures of individual differences.

    3. The observers' impression was that in autocracy there was some loss of individuality.

F. There was more group-mindedness, and also more friendliness, in democracy.

    1. The pronoun "I" was relatively less frequent in the democratic group.

    2. Spontaneous subgroups were larger.

    3. Group-minded remarks were much more frequent in democracy.

    4. Friendly remarks were slightly more frequent.

    5. Mutual praise was more frequent in democracy.

    6. Friendly playfulness was more frequent in democracy.

    7. The democratic group showed more readiness to share group property.

. . .

15

Conceptual Contributions of the Ohio State Leadership Studies

Chester A. Schriesheim and Barbara J. Bird

The Ohio State studies comprise one of the most important and comprehensive research programs in the fields of management and organizational behavior. In fact, the leader behavior scales that were developed by the Ohio State research group have been used in literally hundreds of investigations, and the terms *consideration* and *initiating structure* have earned a special niche in the annals of leadership research (Fleishman, 1973; Kerr, Schriesheim, Murphy, & Stogdill, 1974).

Because the Ohio State Leadership Studies were conducted over a quarter-century ago, it seems very likely that time has eroded general knowledge of the contributions of this research program to the field of leadership. Clearly, the contribution made by the development of the Ohio State Leadership Scales (the measures of consideration and initiating structure) is well known and remembered. However, a number of other important contributions, including those related to research methodology and rigor, are probably less well known and, perhaps, even forgotten. . . .

Changing Conception of Leadership

Prior to about 1950, leadership was thought of as a personality trait or a combination of traits. "To pick leaders, the trick was to find people who had these traits well developed. The catch was that it was difficult to get hold of what the traits were" (Fleishman, 1973, p. 2). In 1948 Stogdill reviewed over

Excerpt reprinted with permission of Sage Publications Inc. from *Journal of Management*, Vol. 5, No. 2, pp. 135–145. Originally titled "Contributions of the Ohio State Studies to the Field of Leadership." Copyright © 1979 by Sage Publications Inc. Journals.

one hundred studies that attempted to identify general leadership traits. He concluded that, while some traits were generally found across leaders, leadership might more profitably "be considered in terms of the interaction of variables which are in constant flux and change" (p. 64).

Shortly after Stogdill's (1948) review, Carter and Nixon (1949) produced empirical evidence that, depending upon the type of task involved, the emergence of different leaders from the same groups of people can occur. That evidence, along with a number of additional studies, reinforced Stogdill's conclusions and led to a new approach to the study of leadership: The study of leader behavior and its effects on various individual, group, and organizational outcomes (Jacobs, 1970).

As Fleishman (1973) notes, "The shift in emphasis during that period was from thinking about leadership in terms of traits that someone 'has' to the conceptualization of leadership as a form of activity" (p. 3). However, "at the time the prevalent concepts and behaviorally oriented research were from the University of Michigan Institute for Social Research, which referred to 'employee-centered' versus 'production-centered' supervision"—a one-dimensional conceptualization of leader behavior (Fleishman, 1973, p. 8).

As the Ohio State researchers began to develop their own methods of performing leadership research, it became clear that a one-dimensional conceptualization of leader behavior was inadequate and that a more fruitful conceptualization involved at least two dimensions—consideration and initiating structure.* Fleishman (1973) made this observation:

> The identification of these two factors of consideration and structure pointed to a new method of conceptualizing leadership in which supervisors could, in fact, rank high on both dimensions or have various combinations of these. . . . These were complementary and not necessarily conflicting aspects. (p. 8)

Thus, the Ohio State Leadership Studies played an important role in first changing the conceptual foundations of leadership research from a trait-based approach to a behavioral base. That, of course, was in addition to shifting conceptions of leader behavior from a one-dimensional to a bi- or multi-dimensional perspective.

Production of Situational Theories

A second conceptual contribution of the Ohio State Leadership Studies is that they either produced or led to the formulation of a number of modern situational theories. This contribution had its roots in the early recognition by Ohio State researchers that leadership is, in fact, situational. For example, Fleishman (1953) wrote that "what is effective leadership in one situation

---

*Editor's note: *Consideration* reflects the extent to which an individual is likely to have job relationships characterized by mutual trust, respect for subordinates' ideas, and consideration of their feelings. *Initiating structure* reflects the extent to which an individual is likely to define and structure his role and the roles of his subordinates toward goal attainment.

may be ineffective in another" (p. 2). Similar remarks were made by Stogdill (1948), Hemphill (1950), and other members of the Ohio State research staff.

Building on that early recognition, the Ohio State program developed a highly situational leadership paradigm. The first published version of this model appeared in Morris and Seeman (1950); it was subsequently simplified and clarified by Shartle (1957). Although Shartle's version is far better known than Morris and Seeman's version (perhaps because of its inclusion in the Stogdill and Coons, 1957, monograph), it is a less complete conceptualization of the leadership process. That is due to the omission of "group factors" and "individual factors" as "conditioners" (moderators) of various leader behavior-outcome relationships. However, the Ohio State paradigm was still highly situational in approach, and it included ideas that have only recently become "popular," such as reciprocal causation between leader behavior and various group factors (Kerr & Schriesheim, 1974). Thus, although many subsequent investigators chose to ignore the role of situational factors in leadership research, the Ohio State model clearly pointed out their importance and influenced some individuals to consider various "conditioners," or moderators, of leadership phenomena.

The early Ohio State paradigm also served as an organizing or guiding framework for much of the Ohio State research, and, as such, it was important in organizing Ralph Stogdill's early thoughts on his theory of individuals, groups, and organizations (Stogdill, 1959, 1967). As Jacobs (1970) has noted in his extensive review of the leadership field, this is a "definitive behavioral model of organization" which is based on many of the more important findings in the Ohio State research program (p. 27). Shaw and Costanzo (1970) evaluated this theory very highly.

> Stogdill has provided a useful framework for the analysis of the process through which groups achieve their goals. He has identified the major elements in the group process, thus giving an overall picture of the many variables operating to determine the results achieved by the group. He has avoided both extremes of level of analysis; his concepts are neither so specific as to be unmanageable nor so gross as to be useless. The theory is internally consistent, testable, and in agreement with the evidence concerning group process. (p. 314)

Stogdill's work is clearly a major contribution to theory in management and organizational behavior. However, it should be noted that "the theory appears not to have stimulated research by others" (Shaw & Costanzo, 1970, p. 314), and it has been largely ignored by scholars in the field. Perhaps this is due to lack of knowledge about Stogdill's theory, perhaps not. In any event, although the theory's predictive value is still not established, it continues to have "considerable descriptive appeal" (Shaw & Costanzo, 1970, p. 314).

As a final point about the theoretical contributions of the Ohio State studies to the field of leadership, it seems worthwhile to mention that the two leader behavior dimensions emphasized by the Ohio State research (consideration and initiating structure), as well as the hundreds of studies that have used Ohio State leader behavior description questionnaires, have served as a springboard to a number of other situational theories. For example, even a cursory reading of either the original (House, 1971) or the revised (House & Dessler, 1974) versions of House's Path-Goal Leadership Theory should clearly show the major effects the Ohio State studies had on the formulation of this theory. Yukl's (1971) theory appears similarly affected, as do a number of other theories and approaches. Taking all of these contributions as a whole, it seems clear that the Ohio State Leadership Studies did, in fact, make a substantial conceptual contribution to the field of leadership, both directly and indirectly. . . .

Conclusion

The purpose of this brief article has been to review some of the major contributions of the Ohio State studies to the field of leadership research. It is impossible to adequately cover the achievements of a lengthy and complex research program in a short space; however, it should be apparent that the contribution made by the Ohio State Leadership Studies was substantial.

The interdisciplinary emphasis of the Ohio State program received wide publicity and furthered the cause of interdisciplinary research programs at a time when they were not commonplace. The design and interdisciplinary nature of the program also led to the performance and publication of a large number of quality studies, often in large, integrated volumes, which served to encourage publication of "meaningful chunks" of research.

The Ohio State researchers were central in changing early conceptions of leadership from a set of universal traits to a situation-dependent set of behaviors. They also played a key role in changing conceptions of leader behavior away from a one-dimensional continuum.

The Ohio State studies led to a number of situational theories, directly (Stogdill, 1959) as well as indirectly (e.g., House, 1971). A number of concepts advanced by the Ohio State program (e.g., reciprocal causation) have only recently been "rediscovered," and a number of others are still awaiting "rediscovery."

The methodological contributions of the Ohio State studies are that it served as a methodological model and led to the development of at least one reasonably sound leadership measure (the revised LBDQ).

Taking these contributions as a whole, it can be said with some certainty that the Ohio State studies made a substantial contribution to the field of leadership research and to management and organizational behavior in general.

References

Carter, L. F., & Nixon, M. An investigation of the relationship between four criteria of leadership ability for three different tasks. *Journal of Psychology,* 1949, 23, 245–261.
Fleishman, E. A. The description of supervisory behavior. *Journal of Applied Psychology,* 1953, 37, 1–6.

Fleishman, E. A. Twenty years of consideration and structure. In E. A. Fleishman & J. G. Hunt (Eds.), *Current developments in the study of leadership.* Carbondale: Southern Illinois University Press, 1973.

Hemphill, J. K. Relations between the size of the group and the behavior of superior leaders. *Journal of Social Psychology,* 1950, 32, 11–22.

House, R. J. A path goal theory of leader effectiveness. *Administrative Science Quarterly,* 1971, 16, 321–338.

House, R. J., & Dessler, G. The path-goal theory of leadership: Some post hoc and a priori tests. In J. G. Hunt &. L. L. Larson (Eds.), *Contingency approaches to leadership.* Carbondale: Southern Illinois University Press, 1974.

Jacobs, T. O. *Leadership and exchange in formal organizations.* Alexandria, VA: Human Resources Research Organization, 1970.

Kerr, S., & Schriesheim, C. Consideration, initiating structure, and organizational criteria—An update of Korman's 1966 review. *Personnel Psychology,* 1974, 27, 555–568.

Kerr, S., Schriesheim, C. A., Murphy, C. J., & Stogdill, R. M. Toward a contingency theory of leadership based upon the consideration and initiating structure literature. *Organizational Behavior and Human Performance,* 1974, 12, 62–82.

Morris, R. T., & Seeman, M. The problem of leadership: An interdisciplinary approach. *American Journal of Sociology,* 1950, 56, 149–155.

Shartle, C. L. Introduction. In R. M. Stogdill & A. E. Coons (Eds.), *Leader behavior: Its description and measurement.* Columbus: Bureau of Business Research, Ohio State University, 1957 (Research Monograph 88).

Shaw, M. E., & Costanzo, P. R. *Theories of social psychology.* New York: McGraw-Hill, 1970.

Stogdill, R. M. Personal factors associated with leadership: A survey of the literature. *Journal of Psychology,* 1948, 25, 35–72.

Stogdill, R. M. *Individual behavior and group achievement.* New York: Oxford University Press, 1959.

Stogdill, R. M. Basic concepts for a theory of organization. *Management Science,* 1967, 13, B-866–676.

Stogdill, R. M., & Coons, A. E. (Eds.), *Leader behavior. Its description and measurement.* Columbus: Bureau of Business Research, Ohio State University, 1957 (Research Monograph 84).

Stogdill, R. M., Shartle, C. L., Scott, E. L., Coons, A. E., & Jaynes, W. E. *A predictive study of administrative work patterns.* Columbus: Bureau of Business Research, Ohio State University, 1956 (Research Monograph 85).

Yukl, G. Toward a behavioral theory of leadership. *Organizational Behavior and Human Performance,* 1971, 6, 414–440.

16

Leadership Implications of Personality Development

Chris Argyris

In order to make more precise predictions about the problems involved when human beings are considered for employment by the formal organization, it is necessary to be more explicit, if possible, about the demands the former will tend to make upon the latter. Since the human personality is a developing organism, one way to become more precise is to define the basic growth or development trends "inherent" in it (so long as it remains in the same culture). One can then logically assume that, at any given moment in time, the human personality will be predisposed to find expression for these developmental trends. Such an assumption implies another, namely, that there are basic development trends characteristic of a relatively large majority of the population being considered. This assumption might seem strained, especially to the psychologists inclined to stress individual differences. However, individual differences need not necessarily be ignored. As Kluckhohn and Murray point out, people tend to have some similar basic psychological characteristics because of their biological inheritance and the socio-cultural matrix within which they develop.[1] This does not preclude the possibility that each individual can express these basic characteristics in his own idiosyncratic manner. Thus the concept of individual differences is still held.

So much for the logic behind the developmental trends listed below. It is assumed that human beings in our culture:

1. Tend to develop from a state of passivity as infants to a state of increasing activity as adults. (This is what Erikson[2] has called self-initiative and Bronfenbrenner[3] has called self-determination.)

2. Tend to develop from a state of dependence upon others as infants to a state of relative independence as adults. Relative independence is the ability to "stand on one's own two feet" and simultaneously to acknowledge healthy dependencies.[4] It is characterized by the liberation of the individual from his childhood determiners of behavior (e.g., family) and development of his own set of behavioral determiners. This individual does not tend to react to others (e.g., the boss) in terms of patterns learned during childhood.[5]

3. Tend to develop from being capable of behaving only in a few ways as an infant to being capable of behaving in many different ways as an adult.[6] Tend to develop from having erratic, casual, shallow, quickly-dropped interests as an infant to having deeper interests as an adult. The mature state is characterized by an endless series of challenges, where the reward comes from doing something for its own sake. The tendency is to analyze and study phenomena in their full-blown wholeness, complexity, and depth.[7]

4. Tend to develop from having a short time perspective (i.e., the present largely determines behavior) as an infant to a much longer time perspective as an adult (i.e., where the behavior is more affected by the past and the future).[8] Bakke cogently describes the importance of time perspective in the lives of workers and their families and the variety of foresight practices by means of which they seek to secure the future.[9]

5. Tend to develop from being in a subordinate position in the family and society as an infant to aspiring to occupy an equal and/or superordinate position relative to their peers.

6. Tend to develop from a lack of awareness of self as an infant to an awareness of and control over self as an adult. The adult who tends to experience adequate and successful control over his own behavior tends to develop a sense of integrity (Erikson) and feelings of self-worth.[10] Bakke[11,12] shows that one of the most important needs of workers is to enlarge those areas of their lives in which their own decisions determine the outcome of their efforts.

These dimensions are postulated as being descriptive of a basic multidimensional developmental process along which the growth of individuals in our culture may be measured. Presumably, every individual, at any given moment in time, can have his degree of development plotted along these dimensions. The exact location on each dimension will probably vary with each individual and even within the same individual at different times. Self-actualization may now be determined more precisely as the individual's plotted scores (or profile) along the above dimensions.[13]

It may be helpful to add a few words of explanation concerning these dimensions of personality development.

1. They comprise only one aspect of the total personality. All the properties of personality must be used in trying to understand the behavior of a particular individual. Much depends upon the individual's self-concept, his degree of adaptation and adjustment, and the way in which he perceives his private world.

2. The dimensions are continua where the growth to be measured is assumed to be continuously changing in degree. An individual is presumed to develop continuously in degree, from the infant end to the adult end of each continuum.

3. The only characteristic assumed to hold for all individuals is that, barring unhealthy personality development, they will be predisposed toward moving from the infant end to the adult end of each continuum. This is a model (a construct) describing the basic growth trends. As such, it does not make any predictions about any specific individual. It *does,* however, presume to supply the researcher with basic developmental continua along which the growth of any individual in our culture may be described and measured.

4. So long as one develops in a particular culture one will never obtain maximum expression of these developmental trends. Clearly, all individuals cannot be maximally independent, alive, and so forth all the time and still maintain an organized society. It is the function of culture (e.g., norms and mores) and society (e.g., family, friends, schools, churches, and laws) to inhibit maximum expression and to help an individual adjust and adapt by finding his optimum expression.

A second factor that prevents maximum expression and fosters optimum expression is the individual's own finite limits set by his personality. Some people fear the same amount of independence and activity that others desire. Also, it is commonplace to find some people who do not have the necessary abilities to perform specific tasks. No given individual is known to have developed all known abilities to their full maturity.

Finally, defense mechanisms also are important factors operating to help an individual to deviate from the basic developmental trends.

5. The dimensions described above are constructed in terms of latent characteristics. If one states that an individual needs to be dependent, this need will probably be ascertained by clinical inference because it is one that individuals are not usually aware of. Thus, if one observes an employee acting as though he were independent, it is possible that if one goes below the behavioral surface, the individual may be quite dependent. The obvious example is the employee who always seems to behave in a contrary manner to that desired by management. Although his behavior may give the appearance that he is independent, his contrariness may be due to his great need to be dependent upon management, which he dislikes to admit to himself and to others.

It may be said that an independent person is one whose behavior is not unduly dominated by the influence others have over him. Of course, no individual is completely independent. All of us have our healthy dependencies (i.e., those which help us to be creative and to develop).

One operational criterion to ascertain whether an individual's desire to be, let us say, independent and active is truly a mature manifestation is to ascertain the extent to which he permits others to express the same needs. Thus an autocratic leader may say that he needs to be active and independent; he may also say that he wants subordinates who are the same; however, there is ample research to suggest that his leadership pattern only makes him and his subordinates more dependent-ridden.

The model of growth trends is a construct developed to help the researcher to understand the basic dimensions of growth and to measure any given individual's growth at a particular moment in time. Nothing is included in the model that should be interpreted to mean that all individuals strive toward maximum expression of the adult end of the continuum.

To the extent that individuals who are hired to become agents of organizations are predisposed toward maturity, they will want to express needs or predispositions related to the adult end of each specific developmental continuum. Theoretically, this means that healthy adults will tend to obtain optimum personality expression while at work if they are provided with jobs which permit them to be more active than passive; more independent than dependent; to have longer rather than shorter time perspectives; to occupy higher positions than their peers; to have control over their world; and to express many of their deeper, more important abilities.[14] These developmental trends may be considered as basic properties of the human personality. They are the "givens" that an administrator accepts the moment he decides to accept human beings as agents of the organization. . . .

Bringing together the evidence regarding the impact of the formal organizational principles on the individual, it is concluded that there are some basic incongruencies between the growth trends of a healthy personality and the requirements of the formal organization. If the principles of formal organization are used as ideally defined, employees will tend to work in an environment where (1) they are provided minimal control over their workday world, (2) they are expected to be passive, dependent, and subordinate, (3) they are expected to have a short time perspective, (4) they are induced to perfect and value the frequent use of a few skin-surface shallow abilities, (5) they are expected to produce under conditions leading to psychological failure.

All these characteristics are incongruent to the ones *healthy* human beings are postulated to desire. They are much more congruent with the needs of infants in our culture. In effect, therefore, organizations are willing to pay high wages and provide adequate seniority if mature adults will, for eight hours a day, behave in a less than mature manner!

Notes

[1] Kluckhohn, Clyde, and Murray, H. A., "Personality Formation: The Determinants," in *Personality,* (ed.) by above authors (New York: Knopf, 1949), pp. 35–37.

[2] Erikson, E. H., *Childhood and Society* (New York: Norton, 1950). See also Kolinsky, R., *Personality in the Making* (New York: Harper, 1952), pp. 8–25.

[3] Bronfenbrenner, Urie, "Toward an Integrated Theory of Personality," in *Perception,* by Robert R. Blake and Glen B. Ramsey (New York: Ronald Press, 1951), pp. 206–257.

[4] This is similar to Erikson's "sense of autonomy" and Bronfenbrenner's "state of creative interdependence."

[5] White, Robert W., *Lives in Progress* (New York: Dryden Press, 1952), p. 339.

[6] Lewin and Kounin believe that, as the individual develops needs and abilities, the boundaries between them become more rigid. This explains why an adult is better able than a child to be frustrated in one activity and behave constructively in another. See Lewin, Kurt, *A Dynamic Theory of Personality* (New York: McGraw-Hill, 1935); and Kounin, Jacob S., "Intellectual Development and Rigidity," in *Child Behavior and Development* (ed.) Barker, R., Kounin, J. and Wright, H. R. (New York: McGraw-Hill, 1943), pp. 179–198.

[7] White, Robert W., *op. cit.,* p. 347.

[8] Lewin also cites the billions of dollars that are invested in insurance policies. Lewin, Kurt, "Time Perspective and Morale," in *Resolving Social Conflicts* (New York: Harper, 1948), p. 105.

[9] Bakke, E. W., *The Unemployed Worker* (New Haven: Yale University Press, 1940), pp. 23–24.

[10] Rogers, Carl R., *Client-Centered Therapy* (Cincinnati: MHE Foundation, 1951).

[11] Bakke, E. W., *op. cit.,* p. 247.

[12] Bakke, E. W., *op. cit.,* p. 29.

[13] Another related but discrete set of developmental dimensions may be constructed to measure the protective (defense) mechanisms individuals tend to create as they develop from infancy to adulthood. Exactly how these would be related to the above model is not clear.

[14] It is possible that adults may be found who report that they prefer jobs that permit them to be in a world similar to the infant's. These adults could be immature or neurotic or they could be defending themselves by not desiring self-expression while at work.

17

Leadership and
the Nature of Man

Douglas McGregor

It has become trite to say that industry has the fundamental know-how to utilize physical science and technology for the material benefit of mankind, and that we must now learn how to utilize the social sciences to make our human organizations truly effective.

To a degree, the social sciences today are in a position like that of the physical sciences with respect to atomic energy in the thirties. We know that past conceptions of the nature of man are inadequate and, in many ways, incorrect. We are becoming quite certain that, under proper conditions, unimagined resources of creative human energy could be come available within the organization setting.

We cannot tell industrial management how to apply this new knowledge in simple, economic ways. We know it will require years of exploration, much costly development research, and a substantial amount of creative imagination on the part of management to discover how to apply this growing knowledge to the organization of human effort in industry.

Management's Task: The Conventional View

The conventional conception of management's task in harnessing human energy to organizational requirements can be stated broadly in terms of three propositions. In order to avoid the complications introduced by a label, let us call this set of propositions "Theory X":

1. Management is responsible for organizing the elements of productive enterprise—money, materials, and people—in the interest of economic ends.

2. With respect to people, this is a process of directing their efforts, motivating them, controlling their actions, modifying their behavior to fit the needs of the organization.

3. Without this active intervention by management, people would be passive, even resistant, to organizational needs. They must therefore be persuaded, rewarded, punished, controlled—their activities must be directed. This is management's task. We often sum it up by saying that management consists of getting things done through other people.

Behind this conventional theory there are several additional beliefs which are less explicit, but widespread:

4. The average man is by nature indolent—he works as little as possible.

5. He lacks ambition, dislikes responsibility, and prefers to be led.

6. He is inherently self-centered, indifferent to organizational needs.

7. He is by nature, resistant to change.

8. He is gullible, not very bright, the ready dupe of the charlatan and the demagogue.

The human side of economic enterprise today is fashioned from propositions and beliefs such as these. Conventional organization structures and managerial policies, practices, and programs reflect these assumptions.

In accomplishing its task, with these assumptions as guides, management has conceived of a range of possibilities. At one extreme, management can be "hard" or "strong." The methods for directing behavior involve coercion and threat (usually disguised), close supervision and tight controls over behavior. At the other extreme, management can be "soft" or "weak." The methods for directing behavior involve being permissive, satisfying people's demands and achieving harmony. Then they will be tractable and accept direction.

This range has been fairly completely explored during the past half century, and management has learned some things from the exploration. There are difficulties with the "hard" approach. Force breeds counter-forces: restriction of output, antagonism, militant unionism, subtle but effective sabotage of management objectives. This "hard" approach is especially difficult during times of full employment.

There are also difficulties in the "soft" approach. It leads frequently to the abdication of management—to harmony, perhaps, but to indifferent performance. People take advantage of the soft approach. They continually expect more, but they give less and less.

Currently, the popular theme is "firm but fair." This is an attempt to gain the advantages of both the hard and the soft approaches. It is reminiscent of Teddy Roosevelt's "speak softly and carry a big stick."

Is the Conventional View Correct?

The findings which are beginning to emerge from the social sciences challenge this whole set of beliefs about man and human nature and about the task of management. The evidence is far from conclusive, certainly, but it is suggestive. It comes from the laboratory, the clinic, the schoolroom, the home, and even to a limited extent from industry itself.

The social scientist does not deny that human behavior in industrial organizations today is what management perceives it to be. He has, in fact, observed it and studied it fairly extensively. But he is pretty sure that this behavior is not a consequence of man's inherent nature. It is a consequence rather of the nature of industrial organizations, of management philosophy, policy and practice. The conventional approach of Theory X is based on mistaken notions of what is cause and what is effect. . . .

A New Theory of Management

For this, and many other reasons, we require a different theory of the task of managing people based on more adequate assumptions about human nature and human motivation. I am going to be so bold as to suggest the broad dimension of such a theory. Call it "Theory Y," if you will.

1. Management is responsible for productive enterprise—money, materials, the interest of economic ends.

2. People are *not* by nature passive or resistant to organizational needs. They have become so as a result of experience in organizations.

3. The motivation, the potential for development, the capacity for assuming responsibility, the readiness to direct behavior toward organizational goals are all present in people. Management does not put them there. It is a responsibility of management to make it possible for people to recognize and develop these characteristics for themselves.

4. The essential task of management is to arrange organizational conditions and methods of operation so that people can achieve their own goals best by directing their own efforts toward organizational objectives.

Some Difficulties

It is no more possible to create an organization today which will be a full, effective application of this theory than it was to build an atomic power plant in 1945. There are many formidable obstacles to overcome. The conditions imposed by conventional organization theory and by the approach of scientific management for the past half century have tied men to limited jobs which do not utilize their capabilities, have discouraged the acceptance of responsibility, have encouraged passivity and have eliminated meaning from work. Man's habits, attitudes, expectations—his whole conception of membership in an industrial organization—have been conditioned by his experience under these circumstances.

People today are accustomed to being directed, manipulated, controlled in industrial organizations and to finding satisfaction for their social, ego and self-fulfillment needs away from the job. This is true as much of management as of workers. Genuine "industrial citizenship"—to borrow a term from Drucker—is a remote and unrealistic idea, the meaning of which has not even been considered by most members of industrial organizations. . . .

Another way of saying this is that Theory X places exclusive reliance upon external control of human behavior, while Theory Y relies heavily on self-control and self-direction. It is worth noting that this difference is the difference between treating people as children and treating them as mature adults. After generations of the former, we cannot expect to shift to the latter overnight.

Applying the Ideas

Concepts such as decentralization, delegation, job enlargement and participation are certainly congruent with the tenets of Theory Y. However, the not infrequent failure of such ideas as these to work as well as expected is often attributable to the fact that management has "bought the idea" but within the framework of Theory X and its assumptions.

Delegation is not an effective way of exercising management by control. Participation becomes a farce when it is applied as a sales gimmick or a device for kidding people into thinking they are important. Only the management that has confidence in human capacities and is itself directed toward organizational objectives rather than toward the preservation of personal power can grasp the implications of this emerging theory. Such management will find and apply successfully other innovative ideas as we move slowly toward the full implementation of a theory like Y. . . .

18

The Managerial Grid

Robert Blake and Jane Mouton

A variety of theories regarding managerial behavior can be identified. These theories, or sets of assumptions, are based on the way in which three organization universals are connected to one another.[1] One of the three is *concern for production;* the amount of emphasis supervision places on achieving production. A second is *concern for people;* the productive unit of the organization. The third is hierarchy; the *boss* aspect. Whenever a man acts as a manager, he is in some way making assumptions about how to solve problems of achieving organization purposes of production through people.[2]

Dimensions of the Grid

Before going on let's define exactly what we mean by "concern for." This is not meant to indicate *how much* (such as, how much production, meaning quantity), nor is it intended to reflect the degree that the needs of people actually are met. Rather, emphasis here is on the *degree* of "concern for" which is present in the *boss* because his *actions* are rooted in, and flow out of, his own *basic attitudes.* What is significant is *how* a supervisor is concerned about production and *how* he concerns himself about people, and *how* these concerns intertwine.[3,4]

Concern for Production

The words *production* or *people* cover a range of considerations. Attitudes of concern toward production, for example, may be seen in the quality of policy decisions, the number of creative ideas that applied research turns into useful products, procedures or processes; number of accounts processed; quality and thoroughness of staff services; workload and efficiency measurements; volume of sales or units of physical output. Production as used here is not limited to *things*. Its proper meaning covers whatever it is that organizations engage people to accomplish.

At the lowest level, it is true, concern for production may take the form of the number of units of things that can be counted or of time required to attain a certain production schedule. But at the top of an organization, concern for production may be demonstrated in the kind of policies which are established and the character of direction given to major programs of organization effort. Indeed, the concern for production at the top may be expressed through finding new directions or new products to sustain organization growth and development.

Concern for People

In a similar fashion, concern for people can be expressed in a variety of different ways. Included are concern for degree of personal commitment to completing a job one is responsible for; accountability based on trust; self-esteem or the personal worth of an individual; establishing and maintaining good working conditions; maintaining an equitable salary structure and fringe benefits; desire for security in work; social relations or friendships with associates; etc.

As will be seen, *concern for production* and *concern for people* are expressed in vastly different ways, depending on the specific manner in which these two concerns are joined.[5]

"Pure" Theories

The *Managerial Grid,* depicted in Figure 1, shows these two concerns and a range of possible interactions between them. The horizontal axis indicates concern for production while the vertical axis indicates concern for people. Each is expressed as a nine-point scale of concern. The number 1 in each instance represents minimum concern. The 9 stands for maximum concern.

At the lower left corner of the grid is the 1, 1 style. This has a minimum of both concerns; that is, of concern for production and concern for people. Going up the grid from the 1, 1 style to the upper left corner is found the 1, 9 style. Here there is a minimum of concern for production but maximum concern for people. In the lower right corner is 9, 1. This style has a maximum concern for production and a minimum for human aspects. In the upper right corner is the 9, 9 style, where concern for both people and production reaches maximum. Then, in the center is the 5, 5 style, which is a "middle of the road" or an intermediate amount of both kinds of concerns.

It should be emphasized that the manner in which these two concerns are linked together by a manager defines how he uses hierarchy. In addition, the character of *concern for* at different grid positions differs, even though the *degree* may be the same. For example, when high concern for people is coupled with a low concern for production, the type of people concern expressed (*i.e.,* that people be "happy") is far different from the type of high concern for people

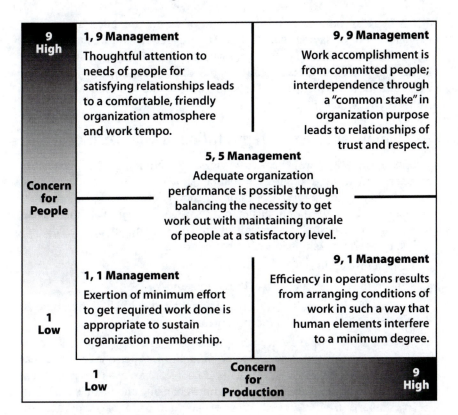

Figure 1   The Managerial Grid

shown when a high concern for production is also evident (*i.e.*, that people be involved in the work and strive to contribute to organization purpose).

A number of additional managerial theories may be shown on this grid. Indeed, in a 9-point system such as is employed here, 81 "mixtures" of these two concerns might be pictured. However, emphasis first will be placed on analyzing the assumptions at the corners and midpoint. Each of these five theories defines a definite but different set of assumptions regarding how individuals, in fact, do orient themselves for managing situations of production that involve people. The important point here is that when a manager confronts a situation in which work is to be accomplished through people, there are, indeed, alternative ways for him to go about supervising. To increase his managerial competence he needs to know them and to be able to select the best course of action for any given situation from among a number of possibilities.[6]

As in any field of applied endeavor, disagreement can arise between what is the best theory and what theory is most realistic for practical application in a "live" situation. However, as in any applied setting, the answer regarding what is best can only be given in the light of existing realities. There is no ideological way of saying what is best without reference to actual circumstances. But the choice is neither arbitrary nor random. The *results* a manager obtains will reflect, in predictable ways, the kinds of assumptions he applied in that situation.[7] If the assumptions do not "fit" the situation well, poorer results will be obtained than if they do.

Significance and Interpretation of Grid Positions

Should the five "pure" theories be viewed as defining a set of personality characteristics? If not, then in what manner should they be considered? One answer is that these positions constitute anchorages for managerial attitudes and practices. Conceived of in this manner, aspects of the grid are more accurately regarded as describing systems of pressures acting on an individual to manage in a certain fashion. Such pressures arise:

1. from inside himself,

2. from the immediate external situation, and/or

3. from characteristics of the organizational system including traditions, established practices and procedures.

Though most people seem to be predisposed to manage in one way or another, points on the grid are *not* to be thought of as personality types that isolate a given individual's behavior. They do not slot him in a rigid and inflexible way into a certain place. Behavior is more changing and flexible than that.

In comparison with a mechanical explanation of managerial behavior, the grid pictures a number of different sets of assumptions about how an individual *can* manage. Any set of assumptions is subject to change. Whenever a person changes his underlying managerial assumptions, his actual managerial practices shift accordingly, or else a gross discrepancy is present between the attitudes he expresses and the actions he takes. A given individual's style, then, may be viewed as a dominant set of assumptions.[8] These assumptions orient his thinking and his behavior in dealing with production/people relationships. Furthermore, he may or may not be aware of the assumptions that are guiding his actions.[9] The purpose of this effort, and of much management training, is to aid an individual to become more knowledgeable regarding his own assumptions about how to manage.

Observe an individual's behavior in a variety of situations. It becomes clear that even the notion of one dominant style, a single set of managerial assumptions, is not sufficient to catch the full implication of a person's managerial approach. In addition to a dominant set of managerial assumptions, which are the most characteristic of the managerial style a person has adopted, the concept of a *backup* set of assumptions is a useful one. An individual's backup theory is the one he uses when his dominant theory fails to get the desired results. It is the style he falls back on. Any style may be a backup to any other theory as a dominant style.

Which managerial style is dominant for any given person in any particular situation can be determined by any one or several sets of conditions in combination.

Organization

Managerial behavior frequently is determined by situational factors, such as the organization in which a person operates. Thus, when organizational practices are so fixed or rigid as to permit only small variations in individual behavior, the managerial style exhibited may reflect little of a man's personal thinking and much of his organization beliefs about "the right way to manage." Therefore, one section within each of the anchor positions is concerned with organization or situational requirements which are likely to call forth various managerial styles.

Situation

The situation itself may be the determining or overriding factor dictating which set of managerial assumptions are employed to deal with it. Management of people in the crisis of an explosive situation is likely to be different than it would be under circumstances that are routine.

Values

Any individual's choice of managerial assumptions may be based on values or beliefs he holds concerning the "right" way to treat people, or the way to manage to achieve "best" results. Any given set of assumptions can have a personal value attached to them which represents an individual's private conviction concerning the desirability of any managerial style as a dominant one.

Personality

The dominant managerial style may, to an important degree, result from deep-rooted personality characteristics which predispose an individual to prefer one approach over another. Thus, in the sections concerned with the five anchor positions (Figure 1), the personality dispositions likely to be found in conjunction with a given managerial style are presented.

Chance

Finally, a set of managerial assumptions may guide a person's behavior because he has not been confronted with, nor has discovered in his own experience, that other sets of assumptions about how to manage are available. "Chance," so to speak, has not helped him learn. But many managers, upon learning the variety of managerial styles available to them, do shift, sometimes rather dramatically, from one style to another, as they seek to integrate people into production. Seeing alternatives, they embrace a different set of assumptions.

The point to be emphasized here is that managerial styles are *not* fixed. They are not unchanging. They are determined by a range of factors. . . .

The 9, 1 Managerial Style

In the lower right-hand corner of the grid is 9, 1. At this position a high concern for production, 9, is coupled with a low concern for people, 1. In the 9, 1 managerial style, the assumption is made that, somehow, there is an inevitable contradiction between organizational needs of production and personal needs of people. If one is met, the other must be sacrificed. Yet, people must be used to attain the production for which the manager feels responsible. If he acts from a 9, 1 orientation, he seeks to resolve the dilemma by arranging conditions of work which minimize feelings and attitudes.[10] He does so in a way that prevents the "human elements from interfering with efficiency and output."

A manager operating at a 9, 1 level, in the extreme, might be characterized as an exacting taskmaster. He drives himself and his people alike. One thought monopolizes his concern and action—*production*. 9, 1 personifies the entrepreneurial spirit.[11]

9, 1 is one of the positions on the grid where concern for people is low. Thus, it is not surprising that topics such as conflict, creativity, and commitment receive little attention. This does not indicate that topics such as conflict, creativity and commitment do not contain managerial assumptions under 9, 1. Indeed, they do. The point is that they are weighted unevenly. Far more attention is given to how to organize work than to the conditions of organizing people in order to make it possible for them to work with maximum productivity.[12]

Management under 9, 1

Under a 9, 1 theory, a manager has a position of authority in the hierarchy and he knows it. He feels his responsibilities are to plan, direct, and control the actions of his subordinates in whatever way is necessary to reach the production objectives of the enterprise. The boss plans, subordinates execute. They carry out the various plans, directions and schedules placed upon them. The aim under this approach is to get production! Schedules are to be met! People are expected to do what they are told to do—no more, no less.[13] A 9, 1 managerial orientation is typified in the following quotations:

Planning.   "I do planning by setting the production quotas and schedules to be followed by each subordinate. Then, I work out the procedures and operating ground rules and I make individual assignments. I also establish check points so I can ascertain that actions I have authorized are being taken as I intended them to be done."

Work Execution.   "I watch the work closely. I criticize as I see the necessity for it and authorize changes as needs for them arise."

Follow-up.   "I have plans laid for the next assignments and move people on to them as operations dictate. Recognition and corrective action are extended to individuals on a one-by-one basis."

These three statements contain a number of 9, 1 assumptions concerning how to manage performance. The above orientations to managerial responsibilities are, in themselves, keys to understanding the 9, 1 style. The success of 9, 1 management is measured solely in terms of production and profit.[14] Personal managerial success in this context, then, has its reward in achieving production goals. *Achievement* becomes the watchword of the 9, 1 approach.[15] Here organization is like a competitive hurdle race. Victory goes to the swiftest, the one able to surmount each hurdle he confronts—without help. To the victor belong the spoils of organization. . . .

The 1, 9 Managerial Style

In the upper left-hand corner of the grid is the 1, 9 managerial orientation. Here a low functional concern for production, 1, is coupled with high concern for people. As with 9, 1, the 1, 9 managerial orientation also is rooted in the assumption that production requirements are contrary to the needs of people.[16] To a manager with a 1, 9 style, however, the attitudes and feelings of people *are* important. They are valuable in their own right. They come first. Within this context, conditions are arranged that personal, social and welfare needs can be met.[17]

Management under 1, 9

When asked to describe his hierarchical responsibilities, a person operating under 1, 9 assumptions is likely to use the same *words* as those the manager operating under 9, 1 might use. He would say that his job is to plan, direct and control the activities of *his* subordinates. His aim as a manager, however, is to avoid pressuring for production at a rate higher than that which would win acceptance from organizational members. He leads by following. By deemphasizing production, the 1, 9 approach avoids some of the conflict that arises from production decisions that disturb people. A deeper 1, 9 attitude is seen in the feeling that, "You can't *push* people for production because if you do, they balk and resist," or "You can lead a horse to water, but you can't make him drink." "When people have turned against you, they are in trouble and you are, too." How he plans and directs subordinates and the way in which follow-up takes place are briefly outlined below.[18]

Planning. "I give broad assignments to my subordinates and convey my confidence by saying, 'I'm sure you know how to do this and that you will do it well.'"

Work Execution. "I see my people frequently and encourage them to visit with me as their time permits. My door is always open. My goal is to see to it that they are able to get the things they want. That's the way to encourage people."

Follow-up. "I hold a meeting with those who are on the job where I place emphasis on congratulating the group as well as individuals. We have fun and when we get down to business our wrap-up sessions usually revolve around why we did as well as we did do and how we can help things to go as smoothly or more so in the future. Criticism rarely helps. My motto is 'don't say anything if you can't say something nice.'"

The 1, 9 managerial style, in other words, focuses on how to arrange conditions of work which will permit people to fit them with comfort, ease and security.[19] Under the 1, 9 set of assumptions, it is felt that organizational demands for production often are harsh, overdemanding and unnecessary. When his people become disturbed, the manager with a 1, 9 orientation also becomes disturbed. To counterbalance the demands of the organization, the manager can lighten work conditions by emphasizing the positive aspects of work, or by giving a bonus of some sort.[20] Informal conversation, a joke, an understanding pat on the back, a smile, coffee together—all help the task to pass a little easier and to make life a little more enjoyable. . . .[21]

The 1, 1 Managerial Style

Low concern for production, 1, is coupled with low concern for people, 1, in the lower left-hand corner of the grid, where the 1, 1 managerial pattern is located. Like 9, 1 or 1, 9, an incompatibility is assumed to exist between production requirements and needs of people. However, since concern for both is low, the manager with a 1, 1 orientation experiences little or no dilemma between production and people—he is more or less "out of it." But, the person managing 1, 1 has learned to "be out of it," while remaining in the organization. Little is expected of him, and little is given by him in return.[22] 1, 1 as an approach is rare in organization situations of nonrepetitive action where each situation presents a different set of problems to be solved. It is far more common in routine operations, and in various staff functions.[23]

The phrase "1, 1 management" of people is an anomaly. A person who has adopted a 1, 1 orientation might better be described as "lost among," rather than "managing" people. Anomalous though it may seem, there are, today, many persons in managerial ranks whose supervision is best pictured as 1, 1.

The 1, 1 approach is unnatural. It comes to those who accepted defeat. To permit oneself again to become involved and concerned over what happens in the work situation can only lead to deeper frustration and discouragement.[24] It is an approach characterized, then, by low involvement with people and the contribution of minimum effort toward organization purpose.[25]

Management under 1, 1

The supervisory approach under 1, 1 is to put people on jobs and to leave them alone. He does this by letting people do their work as they see fit. He does not pester them. "Don't put your hand in a hornet's nest," is a motto characteristic of a manager who operates in the 1, 1 direction. His administrative responses are of minimum movement, enough to get the pressure off his back, but little more. The following show how a 1, 1 supervisor views his managerial responsibilities.[26]

Planning. "I give broad assignments though I don't think in terms of goals or schedules. I do little planning. A way that you might describe my job is I'm a message carrier. I carry the story from those one level above to those one level below me. I put as little 'embroidery' or interpretation on what I pass as possible. I do what my job description requires."

Work Execution. "If I make the rounds, I take little on-the-spot action. People are free to solve their own problems. They like it that way. I do, too."

Follow-up. "If he inquires, I talk to my boss who tells me what is to be done next and to find out how he wants it done and who he wants to do it."

With a 1, 1 orientation, a person takes responsibility for filling his position, but only in a superficial way. His imprint is like a shadow on the sand. It passes over the ground, but leaves no permanent mark. Before judging whether such a prospect is unattractive, however, consider first what this can mean. A person may leave no mark in the organization of which he is a member, but neither does the organization leave its mark on him—a mark which, otherwise, could inflict the pain of anxiety and the frustration of failure. . . .[27]

The 5, 5 Managerial Style

The middle of the grid identifies 5, 5. It is where intermediate concern for production, 5, is linked with moderate concern for people. 5, 5 also assumes conflict between organization purpose of production and needs of people.[28] Rather than resolving the issue in the direction of production as in 9, 1, or of people as in 1, 9, or "leaving the field" as in 1, 1, satisfactory or workable solutions are found through equilibrium or compromise processes.[29] Acceptable, even though not sound, production is possible from this approach without unduly disturbing people.[30] The 5, 5 orientation assumes that people are practical, that they realize *some* effort will have to be exerted on the job. Also, by yielding some push for production and considering attitudes and feelings, people accept the situation and are more or less "satisfied."

The 5, 5 approach is based on a persuasive logic. It says; "What person or movement has ever had its exclusive way? Extreme positions are to be avoided. Doesn't experience show, again and again, that steady progress comes from compromise, trading out, and a willingness to yield some advantages in order to gain others? Democracy, as it has come to be interpreted by many today, operates quite well by yielding to the many and mollifying the few." Realistically, then, the guiding assumption of 5, 5 is *not to seek the best position for either production or people* ("that would be too 'ideal'"), but to find the position that is in between both, about half-way.[31]

Management under 5, 5

The key to 5, 5 is found in placing some emphasis on production. Since recognition is given to the fact that, realistically, people cannot be ignored or disregarded, some deliberate consideration is given to the people side. Yet, this is different than 9, 1, as can be seen in the managerial examples that will follow; the 5, 5 approach holds to the responsibility to plan, direct and control, typical of 9, 1.[32] However, just as important, a major part of this responsibility is seen to be coupled with a need to communicate, to get understanding, and to elicit suggestions from subordinates.[33] This aspect is different from 1, 9. In other ways the 5, 5 style is designed to open up the possibility of subordinates' thinking about their job in more than a 1, 9 social manner.[34] The way in which combining and splitting is done in a 5, 5 orientation can be seen in the following descriptions.[35]

Planning. "I plan work for each subordinate, more in a general way than down to details. After explaining aims and schedules, I make individual assignments. I insure that subordinates are agreeable with what is expected of them and that they feel free to come back if they need help in carrying my assignments out."

Work Execution. "I keep up with each man's job and review his progress with him from time to time or when he asks for it. I give positive suggestions if a subordinate is having difficulty."

Follow-up. "I meet with those involved in the job on a carrot-and-stick approach. I try to get discussion in order to point out good points as well as mistakes and to indicate how people can improve without *telling them.* Each individual gets the opportunity to discuss any reasonable suggestions he might have for improvement before I describe the next assignment."

In other words, there is a mixture, or balance, between taking people into consideration while still emphasizing the relevant aspects of work. In day-by-day activities, if either production or people are suffering, the 5, 5 approach is to fix it by finding a new position that can eliminate the imbalance. The flow of work through people under conditions of 5, 5 is a delicate one. The 5, 5 approach requires constant attention. It demands a delicate "balancing act," combined with the skills of a go-between. . . .

The 9, 9 Managerial Style

In the upper right-hand corner is located 9, 9, where a high concern for production, 9, is coupled with a 9 of high concern for people. Unlike the other basic approaches, it is assumed in the 9, 9 managerial style that there is no necessary and inherent conflict between organization purpose of production requirements and the needs of people. Under 9, 9 effective integration of people with production is possible by involving them and their ideas in determining the conditions and strategies of work.[36,37] Needs of people to think, to apply mental effort in productive work and to establish sound and mature relationships with one another are utilized to accomplish organizational requirements.[38] A basic aim of 9, 9 management, then, is to promote the conditions that integrate creativity, high productivity, and high morale through concerted team action.[39]

The 9, 9 orientation views the integration of people into work from a different perspective than other approaches. In contrast with 9, 1, the solution for a given problem is not necessarily defined by the boss' authority.[40] Unlike 5, 5, the 9, 9 approach is oriented toward discovering the best and most effective solution in a given situation, not the one defined by tradition, etc.[41] By utilizing the mental *and* execution skills of people, this approach aims at the highest attainable level of production. This highest level is only possible through work situations that meet mature needs of people. Sociability for the sake of togetherness, status based on aspects unrelated to work, or power exercised for its own sake, or out of frustration, are not viewed as mature needs. Rather, *accomplishment* and *contribution* are seen as the critical aspect of organization performance and individual motivation. When one is met, the other is gratified automatically.

Management under 9, 9

Mutual understanding and agreement as to what the organizational goals are and of the means by which they are to be attained is at the core of work direction.[42,43] In a real sense people and production *are* interconnected.[44] The manager with a 9, 9 orientation views his responsibility as seeing to it (but not necessarily doing it by himself) that planning, directing and controlling *are* accomplished soundly. Who are best qualified to do it? Those with the most stake in the outcome, regardless of level.

As in the examples following, a boss with a 9, 9 orientation still retains the responsibility for such aspects of work direction as planning. There is no abdication of the 1, 1 variety, nor is there tolerance with "least common denominator" solutions of the kind that crop up under 1, 9, nor of middle-road compromises of divergent interests as in 5, 5. But in the 9, 9 approach others, where indicated, are drawn in on the actual planning of work activities. He might say that, "My job is not necessarily to *make* sound decisions, but it surely is my job to *see* to it that sound decisions are made." The 9, 9 style is seen in the following.[45]

Planning. "I get the people who have relevant facts and/or stakes in the outcome to review the whole picture and to get their reaction and ideas. Then, I, with them, establish goals and flexible schedules as well as procedures and ground rules, and set up individual responsibilities."

Work Execution. "I keep familiar with major points of progress and exert influence on subordinates through identifying problems and revising goals and schedules *with* them as necessary. I lend assistance when needed by helping to remove road blocks."

Follow-up. "I conduct a 'wrap-up' with those responsible. We evaluate how a job went and probe what can be learned from it and how what we learned can be applied in future work. If appropriate, I give recognition on a team basis as well as recognizing outstanding individual contributions."

A general theme in the three excerpts above is that of *creating* conditions of work where people understand the problem, have stakes in the outcome, and where their ideas make a real contribution to the result obtained. This concept of participation is based on the notion that when people can think, when they have influence on outcomes, they *support* rather than comply or resist. Furthermore, with effective leadership, which can arouse *sound* participation, the probability is increased that solutions achieved will be sound and fundamental, not needing constant review and revision. People are able to give the best *of* themselves rather than seeking the best *for* themselves, as is often true when one's contributions are not sought.

Notes

[1] The line of thinking that leads to the generalized version of the Managerial Grid is consistent with work by C. Argyris, *Personality and Organization.* New York: Harper, 1957; K. D. Benne and P. Sheats, Functional Roles of Group Members. *Journal of Social Issues,* 2, 1948, 42–47; E. A. Fleishman, E. F. Harris, & H. E. Burtt, *Leadership and Supervision in Industry.* Columbus, Ohio: Bureau of Educational Research, Ohio State University, 1955; R. Likert, *New Patterns of Management.* New York: McGraw-Hill, 1961; D. McGregor, *The Human Side of Enterprise.* New York: McGraw-Hill, 1960; D. Moment & A. Zaleznik, *Role Development and Interpersonal Competence.* Boston: Harvard University, 1963; and T. Parsons, R. F. Bales & E. A. Shils, *Working Papers in the Theory of Action.* Glencoe, Ill: Free Press, 1953.

[2] Sherif, M. & Sherif, C. *An Outline of Social Psychology.* (Rev.) New York: Harper & Bros., 1956, 143–180.

[3] Simon, H. A. Recent Advances in Organization Theory. *Research Frontiers in Politics and Government,* 1955. Washington, D.C.: Brookings.

[4] Allen, L. A. *Management and Organization.* New York: McGraw, 1958, 58.

[5] Bavelas, A. Communication Patterns in Task-Oriented Groups. *Journal of the Acoustical Society of America,* 22, 1950, 725–730. Also in D. Cartwright & A. Zander, (Eds.), *Group Dynamics: Research and Theory.* Evanston, Ill.: Row, Peterson, 1956, 493–506. Pfeffer, J. M. & Sherwood, F. P. *Administrative Organization.* Englewood Cliffs, N. J.: Prentice-Hall, 1960, 52–73. Kelley, H. H. Communication in Experimentally Created Hierarchies. *Human Relations,* 4, 1951, 39–56.

[6] Appley, L. A. *Management in Action.* New York: American Management Association, 1956, 20–22.

[7] Likert, R. A Motivational Approach to a Modified Theory of Organization and Management. In M. Haire (Ed.), *Modern Organization Theory.* New York: Wiley, 1959, 184–217. Stanton, E. S. Company Policies and Supervisors' Attitudes toward Supervision. *Journal of Applied Psychology,* 44, 1960, 22–26.

[8] In this book, attention is not focused on organization and managerial principles and functions *per se;* such as unity of direction, span of control, delegation of authority, etc. Rather, consideration is limited to the assumptions a manager operates under when, for example, he delegates authority, or plans a given work activity. Organization principles and management functions are treated as neutral or as givens, whereas the *ways* in which they are applied under different managerial styles *are* subject to examination.

[9] Blake, R. R., Mouton, J. S. & Bidwell, A. C. "The Managerial Grid," *Advanced Management-Office Executive,* 1, 1962, 12–15, 36. Blake, R. R., and Mouton, J. S. The Developing Revolution in Management Practices. *ASTD Journal,* 16, 1962, 29–50.

[10] In their early work with small groups, Bales and others identified two distinct roles assumed by various members in problem-solving groups—"task" role and "social" role. Both sets of role behavior are rarely observed in the actions of any one individual, i.e., a person is either concerned for the task (production) or his concern is for the social (people) aspects of a group's activities—seldom both *at the same time.* Representative experimental work and discus-

sion of theory is contained in R. F. Bales, The Equilibrium Problem in Small Groups. In T. Parsons, R. F. Bales & E. A. Shils, *Working Papers in the Theory of Action*. Glencoe, Ill.: Free Press, 1953, 111–161. (Also abridged in A. P. Hare, E. F. Borgatta & R. F. Bales (Eds.), *Small Groups*. New York: Knopf, 1955, 424–456.) Also, see Slater, P. E. Role Differentiations in Small Groups. *American Sociological Review*, 20, 1955, 300–310; Bales, R. F. & Slater, P. Role Differentiation. In T. Parsons, R. F. Bales, et al. *Family, Socialization, and Interaction Process*. Glencoe, Ill.: Free Press, 1955; Slater, P. E. Role Differentiations in Small Groups. *American Sociological Review*, 20, 1955, 300–310.

[11] A recent study by Moment and Zaleznik is in line with the early work of Bales, *et al*. In addition to Task (Technical) and Social roles, Moment and Zaleznik identify a detached, sometimes passive, sometimes hostile and competitive role (Underchosen) and a Fusion role (Star), the latter being high on both task and "congeniality." *Stars* demonstrated a higher combination of task *and* socially relevant behavior. However, a partial dichotomy rather than integration (Fusion) in the two concerns is suggested in some aspects for the roles of the Stars: "Satisfaction comes from engagement in the social-technical process in a way that *balances* progress toward improvement with the disruptions of change." p. 121. Moment, D. & Zaleznik, A. *Role Development and Interpersonal Competence*. Boston: Harvard University, 1963. (Italics, i.e., *balances*, ours). A split between production and people concerns is still assumed under 5, 5 and is contrasted with an *integration* of these two concerns under 9, 9. Since 5, 5 (balancing), *per se*, is not treated by Moment and Zaleznik, it appears that both 5, 5 and 9, 9 (integration) fall into the category of "Stars."

[12] Maier, N. R. F. *Psychology in Industry*. (2nd Ed.). Boston: Houghton, 1955, 139–140.

[13] Marrow, A. J. *Making Management Human*. New York: McGraw-Hill, 1957, 73.

[14] Barnard, C. I. *The Functions of the Executive*. Cambridge: Harvard University, 1938, 67; Urwick, L. *The Elements of Administration*. New York: Harper, 1953, 36–39.

[15] Davis, R. C. *The Fundamentals of Top Management*. New York: Harper and Brothers, 1951. *Working Papers in the Theory of Action*. Glencoe, Ill.: Free Press, 1953, 111–161. Some Philosophies of Management. *Advanced Management*, 24, (7), 1959, 6–8.

[16] McNair, M. P. Thinking Ahead: What Price Human Relations? *Harvard Business Review*, 35, March-April, 1957, 15–39.

[17] Walker, C. R. & Guest, R. H. *The Man on the Assembly Line*. Cambridge: Harvard University Press, 1952, 141–163.

[18] Mayfield, H. The Counseling Function in Management. *The Personnel Administrator*, 3, (1), 1958, 23–24. Also in I. L. Heckmann, Jr., & S. G. Huneryager (Eds.), *Human Relations in Management*. Cincinnati: South-Western, 1960, 513–519.

[19] *The Managerial Grid: A Self-Examination of Managerial Styles*. Austin, Tex.: Scientific Methods, Inc., 1962.

[20] Gellerman, S. W. *People, Problems and Profits*. New York: McGraw-Hill, 1960, 165; Cleeton, G. U. The Human Factor in Industry. *The Annals of the American Academy of Political and Social Sciences*, 274, March, 1951, 17–24. Also in I. L. Heckmann, Jr., & S. G. Huneryager (Eds.), *op. cit.*, 17–26.

[21] Stagner, R. *Psychology of Industrial Conflict*. New York: Wiley, 1956, 327–329.

[22] Shaw, D. M. Size and Share in Task and Motivation in Work Groups. *Sociometry*, 23, 1960, 203–208.

[23] Blau, P. M. *The Dynamics of Bureaucracy*. Chicago: University of Chicago, 1955, 172–179, 184–88; Collins, O., Dalton, M. & Roy, D. Restriction of Output and Social Cleavage in Industry. *Applied Anthropology*, 5, (8), 1946, 1–14; Whyte, W. F. *Money and Motivation*. New York: Harper, 1955; Argyris, C. *Personality and Organization*. New York: Harper, 1957.

[24] McGee, R. *Social Disorganization in America*. San Francisco: Chandler, 1962, 66–78.

[25] Experimental studies and observations of children and adults have demonstrated the reactive and accommodative behavior of individuals in situations of prolonged frustration. The adaptive behavior described in these studies is most like the 1, 1 orientation. Representative studies include: Eisenberg, P. & Lazarsfeld, P. F. The Psychological Effects of Unemployment. *Psychological Bulletin*, 35, 1938, 358–390; Lewin, K., Lippitt, R., & White, R. K. Patterns of Aggres-

sive Behavior in Experimentally Created "Social Climates." *Journal of Social Psychology,* 10, 1939, 271–299; Dollard, J., Doob, L. W., Miller, N. E., Mowrer, O. H., & Sears, R. R. *Frustration and Aggression.* New Haven: Yale University, 1939; Barker, R. G., Dembo, T., & Lewin, K. Frustration and Regression: An Experiment with Young Children. *University of Iowa Studies in Child Welfare,* 18, I, 1941; Merrill, M. A. *Problems of Child Delinquency.* Boston: Houghton, 1947; Marquart, D. I. The Pattern of Punishment and Its Relation to Abnormal Fixation in Adult Human Subjects. *Journal of Genetic Psychology,* 39, 1948, 107–144; Wright, M. E. The Influence of Frustration Upon the Social Relations of Young Children. *Character* & *Personality,* 12, 1943, 111–112; Maier, N. R. F. *Pruetration: The Study of Behavior Without a Goal.* Ann Arbor: University of Michigan, 1949; Heber, R. F. & Heber, M. E. The Effect of Group Failure and Success on Social Status. *Journal of Educational Psychology,* 48, 1957, 129–134; Pepitone, A. & Kleiner, R. The Effects of Threat and Frustration on Group Cohesiveness. *Journal of Abnormal* & *Social Psychology,* 54, 1957, 192–199; Moment, D. & Zaleznik, A. *Role Development and Interpersonal Competence.* Boston: Harvard University, 1963, 124–125. (Lewin, et al., speak of "laissez faire" leadership and Moment and Zaleznik speak of an "Underchosen" role.)

[26] Drucker, P. F. *The New Society.* New York: Harper, 1950, 83; Vitalis, M. *Motivation and Morale in Industry.* New York: Norton, 1953, 51; Argyris, C., *op. cit.,* 89–95; Schutz, W. C. The Interpersonal Underworld. *Harvard Business Review,* 36, (4), 1958, 123–135.

[27] *The Managerial Grid: A Self-Examination of Managerial Styles.* Austin, Tex.: Scientific Methods, Inc., 1962.

[28] Shull, F. A. Administrative Perspectives of Human Relations. *Advanced Management,* March, 1960, 18–22; Roethlisberger, F. J. The Foreman: Master and Victim of Double Talk. *Harvard Business Review,* 23, 1945, 283–298.

[29] Shull, F. A., *op. cit.*

[30] Pfeffer, J. M. & Presthus, R. V. The Role of Human Relations. In K. Davis & W. Scott (Eds.), *Readings in Human Relations.* New York: McGraw-Hill, 1959, 253; Davis, R. C., *op. cit.*

[31] Drucker, P. F. Integration of People and Planning. *Harvard Business Review,* 33, 1955, 35–40; Urwick, L. F. The Purpose of a Business. In K. Davis & W. Scott (Eds.), *op. cit.,* 85–91.

[32] Katz, R. L. Skills of an Effective Administrator. *Harvard Business Review,* 31, 1955, 33–42; Allen, L. A. *Management and Organization.* New York: McGraw-Hill, 1958, 43–44; Tannenbaum, R. & Schmidt, W. H. How to Choose a Leadership Pattern. *Harvard Business Review,* 36, 1958, 95–101.

[33] McCauley, B. G. Accent the Man in Management. *Advanced Management,* August, 1960, 24–27.

[34] *The Managerial Grid: A Self-Examination of Managerial Styles.* Austin, Tex.: Scientific Methods, Inc., 1962.

[35] Allen, L. A., *op. cit.*

[36] Lawrence, P. R., Bailey, J. C., Katz, R. L., Seiler, J. A., Orth, C. D., Clark, J. V., Barnes, L. B. & Turner, A. N. *Organizational Behavior and Administration: Cases, Concepts, and Research Findings.* Homewood, Ill.: Dorsey, 1961, 185; Strauss, G. & Sayles, L. R. *Personnel: The Human Problems of Management.* Englewood Cliffs, N. J.: Prentice-Hall, 1960, 36–41.

[37] The theory and concepts of 9, 9 management find life in the pioneering work of Kurt Lewin and his associates, particularly the concepts of *participation, goal-setting, involvement and commitment, interpersonal relations,* and *strategies for individual and organizational change.* See especially, Lewin, K. *Field Theory in Social Science.* New York: Harper, 1951. Also see Lewin, K. Forces Behind Food Habits and Methods of Change. *Bulletin of National Research Council,* 108, 1943, 35–65; Lewin, K. Frontiers in Group Dynamics: Concept, Method and Reality in Social Science: Social Equilibrium and Social Change. *Human Relations,* 1, 1947, 5–41; Lewin, K. Group Decision and Social Change. In T. M. Newcomb & E. L. Hartley (Eds.), *Readings in Social Psychology.* New York: Holt, 1947, 330–344; Lewin, K. Frontiers in Group Dynamics: II. Channels of Group Life: Social Planning and Action Research. *Human Relations,* 1, 1947, 143–153; Lewin, K. *Resolving Social Conflicts: Selected Papers on Group Dynamics.* New York: Harper, 1948; Lewin, K. Behavior and Development as a Function of the Total Situation. In L. Carmichael (Ed.), *Manual of Child Psychology.* New York: Wiley, 1946, 791–844. (Also see

references in Ch. 3.) For a discussion of and additional relevant references to Lewin's work, see Deutsch, M. Field Theory in Social Psychology. In G. Lindsey (Ed.), *Handbook of Social Psychology. Vol. I.* Reading, Mass.: Addison-Wesley, 1954, 181–222.

38 Wolfe, D. M. Power and Authority in the Family. In D. Cartwright (Ed.), *Studies in Social Power.* Ann Arbor: Institute for Social Research, 1959, 100–101; Vroom, V. H. *Some Personality Determinants of the Effects of Participation.* Englewood Cliffs, NJ:Prentice-Hall, 1960, 1–18.

39 Guest, R. H. *Organizational Change: The Effect of Successful Leadership.* Homewood, Ill.: Dorsey, 1962, 40–81. (This work of Guest is one of the best descriptions in the literature of the managerial actions of a 9, 9 manager. See esp. "Plant Y," post-1953.)

40 See Ch. 3 of *The Managerial Grid* by Blake and Mouton. Also see Ch. 1 and 36–38 of Strauss, G. & Sayles, L. R., *op. cit.*

41 See Ch. 6 of *The Managerial Grid* by Blake and Mouton.

42 The work of Argyris and McGregor has crystallized and put into perspective the more mature needs of individuals in the work situation. See Argyris, C., *Personality and Organization,* Harper & Bros., New York, 1957, esp. pp. 20–53. McGregor, D. *The Human Side of Enterprise.* McGraw-Hill, New York, 1960, esp. pp. 45–58.

43 The work of Herzberg, *et al.,* demonstrates that motivation of a more fundamental and long-lasting character is embedded in the work itself *i.e.,* responsibility, achievement, advancement, and other factors that create a sense of significant accomplishment. Factors not directly related to work, *i.e. hygienic,* take on more importance as work becomes less challenging and meaningful. See Herzberg, F., Mausner, B., & Snyderman, B. B., *The Motivation to Work.* New York: Wiley, 1959, pp. 64, 70, 132, 144. Also see White, R. W., Motivation Reconsidered: The Concept of Competence. *Psychological Review,* 66, 1959, 297–334.

44 Hare, A. P. Small Group Discussions with Participatory and Supervisory Leadership. *Journal of Abnormal & Social Psychology, 48,* 1953, 273–275.

45 Marrow, A. J. *Making Management Human.* New York: McGraw-Hill, 1957, 29. (The work of Marrow, Bavelas and others at Harwood represents the successful attempt of one management group to apply 9, 9 concepts in its organization improvement efforts.)

19

A Four-Factor Theory
of Leadership

David G. Bowers and Stanley E. Seashore

For centuries writers have been intrigued with the idea of specifying predictable relationships between what an organization's leader does and how the organization fares. In our own time, behavioral science has looked extensively at this question, yet incongruities and contradictory or unrelated findings seem to crowd the literature. It is the intent in this paper to locate and integrate the consistencies, to explore some neglected issues, and, finally, to generate and use a network of variables for predicting outcomes of organizational effectiveness.

Leadership has been studied informally by observing the lives of great men and formally by attempting to identify the personality traits of acknowledged leaders through assessment techniques. Review of the research literature from these studies, however, reveals few consistent findings.[1] Since the Second World War, research emphasis has shifted from a search for personality traits to a search for behavior that makes a difference in the performance or satisfaction of the followers. The conceptual scheme to be outlined here is an example of this approach.

In this paper, the primary concern is with leadership in businesses or industrial enterprises, usually termed "supervision" or "management," although most of the constructs of leadership to be used here apply equally well to social groups, clubs, and voluntary associations.

Work situations in business organizations in a technologically advanced society typically involve a comparatively small number of persons who receive direction from one person. This is the basic unit of industrial society and has been called the "organizational family."[2] In this modern organiza-

Excerpt reprinted with permission from *Administrative Science Quarterly*, Vol. 11, No. 2 (September 1966), pp. 238–263. Originally titled "Predicting Organizational Effectiveness with a Four-Factor Theory of Leadership." Copyright © 1966 by Johnson Graduate School of Management, Cornell University.

tional family, there is usually task interdependence and there is frequently social interdependence as well. The ideal is that of a group of people working effectively together toward the accomplishment of some common aim.

This paper presents a review of the conceptual structure resulting from several programs of research in leadership practices, followed by a reconceptualization that attempts to take into consideration all of these earlier findings. In an attempt to assess the usefulness of the reconceptualization, it is then applied to leadership and effectiveness data from a recent study.

It seems useful at the outset to isolate on a common-sense basis certain attributes of "leadership." First, the concept of leadership is meaningful only in the context of two or more people. Second, leadership consists of behavior; more specifically, it is behavior by one member of a group toward another member or members of the group, which advances some joint aim. Not all organizationally useful behavior in a work group is leadership; leadership behavior must be distinguished from the performance of non-interpersonal tasks that advance the goals of the organization. On a common-sense basis, then, leadership is organizationally useful behavior by one member of an organizational family toward another member or members of that same organizational family.

Defined in this manner, leadership amounts to a large aggregation of separate behaviors, which may be grouped or classified in a great variety of ways. Several classification systems from previous research have achieved considerable prominence, and are briefly described here.

Ohio State Leadership Studies

In 1945, the Bureau of Business Research at Ohio State University undertook the construction of an instrument for describing leadership. From extended conversations and discussions among staff members who represented various disciplines, a list of nine dimensions or categories of leadership behavior were postulated. Descriptive statements were then written and assigned to one or another of the nine dimensions, and after further refinement, 150 of these were selected as representing these nine dimensions and were incorporated into the Leader Behavior Description Questionnaire.

Hemphill and Coons'[3] data analysis simplified the conceptual framework and resulted in three variables:

1. *Maintenance of membership character.* Behavior of a leader which allows him to be considered a "good fellow" by his subordinates; behavior which is socially agreeable to group members.

2. *Objective attainment behavior.* Behavior related to the output of the group; for example, taking positive action in establishing goals or objectives, structuring group activities in a way that members may work toward an objective, or serving as a representative of group accomplishment in relation to outside groups, agencies, forces, and so on.

3. *Group interaction facilitation behavior.* Behavior that structures communication among group members, encouraging pleasant group atmosphere, and reducing conflicts among members.

Halpin and Winer[4] made an analysis using data collected from air force crews, revising the original measuring instrument to adapt it to the respondent group. Data analysis produced four variables:

1. *Consideration.* Behavior indicative of friendship, mutual trust, respect, and warmth.

2. *Initiating structure.* Behavior that organizes and defines relationships or roles, and establishes well-defined patterns of organization, channels of communication, and ways of getting jobs done.

3. *Production emphasis.* Behavior which makes up a manner of motivating the group to greater activity by emphasizing the mission or job to be done.

4. *Sensitivity (social awareness).* Sensitivity of the leader to, and his awareness of, social interrelationships and pressures inside or outside the group.

The Halpin and Winer analysis has been the more widely known and used. Because the investigators dropped the third and fourth factors as accounting for too little common variance, "consideration" and "initiating structure" have become to some extent identified as "the Ohio State" dimensions of leadership.

Early Survey Research Center Studies

Concurrent with the Ohio State studies was a similar program of research in human relations at the University of Michigan Survey Research Center. Approaching the problem of leadership or supervisory style by locating clusters of characteristics which (a) correlated positively among themselves and (b) correlated with criteria of effectiveness, this program developed two concepts called "employee orientation" and "production orientation."[5]

Employee orientation is described as behavior by a supervisor, which indicates that he feels that the "human relations" aspect of the job is quite important; and that he considers the employees as human beings of intrinsic importance, takes an interest in them, and accepts their individuality and personal needs. Production orientation stresses production and the technical aspects of the job, with employees as means for getting work done; it seems to combine the Ohio State dimensions of initiating structure and production emphasis. Originally conceived to be opposite poles of the same continuum, employee orientation and production orientation were later reconceptualized on the basis of further data, as representing independent dimensions.[6]

Katz and Kahn,[7] writing from a greater accumulation of findings, presented another conceptual scheme, with four dimensions of leadership:

1. *Differentiation of supervisory role.* Behavior by a leader that reflects greater emphasis upon activities of planning and performing specialized skilled tasks; spending a greater proportion of time in actual

supervision, rather than performing the men's own tasks himself or absorption in impersonal paperwork.

2. *Closeness of supervision.* Behavior that delegates authority, checks upon subordinates less frequently, provides more general, less frequent instructions about the work, makes greater allowance for individuals to perform in their own ways and at their own paces.

3. *Employee orientation.* Behavior that gives major emphasis to a supportive personal relationship, and that reflects a personal interest in subordinates; being more understanding, less punitive, easy to talk to, and willing to help groom employees for advancement.

4. *Group relationships.* Behavior by the leader that results in group cohesiveness, pride by subordinates in their work group, a feeling of membership in the group, and mutual help on the part of those subordinates.

Differentiation of supervisory role corresponds in part to what the Ohio State studies refer to as initiating structure or objective attainment behavior, and clearly derives from the earlier concept of production orientation. Closeness of supervision, on the other hand, has something in common with maintenance of membership character, consideration, and employee orientation, but also with objective attainment behavior, initiating structure, and production orientation. Employee orientation clearly corresponds to the earlier concept by the same name, while group relationships is to some extent similar to the interaction facilitation behavior and social sensitivity of the Ohio State studies.

In still another conceptualization, combining theory with review of empirical data, Kahn postulated four supervisory functions.[8]

1. *Providing direct need satisfaction.* Behavior by a leader, not conditional upon behavior of the employee, which provides direct satisfaction of the employee's ego and affiliation needs.

2. *Structuring the path to goal attainment.* Behavior that cues subordinates toward filling personal needs through attaining organizational goals.

3. *Enabling goal achievement.* Behavior that removes barriers to goal achievement, such as eliminating bottlenecks, or planning.

4. *Modifying employee goals.* Behavior that influences the actual personal goals of subordinates in organizationally useful directions.

Direct need satisfaction clearly resembles consideration and employee orientation; enabling goal achievement seems similar to initiating structure or objective attainment behavior; structuring the path to goal attainment and modifying employee goals are probably closer to the Ohio State production emphasis factor.

Studies at the Research Center for Group Dynamics

Cartwright and Zander[9] at the Research Center for Group Dynamics, on the basis of accumulated findings, described leadership in terms of two sets of group functions.

1. *Group maintenance functions.* Behavior that keeps interpersonal relations pleasant, resolves disputes, provides encouragement, gives the minority a chance to be heard, stimulates self-direction, and increases interdependence among members.

2. *Goal achievement functions.* Behavior that initiates action, keeps members' attention on the goal, develops a procedural plan, evaluates the quality of work done, and makes expert information available.

These descriptive terms clearly refer to broader constructs than consideration or initiating structure. Group maintenance functions, for example, include what has been termed consideration, maintenance of membership character, or employee orientation, but they also include functions concerned with relationships among group members not in formal authority positions. This concept is in some ways similar to group interaction facilitation behavior in the Ohio State factor analysis of Hemphill and Coons.[10] Goal achievement functions seem to encompass what the Ohio State studies referred to as initiating structure and production emphasis or objective attainment behavior, and what early Survey Research Center studies called production orientation.

Mann's Three Skills

In subsequent work at the Survey Research Center built upon earlier findings, a recent classification, proposed by several writers and developed and operationalized by Floyd Mann,[11] treats leadership in terms of a trilogy of skills required of supervisors or managers. Although behaviors requiring particular skills and those skills themselves are not necessarily perfectly parallel, it seems reasonable to assume at least an approximate correspondence between the two. The three skills are:

1. *Human relations skill.* Ability and judgment in working with and through people, including knowledge of principles of human behavior, interpersonal relations, and human motivation.

2. *Technical skill.* Ability to use knowledge, methods, techniques, and equipment necessary for the performance of specific tasks.

3. *Administrative skill.* Ability to understand and act according to the objectives of the total organization, rather than only on the basis of the goals and needs of one's own immediate group. It includes planning, organizing the work, assigning the right tasks to the right people, inspecting, following up, and coordinating the work.

Likert's New Patterns of Management

Rensis Likert of the University of Michigan Institute for Social Research, building upon many of the findings of the Survey Research Center and the Research Center for Group Dynamics as well as upon his own early work in the same area for the Life Insurance Agency Management Association, describes five conditions for effective supervisory behavior:

1. *Principle of supportive relations.* The leadership and other processes of the organization must be such as to ensure a maximum probability that in his interactions and his relationships with the organization, each member will, in the light of his background, values, and expectations, view the experience as supportive, and as one that builds and maintains his sense of personal worth and importance.[12]

2. *Group methods of supervision.* Management will make full use of the potential capacities of its human resources only when each person in an organization is a member of one or more effectively functioning work groups that have a high degree of group loyalty, effective skills of interaction, and high performance goals.[13]

3. *High performance goals.* If a high level of performance is to be achieved, it appears to be necessary for a supervisor to be employee-centered, and at the same time to have high performance goals and a contagious enthusiasm as to the importance of achieving these goals.[14]

4. *Technical knowledge.* The (effective) leader has adequate competence to handle the technical problems faced by his group, or he sees that access to this technical knowledge is fully provided.[15]

5. *Coordinating, scheduling, planning.* The leader fully reflects and effectively represents the views, goals, values, and decisions of his group in those other groups where he is performing the function of linking his group to the rest of the organization. He brings to the group of which he is the leader the views, goals, and decisions of those other groups. In this way, he provides a linkage whereby communication and the exercise of influence can be performed in both directions.[16]

Comparison and Integration

These various research programs and writings make it clear that a great deal of conceptual content is held in common. In fact, four dimensions emerge from these studies, which seem to comprise the basic structure of what one may term "leadership":

1. *Support.* Behavior that enhances someone else's feeling of personal worth and importance.

2. *Interaction facilitation.* Behavior that encourages members of the group to develop close, mutually satisfying relationships.

3. *Goal emphasis.* Behavior that stimulates an enthusiasm for meeting the group's goal or achieving excellent performance.

4. *Work facilitation.* Behavior that helps achieve goal attainment by such activities as scheduling, coordinating, planning, and by providing resources such as tools, materials, and technical knowledge.

This formulation is obviously very close, except in terminology, to that expressed by Rensis Likert and was, in fact, stimulated by it. Table 1 indicates how concepts from the various research programs relate to these four basic concepts of leadership. More important, however, is the fact that each of these four concepts appears, sometimes separately, sometimes in combination, in all but two (Katz, et al., 1950; Kahn, 1958) of the previous formulations listed. These four dimensions are not considered indivisible, but capable of further subdivision according to some regularity of occurrence in social situations or according to the conceptual preferences of investigators.

Traditional leadership research has focused upon the behavior of formally designated or recognized leaders. This is probably due, at least in part, to the historical influence of the hierarchical models of the church and the army. As a result, it has until recently been customary to study leadership either as an attribute of the person of someone who is authority-vested, or as an attribute of his behavior. More recently, attention has been paid to leadership in groups less formally structured, as illustrated by the work of Bass with leaderless group discussion, the work of Sherif, as well as some of the work of other researchers in the area of group dynamics.[17]

In the previous section, leadership was conceptualized in terms of four social-process functions, four kinds of behavior that must be present in work groups if they are to be effective. The performance of these functions was deliberately not limited to formally designated leaders. Instead, it was proposed that leadership, as described in terms of support, goal emphasis, work facilitation, and interaction facilitation, may be provided by anyone in a work group for anyone else in that work group. In this sense, leadership may be either "supervisory" or "mutual"; that is, a group's need for support may be provided by a formally designated leader, by members for each other, or both; goals may be emphasized by the formal leader, by members to each other, or by both; and similarly for work facilitation and interaction facilitation. This does not imply that formally designated leaders are unnecessary or superfluous, for there are both common-sense and theoretical reasons for believing that a formally acknowledged leader through his supervisory leadership behavior sets the pattern of the mutual leadership which subordinates supply each other.

Leadership and Organizational Effectiveness

Leadership in a work situation has been judged to be important because of its connection, to some extent assumed and to some extent demonstrated, to organizational effectiveness. Effectiveness, moreover, although it has been operationalized in a variety of ways, has often been assumed to be a unitary characteristic. These assumptions define a commonly accepted theorem that leadership (if not a unitary characteristic, then a limited roster of closely related ones) is always salutary in its effect and that it always enhances effectiveness.

The pattern of the typical leadership study has been first, to select a criterion of effectiveness: sometimes a rating of overall effectiveness by superiors,

Table 1 Correspondence of leadership concepts of different investigators.

Bowers and Seashore (1964)	Hemphill and Coons (1957)	Halpin and Winer (1957)	Katz et al. (1950)	Katz and Kahn (1951)	Kahn (1958)	Mann (1962)	Likert (1961)	Cartwright and Zander (1960)
Support	Maintenance of membership character	Consideration	Employee orientation	Employee orientation / Closeness of supervision	Providing direct need satisfaction	Human relations skills	Principle of supportive relationships	Group maintenance functions
Interaction facilitation	Group interaction facilitation behavior	Sensitivity		Group relationships			Group methods of supervision	
Goal emphasis		Production emphasis	Production orientation		Structuring path to goal attainment / Modifying employee goals	Administrative skills	High-performance goals	Goal-achievement functions
Work facilitation	Objective attainment behavior	Initiating structure		Differentiation of supervisory role / Closeness of supervision	Enabling goal achievement	Technical skills	Technical knowledge, planning, scheduling	

at other times a questionnaire measure of "morale," on still other occasions a few measures such as output, absence, or accident rates. Next, an attempt is made to relate leadership to the criterion selected. When, in fact, a relationship is obtained, this is accepted. When no relationship or one opposite to that expected is obtained, the investigator often makes some statement referring to "error" or "further research."

It seems that a better strategy would be to obtain: (a) measures reflecting a theoretically meaningful conceptual structure of leadership; (b) an integrated set of systematically derived criteria; and (c) a treatment of these data, which takes account of the multiplicity of relationships and investigates the adequacy of leadership characteristics in predicting effectiveness variables.

In the present study an attempt is made to satisfy these conditions. A conceptual structure of leadership is developed, using empirical evidence. The four concepts of this structure are operationalized in terms of questionnaire items describing behavioral acts and a systematically derived set of criteria of organizational effectiveness is obtained. . . .

The Study*

This study was conducted in 40 agencies of a leading life insurance company. These agencies are independently owned businesses, performing identical functions in their separate parts of the country. Only one or two hierarchical levels intervene between the regional manager, at the top of the hierarchy, and the sales agent at the bottom. . . .

The independent variables include leadership support, goal emphasis, work facilitation, satisfaction, need for affiliation, regional managers' expert power, classical business ideology and rivalry among agents.

The dependent variables include staff/clientele maturity, business growth, business costs, advanced underwriting, business volume, manpower turnover and regional manager's personal performance. . . .

From the data that resulted, the following questions suggest themselves:

1. Are both mutual and supervisory leadership measures useful; that is, are there differential effects from the various leadership dimensions such that some criteria are associated with certain measures or combinations of measures and some with others?

2. In what way are mutual leadership measures related to supervisory measures?

3. How adequately may criteria of effectiveness be predicted from leadership measures as compared to other kinds of measures? . . .

---

*Readers should consult the original article for detailed descriptions of operationalization of the variables and extensive data analysis.

Relation of Peer to Managerial Leadership

It appears that the best predictor of peer support is managerial support; of peer goal emphasis, managerial interaction facilitation; of peer work facilitation, managerial work facilitation; and of peer interaction facilitation, managerial interaction facilitation. With one exception, therefore, the best predictor of the peer characteristic is its managerial complement.

Assuming causation, one may say that if a manager wishes to increase the extent to which his subordinates support one another, he must increase his own support and his own emphasis upon goals.

If he wishes to increase the extent to which his subordinates emphasize goals to one another, he must first increase his own facilitation of interaction and his emphasis upon goals. By increasing his facilitation of the work, he will increase the extent to which his subordinates do likewise, and if, in addition, he increases his facilitation of interaction, his subordinates will in turn facilitate interaction among themselves.

These findings appear to confirm that there is in fact a significant and strong relationship between managerial and peer leadership characteristics. In general, the statement may be made that a forerunner of each peer variable is its managerial complement and that substantial improvement is in most cases made by combining with this another managerial characteristic. . . .

Discussion and Conclusions

To what extent have the findings demonstrated the usefulness of the conceptualization presented at the beginning of this article? It seems reasonable to state the following:

1. Seven of the eight leadership characteristics outlined above in fact play some part in the predictive model generated from the data; only peer interaction facilitation seems to play no unique role.

2. Both managerial and peer leadership characteristics seem important.

3. There are plausible relationships of managerial to peer leadership characteristics.

4. The model is not a simple one of managerial leadership leading to peer leadership, which in turn leads to outcomes separately; instead, different aspects of performance are associated with different leadership characteristics, and, in some cases, satisfaction outcomes seem related to performance outcomes.

5. Some effectiveness measures are related to causal factors other than those tapped in the questionnaire.

6. The ability to predict outcomes with the variables selected varies from .95 to .00.

7. The role of leadership characteristics in this prediction varies in importance from strong, direct relationships in some cases (e.g., satis-

faction with manager) to indirect relationships (e.g., business volume) to no relationship (e.g., advanced underwriting).

8. Leadership, as conceived and operationalized here, is not adequate alone to predict effectiveness: instead, additional and, in some cases, intervening constructs must be included to improve prediction. These "other" constructs are of several distinct types:

   a. *Leadership related.* Regional manager's expert power, regional manager's influence acceptance and rivalry among agents.

   b. *Work patterns.* Percentage of time in miscellaneous activities, in paperwork for clients and in professional development.

   c. *Personal and motivational.* Education, level of aspiration, need for affiliation, goal compatibility of individual and organization and classical business ideology.

Notes

[1] C. A. Gibb, "Leadership," in G. Lindsey, *Handbook of Social Psychology* (Cambridge, Mass.: Addison-Wesley, 1954), 11, 877–917; R. M. Stogdill, "Personal Factors Associated with Leadership: A Survey of the Literature," *Journal of Psychology,* 25 (1948), 35–71.

[2] F. C. Mann, "Toward an Understanding of the Leadership Role in Formal Organization," in R. Dubin, G. C. Homans, F. C. Mann, and D. C. Miller, *Leadership and Productivity* (San Francisco, Calif.: Chandler Publishing Company, 1965), pp. 68–103.

[3] J. K. Hemphill and A. E. Coons, "Development of the Leader Behavior Description Questionnaire," in R. M. Stogdill and A. E. Coons (eds.), *Leader Behavior: Its Description and Measurement* (Research Monograph No. SS, Columbus, Ohio: Bureau of Business Research, the Ohio State University, 1957), pp. 6–38.

[4] A. W. Halpin and J. Winer, "A Factorial Study of the Leader Behavior Description Questionnaire," in R. M. Stogdill and A. E. Coons, *Leader Behavior, op. cit.,* pp. 39–51.

[5] D. Katz, N. Maccoby, and Nancy C. Morse, *Productivity, Supervision, and Morale in an Office Situation* (Detroit, Mich.: The Darel Press, Inc., 1950); D. Katz, N. Maccoby, G. Gurin, and Lucretia G. Floor, *Productivity, Supervision, and Morale Among Railroad Workers* (Ann Arbor, Mich.: Survey Research Center, 1951).

[6] R. L. Kahn, "The Prediction of Productivity," *Journal of Social Issues,* 12 (1956), 41–49.

[7] B. D. Katz and R. L. Kahn, "Human Organization and Worker Motivation," in L. R. Tripp (ed.), *Industrial Productivity* (Madison, WI: Industrial Relations Research Association, 1951), pp. 146–171.

[8] R. L. Kahn, "Human Relations on the Shop Floor," in E. M. Hugh-Jones (ed.), *Human Relations and Modern Management* (Amsterdam: North-Holland Publishing Co., 1958), pp. 43–74.

[9] Cartwright and A. Zander, *Group Dynamics Research and Theory* (Evanston, Ill.: Row, Peterson & Co., 1960).

[10] Hemphill and Coons, *op. cit.*

[11] Mann, *op. cit.*

[12] R. Likert, *New Patterns of Management* (NY: McGraw-Hill, 1961), p.103.

[13] Ibid., p. 104.

[14] Ibid., p. 8.

[15] Ibid., p. 171.

[16] Ibid., p. 171.

[17] B. M. Bass, *Leadership, Psychology, and Organizational Behavior* (New York: Harper & Bros., 1960); Cartwright and Zander, *op. cit.;* M. and Carolyn W. Sherif, *An Outline of Social Psychology* (New York: Harper & Bros., 1956).

20

Servant Leadership
Its Origin, Development and Application

Sen Sendjaya and James C. Sarros

Although the notion of servant leadership has been recognized in the leadership literature since Burns' (1978) and Greenleaf's (1977) publications, the movement has gained momentum only recently. Bowman (1997) argues that to date there is only anecdotal evidence to support a commitment to an understanding of servant leadership. For example, Spears' (1995) identification of ten characteristics of servant leadership (i.e. listening, empathy, healing, awareness, persuasion, conceptualization, foresight, stewardship, commitment to the growth of people, and building community) is based solely on his readings of Greenleaf's essays, and is not grounded in solid research studies.

One reason for the scarcity of research on servant leadership is that the very notion of "servant as leader" is an oxymoron. It may be difficult to think and act both as leader and servant at the same time—a leader who serves and a servant who leads. Nevertheless, the dynamic conceptual relationships and complementary roles between servant-hood and leadership have recently attracted the attention of leadership scholars and practitioners (Bass, 1999; Bowman, 1997; Buchen, 1998; Chappel, 2000; Choi & Mai-Dalton, 1998; De Pree, 1989; Farling, Stone, & Winston, 1999; Graham, 1991; Pollard, 1997; Russell, 2001; Senge, 1990, 1995; Spears, 1995).

Bass (2000) asserts that, as a concept, servant leadership theory requires substantial empirical research. Bass does believe that its profound philosophical foundation provides avenues for its theoretical development: "The strength of the servant leadership movement and its many links to encouraging follower learning, growth, and autonomy, suggests that the untested theory will play a role in the future leadership of the learning organization" (2000:33). Given the current organizational context which puts an emphasis on a sense of community, empowerment, shared authority, and relational power, Bass' (2000) hypothesis on servant leadership suggests it may be a theory with great promise for the future.

Greenleaf's Model of Servant Leadership

According to Greenleaf (1977), servant leaders are leaders who put other people's needs, aspirations and interests above their own. The servant leader's deliberate choice is to serve others. In fact, the servant leader's chief motive is to serve first, as opposed to lead (Greenleaf, 1977). Furthermore, servant leaders seek to transform their followers to "grow healthier, wiser, freer, more autonomous, and more likely themselves to become servants" (Greenleaf, 1977:13–14).

While working as an AT&T executive, Greenleaf (1977) conceptualized the notion of servant leadership and introduced it into the organizational context. Interestingly, his concept has, to a certain extent, some similarities with Burns' (1978) transforming leadership. Greenleaf (1977:13) claimed that:

> The servant leader is a servant *first.* It begins with the natural feeling that one wants to serve, to serve first. Then conscious choice brings one to aspire to lead. The difference manifests itself in the care taken by the servant—first to make sure that other people's highest-priority needs are being served.

Similarly, Burns (1978:20) asserted that:

> Transforming leadership occurs when one or more persons engage with others in such a way that leaders and followers raise one another to higher levels of motivation and morality. But transforming leadership ultimately becomes *moral* in that it raises the level of human conduct and ethical aspiration of both leader and led, thus it has a transforming effect on both.

Greenleaf (1977:7) himself constructed the notion of servant leadership not by studying some top-notch corporate leaders or other high-profile individuals, but through his reading of Herman Hesse's story about a spiritual pilgrimage, *Journey to the East.* In this story we see a band of men on a mythical journey. The central figure of the story is Leo, who accompanies the party as the servant who does their menial chores, but who also sustains them with his spirit and his song. He is a person of extraordinary presence. All goes well until Leo disappears. Then the group falls into disarray and the journey is abandoned. They cannot make it without the servant Leo. The narrator, one of the party, after some years of wandering, finds Leo and is taken into the Order that had sponsored the journey. There he discovers that Leo, whom he had known first as servant, was in fact the titular head of the Order, its guiding spirit, a great and noble leader.

As appealing and refreshing as Greenleaf's conceptualization of servant leadership is, Greenleaf is not the individual who first introduced the notion of servant leadership to everyday human endeavor. It was Christianity's founder, Jesus Christ, who first taught the concept of servant leadership.

From the narrative accounts of his life in the Bible, it is evident that servant leadership was taught and practiced more than two thousand years ago. This practice has been echoed in the lives of ancient monarchs for over 1000 years. Nair (1994:59) asserted that the importance of service to leadership has been acknowledged and practiced for over a thousand years:

> Ancient monarchs acknowledged that they were in the service of their country and their people—even if their actions were not consistent with this.

Modern coronation ceremonies and inaugurations of heads of state all involve the acknowledgement of service to God, country, and the people. Politicians define their role in terms of public service. And service has always been at the core of leadership in the spiritual arena, symbolized at the highest level by Christ washing the feet of his disciples. . . .

The Philosophical Basis of Servant Leadership

These preceding examples highlight the philosophical basis of servant leadership in terms of *who* the servant leader is and *what* the servant leader does. These "being" and "doing" attributes of servant leadership represent a significant paradigm shift in the act of leadership, which comprise the leader's self-concept and primary intent, as shown in Table 1.

Table 1   Servant Leader Constructs

Primary Intent	Serve others first, not lead other first
Self-Concept	Servant and steward, not leader or owner

The Primary Intent of Servant Leaders

There has been a strong tendency among leadership scholars and journalists to treat leaders as isolated heroes controlling and commanding others from within their ivory tower (Gronn, 1995; Yukl, 1999). In the organizational context, the word "leader" has been mostly ascribed to people who hold management positions and are capable of giving orders to other members of the organization (Senge, 1990). The common, principal motive for such larger-than-life Herculean leaders is to lead followers to achieve certain organizational objectives. This role stands in sharp contrast to servant leaders whose chief motive is to serve others to be what they are capable of becoming (Greenleaf, 1977).

The motivational element of servant leadership (i.e. to serve first) portrays a fundamental presupposition which distinguishes the concept from other leadership thoughts. This presupposition forms the mental model of the servant leader, that is the "I serve" as opposed to the "I lead" mentality. The primary reason why leaders exist is to serve first, not to lead first. To put it differently, the servant leader operates on the assumption that "I am the leader, therefore I serve" rather than "I am the leader, therefore I lead." The following case in point outlined by former Herman Miller CEO, Max De Pree (1992:218–219), helps illustrate the difference:

> I arrived at the local tennis club just after high school students had vacated the locker room. Like chickens, they had not bothered to pick up after themselves. Without thinking too much about it, I gathered up all their towels and put them in the hamper. A friend of mine quietly watched me do this and then asked me a question that I've pondered many times over the years. "Do you pick up towels because you're the president of the company? Or are you the president because you pick up the towels?"

Two premises can be derived from the above modest incident: I serve because I am the leader ("I pick up towels because I am the president") and I am the leader because I serve ("I am the president because I pick up the towels"). While both premises imply a linear relationship between the act of service and the position of leader, they stand squarely opposite to each other in terms of cause and effect.

The first premise "I serve because I am the leader" signifies the act of altruism. Greenleaf's delineation of servant leadership put the emphasis on the acts of service, as opposed to the act of leading, of the leader. He (1977:13) posits that the servant leader "begins with the natural feeling that one wants to serve, to serve first." At its core, the nature of servant leadership is serving, not leading (De Pree, 1989). It is through that act of serving that the leaders lead other people to be what they are capable of becoming.

The second premise "I am the leader because I serve" begins with the deep-seated desire that one wants to lead, or ambition to be the foremost among the troop. The desire to be ahead of others may compromise the career endeavors or personal ambitions of leaders.

"Being": The Self-Concept of Servant Leaders

The notion of self-concept has been associated with self-image, self-esteem, self-perception, and self-awareness (Leonard, Beauvais, & Scholl, 1995; Sosik & Dworakivsky, 1998). Using this definition, leaders' self-concept involves the extent to which they are aware of their thoughts, beliefs and values. Like other individuals, leaders behave in ways consistent with their self-concept (Sosik & Dworakivsky, 1998). Therefore, the servant leader's primary intent to serve may emanate from his or her self-concept as an altruistic, moral person.

Servant leaders view themselves as the servant first, as distinguished from the leader first "who later serves out of promptings of conscience or in conformity with normative expectations" (Greenleaf, 1977:14). Viewed this way, servant leaders are natural servants (Farling, Stone & Winston, 1999; Greenleaf, 1977). To recapitulate, servant leadership is not only about "doing" the acts of service but also "being" a servant. It logically implies, therefore, that the leader-follower relationship is that of a client-server, not supervisor-subordinate or master-slave relationship.

Servant leaders also view themselves as stewards (De Pree, 1989; Senge, 1990). The word "stewardship" is derived from the Greek word "oikonomia" whose meaning is rooted in the idea of a house manager (Locyker, 1986). The "oikonomos," which is translated as "steward," was entrusted with the responsibility of managing the business affairs of a household. The word often referred to a servant who was given responsibility over money, property, goods or other servants. In our current terminology, the word carries the idea of a trustee, one to whom something of value is entrusted. Block (1993) asserts that the concept of stewardship essentially is the willingness to be accountable for the well-being of the larger community by operating in the service of those around us. The stewardship for the people they lead is a critical characteristic of servant leaders. As stewards, servant leaders regard their followers as people who have been entrusted to them to be elevated to their better selves and to be what they are capable of becoming.

It is important to note that the servant leader's deliberate choice to serve and be a servant should not be associated with any forms of low self-concept or self-image, in the same way as choosing to forgive should not be viewed as a sign of weakness. Instead, it would take a leader with an accurate understanding of his or her self-image, moral conviction and emotional stability to make such a choice.

Several authors have argued that the source of servant leaders' motivational base lies in their principles, values and beliefs (Farling, Stone, & Winston, 1999) or their humility and spiritual insights (Graham, 1991). These intrinsic motivating factors enable servant leaders to take on the nature and the role of a servant. In fact, they enable servant leaders to engage themselves in self-sacrificial behaviors (Choi & Mai-Dalton, 1998). . . .

Servant Leadership in Organizations

Levering and Moskowitz (2000) contend that servant leadership has been practiced and advocated in some of the best companies to work for in America, on the basis of the *Fortune* survey. Six criteria identify these companies: openness and fairness, camaraderie/friendliness, opportunities, pride in work and company, pay/benefits, and security. Three of the five best places in *Fortune's* January 2000 "Top 100 Best Companies to Work For in America" were held by companies that lived by these criteria, namely, Southwest Airlines (#2 in 2000, #4 in 1999, and #1 in 1998), TD Industries (#4 in 2000, #2 in 1999, and #5 in 1998), and Synovus Financial (#5 in 2000 and #1 in 1999). The latest *Fortune* 2001 annual survey of top employers ranked Southwest Airlines, TD Industries, and Synovus Financial numbers four, six, and eight respectively (Levering & Moskowitz, 2001). The following paragraphs provide more detailed accounts of these companies in view of their servant leadership practices.

As one of the largest mechanical contractors in America, TD Industries has employed servant leadership as an organization-wide leadership development philosophy and program. CEO and Chairman of TD Industries Jack Lowe (1998) asserts that when people become grounded in servant leadership, trust grows and the foundation for organizational excellence is established. The culture of trust is evident in the ownership of TD Industries by the employees (thirty top managers and the founder's widow own 25% of the stock; lower-level employees own the rest), which explains why the company's 1,273 employees are called partners.

In a similar vein, Synovus Financial Corporation, a multibillion-dollar financial services firm, illustrates the servant leadership concept through a strong commitment to family-oriented policies such as work flexibility, leave for new parents, work/life balance, and advancing women in their careers. Chairman and CEO Jimmy Blanchard outlines the company's values in the following way:

> The heart of the servant-leader brings order, brings meaning to employees. When employees feel order and meaning and that they are a part of a team that stands for something good, that there is a higher calling than just working to get a paycheck, that they are improving mankind, there is an energy level that explodes and great things happen. (Chappel, 2000:5)

Under the leadership of founder and CEO Herb Kelleher, Southwest Airlines had one of the most distinguished organizational cultures in America. The company has been recognized as one of the most admired companies in the world and the most admired airline in the world year after year. Servant leadership principles provide the foundation for altruism, defined as the constructive, gratifying service to others, and one of the core values of Southwest's culture (Quick, 1992). Employees of Southwest are notable for their caring approach and appreciation of each other, as well as in the service of others.

Many organizational leaders see themselves as servant leaders today. William Pollard, Chairman of The ServiceMaster, is a case in point. His company has been recognized by *Fortune* as the best service company among the *Fortune* 500 firms over the past ten years. Describing himself as, and encouraging others to be, a leader who leads with a servant's heart, Pollard (1997:49–50) contends that the real leader is not the "person with the most distinguished title, the highest pay, or the longest tenure, but the role model, the risk taker, the servant; not the person who promotes himself or herself, but the promoter of others."

Conclusion

As this paper indicates, the distinctive characteristics of servant leaders lie first and foremost in their primary intent and self-concept. Servant leaders portray a resolute conviction and strong character by taking on not only the role of a servant, but also the nature of a servant. This paper also argues that cases of servant leadership in organizational settings do exist, and will continue to do so. While these accounts are mainly reported in the popular press, at the very least they indicate the proliferation of the servant leadership concept, as well as in practice. . . .

References

Bass, B. M. (1985). *Leadership and performance beyond expectations*. New York: Free Press.

Bass, B. M. (1990). From transactional to transformational leadership: Learning to share the vision. *Organizational Dynamics*, 18(3), 19–31.

Bass, B. M. (1999). On the taming of charisma: A reply to Janice Beyer. *Leadership Quarterly*, 10(4), 541–553.

Bass, B. M. (2000). The future of leadership in learning organizations. *Journal of Leadership Studies*, 7(3), 18–40.

Block, P. (1993). *Stewardship: Choosing service over self-interest*. San Francisco, CA: Barrett Koehler.

Bowman, M. A. (1997). Popular approaches to leadership. In Northouse, P. G. (ed.), *Leadership theory and practice*. Thousand Oaks, CA: Sage Publications.

Buchen, I. H. (1998). Servant leadership: A model for future faculty and future institutions. *The Journal of Leadership Studies*, 5(1), 125–134.

Burns, J. M. (1978). *Leadership*. New York: Harper & Row.

Chappel, D. (2000). Fortune's "Best Companies to Work For" embrace servant leadership. *The Servant Leader*, Spring, 5.

Choi, Y. & Mai-Dalton, R. R. (1998). On the leadership function of self-sacrifice. *Leadership Quarterly*, 9(4), 475–501.

De Pree, M. (1989). *Leadership is an art*. New York: Dell Publishing.

De Pree, M. (1992). *Leadership jazz*. New York: Currency/Doubleday.

Farling, M. L., Stone, A. G., & Winston, B. E. (1999). Servant leadership: Setting the stage for empirical research. *The Journal of Leadership Studies*, 6(1/2), 49–72.

Graham, I. W. (1991). Servant-leadership in organizations: Inspirational and moral. *Leadership Quarterly*, 2(2), 105–119.

Greenleaf, R. K. (1977). *Servant leadership: A journey into the nature of legitimate power and greatness*. Mahwah, NJ: Paulist Press.

Gronn, P. (1995). Greatness re-visited: The current obsession with transformational leadership. *Leading & Managing*, (1), 14–27.

Leonard, N. H., Beauvais, L. L., & Scholl, R. (1995). A self-concept-based model of work motivation. *Academy of Management Journal*, Special Volume I, 322–342.

Levering, R. & Moskowitz, M. (2000). The 100 best companies to work for in America. *Fortune*, 14 (1), 82–110.

Levering, R. & Moskowitz, M. (2001, February 4). The 100 best companies to work for in America [Electronic version]. *Fortune*, 145(3), 60–61.

Locyker, H. (Ed.) (1986). *Nelson's Illustrated Bible Dictionary*. Thomas Nelson Publishers.

Lowe, K. B. (1998). Trust: The invaluable asset. In Spears, L. C. (ed.), *Insights on leadership*. New York: John Wiley & Sons. Inc.

Nair, K. (1994). *A higher standard of leadership: Lessons from the life of Gandhi*. San Francisco, CA: Berrett-Koehler.

Pollard, C. W. (1997, September/October). The leader who serves. *Strategy and Leadership*, 49–51.

Quick, L. C. (1992). Crafting an organizational culture: Herb's hand at Southwest Airlines. *Organizational Dynamics*, 21(2), 45–57.

Russell, R. F. (2001). The role of values in servant leadership. *Leadership & Organizational Development Journal*, 22(2), 76–83.

Senge, P. M. (1990, Fall). The leader's new work: Building learning organizations. *Sloan Management Review*, 32(1), 7–24.

Senge, P. M., (1995). Robert Greenleaf's legacy: A new foundation for twenty-first century institutions. In Spears, L.C. (ed.), *Reflections on leadership*. New York: John Wiley & Sons, Inc.

Sosik, I. J. & Dworakivsky, A. C. (1998). Self-concept based aspects on the charismatic leader: More than meets the eye. *Leadership Quarterly*, 9(4), 503–526.

Spears, L. (1995). Servant leadership and the Greenleaf legacy. In Spears, L. C. (ed.), *Reflections on leadership*. New York: John Wiley & Sons, Inc.

Yukl, G. (1999). An evaluation of conceptual weaknesses in transformational and charismatic leadership theories. *Leadership Quarterly*, 10(2), 285–305.

21

The Leader/Member Attribution Process

Mark J. Martinko and William L. Gardner

Considerable attention has been devoted to understanding the role of attribution processes within the context of leadership. Two important early contributions were made by Green and Mitchell (1979) who emphasized the process by which leaders make attributions for subordinate behavior and Calder (1977) who emphasized subordinate attributions for leadership behavior.

Attention regarding attribution theory and attributional perspectives of leadership processes has focused on attributions for poor performance (Mitchell, Green, & Wood, 1981; Mitchell & Wood, 1980) and learned helplessness (Greenberger & Strasser, 1986; Martinko & Gardner, 1982, 1984). In general, the work of Mitchell and his colleagues has focused almost exclusively on the analysis of the attributional processes of leaders while ignoring those of members. Conversely, research on perspectives of learned helplessness has concentrated on describing the attributional processes of members (Martinko & Gardner, 1982). Although both Green and Mitchell (1979) and Martinko and Gardner (1982) suggest that attributional biases *may* stimulate conflict between leaders' and members' attributions, neither of these perspectives has articulated the dyadic exchange of attributions and behavior which characterize leader/member relations. In view of critiques of the leadership literature which emphasize the need for interactive perspectives (Davis & Luthans, 1979; Graen & Cashman, 1975; Hollander, 1978; Hunt & Osborn, 1978), it is apparent that a comprehensive perspective of the interactive nature of the leader/member attributional processes is needed.

This paper extends the work of Mitchell and his colleagues and that of Martinko and Gardner (1982) by describing the interactive dyadic nature of the leader/member attributional process.

Reprinted with permission from *Academy of Management Review,* Vol. 12, No. 2 (April 1987), pp. 235–248. Copyright © 1987 Academy of Management (NY).

Several comments regarding the focus and perspective of the paper are necessary. In order to reduce scope and increase the precision, attributions for failure rather than attributions for both success and failure are discussed. There are several reasons for this decision. First, an initial intention in developing this paper was to provide a model and set of propositions to guide research and theory development. As Weick's (1979) perspective indicates, although more global treatments of research topics may result in greater simplicity and generalizability, accuracy is diluted. Thus, here, scope was limited to gain precision and to enable more specific predictions regarding the variables of interest.

Second, investigations of dysfunctional behavior simply may be more stimulating and interesting. As theories of cognitive homeostasis suggest, disequilibrium stimulates cognitive reevaluation (Adams, 1965; Festinger, 1957).

Third, both Platt's (1964) notion of theory development through strong inference testing and Mitroff and Pondy's (1974) description of the use of dialectics in theory development suggest that focusing on deviations from normal productive behavior facilitates the identification of problems and the development of normative models of behavior.

A fourth factor which may explain the interest in dysfunctional behavior is the magnitude and severity of its effects. Although dysfunctional and unproductive behavior may account for only a small proportion of the variability in employee behavior, research suggests that the consequences of these behaviors are severe (Bowman, 1984; Clarke & Morris, 1980; Furnham, 1984). Undoubtedly, this last reason accounts for the interest which historically has been devoted to explaining dysfunctional behavior in organizations (Argyris, 1957; Blauner, 1964; March & Simon, 1958).

Finally, it should be emphasized that the narrowed scope of discussion presented here is not intended to limit the generalizability of the processes discussed. Rather, it is hoped that the perspective of the leader/member attribution process presented here will stimulate both research and theoretical development which will result in more generalized conceptualizations of the leader/member interaction process.

An Interactive Attributional Model of Leader/Member Relations

The model which has been developed to depict the interactive nature of leader and member attributions and behavior is illustrated in Figure 1. It builds upon and expands Green and Mitchell's (1979) analysis by incorporating leader attributional processes while simultaneously making member attributions and responses explicit. During this process, both leaders and members make causal attributions by using either covariation analysis or causal schemata (Kelley, 1972). Covariation analysis often is employed to determine the extent to which behavior varies across entities (distinctiveness), contexts (consistency), and people (consensus) in order to form entity, contextual, or dispositional attributions.

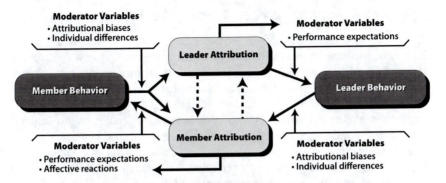

Figure 1   An Interactive Attributional Model of Leader/Member Relations

However, at times, leaders and members may adopt causal schemata (i.e., patterns of assumptions) because they lack the time or motivation or both to perform covariation analysis. As Green and Mitchell (1979) noted, a useful framework for classifying performance attributions has been advanced by Weiner, Frieze, Reed, Rest, and Rosenbaum (1971). This taxonomy includes the causes of ability, effort, task difficulty, and lucky chance which vary along the attributional dimensions of locus of control and stability.

As indicated in the model, attributional processes are moderated by attributional biases and individual difference variables. Depending on whether the leader's attribution is communicated to the member or vice versa, adjustments in the attributions of either or both parties may be made. Once the leader forms an attribution for member performance, this attribution influences both the leader's expectations for future performance and his or her behavior toward the member. For example, a manager who attributes subordinate failure to lack of effort is more likely to expect that disciplinary actions will result in performance gains than is the first leader who attributes failure to lack of ability. Thus, this leader is more likely to employ punitive responses for poor performance.

Depending on the extent to which leaders' responses appear to be appropriate, members may adjust performance attributions. Adjustments are unlikely when leaders' responses are viewed as appropriate. In contrast, members may reevaluate and alter attributions if leader behavior is inconsistent with anticipated responses. Regardless of whether an adjustment is made, the members' attributions for success or failure influence performance expectations and affective reactions. Attributions to unstable causes will create an expectation that future performance can change whereas attributions to stable causes lead to expectations that success or failure will continue. Finally, member performance expectations and affective reactions influence the amount and intensity of subsequent task-directed behaviors.

Reactions to Poor Member Performance

A detailed illustration of the combinations of leader/member attributions and responses is provided in Figure 2. It is recognized that the process depicted in this model is static, whereas the actual process usually is more dynamic and interactive. Although the present model illustrates leader attributions occurring before subordinate attributions, these also could occur simultaneously, or subordinates' attributions could be made before leaders' attributions. In addition, both subordinates and leaders could alter and adjust their attributions several times as a result of leader responses, subordinate responses, or additional performance-related information. Thus, often the performance attribution process is complex and interactive. Clearly, modeling and discussing all possible sequences of interaction would be unwieldy. For this discussion, the present model presents a typical but somewhat simplified account of the leader/member attribution process.

Attributional Biases

It has been found in studies of perceptual congruence within manager-subordinate dyads that similar, as opposed to divergent, perceptions are characterized by (a) higher evaluations of subordinate performance (e.g., Greene, 1972; Wexley, Alexander, Greenawalt, & Couch, 1980), (b) greater subordinate job satisfaction (e.g., Wexley et al., 1980), and (c) higher subordinate evaluations of their managers (Weiss, 1977). This research demonstrates that differences between the perceptions of managers and subordinates can have a profound impact on the nature of their relations. Although, unquestionably, the primary determinant of performance attributions is the objective reality of a specific situation, a number of organizational theorists have proposed that biases in the attributional process may be an important source of perceptual conflict between leaders and members (Green & Mitchell, 1979; Martinko & Gardner, 1982; McElroy, 1982; Mitchell et al., 1981). McElroy (1982, p. 416), for example, suggests that "leader-member conflict may be the direct result of a leader taking action based on his/her own causal analysis of the situation, a causal analysis potentially quite different from that of his/her subordinates."

The Actor/Observer Bias. Jones and Nisbett (1972, p.2) described the actor/observer bias as the "pervasive tendency of actors to attribute their actions to situational requirements, whereas observers tend to attribute the same actions to stable personal dispositions." These authors suggested that bias arises from the actors' more detailed knowledge of the circumstances, history, and experiences surrounding their behavior. In contrast, these cues are less salient to observers who focus on the actor. Subsequent research on the actor/observer bias has demonstrated its occurrence across a variety of situations and subjects (Pruitt & Insko, 1980; Sillars, 1981).

The implication of this bias with respect to poor subordinate performance is that members (actors) *tend* to focus on the situation, invoking environmental explanations of their performance, whereas leaders (observers) *tend* to focus

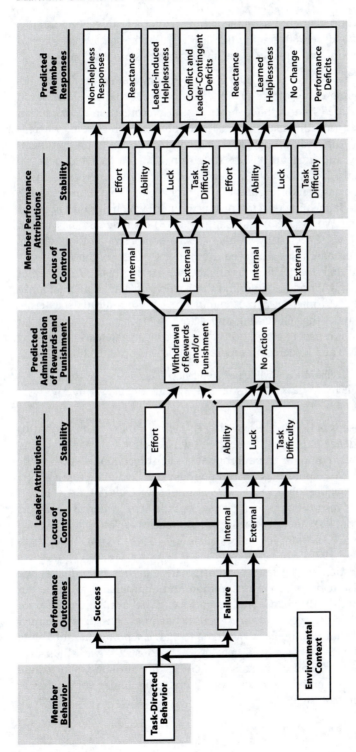

Figure 2   Member and Leader Attributions and Predicted Responses

on the member and, therefore, attribute failure to internal causes. Importantly, Mitchell and Wood's (1980) finding that leaders were biased toward internal attributions for poor performance is consistent with this proposition.

Self-Serving Bias.   Self-serving bias is the tendency to take credit for success while blaming either others or the environment for failure. Reviews of research in this area have resulted in divergent interpretations. Zuckerman (1979) suggested that this bias protects and enhances self-esteem, whereas Bradley (1978) proposed that people take credit for success to present themselves favorably and attribute failure to external causes to avoid negative impressions. Tetlock and Levi (1982) suggested the various interpretations of the self-serving bias are indistinguishable empirically and that future research should focus on delineating the circumstances under which this bias occurs.

Mitchell and Wood (1980) and Soulier (1978) documented bias within leadership contexts. Specifically, Soulier (1978) demonstrated that subjects occupying subordinate roles displayed attributions under conditions of success and failure that are consistent with the self-serving bias. On the other hand, Mitchell and Wood (1980) found that leaders attributed poor subordinate performance to internal causes significantly more often than external causes. Importantly, the self-serving and actor/observer biases have similar implications with respect to attributions for poor subordinate performance by both subordinates and leaders and suggest the following proposition:

> *Proposition 1.* Subordinates will have a tendency to favor external attributions for failure, whereas leaders will tend to blame internal subordinate characteristics.

The False Consensus Effect.   Ross (1977) defined the "false consensus effect" as a tendency of people to "see their own behavioral choices and judgments as relatively common and appropriate to existing circumstances while viewing alternative responses as uncommon, deviant, and inappropriate" (p. 188). As a consequence, observers tend to attribute behavior that they view as unusual to stable dispositional characteristics of the actor, whereas behaviors that are consistent with their own response tendencies are attributed to environmental causes (Gilovich, Jennings, & Jennings, 1983; Major, 1980; Ross, Greene, & House, 1977).

One implication of the false consensus effect is that subordinates are likely to perceive their behavior as common and appropriate given the circumstances. On the other hand, leaders prefer external attributions for poor performance when they perceive a member's behavior as consistent with their own behavioral choices. Similarly, they tend to blame subordinates for failure when they consider the member's behavior as inconsistent with their own response preferences. Thus, it is likely that conflicting attributions for failure will occur among members and leaders who have dissimilar approaches to work. This discussion suggests:

Proposition 2. The degree of congruence between member behaviors and leader behavioral preferences is related positively to the amount of similarity among leader and member attributions.

A final implication of the false consensus effect is that both members and leaders may use "self-based" as opposed to "sample-based" standards when evaluating performance because they perceive their performance as more representative than can be justified statistically. Thus, it is proposed that:

Proposition 3. Members and leaders are biased toward "self-based" as opposed to "sample-based" standards when developing attributions for member performance.

Although this proposition has not been investigated in organizational settings, Hansen and Lowe (1976) and Hansen and Donoghue (1977) documented many situations in which people invoke self-based standards during the attribution process. Assuming that members and leaders have different levels of skill, these findings suggest that the self-based standards of members will conflict with those of the leaders.

Hedonic Relevance.   Another factor that can influence an observer's attribution for actor behavior is the "hedonic relevance" of the behavior for the observer (Jones & Davis, 1965). Behaviors that benefit the observer tend to result in favorable attributions, whereas behaviors that yield adverse consequences may lead to unfavorable inferences. This bias is more pronounced when the outcome of the actor's behavior is serious as opposed to trivial.

Since leaders are ultimately dependent upon their followers for the successful accomplishment of their objectives, the concept of hedonic relevance is especially pertinent to leader/member relations. Thus, leaders are more likely to make negative dispositional attributions about members whose behaviors they perceive as hindering as opposed to facilitating goal attainment. In effect, hedonic relevance amplifies the impact of the biases discussed above.

Proposition 4. The hedonic relevance of member behavior to a leader is related positively to the strength of the attributional biases of leaders.

Leader Attributions, Expectations, and Responses

As a group, the above biases suggest a tendency toward differences in the performance attributions of leaders as opposed to members. As Green and Mitchell (1979) noted, overall, leaders are more likely to make internal as opposed to external attributions for poor member performance. In addition, research on the self-serving bias suggests that leaders tend to view members as much less responsible for success than do the members themselves. Finally, the literature on self-based standards suggests that performance that is perceived as acceptable by subordinates may nevertheless be considered inferior by their superiors. Thus, it appears that leaders are more likely than subordinates to (a) view members' performance as inadequate, (b) discount success, and (c) attribute failures to internal characteristics of subordinates.

Leader attributions for member performance influence both their expectations for future performance and subsequent interactions. Studies by Mitchell and Wood (1980) and Green and Liden (1980) indicate that internal attributions lead to punitive supervisory responses to low performance significantly more often than external attributions. In contrast, leaders with external attributions are less likely to punish member failure since they perceive failure to be beyond the member's control. More specifically, researchers have shown that causal attributions to effort appear to be a primary determinant of performance evaluations and subsequent rewards or punishment, whereas ability attributions are less likely to elicit punitive responses (Mitchell et al., 1981; Weiner & Kukla, 1970). In general, it appears that leaders perceive ability to be less subject to member control and, consequently, less deserving of rewards or punishments. On the other hand, because leaders believe subordinates can control effort, they expect that punishment will lead to improved performance. Of course, some leaders who attribute member failure to ability will, nevertheless, administer punishment.

The relationships between leader attributions for member failure and leader's subsequent responses are depicted schematically in Figure 2. In addition, this discussion suggests the following propositions:

Proposition 5. Leaders have a tendency to attribute poor member performance to internal causes more often than to external causes.

Proposition 6. Leaders who attribute poor member performance to effort as opposed to ability exhibit more punitive responses.

Member Attributions, Expectations, and Individual Differences

The responses exhibited by members following failure are influenced by (a) their performance attributions, (b) their expectations for future task performance, and (c) individual differences (Martinko & Gardner, 1982).

Performance Attributions. As indicated earlier, it has been suggested by both the actor/observer and self-serving biases that members will favor external attributions for failure. Similarly, according to literature on the false consensus effect when the abilities and skills of members and leaders are unequal, attributions for performance will be dissimilar. In general, the above biases suggest that:

Proposition 7. Members have a bias toward attributing poor performance to external as opposed to internal causes.

Unquestionably, the primary sources of member attributions are the actual internal and external contingencies associated with the poor performance and, as Mitchell et al. (1981) noted, there are many situations in which members attribute poor performance to internal causes, thus suggesting:

Proposition 8. Member attributions for poor performance are related positively to the actual external contingencies associated with their behavior.

Performance Expectations. Member attributions for task performance have an impact on their expectations for future performance. Weiner et al. (1971) argued that performance expectations vary directly with the stability dimension of their attributional taxonomy. Indeed, attributional research (Anderson, 1983; Meyer, 1980) indicates that people who make attributions to stable causes expect similar performance outcomes in the future. Conversely, persons with unstable attributions often expect different performance because they anticipate that their luck or effort will change. Thus:

> *Proposition 9.* The degree to which members attribute poor performance to stable versus unstable causes is related negatively to expectations of changes in future performance.

Individual Differences. Individual reactions to failure vary. Attributional style, sex role identity, self-esteem, and need for achievement have been identified as individual differences that moderate attribution processes. Attributional style refers to individual tendencies in the types of attributions made in response to interpersonal success and failure. As noted above, persons who tend to attribute failure to stable internal factors such as ability are more likely to experience motivational and performance deficits than are persons who attribute failure to unstable external causes such as chance (Anderson, 1983; Anderson, Horowitz, & French, 1983). Thus, the style of some individuals predisposes them toward self-defeating attributions, whereas others tend to make attributions which result in more constructive responses. As Martinko and Gardner (1982) noted, objective performance history also plays a role in a person's reactions to failure. Specifically, people who have been exposed repeatedly to failure often become passive and develop self-defeating attributions that persist, even after conditions change so that success is possible. These people are characterized as Learned Helpless (LH).

LH studies have found that females exhibit greater deficits in performance following non-contingent aversive outcomes than do males (e.g., Diener & Dweck, 1980; Dweck & Bush, 1976). Initially, these results were interpreted as indicating that gender is an important individual difference related to LH. However, subsequent research suggests that sex role identity, not gender per se, is the key determinant of LH in these studies (Baucom, 1983; Baucom & Danker-Brown, 1984). More specifically, it appears that persons with both masculine and feminine sex-typed personalities are more vulnerable to LH.

Finally, research indicates that persons with high versus low self-esteem and achievement needs are more resistant to performance deficits that arise from exposure to uncontrollable aversive events (Perez, 1973; Shrauger & Sorman, 1977). Similarly, Krantz, Glass, and Snyder (974) demonstrated that a person whose lifestyle reflects a high need for achievement is less susceptible to LH than others. The research on individual differences and LH suggests the following:

> *Proposition 10.* There is a positive relationship between member conformance to sex-role stereotypes and susceptibility to LH.

Proposition 11. There is a negative relationship between member self-esteem and susceptibility to LH.

Proposition 12. There is a negative relationship between member needs for achievement and susceptibility to LH.

Proposition 13. Members who tend to attribute failure to internal, stable causes are more susceptible to LH than members who tend to attribute failure to other causes.

Member Responses

As noted above, performance attributions, expectations, and individual differences of members have a direct impact on the members' responses to poor performance and punitive leader behavior. Figure 2 delineates probable member responses to various combinations of leader behaviors and member attributions.

Conflict and Leader Contingent Deficits. The discussion of attributional biases indicated that members are biased toward external attributions for their failure whereas leaders tend to attribute member failure to internal causes. In situations where these biases are pronounced, leader/member conflict is particularly likely (Green & Mitchell, 1979; McElroy, 1982). Indeed, if the leader attributes failure to a lack of effort and responds by punishing the subordinate, the member probably will view the leader's response as inappropriate and conflict could occur. Superiors who continue to respond to failure with punishment eventually may be viewed as another external cause of poor performance. As such, the leader's behavior will appear arbitrary to the subordinate and it will yield results that are opposite of those desired. Research on punishment confirms that leaders who are perceived as administering rewards and punishment non-contingently encounter a number of dysfunctional outcomes including declining productivity, dissatisfaction, feelings of inequity, and negative affect among their subordinates (Arvey & Ivancevich, 1980; Podsakoff, 1982).

It is important to note that members who attribute failure to external causes, such as the behavior of their superior, are not as susceptible to LH (Abramson, Seligman, & Teasedale, 1978; Klein, Fencil-Morse, & Seligman, 1976; Tennen & Eller, 1977). Recall that helpless individuals exhibit passive behavior after repeated failure despite the occurrence of environmental changes that make success possible. On the other hand, people who attribute poor performance to external causes tend to exhibit performance deficits that are contingent upon the situation. This implies that when the variables related to failure change, these people will display increased levels of motivation. Thus, members who attribute failure to the leader may respond positively to changes in leadership and exhibit improved performance. This discussion suggests:

Proposition 14. The degree of congruence between leader and member attributions is related negatively to the amount of leader/member conflict.

Proposition 15. The degree to which members attribute poor performance to stable causes is related negatively to subsequent task-related effort.

Proposition 16. The degree to which members attribute poor performance to external causes is related negatively to LH.

Reactance. It has been demonstrated in a number of studies that persons who experience small to moderate exposure to failure actually exhibit improved performance on subsequent tasks (Brockner et al., 1983; Tennen & Eller, 1977). To explain this finding, Wortman and Brehm (1975) postulated that, upon encountering failure, people initially attempt to regain control of their performance through increased effort. This explanation implies:

Proposition 17. Member exposure to small to moderate amounts of failure may result in increased effort.

However, after repeated failures, individuals may become convinced that they lack control and reduce the amount of effort expended. Subsequent research on the Wortman-Brehm model has revealed that reactance is most likely to occur when failure is attributed to internal as opposed to external causes. Brockner et al. (1983) suggested that internal attributions amplify reactance effects because subjects attach greater psychological significance to internally, rather than externally, caused failure.

As Figure 2 indicates, the above findings imply that the initial response to failure may be increased effort, particularly when failure is attributed to internal causes. However, after repeated exposure to failure, members may make other attributions that lead to performance deficits and LH. Thus:

Proposition 18. Increased amounts of exposure to noncontingent failure are related negatively to subsequent task-related efforts.

Learned Helplessness. Earlier sections have noted that people who make stable, internal attributions for failure are particularly vulnerable to LH (Abramson et al., 1978; Anderson, 1983; Dweck, 1975). According to Abramson et al. (1978), these people are more susceptible because they believe their ineffectiveness is due to personal and relatively permanent shortcomings. Ironically, the passive maladaptive behavior of helpless members and the negative affective reactions such as anxiety, hostility, frustration, stress, apathy, and shame, which typically accompany LH (Seligman, 1975), often result in additional decrements in performance (Martinko & Gardner, 1982).

Figure 2 indicates two combinations of leader/member attributions and responses for which helpless behavior is probable. In the first, members attribute their failure to ability, whereas leaders attribute failure to member ability, task difficulty, or bad luck. Although the leader probably will refrain from punishment since the failure appears to be due to factors beyond member control, it is predicted that these members will become helpless since they believe it is unlikely that their ability will change.

In the second set of circumstances, the member attributes failure to ability, whereas the leader blames it on low effort. In this situation, the leader probably will withdraw rewards, punish the subordinate, or both. The member is likely to view punishment as inappropriate since he or she has attributed the failure to a lack of ability rather than to a lack of effort. In effect, the leader has added punishment to the experience of uncontrollable failure. Thus, the leader's behavior increases the probability that the member will become helpless. When LH results under these circumstances it has been labeled "leader-induced helplessness" since the leader plays a key role in its development (Martinko & Gardner, 1982).

From the above discussion, it is apparent that subordinates who experience leader-induced helplessness will have difficulty in responding effectively. Indeed, these members may conclude that no matter what they do, they are unable to meet the leader's expectations. Conversely, managers of helpless members probably will perceive them as low achievers who do not deserve organizational rewards. Vertical dyad linkage theory (Graen & Cashman, 1975) suggests that inevitably such members will find themselves in an "out-group" of subordinates who cannot establish an exchange relationship with their superiors. As a consequence, there is the tendency for these members to remain low performers until they are either dismissed or leave the organization voluntarily. Thus:

> *Proposition 19.* The degree to which leaders inappropriately attribute failure to effort and punish subordinates is related positively to LH.

> *Proposition 20.* LH is associated positively with membership in organizational "out-groups."

Toward Productive Leader/Member Relations

Reducing Divergent Perspectives

Research on attributional biases indicates that the impact of these biases is reduced as the observer gains knowledge and experiences empathy toward the actor (Jones & Nisbett, 1972; Regan & Totten, 1975). This implies that the more a leader feels psychologically close to a subordinate, the more his or her attributions will be in agreement. Conversely, greater psychological distance increases the probability of conflicting attributions and passive behavior characterized by LH. Thus, the following propositions are advanced:

> *Proposition 21.* Decreasing the level of psychological distance between leaders and members is related positively to the degree of congruence within leader/member dyads.

> *Proposition 22.* Increasing the level of psychological distance between leaders and members is related positively to the divergence of attributional perspectives and the emergence of passive maladaptive behavior.

Interaction. In his classic work on group dynamics, Homans (1950) asserted that increasing levels of interaction and communication among group members results in a greater homogeneity of sentiments. This implies that leaders may reduce psychological distance between themselves and their members considerably through planned interactions such as meetings, work sessions, and conferences. Similar propositions are provided in more contemporary works. For example, Rogers and Rogers (1976) suggested that open communication channels provide both the leader and member with a greater appreciation of each other's point of view. Similarly, Carroll and Schneier (1982) suggested that managers can become more aware of the underlying causes of failure by learning to actively listen and by using more productive communication interactions.

Accounts. Accounts are explanations for predicament-creating events (Schlenker, 1980). Actors attempt to reduce responsibility for predicaments by providing accounts which show that the dilemma is beyond their control. Wood and Mitchell (1981) found that when leaders take into consideration member accounts, they make fewer internal attributions and engage in less punitive responses.

Leaders can be encouraged to use accounts through training and recording procedures. Leadership training should include segments on performance analysis that emphasize the consideration of member accounts of performance (Carroll & Schneier, 1982). Similarly, it should be required that records and documentation of important events contain detailed accounts of the event by the subordinate. Such interventions should help reduce the attributional biases of leaders by requiring consideration of the accounts of members.

Behavioral Observation. Several reviews have concluded that evaluators routinely should perform behavior sampling as part of the appraisal process to reduce evaluation biases (Cederblom, 1982; Feldman, 1981; Lee, 1985). Additional support for this proposition is provided by Strickland (1958) and Kruglanski (1970), who indicated that closer monitoring by supervisors results in increased external attributions. Thus, it appears that regular observation of member behavior provides leaders with greater knowledge of the external factors that influence performance and lessens the negative consequences which result from unrealistic internal attributions.

Attribution Training. Several researchers have demonstrated that training using videotapes of ratee behavior, role plays, and experiential exercises can reduce evaluation errors (e.g., Latham & Wexley, 1981; Latham, Wexley, & Pursell, 1975). Workshops devoted to reducing attributional errors easily could be developed to help leaders gain an awareness of how their own personalities and values relate to attributional biases and potentially inappropriate behavior. Similar training also could be provided for subordinates to encourage realistic attributions for both success and failure. Specific guidelines for such training have been provided by Martinko and Gardner (1982).

Multiple Raters. Another approach for identifying and minimizing biases is to obtain input from multiple rating groups (Carroll & Schneier, 1982; Feldman, 1981). Peer ratings, subordinate evaluations of superiors, and self-appraisals are useful means for obtaining alternative perspectives of member performance. These techniques provide leaders with information regarding the circumstances surrounding subordinate performance which they normally would not acquire and, consequently, the awareness of this information results in a reduced tendency to make internal attributions. Importantly, self-appraisals easily could be designed to incorporate member accounts of poor performance. Thus, multiple raters represent another means for reducing gaps between the perspectives of leaders and members and, subsequently, for lowering the probability of dysfunctional attributional conflicts.

Attention to Individual Differences

The literature on individual differences reviewed earlier suggested that organizational members who (a) conform to sex-role stereotypes, (b) possess low self-esteem, (c) have low achievement needs, and/or (d) tend to attribute interpersonal failure to internal stable causes such as ability, are especially vulnerable to particular attributional biases and styles. These findings imply that leaders should be especially aware during interactions with these members and should avoid providing feedback that might result in self-deprecating biases. Training to assist leaders in recognizing these characteristics coupled with the attributional training processes described above could greatly facilitate more congruent attributions and productive leader/member interactions.

Conclusion

The primary objective of this paper has been the articulation and description of the interactive dyadic exchange of leader and member attributions and behavior. During this process, it was necessary to narrow the scope of the discussion so that testable propositions and hypotheses could be developed. Although the primary concentration was on attributions for poor performance, a more general model depicting a broader range of leader and member attributions and behaviors also has been proposed. Several directions are possible for future work in this area. First, both basic laboratory research and field experiments are necessary to validate the propositions that have been advanced. Unfortunately, too few of the studies cited here were conducted in organizational settings. Second, more work should be done to specify the relationships between attributions and behavior. Although this paper provides some suggestions and propositions, the relationship between particular attributions and specific types of behavioral responses has not been investigated thoroughly in either the laboratory or the field. Third, the dyadic exchange of attributions and behavior associated with success needs to be articulated. Researchers who have investigated the impact of success on subject reactions to subsequent failure have found that continuous success also can have debilitating effects (Clifford, 1978; Jones, Nation, & Massad, 1977). This finding suggests that inaccurate and conflicting attributions for success may be as potentially damaging to leader/member relations as those associated with failure. Finally, *practical* guidelines for managing leader/member relations are desirable. It is hoped that the attributional research and theoretical development described above will enable more practical prescriptions for leader/member interactions.

References

Abramson, L. Y., Seligman, M. E. P., & Teasedale, J. D. (1978) Learned helplessness in humans: Critique and reformulation. *Journal of Abnormal Psychology,* 87, 49–74.

Adams, J. C. (1965) Inequity in social exchange. In L. Berkowitz (Ed.), *Advances in experimental social psychology* (Vol. 2, pp. 267–299). New York: Academic Press.

Anderson, C. A. (1983) Motivational and performance deficits in interpersonal settings: The effect of attributional style. *Journal of Personality and Social Psychology,* 45, 1136–1141.

Anderson, C. A., Horowitz, L. M., & French, R. De S. (1983) Attributional style of lonely and depressed people. *Journal of Personality and Social Psychology,* 45, 127–136.

Argyris, C. (1957) *Personality and organization.* New York: Harper.

Arvey, R. D., & Ivancevich, J. M. (1980) Punishment in organizations: A review, propositions, and research suggestions. *Academy of Management Review,* 5, 123–132.

Baucom, D. H. (1983) Sex role identity and the decision to regain control among women: A learned helplessness investigation. *Journal of Personality and Social Psychology,* 44, 334–343.

Baucom, D. H., & Danker-Brown, P. (1984) Sex role identity and sex-stereotyped tasks in the development of learned helplessness in women. *Journal of Personality and Social Psychology,* 46, 422–430.

Blauner, R. (1964) *Alienation and freedom: The factory worker and his industry.* Chicago: University of Chicago Press.

Bowman, P. J. (1984) A discouragement centered approach to studying unemployment among black youth: Hopelessness, attributions, and psychological distress. *International Journal of Mental Health,* 13(1–2), 68–91.

Bradley, G. W. (1978) Self-serving biases in the attribution process: A reexamination of the fact or fiction question. *Journal of Personality and Social Psychology,* 36, 56–71.

Brockner, J., Gardner, M., Bierman, J., Mahan, T., Thomas, B., Weiss, W., Winters, L., & Mitchell, A. (1983) The roles of self-esteem and self-consciousness in the Wortman-Brehm model of reactance and learned helplessness. *Journal of Personality and Social Psychology,* 45, 199–209.

Calder, B. J. (1977) An attribution theory of leadership. In B. M. Staw & G. R. Salancik (Eds.), *New directions in organizational behavior* (pp. 179–204). Chicago: St. Clair Press.

Carroll, S. J., & Schneier, C. E. (1982) *Performance appraisal and review systems: The identification, measurement, and development of performance in organizations.* Glenview, IL: Scott Foresman.

Cederblom, D. (1982) The performance appraisal interview: A review, implications, and suggestions. *Academy of Management Review,* 7, 219–227.

Clifford, M. M. (1978) Have we underestimated the facilitative effects of failure? *Canadian Journal of Behavioral Science,* 10, 308–316.

Clarke, R., & Morris, R. (1980) *Worker's attitudes toward productivity.* Washington, DC: U.S. Chamber of Commerce.

Davis, R. E. V., & Luthans, F. (1979) Leadership reexamined: A behavioral approach. *Academy of Management Review,* 4, 237–248.

Diener, C. I., & Dweck, C. S. (1980) An analysis of learned helplessness: II. The processing of success. *Journal of Personality and Social Psychology*, 39, 940–952.

Dweck, C. S. (1975) The role of expectations and attributions in the alleviation of learned helplessness. *Journal of Personality* and *Social Psychology*, 31, 674–685.

Dweck, C. S., & Bush, E. S. (1976) Sex differences in learned helplessness: I. Differential debilitation with peer and adult evaluators. *Developmental Psychology*, 12, 147–156.

Feldman, J. M. (981) Beyond attribution theory: Cognitive processes in performance appraisal. *Journal of Applied Psychology*, 66, 127–148.

Festinger, L. (1957) *A theory of cognitive dissonance.* Stanford, CA: Stanford University Press.

Furnham, A. (1984) Unemployment, attribution theory, and mental health: A review of the British literature. *International Journal of Mental Health*, 13(1–2), 51–67.

Gilovich, T., Jennings, S., & Jennings, D. L. (1983) Causal focus and estimates of consensus: An examination of the false-consensus effect. *Journal of Personality and Social Psychology*, 45, 550–559.

Graen, G., & Cashman, J. (1975) A role-making model of leadership in formal organizations. In J. G. Hunt & L. L. Larson (Eds.), *Leadership frontiers* (pp. 143–165). Kent, OH: Comparative Administration Research Institute.

Green, S. G., & Liden, R. C. (1980) Contextual and attributional influences on control decisions. *Journal of Applied Psychology*, 65, 453–458.

Green, S. G., & Mitchell, T. R. (1979) Attributional processes of leader-member interactions. *Organizational Behavior and Human Performance*, 23, 429–458.

Greenberger, D. B., & Strasser, S. (1986) Development and application of a model of personal control in organizations. *Academy of Management Review*, 11, 164–177.

Greene, C. N. (1972) Relationships among role accuracy, compliance, performance evaluation and satisfaction within managerial dyads. *Academy of Management Journal*, 15, 205–215.

Hansen, R. D., & Donoghue, J. M. (1977) The power of consensus: Information derived from one's own and other's behavior. *Journal of Personality and Social Psychology*, 35, 294–302.

Hansen, R. D., & Lowe, C. A. (1976) Distinctiveness and consensus: The influence of behavioral information on actors' and observers' attributions. *Journal of Personality and Social Psychology*, 34, 425–433.

Hollander, E. P. (1978) *Leadership dynamics: A practical guide to effective relationships.* New York: Free Press.

Homans, G. C. (1950) *The human group.* New York: Harcourt, Brace & World.

Hunt, J. G., & Osborn, R. N. (1978) A multiple approach to leadership for managers. In J. Stinson & P. Hersey (Eds.), *Leadership for practitioners.* Athens, OH: Center for Leadership Studies, Ohio University.

Jones, E. E., & Davis, K. E. (1965) From acts to dispositions: The attribution process in person perception. In L. Berkowitz (Ed.), *Advances in experimental social psychology* (pp. 219–266). New York: Academic Press.

Jones, E. E., & Nisbett, R. E. (1972) The actor and the observer: Divergent perceptions of the causes of behavior. In E. Jones, D. Kanouse, H. Kelley, R. Nisbett, S. Valins, & B. Weiner (Eds.), *Attribution: Perceiving the causes of behavior* (pp. 79–94). Morristown, NJ: General Learning Press.

Jones, S. L., Nation, J. R., & Massad, P. (1977) Immunization against learned helplessness in man. *Journal of Abnormal Psychology*, 86, 75–83.

Kelley, H. H. (1972) Attribution in social interaction. In E. Jones, D. Kanouse, H. Kelley, R. Nisbett, S. Valins, & B. Weiner (Eds.), *Attribution: Perceiving the causes of behavior* (pp. 1–26). Morristown, NJ: General Learning Press.

Klein, D. C., Fencil-Morse, E., & Seligman, M. E. P. (1976) Learned helplessness, depression, and the attribution of failure. *Journal of Personality and Social Psychology, 33,* 11–26.

Krantz, D. S., Glass, D. C., & Snyder, M. L. (1974) Helplessness, stress level, and the coronary-prone behavior pattern. *Journal of Experimental Social Psychology,* 10, 284–300.

Kruglanski, A. W. (1970) Attributing trustworthiness in supervisor-worker relations. *Journal of Experimental Social Psychology,* 6, 214–232.

Latham, G. P., & Wexley, K. N. (1981) *Increasing productivity through performance appraisal.* Reading, MA: Addison-Wesley.

Latham, G. P., Wexley, K. N., & Pursell, E. D. (1975) Training managers to minimize rating errors in the observation of behavior. *Journal of Applied Psychology,* 50, 550–555.

Lee, C. (1985) Increasing performance appraisal effectiveness: Matching task types, appraisal process, and rater training. *Academy of Management Review,* 10, 322–331.

Major, B. (1980) Information acquisition and attribution processes. *Journal of Personality and Social Psychology,* 39, 1010–1023.

March, J. G., & Simon, H. H. (1958) *Organizations.* New York: Wiley.

Martinko, M. J., & Gardner, W. L. (1982) Learned helplessness: An alternative explanation for performance deficits. *Academy of Management Review,* 7, 413–417.

Martinko, M. J., & Gardner, W. L. (1984) An interactive learned helplessness perspective of the leader/member attribution process. In W. D. Terpening & K. R. Thompson (Eds.), *Proceedings of the 27th Annual Conference of the Midwest Academy of Management* (pp. 251–262). South Bend, IN: University of Notre Dame Press.

McElroy, J. C. (1982) A typology of attribution leadership research. *Academy of Management Review,* 7, 413–417.

Meyer, J. P. (1980) Causal attribution for success and failure: A multivariate investigation of dimensionality, formation, and consequences. *Journal of Personality and Social Psychology,* 38, 704–718.

Mitchell, T. R., Green, S. G., & Wood, R. E. (1981) An attributional model of leadership and the poor performing subordinate: Development and validation. In L. L. Cummings & B. M. Staw (Eds.), *Research in organizational behavior* (Vol. 3, pp. 197–234). Greenwich, CT: JAI Press.

Mitchell, T. R., & Wood, R. E. (1980) Supervisor's responses to subordinate's poor performance: A test of an attributional model. *Organizational Behavior and Human Performance,* 25, 123–128.

Mitroff, I. I., & Pondy, L. R. (1974) On the organization of inquiry: A comparison of some radically different approaches to policy analysis. *Public Administration Review,* 35, 471–479.

Perez, R. C. (1973) The effect of experimentally induced failure, self-esteem, and sex on cognitive differentiation. *Journal of Abnormal Psychology,* 81, 74–79.

Platt, J. (1964) Strong inference. *Science,* 146, 347–353.

Podsakoff, P. M. (1982) Determinants of supervisor's use of rewards and punishments: A literature review and suggestions for further research. *Organizational Behavior and Human Performance,* 29, 58–83.

Pruitt, D. J., & Insko, C. A. (1980) Extension of the Kelley attribution model: The role of comparison-object consensus, target-object consensus, distinctiveness, and consistency. *Journal of Personality and Social Psychology,* 39, 39–58.

Regan, D., & Totten, J. (1975) Empathy and attribution: Turning observers into actors. *Journal of Personality and Social Psychology,* 32, 850–856.

Rogers, E. M., & Rogers, R. A. (1976) *Communications in organizations.* New York: Free Press.

Ross, L. (1977) The intuitive psychologist and his shortcomings: Distortions in the attribution process. In L. Berkowitz (Ed.), *Advances in experimental social psychology* (Vol. 10, pp. 173–219). New York: Academic Press.

Ross, L., Greene, D., & House, P. (1977) The false consensus phenomenon: An attributional bias in self-perception and social perception processes. *Journal of Experimental Social Psychology, 13,* 279–301.

Schlenker, B. R. (1980) *Impression management: The self-concept, social identity, and interpersonal relations.* Monterey, CA: Brooks/Cole.

Shrauger, J. S., & Sorman, P. B. (1977) Self-evaluations, initial success and failure, and improvement as determinants of persistence. *Journal of Consulting and Clinical Psychology, 45,* 784–795.

Seligman, M. E. P. (1975) *Helplessness: On depression, development and death.* San Francisco: Freeman.

Sillars, A. L. (1981) Attributions and interpersonal conflict-resolution. In J. H. Harvey, W. Ickes, & R. F. Kidd (Eds.), *New directions in attributional research* (Vol. 3, pp. 279–305). Hillsdale, NJ: Erlbaum.

Soulier, M. (1978) *The effects of success, failure, and accountability on the content of worker attributions.* Unpublished doctoral dissertation, University of Washington, Seattle.

Strickland, T. H. (1958) Surveillance and trust. *Journal of Personality and Social Psychology, 27,* 165–175.

Tennen, H., & Eller, S. I. (1977) Attributional components of learned helplessness and facilitation. *Journal of Personality and Social Psychology, 35,* 265–271.

Tetlock, P. E., & Levi, A. (1982) Attribution bias: On the inconclusiveness of the cognition-motivation debate. *Journal of Experimental Social Psychology, 18,* 68–88.

Weick, K. (1979) *The social psychology of organizing* (2nd ed.). Reading, MA: Addison-Wesley.

Weiner, B., Frieze, I., Kukla, A., Reed, L., Rest, S., & Rosenbaum, R. M. (1971) *Perceiving the causes of success and failure.* Morristown, NJ: General Learning Press.

Weiner, B., & Kukla, A. (1970) An attributional analysis of achievement motivation. *Journal of Personality and Social Psychology, 15,* 1–20.

Weiss, H. M. (1977) Subordinate imitation of supervisor behavior: The role of modeling in organizational socialization. *Organizational Behavior and Human Performance, 19,* 89–105.

Wexley, K. N., Alexander, R. A., Greenawalt, J. P., & Couch, M. A. (1980) Attitudinal congruence and similarity as related to interpersonal evaluations in manager-subordinate dyads. *Academy of Management Journal, 23,* 320–330.

Wood, R. E., & Mitchell, T. R. (1981) Managerial behavior in a social context: The impact of impression management on attributions and disciplinary actions. *Organizational Behavior and Human Performance, 28,* 356–378.

Wortman, C. B., & Brehm, J. W. (1975) Responses to uncontrollable outcomes: An integration of reactance theory and the learned helplessness model. In L. Berkowitz (Ed.), *Advances in experimental social psychology* (Vol. 8, pp. 277–336). New York: Academic Press.

Zuckerman, M. (1979) Attribution of success and failure revisited, or: The motivational bias is alive and well in attribution theory. *Journal of Personality, 47,* 245–287.

22

A 1976 Theory of
Charismatic Leadership

Robert J. House

Charisma is the term commonly used in the sociological and political science literature to describe leaders who by force of their personal abilities are capable of having profound and extraordinary effects on followers.[1] These effects include commanding loyalty and devotion to the leader and of inspiring followers to accept and execute the will of the leader without hesitation or question or regard to one's self-interest. The term *charisma*, whose initial meaning was "gift," is usually reserved for leaders who by their influence are able to cause followers to accomplish outstanding feats. Frequently such leaders represent a break with the established order and through their leadership major social changes are accomplished.

Most writers concerned with charisma or charismatic leadership begin their discussion with Max Weber's conception of charisma. Weber describes as charismatic those leaders who "reveal a transcendent mission or course of action which may be in itself appealing to the potential followers, but which is acted on because the followers believe their leader is extraordinarily gifted" (Weber, 1947, p. 358). Transcendence is attributed implicitly to both the qualities of the leader and the content of his mission, the former being variously described as "supernatural, superhuman or exceptional" (Weber, 1947, p. 358).

Shils (1965) points out that Weber conceived of charismatic leadership as one of the processes through which routinized social processes, norms and legal rules are changed. Weber distinguished innovators and creators from maintainers and attributed the "gift" of charisma in part to the creative or innovative quality of the leader's goals.

Several writers contend that charismatic leadership can and does exist in formal complex organizations (Dow, 1969; Oberg, 1972; Runciman, 1963;

Shils, 1965). Yet despite the profound effects that charismatic leaders are presumed to have on followers' commitment, motivation, and performance, discussions of charisma have been speculative in nature and almost exclusively theoretical. To the knowledge of this writer none of the theoretical notions in the sociological or political science literature have been subjected to empirical test, despite the fact that many of these notions are implicitly testable.

In this chapter the sociological and political science literature on charisma will be reviewed and, where possible, the major assertions in this literature will be restated as propositions in an attempt to make them testable. In addition, selected literature from the discipline of social psychology will be reviewed and propositions which the writer believes are relevant to the concept of charisma will be inferred from the literature.

The outcome of this analysis is a speculative theoretical explanation of charisma from a psychological perspective rather than from a sociological or political science perspective. Hopefully, such an explanation will help us to have greater insight into how charismatic leadership emerges and its effects in modern organizations. Further, it is hoped that such an explanation will provide testable propositions with which to further leadership research.

In the remainder of this presentation the concept of charisma will be examined under the following topics: charismatic effects, characteristics of charismatic leaders, behavior of charismatic leaders, and situational factors associated with the emergence and effectiveness of charismatic leaders. While these topics will be addressed separately, they are necessarily intertwined. Thus, at times a discussion of one topic will have implications for the other topics, and reference will be made to such implications.

The Effects of Charismatic Leadership

In the current literature the term *charismatic leadership* is generally defined and described in terms of the effects of the leader on followers, or in terms of the relationship between leaders and followers. For example, Oberg (1972) states that "the test for charisma . . . is the degree of devotion and trust the object (charismatic leader) inspires and the degree to which it enables the individual to transcend his own finiteness and alienation and feel made whole" (p. 22). Tucker (1968) refers to both "charismatic following" and the "charismatic relationship."

> Often times, the relationship of the followers to the charismatic leader is that of disciples to a master, and in any event he is revered by them. They do not follow him out of fear or monetary inducement, but out of love, passionate devotion, enthusiasm. They are not as a rule concerned with career, promotion, salary, or benefice. The charismatic following is a non-bureaucratic group. (p. 735)

It appears that most, if not all, writers agree that the effects of charismatic leadership are more emotional than calculative in that the follower is inspired enthusiastically to give unquestioned obedience, loyalty, commitment and devotion to the leader and to the cause that the leader represents.

The charismatic leader is also implicitly assumed to be an object of identification by which the followers emulate the leader's values, goals, and behavior. Thus, one of the effects of the charismatic leader is to cause followers to model their behavior, feelings, and cognitions after the leader (Friedrich, 1961). Through the articulation of a transcendent goal the leader is assumed to clarify or specify a mission for the followers. By the leader's expression of self-confidence, and through the exhibition of confidence in followers, the leader is also assumed to inspire self-confidence in the followers. Thus the charismatic leader is asserted to clarify followers' goals, cause them to set or accept higher goals, and have greater confidence in their ability to contribute to the attainment of such goals.

Finally, according to the political science and sociological literature on charisma, the charismatic leader is assumed to have the effect of bringing about rather radical change by virtue of beliefs and values that are different from the established order. Thus Oberg (1972) speaks of the "change agent" function of the charismatic leader.

The above review of the effects of charismatic leadership suggests several dependent variables for a theory of charisma. Some of these effects are: follower trust in the correctness of the leader's beliefs, similarity of followers' beliefs to those of the leader, unquestioning acceptance of the leader, affection for the leader, willing obedience to the leader, identification with and emulation of the leader, followers' emotional involvement in the mission, heightened goals of the follower, and the feeling of followers that they will be able to accomplish, or contribute to the accomplishment of, the mission. This large number of charismatic effects is consistent with Etzioni's definition of charisma as "the ability of an actor to exercise diffuse and intensive influence over the normative (ideological) orientations of other actors" (1961, p. 203).

The charismatic effects listed above constitute an *initial* list of variables that can be used as preliminary dependent variables for a theory of charisma. While this number of variables lack parsimony as the defining criteria of a charismatic leader, this list of presumed "charismatic effects" provides a starting point for empiric research on charisma. If one were to identify a number of persons in a population (say military or industrial leaders in a given population) who informed observers (such as superiors or peers) could agree on as being clearly charismatic, it would be possible to identify these leaders' effects by measuring the degree to which their followers' responses to them are different from responses of followers of other leaders randomly selected from the same population. The major differences in follower responses could then be clustered into primary groups and scaled. The scores of the followers on these groups could then serve as the basis for a more accurate, complete and parsimonious operational definition of charismatic effects. Leaders who have such effects on followers could be identified as charismatic leaders. Their personality characteristics and behaviors could be compared with those of other leaders (who do not have such effects) to identify characteristics and behaviors which differentiate the charismatic leaders from others. This process of operationally defining charismatic leadership permits one to identify leaders in a population who have the charismatic effects described in the political science and sociological literature and thereby specify an operational set of dependent variables for a theory of leadership.

Some of the above effects have also been the dependent variables in social-psychological research. Specifically, the ability of one person to arouse needs and enhance self-esteem of others, and the ability of one person to serve successfully as a behavioral model for another have been the subject of substantial empirical investigation by psychologists. Later in this chapter we will review this research in an attempt to identify and describe the specific situational factors and the leader behaviors that result in such "charismatic" effects.

Defining charismatic leadership in terms of its effects permits one to identify charismatic leaders only after they have had an impact on followers. Such a definition says nothing about the personal characteristics, behaviors, or situational factors that bring about the charismatic effects. This is the scientific challenge that must be addressed if the mysterious quality of charismatic leadership is to be explained and charismatic effects are to be made predictable. We now turn to a discussion of these issues.

Definition of Charismatic Leadership

Throughout this effort the term *charismatic leadership* will be used to refer to any leader who has the above "charismatic effects" on followers to an unusually high degree.[2] The operational definition of a given charismatic leader awaits research which will allow one to scale the above specific "charismatic effects." While it is not likely that all charismatic leaders have all of the above "charismatic effects," there are many possibilities that can be examined. For example, such effects may be present in a complex interacting manner. Alternatively it may be the sum of, or some absolute level of, selected effects that do indeed differentiate charismatic leaders from others.

Characteristics of the Charismatic Leader

Both the literature concerning charismatic leadership and the opinions of laymen seem to agree that the charismatic leader can be described by a specific set of personal characteristics. According to Weber (1947), the charismatic leader is accepted by followers because both the leader and the follower perceive the leader as possessing a certain extraordinary gift. This "gift" of charisma is seldom specified and generally held to be some mysterious quality that defies definition. In actuality the "gift" is likely to be a complex interaction of personal characteristics, the behavior the leader employs, characteristics of followers, and certain situational factors prevailing at the time of the assumption of the leadership role.

The literature on charismatic leadership repeatedly attributes three personal characteristics to leaders who have charismatic effects, namely:

extremely high levels of self-confidence, dominance, and a strong conviction in the moral righteousness of his/her beliefs.[3] It is interesting to note that these three characteristics are also attributed to charismatic leaders by laymen as well as by scholars. As a classroom exercise I have on three occasions asked students to form into small groups and to discuss the characteristics of some charismatic leader that they have personally known or to whom they have been exposed. These groups repeatedly described the charismatic leaders that they selected for discussion as possessing dominance, self-confidence, and a strong conviction in their beliefs and ideals.

While the consensus of political science and sociological writers and the results of my own informal experiment are not evidence that leaders who have charismatic effects do indeed possess these characteristics, the argument is certainly subject to an empirical test with self-report measures of personality traits, beliefs, and values.

In addition to the characteristics discussed above, it is hypothesized here that leaders who have charismatic effects have a high need to have influence over others. Such a need seems intuitively likely to characterize leaders who have such effects because without such a need they are unlikely to have developed the necessary persuasive skills to influence others and also are unlikely to obtain satisfaction from the leadership role. Uleman (1972) has developed a measure of the need for influence that can be used to test the above hypotheses.

The following proposition summarizes the above discussion:

> *Proposition 1.* Characteristics that differentiate leaders who have charismatic effects on subordinates from leaders who do not have such charismatic effects are dominance and self-confidence, need for influence, and a strong conviction in the moral righteousness of their beliefs.[4]

Behavior of Charismatic Leaders

The sociological and political science literature offer some hints about the behavior of charismatic leaders.

Role Modeling

First it is suggested that leaders who have charismatic effects express, by their actions, a set of values and beliefs to which they want their followers to subscribe. That is, the leader "role models" a value system for the followers. Gandhi constitutes an outstanding example of such systematic and intentional role modeling. He preached self-sacrifice, brotherly love, and nonviolent resistance to British rule. Repeatedly he engaged in self-sacrificing behaviors, such as giving up his lucrative law practice to live the life of a peasant, engaging in civil disobedience, fasting, and refusing to accept the ordinary conveniences offered to him by others.

The importance of the role modeling as a leadership strategy is illustrated by Gandhi's proposed leadership policies for the self-governance of India. "Most important for Gandhi was the example that leaders set for their followers. . . . 'No leader of an independent India will hesitate to give an example by cleaning out his own toilet box'" (Collins & LaPierre, 1975, 234–35).

Concerning role modeling, a study by Joestling and Joestling (1972) is suggestive of the effects that a high-status role model can have on the self-esteem of observers. Male and female students were asked to rate the value of being a woman. Half of the students were enrolled in the class taught by a qualified female instructor. Twenty-six percent of the women subjects in the class taught by a male thought there was nothing good about being a woman. In contrast, only five percent of the women subjects in the class taught by a qualified female had similar negative attitudes toward being a woman.

While role modeling often proves successful, success does not always occur. The question then is what permits a leader to be a successful role model, i.e., to be emulated by the followers. There is substantial evidence that a person is more likely to be modeled to the extent that that person is perceived as nurturing (i.e., helpful, sympathetic, approving) and as being successful or possessing competence. There is evidence that role modeling can have profound effects. Behavior resulting from modeling may be very specific such that the individual can be said to imitate or mimic the behavior of the model. Or, the behavior may be more general, taking the form of innovative behavior, generalized behavior orientations, and applications of principles for generating novel combinations of responses (Bandura, 1968).

Bandura (1968) reviews a substantial body of experimental evidence that shows that: (a) a model's emotional responses to rewards or punishments elicit similar emotional responses in observers (p. 240); (b) stable changes in the valences (a measure of attractiveness) subjects assign to outcomes and changes in long-standing attitudes often result from the role modeling (pp. 243–44); and (c) modeling is capable of developing generalized conceptual and behavioral properties of observers such as moral judgment orientations and delay-of-gratification patterns of behavior (p. 252).

Of particular significance for the study of leadership are the diverse kinds of attitudes, feelings, and behavior and the diversity of subjects involved in prior studies. Role modeling has been shown to influence the degree to which: (a) undergraduate females learn assertive behaviors in assertiveness training programs (Young, Rimm & Kennedy, 1973); (b) mentally disturbed patients assume independence in their personal life (Goldstein, Martins, Hubben, VanBelle, Schaaf, Wiersma & Goedharf, 1973); (c) individuals relate information to others (Sarason, Ganzer & Singer, 1972); (d) personal changes and learning outcomes result from adult t-groups (Peters, 1973); (e) individuals are willing to induce punishment (electric shock) to others (Baron, 1971); (f) nurses experience fear of tuberculosis (DeWolfe, 1967); and (g) subjects adopt biased attitudes toward minority ethnic groups (Kelman, 1958; Stotland and Patchen, 1961).

Many of the subjects in the above studies were either college students or adults. Thus, the findings are not limited to young children but are also relevant to persons in full-time occupations. Further, the dependent variables are all of significance for effective organizational or group performance. Feelings of fear, willingness to disclose information unfavorable to self, stereotyping, willingness to administer punishment, prejudicial attitudes, learning of interpersonal skills, and learning independence are relevant to interpersonal relations within organizations. Similarly, conditions and behaviors are relevant to the establishment of trust, to adequacy of communication, and to experiences that are satisfying in organizational life.

Thus it is argued here that role modeling is one of the processes by which leaders bring about charismatic effects. Furthermore, it is likely that the feelings, cognitions, and behavior that are modeled frequently determine subordinates' adjustment to organizational life, their job satisfaction, and their motivation to work. With respect to motivation, research findings suggest that leaders can have an effect on the values (or valences) subordinates attach to the outcomes of their effort as well as their expectations. And, as will be discussed below, leaders can also have an effect on subordinates' self-esteem, and their goal levels. Based on the above review of the literature concerned with role modeling, the following proposition is advanced:

> *Proposition 2.* The more favorable the perceptions of the potential follower toward a leader the more the follower will model: (a) the valences of the leader; (b) the expectations of the leader that effective performance will result in desired or undesired outcomes for the follower; (c) the emotional responses of the leader to work related stimuli; (d) the attitudes of the leader toward work and toward the organization. Here "favorable perceptions" are defined as the perceptions of the leader as attractive, nurturing, successful, or competent.

Image Building

If proposition 2 is valid, then it can be speculated that leaders who have charismatic effects not only model the values and beliefs they want followers to adopt, but also that such leaders take actions consciously designed to be viewed favorably by followers. This speculation leads to the following proposition:

> *Proposition 3.* Leaders who have charismatic effects are more likely to engage in behaviors designed to create the impression of competence and success than leaders who do not have such effects.

This proposition is consistent with the traditional literature on charismatic leadership. Weber (1947) speaks of the necessity of the charismatic leader to "prove" his extraordinary powers to the followers. Only as long as he can do so will he be recognized. While Weber and others have argued that such "proof" lies in actual accomplishments, the above proposition stresses the *appearance* of accomplishments and asserts that charismatic leaders engage in behaviors to gain such an appearance.

Goal Articulation

In the traditional literature on charisma it is frequently asserted that charismatic leaders articulate a "transcendent" goal which becomes the basis of a movement or a cause. Such a goal is ideological rather than pragmatic and is laden with moral overtones. Alternatively, if a movement is already in effect, one behavior of the emergent leader is the articulation of the goal of the movement with conviction and exhortation of the moral rightness of the goal (Tucker, 1968, p. 738).

Examples of such goals are Martin Luther King's "I have a dream," Hitler's "Thousand-year Reich" and his "lebensraum," or Gandhi's vision of an India in which Hindus and Moslems would live in brotherly love, independent from British rule. Berlew (1974, p. 269) states:

> The first requirement for charismatic leadership is a common or shared vision for what the future *could be*. To provide meaning and generate excitement, such a common vision must reflect goals or a future state of affairs that is valued by the organizations' members and thus important to them to bring about. All inspirational speeches or writings have the common element of some vision or dream of a better existence which will inspire or excite those who share the author's values. This basic wisdom too often has been ignored by managers.

The following proposition is advanced:

> *Proposition 4.* Leaders who have charismatic effects are more likely to articulate ideological goals than leaders who do not have such effects.

Exhibiting High Expectations and Showing Confidence

Leaders who communicate high performance expectations for subordinates and exhibit confidence in their ability to meet such expectations are hypothesized to enhance subordinates' self-esteem and to affect the goals subordinates accept or set for themselves. Some examples of this kind of charismatic leader behavior are Churchill's statement that England's air defense in World War II was "England's finest hour," Hitler's claim that aryans were "the master race," black leaders' exhortation that "Black is beautiful," and Martin Luther King's prediction that "We shall overcome." All of these statements imply high expectations and confidence in the followers.

There is substantial evidence that the expectation that one can accomplish one's goals is positively related to motivation and goal attainment. Persons with high self-esteem are more likely than persons with low self-esteem to seek higher personal rewards for performance (Pepitone, 1964), and to choose occupations that are congruent with self-perceived traits (Korman, 1966) and self-perceived ability level (Korman, 1967). Further, Korman (1968) has shown experimentally that for high self-esteem subjects there is a positive relationship between task performance and satisfaction, but that no such relationship exists for low self-esteem subjects. Raben and Klimoski (1973) have also shown experimentally that high self-esteem subjects are more likely than low self-esteem subjects to rise to the challenge of doing a task for which they believe they are not qualified. Thus, it is argued here that, to the extent the leader can affect the self-esteem of subordinates, leader behavior will have an effect on the kinds of rewards subordinates seek, their satisfaction with the rewards they obtain, and their motivation to perform effectively. The effect of leader behavior on subordinate self-esteem has been given little attention in the leadership literature.[5] The assertion that leaders can affect subordinates' self-esteem is derived from two lines of research: research concerning the role-modeling effects and research concerned with reality testing.

We have already argued that through role modeling leaders can have a rather profound effect on subordinates' beliefs. One of these beliefs is self-esteem, which is defined by Lawler (1971, p. 107) as the belief that subordinates have with respect to their own general level of ability to cope with and control their environment. It is argued here that subordinates' self-perceptions are likely to be modeled after the leader's perceptions of subordinates.[6] Thus if the leader communicates high performance expectations and shows confidence in subordinates, they will in turn set or accept a higher goal for themselves and have greater confidence in themselves.[7]

The second line of research suggesting that leaders affect subordinates' self-esteem is that research concerned with "reality testing." In social situations where interpersonal evaluation is highly subjective, individuals tend to "reality test," i.e., to test their notions of reality against the opinions of others (Deutsch & Gerard, 1955; Festinger, 1950). Consequently, to the extent that the leader shows followers that he/she believes them to be competent and personally responsible, the followers are hypothesized also to perceive themselves as competent. This self-perception is hypothesized to enhance motivation, performance, and satisfaction. Some indirect evidence in support of this line of reasoning is found in the results of studies by Berlew and Hall (1966), Stedry and Kay (1966), Korman (1971), Rosenthal and Jacobson (1968), Seaver (1973), and Meichenbaum, Bowers and Ross (1969). Berlew and Hall (1966) and Stedry and Kay (1966) in field studies both found that individual performance increased as a function of the level of expectation superiors communicated to the individuals. Similarly, Korman (1971) showed in a laboratory study that the performance of students on creative tasks was a direct positive function of the expectations that other college students had for the laboratory subjects. Korman (1971) also showed that ratings of subordinates' performance in two field settings and self-ratings of motivation in three field settings were all significantly correlated with the degree to which subordinates perceived their leaders' practices to reflect confidence in the subordinates.

These findings are consistent with those conducted in educational settings in which the expectations of teaching have been shown to be reflected in the performance of students (Meichenbaum, et al., 1969; Rosenthal & Jacobson, 1968; Seaver, 1973). In these studies teachers were induced to believe that certain students were more competent than others. This belief or expectancy on the part of the teacher was shown to be associated with higher student performance. However, there are also studies conducted in educational settings which have failed to demonstrate an effect of teachers' expectations of students' performance (Anderson & Rosenthal, 1968; Collins, 1969; Conn, Edwards, Rosenthal & Crowne, 1968; Evans and Rosenthal, 1969; Fiedler, Cohen & Finney, 1971). Seaver (1973) points out that in all of these disconfirming studies and also in the Rosenthal and Jacobson study, which is the subject of much controversy, the means of inducing teacher expectations were weak and thus "failure to find expectancy effects may be attributable solely to their failure to induce the desired expectancy in teachers" (p. 341).

If it is assumed that the leader's expectation of subordinates affects the subordinates' self-esteem and their self-esteem in turn affects their performance, then earlier research provides indirect support for the assertion that leaders' expectations affect subordinates' performance.

The *combination* of leaders' confidence and high expectations, rather than high expectations alone, should be emphasized here. It is possible that leaders might set high performance standards, thus implying high expectations of subordinates, while at the same time showing low confidence in the subordinates' ability to meet such expectations. An example of this would be the leader who scores high on such questionnaire items as "he needles foremen for production."[8] While such leader behavior may motivate subordinates to strive for high performance in order to avoid punishment, it is also likely to induce fear of failure. Such a state in turn will likely be accompanied by efforts to avoid accountability on the part of the subordinates, strong feelings of dissatisfaction, low acceptance of the leader, and resistance to the leader's influence attempts in the long run.

Thus while leader expectations are considered to have a significant effect on the reactions of subordinates, high expectations are hypothesized to have a positive effect only when subordinates' perceive the superior to also have confidence in their (the subordinates') ability to meet such expectations.

Effect on Followers' Goals

In addition to affecting the self-esteem of subordinates, leader expectations and confidence are also hypothesized to affect several important characteristics of the subordinates' goals.

In a series of laboratory studies, Locke and his associates (Bryan & Locke, 1967a, 1967b; Locke & Bryan, 1966a, 1966b) have demonstrated that when subjects are given specific goals by the experimenter they perform at significantly higher levels than those given the instruction to "do your best." Two field studies (Mace, 1935; Mendleson, 1971) also offer support for the external validity of these laboratory findings to natural field settings. Thus, it is argued here that, if laboratory experimenters can influence the goal characteristics of experimental subjects, it seems reasonable that leaders can have similar influence on the goal characteristics of subordinates.

Specific and high expectations of leaders are hypothesized to clarify subordinates' performance goals. Further, it is hypothesized that the more the leader shows confidence in the subordinates' ability to meet goals, the more subordinates are likely to accept them as realistic and attainable. Specific and high leader expectations are likely to provide a standard against which subordinates can evaluate their own performance. Accordingly, it is hypothesized here that leaders' expectations also serve as a basis on which subordinates may derive feedback. Finally, it is hypothesized that, when the leader's expectations are both high and clear to the subordinate and when the leader shows confidence in the subordinate's ability to meet such expectations, the subordinates will set and/or accept higher goals for themselves than would otherwise be the case, and will have more confidence that they will be able to meet the goals.

The above hypotheses concerning the leaders' effect on followers' self-esteem and goals can be summarized in the following proposition:

> *Proposition 5.* Leaders who simultaneously communicate high expectations of and confidence in followers are more likely to have followers who accept the goals of the leader and believe that they can contribute to goal accomplishment and are more likely to have followers who strive to meet specific and challenging performance standards.

Motive Arousal Leader Behavior

One explanation for the emotional appeal of the charismatic leader may be the specific content of the messages he communicates to followers. It is speculated here that charismatic leaders communicate messages that arouse motives that are especially relevant to mission accomplishment. For example, Gandhi's exhortations of love and acceptance of one's fellow man likely aroused the need for affiliation, a need (or motive) especially relevant to the goal of uniting Hindus, Moslems, and Christians.

Military leaders often employ symbols of authoritarianism and evoke the image of the enemy, thus arousing the power motive, a motive especially relevant to effective combat performance. For example, Patton, when addressing infantry recruits, would do so against the background of a large American flag, dressed with medals of his accomplishments, and wearing a shining helmet displaying the four stars indicating the status of general.

Miner's research is relevant to defining some of the conditions under which the arousal of the need for power is associated with successful performance. Miner found that individuals who were high on a projective (sentence completion) measure of the power need were more likely to be successful in hierarchical bureaucratic organizations than individuals low on the power need. These findings did not hold true in egalitarian non-bureaucratic organizations, however (Miner, 1965).

Industrial leaders and leaders of scientists frequently stress excellence of performance as a measure of one's worth, thus arousing the need for achievement, a motive especially relevant to the assumption of personal responsibility, persistence, and pride in high-quality work performance. Varga (1975) has shown that the need for achievement is positively associated with economic and technical performance among research and development project leaders. He has also shown that the need for power is a strong factor contributing to such success when in conjunction with the need for achievement, but a factor making for failure when possessed by leaders low on the need for achievement.

There is some evidence that formally appointed leaders in a laboratory situation are capable of arousing subordinates' need for achievement (Litwin & Stringer, 1968). There is also a substantial amount of evidence that the achievement, affiliation, and power needs can be aroused from experimental inductions. For example, the need for achievement has been aroused for males by suggesting to subjects that the experimental task is a measure of personal competence, or that the task is a standard against which one can measure his general level of ability (Heckhausen, 1967; McClelland, 1953; McClelland, Clarke, Roby & Atkinson, 1958; Raynore, 1974).

The need for affiliation has been aroused by having fraternity members rate one another, while all were present, on a sociometric friendship index (Shipley & Veroff, 1952) while at the same time requiring each brother to stand and be rated by the other members of the fraternity on a list of trait adjectives for achievement.

The power need has been aroused experimentally by (a) evoking the image of, or reminding one of, an enemy, (b) having subjects observe the exercise of power by one person over another, or (c) allowing subjects to exercise power over another (Winter, 1973). Thus it is hypothesized that needs can be, and often are, similarly aroused by leaders in natural settings. By stressing the challenging aspects of tasks, making group members' acceptance of each other salient to performance appraisal, or talking about competition from others, it is hypothesized that leaders can and frequently do arouse the needs for achievement, affiliation, and power. Further, it is hypothesized that, to the extent that such motives are associated with task-required performance, the arousal of these motives will result in increased effectiveness on the part of subordinates. Thus the performance consequence of motive arousal is contingent on the task contingencies. For example, when task demands of subordinates require assumption of calculated risks, achievement-oriented initiative, assumption of personal responsibility, and persistence toward challenging goals, the arousal of the need for achievement will facilitate task accomplishment. Further, there is ample evidence that when subordinates' need for achievement is high, task accomplishment will lead to satisfaction. When subordinates' need for achievement is low, task accomplishment will not be related to satisfaction (Steers, 1975).

When the task demands of subordinates require them to be persuasive, assert influence over or exercise control of others, or be highly competitive or combative, the arousal of the power motive is hypothesized to be related to effective performance and satisfaction. For example, on competitive tasks, or tasks requiring persuasion or aggression, the arousal of the power motive is hypothesized to lead to effective performance.

Finally, when task demands require affiliation behavior, as in the case of tasks requiring cohesiveness, teamwork, and peer support, the arousal of the affiliation motive becomes highly relevant to performance and satisfaction.

An example of such tasks would be tasks that are enriched by assignment of major work goals to groups rather than individuals (Trist & Bamforth, 1951).

These speculations are summarized with the following proposition:

> *Proposition 6.* Leaders who have charismatic effects are more likely to engage in behaviors that arouse motives relevant to the accomplishment of the mission than are leaders who do not have charismatic effects.[9]

Social Determinants of Charismatic Leadership

The sociological literature stresses that charismatic leadership is born out of stressful situations. It is argued that such leaders express sentiments deeply held by followers. These sentiments are different from the established order and thus their expression is likely to be hazardous to the leader (Friedland, 1964). Since their expression is hazardous, the leader is perceived as courageous. Because of other "gifts" attributed to the leader, such as extraordinary competence, the followers believe that the leader will bring about social change and will thus deliver them from their plight.

Thus it can be hypothesized that a strong feeling of distress on the part of followers is one situational factor that interacts with the characteristics and behavior of leaders to result in charismatic effects.

However, Shils (1965) argues that charisma need not be born out of distress. Rather, according to Shils, charisma is dispersed throughout the formal institutions of society. Accordingly, persons holding positions of great power will be perceived as charismatic because of the "awe-inspiring" quality of power. Shils' only requirement is that the expression of power must appear to be integrated with a transcendent goal.

The above controversy suggests the hypothesis that leaders are more likely to have charismatic effects in situations stressful for followers than in nonstressful situations. Further, it can be hypothesized that persons with the characteristics of dominance, self-confidence, need for influence, and strong convictions will be more likely to emerge as leaders under stressful conditions. Whether or not follower distress is a necessary condition for leaders to have charismatic effects or for persons with such characteristics to emerge as leaders is an empirical question that remains to be tested.

While there is lack of agreement as to whether or not leaders can have charismatic effects under nonstressful situations, all writers do seem to agree that charisma must be based on the articulation of an ideological goal. Opportunity to articulate such a goal, whether in stressful or nonstressful situations, thus can be hypothesized as one of the situational requirements for a person to have charismatic effects. This hypothesis suggests that, whenever the roles of followers can be defined as contributing to ideological values held by the followers, a leader can have some degree of charismatic effect by stressing such values and engaging in the specific behaviors described in the above propositions.

The question then is under what circumstances are roles definable in terms of ideological values. Clearly the roles of followers in political or religious movements can be defined in terms of ideological values. In addition, Berlew (1974) argues that since man seeks meaning in work there are many such ideological values to be stressed in modern formal organizations. Specifically, he argues that any of the value-related opportunities listed in Table 1 can have a charismatic effect.

There are some work roles in society which do not lend themselves to ideological value orientation. These are generally the roles requiring highly routine, nonthinking effort in institutions directed exclusively to economic ends. It is hard to conceive of clerks or assembly-line workers in profit-making firms as perceiving their roles as ideologically oriented. However, the same work when directed toward an ideological goal could lend itself to charismatic leadership. For example, in World War II, "Rosie the Riveter" expressed the ideological contribution of an assembly-line worker. And such menial efforts as stuffing envelopes frequently are directed toward ideological goals in political or religious organizations. The following proposition summarizes the above argument:

> *Proposition 7.* A necessary condition for a leader to have charismatic effects is that the role of followers be definable in ideological terms that appeal to the follower.

Summary and Overview

Figure 1 presents an overview of the theory presented above. It is hypothesized that leaders who have charismatic effects are differentiated from others by some combination (possibly additive and possibly interactive) of the four personal characteristics shown in the upper right box: dominance, self-confidence, need for influence, and a strong conviction in the moral righteousness of

Table 1   Sources of Meaning in Organizations: Opportunities & Related Values

Type of Opportunity	Related Need or Value
1. A chance to be tested; to make it on one's own	Self-reliance Self-actualization
2. A social experiment to combine work, family, and play in some new way	Community Integration of life
3. A chance to do something *well*—e.g., real craftsmanship; to be really creative	Excellence Unique accomplishment
4. A chance to do something *good*—e.g., run an honest, no rip-off business, or a youth counseling center	Consideration Service
5. A chance to change the way things are—e.g., from Republican to Democrat or Socialist, from war to peace, from unjust to just	Activism Social responsibility Citizenship

Source: Berlew, 1974.

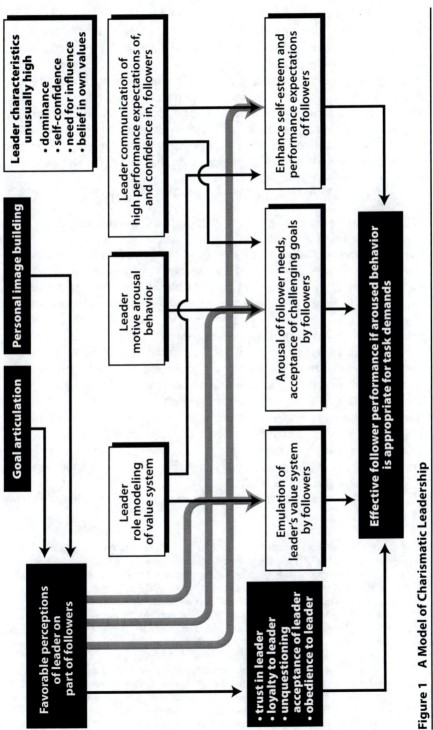

Figure 1   A Model of Charismatic Leadership

his or her beliefs. Charismatic leaders are hypothesized to employ these characteristics with the following specific behaviors: goal articulation, role modeling, personal image building, demonstration of confidence and high expectations of followers, and motive arousal behaviors. Goal articulation and personal image-building are hypothesized to result in favorable perceptions of the leader by followers. These favorable perceptions are asserted to enhance followers' trust, loyalty, and obedience to the leader and also to moderate the relationships between the remaining leader behaviors and the follower responses to the leader. The follower responses are hypothesized to result in effective performance if the aroused behavior is appropriate for their task demands.

Conclusion—Why a 1976 Theory?

This chapter presents a "1976" theory of charismatic leadership. The date, 1976, is attached to the title to reflect the philosophy of science of the writer. The theory is advanced for the purpose of guiding future research and not as a conclusive explanation of the charismatic phenomenon. As such it includes a set of propositions that are hopefully testable. Admittedly, test of the theory will require the development and validation of several new scales. However, it is hoped that the propositions are at least presently testable in principle. "A theory that cannot be mortally endangered cannot be alive" (cited in Platt, 1964, from personal communication by W. A. H. Rustin).

The results of empiric tests of the theory will undoubtedly require revision of the theory. It is believed by the writer that theories, no matter how good at explaining a set of phenomena, are ultimately incorrect and consequently will undergo modification over time. Thus, as MacKenzie and House (1975) have stated, "The fate of the better theories is to become explanations that hold for some phenomena in some limited condition." Or, as Hebb (1969, p. 21) asserts, "A good theory is one that holds together long enough to get you to a better theory."

Hopefully at some future date this theory will have led to a better theory.

Notes

[1] The author is indebted to Hugh J. Arnold, Martin G. Evans, Harvey Kolodny, Stephan J. Motowidlo, John A. Dearness, and William Cooper for their helpful critiques of this chapter. The literature review on which this chapter is based was conducted while the author was visiting professor at Florida International University, April–July, 1975.

[2] This definition would be tautological if the "charismatic effects" were not operationally discovered using two independent operations. However, since the discovery of the "charismatic effects" involves having charismatic leaders identified by one set of observers (peers or superiors) and specification of their effects by an independent set of observers (namely their followers), such a definition avoids the tautological problem.

[3] It is entirely possible that the charismatic leaders present themselves as highly confident and as having a strong conviction in the moral righteousness of their beliefs but do not indeed believe in either themselves or their beliefs. Some leaders may thus have charismatic effects because of their ability to *act as though* they have such confidence and conviction. The writer is indebted to Ed Locke for pointing out this alternative hypothesis.

[4] Sashkin, in his commentary on the present chapter, points out that earlier research has shown eminent leaders possess the traits of "intellectual fortitude and integrity of character and speech fluency (or capacity for ready communication)." These traits were not in contradiction to the earlier literature on charismatic leadership and rather were consistent with the general description of the charismatic personality advanced in this literature. Thus I would accept these characteristics, along with those in proposition 1, as possible characteristics that differentiate leaders who have charismatic effects from other leaders.

[5] The argument that the enhancement of subordinate self-esteem is an important charismatic effect grew out of earlier conversations between the writer and David E. Berlew. See Berlew (1974) for further elaboration of this argument.

[6] Such modeling, of course, will be a function of the degree to which the subordinate holds favorable perceptions of the leader, as specified in proposition 2.

[7] It is possible that such leader behavior will have a positive effect on subordinates' task-related self-esteem only (i.e., on the subordinates' confidence in their ability to accomplish task goals). It is also possible that such leader behavior will result in enhanced chronic and generalized self-esteem of subordinates. Whether leaders can indeed have such a powerful effect on subordinates' self-perceptions is of course a question that requires empiric investigation.

[8] Fleishman, E. A. *Manual for the Supervisory Behavior Description Questionnaire*, Washington, DC: American Institute for Research, 1972.

[9] The ability of the leader to arouse motives of subordinates is hypothesized to be a function of the degree to which subordinates hold favorable perceptions of the leader, as specified in proposition 2.

References

Anderson, D. F., & Rosenthal, R. Some effects of interpersonal expectancy and social interaction on institutionalized retarded children. *Proceedings of the 76th Annual Convention of the American Psychological Association,* 1983, 3, 479–80.

Bandura, A. Social learning theory of indentificatory process. In David A. Goslin (Ed.), *Handbook of socialization theory and research.* Chicago: Rand McNally, 1968.

Baron, Robert A. Exposure to an aggressive model and apparent probability of retaliation from the victim as determinants of adult aggressive behavior. *Journal of Experimental and Social Psychology,* 1971, 1, 343–55.

Berlew, D. E. Leadership and organizational excitement. In D. A. Kolb, I. M. Rubin, and J. M. McIntyre (Eds.), *Organizational psychology: A book of readings* (2nd ed.). Englewood Cliffs, NJ: Prentice Hall, 1974.

Berlew, D. E., & Hall, D. T. The socialization of managers: Effects of expectations on performance. *Administrative Science Quarterly,* 1966, 11, 207–23.

Bryan, J. F., & Locke, E. A. Parkinson's Law as a goal-setting phenomenon. *Organizational Behavior and Human Performance,* 1967, 2, 258–75.

Bryan, J. F., & Locke, E. A. Goal-setting as a means of increasing motivation. *Journal of Applied Psychology,* 1967, 51, 274–77.

Collins, W. L. Expectancy effects in the classroom: A failure to replicate. *Journal of Educational Psychology,* 1969, 60, 377–83.

Collins, L., & LaPierre, D. *Freedom at midnight.* New York: Simon and Schuster, 1975.

Conn, L. K., Edwards, C. N., Rosenthal, R., & Crowne, D. Perception of emotion and response to teachers' expectancy by elementary school children. *Psychological Reports,* 1968, 22, 27–34.

Deutsch, M., & Gerard, H. A study of normative and informational social influence upon individual judgment. *Journal of Abnormal and Social Psychology,* 1955, 51, 629–63.

DeWolfe, A. S. Identification and fear decrease. *Journal of Consulting Psychology,* 1967, 31, 259–83.

Dow, T. E. The theory of charisma. *Sociological Quarterly,* 1969, 10, 306–18.

Etzioni, A. *A comparative analysis of complex organizations.* New York: Free Press, 1961.

Evans, J. T., & Rosenthal, R. Interpersonal self-fulfilling prophecies: Further extrapolation from the laboratory to the classroom. *Proceedings of the 77th Annual Convention of the American Psychological Association,* 1969, 4, 371–72.

Festinger, L. Informal social communication. *Psychological Review,* 1950, 57, 271–82.

Fiedler, F. E., Cohen, R. D., & Finney, S. An attempt to replicate the teacher expectancy effect. *Psychological Reports,* 1971, 29, 1223–28.

Friedland, W. H. For a sociological concept of charisma. *Social Forces,* 1964, 43, 18–26.

Friedrich, C. J. Political leadership and the problem of the charismatic power. *The Journal of Politics,* 1961, 23, 3–24.

Goldstein, A. P., Martins, J., Hubben, J., Van Belle, H. A., Schaaf, W., Wiersma, H., & Goedhart, A. The use of modeling to increase independent behavior. *Behavior Research and Therapy,* 1973, 11, 31–42.

Heckhausen, H. *The anatomy of achievement motivation.* New York: Academic Press, 1967.

Joestling, J., & Joestling, R. Sex differences in group belongingness as influenced by instructor's sex. *Psychological Reports,* 1972, 31, 717–18.

Kelman, H. C. Compliance, identification, and internalization: Three processes of attitude change. *Journal of Conflict Resolution,* 1958, 2, 51–61.

Korman, A. K. Self-esteem variable in vocational choice. *Journal of Applied Psychology,* 1966a, 50, 479–86.

Korman, A. K. Consideration, initiating structure and organizational criteria: A review. *Personnel Psychology,* 1966b, 19, 349–61.

Korman, A. K. Self-esteem as a moderator of the relationship between perceived abilities and vocational choice. *Journal of Applied Psychology,* 1967, 51, 65–67.

Korman, A. K. Task success, task popularity, and self-esteem. *Journal of Applied Psychology,* 1968, 52, 484–90.

Korman, A. K. Expectancies as determinants of performance. *Journal of Applied Psychology,* 1971, 55, 218–22.

Hebb, D. O. Hebb on hocus-pocus: A conversation with Elizabeth Hall. *Psychology Today,* 1969, 3(6), 20–28.

Lawler, E. E., III. *Pay and organizational effectiveness: A psychological view.* New York: McGraw-Hill, 1971.

Litwin, G. H., & Stringer, R. A. Jr. *Motivation and organization climate.* Graduate School of Business Administration, Harvard University, 1958.

Locke, E. A., & Bryan, J. F. Cognitive aspects of psychomotor performance: The effects of performance goals on level of performance. *Journal of Applied Psychology,* 1966a, 50, 286–91.

Locke, E. A., & Bryan, J. F. The effects of goal-setting, rule-learning and knowledge of score on performance. *American Journal of Psychology,* 1966b, 79, 451–57.

Mace, C. A. Incentives: Some experimental studies. Report No. 72. London: Industrial Health Research Board, 1935.

Mackenzie, K. D., & House, R. J. Paradigm development in the social sciences: A proposed research strategy. Working Paper No. 75–03, Faculty of Management Studies, University of Toronto, 1975.

McClelland, D. C. *The achievement motive.* New York: Appleton-Century-Crofts, 1953.

McClelland, D. C., Clarke, R. A., Roby, T. B., & Atkinson, J. W. The effect of the need for achievement on thematic apperception. In J. W. Atkinson (Ed.), *Motives in fantasy, action, and society.* New York: Van Nostrand, 1958.

Meichenbaum, D. H., Bowers, K. S., & Ross, R. R. A behavioral analysis of teacher expectancy effect. *Journal of Personality and Social Psychology,* 1969, 13, 306–16.

Mendleson, J. Managerial goal setting: An exploration into its meaning and measurement. Unpublished doctoral dissertation, Michigan State University, 1971.

Miner, J. B. *Studies in managerial education.* New York: Springer, 1965.

Oberg, W. Charisma, commitment, and contemporary organization theory. *Business Topics,* 1972, 20(2), 18–32.

Pepitone, A. *Attraction and hostility.* New York: Atherton, 1964.

Peters, D. R. Identification and personal learning in t-groups. *Human Relations,* 1973, 26, 1–21.

Platt, J. R. Strong inference. *Science,* 1964, 146, 347–53.

Raben, C. S., & Klimoski, R. J. The effects of expectations upon task performance as moderated by levels of self-esteem. *Journal of Vocational Behavior,* 1973, 3, 475–83.

Raynor, J. O. Future orientation in the study of achievement motivation. In J. W. Atkinson, and J. O. Raynor (Eds.), *Motivation and achievement.* New York: Wiley, 1974.

Rosenthal, R., & Jacobson, I. *Pygmalion in the classroom: Teacher expectation and pupils' intellectual development.* New York: Holt, Reinhardt, and Winston, 1968.

Runciman, W. G. Charismatic legitimacy and one-party rule in China. *Archives Europeenes de Sociologic,* 1963, 4, 148–65.

Sarason, I. G., Ganzer, V. J., & Singer, M. Effects of modeled self-disclosure on the verbal behavior of persons differing in defensiveness. *Journal of Counseling and Clinical Psychology,* 1972, 39, 483–90.

Seaver, W. B. Effects of naturally induced teacher expectancies. *Journal of Personality and Social Psychology,* 1973, 28, 333–42.

Shipley, T. E., & Veroff, J. A projective measure of need affiliation. *Journal of Experimental Psychology,* 1952, 43, 349–56.

Shils, E. A. Charisma, order, and status. *American Sociological Review,* 1965, 30, 199–213.

Stedry, A. C., & Kay, E. The effects of goal difficulty on performance: A field experiment. *Behavioral Science,* 1966, 11, 459–70.

Steers, R. M. Task-goal attributes, n-achievement, and supervisory performance. *Organizational Behavior and Human Performance,* 1975, 13, 392–403.

Stotland, E., & Patchen, M. Identification and changes in prejudice and authoritarianism. *Journal of Abnormal and Social Psychology,* 1961, 62, 265–74.

Trist, E. L., & Bamforth, K. W. Some social and psychological consequences of the longwall method of coal-getting. *Human Relations,* 1951, 4, 3–38.

Tucker, R. C. The theory of charismatic leadership. *Daedulus,* 1968, 97, 731–56.

Uleman, J. S. The need for influence: Development and validation of a measure and comparison with the need for power. *Genetic Psychology Monographs,* 1972, 85, 157–214.

Varga, K. n-Achievement, n-Power and effectiveness of research and development. *Human Relations,* 1975, 28, 571–90.

Weber, M. *The theory of social and economic organization.* A. M. Henderson and T. Parsons (Trs.). Glencoe, Ill.: Free Press, 1947.

Winter, D. G. *The power motive.* New York: Free Press, 1973.

Young, E. R., Rimm, D. C., & Kennedy, T. D. An experimental investigation of modeling and verbal reinforcement in the modification of assertive behavior. *Behavior Research and Therapy,* 1973, 11(3), 317–19.

23

From Transactional to Transformational Leadership
Learning to Share the Vision

Bernard M. Bass

Sir Edmund Hillary of Mount Everest fame liked to tell a story about one of Captain Robert Falcon Scott's earlier attempts, from 1901 to 1904, to reach the South Pole. Scott led an expedition made up of men from the Royal Navy and the merchant marine, as well as a group of scientists. Scott had considerable trouble dealing with the merchant marine personnel, who were unaccustomed to the rigid discipline of Scott's Royal Navy. Scott wanted to send one seaman home because he would not take orders, but the seaman refused, arguing that he had signed a contract and knew his rights. Since the seaman was not subject to Royal Navy disciplinary action, Scott did not know what to do. Then Ernest Shackleton, a merchant navy officer in Scott's party, calmly informed the seaman that he, the seaman, was returning to Britain. Again the seaman refused—and Shackleton knocked him to the ship's deck. After another refusal, followed by a second flooring, the seaman decided he would return home. Scott later became one of the victims of his own inadequacies as a leader in his 1911 race to the South Pole. Shackleton went on to lead many memorable expeditions; once, seeking help for the rest of his party, who were stranded on the Antarctic Coast, he journeyed with a small crew in a small open boat from the edge of Antarctica to South Georgia Island.

Leadership Today

Most relationships between supervisors and their employees are quite different today. Few managers depend mainly on their legitimate power, as

Reprinted with permission of Elsevier from *Organizational Dynamics,* Vol. 18, No. 3 (Winter 1990), pp. 19–31. Copyright © 1990 Elsevier Science Publishing Inc.

Scott did, or on their coercive power, as Shackleton did, to persuade people to do as they're told. Rather, managers engage in a transaction with their employees: They explain what is required of them and what compensation they will receive if they fulfill these requirements.

A shift in management style at Xerox's Reprographic Business Group (RBG) provides a good example. In the first step toward establishing management in which managers take the initiative and show consideration for others, 44 specific, effective management behaviors were identified. Two factors that characterize modern leadership were found in many of these behaviors. One factor—initialing and organizing work—concentrates on accomplishing the tasks at hand. The second factor—showing consideration for employees—focuses on satisfying the self-interest of those who do good work. The leader gets things done by making, and fulfilling, promises of recognition, pay increases, and advancement for employees who perform well. By contrast, employees who do not do good work are penalized. This transaction or exchange—this promise and reward for good performance, or threat and discipline for poor performance—characterizes effective leadership. These kinds of transactions took place in most of the effective 44 leadership behaviors identified at Xerox's RBG. This kind of leadership, which is based on transactions between manager and employees, is called "transactional leadership."

In many instances, however, such transactional leadership is a prescription for mediocrity. This is particularly true if the leader relies heavily on passive management-by-exception, intervening with his or her group only when procedures and standards for accomplishing tasks are not being met. My colleagues and I have arrived at this surprising but consistent finding in a number of research analyses. Such a manager espouses the popular adage, "If it ain't broken, don't fix it." He or she stands in back of the caboose of a moving freight train and says, "Now I know where we are going." This kind of manager may use disciplinary threats to bring a group's performance up to standards—a technique that is ineffective and, in the long run, likely to be counterproductive.

Moreover, whether the promise of rewards or the avoidance of penalties motivates the employees depends on whether the leader has control of the rewards or penalties, and on whether the employees want the rewards or fear the penalties. In many organizations, pay increases depend mainly on seniority, and promotions depend on qualifications and policies about which the leader has little to say. The breaking of regulations may be the main cause of penalties. Many an executive has found his or her hands tied by contract provisions, organizational politics, and inadequate resources.

Transformational Leadership

Superior leadership performance—transformational leadership—occurs when leaders broaden and elevate the interests of their employees, when they generate awareness and acceptance of the purposes and mission of the group, and when they stir their employees to look beyond their own self-interest for the good of the group. Transformational leaders achieve these results in one or more ways: They may be charismatic to their followers and thus inspire them; they may meet the emotional needs of each employee; and/or they may intellectually stimulate employees. Exhibit 1 lists the characteristics of transformational and transactional leadership; these listings are based on the findings of a series of surveys and on clinical and case evidence.

Attaining charisma in the eyes of one's employees is central to succeeding as a transformational leader. Charismatic leaders have great power and influence. Employees want to identify with them, and they have a high degree of trust and confidence in them. Charismatic leaders inspire and excite their employees with the idea that they may be able to accomplish great things with extra effort. Further, transformational leaders are individually considerate, that is, they pay close attention to differences among their employees; they act as mentors to those who need help to grow and develop. Intellectual stimulation of employees is a third factor in transformational leadership. Intellectually stimulating leaders are willing and able to show their employees new ways of looking at old problems, to teach them to see difficulties as problems to be solved, and to emphasize rational solutions. Such a leader was Lorenz Iversen, the former president of the Mesta Machine Company, who said to his employees, "We got this job because you're the best mechanics in the world!" He practiced management-by-walking-around and stimulated the development of many of Mesta's patented inventions. He is remembered for instilling pride and commitment in his employees.

Exhibit 1
Characteristics of Transformational and Transactional Leaders

Transformational Leader

Charisma: Provides vision and sense of mission, instills pride, gains respect and trust.

Inspiration: Communicates high expectations, uses symbols to focus efforts, expresses important purposes in simple ways.

Intellectual Stimulation: Promotes intelligence, rationality, and careful problem solving.

Individualized Consideration: Gives personal attention, treats each employee individually, coaches, advises.

Transactional Leader

Contingent Reward: Contracts exchange of rewards for effort, promises rewards for good performance, recognizes accomplishments.

Management by Exception (active): Watches and searches for deviations from rules and standards, takes corrective action.

Management by Exception (passive): Intervenes only if standards are not met.

Laissez-Faire: Abdicates responsibilities, avoids making decisions.

The Big Payoff

Managers who behave like transformational leaders are more likely to be seen by their colleagues and employees as satisfying and effective leaders than are those who behave like transactional leaders, according to their colleagues', supervisors', and employees' responses on the Multifactor Leadership Questionnaire (MLQ). Similar results have been found in various organizational settings. Leaders studied have come from an extremely broad variety of organizations: chief executive officers and senior and middle level managers in business and industrial firms in the United States, Canada, Japan, and India; research and development project leaders; American, Canadian, and British Army field grade officers; United States Navy senior officers and junior surface fleet officers; Annapolis midshipmen; educational administrators; and religious leaders.

Moreover, various types of evaluations—including performance ratings by both supervisors and direct reports, as well as standard financial measures—have produced a similar correlation between transformational behavior and high ratings. Managers tagged as high performers by their supervisors were also rated, in a separate evaluation by their followers, as more transformational than transactional. Their organizations do better financially. The same pattern emerged between followers' descriptions of shipboard naval officers and those officers' supervisors' performance appraisals and recommendations for early promotion. And among Methodist ministers, transformational—not transactional—leadership behavior was positively related to high church attendance among congregants and growth in church membership.

Results were the same for evaluation of team performance in complex business simulations. Considerable credit for Boeing's turnaround since its 1969 crisis can be given to its chief executive, T. A. Wilson, who has emphasized technological progress, aggressive marketing, and a willingness to take calculated business risks. The confidence that Boeing employees have in Wilson, and their respect for him as a brilliant engineer and an outstanding leader, have instilled in them great pride in the company and its products.

Extra Effort from Below

Transformational leaders have better relationships with their supervisors and make more of a contribution to the organization than do those who are only transactional. Moreover, employees say that they themselves exert a lot of extra effort on behalf of managers who are transformational leaders. Organizations whose leaders are transactional are less effective than those whose leaders are transformational—particularly if much of the transactional leadership is passive management-by-exception (intervening only when standards are not being met). Employees say they exert little effort for such leaders. Nevertheless, leader-follower transactions dependent on contingent reward may also work reasonably well if the leaders can provide rewards that are valued by the followers.

Figure 1 illustrates the effect that transformational, as compared with transactional, leadership has on employee effort. The data were collected from 228 employees of 58 managers in a large engineering firm. The managers were ranked according to their leadership factor scores, which were based on descriptions of leaders by their employees and colleagues on the Multifactor Leadership Questionnaire. "Four-star" leaders were those who ranked in the top 25% on a leadership factor score; "one-star" leaders were among the bottom 25% of managers on the leadership factor score. From 75% to 82% of the "four-star" transformational managers had employees who indicated they frequently exerted extra effort on their jobs. Of the "one-star" transformational managers, only 22% to 24% had employees who said they frequently exerted extra effort.

It is interesting to note that, as Figure 1 illustrates, being rated as "four-star" rather than "one-star" in *transactional* leadership did not have the same impact on employees' extra effort as a high rating had for the transformational leaders. Similar findings have emerged from studies of leaders and their immediate employees at a diverse range of organizations, including Digital Equipment Corporation and Federal Express.

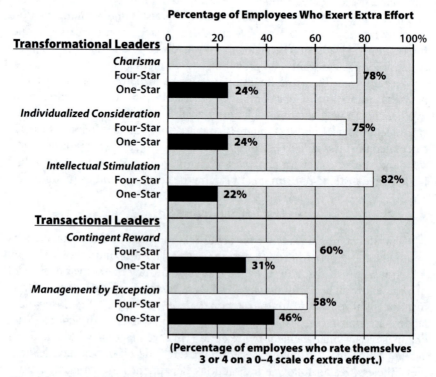

Percentage of Employees Who Exert Extra Effort

(Percentage of employees who rate themselves 3 or 4 on a 0–4 scale of extra effort.)

Figure 1   Employees' Efforts under Various Leaders

Different Styles of Transformational Leadership

As noted earlier, certain types of behavior characterize the transformational leader. Yet transformational leaders vary widely in their personal styles. H. Ross Perot is self-effacing: "I don't look impressive," he says. "To a lot of guys I don't look like I could afford a car." But Perot created the $2.5 billion EDS organization from his vision, initiative, emphasis on hard work, and a special organizational culture with strict codes of morality and dress and quasi-military management. His personal involvement in the rescue of two of his employees trapped as hostages in Iran in 1979 is an extreme example of individualized consideration, a transformational factor. Leslie Wexner of The Limited, Inc. enjoys a more flamboyant lifestyle. But like Perot, Wexner converted his vision of a nationwide chain of women's sportswear stores into reality through his own hard work. He stimulates employee participation in discussions and decisions and encourages them to share his vision of the company's future.

Many on *Fortune*'s list of the ten toughest bosses would not live up to modern behavioral science's prescriptions for the good leader: one who initiates the structure for interaction among his colleagues, and who does so with consideration for their welfare. Nevertheless, these tough bosses are highly successful as a consequence of the transformational qualities they display; Boeing's Wilson is a case in point. Although they do initiate structure and may be considerate of their employees, these leaders succeed through such transformational factors as charisma and the ability and willingness to treat different subordinates differently, as well as by providing intellectual stimulation for the employees. They frequently raise standards, take calculated risks, and get others to join them in their vision of the future. Rather than work within the organizational culture, they challenge and change that culture, as Roger Smith of General Motors Corporation did. Self-determination and self-confidence are characteristic of them. They succeed because of these transformational elements—even if they, like Wilson, have authoritarian tendencies.

Transformational Leaders Make the Difference between Success and Failure

Fighting with far fewer men and tanks than his enemy had, against superior equipment, Ernst Rommel, the Desert Fox, won a series of victories in 1941 and 1942 against the British in North Africa, until he was overwhelmed at El Alamein. Because he was up front at the scene of the action, he could make more rapid assessments and decisions than could his British counterparts, who stayed miles back in headquarters. This, and his willingness to accept calculated risks, contributed to his legendary speed, surprise, and boldness, as well as to the continuing high morale of his troops.

Napoleon declared that an army of rabbits commanded by a lion could do better than an army of lions commanded by a rabbit. He was not far from the truth. With all due respect to social, economic, political, and market forces, and to human resources policies that affect an organization's health, having a lion—or, in Rommel's case, a fox—in command rather than a rabbit frequently means success for the organization. Lee Iacocca of Chrysler Corporation and John Welch of General Electric, who have become folk heroes (or folk devils, to some), are contemporary examples of the importance of transformational leaders to their organizations.

Leadership makes its presence felt throughout the organization and its activities. We have found that employees not only do a better job when they believe their supervisors are transformational leaders, but they also are much more satisfied with the company's performance appraisal system. Likewise, mass communications directed toward individual employees are much more likely to have an impact if the messages are reinforced face-to-face by their supervisors at all organizational levels.

Transformational leadership should be encouraged, for it can make a big difference in the firm's performance at all levels. Managers need to do more than focus on the exchange of material, social, and personal benefits for services satisfactorily rendered. The charismatic leader, like the flamboyant Ted Turner of Turner Broadcasting System, Inc., can instill a sense of mission; the individually considerate leader, like the shy and self-effacing Roberto Goizueta of the Coca-Cola Corporation, can lead employees to take an interest in higher-level concerns; the intellectually stimulating leader, like the innovative Roger Smith at General Motors Corporation, can articulate a shared vision of jointly acceptable possibilities. This is not to say that transformational leaders are always prosocial in their efforts, for some fulfill grandiose dreams at the expense of their followers.

Despite the many successes with management development programs and the leadership development programs in our military academies, many executives still feel that leadership is like the weather—something to talk about, but about which not much can be done. Others say leadership ability is mystical—one needs to be born with it.

In fact, much can be done to improve leadership in an organization and to change the presiding style from transactional to transformational. The overall amount of transformational leadership in an organization can be increased substantially by suitable organizational and human resources policies. The new model of transformational leadership presents opportunities for enhancing a corporation's image and for improving its success in recruitment, selection, and promotion. This model also has implications for the organization's training and development activities and for the design of its jobs and organizational structure.

Implications for Corporate Image

It is no accident that many of the firms identified in Tom Peters and Robert Waterman's *In Search of Excellence* (Warner Books, 1982) as excellently managed have large numbers of transformational leaders. Conversely, the poorly managed "dinosaurs" among the firms they describe need to implement a lot more transformational leadership. A firm that is permeated with transformational leadership from top to bottom conveys to its own personnel as well as to customers, suppliers, financial backers, and the community at large that it has its eyes on the future; is confident; has personnel who are pulling together for the common good; and places a premium on its intellectual resources and flexibility and the development of its people.

Implications for Recruiting

Increasing transformational leadership within the organization may help in recruitment. Candidates are likely to be attracted to an organization whose CEO is charismatic and enjoys a public image as a confident, successful, optimistic, dynamic leader. In addition, prospects are likely to be attracted by interview experiences with other members of management who exhibit individualized consideration. More intelligent prospects will be particularly impressed with intellectually stimulating contacts they make during the recruiting and hiring process.

Implications for Selection, Promotion, and Transfer

Since we can identify and measure the factors associated with transformational leadership, these factors should be incorporated into managerial assessment, selection, placement, and guidance programs—along with related assessments of relevant personal dimensions and individual differences. Somewhat more transformational leadership is generally expected and found as managers move to successively higher levels in the organization, but it is reasonable to expect that an individual's performance at one level will be similar to his or her performance at the next. Direct reports, peers, and/or supervisors can be asked to describe the manager's current leadership with the Multifactor Leadership Questionnaire; their responses should be considered when decisions are made regarding a manager's promotion or transfer into a position of greater supervisory responsibility. Feedback from these results can also be used for counseling, coaching, and mentoring.

Further, the organization can tap the personal characteristics and strengths that underlie the manager's transformational behavior. Charismatic leaders are characterized by energy, self-confidence, determination, intellect, verbal skills, and strong ego ideals. Each of these traits can be assessed in individual managers. Similarly, we can assess some of the traits underlying individualized consideration, such as coaching skills; preference for two-way, face-to-face communication; and willingness to delegate. Again, in the area of intellectual stimulation, candidates for promotion could be assessed with an eye toward the type of intellectual stimulation—general, creative, or mathematical—that would be most effective at the higher level of management. Appropriate intelligence tests may be used to select intellectually stimulating candidates.

Research findings indicate that when employees rate their managers on the MLQ, they describe new business leaders as significantly more transformational than established business leaders. Thus MLQ scores can be used profitably to identify executives to head new ventures.

Implications for Development

A management trainee's first supervisor can make a big difference in his or her subsequent career success. For example, six years after they joined Exxon, many managers who were highly rated by their supervisors reported that they had been given challenging assignments by their initial supervisor (i.e., they had received individualized consideration). Many had been assigned to supervisors with good reputations in the firm. It is important to note that managers tend to model their own leadership style after that of their immediate supervisors. Thus if more higher-ups are transformational, more lower-level employees will emulate transformational behavior—and will be likely to act as transformational leaders as they rise in the organization.

Organizational policy needs to support an understanding and appreciation of the maverick who is willing to take unpopular positions, who knows when to reject the conventional wisdom, and who takes reasonable risks. For example, when R. Gordon McGovern took over as president of Campbell Soup, he introduced the "right to fail" policy, which shook up the stodgy organization. On the other hand, the fine line between self-confidence and obstinacy needs to be drawn. The determined Winston Churchill who contributed so much to the survival of Britain in 1940 was the same Churchill whose obstinacy contributed to the mistakes in 1941 of failing to prepare Singapore adequately and of committing British troops to unnecessary disaster in Crete and Greece.

Intellectual stimulation also needs to be nurtured and cultivated as a way of life in the organization. The "best and the brightest" people should be hired, nourished, and encouraged. Innovation and creativity should be fostered at all levels in the firm.

Implications for Training

Despite conventional wisdom to the contrary, transformational leadership is a widespread phenomenon. True, more of it occurs at the top than at the bottom of an organization; but it has also been observed by many employees in their first-level supervisors. Transformational leadership can be learned, and it can—and should—be the subject of management training and development. Research has shown that leaders at all levels can be trained to be charismatic in both verbal and nonverbal performance. Successful programs have been conducted for first-level project leaders in hi-tech computer firms as well as for senior executives of insurance firms.

That transformational leadership can be increased through training was verified in an experiment when Multifactor Leadership Questionnaire scores were obtained on shop supervisors from their trainees, who were inmates in minimum, medium, and maximum security prisons. The supervisors worked directly with the inmates in industrial shops to produce various products for sale within and outside the prison system. The experiment compared four groups of supervisors on their pre- and post-training effectiveness in various industrial and vocational shops in the prison. One group was trained in transformational leadership, one group was trained in transactional leadership, one was untrained but measured "before and after," and one was untrained and measured only "after." The performances of both trained groups improved, but in comparison to the three other groups of supervisors, those who were trained in transformational leadership did as well or better at improving productivity, absenteeism, and "citizenship" behavior among the inmates; they also won more respect from the inmates.

Training Managers

Practical training that teaches people how to be transformational is similar to that used in the Xerox RPG strategy to modify management style. A counselor, mediator, or supervisor gives a manager a detailed, standardized description of his or her transformational and transactional leadership performance as rated by the manager's employees and/or colleagues. The Multifactor Leadership Questionnaire is used for this purpose. The manager also sees a chart showing the effects of his or her leadership on employee satisfaction, motivation, and perception of organizational effectiveness. Anonymity is maintained, although the manager sees the individual differences among the responses.

Participating managers complete a parallel questionnaire about their own leadership. The discrepancies between how they rate themselves and how their employees rate them may be examined scale-by-scale and item-by-item. The counselor may pose such questions as: "Why do you think you gave yourself a much higher score than your employees gave you in individualized consideration?" and "Why did your employees disagree with you on how rapidly you get to the heart of complex problems or the extent to which they trust you to overcome any obstacles?" It is important for managers to be aware of and accept their employees' view of their performance. A study of United States Naval officers found that those who agreed with their direct reports about their transformational leadership behavior were also likely to earn higher fitness ratings and recommendations for early promotion from their supervisors.

The manager and the counselor discuss in detail why certain results may have appeared and what can be done to improve ratings. For example, a manager may be asked: "What specific behavior on your part makes your employees say they are proud to work with you?" or "What have you done that results in your colleagues' saying you foster a sense of mission?" The collected responses to these questions can create a useful picture of what the manager can do to raise his or her performance on particular items.

In addition to working individually with a counselor, the manager also may participate in a workshop with other managers who are working toward becoming more transformational leaders. Workshop participants who received high ratings from their employees on a particular item are asked what they, the participants, specifically did to achieve these ratings. Questions might include "Why did all of your employees say that you frequently enabled them to think about old problems in new ways?" or "Why did they all say that you increased their optimism for the future?"

Conversely, questions may focus on why a participant's employees varied widely in their ratings. If the data printout shows a wide divergence of opinion about whether a manager made the employees enthusiastic about assignments, he or she might be asked to suggest possible reasons for such differences of opinion among the employees.

Other Approaches to Training

Several other approaches to teaching transformational leadership make use of the specific data gathered in the workshop. For instance, participants are asked to think of an effective leader they have known and the behavior the leader displayed. Many examples of charisma, individualized consideration, and intellectual stimulation are usually noted. The effective leaders who are mentioned typically come from many levels inside and outside the organization; the workshop leader may point out that transformational leadership is neither particularly uncommon nor limited only to world class leaders. Moreover, these leaders' specific behaviors can be described, observed, and adopted. After viewing videotapes of charismatic, individually considerate, and intellectually stimulating managers in action, workshop participants may be asked to create their own scenarios and videotapes, in which they emulate the transformational leaders they have observed. The other participants may then offer critiques and suggest improvements.

The workshop also aims to increase other aspects of transformational leadership. The transformational leader develops and changes the organizational culture, and to show participants that they have such capabilities, the workshop leader asks them to imagine what the organization might be like in two to five years if it were fully aligned with their own ideas and interests. Then, in small teams based on their actual functions at work, they proceed to redesign the organization.

Similarly, training in mentoring can be used to promote the transformational factor of individualized consideration. For example, one participant can counsel another while a third acts as an observer and a source of feedback about the performance. And many creativity exercises show a manager how he or she can be more intellectually stimulating. Action plans emerge from workshop sessions. Examples include the following:

- I am going to sit down with all my employees and review these data with them.
- I am going to ask for another "reading" in a year; in the meantime I will try to reduce the discrepancies between where I am and where I should be.
- I'm going to talk with my mentor about these results and ask him what he thinks I should do about them.

Implications for Leadership Education

Military academies have traditionally emphasized leadership education, and today we are seeing a surge of interest in leadership courses in liberal arts colleges as well. At least 600 such courses were being offered, according to a recently completed survey of colleges. The Center for Creative Leadership holds conferences on leadership courses in undergraduate education, most recently in the summer of 1986. The subject of transformational leadership also has been added to leadership courses at the U.S. Air Force Academy at Colorado Springs. In one such course, both faculty and students examined how Air Force officers who are transformational leaders serve as role models for cadets. Scales from the Multifactor Leadership Questionnaire were used to show that the transformational leaders among the instructors and staff provided role models for their students. The faculty and students discussed the questionnaire results and their implications.

Clearly, training cannot turn a purely transactional leader into a transformational leader. Moreover, some managers, while striving to be transformational leaders, misuse their training; their pseudotransformational efforts only further the manager's self-interest and values. Under the influence of such a manager, employees can be misdirected away from their own best interests and those of the organization as a whole. In one such case, Donald Burr of People's Express Airlines displayed many transformational qualities that rapidly built and then rapidly ruined the firm.

For too long, leadership development has been seen as mainly a matter of skill development. But leadership—particularly transformational leadership—should be regarded as an art and a science. It is encouraging to see that the Council for Liberal Learning of the Association of American Colleges now sponsors week-long conferences on leadership for scholars, prominent citizens, and national leaders.

Implications for Job Design and Job Assignment

As we have noted earlier, the results of a study of Exxon managers showed that highly rated managers had had challenging tasks delegated to them by their supervisors when they first joined the company. Jobs can—and should—be designed to provide greater challenges. Delegation with guidance and follow-up can become an individualizing and developmental way of life in a firm.

Transformational leaders show individualized consideration by paying attention to the particular development needs of each of their employees. Employees' jobs are designed with those needs in mind, as well as the needs of the organization. One employee needs experience leading a project team. Another needs an opportunity to reinforce what she has learned in an advanced computer programming class. Their transformational leader assigns them tasks accordingly.

Leaders can be intellectually stimulating to their employees if their own jobs allow them to explore new opportunities, to diagnose organizational problems, and to generate solutions. Leaders whose jobs force them to focus on solving small, immediate problems are likely to be less intellectually stimulating than those who have time to think ahead and in larger terms.

Implications for Organizational Structure

Transformational leadership is not a panacea. In many situations, it is inappropriate and transactional processes are indicated. In general, firms that are functioning in stable markets can afford to depend on their "one-minute" managers to provide the necessary, day-to-day leadership. If the technology, workforce, and environment are stable as well, then things are likely to move along quite well with managers who simply promise and deliver rewards to employees for carrying out assignments. And in stable organizations, even management-by-exception can be quite effective if the manager monitors employee performance and takes corrective action as needed. Rules and regulations for getting things done, when clearly understood and accepted by the employees, can eliminate the need for leadership under some circumstances.

But when the firm is faced with a turbulent marketplace; when its products are born, live, and die within the span of a few years; and/or when its current technology can become obsolete before it is fully depreciated; then transformational leadership needs to be fostered at all levels in the firm. In order to succeed, the firm needs to have the flexibility to forecast and meet new demands and changes as they occur—and only transformational leadership can enable the firm to do so.

Problems, rapid changes, and uncertainties call for a flexible organization with determined leaders who can inspire employees to participate enthusiastically in team efforts and share in organizational goals. In short, charisma, attention to individualized development, and the ability and willingness to provide intellectual stimulation are critical in leaders whose firms are faced with demands for renewal and change. At these organizations, fostering transformational leadership through policies of recruitment, selection, promotion, training, and development is likely to pay off in the health, well-being, and effective performance of the organization.

Selected Bibliography

For nontechnical reading about transformational and transactional leadership, the following are suggested: James MacGregor Burns's *Leadership* (Harper, 1978); Bernard M. Bass's *Leadership and Performance Beyond Expectations* (Free Press, 1985) and "Leadership: Good, Better, Best" (*Organizational Dynamics,* 1985); Noel Tichy and Michelle Devanna's *Transformational Leadership* (Wiley, 1986); Warren G. Bennis and B. Nanus's *Leaders: The Strategies for Taking Charge* (Harper & Row, 1985); and Jan M. Kouzes and Barry Z. Posner's *The Leadership Challenge: How to Get Extraordinary Things Done in Organizations* (Jossey-Bass, 1987).

For more on transformational leadership that is selfish or antisocial, see Bernard M. Bass's "The Two Faces of Charismatic Leadership" *(Leaders Magazine,* forthcoming) and Jane Howell's "Two Faces of Charisma: Socialized and Personalized Leadership in Organizations" in *Charismatic Leadership: The Illusive Factor in Organizational Effectiveness* (Jossey-Bass, 1988), edited by Jay A. Conger and Rabindra N. Kanungo and Associates.

Several articles provide more specific evidence about and applications of transformational leadership. These include Bruce J. Avolio and Bernard M. Bass's "Charisma and Beyond," in *Emerging Leadership Vistas,* edited by Jerry G. Hunt (Lexington Books, 1988); Bernard M. Bass, Bruce J. Avolio, and Laurie Goodheim's "Biography and the Assessment of Transformational Leadership at the World Class Level" *(Journal of Management,* Volume 13, 1987); and John Hater and Bernard M. Bass's "Superiors' Evaluations and Subordinates' Perceptions of Transformational and Transactional Leadership" *(Journal of Applied Psychology,* November 1988).

Other very useful articles include Richard Crookall's "Management of Inmate Workers: A Field Test of Transformational and Situational Leadership" (Ph.D. dissertation, University of Western Ontario, 1989); and David A. Waldman, Bernard M. Bass, and Francis J. Yammarino's "Adding to Leader-Follower Transactions: The Augmenting Effect of Charismatic Leadership" (Technical Report 3, Center for Leadership Studies, State University of New York, Binghamton, 1988). A detailed review of findings is presented in Bernard M. Bass and Bruce J. Avolio's "Implications of Transactional and Transformational Leadership for Individual, Team and Organizational Development" in *Research in Organizational Change and Development,* edited by Richard W. Woodman and William A. Pasmore (JAI Press, 1989).

Questions and Learning Activities

Section III

Questions

1. The study described in the first entry in this section was done more than 75 years ago with 11-year-olds. Highlight the findings. Is there anything that surprises you? What are the implications of this research?

2. Would White and Lippitt's findings hold true for today's adult workers? Can you think of elements of today's world that might change the results?

3. Is initiating structure equivalent to autocratic leadership? Is consideration the same as democratic leadership?

4. Do the Ohio State constructs of consideration and initiating structure capture all we need to know about leadership style? Why or why not?

5. What would you say to a leader/manager who says that research designed to develop measures of leadership style is not practically relevant?

6. The Argyris reading is more than 50 years old. Is it more or less relevant today? Provide justification for your position.

7. How do people express their frustration at work when confronted with the type of conflict that Argyris describes? Are these behaviors a problem or a symptom of a problem?

8. Our culture values democracy. Why is it, then, that we have so many autocratic leaders in our organizations?

9. What are the likely generational differences regarding belief in Theory X or Theory Y? Provide a couple of examples.

10. Describe how a leader/manager who believes in Theory X, and whose management style reflects that belief, is likely to generate a self-fulfilling prophecy.

11. Bowers and Seashore summarize the contributions of a number of researchers and highlight the importance of *peer leadership*—the idea that certain leadership functions are important and members of the group can carry them out just as well as the formal leader. This is obviously a major shift from models that focus on "the" leader. What are the advantages and disadvantages of this?

12. Leadership style, in *The Managerial Grid*, is defined as "concern for" people and production, and the degree to which these concerns are linked. Some would say, therefore, that this is a model based upon attitudes. Is this a strength or a weakness of this model? Why?

13. How might learning and applying the managerial grid help leader/managers become more effective? Are there aspects of this model that might diminish effectiveness?

14. The idea of servant leadership has considerable appeal, especially to followers. For some leader/managers, however, there may be reluctance to practice servant leadership. What information presented in this section could serve to reduce this reluctance?

15. Does the concept of servant leadership conflict or concur with the implications of the managerial grid model?

16. What are two practical implications for leader/managers that can be derived from attribution theory?

17. When we say a leader/manager makes an attribution error, what do we mean? What types of problems do attribution errors lead to?

18. Is the charismatic theory of leadership useful for someone who does not appear to have any demonstrated attributes of charisma? Explain your answer.

19. Charismatic leaders are characterized by very specific behaviors. Are these behaviors available to any leader/manager?

20. Compare and contrast charismatic and transformational leadership as they are described in the final two readings of this section.

21. Differentiate transactional and transformational leadership. What differences would you expect in performance and satisfaction for the followers of each style?

22. Under what conditions might transactional leadership be effective?

23. What commonalities related to leadership exist among the readings in this section?

24. What conflicts related to leadership exist among the readings in this section?

25. If you had to choose only one model from this section to guide your leadership, which one would it be, and why?

Activities

1. Identify your preferences for the leadership styles examined in the first reading in this section—autocratic, democratic, and laissez faire. See the editor's Web site (www.waveland.com/McMahon/) for this self-awareness suggestion.

2. Find out how you score on the Ohio State constructs of initiating structure and consideration. See the Web site for this self-awareness suggestion.

3. Discuss with classmates or colleagues instances in which you experienced or observed the conflict between the mature personality and the organization, as described by Argyris. What happened as a result of the conflict? How could it have been avoided?

4. Ask 30 people of different ages whether they subscribe more to Theory X or Theory Y. Attempt to determine if age plays a role in their views.

5. Discover the extent to which you agree with Theory X and Theory Y. See the Web site for this self-awareness suggestion.

6. Identify several leaders or leader/managers that you know now or have known in the past. Classify the style of each according to the managerial grid and indicate how effective you think each was. Did the style they employ have an impact on their degree of effectiveness, or ineffectiveness?

7. Refer back to the managerial grid and predict where you think you fall on this model. Complete the self-awareness suggestion on the Web site and compare your prediction with the outcome of the assessment.

8. Discuss with classmates/colleagues charismatic leaders from your collective experiences. What characteristics or qualities prompted you to label the person as charismatic? Why did you choose to follow this person? How did you feel?

9. Compare the outcomes of the self-awareness suggestions in items 1, 2, 5, and 7 above. What conclusion do you draw from this comparison?

10. Write an essay entitled "Servant Leadership—Realistic or Unrealistic?"

SECTION IV

SITUATIONAL APPROACHES TO LEADERSHIP

The flow of theory, research, and thought about leadership style initiated by the work at Ohio State and the University of Michigan continued through the 1960s, focusing on the relationship between leader behaviors and outcomes such as performance and satisfaction as well as correlates of satisfaction such as turnover, absenteeism, and grievances. Although Stogdill noted the importance of situational elements in 1948, serious attempts to account for the impact of situational circumstances did not begin in earnest until the late 1960s. As leadership theory evolved, attention focused on the moderating impact of situational elements on the relationship between leader behaviors, style, and outcomes. In other words, rather than suggesting that a certain style is always effective (a normative approach), the issue became *under what conditions* are different styles effective (a contingency approach).

Robert Tannenbaum and Warren Schmidt were a decade ahead of the emergence of contingency theory developments with their classic *How to Choose a Leadership Pattern.* This article is surely one of the most popular articles in the history of *Harvard Business Review.* The authors present a range of leadership approaches, from boss-centered leadership at one extreme to subordinate-centered leadership at the other, with five alternatives in between. The discussion of deciding how to lead focuses upon contingent or situational factors with regard to the manager, the subordinates, and the situation.

In *Contingency Theory of Leadership,* Roya Ayman, Martin Chemers, and Fred Fiedler discuss new and old evidence in an attempt to clarify misunderstandings about the model, which was first introduced by Fiedler in 1967. Since then, the model has undergone numerous reviews and has generated significant controversy—about the model itself and the measurement of its variables. The model predicts that task-oriented leaders will be more effective in situations highly favorable or highly unfavorable to the leader. Relationship-oriented leaders are predicted to be more effective in situations of intermediate favorableness. Situational favorableness is assessed by task structure, position power of the leader, and leader-member relations. As the model evolved, "leadership style" became "motivational orientation" and "situa-

273

tional favorableness" became "leader's situational control." Nevertheless, the basics are the same, and the leader is considered "in match" in situations where the model predicts high group performance and "out of match" when it predicts low group performance. An intriguing aspect of this approach is the possibility of the leader changing the situation to match his or her style (motivational orientation).

The Hersey-Blanchard contingency model of leadership, referred to today as "situational leadership" was introduced in 1969 in *Life Cycle Theory of Leadership*. The essence of this model is that effectiveness will be determined by the extent to which the leader's style is appropriate for the development level of the employee. The term "life cycle" was derived from parent-child interactions over time and is no longer used. This model has evolved considerably in terms of the dynamics involved and prescriptions for leader/managers. While research on this model is scarce, it is very popular in the management and leadership development arena. It is intuitively appealing and relatively easy to apply for leaders who have good self-awareness and are flexible enough to modify their style as needed. Hersey and Blanchard parted ways some time ago and each now has his own model with unique characteristics, although the essence of each of their models is true to the original.

W. J. Reddin's 3-D model of managerial effectiveness was introduced in his 1970 book *Managerial Effectiveness*. This is a work of significant depth and detail. The situational assessment is more comprehensive than in the previous selection as it considers technology, superiors, coworkers, and the organization. Like the preceding two selections, leadership style in Reddin's model has its roots in the work done at Ohio State. Reddin's approach also requires diagnostic skill and leadership flexibility in order to adopt the most effective style required by the situation. In a manner similar to Fiedler, Reddin also introduces the possibility of the leader changing the situation so that the style in use is appropriate. Reddin's approach, despite its comprehensiveness and depth, has not been as widely embraced by American leader/managers as by those in other countries.

Path-Goal Theory of Leadership by Robert J. House was stimulated by the mixed results of studies investigating the relationship between leadership style and outcome measures such as performance and satisfaction. Like the Hersey-Blanchard model, the path-goal theory focuses exclusively on the relationship between the leader and follower; it does not consider additional situational elements such as those incorporated by Fiedler and Reddin. In House's model, the behavior of the leader is deemed appropriate if it is viewed by the subordinate as facilitating current or future performance and satisfaction. There are four components to leader behavior: directive path-goal clarifying behavior, supportive leader behavior, participative leader behavior, and achievement-oriented leader behavior. This important work is often not categorized as a contingency theory but is treated as such here because what the leader needs to do will differ depending on the situation of different employees.

Leadership and Decision Making by Victor Vroom and Arthur Jago summarizes and extends the groundbreaking model introduced in 1973 by Vroom and Phillip Yetton. This sophisticated, research-based, decision-making model has evolved over the years and now includes software to help the leader determine which style is most appropriate for a specific decision/problem. The model considers five leadership styles that vary according to the degree of participation exercised by the leader; ranging from autocratic with no participation by group members at one extreme to delegating the decision to the group at the other. In the original model, the situation is defined by 11 variables directly related to the decision/problem at hand. The current computer-based model increases the situational variables to 15. The model's output tells the leader which style is most appropriate for the problem described. Like all contingency approaches, it is subject to an accurate assessment of the situation and requires leaders to have the flexibility to employ different styles.

Leadership theory, research, and development generally ignored cultural variables until the seminal work of Geert Hofstede was published. His body of work, which includes several books, is represented here with the 1980 article *Motivation, Leadership, and Organization: Do American Theories Apply Abroad?* Four cultural variables are discussed: individualism-collectivism, uncertainty avoidance, power distance, and masculinity-femininity. While all of these situational variables are relevant to leadership, the most important one is clearly power distance. Mistakes made by leader/managers who did not understand or appreciate that power distance varies across cultures are legendary. Hofstede's work, which stimulated much research and writing, is especially relevant today given globalization trends.

24

How to Choose
a Leadership Pattern

Robert Tannenbaum and Warren H. Schmidt

- "I put most problems into my group's hands and leave it to them to carry the ball from there. I serve merely as a catalyst, mirroring back the people's thoughts and feelings so that they can better understand them."

- "It's foolish to make decisions oneself on matters that affect people. I always talk things over with my subordinates, but I make it clear to them that I'm the one who has to have the final say."

- "Once I have decided on a course of action, I do my best to sell my ideas to my employees."

- "I'm being paid to lead. If I let a lot of other people make the decisions I should be making, then I'm not worth my salt."

- "I believe in getting things done. I can't waste time calling meetings. Someone has to call the shots around here, and I think it should be me."

Each of these statements represents a point of view about "good leadership." Considerable experience, factual data, and theoretical principles could be cited to support each statement, even though they seem to be inconsistent when placed together. Such contradictions point up the dilemma in which the modern manager frequently finds himself.

New Problem

The problem of how the modern manager can be "democratic" in his relations with subordinates and at the same time maintain the necessary authority and control in the organization for which he is responsible has come into focus increasingly in recent years.

Earlier in the century this problem was not so acutely felt. The successful executive was generally pictured as possessing intelligence, imagination, initiative, the capacity to make rapid (and generally wise) decisions, and the ability to inspire subordinates. People tended to think of the world as being divided into "leaders" and "followers."

New Focus

Gradually, however, from the social sciences emerged the concept of "group dynamics" with its focus on *members* of the group rather than solely on the leader. Research efforts of social scientists underscored the importance of employee involvement and participation in decision making. Evidence began to challenge the efficiency of highly directive leadership, and increasing attention was paid to problems of motivation and human relations.

Through training laboratories in group development that sprang up across the country, many of the newer notions of leadership began to exert an impact. These training laboratories were carefully designed to give people a firsthand experience in full participation and decision making. The designated "leaders" deliberately attempted to reduce their own power and to make group members as responsible as possible for setting their own goals and methods within the laboratory experience.

It was perhaps inevitable that some of the people who attended the training laboratories regarded this kind of leadership as being truly "democratic" and went home with the determination to build fully participative decision making into their own organizations. Whenever their bosses made a decision without convening a staff meeting, they tended to perceive this as authoritarian behavior. The true symbol of democratic leadership to some was the meeting—and the less directed from the top, the more democratic it was.

Some of the more enthusiastic alumni of these training laboratories began to get in the habit of categorizing leader behavior as "democratic" or "authoritarian." The boss who made too many decisions himself was thought of as authoritarian, and his directive behavior was often attributed solely to his personality.

New Need

The net result of the research findings and of the human relations training based upon them has been to call into question the stereotype of an effective leader. Consequently, the modern manager often finds himself in an uncomfortable state of mind.

Often he is not quite sure how to behave; there are times when he is torn between exerting "strong" leadership and "permissive" leadership. Sometimes new knowledge pushes him in one direction ("I should really get the group to help make this decision"), but at the same time his experience pushes him in another direction ("I really understand the problem better than the group and therefore I should make the decision"). He is not sure when a group decision is really appropriate or when holding a staff meeting serves merely as a device for avoiding his own decision-making responsibility.

The purpose of our article is to suggest a framework which managers may find useful in grappling with this dilemma. First, we shall look at the different patterns of leadership behavior that the manager can choose from in relating himself to his subordinates. Then, we shall turn to some of the questions suggested by this range of patterns. For instance, how important is it for a manager's subordinates to know what type of leadership he is using in a situation? What factors should he consider in deciding on a leadership pattern? What difference do his long-run objectives make as compared to his immediate objectives?

Range of Behavior

Figure 1 presents the continuum or range of possible leadership behavior available to a manager. Each type of action is related to the degree of authority used by the boss and to the amount of freedom available to his subordinates in reaching decisions. The actions seen on the extreme left characterize the manager who maintains a high degree of control while those seen on the extreme right characterize the manager who releases a high degree of control. Neither extreme is absolute; authority and freedom are never without their limitations.

Now let us look more closely at each of the behavior points occurring along this continuum.

The Manager Makes the Decision and Announces It

In this case the boss identifies a problem, considers alternative solutions, chooses one of them, and then reports this decision to his subordinates for implementation. He may or may not give consideration to what he believes his subordinates will think or feel about his decision; in any case, he provides

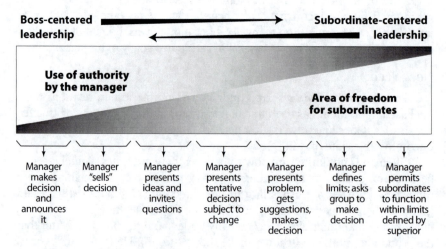

Figure 1   Continuum of Leadership Behavior

no opportunity for them to participate directly in the decision-making process. Coercion may or may not be used or implied.

The Manager "Sells" His Decision

Here the manager, as before, takes responsibility for identifying the problem and arriving at a decision. However, rather than simply announcing it, he takes the additional step of persuading his subordinates to accept it. In doing so, he recognizes the possibility of some resistance among those who will be faced with the decision, and seeks to reduce this resistance by indicating, for example, what the employees have to gain from his decision.

The Manager Presents His Ideas, Invites Questions

Here the boss who has arrived at a decision and who seeks acceptance of his ideas provides an opportunity for his subordinates to get a fuller explanation of his thinking and his intentions. After presenting the ideas, he invites questions so that his associates can better understand what he is trying to accomplish. This "give and take" also enables the manager and the subordinates to explore more fully the implications of the decision.

The Manager Presents a Tentative Decision Subject to Change

This kind of behavior permits the subordinates to exert some influence on the decision. The initiative for identifying and diagnosing the problem remains with the boss. Before meeting with his staff, he has thought the problem through and arrived at a decision—but only a tentative one. Before finalizing it, he presents his proposed solution for the reaction of those who will be affected by it. He says in effect, "I'd like to hear what you have to say about this plan that I have developed. I'll appreciate your frank reactions, but will reserve for myself the final decision."

The Manager Presents the Problem, Gets Suggestions, and Then Makes His Decision

Up to this point the boss has come before the group with a solution of his own. Not so in this case. The subordinates now get the first chance to suggest solutions. The manager's initial role involves identifying the problem. He might, for example, say something of this sort: "We are faced with a number of complaints from newspapers and the general public on our service policy. What is wrong here? What ideas do you have for coming to grips with this problem?"

The function of the group becomes one of increasing the manager's repertory of possible solutions to the problem. The purpose is to capitalize on the knowledge and experience of those who are on the "firing line." From the expanded list of alternatives developed by the manager and his subordinates, the manager then selects the solution that he regards as most promising.[1]

The Manager Defines the Limits and Requests the Group to Make a Decision

At this point the manager passes to the group (possibly including himself as a member) the right to make decisions. Before doing so, however, he defines the problem to be solved and the boundaries within which the decision must be made.

An example might be the handling of a parking problem at a plant. The boss decides that this is something that should be worked on by the people involved, so he calls them together and points up the existence of the problem. Then he tells them: "There is the open field just north of the main plant which has been designated for additional employee parking. We can build underground or surface multilevel facilities as long as the cost does not exceed $100,000. Within these limits we are free to work out whatever solution makes sense to us. After we decide on a specific plan, the company will spend the available money in whatever way we indicate."

The Manager Permits the Group to Make Decisions within Prescribed Limits

This represents an extreme degree of group freedom only occasionally encountered in formal organizations, as, for instance, in many research groups. Here the team of managers or engineers undertakes the identification and diagnosis of the problem, develops alternative procedures for solving it, and decides on one or more of these alternative solutions. The only limits directly imposed on the group by the organization are those specified by the superior of the team's boss. If the boss participates in the decision-making process, he attempts to do so with no more authority than any other member of the group. He commits himself in advance to assist in implementing whatever decision the group makes.

Key Questions

As the continuum in Figure 1 demonstrates, there are a number of alternative ways in which a manager can relate himself to the group or individuals he is supervising. At the extreme left of the range, the emphasis is on the manager—on what *he* is interested in, how *he* sees things, how *he* feels about them. As we move toward the subordinate-centered end of the continuum, however, the focus is increasingly on the subordinates—on what *they* are interested in, how *they* look at things, how *they* feel about them.

When business leadership is regarded in this way, a number of questions arise. Let us take four of especial importance:

Can a boss ever relinquish his responsibility by delegating it to someone else?   Our view is that the manager must expect to be held responsible by his superior for the quality of the decisions made, even though operationally these decisions may have been made on a group basis. He should, therefore, be ready to accept whatever risk is involved whenever he delegates decision-making power to his subordinates. Delegation is not a way of "passing the buck." Also, it should be emphasized that the amount of freedom the boss gives to his subordinates cannot be greater than the freedom which he himself has been given by his own superior.

Should the manager participate with his subordinates once he has delegated responsibility to them?   The manager should carefully think over this question and decide on his role prior to involving the subordinate group. He should ask if his presence will inhibit or facilitate the problem-solving process. There may be some instances when he should leave the group to let it solve the problem for itself. Typically, however, the boss has useful ideas to contribute, and should function as an additional member of the group. In the latter instance, it is important that he indicate clearly to the group that he sees himself in a *member* role rather than in an authority role.

How important is it for the group to recognize what kind of leadership behavior the boss is using?   It makes a great deal of difference. Many relationship problems between boss and subordinate occur because the boss fails to make clear how he plans to use his authority. If, for example, he actually intends to make a certain decision himself, but the subordinate group gets the impression that he has delegated this authority, considerable confusion and resentment are likely to follow. Problems may also occur when the boss uses a "democratic" facade to conceal the fact that he has already made a decision which he hopes the group will accept as its own. The attempt to "make them think it was their idea in the first place" is a risky one. We believe that it is highly important for the manager to be honest and clear in describing what authority he is keeping and what role he is asking his subordinates to assume in solving a particular problem.

Can you tell how "democratic" a manager is by the number of decisions his subordinates make?   The sheer number of decisions is not an accurate index of the amount of freedom that a subordinate group enjoys. More important is the *significance* of the decisions which the boss entrusts to his subordinates. Obviously a decision on how to arrange desks is of an entirely different order from a decision involving the introduction of new electronic data-processing equipment. Even though the widest possible limits are given in dealing with the first issue, the group will sense no particular degree of responsibility. For a boss to permit the group to decide equipment policy, even within rather narrow limits, would reflect a greater degree of confidence in them on his part.

Deciding How to Lead

Now let us turn from the types of leadership which are possible in a company situation to the question of what types are *practical* and *desirable*. What factors or forces should a manager consider in deciding how to manage? Three are of particular importance: forces in the manager, forces in the subordinates, and forces in the situation.

We should like briefly to describe these elements and indicate how they might influence a manager's action in a decision-making situation.[2] The strength of each of them will, of course, vary from instance to instance, but the manager who is sensitive to them can better assess the problems which face him and determine which mode of leadership behavior is most appropriate for him.

Forces in the manager.   The manager's behavior in any given instance will be influenced greatly by the many forces operating within his own personality. He will, of course, perceive his leadership problems in a unique way on the basis of his background, knowledge, and experience. Among the important internal forces affecting him will be the following:

1. *His value system.*   How strongly does he feel that individuals should have a share in making the decisions which affect them? Or, how convinced is he that the official who is paid to assume responsibility should personally carry the burden of decision making? The strength of his convictions on questions like these will tend to move the manager to one end or the other of the continuum shown in Figure 1. His behavior will also be influenced by the relative importance that he attaches to organizational efficiency, personal growth of subordinates, and company profits.[3]

2. *His confidence in his subordinates.*   Managers differ greatly in the amount of trust they have in other people generally, and this carries over to the particular employees they supervise at a given time. In viewing his particular group of subordinates, the manager is likely to consider their knowledge and competence with respect to the problem. A central question he might ask himself is: "Who is best qualified to deal with this problem?" Often he may, justifiably or not, have more confidence in his own capabilities than in those of his subordinates.

3. *His own leadership inclinations.*   There are some managers who seem to function more comfortably and naturally as highly directive leaders. Resolving problems and issuing orders come easily to them. Other managers seem to operate more comfortably in a team role, where they are continually sharing many of their functions with their subordinates.

4. *His feelings of security in an uncertain situation.*   The manager who releases control over the decision-making process thereby reduces the predictability of the outcome. Some managers have a greater need than others for predictability and stability in their environment. This "tolerance for ambiguity" is being viewed increasingly by psychologists as a key variable in a person's manner of dealing with problems.

The manager brings these and other highly personal variables to each situation he faces. If he can see them as forces which, consciously or unconsciously, influence his behavior, he can better understand what makes him prefer to act in a given way. And understanding this, he can often make himself more effective.

Forces in the subordinate.   Before deciding how to lead a certain group, the manager will also want to consider a number of forces affecting his subordinates' behavior. He will want to remember that each employee, like himself, is influenced by many personality variables. In addition, each subordinate has a set of expectations about how the boss should act in relation to him. The better the manager understands these factors, the more accurately he can determine what kind of behavior on his part will enable his subordinates to act most effectively.

Generally speaking, the manager can permit his subordinates greater freedom if the following essential conditions exist:

- If the subordinates have relatively high needs for independence. (As we all know, people differ greatly in the amount of direction that they desire.)
- If the subordinates have a readiness to assume responsibility for decision making. (Some see additional responsibility as a tribute to their ability; others see it as "passing the buck.")
- If they have a relatively high tolerance for ambiguity. (Some employees prefer to have clear-cut directives given to them; others prefer a wider area of freedom.)
- If they are interested in the problem and feel that it is important.
- If they understand and identify with the goals of the organization.
- If they have the knowledge and experience to deal with the problem.
- If they have learned to expect to share in decision making. (Persons who have come to expect strong leadership and are then suddenly confronted with the request to share more fully in decision making are often upset by this new experience. On the other hand, persons who have enjoyed a considerable amount of freedom resent the boss who begins to make all the decisions himself.)

The manager will probably tend to make fuller use of his own authority if the above conditions do *not* exist; at times there may be no realistic alternative to running a "one-man show."

The restrictive effect of many of the forces will, of course, be greatly modified by the general feeling of confidence which subordinates have in the boss. Where they have learned to respect and trust him, he is free to vary his behavior. He will feel certain that he will not be perceived as an authoritarian boss on those occasions when he makes decisions by himself. Similarly, he will not be seen as using staff meetings to avoid his decision-making responsibility. In a climate of mutual confidence and respect, people tend to feel less threatened by deviations from normal practice, which in turn makes possible a higher degree of flexibility in the whole relationship.

Forces in the situation.   In addition to the forces which exist in the manager himself and in his subordinates, certain characteristics of the general situation will also affect the manager's behavior. Among the more critical environmental pressures that surround him are those which stem from the organization, the work group, the nature of the problem, and the pressures of time. Let us look briefly at each of these:

1. *Type of organization.*   Like individuals, organizations have values and traditions which inevitably influence the behavior of the people who work in them. The manager who is a newcomer to a company quickly discovers that certain kinds of behavior are approved while others are not. He also discovers that to deviate radically from what is generally accepted is likely to create problems for him.

These values and traditions are communicated in numerous ways—through job descriptions, policy pronouncements, and public statements by top executives. Some organizations, for example, hold to the notion that the desirable executive is one who is dynamic, imaginative, decisive, and persuasive. Other organizations put more emphasis upon the importance of the executive's ability to work effectively with people—his human relations skills. The fact that his superiors have a defined concept of what the good executive should be will very likely push the manager toward one end or the other of the behavioral range.

In addition to the above, the amount of employee participation is influenced by such variables as the size of the working units, their geographical distribution, and the degree of inter- and intra-organizational security required to attain company goals. For example, the wide geographical dispersion of an organization may preclude a practical system of participative decision making, even though this would otherwise be desirable. Similarly, the size of the working units or the need for keeping plans confidential may make it necessary for the boss to exercise more control than would otherwise be the case. Factors like these may limit considerably the manager's ability to function flexibly on the continuum.

2. *Group effectiveness.*   Before turning decision-making responsibility over to a subordinate group, the boss should consider how effectively its members work together as a unit.

One of the relevant factors here is the experience the group has had in working together. It can generally be expected that a group which has functioned for some time will have developed habits of cooperation and thus be able to tackle a problem more effectively than a new group. It can also be expected that a group of people with similar backgrounds and interests will work more quickly and easily than people with dissimilar backgrounds, because the communication problems are likely to be less complex.

The degree of confidence that the members have in their ability to solve problems as a group is also a key consideration. Finally, such group variables as cohesiveness, permissiveness, mutual acceptance, and commonality of purpose will exert subtle but powerful influence on the group's functioning.

3. *The problem itself.*   The nature of the problem may determine what degree of authority should be delegated by the manager to his subordinates. Obviously he will ask himself whether they have the kind of knowledge which is needed. It is possible to do them a real disservice by assigning a problem that their experience does not equip them to handle.

Since the problems faced in large or growing industries increasingly require knowledge of specialists from many different fields, it might be inferred that the more complex a problem, the more anxious a manager will be to get some assistance in solving it. However, this is not always the case. There will be times when the very complexity of the problem calls for one person to work it out. For example, if the manager has most of the background and factual data relevant to a given issue, it may be easier for him to think it through himself than to take the time to fill in his staff on all the pertinent background information. The key question to ask, of course, is: "Have I heard the ideas of everyone who has the necessary knowledge to make a significant contribution to the solution of this problem?"

4. *The pressure of time.* This is perhaps the most clearly felt pressure on the manager (in spite of the fact that it may sometimes be imagined). The more that he feels the need for an immediate decision, the more difficult it is to involve other people. In organizations which are in a constant state of "crisis" and "crash programming" one is likely to find managers personally using a high degree of authority with relatively little delegation to subordinates. When the time pressure is less intense, however, it becomes much more possible to bring subordinates in on the decision-making process.

These, then, are the principal forces that impinge on the manager in any given instance and tend to determine his tactical behavior in relation to his subordinates. In each case his behavior ideally will make possible the most effective attainment of his immediate goal within the limits facing him.

Long-Run Strategy

As the manager works with his organization on the problems that come up day by day, his choice of a leadership pattern is usually limited. He must take account of the forces just described and, within the restrictions they impose on him, do the best that he can. But as he looks ahead months or even years, he can shift his thinking from tactics to large-scale strategy. No longer need he be fettered by all of the forces mentioned, for he can view many of them as variables over which he has some control. He can, for example, gain new insights or skills for himself, supply training for individual subordinates, and provide participative experiences for his employee group.

In trying to bring about a change in these variables, however, he is faced with a challenging question: At which point along the continuum *should* he act? The answer depends largely on what he wants to accomplish. Let us suppose that he is interested in the same objectives that most modern managers seek to attain when they can shift their attention from the pressure of immediate assignments:

1. To raise the level of employee motivation.
2. To increase the readiness of subordinates to accept change.
3. To improve the quality of all managerial decisions.
4. To develop teamwork and morale.
5. To further the individual development of employees.

In recent years the manager has been deluged with a flow of advice on how best to achieve these longer-run objectives. It is little wonder that he is often both bewildered and annoyed. However, there are some guidelines which he can usefully follow in making a decision.

Most research and much of the experience of recent years give a strong factual basis to the theory that a fairly high degree of subordinate-centered behavior is associated with the accomplishment of the five purposes mentioned.[4] This does not mean that a manager should always leave all decisions to his assistants. To provide the individual or the group with greater freedom than they are ready for at any given time may very well tend to generate anxieties and therefore inhibit rather than facilitate the attainment of desired objectives. But this should not keep the manager from making a continuing effort to confront his subordinates with the challenge of freedom.

Conclusion

In summary, there are two implications in the basic thesis that we have been developing. The first is that the successful leader is one who is keenly aware of those forces which are most relevant to his behavior at any given time. He accurately understands himself, the individuals and group he is dealing with, and the company and broader social environment in which he operates. And certainly he is able to assess the present readiness for growth of his subordinates.

But this sensitivity or understanding is not enough, which brings us to the second implication. The successful leader is one who is able to behave appropriately in the light of these perceptions. If direction is in order, he is able to direct; if considerable participative freedom is called for, he is able to provide such freedom.

Thus, the successful manager of men can be primarily characterized neither as a strong leader nor as a permissive one. Rather, he is one who maintains a high batting average in accurately assessing the forces that determine what his most appropriate behavior at any given time should be and in actually being able to behave accordingly. Being both insightful and flexible, he is less likely to see the problems of leadership as a dilemma.

Notes

[1] For a fuller explanation of this approach, see Leo Moore, "Too Much Management, Too Little Change," *HBR* January–February 1936, p. 41.

[2] See Robert Tannenbaum and Fred Massarik, "Participation by Subordinates in the Managerial Decision-Making Process," *Canadian Journal of Economics and Political Science,* August 1950, p. 413.

[3] See Chris Argyris, "Top Management Dilemma: Company Needs vs. Individual Development," *Personnel,* September 1955, pp. 123–134.

[4] For example, see Warren H. Schmidt and Paul C. Buchanan, *Techniques that Produce Teamwork* (New London, Arthur C. Croft Publications, 1954); and Morris S. Viteles, *Motivation and Morale in Industry* (New York, W.W. Norton & Company, Inc., 1953).

25

Contingency Theory of Leadership

Roya Ayman, Martin M. Chemers, and Fred Fiedler

The contingency model of leadership effectiveness was presented in its most complete form in Fiedler (1967) and Fiedler and Chemers (1974). The evolution of the model and the development of its constructs covers three decades of research.

The model predicts that a leader's effectiveness is based on two main factors: a leader's attributes, referred to as task or relationship motivational orientation (formerly referred to as style), and a leader's situational control (formerly referred to as situational favorability). The model predicts that leaders who have a task motivational orientation compared to those who have a relationship orientation or motivation will be more successful in high- and low-control situations. Relationship-oriented leaders compared to task-oriented leaders will be more effective in moderate control situations (Fiedler, 1978). A leader is designated as "in match" in situations where the model predicts high group performance and "out of match" in situations of low group performance (Fiedler & Chemers, 1984). . . .

The model has been the target of numerous criticisms through its evolution (e.g., Ashour, 1973; Graen, Alvares, Orris, & Martella, 1971; Graen, Orris, & Alvares, 1971; Schriesheim & Kerr, 1977; Vecchio, 1977) and has been an impetus for over 200 empirical studies. After three decades of research, two meta-analyses (i.e., Peters, Hartke, & Pohlmann, 1985; Strube & Garcia, 1981) have tested its criteria-related validity. The results, overall, have supported the model. . . .

Although there have been several reviews of the model, it has been about 16 years since the last complete review (Fielder, 1978). Confusion still exists

Excerpt reprinted with permission of Elsevier Science & Technology Journals from "The Contingency Model of Leadership Effectiveness," *Leadership Quarterly,* Vol. 6, No. 2 (Summer 1995), pp. 147–167. Copyright ©1995 by Elsevier Science & Technology Journals.

regarding the model's components and their relationship with each other. In this article, new and old evidence is discussed to clarify these misunderstandings. The model's constructs are: (1) leader's characteristics, (2) situational control, and (3) leadership effectiveness. Table 1 gives a summary of the way each of these variables in the model has been defined and measured.

This article seeks to demonstrate that the strength of the contingency model lies in its use of a multi-level and multiple-sources approach in defin-

Table 1   Summary of Contingency Model's Variables with Their Conceptual Level of Analysis, Measure, and Source of Information

Variables	Level	Measure	Source
Leader's Motivational Orientation	Individual	Least Preferred Coworker (LPC) Scale	Leader
Situational Control			
Group Atmosphere	Group	Group Atmosphere (GA), Leader-Member Relations Sociometric Method	Leader or Averaged Group Score
Task Structure	Individual	Task Structure Scale or Type of Job	Leader or Experimenter
Authority	Individual	Position Power Scale	Leader, Experimenter, Superior
Effectiveness			
Satisfaction	Group or dyadic	Job Description Index (JDI)	Subordinate
Performance	Group	Supervisory Ratings, Archival Data	Superior, Experimenter, Original Records
Stress	Individual	Fiedler's Job Stress Scale	Leader

ing leadership effectiveness. Specifically, as presented in Table 1, measures of the leader's orientation are drawn from the leader; outcome measures are typically taken from sources independent of the leader, such as supervisor ratings or objective performance measures.

Situational variables have been specified in a number of ways, many of which are conceptually and operationally independent both from leader variables and sources of the outcome criteria (e.g., experimental manipulations, observer ratings of organizational characteristics). . . .

Leadership Motivational Orientation

Although past reviews (e.g., Rice 1978a, 1978b) have been quite thorough, there are a few issues regarding the conceptualization of the scale and its use that were not clarified.

The leader's orientation is measured by a scale referred to as "least preferred coworker" (LPC) scale. The scale's instructions ask the respondent to identify within the context of all the persons with whom the respondent has ever worked the one person in your life with whom you could work least well. This individual may or may not be the person you also dislike most. It must be the one person with whom you had the most difficulty getting a job done, the one single individual with whom you would least want to work—a boss, a subordinate, or a peer (Fiedler & Chemers, 1984, p. 17). . . .

Based on the existing evidence, it is safe to say that the LPC scale is a measure of the internal state of the leader. Whether it measures values, motivation attitude, or goals is not totally resolved. However, based on Markus and Wurf (1987), all of these concepts are variables that operate in determining the working self, though they vary in their level of specificity.

Situational Control

The other central construct in contingency model research, situational control, has been operationalized in various ways. It is conceptually defined as the leader's sense of influence and control afforded by the situation (Fiedler, 1978). In most of the research, three components of the situation have been identified as contributors to a sense of predictability and control: Leader-member relationship (formerly referred to as group atmosphere), task structure, and position power.

Leader-Member Relations

This construct refers to the amount of cohesiveness in the work team and the support of the team for the leader. Leader-member relations is the most important aspect of the situation, because if the leader lacks group support, energy is diverted to controlling the group rather than toward planning, problem-solving, and productivity. Under these conditions, the leader's influence is weakened, and he or she cannot rely on the team to achieve and implement the goal. . . .

Task Structure

This second component of situational control represents the clarity and certainty in task goals and procedures that allow the leader confidently to guide the group's activities. In laboratory studies, the variable was usually manipulated by the choice of assigned tasks that varied on Shaw's (1963) criteria for task structure (Fiedler, 1978). In field studies, task structure ratings can be provided by a knowledgeable observer, such as a superior. A scale for rating task structure by a supervisor or investigator was developed by Hunt (1967). . . .

Position Power

This component of situational control is defined as the administrative authority bestowed on the leader by the organization or other source of authority—for example, the experimenter. Fiedler (1978) advised that position power assessments should be supplied by the leader's supervisor, due to the possibility of distortion of information by self-report. . . .

Summary of Situational Control and Social Power

The three components of situational control parallel French and Raven's (1959) five bases of power. Power has been defined as the ability to influence others. Situational control has also been defined as providing the leader with the ability to influence and gain control (Bass, 1991). French and Raven identified the expert and referent sources of power as sources based on knowledge and expertise regarding the task and the strength or solidity of the social relationships. Research has indicated that these two sources of power have the most efficacious and lasting effects in social influence (Podsakoff & Schriesheim, 1985; Yukl & Taber, 1983). Referent power based on the quality of the social relationship is most similar to the contingency model variable of "Leader-Member Relations." Expert power with its emphasis on task knowledge bears much in common with "Task Structure." The three other sources of power—coercive, reward, and legitimate—reflect an individual's authority. These three sources have shown to be inter-correlated to the point that some have referred to it as position power (Bass, 1991). Their effects have been debated. Thus, they do not seem to have as robust and lasting effect as the referent and expert sources (Podsakoff & Schriesheim, 1985). In the contingency model, these power sources are given the least weight in the assessment of situational control. . . .

The Relationship among the Independent Variables within the Contingency Model

The variables that define the leader's personal characteristic (the LPC) and the leader's situational control (leader-member relations, task structure, and position power) are both conceptually and psychometrically independent. This is one of the most valuable and unique properties of the contingency model. In studies where the leader is the only source of information for both personal and situational variables, or where the situation is defined by an independent observer, the LPC and situational control scores are not statistically related. Problems of multicolinearity and single-source biases, which bedevil much current leadership-research methodology (Podsakoff & Organ, 1986; Spector, 1987), are not a serious problem for contingency model research. Although LPC and situational control are uncorrelated, some dependency does appear among the three situational variables. . . .

Relationship of the Model to Outcome (Dependent) Variables

The contingency model of leadership effectiveness has defined its criterion of effectiveness primarily as work group performance. However, some studies have examined effects on other criteria, such as subordinate satisfaction or leader's reported symptoms of stress.

The operational definition of performance has been based partially on the nature of the task and the level of the leader's position. Wherever possible, productivity was defined by objective measures, such as win-lose records for basketball teams, tons per person-hour for steel production crews, and accuracy for bombing crews. In cases where the nature of the tasks required a subjective evaluation, at least two raters evaluated the quality of performance. Such tasks typically consisted of composing a story, developing a report, or recommending a program. In most of the organizational field studies, the manager's performance was rated by a superior. . . .

Summary and Conclusions

The contingency model of leadership has stimulated and guided research for more than 30 years. The greatest strengths of the model reside in: (1) the conceptual and statistical independence of its central constructs, LPC and situational control; (2) its emphasis on independent and, where possible, objective measures of important organizational outcomes such as group productivity; (3) its relatively lesser vulnerability to the invalidation of its constructs and findings as a result of information-processing biases and methodological weaknesses; and, of course, (4) its proven predictive validity.

The model's greatest weaknesses arise from its inductive development. The LPC construct has little face or concurrent validity, and even evidence for its construct validity requires some faith. The lack of process-based explanations for performance effects makes both the understanding and application of the model more difficult.

One of the major strengths of the contingency model in practical application is that about 15 minutes worth of questionnaire administration provides a multilevel analysis of person-situation match that can be used in selection, placement, training, and organizational development. Based on the contingency model, the Leader Match training program (Fiedler & Chemers, 1984) provides a framework for organizational intervention at the individual, dyadic, and group levels.

Through training such as Leader Match, which is based on the contingency model of leadership effectiveness, the leader uses both personal and group data to assess his or her match in the situation. The validity of this training program has been presented in numerous documents (Fiedler & Mahar, 1979; Burke & Day, 1986). Using the model's existing research, the leader can then anticipate his or her effectiveness both at a personal and dyadic level (i.e., experienced stress or subordinate satisfaction) and at a group level (i.e., performance, subordinates' satisfaction and morale). With access to such wisdom, the leader can do "job engineering." This does not require major changes in the way the work is done but, through modifying the three situational control constructs, the leader can affect all levels of work team dynamics and alter group functioning.

Because the model is multilevel (that is, it represents leadership as a dynamic exchange of various levels of analyses present in a natural team-building setting instead of an individually focused model—only the leader or the subordinates), it allows for interventions at different levels. For example, at the individual level, the leader is made aware of his or her strengths and the environmentally available resources, and learns job engineering. This is helpful for leadership development programs. A focus on the dyadic level will assist in arranging work teams for the highest yield.

Similar to some other leadership theories, the contingency model has also been tested for validity in other countries (e.g., Ayman & Chemers, 1991; Rubio, 1986; Shima, 1968). In addition, cross-cultural research with the contingency model has incorporated the effects of work team diversity (e.g., Fiedler, 1966). The employment of a multilevel approach in which group-level variables, such as leader-member relations, are conceptualized and measured at the group level of analysis provides a basis for the inclusion of work team diversity. Diverse group affiliations between leader and followers (e.g., with respect to religion, language, ethnicity, gender, functional specialization, etc.) can be addressed in terms of effects on the situational control constructs. Groups marked by diversity may have lower leader-member relations. Diversity might also affect the leader's power and authority or task structure, as cultural differences in customs and norms affect expectations about the acceptable forms of leadership influence (Triandis, 1993). The ability of the contingency model to incorporate the effects of cultural differences and diversity provides the potential for building a universal leadership theory.

Although the contingency model is almost 40 years old, its basic premise, the interaction of person and situation in the study of leadership effectiveness, provides a flexibility that allows the model to grow and develop. The levels-of-analysis approach offers a framework for utilizing the flexibility that may render productive avenues for future research. . . .

References

Ashour, A. S. (1973). The contingency model of leadership effectiveness: An evaluation. *Organizational Behavior and Human Performance, 9,* 339–355.

Ayman, R., & Chemers, M. M. (1991). The effect of leadership match on subordinate satisfaction in Mexican organizations: Some moderating influences of self-monitoring. *Applied Psychology: An International Review, 40,* 299–314.

Bass, B. M. (1991). *Bass & Stogdill's handbook of leadership: Theory, research, & managerial applications.* 3rd edition. New York: Free Press.

Burke, M. J., & Day, R. R. (1986). Accumulative study of the effectiveness of managerial training. *Journal of Applied Psychology, 71,* 232–246.

Fiedler, F. E. (1966). The effect of leadership and cultural heterogeneity on group performance. *Journal of Experimental Social Psychology, 2,* 237–264.

Fiedler, F. E. (1967). *A theory of leadership effectiveness.* New York: McGraw-Hill.

Fiedler, F. E. (1978). The contingency model and the dynamics of the leadership process. In L. Berkowitz (Ed.), *Advances in Experimental Social Psychology* (Vol. 11, pp. 59–96). New York: Academic Press.

Fiedler, F. E., & Chemers, M. M. (1974). *Leadership and effective management.* Glenview, IL: Scott-Foresman.

Fiedler, F. E., & Chemers, M. M. (1984). *Improving leadership effectiveness: The leader match concept.* 2nd edition. New York: Wiley.

Fiedler, F. E., & Mahar, L. (1979). A field experiment validating contingency model leadership training. *Journal of Applied of Psychology,* 64, 247–254.

French, J. R., & Raven, B. (1959). The basis of social power. In D. Cartwright (Ed.), *Studies in social power.* Ann Arbor: Institute for Social Research, Univ. of Michigan.

Graen, G., Alvares, K. M., Orris, J. B., & Martella, J. A. (1971). Contingency model of leadership effectiveness: Antecedent and evidential results. *Psychological Bulletin,* 74, 285–296.

Graen, G., Orris, J. B., & Alvares, K. M. (1971). Contingency model of leadership effectiveness: Some experimental results. *Journal of Applied Psychology,* 55, 196–201.

Hunt, J. G. (1967). Fiedler's leadership contingency model: An empirical test in three organizations. *Organizational Behavior and Human Performance,* 2, 290–308.

Markus, H., and Wurf, E. (1987). The dynamic self-concept: A social psychological perspective. *Annual Review of Psychology,* 38, 299–337.

Peters, L. H., Harke, D. D., & Pohlmann, J. F. (1985). Fiedler's contingency theory of leadership: An application of the meta-analysis procedures of Schmitt and Hunter. *Psychological Bulletin,* 97, 274–285.

Podsakoff, P. M., and Organ, D. W. (1986). Self-reports in organizational research: Problems and prospects. *Journal of Management,* 12, 31–41.

Podsakoff, P. M., and Schriesheim, C. A. (1985). Field studies of French and Raven's bases of power: Critique, reanalysis, and suggestions for future research. *Psychological Bulletin,* 97, 387–411.

Rubio, J. (1986). Estudio empirico sobre la validez del Modelo de la Contingencia de Fiedler [An empirical study of the validity of Fiedler's contingency model.] *Revista de Psicologia General y Aplicada,* 41, 601–614.

Schriesheim, C. A., & Kerr, S. (1977). Theories and measures of leadership: A critical appraisal of current and future directions. In J. G. Hunt and L. L. Larson (Eds.), *Leadership: The cutting edge* (pp. 9–44). Carbondale: Southern Illinois Univ. Press.

Shaw, M. E. (1963). Scaling group tasks: A method of dimensional analysis. *JSAS Catalogue of Selected Documents in Psychology,* 3(8).

Shima, H. (1968). The leadership between the leader's modes of interpersonal cognition and the performance of the group. *Japanese Psychological Research,* 10, 13–30.

Spector, P. E. (1987). Method variance as an artifact in self-report affect and perceptions at work: Myth or significant problem? *Journal of Applied Psychology,* 72, 438–443.

Strube, M. J., & Garcia, J. E. (1981). A meta-analytic investigation of Fiedler's contingency model of leadership effectiveness. *Psychological Bulletin,* 90, 307–321.

Triandis, H. C. (1993). The contingency model in cross-cultural perspective. In M. M. Chemers & R. Ayman (Eds.), *Leadership theory and research: Perspectives and directions* (pp. 167–188). New York: Academic Press.

Vecchio, R. P. (1977). An empirical examination of the validity of Fiedler's model of leadership effectiveness. *Organizational Behavior and Human Performance,* 19, 180–206.

Yukl, G., & Taber, T. (1983). The effective use of managerial power. *Personnel,* 60, 37–44.

26

Life Cycle Theory
of Leadership

Paul Hersey and Kenneth H. Blanchard

The recognition of task and relationships as two important dimensions of leader behavior has pervaded the works of management theorists[1] over the years. These two dimensions have been variously labeled as "autocratic" and "democratic"; "authoritarian" and "equalitarian"; "employee-oriented" and "production-oriented"; "goal achievement" and "group maintenance"; "task-ability" and "likeability"; "instrumental and expressive"; "efficiency and effectiveness." The difference between these concepts and task and relationships seems to be more semantic than real.

For some time, it was believed that task and relationships were either/or styles of leader behavior and, therefore, should be depicted as a single dimension along a continuum, moving from very authoritarian (task) leader behavior at one end to very democratic (relationships) leader behavior at the other.[2]

Ohio State Leadership Studies

In more recent years, the feeling that task and relationships were either/or leadership styles has been dispelled. In particular, the leadership studies initiated in 1945 by the Bureau of Business Research at Ohio State University[3] questioned whether leader behavior could be depicted on a single continuum.

In attempting to describe *how* a leader carries out his activities, the Ohio State staff identified "initiating structure" (task) and "consideration" (relationships) as the two most important dimensions of leadership. "Initiating structure" refers to "the leader's behavior in delineating the relationship between himself and members of the work-group and in endeavoring to establish well-defined patterns of organization, channels of communication, and methods of procedure." On the other hand, "consideration" refers to "behavior indicative of friendship, mutual trust, respect, and warmth in the relationship between the leader and the members of his staff."[4]

In the leadership studies that followed, the Ohio State staff found that leadership styles vary considerably from leader to leader. The behavior of some leaders is characterized by rigidly structuring activities of followers in terms of *task* accomplishments, while others concentrate on building and maintaining good personal *relationships* between themselves and their followers. Other leaders have styles characterized by both task and relationships behavior. There are even some individuals in leadership positions whose behavior tends to provide little structure or development of interpersonal relationships. No dominant style appears. Instead, various combinations are evident. Thus, task and relationships are not either/or leadership styles as an authoritarian-democratic continuum suggests. Instead, these patterns of leader behavior are separate and distinct dimensions which can be plotted on two separate axes, rather than a single continuum. Thus, the Ohio State studies resulted in the development of four quadrants to illustrate leadership styles in terms of initiating structure (task) and consideration (relationships) as shown in Figure 1.

The Managerial Grid

Robert R. Blake and Jane S. Mouton[5] in their Managerial Grid have popularized the task and relationships dimensions of leadership and have used them extensively in organization and management development programs.

In the Managerial Grid, five different types of leadership based on concern for production (task) and concern for people (relationships) are located in the four quadrants identified by the Ohio State studies.

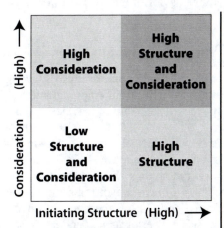

Figure 1   The Ohio State Leadership Quadrants

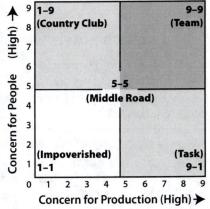

Figure 2   The Managerial Grid Leadership Styles

Concern for *production* is illustrated on the horizontal axis. Production becomes more important to the leader as his rating advances on the horizontal scale. A leader with a rating of 9 has a maximum concern for production.

Concern for people is illustrated on the vertical axis. People become more important to the leader as his rating progresses up the vertical axis. A leader with a rating of 9 on the vertical axis has a maximum concern for people.

The Managerial Grid, in essence, has given popular terminology to five points within the four quadrants identified by the Ohio State studies.

Suggesting a "Best" Style of Leadership

After identifying task and relationships as two central dimensions of any leadership situation, some management writers have suggested a "best" style of leadership. Most of these writers have supported either an integrated leader behavior style (high task and high relationships) or a permissive, democratic, human relations approach (high relationships).

Andrew W. Halpin,[6] of the original Ohio State staff, in a study of school superintendents, pointed out that according to his findings "effective or desirable leadership behavior is characterized by high ratings on both initiating structure and consideration. Conversely, ineffective or undesirable leadership behavior is marked by low ratings on both dimensions." Thus, Halpin seemed to conclude that the high consideration and high initiating structure style is theoretically the ideal or "best" leader behavior, while the style low on both dimensions is theoretically the "worst."

Blake and Mouton in their Managerial Grid also imply that the most desirable leadership style is "team management" (maximum concern for production and people) and the least desirable is "impoverished management" (minimum concern for production and people). In fact, they have developed training programs designed to change the behavior of managers toward this "team" style.[7]

Leadership Style Should Vary With the Situation

While the Ohio State and the Managerial Grid people seem to suggest there is a "best" style of leadership,[8] recent evidence from empirical studies clearly shows that there is no single all-purpose leadership style which is universally successful.

Some of the most convincing evidence which dispels the idea of a single "best" style of leader behavior was gathered and published by A. K. Korman[9] in 1966. Korman attempted to review all the studies which examined the relationship between the Ohio State behavior dimensions of initiating structure (task) and consideration (relationships) and various measures of effectiveness, including group productivity, salary, performance under stress, administrative reputation, work group grievances, absenteeism, and turnover. Korman reviewed over twenty-five studies and concluded that:

Despite the fact that "consideration" and "initiating structure" have become almost bywords in American industrial psychology, it seems apparent that very little is now known as to how these variables may predict work group performance and the conditions which affect such predictions. At the current time, we cannot even say whether they have any predictive significance at all.

Thus, Korman found the use of consideration and initiating structure had no significant predictive value in terms of effectiveness as situations changed. *This suggests that since situations differ, so must leader style.*

Fred E. Fiedler,[10] in testing his contingency model of leadership in over fifty studies covering a span of fifteen years (1951–1967), concluded that both directive, task-oriented leaders and non-directive, human relations-oriented leaders are successful under some conditions. Fiedler argues:

While one can never say that something is impossible, and while someone may well discover the all-purpose leadership style or behavior at some future time, our own data and those which have come out of sound research by other investigators do not promise such miraculous cures.

A number of other investigators[11] besides Korman and Fiedler have also shown that different leadership situations require different leader styles.

In summary, empirical studies tend to show that there is no normative (best) style of leadership; that successful leaders are those who can adapt their leader behavior to meet the needs of their followers and the particular situation. Effectiveness is dependent upon the leader, the followers, and other situational elements. In managing for effectiveness a leader must be able to diagnose his own leader behavior in light of his environment. Some of the variables other than his followers which he should examine include the organization, superiors, associates, and job demands. This list is not all inclusive, but contains interacting components which tend to be important to a leader in many different organizational settings.

Adding an Effectiveness Dimension

To measure more accurately how well a leader operates within a given situation, an "effectiveness dimension" should be added to the two-dimension Ohio State model. This is illustrated in Figure 3.

By adding an effectiveness dimension to the Ohio State model, a three-dimensional model is created.[12] This Leader Effectiveness Model attempts to integrate the concepts of leader style with situational demands of a specific environment. When the leader's style is appropriate to a given environment measured by results, it is termed *effective*; when his style is inappropriate to a given environment, it is termed *ineffective*.

If a leader's effectiveness is determined by the interaction of his style and environment (followers and other situational variables), it follows that any of the four styles depicted in the Ohio State model may be effective or ineffective depending on the environment.

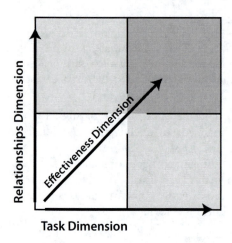

Figure 3   Adding an Effectiveness Dimension

Thus, there is *no* single ideal leader behavior style which is appropriate in all situations. For example, the high task and high relationships style is appropriate only in certain situations, but is inappropriate in others. In basically crisis-oriented organizations like the military or the police, there is considerable evidence that the most appropriate style would be high task, since under combat or riot conditions success often depends upon immediate response to orders. Time demands do not permit talking things over or explaining decisions. For success, behavior must be automatic.

While a high task style might be effective for a combat officer, it might not be effective in other situations even within the military. This was pointed out when line officers trained at West Point were sent to command outposts in the Dew Line, which was part of an advanced warning system. The scientific personnel involved, living in close quarters in an Arctic region, did not respond favorably to the task-oriented behavior of these combat trained officers. The level of education and maturity of these people was such that they did not need a great deal of structure in their work. In fact, they tended to resent it.

Other studies of scientific and research-oriented personnel show also that many of these people desire, or need, only a limited amount of socio-emotional support. Therefore, there are situations in which the low task and relationships style, which has been assumed by some authors to be theoretically a poor leadership style, may be an appropriate style.

In summary, an effective leader must be able to *diagnose* the demands of the environment and then either *adapt* his leader style to fit these demands, or develop the means to *change* some or all of the other variables.

Attitudinal vs. Behavioral Models

In examining the dimensions of the Managerial Grid (*concern* for production and *concern* for people), one can see that these are attitudinal dimensions. That is, concern is a feeling or emotion toward something. On the other hand, the dimensions of the Ohio State Model (initiating structure and consideration) and the Leader Effectiveness Model (task and relationships) are dimensions of *observed* behavior. Thus, the Ohio State and Leader Effectiveness models measure *how* people behave, while the Managerial Grid measures *predisposition* toward production and people. As discussed earlier, the Leader Effectiveness Model is an outgrowth of the Ohio State Model but is distinct from it in that it adds an effectiveness dimension to the two dimensions of behavior.

Although the Managerial Grid and the Leader Effectiveness Model measure different aspects of leadership, they are not incompatible. A conflict develops, however, because behavioral assumptions have often been drawn from analysis of the attitudinal dimensions of the Managerial Grid.[13] While high *concern* for both production and people is desirable in many organizations, managers having a high concern for both people and production do not always find it appropriate in all situations to initiate a high degree of structure and provide a high degree of socio-emotional support.

For example, if a manager's subordinates are emotionally mature and can take responsibility for themselves, his appropriate style of leadership may be low task and low relationships. In this case, the manager permits these subordinates to participate in the planning, organizing and controlling of their own operation. He plays a background role, providing socio-emotional support only when necessary. Consequently, it is assumptions about behavior drawn from the Managerial Grid and not the Grid itself that are inconsistent with the Leader Effectiveness Model.

Life Cycle Theory

Korman,[14] in his extensive review of studies examining the Ohio State concepts of initiating structure and consideration, concluded that:

> What is needed . . . in future concurrent (and predictive) studies is not just recognition of this factor of "situational determinants" but, rather, a systematic conceptualization of situational variance as it might relate to leadership behavior (initiating structure and consideration).

In discussing this conclusion, Korman suggests the possibility of a curvilinear relationship rather than a simple linear relationship between structure and consideration and other variables. The Life Cycle Theory of Leadership which we have developed is based on a curvilinear relationship between task and relationships and "maturity." This theory will attempt to provide a leader with some understanding of the relationship between an effective style of leadership and the level of maturity of one's followers. The emphasis in the Life Cycle Theory of Leadership will be on the followers. As Fillmore H. Sanford has indicated, there is some justification for regarding the followers "as the most crucial factor in any leadership event."[15] Followers in any situation are vital, not only because individually they accept or reject the leader, but as a group they actually determine whatever personal power he may have.

According to Life Cycle Theory, as the level of maturity of one's followers continues to increase, appropriate leader behavior not only requires less and less structure (task) but also less and less socio-emotional support (relationships). This cycle can be illustrated in the four quadrants of the basic

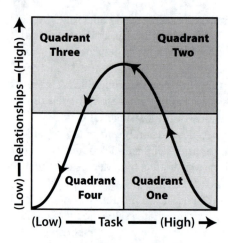

Figure 4   Life Cycle Theory of Leadership

styles portion of the Leader Effectiveness Model as shown in Figure 4.

Maturity is defined in Life Cycle Theory by the relative independence,[16] ability to take responsibility, and achievement-motivation[17] of an individual or group. These components of maturity are often influenced by level of education and amount of experience. While age is a factor, it is not directly related to maturity as used in the Life Cycle. Our concern is for psychological age, not chronological age. Beginning with structured task behavior which is appropriate for working with immature people, Life Cycle Theory suggests that leader behavior should move from: (1) high task/low relationships behavior to (2) high task/high relationships and (3) high relationships/low task behavior to (4) low task/low relationships behavior, if one's followers progress from immaturity to maturity.

Parent-Child Example

An illustration of this Life Cycle Theory familiar to everyone is the parent-child relationship. As a child begins to mature, it is appropriate for the parent to provide more socio-emotional support and less structure. Experience shows us that if the parent provides too much relationships before a child is somewhat mature, this behavior is often misinterpreted by the child as permissiveness. Thus it is appropriate to increase one's relationships behavior as the child is able to increase his maturity or capacity to take responsibility.

A child when first born is unable to control much of his own environment. Consequently, his parents must initiate almost all structure, i.e., dress the child, feed the child, bathe the child, turn the child over, etc. While it is appropriate for a parent to show love and affection toward a child, this is different than the mutual trust and respect which characterizes relationships behavior. Consequently, the most appropriate style for a parent to use with his children during the early preschool years may be high task/low relationships (quadrant 1).

Even when the child begins to attend school, the parent must provide a great deal of structure. The child is still not mature enough to accept much responsibility on his own. It may become appropriate at this state, as the child matures, for the parent to increase his relationships behavior by showing more trust and respect for his child. At this point, the parent's behavior could be characterized as high task/high relationships (quadrant 2).

Gradually as the child moves into high school and/or college, he begins to seek and accept more and more responsibility for his own behavior. It is during this time that a parent should begin to engage in less structured behavior and provide more socio-emotional support (quadrant 3). This does not mean that the child's life will have less structure, but it will now be internally imposed by the "young man" rather than externally by the parent. When this happens, the cycle as depicted on the Leader Effectiveness Model begins to become a backward bending curve. The child is not only able to structure many of the activities in which he engages, but is also able to provide self-control over his interpersonal and emotional needs.

As the child begins to make his own living, start his own family, and take full responsibility for his actions, a decrease in structure and socio-emotional support by the parents becomes appropriate. In reality, the umbilical cord has been severed and the child is now "on his own." At this stage of the parent-child relationship, a low task/low relationships style seems to be most appropriate (quadrant 4).

Although the Life Cycle suggests a basic style for different levels of maturity in meeting specific contingencies, it may be necessary to vary one's style anywhere within the four quadrants to deal appropriately with this event. For example, even when a young man is away at college and his parents are using a high relationships style with him, it might be appropriate for them to initiate some structure with their son if they discover that he is not behaving in as mature a way as expected (he has become a discipline problem). A change in parental behavior might even be necessary later in life after a son (or daughter) has had a family of his own for a number of years. If this son, for example, suddenly begins to experience marital difficulties and his family begins to disintegrate, it might be appropriate for his parents temporarily to increase their socio-emotional support.

Other Aspects of the Life Cycle

The parent-child relationship is only one example of the Life Cycle. This cycle is also discernible in other organizations in the interaction between superiors and subordinates. An interesting example is found in research and development work. In working with highly trained and educated research and development personnel, the most effective leader behavior style might be low task/low relationships. However, during the early stages of a particular project, the director must impose a certain amount of structure as the requirements and limitations of the project are established. Once these limitations are understood, the R & D director moves rapidly through the *project cycle* back to the mature low task/low relationships style.

In a college setting, the Life Cycle Theory has been validated in studying the teacher-student relationship. Effective teaching of lower division students (freshmen and sophomores) has been characterized by structured behavior on the part of the teacher as he reinforces appropriate patterns in attendance and study habits, while more relationships behavior seems to be appropriate for working with upper division undergraduates and Master's students. And finally the cycle seems to be completed as a teacher begins to work with mature Ph.D. candidates, who need very little guidance or socio-emotional support.

We realize that most groups in our society do not reach the backward bending aspect of the cycle. But there is some evidence that as the level of education and experience of a group increases, appropriate movement in this direction will take place. However, the demands of the job may often be a limiting factor on the development of maturity in workers. For example, an assembly line operation in an automobile plant is so highly structured that it offers little opportunity for the maturing process to occur. With such monotonous tasks, workers are given minimal control over their environment and are often encouraged to be passive, dependent, and subordinate.

Life Cycle and Span of Control

For years it has been argued by many management writers that one man can supervise only a relatively few people; therefore, all managers should have a limited span of control. For example, Harold Koontz and Cyril O'Donnell[18] state that:

> In every organization it must be decided how many subordinates a superior can manage. Students of management have found that this number is usually four to eight subordinates at the upper levels of organization and eight to fifteen or more at the lower levels.

While the suggested number of subordinates which one can supervise varies anywhere from three to thirty, the principle usually states that the number should decrease as one moves higher in the organization. Top management should have fewer subordinates to supervise than lower level managers. Yet the Life Cycle Theory of Leadership suggests that span of control may not depend on the level of the management hierarchy but should be a function of the maturity of the individuals being supervised. The more independent, able to take responsibility, and achievement-motivated one's subordinates are, the more people a manager can supervise. It is theoretically possible to supervise an infinite number of subordinates if everyone is completely mature and able to be responsible for his own job. This does not mean there is less control, but these subordinates are self-controlled rather than externally controlled by their superior. Since people occupying higher level jobs in an organization tend to be more "mature" and therefore need less close supervision than people occupying lower level jobs, it seems reasonable to assume that top managers should be able to supervise more subordinates than their counterparts at lower levels.[19]

Conclusions

Rensis Likert[20] found in his research that supervisors with the best records of performance were employee-centered (high relationships), while job-centered (high task) supervisors were found more often to have low-producing sections. While this relationship seemed to exist, Likert raised the question of which variable was the causal factor. Is the style of the supervisor causing the level of production or is the level of production encouraging the style of the managers? As Likert suggests, it may very well be that high-producing sections allow for general supervision rather than close supervision and relationship behavior rather than task behavior. The supervisor soon learns that his subordinates are mature enough to structure their own environment, thus leaving him time for other kinds of activities. At the same time a low-producing section may leave the supervisor with no choice but to be job-centered. If he attempted to use a relationships style this may be misunderstood and interpreted as reinforcement for their low level of performance. The point is, the supervisor must change appropriately.

Changing Style

The problem with the conclusions of Likert and other behavioral scientists comes in implementation. Practitioners read that employee-centered supervisors tend to have higher-producing sections than job-centered supervisors. Wanting to implement these findings overnight, they encourage all supervisors to become more employee-oriented. Consequently, a foreman who has been operating as a task-oriented, authoritarian leader for many years may be encouraged to change his style—"get in step with the times." Upon returning from a "human relations" training program, the foreman will probably try to utilize some of the new relationships techniques he has recently been taught. The problem is that his personality is not compatible with the new concepts, but he tries to use them anyway. As long as things are running smoothly, there is no difficulty. However, the minute an important issue or crisis develops he tends to revert to his old basic style and becomes inconsistent, vacillating between the new relationships style he has been taught, and his old task style which has the force of habit behind it.

This idea was supported in a study conducted by the General Electric Company at one of its turbine and generator plants. In this study, the leadership styles of about 90 foremen were analyzed and rated as "democratic," "authoritarian" or "mixed." In discussing the findings, Saul W. Gellerman[21] reported that:

> The lowest morale in the plant was found among those men whose foremen were rated *between* the democratic and authoritarian extremes. The GE research team felt that these foremen might have varied inconsistently in their tactics, permissive at one moment and hard-fisted the next, in a way that left their men frustrated and unable to anticipate how they would be treated. The naturally autocratic supervisor who is exposed to human relations training may behave in exactly such a manner . . . a pattern which will probably make him even harder to work for than he was before being "enlightened."

Thus, changing the style of managers is a difficult process, and one that takes considerable time to accomplish. Expecting miracles overnight will only lead to frustration and uneasiness for both managers and their subordinates. Yet industry invests many millions of dollars annually for training and development programs which concentrate on effecting change in the style of managers. As Fiedler[22] suggests:

> A person's leadership style . . . reflects the individual's basic motivational and need structure. At best it takes one, two, or three years of intensive psychotherapy to effect changes in personality structure. It is difficult to see how we can change in more than a few cases an equally important set of core values in a few hours of lectures and role playing or even in the course of a more intensive training program of one or two weeks.

Fiedler's point is well-taken. It is indeed difficult to effect changes in the styles of managers overnight. However, it is not completely hopeless. But, at best, it is a slow and expensive process which requires creative planning and patience. In fact, Likert[23] found that it takes from three to seven years, depending on the size and complexity of the organization, to effectively implement a new management theory.

> Haste is self-defeating because of the anxieties and stresses it creates. There is no substitute for ample time to enable the members of an organization to reach the level of skillful and easy, habitual use of the new leadership . . .

Changing Performance

Not only is it difficult to effect changes in the styles of managers overnight, but the question that we raise is whether it is even appropriate. It is questionable whether a work group whose performance has been continually low would suddenly leap to high productivity with the introduction of an employee-centered supervisor. In fact, they might take advantage of him and view him as a "soft-touch." These workers lack maturity and are not ready for more responsibility. Thus the supervisor must bring them along slowly, becoming more employee-centered and less job-centered as they mature. When an individual's performance is low, one cannot expect drastic changes overnight, regardless of changes in expectations or other incentives. The key is often reinforcing positively "successive approximations." By successive approximations we mean behavior which comes closer and closer to the supervisor's expectations of good performance. Similar to the child learning some new behavior, a manager should not expect high levels of performance at the outset. As a parent or teacher, we would use positive reinforcement as the child's behavior approaches the desired level of performance. Therefore, the manager must be aware of any progress of his subordinates so that he is in a position to reinforce appropriately improved performance.

Change through the cycle from quadrant 1 to quadrant 2, 3, and then 4 must be gradual. This process by its very nature cannot be revolutionary but must be evolutionary—gradual developmental changes, a result of planned growth and the creation of mutual trust and respect.

Notes

[1] As examples see the following: Robert F. Bales, "Task Roles and Social Roles in Problem-Solving Groups," in *Readings in Social Psychology*, E. E. Maccoby, T. M. Newcomb and E. L. Hartley (eds.), Holt, Rinehart and Winston, 1958; Chester I. Barnard, *The Functions of the Executive*, Harvard University Press, 1938; Dorwin Cartwright and Alvin Zander (eds.), *Group Dynamics: Research and Theory*, second edition, Row, Peterson and Co., 1960; D. Katz, N. Maccoby, and Nancy C. Morse, *Productivity, Supervision, and Morale in an Office Situation*, The Darel Press, Inc., 1950; Talcott Parsons, *The Social System*, The Free Press, 1951.

[2] Robert Tannenbaum and Warren H. Schmidt, "How to Choose a Leadership Pattern," *Harvard Business Review*, Mar.–Apr. 1957, pp. 95–101.

[3] Roger M. Stogdill and Alvin E. Coons (eds.), *Leader Behavior: Its Description and Measurement*, Research Monograph No. 88, Bureau of Business Research, The Ohio State Univ., 1957.

[4] Ibid; See also Andrew W. Halpin, *The Leadership Behavior of School Superintendents*, Midwest Administration Center, The University of Chicago, 1959.

[5] Robert R. Blake and Jane S. Mouton, *The Managerial Grid*, Gulf Publishing, 1964.

[6] Halpin, *The Leadership Behavior of School Superintendents*.

[7] Robert R. Blake et al., "Breakthrough in Organization Development," *Harvard Business Review*, Nov.–Dec. 1964.

[8] See also, Rensis Likert, *New Patterns of Management*, McGraw-Hill, 1961.

[9] A. K. Korman, "'Consideration,' 'Initiating Structure,' and Organizational Criteria—A Review," *Personnel Psychology*, Vol. 19, No. 4, (Winter 1966), pp. 349–361.

[10] Fred E. Fiedler, *A Theory of Leadership Effectiveness*, McGraw-Hill, 1967.

[11] See C. A. Gibb, "Leadership"; A. P. Hare, *Handbook of Small Group Research*, Wiley, 1965; and D. C. Pelz, "Leadership Within a Hierarchical Organization," *Journal of Social Issues*, 1961, 7, pp. 49–55.

[12] Paul Hersey and Kenneth H. Blanchard, *Leader Behavior*, Management Education & Development, Inc., 1967; see also Hersey and Blanchard, *Management of Organizational Behavior: Utilizing Human Resources*, Prentice-Hall, Inc.; and William J. Reddin, "The 3-D Management Style Theory," *Training and Development Journal*, Apr. 1967.

[13] Fred E. Fiedler in his Contingency Model of Leadership Effectiveness (Fiedler, *A Theory of Leadership Effectiveness*) tends to make behavioral assumptions from data gathered from an attitudinal measure of leadership style. A leader is asked to evaluate his least preferred co-worker (LPC) on a series of Semantic Differential type scales. Leaders are classified as high or low LPC depending on the favorableness with which they rate their LPC.

[14] Korman, "'Consideration,' 'Initiating Structure,' and Organizational Criteria—A Review."

[15] F. H. Sanford, *Authoritarianism and Leadership*, Inst. for Research in Human Relations, 1950.

[16] Chris Argyris, *Personality and Organization*, Harper & Row, 1957; *Interpersonal Competence and Organizational Effectiveness*, Dorsey Press, 1962; and *Integrating the Individual and the Organization*, Wiley, 1964.

[17] David C. McClelland, J. W. Atkinson, R. A. Clark, and E. L. Lowell, *The Achievement Motive*, Appleton-Century-Crafts, Inc., 1953, and *The Achieving Society*, D. Van Nostrand Co., 1961.

[18] Harold Koontz and Cyril O'Donnell, *Principles of Management*, fourth edition, McGraw-Hill, 1968.

[19] Support for this is provided by Peter F. Drucker, *The Practice of Management*, Harper, 1954, pp. 139–40.

[20] Rensis Likert, *New Patterns of Management*, McGraw-Hill, 1961.

[21] Saul Gellerman, *Motivation and Productivity*, American Management Assn., 1963.

[22] Fiedler, *A Theory of Leadership Effectiveness*.

[23] Likert, *New Patterns of Management*.

27

3-D Theory of
Managerial Effectiveness

W. J. Reddin

By learning to apply the 3-D Theory, any manager can learn to become more effective. It was designed with that single specific purpose in mind. At the heart of the 3-D Theory is a very simple idea. It was discovered in a long series of research studies conducted by psychologists in the United States. They discovered that the two main elements in managerial behavior concerned the task to be done and relationships with other people. They also found that managers sometimes emphasized one and sometimes emphasized the other, and that these two elements of behavior could be used in small or large amounts. For instance, a manager could be very much task-oriented or only a small amount. Also, both behaviors could be used together (the 3-D term is integrated style), task could be used alone (dedicated style), relationships could be used alone (related style), or each could be used to only a small degree (separated style). The four basic styles are arranged as shown in Figure 1. The TO and RO along the sides stand for Task Orientation (TO) and Relationships Orientation (RO) respectively. These four basic styles represent four types of behavior. Not all types of managerial behavior will fit neatly into these four types, but they are very useful as a general framework. A clear set of indicators and characteristics for each type has been developed which enables each style to be fully understood.

No One Style is Always Effective

Further research conducted at several universities clearly established that any of these four basic styles of behavior could be effective in certain situations and not effective in others. None are more or less effective in themselves. Their effectiveness depends on the situation in which they are used. This means that each one of the four basic styles has a less effective equivalent and a more effective equivalent, resulting in eight managerial styles. For example, when the high task orientation of the dedicated style is used inappropriately, the popular, as well as the 3-D term applied is "autocrat." When used appropriately the term is "benevolent autocrat." These eight managerial styles *are not* eight additional kinds of behavior. They are simply the names given to the four basic styles when they are used appropriately or inappropriately. 3-D Theory distinguishes sharply between the behavior and the effectiveness of the behavior.

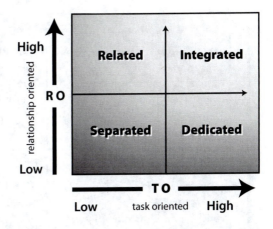

Figure 1 Four Basic Styles of Managerial Behavior

These eight managerial styles can be arranged around the four basic styles by using a third dimension of effectiveness as shown in Figure 2. The four basic styles are in the center, the four less effective equivalents to the left and the four more effective equivalents to the right. The third dimension is effectiveness. One of the contributions of 3-D is that it gives this term a clear, usable definition. Managerial effectiveness is measured by the extent to which a manager achieves the output requirements of his position. Clearly, managers must understand, and then work to achieve, the outputs, not the inputs, of their jobs. The introduction of 3-D knowledge associated with management by objectives ensures that they do. The managers involved play a large part in setting these output requirements. Figure 3 provides some behavioral indicators of the basic styles for a selection of variables. . . .

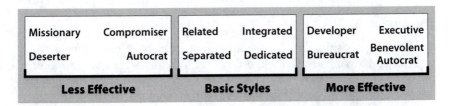

Figure 2 Basic Styles with More Effective and Less Effective Counterparts

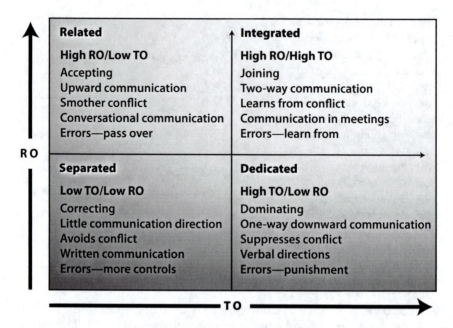

Related	**Integrated**
High RO/Low TO	**High RO/High TO**
Accepting	Joining
Upward communication	Two-way communication
Smother conflict	Learns from conflict
Conversational communication	Communication in meetings
Errors—pass over	Errors—learn from
Separated	**Dedicated**
Low TO/Low RO	**High TO/Low RO**
Correcting	Dominating
Little communication direction	One-way downward communication
Avoids conflict	Suppresses conflict
Written communication	Verbal directions
Errors—more controls	Errors—punishment

Figure 3   Basic Styles Behavioral Indicators, a Sample of Examples

Three Managerial Skills

If effectiveness depends on using the appropriate behavior to match the situation, what skills besides style flexibility will an effective manager have? He must know how to read a situation (situational sensitivity), and he must have the skill to change the situation if it needs to be changed (situational management skill). An effective manager, then, needs not simply an ability to use a high or low task or relationships orientation, or any particular style, but these three: situational sensitivity skill, style flexibility skill, situational management skill. The acquisition of these three skills is usually called experience. Some very young managers have them to a high degree while some much older managers have hardly acquired them in even minimal amounts.

The Situation

Clearly the "situation" is very important for a manager to consider. Just what is it? How can it be broken down into manageable units in order to observe or change it? The 3-D Theory breaks the situation into five elements which contain all aspects of it: organization, technology, superior, coworkers and subordinates.

Organization, short for organization philosophy, is all those influences on behavior that come from outside the manager's work itself and from outside his department or division. Organization philosophy is usually reflected in systems design, in operating procedures, and in who does and does not get promoted. It is an expression of "How we do things around here." A manager in a firm staffed heavily by engineers may have quite different demands on his behavior than one in a firm staffed by accountants. In the same way, the organization philosophy behind a government department is often quite different from the military. These differences are real, and understanding how they operate is important to managerial effectiveness.

The second element, technology, is how the work is done. Some technologies need a dedicated style of management, some separated, and so on. For instance, if the work a manager is doing has the following elements he should use the dedicated, highly task-oriented style:

- Subordinates have to put physical effort into their work
- The manager knows more about the job than the subordinates
- Unscheduled events are likely to occur
- Directions must be given
- The subordinates' performance is easily measurable

Analysis of work along these lines can help managers to decide which style to use. It is particularly helpful for a manager when he is moving into a new position or when he is redesigning the technology of his department.

To take an example, suppose a particular technology demanded dedicated behavior from the manager, yet the manager could only use the separated style. Clearly this situation is a problem. The manager is unable to use the style the technology demands. He has two alternatives, increase his flexibility or change the technology. Only if he does one or both of these will the situation be rectified. The 3-D Theory teaches him how to do each and how to decide which to try first. More important, it teaches him to recognize the situation to begin with. This helps managers really think about what is going on and how they might improve things. . . . Figure 4 shows technology demand indicators for the four basic styles.

Subordinates, coworkers, and superiors round out the elements of the situation. Figure 5 contains descriptors to help identify the demands of the organization, subordinates, coworkers and superiors.

These demands can be expressed in terms of one or more of the basic styles required to satisfy them. Anything that affects a manager's effectiveness can be said to be expressed through one or more of them. They are, in effect, the sum of all the demands of his position. This means that a manager need only to appraise these five elements accurately in order to make a comprehensive situation diagnosis. Further, if he learns how to change each, he can manage the total situation. The manager is not listed as one of the five elements in the situation, yet he is obviously in it. Why is this? The 3-D Theory sees managers as being active rather than passive, as being flexible rather than adaptable. It is the manager's job to control the situation, and by doing so, he must first control himself. Keeping the situation and the manager separate under-

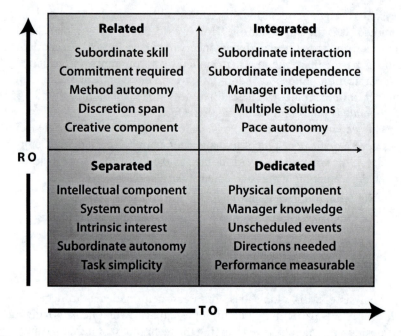

Figure 4   Technology Demand Indicators

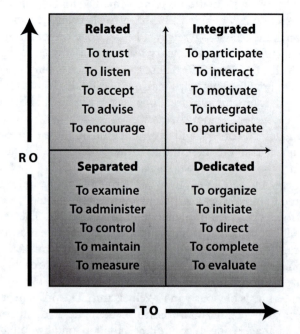

Figure 5   Human Element and Organization Demand Indicators

lines the fact that situations exist for managers to work in them and to increase their managerial effectiveness. Managers obviously need to know the nature of the demands of these five elements, and how they can be appraised. . . .

Theory and research on each of the five situational elements has a unique point of view and has provided valuable insights and opportunities for improving effectiveness. Each has strong adherents and practitioners today, and each is being taught at management development courses and at universities all over the world. While each has strengths and has been found useful, no impartial observer would seriously claim that any one offers solutions for all management problems. They each tend to deal with different aspects of the total situation a manager is concerned with. Thus, the opportunity that managers should seek is to take the best of all these approaches and not focus unduly on any one. Today managers want to focus on the total situation rather than solely on the technology, subordinates, coworkers, superior, or organization. The growing emphasis on situational theory will help managers to do this.

Style Flex

If any one of four styles may lead to higher outputs, then style flexibility is clearly a skill most managers would want to acquire. It is the skill to use a variety of styles to match a variety of situations. Style flexibility needs to be distinguished sharply from style drift; that is, changing one's own style to keep the peace or to lower pressure on oneself; this is clearly not effective behavior. Style resilience though is a positive quality. It is maintaining an appropriate style under stress; it is sharply distinguished from style rigidity, which is maintaining an inappropriate style. The dividing line along some of these is clearly thin. The 3-D Theory makes the distinction clearer by teaching how to recognize all four types of behavior and how to use two of them. Some indicators of style resilience, for instance, are:

- Low ambiguity tolerance (comfortable in structured situations)
- Power sensitive (control oriented)
- Firm belief system (fixed ideas)
- Inner directed (interested in self)

. . .

Situational Management Skill

The professional manager is a manager of total situations. Situational management skill is nothing more than changing the demands of the situational elements so that managerial effectiveness is increased. As this always involves change, a central skill in management is the smooth introduction of change, or put another way, overcoming resistance to change.

A manager's situational sensitivity can help him determine the existing conditions in the social systems he manages. It will also lead him to decide what problems require solutions and what the solution, or ideal state, should be. All this requires intellectual skill. To apply this knowledge to reality he must devise an action plan program to increase acceptance for the change and then see that the change is implemented. The change to be made may be reassigning duties, modifying a work process, changing the role of a staff unity, or perhaps changing an organization structure that has not been touched in years.

Professional managers have no need to passively adapt to situations in which they find themselves. At times, of course, they must, but usually some form of situational management is desirable. Managers should, in fact, seek opportunities to change the demands of one or more situational elements. They should change them only with the view to increasing their own managerial effectiveness. It may be that subordinates' expectations are unrealistic in the face of the job to be done. They may expect to be treated in a related fashion, yet the work system may virtually demand that they be treated in a dedicated fashion. Obviously these are in conflict, and one or both must be changed if managerial effectiveness is to be maximized.

The objective of situational management is to arrange a situation that those in it cooperate of their own accord. It produces motivation to work and effectiveness. Motivation is not best seen as being produced by what a manager does to someone. Instead it is best seen as arising from a matching of all the demands of the situation. Situational management has nothing to do with speeches on the year AD 2000 or sermons on the virtues of accepting change. It is, instead, concerned with a planned, tested, rational, logical approach that considers as its central issue how change can be effectively implemented. . . .

28

Path-Goal Theory
of Leadership

Robert J. House

The path-goal theory of leader effectiveness was developed to reconcile prior findings and anomalies resulting from empirical investigations of the effects of leader task orientation and leader person orientation on subordinate satisfaction and performance. Prior to the introduction of the theory, the leadership literature was dominated by concerns with, and research on, task and person orientation. The most frequently used measures were the Ohio State leader initiating structure and leader consideration scales (Stogdill & Coons, 1957). The findings were mixed. Some studies showed positive relationships between these two variables and leader, work-unit, or subordinate performance and satisfaction. Some studies found either no such relationships, or a positive relationship between only one of the two leader behaviors and dependent variables. Further, several studies showed negative relationships between leader initiating structure and various indicators of subordinate satisfaction (Bass, 1990; Korman, 1966).

The theory was stimulated by Evans' (1970) paper in which the relationships between the Ohio State measures of leader consideration and leader initiating structure and follower perceptions of path-goal relationships (instrumentalities and expectancies) were assessed. Evans found support for the hypothesis that the leader behaviors would be positively related to follower path-goal perceptions in one organization, but not in a second organization. At the time I read the paper by Evans, I was struggling to make sense of a set of findings that indicated that the same leader behaviors had different effects from sample to sample. The findings by Evans suggested to me that the effects of the two leader behaviors are likely contingent on the organizational context in which the leaders and followers worked.

Excerpt reprinted with permission from *Leadership Quarterly*, Vol. 7, Issue 3 (Autumn 1996), pp. 323–352. Copyright © 1996 by Elsevier Science and Technology Journals.

More specifically, at the time I read Evans' 1970 paper, I was thinking about some of my own recently computed findings that showed a positive relationship between leader initiating structure and satisfaction of subordinate white-collar professional employees in research and engineering departments of large manufacturing organizations. Such a relationship was not found in prior studies. Rather, the literature at that time included only reports of negative relationships between leader initiating structure and subordinate satisfaction (Korman, 1966). Thus I was faced with an anomaly for which I had no explanation until I read the paper by Evans. Evans' paper suggested to me that the relationship between structure and subordinate satisfaction and motivation is contingent on the degree to which subordinates needed clarification of the behaviors required of them in order to perform effectively. Once I began thinking in terms of such contingencies and the effect of leaders on subordinate motivation, a number of hypotheses came to mind. I called Evans and asked him how he felt about my publishing a paper entitled, "Path-Goal Theory of Leadership." He replied that his paper did not present a theory, and encouraged me to develop one. Thus the theory was born.

The Scope of the Theory

The scope of path-goal theory reflects the dominant paradigm of the study of leadership through about 1975. Path-goal theory is a dyadic theory of supervision. It concerns relationships between formally appointed superiors and subordinates in their day-to-day functioning. It is concerned with how formally appointed superiors affect the motivation and satisfaction of subordinates. It is a dyadic theory of supervision in that it does not address the effect of leaders on groups or work units, but rather the effects of superiors on subordinates.

Consistent with the dominant leadership paradigm of the time, path-goal theory is primarily a theory of task- and person-oriented supervisory behavior. Also consistent with the dominant paradigm, it does not concern the leadership of entire organizations, emergent-informal leadership, leadership as it affects several levels of managers and subordinates, political behavior of leaders, strategic leadership of organizations, or leadership as it relates to change.

Essential Notions

In the initial version of the theory it was asserted that "the motivational function of the leader consists of increasing personal payoffs to subordinates for work-goal attainment and making the path to these payoffs easier to travel by clarifying it, reducing roadblocks and pitfalls, and increasing the opportunities for personal satisfaction en route" (House, 1971, p. 324). In a later version of path-goal theory House and Mitchell (1974) advanced two general propositions:

> Leader behavior is acceptable and satisfying to subordinates to the extent
> that the subordinates see such behavior as either an immediate source of
> satisfaction or instrumental to future satisfaction. (p. 84)

Leader behavior is motivational, i.e., increases effort, to the extent that (1) such behavior makes satisfaction of subordinates' needs contingent on effective performance and (2) such behavior complements the environment of subordinates by providing coaching, guidance, support and rewards necessary for effective performance. (p. 84)

The essential notion underlying the path-goal theory is that individuals in positions of authority, superiors, will be effective to the extent that they complement the environment in which their subordinates work by providing the necessary cognitive clarifications to ensure that subordinates expect that they can attain work goals and that they will experience intrinsic satisfaction and receive valent rewards as a result of work goal attainment. To the extent that the environment does not provide for clear causal linkages between effort and goal attainment, and between goal attainment and extrinsic rewards, it is the leader's function to arrange such linkages. To the extent that subordinates do not perceive such linkages when they do indeed exist, it is the leader's function to clarify such perceptions. Finally, to the extent that subordinates lack support or resources required to accomplish work goals, it is the leader's function to provide such support and resources. Thus, consistent with Katz and Kahn's (1978) definition of leadership, the role of the leader is to provide the necessary incremental information, support, and resources, over and above those provided by the formal organization or the subordinate's environment, to ensure both subordinate satisfaction and effective performance. According to the theory, leaders are justified in their role by being instrumental to the performance and satisfaction of subordinates.

Independent Variables: Leader Behaviors

The independent variables of the theory are leader behaviors. The seminal paper in which the theory was advanced (House, 1971) made assertions about two general classes of leader behavior: path-goal clarifying behavior and behavior directed toward satisfying subordinate needs. These behaviors were described generally but not defined operationally as part of the theory. However, in the tests reported in that paper, the Ohio State measures of leader initiating structure and consideration (Stogdill, 1965) were used as approximate measures of path-goal clarifying behavior and behavior directed toward satisfying subordinate needs. Subsequently, House and Mitchell (1974) defined four kinds of behavior in more specific terms:

1. *Directive path-goal clarifying leader behavior* is behavior directed toward providing psychological structure for subordinates: letting subordinates know what they are expected to do, scheduling and coordinating work, giving specific guidance, and clarifying policies, rules, and procedures. Directive behavior is one form of path-goal clarifying behavior. Non-authoritarian and non-punitive directive leader behavior was asserted in the seminal path-goal theory paper to reduce subordinate role ambiguity, clarify follower perceptions concerning the degree to which their effort would result in successful perfor-

mance (goal attainment), and the degree to which performance would be extrinsically rewarded with recognition by the leader through pay, advancement, job security and the like.

2. *Supportive leader behavior* is behavior directed toward the satisfaction of subordinates' needs and preferences, such as displaying concern for subordinates' welfare and creating a friendly and psychologically supportive work environment. Supportive leader behavior was asserted to be a source of self-confidence and social satisfaction and a source of stress reduction and alleviation of frustration for subordinates (House & Mitchell, 1974). Supportive leader behavior was asserted to increase performance of subordinates to the extent that it increases the net positive valences associated with goal-directed effort (House, 1971). Thus supportive leader behavior was expected to increase performance when such behavior was *contingent* on goal-directed effort.

3. *Participative leader behavior* is behavior directed toward encouragement of subordinate influence on decision making and work unit operations: consulting with subordinates and taking their opinions and suggestions into account when making decisions. Participative leader behavior was asserted to have four effects: first, to clarify path-goal relationships concerning effort and work-goal attainment and work-goal attainment and extrinsic rewards; second, to increase congruence between subordinate goals and organizational goals, because under participative leadership subordinates would have influence concerning their assigned goals and therefore would select goals they highly value; third, to increase subordinate autonomy and ability to carry out their intentions thus leading to greater effort and performance; fourth, to increase the amount of pressure for organizational performance by increasing subordinate involvement and commitment and by increasing social pressure of peers.

4. *Achievement-oriented behavior* is behavior directed toward encouraging performance excellence: setting challenging goals, seeking improvement, emphasizing excellence in performance, and showing confidence that subordinates will attain high standards of performance. Achievement-oriented leader behavior was asserted to cause subordinates to strive for higher standards of performance and to have more confidence in their ability to meet challenging goals.

Implicit Assumptions and Boundary Conditions

The initial version of the theory made four implicit assumptions. First, it was assumed that individuals choose the level of effort they will devote to their tasks on the basis of the degree to which they expect to receive, or experience, valued outcomes as a result of their effort. Thus, the theory makes a strong self-interest-driven assumption about the nature of subordinates' work motivation. Second, the theory assumed that the propositions of valence-expectancy theory of motivation (Vroom, 1964) were adequate to account for individual work motivation. Valence-expectancy theory, on which path-goal theory of leadership rests, implicitly assumes that individuals cognitively calculate work outcomes contingent on the level of effort they put forth and that they consciously choose the level of effort to be expended which will maximize the attainment of valent outcomes. Thus path-goal theory of leadership made a strong rationality assumption about individual work motivation. In the reformulated theory advanced below, we define the first two assumptions as boundary conditions for the path-goal clarifying propositions of the reformulated theory.

The initial theory further assumed that the experience of role ambiguity is stressful and unpleasant and that reducing ambiguity will lead to subordinate satisfaction and effective performance. Role ambiguity is experiencing lack of clarity about what is expected of one, how one will be evaluated, and criteria for evaluation. Stinson and Johnson (1975) and Yukl (1994a) note that some people like jobs in which duties and responsibilities are not defined in detail and there is ample opportunity to define their own work role. They therefore argue that path-goal theory rests on a questionable assumption that role ambiguity is stressful. What Stinson and Johnson, and Yukl, are talking about has little to do with role ambiguity as defined in path-goal theory. Rather, they are concerned with latitude for description, not ambiguity about evaluation criteria and process. I continue to assume that role ambiguity, as defined in the original path-goal theory, is unpleasant and stressful. Substantial evidence and managerial implications of this assumption were reviewed in House (1970). Original data in support of this assumption were presented in the seminal path-goal theory paper and in two additional papers (House & Rizzo, 1972; Rizzo, House, & Lirtzman, 1970). An abundance of empirical evidence in support of this assumption has been subsequently reviewed by Jackson and Schuler (1985), whose meta-analysis of over 30 studies clearly shows that the experience of role ambiguity is dissatisfying and stressful.

Yukl also notes that the theory assumes that reduction of role ambiguity will result in increased expectancies and that sometimes role clarification may make it clear to individuals that successful task performance and goal attainment is more difficult than the individual initially expected (1994a, p. 290). . . .

The mixed findings with respect to empirical tests of the theory are in part likely due to the strong self-interest and rationality assumptions of the theory. Clearly individuals engage in behaviors that are not self-interest driven. One example of such behavior is organizational citizenship behavior (Organ, 1988). The rationality assumption has been shown to hold only under rather limited conditions. It is likely that the propositions concerning path-goal clarifying behavior hold and are most predictive when it is possible to rather accurately assess the probability of attaining valued outcomes, contingent on high, medium, or low levels of effort. Thus, the propositions concerning path-goal clarifying behavior are most likely invalid when subordinates are under conditions of substantial stress (Fiedler & Garcia, 1987) or uncertainty (Simon, 1987). Such conditions make it impossible to formulate accurate, confident, and rational expectations of rewards contingent on effort expended. It is most likely that propositions concerning path-goal clarifying behavior hold under conditions of certainty or risk, and when subordinates are not highly stressed. Under such conditions probabilities can be assessed rationally. Therefore, these conditions satisfy the underlying rationality assumptions of the theory. These are the boundary conditions of the path-goal clarifying propositions of the theory. . . .

Legacy

Path-goal theory has given us a two-fold legacy. First, the framework for analysis of leadership in terms of substitutes for leadership offered by Kerr and Jermier (1978) grew out of early work conducted by House, Filley and Kerr (1971). In the speculative discussion of that paper we advanced notions of organizational formalization and occupational level as moderators (substitutes) of the effects of leader behaviors. These notions were further elaborated in the original statement of path-goal theory (House, 1971, p. 326). Substitutes theory is an extension of path-goal theory in that it elaborates in substantial detail many of the moderating variables suggested by path-goal theory. The evidence relative to substitutes theory is mixed (Podsakoff, Mackenzie, & Fetter, 1993). Yet it is widely cited in the organizational behavioral literature and represented in most organizational behavior textbooks.

Second, path-goal theory led to the formulation of the 1976 theory of charismatic leadership (House, 1977). In contrast to earlier leadership theory which primarily addressed the effects of leaders on follower cognitions and behaviors, charismatic leadership theory primarily addresses the effects of leaders on followers' valences, emotions, nonconscious motivation, and self-esteem. Charismatic theory has enjoyed considerable support from a number of studies using a wide variety of methods and samples. (See Yukl, 1994b for a review of the empirical evidence and House & Shamir, 1993 for the most recent version of charismatic theory). Charismatic theory grew out of path-goal theory notions as a result of lengthy discussions between David Berlew and me. About two years after the seminal path-goal theory paper was published, I began a rather ambitious consulting project together with David Berlew. Having been a student of David McClelland's about 15 or so years earlier, Dave Berlew had naturally mastered McClelland's theory of personality. According to this theory, the psychological nature of human beings can be explained fairly well by the operation of three motives: achievement, affiliation, and power. These motives are conceived as nonconscious motivators that can be aroused by a select set of stimuli relevant to each motive.

I had read this literature prior to meeting Dave. I was impressed with the achievement motivation training that had been conducted by McClelland and Winter (1971) in India. Dave and I had many long discussions concerning the McClelland theory of personality. Dave believed that effective leaders articulate visions and empower followers by building their sense of self-efficacy.

From my discussions with him, I concluded that effective leaders also arouse motives that are relevant to particular followers' tasks. Thus, I speculated that effective military combat leaders arouse the power motive; effective leaders of social groups arouse the affiliation motive; and effective leaders of salespersons, profit center managers, entrepreneurial firms, and scientists and engineers arouse the achievement motive.

Motive arousal is equivalent to powerfully enhancing valence (attraction) of particular kinds of behaviors and outcomes. As a result of motive arousal, the intrinsic valence of selected behaviors and outcomes is substantially increased. From this line of reasoning, and discussions with Berlew, I developed the theoretical notion that path-goal theory needed to be supplemented with a set of propositions concerning leaders who empower followers and arouse motives to enhance intrinsic valences.

If an image of such a leader is formed in the mind's eye, that image is likely to be strikingly similar to the stereotypic charismatic leader. Leaders who enhance follower self-esteem and arouse follower motives appeared to me to be similar to charismatic leaders as commonly perceived. I learned a great deal from my conversations with Dave Berlew. He was a major influence on my thinking and the stimulus for the development of the 1976 theory. Thus, the 1976 theory of charismatic leader was conceived. It had yet to be nurtured and brought to birth.

Later, while at the University of Toronto, I was visited by an elderly gentleman who was very high up in the government of the People's Republic of China. His position was something like the equivalent to that of the head of the National Science Foundation in the United States. When he met me, he stated, "I've been looking forward to meeting you because there are so few Marxists in the field of organizational behavior." I asked, "Whatever led you to believe that I'm a Marxist?" He said, "The path-goal theory. It is a theory of the people! In your theory it is the needs and the conditions of the people that determine the behavior of the leaders. According to the theory leaders are justified only to the extent to which they are instrumental to follower satisfaction and performance. It is clearly a Marxist theory." I now wonder what he would say about the 1976 theory of charismatic leadership, which is clearly a theory about how leaders change people rather than respond to them.

From this story, one can see how path-goal theory led to charismatic theory. D.O. Hebb, a famous psychologist, stated that "A good theory is one that holds together long enough to get you to a better theory" (1969, p. 21). Clearly, path-goal theory held together long enough (in my mind) to set the stage for charismatic theory. Whether charismatic theory is a better theory is still an open question. However, our recent research, and that of at least 20 other investigators, much to my pleasant surprise, shows rather strong support for the theory (Yukl, 1994b). . . .

References

Bass, B. M. (1990). *Bass and Stogdill's handbook of leadership*, 3rd ed. New York: Free Press.

Evans, G. (1970). The effects of supervisory behavior on the path-goal relationship. *Organizational Behavior and Human Performance*, 5, 277–298.

Fiedler, F. E., & Garcia, J. E. (1987). *New approaches to effective leadership.* New York: Wiley.

Hebb, D. O. (1969). Hebb on hocus-pocus: A conversation with Elizabeth Hall. *Psychology Today,* 3(6), 20–28.

House, R. J. (1970). Role conflict and multiple authority in complex organizations. *California Management Review,* 12(4) (Summer), 53–60.

House, R. J. (1971). A path-goal theory of leader effectiveness. *Administrative Science Quarterly,* 16, 321–338.

House, R. J. (1977). A 1976 theory of charismatic leadership. In J. G. Hunt & L. L. Larson (Eds.), *Leadership: The cutting edge* (pp. 189–207). Carbondale: Southern Illinois University Press.

House, R. J., Filley, A. C., & Kerr, S. (1971). Relation of leader consideration and initiating structure to R and D subordinates' satisfaction. *Administrative Science Quarterly,* 16, 19–30.

House, R. J., & Mitchell, T. R. (1974). Path-goal theory of leadership. *Journal of Contemporary Business,* 3, 81–97.

House, R. J., & Rizzo, J. R. (1972). Role conflict and ambiguity as critical variables in a model of organizational behavior. *Organizational Behavior and Human Performance,* 7, 467–505.

House, R. J., & Shamir, B. (1993). Toward the integration of transformational, charismatic, and visionary theories. In M. Chemers & R. Ayman (Eds.), *Leadership theory and research: Perspectives and directions* (pp. 81–107). Orlando, FL: Academic Press.

Jackson, S. E., & Schuler, R. S. (1985). A meta-analysis and conceptual critique of research on role ambiguity and role conflict in work settings. *Organizational Behavior and Human Decision Processes,* 36, 16–78.

Katz, D., & Kahn, R. L. (1978). *The social psychology of organizations.* New York: Wiley.

Kerr, S., & Jermier, J. M. (1978). Substitutes for leadership: Their meaning and measurement. *Organizational Behavior and Human Performance,* 22, 375–403.

Korman, A. K. (1966). Consideration, initiating structure and organizational criteria—A review. *Personnel Psychology,* 19, 349–361.

McClelland, D. C., & Winter, D. G. (1971). *Motivating economic achievement.* New York: Free Press.

Organ, D.W. (1988). *Organizational citizenship behavior.* Lexington, MA: Lexington Press.

Podsakoff, P. M., Mackenzie, S. B., & Fetter, R. (1993). Substitutes for leadership and management of professionals. *Leadership Quarterly,* 4(1), 1–44.

Rizzo, J. R., House, R. J., & Lirtzman, S. I. (1970). Role conflict and ambiguity in complex organizations. *Administrative Science Quarterly,* June, 150–163.

Simon, H.A. (1987) Making management decisions: The role of intuition and emotion. *Academy of Management Executive,* 57–64.

Stinson, J. E., & Johnson, T. W. (1975). The path-goal theory of leadership: A partial test and suggested refinement. *Academy of Management Journal,* 18, 242–252.

Stogdill, R. M., & Coons, A. E. (1957). *Leader behavior: Its description and measurement.* Columbus: Ohio State University, Bureau of Business Research.

Stogdill, R. M. (1965). *Manual for the job satisfaction and expectations scales.* Columbus: Ohio State University, Bureau of Business Research.

Vroom, V. H. (1964). *Work and motivation.* New York: Wiley.

Yukl, G. (1994a). *Leadership in Organizations,* 3rd ed. Englewood Cliffs, NJ: Prentice Hall.

Yukl, G. (1994b). A retrospective on Robert House's 1976 theory of charismatic leadership and recent revisions. *Leadership Quarterly,* 4, 367–373.

29

Leadership and Decision Making

Victor H. Vroom and Arthur G. Jago

Introduction

Several scholarly disciplines share an interest in the decision-making process. On one hand, there are related fields of operations research and management science, both concerned with how to improve the decisions which are made. Their models of decision making, aimed at providing a rational basis for selecting among alternative courses of action, are termed *normative* or *prescriptive* models. On the other hand, there have been attempts by psychologists, sociologists, and political scientists to understand the decisions and choices that people do make. March and Simon (1958) were among the first to suggest that an understanding of the decision-making process could be central to an understanding of the behavior of organizations—a point of view that was later amplified by Cyert and March (1963) in their behavioral theory of the firm. In this tradition, the goal is understanding rather than improvement, and the models are descriptive rather than normative.

Whether the models are normative or descriptive, the common ingredient is a conception of decision making as an information-processing activity, frequently one which takes place within a single manager. Both sets of models focus on the set of alternative decisions or problem solutions from which the choice is, or should be, made. The normative models are based on the consequences of choices among these alternatives, the descriptive models on the determinants of these choices.

In this article, the authors take a somewhat different, although complementary, view of managerial decision making. They view decision making as

Reprinted with permission of the Decision Sciences Institute from *Decision Sciences*, Vol. 5, 1974, pp. 743–755. Originally titled "Decision Making as a Social Process." Copyright © 1974, Decision Sciences Institute, George State University, Atlanta.

a social process, with the elements of the process presented in terms of events between people, rather than events that occur within a person. When a problem or occasion for decision making occurs within an organization, there are typically several alternative social mechanisms available for determining what solution is chosen or decision reached. These alternatives vary in the person or persons participating in the problem-solving and decision-making process, and in the relative amounts of influence that each has on the final solution or decision reached.

There are both descriptive and normative questions to be answered about the social processes used for decision making in organizations. The normative questions hinge on knowledge concerning the consequences of alternatives for the effective performance of the system. The dimensions on which social processes can vary constitute the independent variables, and criteria of the effectiveness of the decisions constitute dependent variables. Ultimately, such knowledge could provide the foundation for a specification of the social and interpersonal aspects of how decisions *should be* made within organizations.

Similarly, the descriptive questions concern the circumstances under which alternative social processes for decision making *are* used in organizations. The dimensions on which social processes vary become the dependent variables, and characteristics of the manager who controls the process and the nature of the decision itself provide the basis for the specification of independent variables.

Vroom and Yetton (1973) provided a start to an examination of both normative and descriptive questions through an examination of one dimension of decision making—the extent to which a leader encourages the participation of his subordinates in decision making. Participation in decision making was a logical place to start since there is substantial evidence of its importance and of the circumstances surrounding different consequences of it (Lowin, 1968; Vroom, 1970; Wood, 1973).

The purpose of this article is twofold: (1) to provide a brief summary of the objectives, methods, and results of the research pertaining to both normative and descriptive models of decision processes used in organizations (described in detail in Vroom and Yetton, 1973); (2) to describe some recent extensions of the previous work, including an empirical investigation designed to explore facets of decision making not previously studied.

Vroom and Yetton concern themselves primarily with problems or decisions to be made by managers with a formally defined set of subordinates reporting to them. In each problem or decision, the manager must have some area of freedom or discretion in determining the solution adopted, and the solution must affect at least one of the manager's subordinates. Following Maier, Solem, and Maier (1957), they further make a distinction between group problems and individual problems. If the solution adopted has potential effects on all immediate subordinates or some readily identifiable subset of them, it is classified as a group problem. If the solution affects only one of the subordinates, it is called an *individual problem*. This distinction is an important one because it determines the range of decision-making processes available to the manager. Table 1 shows a taxonomy of decision processes for both types of problems. Each process is represented by a symbol (e.g., AI, CI, GII, DI), which provides a convenient method of referring to each process. The letters in the code signify the basic properties of the process (A stands for autocratic; C for consultative; G for group; and D for delegated). The roman numerals that follow the letters constitute variants on that process. Thus, AI represents the first variant on an autocratic process; AII the second variant, and so on.

The processes shown in Table 1 are arranged in columns corresponding to their presumed applicability to either group or individual problems and are arranged within columns in order of increasing opportunity for the subordinate to influence the solution to the problem.

The discrete alternative processes shown in Table 1 can be used both normatively and descriptively. In the former use, they constitute discrete alternatives available to the manager or decision maker, who presumably is motivated to choose that alternative which has the greatest likelihood of producing effective results for his organization. In the latter use, the processes constitute forms of behavior on the part of individuals which require explanation. In the balance of this paper, we will attempt to keep in mind these two uses of the taxonomy and will discuss them separately.

Table 1 Decision-Making Processes

For Individual Problems	For Group Problems
AI You solve the problem or make the decision yourself, using information available to you at that time.	AI You solve the problem or make the decision yourself, using information available to you at that time.
AII You obtain any necessary information from the subordinate, then decide on the solution to the problem yourself. You may or may not tell the subordinate what the problem is, in getting the information from him. The role played by your subordinate in making the decision is clearly one of providing specific information which you request, rather than generating or evaluating alternative solutions.	AII You obtain any necessary information from subordinates, then decide on the solution to the problem yourself. You may or may not tell subordinates what the problem is, in getting the information from them. The role played by your subordinates in making the decision is clearly one of providing specific information which you request, rather than generating or evaluating solutions.
CI You share the problem with the relevant subordinate, getting his ideas and suggestions. Then *you* make the decision. The decision may or may not reflect your subordinate's influence.	CI You share the problem with the relevant subordinates individually, getting their ideas and suggestions without bringing them together as a group. Then *you* make the decision. This decision may or may not reflect your subordinates' influence.
GI You share the problem with one of your subordinates and together you analyze	

(continued)

the problem and arrive at a mutually satisfactory solution in an atmosphere of free and open exchange of information and ideas. You both contribute to the resolution of the problem with the relative contribution of each being dependent on knowledge, rather than formal authority.

DI You delegate the problem to one of your subordinates, providing him with any relevant information that you possess, but giving him responsibility for solving the problem by himself. Any solution which the person reaches will receive your support.

CII You share the problem with your subordinates in a group meeting. In this meeting you obtain their ideas and suggestions. Then *you* make the decision which may or may not reflect your subordinates' influence.

GII You share the problem with your subordinates as a group. Together you generate and evaluate alternatives and attempt to reach agreement (consensus) on a solution. Your role is much like that of chairman; coordinating the discussion, keeping it focused on the problem, and making sure that the critical issues are discussed. You do not try to influence the group to adopt "your" solution and are willing to accept and implement any solution which has the support of the entire group.

A Normative Model of Decision Processes

What would be a rational way of deciding on the form and amount of participation in decision making to be used in different situations? Neither debates over the relative merits of Theory X and Theory Y (McGregor, 1960) nor the apparent truism that leadership depends on the situation are of much help here. The aim in this portion of the research is to develop a framework for matching a leader's behavior, as expressed in the alternatives presented in Table 1, to the demands of his situation. Any framework developed must be consistent with empirical evidence concerning the consequences of participation and be so operational that a trained leader could use it to determine how he should act in a given situation.

The normative model should provide a basis for effective problem solving and decision making by matching the desired decision process with relevant properties of particular problems or decisions to be made. Following Maier (1963), the effectiveness of a decision is thought to be a function of three classes of outcomes, each of which may be expected to be affected by the decision process used. These are:

1. The quality or rationality of the decision.

2. The acceptance or commitment on the part of subordinates to execute the decision effectively.

3. The amount of time required to make the decision.

Space prevents an exposition of the empirical evidence concerning the consequences of participation, but the reader interested in these questions is referred to Vroom (1970) and to Vroom and Yetton (1973, pp. 20–31) for a presentation of that evidence. Since the research program began, a number of normative models for choosing among alternative decision processes have been developed. Each revision is slightly more complex than its predecessor but, in the minds of both developers and users, also is more accurate in forecasting the consequences of alternatives. Most of these models have been concerned solely with group problems (the right-hand column in Table 1). In Vroom and Yetton (1973) virtually all of the discussion of normative models is oriented toward group problems; although, in their discussion of further revisions and extensions of the model, they discuss the possibility of a model for both individual and group problems and present a tentative model which governs choice of decision processes for both types.

Figure 1 shows the latest version of a model intended to deal with both types of problems. Like previous models, it is expressed in the form of a decision tree. Arranged along the top of the tree are a set of eight problem attributes, expressed here in the form of simple yes–no questions that a leader could ask himself about the decision-making situation he is presently confronting.[1] To use the model, one starts at the left-hand side of the tree and works toward the right-hand side, asking oneself the questions pertaining to any box that is encountered. When a terminal node is reached, a number will be found designating the problem type and one or more decision-making processes considered appropriate for that problem. Within each problem type there are both individual and group problems, and the feasible set of methods is different for each.

The decision processes specified for each problem type are not arbitrary. The specification of the feasible set of decision processes for each problem type is governed by a set of 10 rules that serve to protect the quality and acceptance of the decision by eliminating alternatives that risk one or the other of these decision outcomes. These rules, consistent with existing empirical evidence concerning the consequences of participation, are shown in Table 2 in both verbal and set-theoretic form. It should be noted that the rules are of three distinct types. Rules 1 through 4 are designed to protect the quality or rationality of the decision; Rules 5 through 8 are designed to protect the acceptance of or commitment to the decision; and Rules 9 through 10 eliminate the use of group methods for individual problems and vice versa. The decision tree is merely a convenient structure for applying these rules, and, once the problem type has been determined, the rules have all been applied. It can be seen that there are some problem types for which only one method remains in the feasible set, and others for which two, three, four, or even five methods remain in the feasible set.

When more than one method remains in the feasible set, there are a number of ways in which one might choose among them. One method, called Model A and discussed at length by Vroom and Yetton, uses the number of man-hours required by the process of decision making. They argue that if the alternatives within the feasible set are equal in the probability of generating a rational decision which subordinates will accept, a choice among them based on the time requirement of each will be of maximum short-run benefit to the organization.

The basis for estimating the relative requirements in man-hours for the alternatives given for group problems is simple. Vroom and Yetton argue that

A. Is there a quality requirement such that one solution is likely to be more rational than another?
B. Do I have sufficient info to make a high-quality decision?
C. Is the problem structured?
D. Is acceptance of decision by subordinates critical to effective implementation?
E. If I were to make the decision by myself, is it reasonably certain that it would be accepted by my subordinates?
F. Do subordinates share the organizational goals to be attained in solving this problem?
G. Is conflict among subordinates likely in preferred solutions? (This question is irrelevant to individual problems.)
H. Do subordinates have sufficient info to make a high-quality decision?

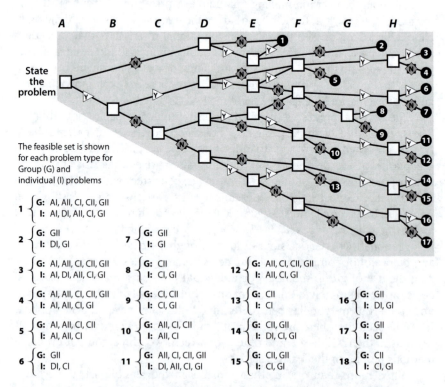

Figure 1   Decision-Process Flow Chart for Both Individual and Group Problems

Table 2   Rules Underlying the Normative Model

1. The Leader Information Rule: $A \cap \bar{B} \rightarrow \overline{AI}$
If the quality of the decision is important and the leader does not possess enough information or expertise to solve the problem by himself, then AI is eliminated from the feasible set.

2. The Subordinate Information Rule: $A \cap \bar{H} \rightarrow \overline{DI}$ (applicable to individual problems only)
If the quality of the decision is important and the subordinate does not possess enough information or expertise to solve the problem himself, then DI is eliminated from the feasible set.

3a. The Goal Congruence Rule: $A \cap \bar{F} \rightarrow \overline{GII, DI}$
If the quality of the decision is important and the subordinates are not likely to pursue organization goals in their efforts to solve this problem, then GII and DI are eliminated from the feasible set.

3b. The Augmented Goal Congruence Rule: $A \cap (\bar{D} \cap E) \cap \bar{F} \rightarrow \overline{GI}$ (applicable to individual problems only)
Under the conditions specified in the previous rule (i.e., quality of decision is important, and the subordinate does not share the organizational goals to be attained in solving the problem) GI may also constitute a risk to the quality of the decision taken in response to an individual problem. Such a risk is a reasonable one to take only if the nature of the problem is such that the acceptance of the subordinate is critical to the effective implementation and prior probability of acceptance of an autocratic solution is low.

4a. The Unstructured Problem Rule (Group): $A \cap \bar{B} \cap \bar{C} \rightarrow \overline{AI, AII, CI}$
In decisions in which the quality of the decision is important, if the leader lacks the necessary information or expertise to solve the problem by himself and if the problem is unstructured, the method of solving the problem should provide for interaction among subordinates. Accordingly, AI, AII, and CI are eliminated from the feasible set.

4b. The Unstructured Problem Rule (Individual): $A \cap \bar{B} \cap \bar{C} \rightarrow \overline{AI, AII}$
In decisions in which the quality of the decision is important, if the leader lacks the necessary information to solve the problem by himself and if the problem is unstructured, the method of solving the problem should permit the subordinate to generate solutions to the problem. Accordingly, AI and AII are eliminated from the feasible set.

5. The Acceptance Rule: $D \cap \bar{E} \rightarrow \overline{AI, AII}$
If the acceptance of the decision by subordinates is critical to effective implementation and if it is not certain that an autocratic decision will be accepted, AI and AII are eliminated from the feasible set.

6. The Conflict Rule: $D \cap \bar{E} \cap G \rightarrow \overline{AI, AII, CI}$ (applicable to group problems only)
If the acceptance of the decision is critical, an autocratic decision is not certain to be accepted, and disagreement among subordinates in methods of attaining the organizational goal is likely, the methods used in solving the problem should enable those in disagreement to resolve their differences with full knowledge of the problem. Accordingly, AI, AII, and CI, which permit no interaction among subordinates, are eliminated from the feasible set.

(continued)

7. The Fairness Rule: $\overline{A} \cap D \cap \overline{E} \rightarrow \overline{AI}, \overline{AII}, \overline{CI}, \overline{CII}$
If the quality of the decision is unimportant, but acceptance of the decision is critical and not certain to result from an autocratic decision, the decision process used should permit the subordinates to interact with one another and negotiate over the fair method of resolving any differences with full responsibility on them for determining what is equitable. Accordingly, AI, AII, CI, and CII are eliminated from the feasible set.

8. The Acceptance Priority Rule: $D \cap \overline{E} \cap F \rightarrow \overline{AI}, \overline{AII}, \overline{CI}, \overline{CII}$
If acceptance is critical, not certain to result from an autocratic decision and if (the) subordinate(s) is (are) motivated to pursue the organizational goals represented in the problem, then methods which provide equal partnership in the decision-making process can provide greater acceptance without risking decision quality. Accordingly, AI, AII, CI, and CII are eliminated from the feasible set.

9. The Group Problem Rule: $Group \rightarrow \overline{GI}, \overline{DI}$
If a problem has approximately equal effects on each of a number of subordinates (i.e., is a group problem) the decision process used should provide them with equal opportunities to influence that decision. Use of a decision process, such as GI or DI, which provides opportunities for only one of the affected subordinates to influence that decision, may in the short run produce feelings of inequity reflected in lessened commitment to the decision on the part of those "left out" of the decision process and, in the long run, be a source of conflict and divisiveness.

10. The Individual Problem Rule: $Individual \rightarrow \overline{CII}, \overline{GII}$
If a problem affects only one subordinate, decision processes which unilaterally introduce other (unaffected) subordinates as equal partners constitute an unnecessary use of time of the unaffected subordinates and can reduce the amount of commitment of the affected subordinate to the decision by reducing the amount of his opportunity to influence the decision. Thus, CII and GII are eliminated from the feasible set.

---

more participative processes require more time. Therefore, the ordering of the methods shown for group problems in terms of man-hours is perfectly correlated with the degree of participation they permit (AI<AII<CICII<GII). However, the extension of the model to cover individual problems complicates this picture, since the decision process which provides greatest opportunity for subordinate influence, DI, is certainly less time consuming than GI, which requires reaching a solution that has the agreement of both superior and subordinate. While the differences in time requirements of the alternatives for individual problems is not nearly so great as the differences in the alternatives for group problems, we have assumed an ordering such that AI<DI<AII<CI<GI. The reader will note that the ordering of alternatives from left to right within the feasible sets for each problem type in Figure 1 reflects this assumption. Thus, for both group and individual problems, the minimum-man-hours solution is assumed to be the alternative furthest to the left within the feasible set.

There are, however, other bases for choice within the feasible set. A manager may wish to choose the most participative alternative that can be used while still producing rational and acceptable solutions to organizational problems. Such a position could be grounded in humanistic considerations, emphasizing the intrinsic value of participation, or on pragmatic considerations, such as the utility of participation in developing informed and responsible behavior (Vroom and Yetton, 1973). A model based on these considerations is termed *Model B.*

The reader should note that both Models A and B are consistent with the rules which generate the feasible set. They merely represent different bases for choice within it. Model A chooses the method within the feasible set which is the most economical method in terms of man-hours. Its choice is always the method furthest to the left in the set shown in Figure 1. Model B chooses the most participative method available within the feasible set, which is that method closest to the bottom of Table 1. Model A seeks to minimize man-hours, subject to quality and acceptance constraints, while Model B seeks to maximize participation, subject to quality and acceptance constraints. Of course, when only one process exists within the feasible set, the choices of Model A and B are identical. Perhaps the best way of illustrating the model is to show how it works in sample situations. Following are a set of actual leadership problems,[2] each based on a retrospective account by a manager who experienced the problem. The reader may wish, after reading each case, to analyze it himself using the model and then to compare his analysis with that of the authors.

Case I.   You are president of a small but growing midwestern bank, with its head office in the state's capital and branches in several nearby market towns. The location and type of business are factors which contribute to the emphasis on traditional . . . and conservative banking practices at all levels.

When you bought the bank five years ago, it was in poor financial shape. Under your leadership, much progress has been made. This progress has been achieved while the economy has moved into a mild recession, and, as a result, your prestige among your bank managers is very high. Your success, which you are inclined to attribute principally to good luck and to a few timely decisions on your part, has, in your judgment, one unfortunate by-product. It has caused your subordinates to look to you for leadership and guidance in decision making beyond what you consider necessary. You have no doubts about the fundamental capabilities of these men but wish that they were not quite so willing to accede to your judgment.

You have recently acquired funds to permit opening a new branch. Your problem is to decide on a suitable location. You believe that there is no "magic formula" by which it is possible to select an optimal site. The choice will be made by a combination of some simple common-sense criteria and "what feels right." You have asked your managers to keep their eyes open for commercial real estate sites that might be suitable. Their knowledge about the communities in which they operate should be extremely useful in making a wise choice.

Their support is important because the success of the new branch will be highly dependent on your managers' willingness to supply staff and technical assistance during its early days. Your bank is small enough for everyone to feel like part of a team, and you feel that this has been and will be critical to the bank's prosperity.

The success of this project will benefit everybody. Directly, they will benefit from the increased base of operations, and, indirectly, they will reap the personal and business advantages of being part of a successful and expanding business.

Analysis:		Synthesis:	
A	(Quality?) = Yes	Problem type	14-Group
B	(Leader's information?) = No	Feasible set	CII, GII
C	(Structured?) = No	Model A behavior	CII
D	(Acceptance?) = Yes	Model B behavior	GII
E	(Prior probability of acceptance?) = Yes		
F	(Goal congruence?) = Yes		
G[3]	(Conflict?) = No		
H[3]	(Subordinate information?) = Yes		

Case II. You are regional manager of an international management consulting company. You have a staff of six consultants reporting to you, each of whom enjoys a considerable amount of autonomy with clients in the field.

Yesterday you received a complaint from one of your major clients to the effect that the consultant whom you assigned to work on the contract with them was not doing his job effectively. They were not very explicit about the nature of the problem, but it was clear that they were dissatisfied and that something would have to be done if you were to restore the client's faith in your company.

The consultant assigned to work on that contract has been with the company for six years. He is a systems analyst and is one of the best in that profession. For the first four or five years his performance was superb, and he was a model for the other more junior consultants. However, recently he has seemed to have a "chip on his shoulder," and his previous identification with the company and its objectives has been replaced with indifference. His negative attitude has been noticed by other consultants, as well as by clients. This is not the first such complaint that you have had from a client this year about his performance. A previous client even reported to you that the consultant reported to work several times obviously suffering from a hangover and that he had been seen around town in the company of "fast" women.

It is important to get to the root of this problem quickly if that client is to be retained. The consultant obviously has the skill necessary to work with the clients effectively. If only he were willing to use it!

Analysis:		Synthesis:	
A	(Quality?) = Yes	Problem type	18-Individual
B	(Leader's information?) = No	Feasible set	CI, GI
C	(Structured?) = No	Model A behavior	CI
D	(Acceptance?) = Yes	Model B behavior	GI

E   (Prior probability of
       acceptance?) = No
F   (Goal congruence?) = No
H^3 (Subordinate information?) = Yes

Case III. You have recently been appointed manager of a new plant which is presently under construction. Your team of five department heads has been selected, and they are now working with you in selecting their own staffs, purchasing equipment, and generally anticipating the problems that are likely to arise when you move into the plant in three months.

Yesterday, you received from the architect a final set of plans for the building, and, for the first time, you examined the parking facilities that are available. There is a large lot across the road from the plant intended primarily for hourly workers and lower-level supervisory personnel. In addition, there are seven spaces immediately adjacent to the administrative offices, intended for visitor and reserved parking. Company policy requires that a minimum of three spaces be made available for visitor parking, leaving you only four spaces to allocate among yourself and your five department heads. There is no way of increasing the total number of such spaces without changing the structure of the building.

Up to now, there have been no obvious status differences among your team, who have worked together very well in the planning phase of the operation. To be sure, there are salary differences, with your administrative, manufacturing, and engineering managers receiving slightly more than the quality control and industrial relations managers. Each has recently been promoted to his new position and expects reserved parking privileges as a consequence of his new status. From past experience, you know that people feel strongly about things which would be indicative of their status. So you and your subordinates have been working together as a team, and you are reluctant to do anything which might jeopardize the team relationship.

Analysis:	Synthesis:	
A (Quality?) = No	Problem type	2-Group
D (Acceptance?) = Yes	Feasible set	GII
E (Prior probability of	Model A behavior	GII
acceptance?) = No	Model B behavior	GII
G^3 (Conflict?) = Yes		

Case IV. You are executive vice president for a small pharmaceutical manufacturer. You have the opportunity to bid on a contract for the Defense Department pertaining to biological warfare. The contract is outside the mainstream of your business; however, it could make economic sense since you do have unused capacity in one of your plants, and the manufacturing processes are not dissimilar.

You have written the document to accompany the bid and now have the problem of determining the dollar value of the quotation which you think will win the job for your company. If the bid is too high, you will undoubt-edly lose to one of your competitors; if it is too low, you would stand to lose money on the program.

There are many factors to be considered in making this decision, includ-ing the cost of the new raw materials and the additional administrative bur-den of relationships with a new client, not to speak of factors which are likely to influence the bids of your competitors, such as how much they *need* this particular contract. You have been busy assembling the necessary data to make this decision but there remain several "unknowns," one of which involves the manager of the plant in which the new products will be manufac-tured. Of all your subordinates, only he is in the position to estimate the costs of adapting the present equipment to their new purpose, and his cooperation and support will be necessary in ensuring that the specifications of the con-tract will be met.

However, in an initial discussion with him when you first learned of the possibility of the contract, he seemed adamantly opposed to the idea. His pre-vious experience has not particularly equipped him with the ability to evalu-ate projects like this one, so you were not overly influenced by his opinions. From the nature of his arguments, you inferred that his opposition was ideo-logical, rather than economic. You recall that he was actively involved in a local "peace organization" and, within the company, was one of the most vocal opponents to the war in Vietnam.

Analysis:		Synthesis:	
A	(Quality?) = Yes	Problem type	8- or 9-Individual
B	(Leader's information?) = No	Feasible set	CI, GI
C	(Structured?) = Yes	Model A behavior	CI
D	(Acceptance?) = Yes	Model B behavior	GI
E	(Prior probability of acceptance?) = No		
F	(Goal congruence?) = No		
H^3	(Subordinate information?) = No		

Toward a Descriptive Model

So far, we have been concerned only with normative or prescriptive ques-tions. But, how do managers really behave? What decision rules underlie their willingness to share their decision-making power with their subordi-nates? In what respects are these decision rules similar to or different from those employed in the normative model?

The manner in which these questions are posed is at variance with much of the conventional treatment of such issues. Frequently, leaders are typed as autocratic or participative or as varying on a continuum between these extremes. In effect, autocratic or participative behavior is assumed to be con-trolled by a personality trait, the amount of which varies from one person to another. The trait concept is a useful one for summarizing differences among people but allows no room for the analysis of intra-individual differences in behavior. Following Lewin's (1951) classic formation $B = f(P,E)$, we assumed that a leader's behavior in a given situation reflects characteristics of that leader, properties of the situation, and the interaction of the two.

Two somewhat different research methods have been used in studying the situational determinants of participative behavior. The first method (Vroom and Yetton, 1973, chapter 4) utilized what we have come to refer to as "recalled problems." Over 500 managers, all of whom were participants in management development programs, provided written descriptions of a group problem which they encountered recently. These descriptions ranged in length from one paragraph to several pages and covered virtually every facet of managerial decision making. Each manager was then asked to indicate which of the methods shown on the right-hand side of Table 1 (AI, AII, CI, CII, GII) he had used in solving the problem. Finally, each manager was asked a set of questions concerning the problem he had selected. These questions corresponded to attributes in the normative model.

Preliminary investigation revealed that managers perceived the five alternatives as varying (in the order shown in Table 1) on a scale of participation, but that the four intervals separating adjacent processes were not seen as equal. On the basis of the application of several scaling methods (Vroom and Yetton, 1973, pp. 65–71), the following values on a scale of participation were assigned to each process: AI = 0; AII = .625; CI = 5.0; CII = 8.125; GII = 10.

Using the managers' judgments of the status of the problems they described on the problem attributes as independent variables and the scale values of their behavior on the problem as a dependent variable, it is possible to use the method of multiple regression to determine the properties of situations (i.e., problems), which are associated with autocratic or participative behavior. It is also possible to insert the managers' judgments concerning their problems into the normative model and to determine the degree of correspondence between managerial and model behavior.

Several investigations have been conducted using this method—all of which have been restricted to group problems and the decision processes corresponding to them. The results are consistent with the view that there are important differences in the processes used for different kinds of problems. Specifically, managers were more likely to exhibit autocratic behavior on structured problems in which they believed that they had enough information, their subordinates lacked information, their subordinates' goals were incongruent with the organizational goals, their subordinates' acceptance of the decision was not critical to its effective implementation, and the prior probability that an autocratic decision would be accepted was high. Thus, many (but not all) of the attributes contained in the normative model had an effect on the decision processes which managers employed, and the directions of these effects are similar to those found in the model. However, it would be a mistake to conclude that the managers' behavior was always identical to that of the model. In approximately two-thirds of the problems, nevertheless, the behavior which the manager reported was within the feasible set of methods prescribed for that problem, and in about 40 percent of the cases it corresponded exactly to the minimum man-hours (Model A) solution.

Several observations help to account for differences between the model and the typical manager in the sample. First, as is apparent from an inspection of Figure 1, the normative model incorporates a substantial number of interactions among attributes, whereas no such interactions appeared in the results of the regression analysis. Second, the magnitude of the effects of two attributes pertaining to the acceptance or commitment of subordinates to decisions was considerably weaker in the descriptive than in the normative model, suggesting that these considerations play less of a role in determining how people behave. This inference was further supported by the fact that rules designed to protect the acceptance of the decision in the normative model were violated far more frequently than rules designed to protect decision quality.

The results of this research were supportive of the concept of intrapersonal variance in leadership style and helped to identify some of the situational factors influencing leaders' choices of decision processes. There were, however, some key methodological weaknesses to this research. Limited variance in and intercorrelations among the problem attributes restricted the extent to which situational effects could be determined with precision. Furthermore, the fact that subjects selected and scored their own problems may have led to confounding of individual differences and situational effects. Finally, since only one problem was obtained from each manager, it was impossible to identify interactions between person and situational variables (i.e., idiosyncratic rules for deciding when and to what extent to encourage participation by subordinates).

The methodological problems inherent in the use of "recalled problems" dictated a search for another method with which to explore the same phenomenon. The technique selected involved the development of a standardized set of administrative problems or cases, each of which depicted a leader faced with some organizational requirement for action or decision making. Managers were asked to assume the role of leader in each situation and to indicate which decision process they would employ.

Several standardized sets of cases were developed, using rewritten accounts of actual managerial problems obtained from the previous method. These sets of cases, or problem sets, were developed in accordance with a multi-factorial experimental design, within which the problem attributes were varied orthogonally. Each case corresponded to a particular combination of problem characteristics, and the entire set of cases permitted the simultaneous variation of each problem attribute. To ensure conformity of a given case or problem with the specifications of a cell in the experimental design, an elaborate procedure for testing cases was developed (Vroom and Yetton, 1973, pp. 97–101), involving coding of problems by expert judges and practicing managers.

This method showed promise of permitting the replication of the results using recalled problems with a method that avoided spurious effects stemming from the influence of uncontrolled variables on problem selection. Since the use of a "repeated measures design" permitted a complete experiment to be performed on each subject, the main effects of each of the problem attributes on the decision processes used by the subject could be identified. By comparing the results for different subjects, the similarities and differences in these main effects and the relative importance of individual differences and of situational variables could be ascertained.

Vroom and Yetton worked exclusively with group problems and with an experimental design which called for 30 cases. The results, obtained from investigations of eight distinct populations comprising over 500 managers, strongly support the major findings from the use of recalled problems, both in terms of the amount of correspondence with the normative model and the specific attributes of situations which tended to induce autocratic and participative decision processes. Moreover, the nature of the methods used made it possible also to obtain precise estimates of the amount of variance attributable to situational factors and individual differences. Only 10 percent of the total variance could be accounted for in terms of general tendencies to be autocratic or participative (as expressed in differences among individuals in mean behavior on all 30 problems), while about 30 percent was attributable to situational effects (as expressed in differences in mean behavior among situations).

What about the remaining 60 percent of the variance? Undoubtedly, some of it can be attributed to errors of measurement, but Vroom and Yetton were able to show that a significant portion of that variance can be explained in terms of another form of individual differences (i.e., differences among managers in ways of "tailoring" their approach to the situation). Theoretically, these can be thought of as differences in decision rules that they employ concerning when to encourage participation.

Notes

[1] For a detailed definition of these attributes and of criteria to be used in making Yes-No judgments, see Vroom and Yetton (1973, pp. 21–31).

[2] For additional problems and their analysis, see Vroom and Yetton (1973, pp. 40–44).

[3] The question pertaining to this attribute is asked in the decision tree but is irrelevant to the prescribed behavior.

References

Cyert, R. M., and J. G. March. *A Behavioral Theory of the Firm.* Englewood Cliffs, NJ: Prentice-Hall, 1963.

Lewin, K. "Frontiers in Group Dynamics." *Field Theory in Social Science,* ed. D. Cartwright. New York: Harper & Row, 1951, pp. 188–237.

Lowin, A. "Participative Decision Making: A Model, Literature Critique, and Prescriptions for Research." *Organizational Behavior and Human Performance* 3 (1968), pp. 68–106.

Maier, N. R. F., A. R. Solem, and A. A. Maier. *Supervisory and Executive Development: A Manual for Role Playing.* New York: John Wiley & Sons, 1957.

Maier, N. R. F. "Problem-Solving Discussions and Conferences." *Leadership Methods and Skills.* New York: McGraw-Hill, 1963.

March, J. G., and H. A. Simon. *Organizations.* New York: John Wiley & Sons, 1958.

McGregor, D. *The Human Side of Enterprise.* New York: McGraw-Hill, 1960.

Overall, J. E., and D. K. Spiegel. "Concerning Least Squares Analysis of Experimental Data." *Psychological Bulletin* 72 (1969), pp. 311–22.

Vroom, V. H. "Industrial Social Psychology." *Handbook of Social Psychology,* ed. L. G. Lindzey and E. Aronson. Reading, MA: Addison-Wesley, 1970, chap. 5, pp. 196–268.

Vroom, V. H., and P. W. Yetton. *Leadership and Decision-Making.* Pittsburgh: University of Pittsburgh Press, 1973.

Wood, M. T. "Power Relationships and Group Decision Making in Organizations." *Psychological Bulletin* 79 (1973), pp. 280–93.

30

Motivation, Leadership, and Organization
Do American Theories Apply Abroad?

Geert Hofstede

A well-known experiment used in organizational behavior courses involves showing the class an ambiguous picture—one that can be interpreted in two different ways. One such picture represents either an attractive young girl or an ugly old woman, depending on the way you look at it. Some of my colleagues and I use the experiment, which demonstrates how different people in the same situation may perceive quite different things. We start by asking half of the class to close their eyes while we show the other half a slightly altered version of the picture—one in which only the young girl can be seen—for only five seconds. Then we ask those who just saw the young girl's picture to close their eyes while we give the other half of the class a five-second look at a version in which only the old woman can be seen. After this preparation we show the ambiguous picture to everyone at the same time.

The results are amazing—most of those "conditioned" by seeing the young girl first see only the young girl in the ambiguous picture, and those "conditioned" by seeing the old woman tend to see only the old woman. We then ask one of those who perceive the old woman to explain to one of those who perceive the young girl what he or she sees, and vice versa, until everyone finally sees both images in the picture. Each group usually finds it very difficult to get its views across to the other one and sometimes there's considerable irritation at how "stupid" the other group is.

Reprinted with permission of Geert Hofstede from *Organizational Dynamics*, Vol. 9, Issue 1 (Summer 1980), pp. 42–63.

Cultural Conditioning

I use this experiment to introduce a discussion on cultural conditioning. Basically, it shows that in five seconds I can condition half a class to see something different from what the other half sees. If this is so in the simple classroom situation, how much stronger should differences in perception of the same reality be between people who have been conditioned by different education and life experience—not for five seconds, but for twenty, thirty, or forty years?

I define culture as the collective mental programming of the people in an environment. Culture is not a characteristic of individuals; it encompasses a number of people who were conditioned by the same education and life experience. When we speak of the culture of a group, a tribe, a geographical region, a national minority, or a nation, culture refers to the collective mental programming that these people have in common; the programming that is different from that of other groups, tribes, regions, minorities or majorities, or nations.

Culture, in this sense of collective mental programming, is often difficult to change; if it changes at all, it does so slowly. This is so not only because it exists in the minds of the people but, if it is shared by a number of people, because it has become crystallized in the institutions these people have built together: their family structures, educational structures, religious organizations, associations, forms of government, work organizations, law, literature, settlement patterns, buildings and even, as I hope to show, scientific theories. All of these reflect common beliefs that derive from the common culture.

Although we are all conditioned by cultural influences at many different levels—family, social, group, geographical region, professional environment—this article deals specifically with the influence of our national environment: that is, our country. Most countries' inhabitants share a national character that's more clearly apparent to foreigners than to the nationals themselves; it represents the cultural mental programming that the nationals tend to have in common.

National Culture in Four Dimensions

The concept of national culture or national character has suffered from vagueness. There has been little consensus on what represents the national culture of, for example, Americans, Mexicans, French, or Japanese. We seem to lack even the terminology to describe it. Over a period of six years, I have been involved in a large research project on national cultures. For a set of 40 independent nations, I have tried to determine empirically the main criteria by which their national cultures differed. I found four such criteria, which I label dimensions; these are Power Distance, Uncertainty Avoidance, Individualism-Collectivism, and Masculinity-Femininity. To understand the dimensions of national culture, we can compare it with the dimensions of personality we use when we describe individuals' behavior. In recruiting, an organization often tries to get an impression of a candidate's dimensions of personality, such as intelligence (high-low); energy level (active-passive); and emotional stability (stable-unstable). These distinctions can be refined through the use of certain tests, but it's essential to have a set of criteria whereby the characteristics of individuals can be meaningfully described. The dimensions of national culture I use represent a corresponding set of criteria for describing national cultures.

The Research Data

The four dimensions of national culture were found through a combination of theoretical reasoning and massive statistical analysis, in what is most likely the largest survey material ever obtained with a single questionnaire. This survey material was collected between 1967 and 1973 among employees of subsidiaries of one large U.S.-based multinational corporation (MNC) in 40 countries around the globe. The total data bank contains more than 116,000 questionnaires collected from virtually everyone in the corporation, from unskilled workers to research Ph.D.s and top managers. Moreover, data were collected twice—first during a period from 1967 to 1969 and a repeat survey during 1971 to 1973. Out of a total of about 150 different survey questions (of the precoded answer type), about 60 deal with the respondents' beliefs and values; these were analyzed for the present study. The questionnaire was administered in the language of each country; a total of 20 language versions had to be made. On the basis of these data, each of the 40 countries could be given an index score for each of the four dimensions.

I was wondering at first whether differences found among employees of one single corporation could be used to detect truly national culture differences. I also wondered what effect the translation of the questionnaire could have had. With this in mind, I administered a number of the same questions in 1971–1973 to an international group of about 400 managers from different public and private organizations following management development courses in Lausanne, Switzerland. This time, all received the questionnaire in English. In spite of the different mix of respondents and the different language used, I found largely the same differences between countries in the manager group that I found among the multinational personnel. Then I started looking for other studies, comparing aspects of national character across a number of countries on the basis of surveys using other questions and other respondents (such as students) or on representative public opinion polls. I found 13 such studies; these compared between 5 and 19 countries at a time. The results of these studies showed a statistically significant similarity (correlation) with one or more of the four dimensions. Finally, I also looked for national indicators (such as per capita national income, inequality of income distribution, and government spending on development aid) that could logically be supposed to be related to one or more of the dimensions. I found 31 such indicators—of which the values were available for between 5 and 40 countries—that were correlated in a statistically significant

(continued)

way with at least one of the dimensions. All these additional studies (for which the data were collected by other people, not by me) helped make the picture of the four dimensions more complete. Interestingly, very few of these studies had even been related to each other before, but the four dimensions provide a framework that shows how they can be fit together like pieces of a huge puzzle. The fact that data obtained within a single MNC have the power to uncover the secrets of entire national cultures can be understood when it's known that the respondents form well-matched samples from their nations: They are employed by the same firm (or its subsidiary); their jobs are similar (I consistently compared the same occupations across the different countries); and their age categories and sex composition were similar—only their nationalities differed. Therefore, if we look at the differences in survey answers between multinational employees in countries A, B, C, and so on, the general factor that can account for the differences in the answers is national culture.

Characterizing a national culture does not, of course, mean that every person in the nation has all the characteristics assigned to that culture. Therefore, in describing national cultures we refer to the common elements within each nation—the national norm—but we are not describing individuals. This should be kept in mind when interpreting the four dimensions explained in the following paragraphs.

Power Distance

The first dimension of national culture is called *Power Distance*. It indicates the extent to which a society accepts the fact that power in institutions and organizations is distributed unequally. It's reflected in the values of the less powerful members of society as well as in those of the more powerful ones. A fuller picture of the difference between small Power Distance and large Power Distance societies is shown in Table 1. Of course, this shows only the extremes; most countries fall somewhere in between.

Table 1 The Power Distance Dimension

Small Power Distance	Large Power Distance
Inequality in society should be minimized.	There should be an order of inequality in this world in which everybody has a rightful place; high and low are protected by this order.
All people should be interdependent.	A few people should be independent; most should be dependent.
Hierarchy means an inequality of roles, established for convenience.	Hierarchy means existential inequality.

Small Power Distance	Large Power Distance
Superiors consider subordinates to be "people like me."	Superiors consider subordinates to be a different kind of people.
Subordinates consider superiors to be "people like me."	Subordinates consider superiors as a different kind of people.
Superiors are accessible.	Superiors are inaccessible.
The use of power should be legitimate and is subject to the judgment as to whether it is good or evil.	Power is a basic fact of society that antedates good or evil. Its legitimacy is irrelevant.
All should have equal rights.	Power-holders are entitled to privileges.
Those in power should try to look less powerful than they are.	Those in power should try to look as powerful as possible.
The system is to blame.	The underdog is to blame.
The way to change a social system is to redistribute power.	The way to change a social system is to dethrone those in power.
People at various power levels feel less threatened and more prepared to trust people.	Other people are a potential threat to one's power and can rarely be trusted.
Latent harmony exists between the powerful and the powerless.	Latent conflict exists between the powerful and the powerless.
Cooperation among the powerless can be based on solidarity.	Cooperation among the powerless is difficult to attain because of their low-faith-in-people norm.

Uncertainty Avoidance

The second dimension, *Uncertainty Avoidance,* indicates the extent to which a society feels threatened by uncertain and ambiguous situations and tries to avoid these situations by providing greater career stability, establishing more formal rules, not tolerating deviant ideas and behaviors, and believing in absolute truths and the attainment of expertise. Nevertheless, societies in which uncertainty avoidance is strong are also characterized by a higher level of anxiety and aggressiveness that creates, among other things, a strong inner urge in people to work hard. (See Table 2.)

Individualism–Collectivism

The third dimension encompasses *Individualism* and its opposite, *Collectivism.* Individualism implies a loosely knit social framework in which people are supposed to take care of themselves and of their immediate families only, while collectivism is characterized by a tight social framework in which people distinguish between in-groups and out-groups; they expect their in-group (relatives, clan, organizations) to look after them, and in exchange for that they feel they owe absolute loyalty to it. A fuller picture of this dimension is presented in Table 3.

Table 2   The Uncertainty Avoidance Dimension

Weak Uncertainty Avoidance	Strong Uncertainty Avoidance
The uncertainty inherent in life is more easily accepted and each day is taken as it comes.	The uncertainty inherent in life is felt as a continuous threat that must be fought.
Ease and lower stress are experienced.	Higher anxiety and stress are experienced.
Time is free.	Time is money.
Hard work, as such, is not a virtue.	There is an inner urge to work hard.
Aggressive behavior is frowned upon.	Aggressive behavior of self and others is accepted.
Less showing of emotions is preferred.	More showing of emotions is preferred.
Conflict and competition can be contained on the level of fair play and used constructively.	Conflict and competition can unleash aggression and should therefore be avoided.
More acceptance of dissent is entailed.	A strong need for consensus is involved.
Deviation is not considered threatening; greater tolerance is shown.	Deviant persons and ideas are dangerous; intolerance holds sway.
The ambiance is one of less nationalism.	Nationalism is pervasive.
More positive feelings toward younger people are seen.	Younger people are suspect.
There is more willingness to take risks in life.	There is great concern with security in life.
The accent is on relativism, empiricism.	The search is for ultimate, absolute truths and values.
There should be as few rules as possible.	There is a need for written rules and regulations.
If rules cannot be kept, we should change them.	If rules cannot be kept, we are sinners and should repent.
Belief is placed in generalists and common sense.	Belief is placed in experts and their knowledge.
The authorities are there to serve the citizens.	Ordinary citizens are incompetent compared with the authorities.

Masculinity

The fourth dimension is called *Masculinity* even though, in concept, it encompasses its opposite pole, *Femininity*. Measurements in terms of this dimension express the extent to which the dominant values in society are "masculine"—that is, assertiveness, the acquisition of money and things, and *not* caring for others, the quality of life, or people. These values were labeled "masculine" because, *within* nearly all societies, men scored higher in terms of the values' positive sense than of their negative sense (in terms of assertive-

Table 3   The Individualism Dimension

Collectivist	Individualist
In society, people are born into extended families or clans who protect them in exchange for loyalty.	In society, everybody is supposed to take care of himself/herself and his/her immediate family.
"We" consciousness holds sway.	"I" consciousness holds sway.
Identity is based in the social system.	Identity is based in the individual.
There is emotional dependence of individual on organizations and institutions.	There is emotional independence of individual from organizations or institutions.
The involvement with organizations is moral.	The involvement with organizations is calculative.
The emphasis is on belonging to organizations; membership is the ideal.	The emphasis is on individual initiative and achievement; leadership is the ideal.
Private life is invaded by organizations and clans to which one belongs; opinions are predetermined.	Everybody has a right to a private life and opinion.
Expertise, order, duty, and security are provided by organization or clan.	Autonomy, variety, pleasure, and individual financial security are sought in the system.
Friendships are predetermined by stable social relationships, but there is need for prestige within these relationships.	The need is for specific friendships.
Belief is placed in group decisions.	Belief is placed in individual decisions.
Value standards differ for in-groups and out-groups (particularism).	Value standards should apply to all (universalism).

ness, for example, rather than its lack)—even though the society as a whole might veer toward the "feminine" pole. Interestingly, the more an entire society scores to the masculine side, the wider the gap between its "men's" and "women's" values (see Table 4).

A Set of Cultural Maps of the World

Research data were obtained by comparing the beliefs and values of employees within the subsidiaries of one large multinational corporation in 40 countries around the world. These countries represent the wealthy countries of the West and the larger, more prosperous of the Third World countries. The Socialist block countries are missing, but data are available for Yugoslavia (where the corporation is represented by a local, self-managed company under Yugoslavian law). It was possible, on the basis of mean answers of employees on a number of key questions, to assign an index value to each country on each dimension. As described in the box on pp. 339–340,

Table 4   The Masculinity Dimension

Feminine	Masculine
Men needn't be assertive, but can also assume nurturing roles.	Men should be assertive. Women should be nurturing.
Sex roles in society are more fluid.	Sex roles in society are clearly differentiated.
There should be equality between the sexes.	Men should dominate in society.
Quality of life is important.	Performance is what counts.
You work in order to live.	You live in order to work.
People and environment are important.	Money and things are important.
Interdependence is the ideal.	Independence is the ideal.
Service provides the motivation.	Ambition provides the drive.
One sympathizes with the unfortunate.	One admires the successful achiever.
Small and slow are beautiful.	Big and fast are beautiful.
Unisex and androgyny are ideal.	Ostentatious manliness ("machismo") is appreciated.

these index values appear to be related in a statistically significant way to a vast amount of other data about these countries, including both research results from other samples and national indicator figures.

Because of the difficulty of representing four dimensions in a single diagram, the position of the countries on the dimensions is shown in Figures 1, 2, and 3 for two dimensions at a time. The vertical and horizontal axes and the circles around clusters of countries have been drawn subjectively, in order to show the degree of proximity of geographically or historically related countries. The three diagrams thus represent a composite set of cultural maps of the world.

Of the three "maps," those in Figure 1 (Power Distance × Uncertainty Avoidance) and Figure 3 (Masculinity × Uncertainty Avoidance) show a scattering of countries in all corners—that is, all combinations of index values occur. Figure 2 (Power Distance × Individualism), however, shows one empty corner: The combination of Small Power Distance and Collectivism does not occur. In fact, there is a tendency for Large Power Distance to be associated with Collectivism and for Small Power Distance with Individualism. However, there is a third factor that should be taken into account here: national wealth. Both Small Power Distance and Individualism go together with greater national wealth (per capita gross national product). The relationship between Individualism and Wealth is quite strong, as Figure 2 shows. In the upper part (Collectivist) we find only the poorer countries, with Japan as a borderline exception. In the lower part (Individualism), we find only the wealthier countries. If we look at the poorer and the wealthier countries separately, there is no longer any relationship between Power Distance and Individualism.

The Cultural Relativity of Management Theories

Of particular interest in the context of this discussion is the relative position of the United States on the four dimensions. Here is how the United States rates:

- On *Power Distance* at rank 15 out of the 40 countries (measured from below), it is below average but it is not as low as a number of other wealthy countries.
- On *Uncertainty Avoidance* at rank 9 out of 40, it is well below average.
- On *Individualism* at rank 40 out of 40, the United States is the single most individualist country of the entire set (followed closely by Australia and Great Britain).
- On *Masculinity* at rank 28 out of 40, it is well above average.

For about 60 years, the United States has been the world's largest producer and exporter of management theories covering such key areas as motivation, leadership, and organization. Before that, the centers of theorizing about what we now call "management" lay in the Old World. We can trace the history of management thought as far back as we want—at least to parts of the Old Testament of the Bible, and to ancient Greece (Plato's *The Laws* and *The Republic*, 350 B.C.). Sixteenth-century European "management" theorists include Niccoló Machiavelli (Italy) and Thomas More (Great Britain); early twentieth-century theorists include Max Weber (Germany) and Henri Fayol (France).

Today we are all culturally conditioned. We see the world in the way we have learned to see it. Only to a limited extent can we, in our thinking, step out of the boundaries imposed by our cultural conditioning. This applies to the author of a theory as much as it does to the ordinary citizen: Theories

The 40 Countries
(Showing Abbreviations used in Figures 1, 2, and 3.)

ARG	Argentina	HOK	Hong Kong	PHI	Philippines
AUL	Australia	IND	India	POR	Portugal
AUT	Austria	IRA	Iran	SAF	South Africa
BEL	Belgium	IRE	Ireland	SIN	Singapore
BRA	Brazil	ISR	Israel	SPA	Spain
CAN	Canada	ITA	Italy	SWE	Sweden
CHL	Chile	JAP	Japan	SWI	Switzerland
COL	Colombia	MEX	Mexico	TAI	Taiwan
DEN	Denmark	NET	Netherlands	THA	Thailand
FIN	Finland	NOR	Norway	TUR	Turkey
FRA	France	NZL	New Zealand	USA	United States
GBR	Great Britain	PAK	Pakistan	VEN	Venezuela
GER	Germany (West)	PER	Peru	YUG	Yugoslavia
GRE	Greece				

reflect the cultural environment in which they were written. If this is true, Italian, British, German, and French theories reflect the culture of Italy, Britain, Germany, and France of their day, and American theories reflect the culture of the United States of its day. Since most present-day theorists are middle-class intellectuals, their theories reflect a national intellectual middle-class culture background.

Now we ask the question: To what extent do theories developed in one country and reflecting the cultural boundaries of that country apply to other countries? Do American management theories apply in Japan? In India? No management theorist, to my knowledge, has ever explicitly addressed himself or herself to this issue. Most probably assume that their theories are universally valid. The availability of a conceptual framework built on four dimensions of national culture, in conjunction with the cultural maps of the world, makes it possible to see more clearly where and to what extent theories developed in one country are likely to apply elsewhere. In the remaining sections of this article I shall look from this viewpoint at most popular American theories of management in the areas of motivation, leadership, and organization.

Motivation

Why do people behave as they do? There is a great variety of theories of human motivation. According to Sigmund Freud, we are impelled to act by unconscious forces within us, which he called our id. Our conscious conception of ourselves—our ego—tries to control these forces, and an equally unconscious internal pilot—our superego—criticizes the thoughts and acts of our ego and causes feelings of guilt and anxiety when the ego seems to be giving in to the id. The superego is the product of early socialization, mainly learned from our parents when we were young children.

Freud's work has been extremely influential in psychology, but he is rarely quoted in the context of management theories. The latter almost exclusively refer to motivation theories developed later in the United States, particularly those of David McClelland, Abraham Maslow, Frederick Herzberg, and Victor Vroom. According to McClelland, we perform because we have a need to achieve (the achievement motive). More recently, McClelland has also paid a lot of attention to the power motive. Maslow has postulated a hierarchy of human needs, from more "basic" to "higher": most basic are physiological needs, followed by security, social needs, esteem needs and, finally, a need for "self-actualization." The latter incorporates McClelland's theory of achievement, but is defined in broader terms. Maslow's theory of the hierarchy of needs postulates that a higher need will become active only if the lower needs are sufficiently satisfied. Our acting is basically a rational activity by which we expect to fulfill successive levels of needs. Herzberg's two-factor theory of motivation distinguishes between hygienic factors (largely corresponding to Maslow's lower needs—physiological, security, social) and motivators (Maslow's higher needs—esteem, self-actualization);

the hygienic factors have only the potential to motivate negatively (demotivate—they are necessary but not sufficient conditions), while only the motivators have the potential to motivate positively. Vroom has formalized the role of "expectancy" in motivation; he opposes "expectancy" theories and

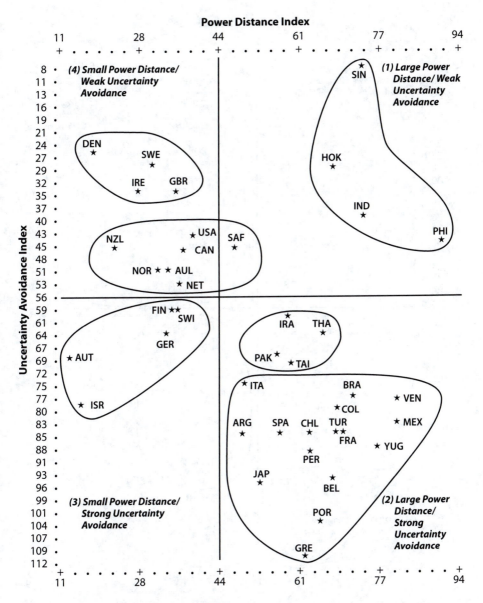

Figure 1   **The Position of the 40 Countries on the Power Distance and Uncertainty Avoidance Scales**

"drive" theories. The former see people as being *pulled* by the expectancy of some kind of result from their acts, mostly consciously. The latter (in accordance with Freud's theories) see people as *pushed* by inside forces—often unconscious ones.

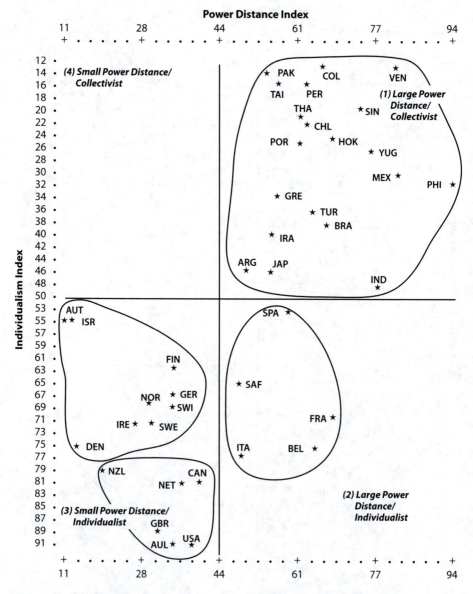

Figure 2   The Position of the 40 Countries on the Power Distance and Individualism Scales

Let us now look at these theories through culture-conscious glasses. Why has Freudian thinking never become popular in U.S. management theory, as has the thinking of McClelland, Maslow, Herzberg, and Vroom? To what extent do these theories reflect different cultural patterns? Freud was part of an Austrian middle-class culture at the turn of the century. If we compare present-day Austria and the United States on our cultural maps, we find the following:

- Austria scores considerably lower on Power Distance.
- Austria scores considerably higher on Uncertainty Avoidance.
- Austria scores considerably lower on Individualism.
- Austria scores considerably higher on Masculinity.

We do not know to what extent Austrian culture has changed since Freud's time, but evidence suggests that cultural patterns change very slowly. It is, therefore, not likely to have been much different from today's culture. The most striking thing about present-day Austrian culture is that it combines a fairly high Uncertainty Avoidance with a very low Power Distance (see Figure 1). Somehow the combination of high Uncertainty Avoidance with high Power Distance is more comfortable (we find this in Japan and in all Latin and Mediterranean countries—see Figure 1). Having a powerful superior whom we can both praise and blame is one way of satisfying a strong need for avoiding uncertainty. The Austrian culture, however (together with the German, Swiss, Israeli, and Finnish cultures), cannot rely on an external boss to absorb its uncertainty. Thus Freud's superego acts naturally as an inner uncertainty-absorbing device, an internalized boss. For strong Uncertainty Avoidance countries like Austria, working hard is caused by an inner urge—it is a way of relieving stress (see Table 2). The Austrian superego is reinforced by the country's relatively low level of Individualism (see Figure 2). The inner feeling of obligation to society plays a much stronger role in Austria than in the United States. The ultrahigh Individualism of the United States leads to a need to explain every act in terms of self-interest, and expectancy theories of motivation do provide this explanation—we always do something *because* we expect to obtain the satisfaction of some need.

The comparison between Austrian and U.S. culture has so far justified the popularity of expectancy theories of motivation in the United States. The combination in the United States of weak Uncertainty Avoidance and relatively high Masculinity can tell us more about why the achievement motive has become so popular in that country. David McClelland, in his book *The Achieving Society*, sets up scores reflecting how strong achievement need is in many countries by analyzing the content of children's stories used in those countries to teach the young to read. It now appears that there is a strong relationship between McClelland's need for achievement country scores and the combination of weak Uncertainty Avoidance and strong Masculinity charted in Figure 3. (McClelland's data were collected for two historic years—1925 and 1950—but only his 1925 data relate to the cultural map in

Figure 3. It is likely that the 1925 stories were more traditional, reflecting deep underlying cultural currents; the choice of stories in 1950 in most countries may have been affected by modernization currents in education, often imported from abroad.)

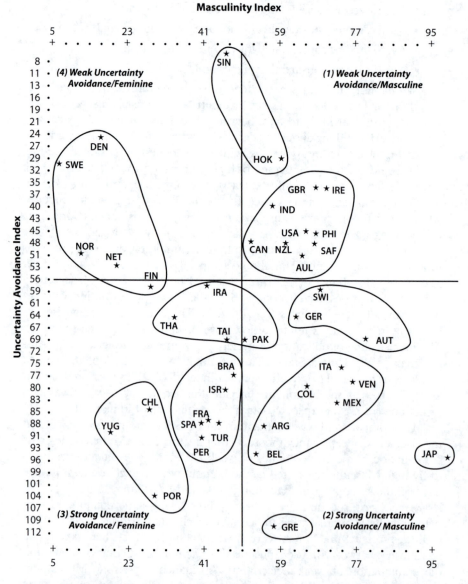

Figure 3   The Position of the 40 Countries on the Uncertainty Avoidance and Masculinity Scales

Countries in the upper right-hand corner of Figure 3 received mostly high scores on achievement need in McClelland's book; countries in the lower left-hand corner of Figure 3 received low scores. This leads us to the conclusion that the concept of the achievement motive presupposes two cultural choices—a willingness to accept risk (equivalent to weak Uncertainty Avoidance; see Table 2) and a concern with performance (equivalent to strong Masculinity; see Table 4). This combination is found exclusively in countries in the Anglo-American group and in some of their former colonies (Figure 3). One striking thing about the concept of achievement is that the word itself is hardly translatable into any language other than English; for this reason, the word could not be used in the questionnaire of the multinational corporation used in my research. The English-speaking countries all appear in the upper right-hand corner of Figure 3.

If this is so, there is reason to reconsider Maslow's hierarchy of human needs in the light of the map shown in Figure 3. Quadrant 1 (upper right-hand corner) in Figure 3 stands for *achievement motivation, as* we have seen (performance plus risk). Quadrant 2 distinguishes itself from quadrant 1 by strong Uncertainty Avoidance, which means *security motivation* (performance plus security). The countries on the feminine side of Figure 3 distinguish themselves by focusing on quality of life rather than on performance and on relationships between people rather than on money and things (see Table 4). This means *social motivation:* quality of life plus security in quadrant 3, and quality of life plus risk in quadrant 4. Now, Maslow's hierarchy puts self-actualization (achievement) plus esteem above social needs above security needs. This, however, is not the description of a universal human motivation process—it is the description of a value system, the value system of the U.S. middle class to which the author belonged. I suggest that if we want to continue thinking in terms of a hierarchy for countries in the lower right-hand corner of Figure 3 (quadrant 2), security needs should rank at the top; for countries in the upper left-hand corner (quadrant 4), social needs should rank at the top, and for countries in the lower left-hand corner (quadrant 3) *both* security and social needs should rank at the top.

One practical outcome of presenting motivation theories is the movement toward humanization of work—an attempt to make work more intrinsically interesting to the workers. There are two main currents in humanization of work—one, developed in the United States and called *job enrichment,* aims at restructuring individual jobs. A chief proponent of job enrichment is Frederick Herzberg. The other current, developed in Europe and applied mainly in Sweden and Norway, aims at restructuring work into group work—forming, for example, such semiautonomous teams as those seen in the experiments at Volvo. Why the difference in approaches? What is seen as a "human" job depends on a society's prevailing model of humankind. In a more masculine society like the United States, humanization takes the form of masculinization, allowing individual performance. In the more feminine societies of Sweden and Norway, humanization takes the form of feminization—it is a means toward more wholesome interpersonal relationships in its de-emphasis of interindividual competition.

Leadership

One of the oldest theorists of leadership in world literature is Machiavelli (1468–1527). He described certain effective techniques for manipulation and remaining in power (including deceit, bribery, and murder) that gave him a bad reputation in later centuries. Machiavelli wrote in the context of the Italy of his day, and what he described is clearly a large Power Distance situation. We still find Italy on the larger Power Distance side of Figure 1 (with all other Latin and Mediterranean countries), and we can assume from historical evidence that Power Distances in Italy during the sixteenth century were considerably larger than they are now. When we compare Machiavelli's work with that of his contemporary, Sir Thomas More (1478–1535), we find cultural differences between ways of thinking in different countries even in the sixteenth century. The British More described in *Utopia* a state based on consensus as a "model" to criticize the political situation of his day. But practice did not always follow theory, of course: More, deemed too critical, was beheaded by order of King Henry VIII, while Machiavelli the realist managed to die peacefully in his bed. The difference in theories is nonetheless remarkable.

In the United States a current of leadership theories has developed. Some of the best known were put forth by the late Douglas McGregor (Theory X versus Theory Y), Rensis Likert (System 4 management), and Robert R. Blake with Jane S. Mouton (the Managerial Grid®). What these theories have in common is that they all advocate participation in the manager's decisions by his/ her subordinates (participative management); however, the initiative toward participation is supposed to be taken by the manager. In a worldwide perspective (Figure 1), we can understand these theories from the middle position of the United States on the Power Distance side (rank 15 out of 40 countries). Had the culture been one of larger Power Distance, we could have expected more "Machiavellian" theories of leadership. In fact, in the management literature of another country with a larger Power Distance index score, France, there is little concern with participative management American style, but great concern with who has the power. However, in countries with smaller Power Distances than the United States (Sweden, Norway, Germany, Israel), there is considerable sympathy for models of management in which even the initiatives are taken by the subordinates (forms of industrial democracy) and with which there's little sympathy in the United States. In the approaches toward "industrial democracy" taken in these countries, we notice their differences on the second dimension, Uncertainty Avoidance. In weak Uncertainty Avoidance countries like Sweden, industrial democracy was started in the form of local experiments and only later was given a legislative framework. In strong Uncertainty Avoidance countries like Germany, industrial democracy was brought about by legislation first and then had to be brought alive in the organizations ("Mitbestimmung").

The crucial fact about leadership in any culture is that it is a complement to subordinateship. The Power Distance index scores in Figure 1 are, in fact, based on the values of people as *subordinates,* not on the values of superiors. Whatever a naïve literature on leadership may give us to understand, leaders cannot choose their styles at will; what is feasible depends to a large extent on the cultural conditioning of a leader's subordinates. Along these lines, Table 5 describes the type of subordinateship that, other things being equal, a leader can expect to meet in societies at three different levels of Power Distance—subordinateship to which a leader must respond. The middle level represents what is most likely found in the United States.

Neither McGregor, nor Likert, nor Blake and Mouton allow for this type of cultural proviso—all three tend to be prescriptive with regard to a leadership style that, at best, will work with U.S. subordinates and with those in cultures—such as Canada or Australia—that have not too different Power Distance levels (Figure 1). In fact, my research shows that subordinates in larger Power Distance countries tend to agree more frequently with Theory Y.

A U.S. theory of leadership that allows for a certain amount of cultural relativity, although indirectly, is Fred Fiedler's contingency theory of leadership. Fiedler states that different leader personalities are needed for "difficult" and "easy" situations, and that a cultural gap between superior and subordinates is one of the factors that makes a situation "difficult." However, this theory does not address the kind of cultural gap in question.

In practice, the adaptation of managers to higher Power Distance environments does not seem to present too many problems. Although this is an unpopular message—one seldom professed in management development courses—managers moving to a larger Power Distance culture soon learn that they have to behave more autocratically in order to be effective, and tend to do so; this is borne out by the colonial history of most Western countries. But it is interesting that the Western ex-colonial power with the highest Power Distance norm—France—seems to be most appreciated by its former colonies and seems to maintain the best postcolonial relationships with most of them. This suggests that subordinates in a large Power Distance culture feel even more comfortable with superiors who are real autocrats than with those whose assumed autocratic stance is out of national character.

The operation of a manager in an environment with a Power Distance norm lower than his or her own is more problematic. U.S. managers tend to find it difficult to collaborate wholeheartedly in the "industrial democracy" processes of such countries as Sweden, Germany, and even the Netherlands. U.S. citizens tend to consider their country as the example of democracy, and find it difficult to accept that other countries might wish to develop forms of democracy for which they feel no need and that make major inroads upon managers' (or leaders') prerogatives. However, the very idea of management prerogatives is not accepted in very low Power Distance countries. This is, perhaps, best illustrated by a remark a Scandinavian social scientist is supposed to have made to Herzberg in a seminar: "You are against participation for the very reason we are in favor of it—one doesn't know where it will stop. We think that is good."

One way in which the U.S. approach to leadership has been packaged and formalized is management by objectives (MBO), first advocated by Peter Drucker in 1955 in *The Practice of Management*. In the United States, MBO has been used to spread a pragmatic results orientation throughout the organization. It has been considerably more successful where results are objectively measurable than where they can only be interpreted subjectively, and, even in the United States, it has been criticized heavily. Still, it has been perhaps the single most popular management technique "made in U.S.A." Therefore, it can be accepted as fitting U.S. culture. MBO presupposes:

- That subordinates are sufficiently independent to negotiate meaningfully with the boss (not-too-large Power Distance).
- That both are willing to take risks (weak Uncertainty Avoidance).
- That performance is seen as important by both (high Masculinity).

Let us now take the case of Germany, a below-average Power Distance country. Here, the dialogue element in MBO should present no problem. However, since Germany scores considerably higher on Uncertainty Avoidance, the tendency toward accepting risk and ambiguity will not exist to the same extent. The idea of replacing the arbitrary authority of the boss with the impersonal authority of mutually agreed-upon objectives, however, fits the small Power Distance/strong Uncertainty Avoidance cultural cluster very well. The objectives become the subordinates' "superego." In a book of case studies about MBO in Germany, Ian R. G. Ferguson states that

> MBO has acquired a different flavor in the German-speaking area, not least because in these countries the societal and political pressure towards increasing the value of man in the organization on the right to co-determination has become quite clear. Thence, MBO has been transliterated into Management by Joint Goal Setting (Führung durch Zielvereinbarung).

Ferguson's view of MBO fits the ideological needs of the German-speaking countries of the moment. The case studies in his book show elaborate formal systems with extensive ideological justification; the stress on *team* objectives is quite strong, which is in line with the lower individualism in these countries.

The other area in which specific information on MBO is available is France. MBO was first introduced in France in the early 1960s, but it became extremely popular for a time after the 1968 student revolt. People expected that this new technique would lead to the long-overdue democratization of organizations. Instead of DPO (Direction par Objectifs), the French name for MBO became DPPO (Direction *Participative* par Objectifs). So in France, too, societal developments affected the MBO system. However, DPPO remained, in general, as much a vain slogan as did Liberté, Egalité, Fraternité (Freedom, Equality, Brotherhood) after the 1789 revolt. G. Franck wrote in 1973

> . . . I think that the career of DPPO is terminated, or rather that it has never started, and it won't ever start as long as we continue in France our tendency to confound ideology and reality. . . .

In a postscript to Franck's article, the editors of *Le Management* write:

> French blue- and white-collar workers, lower-level and higher-level managers, and "patrons" all belong to the same cultural system which maintains dependency relations from level to level. Only the deviants really dislike this system. The hierarchical structure protects against anxiety; DPO, however, generates anxiety . . .

The reason for the anxiety in the French cultural context is that MBO presupposes a depersonalized authority in the form of internalized objectives; but French people, from their early childhood onward, are accustomed to large Power Distances, to an authority that is highly personalized. And in spite of all attempts to introduce Anglo-Saxon management methods, French superiors do not easily decentralize and do not stop short-circuiting intermediate hierarchical levels, nor do French subordinates expect them to. The developments of the 1970s have severely discredited DPPO, which probably does injustice to the cases in which individual French organizations or units, starting from less exaggerated expectations, have benefited from it.

In the examples used thus far in this section, the cultural context of leadership may look rather obvious to the reader. But it also works in more subtle, less obvious ways. Here's an example from the area of management decision making: A prestigious U.S. consulting firm was asked to analyze the decision-making processes in a large Scandinavian "XYZ" corporation. Their report criticized the corporation's decision-making style, which they characterized as being, among other things, "intuitive" and "consensus based." They compared "observations of traditional XYZ practices" with "selected examples of practices in other companies." These "selected examples," offered as a model, were evidently taken from their U.S. clients and reflect the U.S. textbook norm—"fact based" rather than intuitive management, and "fast decisions based on clear responsibilities" rather than the use of informal, personal contacts and the concern for consensus.

Is this consulting firm doing its Scandinavian clients a service? It follows from Figure 3 that where the United States and the Scandinavian culture are wide apart is on the Masculinity dimension. The use of intuition and the concern for consensus in Scandinavia are "feminine" characteristics of the culture, well embedded in the total texture of these societies. Stressing "facts" and "clear responsibilities" fits the "masculine" U.S. culture. From a neutral viewpoint, the reasons for criticizing the U.S. decision-making style are as good as those for criticizing the Scandinavian style. In complex decision-making situations, "facts" no longer exist independently from the people who define them, so "fact-based management" becomes a misleading slogan. Intuition may not be a bad method of deciding in such cases at all. And if the implementation of decisions requires the commitment of many people, even a consensus process that takes more time is an asset rather than a liability. But the essential element overlooked by the consultant is that decisions have to be made in a way that corresponds to the values of the environment in which they have to be effective. People in this consulting firm lacked insight into their own cultural biases. This does not mean that the Scandinavian corporation's management need not improve its decision making and could not learn from the consultant's experience. But this can be done only through a mutual recognition of cultural differences, not by ignoring them.

Organization

The Power Distance/Uncertainty Avoidance map (Figure 1) is of vital importance for structuring organizations that will work best in different countries. For example, one U.S.-based multinational corporation has a worldwide policy that salary-increase proposals should be initiated by the employee's direct superior. However, the French management of its French subsidiary interpreted this policy in such a way that the superior's superior's superior—three levels above—was the one to initiate salary proposals. This way of working was regarded as quite natural by both superiors and subordinates in France. Other factors being equal, people in large Power Distance cultures prefer that decisions be centralized because even superiors have strong dependency needs in relation to their superiors; this tends to move decisions up as far as they can go (see Table 5). People in small Power Distance cultures want decisions to be decentralized.

While Power Distance relates to centralization, Uncertainty Avoidance relates to formalization—the need for formal rules and specialization, the assignment of tasks to experts. My former colleague O. J. Stevens at INSEAD has done an interesting research project (as yet unpublished) with M.B.A. students from Germany, Great Britain, and France. He asked them to write their own diagnosis and solution for a small case study of an organizational problem—a conflict in one company between the sales and product development departments. The majority of the French referred the problem to the next higher authority (the president of the company); the Germans attributed it to the lack of a written policy, and proposed establishing one; the British attributed it to a lack of interpersonal communication, to be cured by some kind of group training.

Stevens concludes that the "implicit model" of the organization for most French was a pyramid (both centralized and formal); for most Germans, a well-oiled machine (formalized but not centralized); and for most British, a village market (neither formalized nor centralized). This covers three quadrants (2, 3, and 4) in Figure 1. What is missing is an "implicit model" for quadrant 1, which contains four Asian countries, including India. A discussion with an Indian colleague leads me to place the family (centralized, but not formalized) in this quadrant as the "implicit model" of the organization. In fact, Indian organizations tend to be formalized as far as relationships

Table 5   Subordinateship for Three Levels of Power Distance

Small Power Distance	Medium Power Distance (United States)	Large Power Distance
Subordinates have weak dependence needs.	Subordinates have medium dependence needs.	Subordinates have strong dependence needs.
Superiors have weak dependence needs toward their superiors.	Superiors have medium dependence needs toward their superiors.	Superiors have strong dependence needs toward their superiors.
Subordinates expect superiors to consult them and may rebel or strike if superiors are not seen as staying within their legitimate role.	Subordinates expect superiors to consult them but will accept autocratic behavior as well.	Subordinates expect superiors to act autocratically.
Ideal superior to most is a loyal democrat.	Ideal superior to most is a resourceful democrat.	Ideal superior to most is a benevolent autocrat or paternalist.
Laws and rules apply to all and privileges for superiors are not considered acceptable.	Laws and rules apply to all, but a certain level of privileges for superiors is considered normal.	Everybody expects superiors to enjoy privileges; laws and rules differ for superiors and subordinates.
Status symbols are frowned upon and will easily come under attack from subordinates.	Status symbols for superiors contribute moderately to their authority and will be accepted by subordinates.	Status symbols are very important and contribute strongly to the superior's authority with the subordinates.

between people go (this is related to Power Distance), but not as far as work-flow goes (this is Uncertainty Avoidance).

The "well-oiled machine" model for Germany reminds us of the fact that Max Weber, author of the first theory of bureaucracy, was a German. Weber pictures bureaucracy as a highly formalized system (strong Uncertainty Avoidance), in which, however, the rules protect the lower-ranking members against abuse of power by their superiors. The superiors have no power by themselves, only the power that their bureaucratic roles have given them as incumbents of the roles—the power is in the role, not in the person (small Power Distance).

The United States is found fairly close to the center of the map in Figure 1, taking an intermediate position between the "pyramid," "machine," and "market" implicit models—a position that may help explain the success of U.S. business operations in very different cultures. However, according to the common U.S. conception of organization, we might say that *hierarchy is not a goal by itself* (as it is in France) and that *rules are not a goal by themselves.* Both are means toward obtaining results, to be changed if needed. A breaking away from hier-archic and bureaucratic traditions is found in the development toward matrix organizations and similar temporary or flexible organization systems.

Another INSEAD colleague, André Laurent, has shown that French managers strongly disbelieve in the feasibility of matrix organizations, because they see them as violating the "holy" principle of unit of command. However, in the French subsidiary of a multinational corporation that has a long history of successful matrix management, the French managers were quite positive toward it; obviously, then, cultural barriers to organizational innovation can be overcome. German managers are not too favorably disposed toward matrix organizations either, feeling that they tend to frustrate their need for organiza-tional clarity. This means that matrix organizations will be accepted *if* the roles of individuals within the organization can be defined without ambiguity.

The extreme position of the United States on the Individualism scale leads to other potential conflicts between the U.S. way of thinking about orga-nizations and the values dominant in other parts of the world. In the U.S. Individualist conception, the relationship between the individual and the organization is essentially calculative, being based on enlightened self-inter-est. In fact, there is a strong historical and cultural link between Individual-ism and Capitalism. The capitalist system—based on self-interest and the market mechanism—was "invented" in Great Britain, which is still among the top three most Individualist countries in the world. In more Collectivist societies, however, the link between individuals and their traditional organi-zations is not calculative, but moral: It is based not on self-interest, but on the individual's loyalty toward the clan, organization, or society—which is sup-posedly the best guarantee of that individual's ultimate interest. "Collectiv-ism" is a bad word in the United States, but "individualism" is as much a bad word in the writings of Mao Tse-tung, who writes from a strongly Collectivist cultural tradition (see Figure 2 for the Collectivist scores of the Chinese majority countries Taiwan, Hong Kong, and Singapore). This means that U.S. organizations may get themselves into considerable trouble in more Col-lectivist environments if they do not recognize their local employees' needs for ties of mutual loyalty between company and employee. "Hire and fire" is very ill perceived in these countries, if firing isn't prohibited by law altogether. Given the value position of people in more Collectivist cultures, it should not be seen as surprising if they prefer other types of economic order to capital-ism—if capitalism cannot get rid of its Individualist image.

Consequences for Policy

So far we have seriously questioned the universal validity of management theories developed in one country—in most instances here, the United States.

On a practical level, this has the least consequence for organizations oper-ating entirely within the country in which the theories were born. As long as the theories apply within the United States, U.S. organizations can base their policies for motivating employees, leadership, and organization development on these policies. Still, some caution is due. If differences in environmental culture can be shown to exist between countries, and if these constrain the validity of management theories, what about the subcultures and countercultures within the country? To what extent do the familiar theories apply when the organization employs people for whom the theories were not, in the first instance, conceived—such as members of minority groups with a different educational level, or belonging to a different generation? If culture matters, an organization's policies can lose their effectiveness when its cultural environment changes.

No doubt, however, the consequences of the cultural relativity of management theories are more serious for the multinational organization. The cultural maps in Figures 1, 2, and 3 can help predict the kind of culture difference between subsidiaries and mother company that will need to be met. An important implication is that identical personnel policies may have very different effects in different countries—and within countries for different subgroups of employees. This is not only a matter of different employee values; there are also, of course, differences in government policies and legislation (which usually reflect quite clearly the country's different cultural position). And there are differences in labor market situations and labor union power positions. These differences—tangible as well as intangible—may have consequences for performance, attention to quality, cost, labor turnover, and absenteeism. Typical universal policies that may work out quite differently in different countries are those dealing with financial incentives, promotion paths, and grievance channels.

The dilemma for the organization operating abroad is whether to adapt to the local culture or try to change it. There are examples of companies that have successfully changed local habits, such as in the earlier mention of the introduction of matrix organization in France. Many Third World countries want to transfer new technologies from more economically advanced countries. If they are to work at all, these technologies must presuppose values that may run counter to local traditions, such as a certain discretion of subordinates toward superiors (lower Power Distance) or of individuals toward in-groups (more Individualism). In such a case, the local culture has to be changed; this is a difficult task that should not be taken lightly. Since it calls for a conscious strategy based on insight into the local culture, it's logical to involve acculturated locals in strategy formulations. Often, the original policy will have to be adapted to fit local culture to lead to the desired effect. We saw earlier how, in the case of MBO, this has succeeded in Germany, but generally failed in France.

A final area in which the cultural boundaries of home-country management theories are important is the training of managers for assignments abroad. For managers who have to operate in an unfamiliar culture, training based on home-country theories is of very limited use and may even do more harm than good. Of more importance is a thorough familiarization with the other culture, for which the organization can use the services of specialized cross-cultural training institutes—or it can develop its own program by using host-country personnel as teachers.

Acknowledgments

This article is based on research carried out in the period 1973–78 at the European Institute for Advanced Studies in Management, Brussels. The article itself was sponsored by executive search consultants Berndtson International S.A., Brussels. The author acknowledges the helpful comments of Mark Cantley, Andre Laurent, Ernest C. Miller, and Jennifer Robinson on an earlier version of it.

Selected Bibliography

The first U.S. book about the cultural relativity of U.S. management theories is still to be written, I believe—which lack in itself indicates how difficult it is to recognize one's own cultural biases. One of the few U.S. books describing the process of cultural conditioning for a management readership is Edward T. Hall's *The Silent Language* (Fawcett, 1959, but reprinted since). Good reading also is Hall's article "The Silent Language in Overseas Business" *(Harvard Business Review,* May-June 1960). Hall is an anthropologist and therefore a specialist in the study of culture. Very readable on the same subject are two books by the British anthropologist Mary Douglas, *Natural Symbols: Exploration in Cosmology* (Vintage, 1973) and the reader *Rules and Meanings: The Anthropology of Everyday Knowledge* (Penguin, 1973). Another excellent reader is Theodore D. Weinshall's *Culture and Management* (Penguin, 1977).

On the concept of national character, some well-written professional literature is Margaret Mead's "National Character," in the reader by Sol Tax, *Anthropology Today* (University of Chicago Press, 1962), and Alex Inkeles and D. J. Levinson's, "National Character," in Lindzey and Aronson's *Handbook of Social Psychology,* second edition, volume 4 (Addison-Wesley, 1969). Critique on the implicit claims of universal validity of management theories comes from some foreign authors: An important article is Michel Brossard and Marc Maurice's "Is There a Universal Model of Organization Structure?" *(International Studies of Management and Organization,* Fall 1976). This journal is a journal of translations from non-American literature, based in New York, that often contains important articles on management issues by non-U.S. authors that take issue with the dominant theories. Another article is Gunnar Hjelholt's "Europe Is Different," in Geert Hofstede and M. Sami Kassem's reader, *European Contributions to Organization Theory* (Assen Netherlands: Von Gorcum, 1976).

Some other references of interest: Ian R. G. Ferguson's *Management by Objectives in Deutschland* (Herder and Herder, 1973) (in German); G. Franck's "Epitaphe pour la DPO," in *Le Management,* November 1973 (in French); and D. Jenkins's *Blue- and White-Collar Democracy* (Doubleday, 1973).

Note: Details of Geert Hofstede's study of national cultures has been published in his book, *Culture's Consequences: International Differences in Work-Related Values* (Beverly Hills: Sage Publications, 1980).

Questions and Learning Activities

Section IV

Questions

1. At first glance, the idea of "situational" leadership appears to be in conflict with what could be called the general guidelines in readings 1–23; for example, being supportive, being a servant leader, and engaging in the leader behaviors that Kotter describes. How would you reconcile this apparent conflict?

2. Do you think that Tannenbaum and Schmidt's classic article of 50 years ago makes sense in today's world? What variables would you add or delete to make their model more contemporary?

3. Tannenbaum and Schmidt view leader behavior on a continuum ranging from authoritarian to democratic. According to this model, under what circumstances would authoritarian leadership be more effective? Under what circumstances would democratic leadership be more effective?

4. Several of the readings view leadership style as two independent sets of behaviors—one that relates to the people and one to the task. In the Tannenbaum and Schmidt reading, style is essentially one variable on a continuum from autocratic to democratic. In the Fiedler model, style is either task-oriented or relationship-oriented. Comment on the relative advantages and disadvantages of these different conceptualizations of style.

5. Reddin's 3-D model indicates that any combination of task behavior and relationships behavior can be effective or ineffective depending on the situation. Briefly describe situations where each of the four leadership styles would be predicted to be effective.

6. Fiedler's approach suggests that it may be advantageous to design jobs to fit leaders' styles rather than attempting to change leaders' behavior to fit the situation. What are the possible advantages to this approach and potential difficulties in implementing it?

7. How might the prevalent leadership styles in cultures that rank high in power distance make it difficult for organizations to cope with today's business environment?

8. Some people believe that the application of contingency theories of leadership will result in perceived favoritism. Do you agree? Why or why not? If, indeed, the potential for such a problem exists, how can it be overcome?

9. A successful leader/manager is moving from an individualistic culture, in which she has worked for many years, to a collectivist culture with

which she is unfamiliar. How should she consider modifying her leadership style?

10. Hersey and Blanchard's *Life Cycle Theory of Leadership* indicates that the appropriate leadership style depends on the maturity level of the follower. What are the advantages of this recommendation? What does it not consider that may be important?

11. What problems could result from using a leadership style that does not match the follower's maturity level?

12. What might happen if a leader believed a follower's maturity level to be very low but the follower believed it to be very high? What would remedy this situation?

13. What leadership skills are shared by Reddin's 3-D model, Fiedler's model, and the Hersey-Blanchard model?

14. According to Reddin, what important contingency factors are missing in the Hersey-Blanchard model? Do you agree that they are important?

15. House discusses four types of leadership behavior: directive, supportive, participative, and achievement oriented. Does this make his model more complete than the others in this section as far as leadership style is concerned?

16. Some people would say that the path-goal approach to leadership is not truly a contingency or situational theory of leadership. Do you agree? Why or why not?

17. How does the Vroom-Jago model of leadership decision making differ from the other contingency approaches included in this section?

18. How would you react to a leader/manager who said "I am who I am and I can't change who I am, so these contingency approaches to leadership are of no use to me"?

19. Hofstede discusses how cultural differences impact leadership effectiveness. What are the implications for using the contingency models described in this section in non-Western cultures?

20. A leader/manager who has a very participative style is scheduled to move from the USA to South America. How will she most likely have to modify her style?

Activities

1. Compare and contrast the models presented in this section by identifying (1) how each conceptualizes or defines leadership style and (2) the situational or contingency variables included. Based upon this, indicate the potential strengths or weaknesses of each, and note your preferences.

2. Identify a classmate or colleague who is from Mexico, South America, or Asia. Discuss with this person Hofstede's concept of power distance. What did you learn?

3. Write a paper where you select two models from this section and use each to explain instances where outcomes you experienced or observed were positive—i.e., how specific leader behaviors facilitated the outcomes. Now do the opposite—where not following the models resulted in poor outcomes.

4. Discuss with classmates/colleagues situations where you were very unhappy with a leader's style. Which model in this section does the best job of explaining why this person's style provoked your negative reaction?

5. Think of decisions that you have been a party to or observed that turned out very wrong for the unit or organization. What information in *Leadership and Decision Making* offers possible explanations for the less than desirable outcomes?

6. Think about your work experiences in relation to the path-goal theory of leadership. Can you describe an example where the leader/manager took actions related to the model and your performance was good. Now describe an example where your leader/manager did not take the appropriate actions and your performance was poor.

7. Conduct short interviews with 10 leader/managers about their style. Ask them: (1) to describe it; (2) if they change it from time to time; and (3) if they do change it, why. Summarize your findings in light of the readings in this section.

8. The life cycle theory of leadership evolved over the years and is now referred to as "Situational Leadership." Hersey and Blanchard parted ways some time ago and each has his own version of the model. Write a paper that compares each version to the original and to each other. Conclude by indicating which version you prefer and why.

9. Self-awareness suggestion—assess your leadership style using the Fiedler approach. See the editor's Web site at www.waveland.com/McMahon/.

10. Behavior change and flexibility are key to all situational approaches. Some view this as difficult, if not impossible. Write a paper with this title: "Changing Leaders' Behaviors: An Achievable Goal?"

LEADERSHIP, POWER, AND INFLUENCE

Leadership involves, among other things, influencing followers. And nothing is more central to influence than power. Much of the literature on power is dense, theoretical, and quite "academic." The resolution of this complexity for students and practitioners of leadership is as follows: leadership involves influencing others to behave and perform in ways that contribute to organizational goals and objectives; power is a "commodity" that the leader uses to influence. Examples of this power include, but are surely not limited to, authority, expertise, and charisma. Over recent history, the developments in this area have focused on the benefits accruing to the organization and the leader/manager who empowers subordinates.

It is nearly impossible to discuss power without considering the work of Niccolo Machiavelli. His most popular work on the subject is *The Prince,* written in the period of 1513–1516. The selection included here, *Machiavelli and Leadership* by Richard Calhoon, provides an excellent overview of this work. There is no question that Machiavelli was directly concerned about the challenges of leadership. The term "Machiavellian behavior" in today's jargon connotes scheming, manipulation, absolute control, and so forth. Yet the depth and sophistication of Machiavelli's work have surely contributed to its relevance some 500 years later.

Leadership Power Bases continues to be an essential element of all current discussions about leadership and power some 50 years after it first appeared. John French and Bertram Raven identify five types of power; three are organization based and two are person based. The discussion of which types of power are more likely to lead to higher performance and satisfaction has important implications for all leader/managers, regardless of the organizational level they occupy.

The third reading in this section, *Leadership Role-Making and Leader-Member Exchange*, examines power as arising from agreements on role definitions and exchanges between leaders and members. A simple example of exchange is an employee who agrees to expend great effort and commitment in return for a favorable assignment. The focus of this article is on the leader-follower dyad (pair). The process by which roles are defined and exchanges take place between leader and follower will resonate with readers who have been in either position. In particular, the insights of this work heighten awareness of the role-making process, in-group and out-group dynamics, and the power of leader-member exchange. Practical implications for organizations interested in team building are clearly articulated.

The selection titled *Power Acquisition and Retention* highlights the classic work of Gerald R. Salancik and Jeffrey Pfeffer, which explores power as a function of strategic contingencies. Specifically, these authors view power as something that accrues to organizational subunits (individuals, departments) that cope with critical organizational problems. Their model provides explanations and guidance regarding power in organizations that go beyond those which restrict power to an interpersonal process. Moreover, it holds a number of practically relevant implications for all leader/managers.

The "empowerment" movement was born with Bandura's work on the concept of self-efficacy (sense of self power) and its consequences. In *Leadership: The Art of Empowering Others,* Jay A. Conger provides a lucid explanation of the process of empowerment, its relevance and probable advantages, and implementation issues. Although the promise of empowerment has not materialized for many organizations that initially bought into the concept, this has more to do with ill-advised methods of implementation and the weakness of top leader/managers than it has to do with the integrity, relevance, and applicability of the concept. Conger's excellent article provides clear direction to leader/managers.

The final reading in this section is *Goodbye, Command and Control*, an insightful and timely essay by Margaret Wheatley. Wheatley notes that the relevance and implications of self-organizing systems, so prevalent in nature, cannot be overlooked. The environment in which all organizations operate is more complex, interdependent, and rapidly changing than ever before. Is it possible for leader/managers to be effective by behaving as though events are predictable when they are no longer so? How do we, as leader/managers, capture the hearts, minds, and creativity of our members? And how do organizations that attempt to incorporate participation and self-management deal with such issues as the fear of losing control and trust? Wheatley's cogent analysis addresses these and other questions relating to self-organizing systems.

31

Machiavelli and Leadership

Richard P. Calhoon

Niccolo Machiavelli would applaud the widespread application of his precepts of leadership in today's organizations and the sophisticated refinements added as a consequence of changing culture and increased knowledge. That his keen, insightful observations have continued to live for five hundred years is a testimonial to two facts: (1) tactics that are sound, based on a realistic knowledge of behavior, and (2) ploys that are "natural" courses of action, undertaken by leaders of any period to acquire power, resist aggression, and control subordinates.

The full extent and ubiquity of Machiavelli's concepts relevant to present day organizational administrators have largely escaped notice. Emphasis on "good" practices and "principles" of management on the one hand have tended to obscure the action of leaders that are unsavory but effective. On the other hand, the prevailing connotation of "Machiavellian" as a conniving, manipulative, cold-blooded means for arriving at selfish ends has completely overshadowed the need for and validity of his concepts. Actually, modern organizational leaders operate much more according to the various teachings of Machiavelli than anyone might care to admit. Moreover, they have developed gambits, machinations, and pressures far beyond those that Machiavelli ever dreamed of advancing.

Machiavellian concepts and actions are much more germane to the "guts" of interactions in business than social scientists and/or management analysts care to recognize. Responsibility for downplaying Machiavellianism in modern organizations is the same as in political science:

> I think that the unpleasant but realistic picture of politics that Machiavelli saw in his reading of history and formulation into a science, is the principal reason for the aversion in which he is generally held. No one likes to be told of shortcomings.[1]

Reprinted with permission of Academy of Management (NY) from *Academy of Management Journal*, Vol. 12, No. 2 (June 1969), pp. 205–12. Originally titled "Niccolo Machiavelli and the Twentieth Century Administrator." Copyright © 1969 Academy of Management (NY).

Francis Bacon wrote of Machiavelli: "He set forth openly and sincerely what men are wont to do, and not what they ought to do."

Current analysts of behavior in management are coming to see that "systems" at one pole and the case studies of individual managers at the other are inadequate. Some thoughtful students of management see that somehow writers are passing over much of what is *real* in management action. George Odiorne writes:

> A faint suspicion arises that there may still be room for a couple of books which tell managers what they actually do and how they behave once they have their values, attitudes, and concepts sorted out . . . among the possible areas for research in the future would be a statement of what managers actually are doing.[2]

Journal articles and books on management are, in increasing numbers, referring to *strategies* used in leadership—to pressure tactics and to other aspects of Machiavellianism, as a matter of fact.

A few writers have been intrigued by managerial practices of a less than socially acceptable nature, but no one has undertaken a thorough analysis of this shadowy area, with apologies to noteworthy but incomplete contributions in the Machiavellian vein by writers such as Chester Burger, Irving Goffman, Antony Jay, Eugene Jennings, and Stephen B. Miles, Jr.

Although other writers through the years have written along kindred lines, it was Machiavelli who produced far and away the most thorough analysis of leadership actions pertinent to any type of organization in any age.[3] Why is it that a Renaissance, Florentine writer, Niccolo Machiavelli (May 3, 1469–June 20, 1527) was able to identify so many leadership actions that are widely used today, some five centuries later?

Reasons for Machiavelli's Lasting Impact

A quick examination of his life and times helps to explain why Machiavelli's thinking has had such a living impression despite many efforts over the years to bury his work. Born in Florence, Niccolo Machiavelli's youth included a sound grounding in classical history, as his writings so well demonstrate. From 1498 to 1512, he held numerous diplomatic assignments in Florence which took him to the various Italian city states, to other city states in Western Europe, and to the kingdoms of France and Spain. Exiled from Florence through a change in regime, Machiavelli spent the years from 1512 to 1527 largely in writing although he did eventually receive some rather inconsequential diplomatic assignments. While in exile, he completed his most famous work, *The Prince* (1513–1516), and wrote his *Discourses on the First Ten Books of Titus Livius* (1512–1522). These two works contain the vast bulk of his writings on leadership, although letters and other discourses contain additional thought in this area.

Much the more popular, *The Prince* was in truth:

a slender volume concocted during off-hours while Machiavelli composed his life's work. . . . this booklet . . . is so full of dramatic vigor and the sharp vision which characterized all of Machiavelli's writing that it still reads like a detective story. What wonder then that the self-styled historians of all times and countries have devoured its three-score pages while the same scriveners have felt rebutted both by the scope and by the lack of a conventional plan in Machiavelli's truly great work: *Discourses on the First Ten Books of Titus Livius.*[4] Indeed, it was *The Prince* that made Machiavelli both famous and infamous.[5]

The Prince was an incomplete but vigorous digest of his *Discourses.* Antony Jay says of this shorter work: "Above all it is about leadership; Machiavelli called his book *The Prince* and not something like *The Art of Government* because he saw success and failure for states as stemming directly from the qualities of the leader."[6] By far the richer and fuller work on leadership, *The Discourses* was also a much better example of Machiavelli's extensive historical knowledge. Much more that is applicable to leadership today can be gleaned from *The Discourses* than from *The Prince*. It just takes more digging. A virtual treasure trove of conceptual material in *The Discourses* is available for use by administrators of the twentieth century. As Jay says, ". . . Machiavelli, however marginal his relevance to academic historians, is bursting with urgent advice and acute observations for top management of the great private and public corporations all over the world."[7]

Machiavelli's versatility is seen in his other contributions to history and to political science. *The Art of War* (1520) and *The History of Florence* (unfinished— written c. 1520) bring out his talents for objective analysis. The history is outstanding in showing the sequential vicissitudes that befall a people over a period of time. His advice to heads of states, his aim of a united Italy, and his evaluations of various forms of government are of interest to political scientists.

The *reasons* for the continuing vitality of all of these contributions and especially of his insights into leadership can be seen more clearly in the following:

1. His *scientific* point of view, not in the sense of being experimental but in the sense of orderly, logical, objective analysis of data, earned him the designation, "the first modern man." He had scorn for outdated, preconceived notions and for any unrealistic approach (moralistic or what). His reasoning was pragmatic and practical rather than philosophical.

2. The *laboratory* in which he made his analyses was unique in history. Fifteenth- and sixteenth-century city states were in a constant state of ferment. Leaders came and went (often by the murder route). City states and monarchies expanded and shrank. At no other time in history were so many acts immediately relatable to so many persons and to such immediate consequences. Structure was relatively simple, the framework exposed, so that the actions of leaders in cities, in states, and in armies were relatively easy to observe and to analyze. Machiavelli had both first-hand contact and second-hand knowledge of what was taking place in the French kingdom, the Swiss states and confederacy, the Spanish kingdom, the German states and king-

dom, the major Italian city states of Naples, Venice, Florence, Milan, the Papal State and Rome, and in Sicily.

3. The period of *exile* provided time for reflection, for building on his considerable experience and knowledge of the Renaissance, for relating this to historical happenings, and for formulating his observations of leadership actions that are as apt today as they were 500 years ago.

4. Machiavelli's *observational* method of studying leadership enabled him to cover a range of leadership actions of amazing breadth. And in the process, he exposed numerous facets of leadership that have escaped notice by modern social scientists. Moreover, his observations were action oriented, his conclusions far from irresponsible. Indeed, he followed a "critical incident" approach in his historical associations that has acquired some respectability as a method of research today.

5. Historical *analogy,* the principal method used by Machiavelli to prove his concepts of leadership, is a valuable tool for analysis when properly used. Had he referred solely to events occurring in the Renaissance world, Machiavelli could only have observed what was happening at the time and the actions associated therewith in drawing his conclusions. This he did on occasion, it is true. But his most powerful precepts, the majority indeed, were drawn from comparisons of Renaissance leadership with the wealth of leadership tactics found in classical civilization. His favorite era was the Roman Republic, for which he had tremendous admiration, but Rome was far from being the only historical source used in his analogies. He studied the tactics of Alexander, Cyrus, Darius, and Philip of Macedon, to mention only a few leaders from the Near East and Greece. Not one for quoting the Bible's moral teachings, Machiavelli did occasionally use historical events and personages from the Bible (Moses, for example) in making analogies with Renaissance leaders.

This method of historical analogy has intrigued other writers such as Antony Jay, whose *Management and Machiavelli* applies the historical methods of Machiavelli (but not his concepts) to such unlikely figures as Martin Luther and Walter Chrysler, medieval popes and recent presidents of the U.S., the General Motors Corp. and Emperor Henry IV, William I and General Dynamics Corp., Charles I and Howard Hughes.[8]

Despite the likelihood and consequences of error from drawing historical parallels, Jay contends that "There are far more lessons for those who care to read them, in the long annals of history than in the few published management case studies."[9] It may be true that historians tend to repeat themselves more than history does because of differences in situations, but a study of leaders through the ages reveals parallels in behavior that are illustrative and broadly so of the actions of leaders of any age and any type of organization. If parallels from history can be helpful in understanding leadership behavior, taking parallels from Classical and Renaissance times and extending them to the present should have even more value.

Now what about relevance of the *political* and *military* leaders (with whom Machiavelli dealt) to *business* leaders of today? Jay says: "A corporation . . . is not something different from a state with some interesting similarities; it is a state with few unimportant differences."[10] The point is that corporations and states both have leaders and, although culture, society, circumstances, and organizational structure modify behavior, interactions and tactics have marked similarities within the leadership task regardless of the specific setting—university, city, automobile industry, hospital, U.S. Air Force, or retail store. Systems change, technology changes, organization changes, but there is little alteration in the basics of human behavior despite sociocultural shifts. There is utility in considering these universals of managerial action, especially when the lessons of history show that these tactics and strategies are practiced in virtually every civilized society and age: ". . . by a judicious use of the Machiavelli method we can . . . see the different results that tend to be brought out by different courses of action."[11]

Relevance of Renaissance to Modern Leadership

It would be wrong to say that heads of states in Renaissance Italy operated through the same bureaucratic structures as do twentieth-century organizations. Today's structures in large governmental and business organizations allow executives less freedom of action—they are more circumscribed by policy and procedure and by other levels of authority (even corporation presidents). At the same time, growth and technological change continually alter structure and relationships so that flexibility is required of today's Prince.

Pressures of modern organizations are different from those in Renaissance times but only in severity of consequences. Rivalries, competition for power, fears—of failure, of subordinates, of superiors ("an executive is a guy who walks around with a worried expression on his subordinates' faces"), and problems of motivating people existed in Machiavelli's era, and they are present today. Today's employees, however, are much more sophisticated than was the "populace" in Machiavelli's time. Education is at a higher level; communications media, especially television, introduce people to many and varied leadership tactics. All of which makes it increasingly difficult for today's leaders to "use psychology" on subordinates.

Both the tasks and the interactions of people within organizations at various levels presented much the same dilemmas in Renaissance as in modern times. Either today's executive or a late medieval prince could have made this statement by Machiavelli: "A statesman must accept the heavy duty of forgetting his own personal feelings, his habitual kindness, in order to enter into another sphere of action." Another example by Guiseppe Prezzolini shows by simile and metaphor the major task of Machiavelli's Prince in relation to the state: The statesman "is like the captain of a ship which must reach port. In spite of the complaints, demands and disorders of passengers and crew, the safety of the ship is paramount, not the happiness or satisfaction of this or that individual."[12]

The difference between administrative behavior in Machiavelli's time and today is largely one of degree. Rules of the game are more complicated and restricted (killing off or putting the opposition on the rack is replaced by discharge, and even this modern "industrial capital punishment" has become difficult). Behavior is today smoother, less blatant, more subtle. But feelings, needs for power, and actions to control the behavior of others follow remarkably similar paths, as detailed examination of Machiavelli's writings relative to current leadership actions will reveal.

Why Leaders Today Practice Machiavellianism

According to the 1964 edition of Webster's *Unabridged Dictionary*, Machiavellianism is "characterized by shrewdness" rather than by interest in an individual's welfare. "Manipulation," a term closely identified with Machiavellianism, is ". . . the capacity of an individual to modify the behavior of others in a manner which he desires and at the same time resist modifying his own behavior in a manner which he does not desire."[13]

A definition of the twentieth-century Machiavellian administrator is one who employs aggressive, manipulative, exploiting, and devious moves in order to achieve personal and organizational objectives. These moves are undertaken according to perceived feasibility with secondary consideration (what is necessary under the circumstances) to the feelings, needs, and/or "rights" of others. Not that Machiavellianism is "right" or even particularly "bright," but it exists in today's leadership and needs to be recognized as such.

A number of forces are responsible for Machiavellian actions on the part of leaders today:

1. Ambition—consequent impatience
2. Organizational constraints—on actions or incentives
3. The failure of less directive methods—setting examples or giving cues
4. Operationality—feasibility as observed and as a consequence of trial and error
5. Ignorance—aggressiveness, etc., the only ways known to obtain results
6. Personality of the individual—e.g., compulsive, or at the other extreme, averse to confrontation

One of the pervasive, really significant reasons for application of Machiavellianism in today's organizations centers around the ugly problem of loyalty. Loyalty here refers to dedication or commitment to persons, to task, and to organization. Loyalties today are manifestly at odds with one another—loyalties to the establishment, to oneself, to one's family, to society, to others in the organization (superiors, associates, subordinates). Of the various forces affecting loyalty, self-interest is perhaps the most powerful, influencing both those who employ Machiavellianism and the recipients thereof. Whether called conflict in needs, conflict in values, or what, dedication becomes no simple matter.

Loyalties constituted a serious problem in Renaissance Italy, too, where dedication was far from constant or wholehearted. This is one of the most powerful reasons for the relevance of Machiavelli's thinking today, since his observations took place in an environment in which loyalties switched with astounding facility—allies to enemies *among* city states and vice versa, supporters to opponents *within* city states. Whom could one trust? And for how long? In a much more sophisticated way, the problem of shifting loyalties is widespread in organizations today—e.g., office politics, shifting balance of power, ganging up on a single member, "knifing" someone—preferably an already-wounded member who cannot retaliate and most preferably a critically wounded member on his way out.

As intimated in the foregoing, Machiavellian moves may be warranted and even necessary under many circumstances in today's organizations. Indeed, some maneuverings in the Machiavellian cast may well be partially for the benefit of the "other" person: the long-service employee who has been faithful and diligent but whose work is deteriorating may be moved to a better paying sinecure in the hope of not hurting him; the stubborn but valuable employee who blocks changes may be unobtrusively circumvented or left off committees; the sensitive, useful employee who has grievous shortcomings may be beguiled into taking an assistant whose work will be complementing.

Now for some examples of the many more prevalent Machiavellianisms that are justified or necessary for the "good of the organization" or for protecting oneself in the face of resistive, low motivated, or unprincipled personnel: using deviousness when power is limited and some action is required; inducing a nondelegating superior to expand one's duties; activating the man who is secure in his job, who knows that he is, and who will not do what he should; counteracting the moves of someone who is out to get one's job, to make one look bad, or to make himself look good in comparison with one.

At this point there are some thoughts about Machiavellianism today which are worth injecting so as to provide balance. Awareness of this aggressive sort of leadership can be helpful if the net result is increased understanding of administrative behavior without provoking an inordinate amount of paranoia. It is easy to engage in projection that can be harmful. Mere sensitivity to prospects for devious moves, on the other hand, can increase one's ability to recognize Machiavellian moves and can make possible counteractions that will prevent damage to oneself and to one's organization.

It is likewise worth recognizing that motivation is extremely complicated, that self-interest is a natural source of action, and that there are bound to be degrees of Machiavellianism present in managerial behavior—extreme selfishness or nonfunctionality at one extreme to selfishness plus organizational interest, to concern for both the organization and other individuals or groups, to what is for the good of others and the organization, and to what is for the benefit of the other individual or group as such. And any of these degrees can be Machiavellian depending on methods used and on end objectives.

Notes

[1] Guiseppe Prezzolini, "The Kernel of Machiavelli," *The National Review* (April 8, 1961), p. 217.

[2] George S. Odiorne, "Reality in Management," *Michigan Business Review* (Nov., 1967), p. 23.

[3] The moral tone of Francis Bacon's *Essays* (1597–1623), *The Art of Worldly Wisdom* by Baltazer Gracian y Morales (1653), and the ethics of Friedrich Nietzsche (1844–1900) are spotted examples reflective of the objective, realistic point of view seen in Machiavelli's work.

[4] Livy was born in 59 B.C. and died in 17 A.D. His fame rests upon his history of Rome, some 142 volumes.

[5] Count Carlo Sforza, *The Living Thoughts of Machiavelli* (Longmans, Greene & Co., 1940), p. 13.

[6] Antony Jay, *Management and Machiavelli* (New York: Holt, Rinehart & Winston, 1967), p. 26.

[7] Jay, p. 4.

[8] Jay, p. 4.

[9] Jay, p. 17.

[10] Jay, p. 17.

[11] Jay, p. 28.

[12] Prezzolini, p. 216.

[13] Stephen B. Miles Jr., "The Management Politician," *Harvard Business Review,* 39 (Jan.–Feb., 1961), p. 36.

32

Leadership Power Bases

John R. P. French, Jr. and Bertram Raven

The processes of power are pervasive, complex, and often disguised in our society. Accordingly one finds in political science, in sociology, and in social psychology a variety of distinctions among different types of social power or among qualitatively different processes of social influence.[1] Our main purpose is to identify the major types of power and to define them systematically so that we may compare them according to the changes which they produce and the other effects which accompany the use of power. The phenomena of power and influence involve a dyadic relation between two agents which may be viewed from two points of view: (a) What determines the behavior of the agent who exerts power? (b) What determines the reactions of the recipient of this behavior? We take this second point of view and formulate our theory in terms of the life space of P, the person upon whom the power is exerted. In this way we hope to define basic concepts of power which will be adequate to explain many of the phenomena of social influence, including some which have been described in other less genotypic terms.

Recent empirical work, especially on small groups, has demonstrated the necessity of distinguishing different types of power in order to account for the different effects found in studies of social influence. Yet there is no doubt that more empirical knowledge will be needed to make final decisions concerning the necessary differentiations, but this knowledge will be obtained only by research based on some preliminary theoretical distinctions. We present such preliminary concepts and some of the hypotheses they suggest.

Reprinted with permission of the Institute for Social Research at the University of Michigan from *Studies in Social Power*, D. Cartwright, ed., 1959, pp. 150–167. Originally titled "The Bases of Social Power." Copyright © 1959 by the University of Michigan.

Power, Influence, and Change

Psychological Change

Since we shall define power in terms of influence, and influence in terms of psychological change, we begin with a discussion of change. We want to define change at a level of generality which includes changes in behavior, opinions, attitudes, goals, needs, values and all other aspects of the person's psychological field. We shall use the word "system" to refer to any such part of the life space.[2] Following Lewin, the state of a system at time 1 will be denoted $s_1(a)$.[3]

Psychological change is defined as any alteration of the state of some system a over time. The amount of change is measured by the size of the difference between the states of the system a at time 1 and at time 2: $ch(a) = s_2(a) - s_1(a)$.

Change in any psychological system may be conceptualized in terms of psychological forces. But it is important to note that the change must be coordinated to the resultant force of all the forces operating at the moment. Change in an opinion, for example, may be determined jointly by a driving force induced by another person, a restraining force corresponding to anchorage in a group opinion, and an own force stemming from the person's needs.

Social Influence

Our theory of social influence and power is limited to influence on the person, P, produced by a social agent, O, where O can be either another person, a role, a norm, a group or a part of a group. We do not consider social influence exerted on a group.

The influence of O on system a in the life space of P is defined as the resultant force on system a which has its source in an act of O. This resultant force induced by O consists of two components: a force to change the system in the direction induced by O and an opposing resistance set up by the same act of O.

By this definition the influence of O does not include P's own forces nor the forces induced by other social agents. Accordingly the "influence" of O must be clearly distinguished from O's "control" of P. O may be able to induce strong forces on P to carry out an activity (*i.e.*, O exerts strong influence on P); but if the opposing forces induced by another person or by P's own needs are stronger, then P will locomote in an opposite direction (*i.e.*, O does not have control over P). Thus psychological change in P can be taken as an operational definition of the social influence of O on P only when the effects of other forces have been eliminated.

It is assumed that any system is interdependent with other parts of the life space so that a change in one may produce changes in others. However, this theory focuses on the primary changes in a system which are produced directly by social influence; it is less concerned with secondary changes which are indirectly effected in the other systems or with primary changes produced by nonsocial influences.

Commonly, social influence takes place through an intentional act on the part of O. However, we do not want to limit our definition of "act" to such conscious behavior. Indeed, influence might result from the passive presence of O, with no evidence of speech or overt movement. A policeman's standing on a corner may be considered an act of an agent for the speeding motorist. Such acts of the inducing agent will vary in strength, for O may not always utilize all of his power. The policeman, for example, may merely stand and watch or act more strongly by blowing his whistle at the motorist.

The influence exerted by an act need not be in the direction intended by O. The direction of the resultant force on P will depend on the relative magnitude of the induced force set up by the act of O and the resisting force in the opposite direction which is generated by that same act. In cases where O intends to influence P in a given direction, a resultant force in the same direction may be termed positive influence whereas a resultant force in the opposite direction may be termed negative influence.

If O produces the intended change, he has exerted positive control; but if he produces a change in the opposite direction, as for example in the negativism of young children or in the phenomena of negative reference groups, he has exerted negative control.

Social Power

The *strength of power* of O/P in some system *a* is defined as the maximum potential ability of O to influence P in *a*.

By this definition influence is kinetic power, just as power is potential influence. It is assumed that O is capable of various acts which, because of some more or less enduring relation to P, are able to exert influence on P.[4] O's power is measured by his maximum possible influence, though he may often choose to exert less than his full power.

An equivalent definition of power may be stated in terms of the resultant of two forces set up by the act of O: one in the direction of O's influence attempt and another resisting force in the opposite direction. Power is the maximum resultant of these two forces:

$$\text{Power of O / P(a)} = \left(f_{a,x} - f_{\overline{a,x}} \right)^{\max}$$

where the source of both forces is an act of O.

Thus the power of O with respect to system *a* of P is equal to the maximum resultant force of two forces set up by any possible act of O: (a) the force which O can set up on the system *a* to change in the direction x, (b) the resisting force[5] in the opposite direction. Whenever the first component force is greater than the second, positive power exists; but if the second component force is greater than the first, then O has negative power over P.

It is necessary to define power with respect to a specified system because the power of O/P may vary greatly from one system to another. O may have great power to control the behavior of P but little power to control his opinions. Of course a high power of O/P does not imply a low power of P/O; the two variables are conceptually independent.

For certain purposes it is convenient to define the range of power as the set of all systems within which O has power of strength greater than zero. A husband may have a broad range of power over his wife, but a narrow range of power over his employer. We shall use the term "magnitude of power" to denote the summation of O's power over P in all systems of his range.

The Dependence of s(a) on O

Several investigators have been concerned with differences between superficial conformity and "deeper" changes produced by social influence.[6] The kinds of systems which are changed and the stability of these changes have been handled by distinctions such as "public vs. private attitudes," "overt vs. covert behavior," "compliance vs. internalization," and "own vs. induced forces." Though stated as dichotomies, all of these distinctions suggest an underlying dimension of the degree of dependence of the state of a system on O.

We assume that any change in the state of a system is produced by a change in some factor upon which it is functionally dependent. The state of an opinion, for example, may change because of a change either in some internal factor such as a need or in some external factor such as the arguments of O. Likewise the maintenance of the same state of a system is produced by the stability or lack of change in the internal and external factors. In general, then, psychological change and stability can be conceptualized in terms of dynamic dependence. Our interest is focused on the special case of dependence on an external agent, O.[7]

In many cases the initial state of the system has the character of a quasi-stationary equilibrium with a central force held around $s_1(a)$.[8] In such cases we may derive a tendency toward retrogression to the original state as soon as the force induced by O is removed.[9] Let us suppose that O exerts influence producing a new state of the system, $s_2(a)$. Is $s_2(a)$ now dependent on the continued presence of O? In principle we could answer this question by removing any traces of O from the life space of P and by observing the consequent state of the system at time 3. If $s_3(a)$ retrogresses completely back to $s_1(a)$, then we may conclude that maintenance of $s_2(a)$ was completely dependent on O; but if $s_3(a)$ equals $s_2(a)$, this lack of change shows that $s_2(a)$ has become completely independent of O. In general the degree of dependence of $s_2(a)$ on O, following O's influence, may be defined as equal to the amount of retrogression following the removal of O from the life space of P:

$$\text{Degree of dependence of } s_2(a) \text{ on } O = s_2(a) - s_3(a).$$

A given degree of dependence at time 2 may later change, for example, through the gradual weakening of O's influence. At this later time, the degree of dependence of $s_4(a)$ on O, would still be equal to the amount of retrogression toward the initial state of equilibrium $s_1(a)$. Operational measures of the degree of dependence on O will, of course, have to be taken under conditions where all other factors are held constant.

Consider the example of three separated employees who have been working at the same steady level of production despite normal, small fluctuations in the work environment. The supervisor orders each to increase his production, and the level of each goes up from 100 to 115 pieces per day. After a week of producing at the new rate of 115 pieces per day, the supervisor is removed for a week. The production of employee A immediately returns to 100 but B and C return to only 110 pieces per day. Other things being equal, we can infer that A's new rate was completely dependent on his supervisor whereas the new rate of B and C was dependent on the supervisor only to the extent of 5 pieces. Let us further assume that when the supervisor returned, the production of B and of C returned to 115 without further orders from the supervisor. Now another month goes by during which B and C maintain a steady 115 pieces per day. However, there is a difference between them: B's level of production still depends on O to the extent of 5 pieces whereas C has come to rely on his own sense of obligation to obey the order of his legitimate supervisor rather than on the supervisor's external pressure for the maintenance of his 115 pieces per day. Accordingly, the next time the supervisor departs, B's production again drops to 110 but C's remains at 115 pieces per day. In cases like employee B, the degree of dependence is contingent on the perceived probability that O will observe the state of the system and note P's conformity.[10] The level of observability will in turn depend on both the nature of the system (*e.g.*, the difference between a covert opinion and overt behavior) and on the environmental barriers to observation (*e.g.*, O is too far away from P). In other cases, for example that of employee C, the new behavior pattern is highly dependent on his supervisor, but the degree of dependence of the new state will be related not to the level of observability but rather to factors inside P, in this case a sense of duty to perform an act legitimately prescribed by O. The internalization of social norms is a related process of decreasing degree of dependence of behavior on an external O and increasing dependence on an internal value; it is usually assumed that internalization is accompanied by a decrease in the effects of level of observability.[11]

The concepts "dependence of a system on O" and "observability as a basis for dependence" will be useful in understanding the stability of conformity. In the next section we shall discuss various types of power and the types of conformity which they are likely to produce.

The Bases of Power

By the basis of power we mean the relationship between O and P which is the source of that power. It is rare that we can say with certainty that a given empirical case of power is limited to one source. Normally, the relation between O and P will be characterized by several qualitatively different variables which are bases of power.[12] Although there are undoubtedly many possible bases of power which may be distinguished, we shall here define five which seem especially common and important. These five bases of O's power are: (1) reward power, based on P's perception that O has the ability to mediate rewards for him; (2) coercive power, based on P's perception that O has the ability to mediate punishments for him; (3) legitimate power, based on the perception by P that O has a legitimate right to prescribe behavior for him; (4) referent power, based on P's identification with O; (5) expert power, based on the perception that O has some special knowledge or expertness.

Our first concern is to define the bases which give rise to a given type of power. Next, we describe each type of power according to its strength, range, and the degree of dependence of the new state of the system which is most likely to occur with each type of power. We shall also examine the other effects which the exercise of a given type of power may have upon P and his relationship to O. Finally, we shall point out the interrelationships between different types of power, and the effects of use of one type of power by O upon other bases of power which he might have over P. Thus we shall both define a set of concepts and propose a series of hypotheses. Most of these hypotheses have not been systematically tested, although there is a good deal of evidence in favor of several. No attempt will be made to summarize that evidence here.

Reward Power

Reward power is defined as power whose basis is the ability to reward. The strength of the reward power of O/P increases with the magnitude of the rewards which P perceives that O can mediate for him. Reward power depends on O's ability to administer positive valences and to remove or decrease negative valences. The strength of reward power also depends upon the probability that O can mediate the reward, as perceived by P. A common example of reward power is the addition of piece-work rate in the factory as an incentive to increase production.

The new state of the system induced by a promise of reward (for example the factory worker's increased level of production) will be highly dependent on O. Since O mediates the reward, he controls the probability that P will receive it. Thus P's new rate of production will be dependent on his subjective probability that O will reward him for conformity minus his subjective probability that O will reward him even if he returns to his old level. Both probabilities will be greatly affected by the level of observability of P's behavior. Incidentally, a piece rate often seems to have more effect on production than a merit rating system because it yields a higher probability of reward for conformity and a much lower probability of reward for nonconformity.

The utilization of actual rewards (instead of promises) by O will tend over time to increase the attraction of P toward O and therefore the referent power of O over P. As we shall note later, such referent power will permit O to induce changes which are relatively independent. Neither rewards nor promises will arouse resistance in P, provided P considers it legitimate for O to offer rewards.

The range of reward power is specific to those regions within which O can reward P for conforming. The use of rewards to change systems within the range of reward power tends to increase reward power by increasing the probability attached to future promises. However, unsuccessful attempts to exert reward power outside the range of power would tend to decrease the power; for example if O offers to reward P for performing an impossible act, this will reduce for P the probability of receiving future rewards promised by O.

Coercive Power

Coercive power is similar to reward power in that it also involves O's ability to manipulate the attainment of valences. Coercive power of O/P stems from the expectation on the part of P that he will be punished by O if he fails to conform to the influence attempt. Thus negative valences will exist in given regions of P's life space, corresponding to the threatened punishment by O. The strength of coercive power depends on the magnitude of the negative valence of the threatened punishment multiplied by the perceived probability that P can avoid the punishment by conformity, *i.e.*, the probability of punishment for nonconformity minus the probability of punishment for conformity.[13] Just as an offer of a piece-rate bonus in a factory can serve as a basis for reward power, so the ability to fire a worker if he falls below a given level of production will result in coercive power.

Coercive power leads to dependent change also; and the degree of dependence varies with the level of observability of P's conformity. An excellent illustration of coercive power leading to dependent change is provided by a clothes presser in a factory observed by Coch and French.[14] As her efficiency rating climbed above average for the group the other workers began to "scapegoat" her. That the resulting plateau in her production was not independent of the group was evident once she was removed from the presence of the other workers. Her production immediately climbed to new heights.[15]

At times, there is some difficulty in distinguishing between reward power and coercive power. Is the withholding of a reward really equivalent to a punishment? Is the withdrawal of punishment equivalent to a reward? The answer must be a psychological one—it depends upon the situation as it exists for P. But ordinarily we would answer these questions in the affirmative; for P, receiving a reward is a positive valence as is the relief of suffering. There is some evidence that conformity to group norms in order to gain acceptance (reward power) should be distinguished from conformity as a means of forestalling rejection (coercive power).[16]

The distinction between these two types of power is important because the dynamics are different. The concept of "sanctions" sometimes lumps the two together despite their opposite effects. While reward power may eventually result in an independent system, the effects of coercive power will continue to be dependent. Reward power will tend to increase the attraction of P toward O; coercive power will decrease this attraction.[17] The valence of the region of behavior will become more negative, acquiring some negative valence from the threatened punishment. The negative valence of punishment would also spread to other regions of the life space. Lewin has pointed out this distinction between the effects of rewards and punishment.[18] In the case of threatened punishment, there will be a resultant force on P to leave the field entirely. Thus, to achieve conformity, O must not only place a strong negative valence in certain regions through threat of punishment, but O must also introduce restraining forces, or other strong valences, so as to prevent P from withdrawing completely from O's range of coercive power. Otherwise the probability of receiving the punishment, if P does not conform, will be too low to be effective.

Legitimate Power

Legitimate power is probably the most complex of those treated here, embodying notions from the structural sociologist, the group-norm and role-oriented social psychologist, and the clinical psychologist.

There has been considerable investigation and speculation about socially prescribed behavior, particularly that which is specified to a given role or position. Linton distinguishes group norms according to whether they are universals for everyone in the culture, alternatives (the individual having a choice as to whether or not to accept them), or specialties (specific to given positions).[19] Whether we speak of internalized norms, role prescriptions and expectations,[20] or internalized pressures,[21] the fact remains that each individual sees certain regions toward which he should locomote, some regions toward which he should not locomote, and some regions toward which he may locomote if they are generally attractive for him. This applies to specific behaviors in which he may, should, or should not engage; it applies to certain attitudes or beliefs which he may, should, or should not hold. The feeling of "oughtness" may be an internalization from his parents, from his teachers, from his religion, or may have been logically developed from some idiosyncratic system of ethics. He will speak of such behaviors with expressions like "should," "ought to," or "has a right to." In many cases, the original source of the requirement is not recalled.

Though we have oversimplified such evaluations of behavior with a positive-neutral-negative trichotomy, the evaluation of behaviors by the person is really more one of degree. This dimension of evaluation we shall call "legitimacy." Conceptually, we may think of legitimacy as a valence in a region which is induced by some internalized norm or value. This value has the same conceptual property as power, namely an ability to induce force fields.[22] It may or may not be correct that values (or the super-ego) are internalized parents, but at least they can set up force fields which have a phenomenal "oughtness" similar to a parent's prescription. Like a value, a need can also induce valences (*i.e.*, force fields) in P's psychological environment, but these valences have more the phenomenal character of noxious or attractive properties of the object or activity. When a need induces a valence in P, for example, when a need makes an object attractive to P, this attraction applies to P but not to other persons. When a value induces a valence, on the other hand, it not only sets up forces on P to engage in the activity, but P may feel that all others ought to behave in the same way. Among other things, this evaluation applies to the legitimate right of some other individual or group to prescribe behavior or beliefs for a person even though the other cannot apply sanctions.

Legitimate power of O/P is here defined as that power which stems from internalized values in P which dictate that O has a legitimate right to influence P and that P has an obligation to accept this influence. We note that legitimate power is very similar to the notion of legitimacy of authority which has long been explored by sociologists, particularly by Weber,[23] and more recently by Goldhammer and Shils.[24] However, legitimate power is not always a role relation: P may accept an induction from O simply because he had previously promised to help O and he values his work too much to break the promise. In all cases, the notion of legitimacy involves some sort of code or standard, accepted by the individual, by virtue of which the external agent can assert his power. We shall attempt to describe a few of these values here.

Bases for Legitimate Power. Cultural values constitute one common basis for the legitimate power of one individual over another. O has characteristics which are specified by the culture as giving him the right to prescribe behavior for P, who may not have these characteristics. These bases, which Weber has called the authority of the "eternal yesterday," include such things as age, intelligence, caste, and physical characteristics.[25] In some cultures, the aged are granted the right to prescribe behavior for others in practically all behavior areas. In most cultures, there are certain areas of behavior in which a person of one sex is granted the right to prescribe behavior for the other sex.

Acceptance of the social structure is another basis for legitimate power. If P accepts as right the social structure of his group, organization, or society, especially the social structure involving a hierarchy of authority, P will accept the legitimate authority of O who occupies a superior office in the hierarchy. Thus legitimate power in a formal organization is largely a relationship between offices rather than between persons. And the acceptance of an office as *right* is a basis for legitimate power—a judge has a right to levy fines, a foreman should assign work, a priest is justified in prescribing religious beliefs, and it is the management's prerogative to make certain decisions.[26] However, legitimate power also involves the perceived right of the person to hold the office.

Designation by a legitimizing agent is a third basis for legitimate power. An influencer O may be seen as legitimate in prescribing behavior for P because he has been granted such power by a legitimizing agent whom P accepts. Thus a department head may accept the authority of his vice-president in a certain area because that authority has been specifically delegated by the president. An election is perhaps the most common example of a group's serving to legitimize the authority of one individual or office for other individuals in the group. The success of such legitimizing depends upon the acceptance of the legitimizing agent and procedure. In this case it depends ultimately on certain democratic values concerning election procedures. The election process is one of legitimizing a person's right to an office which already has a legitimate range of power associated with it.

Range of Legitimate Power of O/P.   The areas in which legitimate power may be exercised are generally specified along with the designation of that power. A job description, for example, usually specifies supervisory activities and also designates the person to whom the job-holder is responsible for the duties described. Some bases for legitimate authority carry with them a very broad range. Culturally derived bases for legitimate power are often especially broad. It is not uncommon to find cultures in which a member of a given caste can legitimately prescribe behavior for all members of lower castes in practically all regions. More common, however, are instances of legitimate power where the range is specifically and narrowly prescribed. A sergeant in the army is given a specific set of regions within which he can legitimately prescribe behavior for his men.

The attempted use of legitimate power which is outside of the range of legitimate power will decrease the legitimate power of the authority figure. Such use of power which is not legitimate will also decrease the attractiveness of O.[27]

Legitimate Power and Influence.   The new state of the system which results from legitimate power usually has high dependence on O though it may become independent. Here, however, the degree of dependence is not related to the level of observability. Since legitimate power is based on P's values, the source of the forces induced by O include both these internal values and O. O's induction serves to activate the values and to relate them to the system which is influenced, but thereafter the new state of the system may become directly dependent on the values with no mediation by O. Accordingly this new state will be relatively stable and consistent across varying environmental situations since P's values are more stable than his psychological environment.

We have used the term legitimate not only as a basis for the power of an agent, but also to describe the general behaviors of a person. Thus, the individual P may also consider the legitimacy of the attempts to use other types of power by O. In certain cases, P will consider that O has a legitimate right to threaten punishment for nonconformity; in other cases, such use of coercion would not be seen as legitimate. P might change in response to coercive power of O, but it will make a considerable difference in his attitude and conformity if O is not seen as having a legitimate right to use such coercion. In such cases, the attraction of P for O will be particularly diminished, and the influence attempt will arouse more resistance.[28] Similarly the utilization of reward power may vary in legitimacy; the word "bribe," for example, denotes an illegitimate reward.

Referent Power

The referent power of O/P has its basis in the identification of P with O. By identification, we mean a feeling of oneness of P with O, or a desire for such an identity. If O is a person toward whom P is highly attracted, P will have a desire to become closely associated with O. If O is an attractive group, P will have a feeling of membership or a desire to join. If P is already closely associated with O, he will want to maintain this relationship.[29] P's identification with O can be established or maintained if P behaves, believes, and perceives as O does. Accordingly O has the ability to influence P, even though P may be unaware of this referent power. A verbalization of such power by P might be, "I am like O, and therefore I shall behave or believe as O does," or "I want to be like O, and I will be more like O if I behave or believe as O does." The stronger the identification of P with O, the greater the referent power of O/P.

Similar types of power have already been investigated under a number of different formulations. Festinger points out that in an ambiguous situation, the individual seeks some sort of "social reality" and may adopt the cognitive structure of the individual or group with which he identifies.[30] In such a case, the lack of clear structure may be threatening to the individual and the agreement of his beliefs with those of a reference group will both satisfy his need for structure and give him added security through increased identification with his group.[31]

We must try to distinguish between referent power and other types of power which might be operative at the same time. If a member is attracted to a group and he conforms to its norms only because he fears ridicule or expulsion from the group for nonconformity, we would call this coercive power. On the other hand if he conforms in order to obtain praise for conformity, it is a case of reward power. The basic criterion for distinguishing referent power from both coercive and reward power is the mediation of the punishment and the reward by O: to the extent that O mediates the sanctions (*i.e.,* has means control over P) we are dealing with coercive and reward power; but to the extent that P avoids discomfort or gains satisfaction by conformity based on identification, regardless of O's responses, we are dealing with referent power. Conformity with majority opinion is sometimes based on a respect for the collective wisdom of the group, in which case it is expert power. It is important to distinguish these phenomena, all grouped together elsewhere as "pressures toward uniformity," since the type of change which occurs will be different for different bases of power.

The concepts of "reference group"[32] and "prestige suggestion" may be treated as instances of referent power. In this case, O, the prestigious person or group, is valued by P; because P desires to be associated or identified with O, he will assume attitudes or beliefs held by O. Similarly a negative reference group which O dislikes and evaluates negatively may exert negative influence on P as a result of negative referent power.

It has been demonstrated that the power which we designate as referent power is especially great when P is attracted to O.[33] In our terms, this would mean that the greater the attraction, the greater the identification, and consequently the greater the referent power. In some cases, attraction or prestige may have a specific basis, and the range of referent power will be limited accordingly: a group of campers may have great referent power over a member regarding campcraft, but considerably less effect on other regions.[34] However, we hypothesize that the greater the attraction of P toward O, the broader the range of referent power of O/P.

The new state of a system produced by referent power may be dependent on or independent of O; but the degree of dependence is not affected by the level of observability to O.[35] In fact, P is often not consciously aware of the referent power which O exerts over him. There is probably a tendency for some of these dependent changes to become independent of O quite rapidly.

Expert Power

The strength of the expert power of O/P varies with the extent of the knowledge or perception which P attributes to O within a given area. Probably P evaluates O's expertness in relation to his own knowledge as well as against an absolute standard. In any case expert power results in primary social influence on P's cognitive structure and probably not on other types of systems. Of course changes in the cognitive structure can change the direction of forces and hence of locomotion, but such a change of behavior is secondary social influence. Expert power has been demonstrated experimentally.[36] Accepting an attorney's advice in legal matters is a common example of expert influence; but there are many instances based on much less knowledge, such as the acceptance by a stranger of directions given by a native villager.

Expert power, where O need not be a member of P's group, is called "informational power" by Deutsch and Gerard.[37] This type of expert power must be distinguished from influence based on the content of communication as described by Hovland et al.[38] The influence of the content of a communication upon an opinion is presumably a secondary influence produced after the *primary* influence (*i.e.*, the acceptance of the information). Since power is here defined in terms of the primary changes, the influence of the content on a related opinion is not a case of expert power as we have defined it, but the initial acceptance of the validity of the content does seem to be based on expert power or referent power. In other cases, however, so-called facts may be accepted as self-evident because they fit into P's cognitive structure; if this impersonal acceptance of the truth of the fact is independent of the more or less enduring relationship between O and P, then P's acceptance of the fact is not an actualization of expert power. Thus we distinguish between expert power based on the credibility of O and informational influence which is based on characteristics of the stimulus such as the logic of the argument or the "self-evident facts."

Wherever expert influence occurs it seems to be necessary both for P to think that O knows and for P to trust that O is telling the truth (rather than trying to deceive him).

Expert power will produce a new cognitive structure which is initially relatively dependent on O, but informational influence will produce a more independent structure. The former is likely to become more independent with the passage of time. In both cases the degree of dependence on O is not affected by the level of observability.

The "sleeper effect"[39] is an interesting case of a change in the degree of dependence of an opinion on O. An unreliable O (who probably had negative referent power but some positive expert power) presented "facts" which were accepted by the subjects and which would normally produce secondary influence on their opinions and beliefs. However, the negative referent power aroused resistance and resulted in negative social influence on their beliefs (*i.e.*, set up a force in the direction opposite to the influence attempt), so that there was little change in the subjects' opinions. With the passage of time, however, the subjects tended to forget the identity of the negative communicator faster than they forgot the contents of his communication, so there was a weakening of the negative referent influence and a consequent delayed positive change in the subjects' beliefs in the direction of the influence attempt ("sleeper effect"). Later, when the identity of the negative communicator was experimentally reinstated, these resisting forces were reinstated, and there was another negative change in belief in a direction opposite to the influence attempt.[40]

The range of expert power, we assume, is more delimited than that of referent power. Not only is it restricted to cognitive systems but the expert is seen as having superior knowledge or ability in very specific areas, and his power will be limited to these areas, though some "halo effect" might occur. Recently, some of our renowned physical scientists have found quite painfully that their expert power in physical sciences does not extend to regions involving international politics. Indeed, there is some evidence that the attempted exertion of expert power outside of the range of expert power will reduce that expert power. An undermining of confidence seems to take place.

Summary

We have distinguished five types of power: referent power, expert power, reward power, coercive power, and legitimate power. These distinctions led to the following hypotheses:

1. For all five types, the stronger the basis of power the greater the power.

2. For any type of power the size of the range may vary greatly, but in general referent power will have the broadest range.

3. Any attempt to utilize power outside the range of power will tend to reduce the power.

4. A new state of a system produced by reward power or coercive power will be highly dependent on O, and the more observable P's conformity the more dependent the state. For the other three types of power, the new state is usually dependent, at least in the beginning, but in any case the level of observability has no effect on the degree of dependence.

5. Coercion results in decreased attraction of P toward O and high resistance; reward power results in increased attraction and low resistance.

6. The more legitimate the coercion the less it will produce resistance and decreased attraction.

Notes

[1] S. E. Asch, *Social Psychology* (New York: Prentice-Hall, 1952). L. Festinger, "An Analysis of Compliant Behavior," in *Group Relations at the Crossroads*, eds. M. Sherif and M. O. Wilson (New York: Harper, 1953), pp. 232–56. H. Goldhammer and E. A. Shils, "Types of Power and Status," *Amer. J. Sociol.*, Vol. 45 (1939): 171–78. M. Jahoda, "Psychological Issues in Civil Liberties," *Amer. Psychologist*, Vol. 11 (1956): 234–40. H. Kelman, "Three Processes of Acceptance of Social Influence: Compliance, Identification and Internalization" (Paper read at the meetings of the American Psychological Association, August 1956). R. Linton, *The Cultural Background of Personality* (New York: Appleton-Century-Crofts, 1945). R. Lippitt *et al.*, "The Dynamics of Power," *Hum. Relat.*, Vol. 5 (1952): 37–64. B. Russell, *Power: A New Social Analysis* (New York: Norton, 1938). E. P. Torrance and R. Mason, "Instructor Effort to Influence: An Experimental Evaluation of Six Approaches" (Paper presented at USAF-NRC Symposium on Personnel, Training, and Human Engineering, Washington, DC, 1956).

[2] The word "system" is here used to refer to a whole or to a part of the whole.

[3] K. Lewin, *Field Theory in Social Science* (New York: Harper, 1951).

[4] The concept of power has the conceptual property of *potentiality*; but it seems useful to restrict this potential influence to more or less enduring power relations between O and P by excluding from the definition of power those cases where the potential influence is so momentary or so changing that it cannot be predicted from the existing relationship. Power is a useful concept for describing social structure only if it has a certain stability over time; it is useless if every momentary social stimulus is viewed as actualizing social power.

[5] We define resistance to an attempted induction as a force in the opposite direction which is set up by the same act of O. It must be distinguished from opposition which is defined as existing opposing forces which do not have their source in the same act of O. For example, a boy might resist his mother's order to eat spinach because of the manner of the induction attempt, and at the same time he might oppose it because he didn't like spinach.

[6] Asch, *op. cit.* J. E. Dittes and H. H. Kelley, "Effects of Different Conditions of Acceptance upon Conformity to Group Norms," *J. Abnorm. Soc. Psychol.*, Vol. 53 (1956): 100–107. Festinger, "An Analysis . . .," *op. cit.* J. R. P. French, Jr., G. Levinger, and H. W. Morrison, "The Legitimacy of Coercive Power" (In preparation). J. R. P. French, Jr. and B. H. Raven, "An Experiment in Legitimate and Coercive Power" (In preparation). Jahoda, *op. cit.* D. Katz and R. L. Schank, *Social Psychology* (New York: Wiley, 1938). H. H. Kelley and E. H. Volkart, "The Resistance to Change of Group-Anchored Attitudes," *Amer. Soc. Rev.*, Vol. 17 (1952): 453–65. Kelman, *op. cit.* Lewin, *Field . . . op. cit.* B. H. Raven and J. R. P. French, Jr., "Group Support, Legitimate Power, and Social Influence," *J. Person.*, Vol. 26 (1958): 400–409. R. Rommetveit, *Social Norms and Roles* (Minneapolis: University of Minnesota Press, 1953).

[7] J. G. March, "An Introduction to the Theory and Measurement of Influence," *Amer. Polit. Sci. Rev.*, Vol. 49 (1955): 431–51.

[8] Lewin, *Field . . . op. cit.*, p. 106.

[9] J. G. Miller, "Toward a General Theory for the Behavioral Sciences," *Amer. Psychologist*, Vol. 10 (1955): 513–31 assumes that all living systems have this character. However, it may be that some systems in the life space do not have this elasticity.

[10] Dittes and Kelley, *op. cit.* Festinger, "An Analysis . . ." *op. cit.* French, Levinger, and Morrison, *op. cit.* French and Raven, *op. cit.* Kelman, *op. cit.*

[11] Rommetveit, *op. cit.*

[12] Lippitt *et al.*, *op. cit.*, chapter 11.

[13] French, Levinger, and Morrison, *op. cit.*

[14] L. Coch and J. R. P. French, Jr., "Overcoming Resistance to Change," *Hum. Relat.*, Vol. 1 (1948): 512–32.

[15] Though the primary influence of coercive power is dependent, it often produces secondary changes which are independent. Brainwashing, for example, utilizes coercive power to produce many primary changes in the life space of the prisoner, but these dependent changes can lead to identification with the aggressor and hence to secondary changes in ideology which are independent.

[16] Dittes and Kelley, *op. cit.*

[17] French, Levinger, and Morrison, *op. cit.* French and Raven, *op. cit.*

[18] K. Lewin, *Dynamic Theory of Personality* (New York: McGraw-Hill, 1935), pp. 114–70.

[19] Linton, *op. cit.*

[20] T. M. Newcomb, *Social Psychology* (New York: Dryden, 1950).

[21] P. G. Herbst, "Analysis and Measurement of a Situation," *Hum. Relat.*, Vol. 2 (1953): 113–40.

[22] Lewin, *Field . . . op cit.*, pp. 40–41.

[23] M. Weber, *The Theory of Social and Economic Organization* (Oxford: Oxford University Press, 1947).

[24] Goldhammer and Shils, *op. cit.*

[25] Weber, *op. cit.*

[26] J. R. P. French, Jr., Joachim Israel, and Dagfinn Ås, "Arbeidernes Medvirkning i Industribedriften. En Eksperimentell Undersøkelse." Oslo, Norway: Institute for Social Research, 1957.

[27] French, Levinger, and Morrison, *op. cit.* French and Raven, *op. cit.* Raven and French, *op. cit.*

[28] French, Levinger, and Morrison, *op. cit.*

[29] E. Stotland *et al.*, "Studies on the Effects of Identification" (Forthcoming, University of Michigan, Institute for Social Research). Torrance and Mason, *op. cit.*

[30] L. Festinger, "Informal Social Communication," *Psychol. Rev.*, Vol. 57 (1950): 271–82.

[31] G. M. Hochbaum, "Self-Confidence and Reactions to Group Pressures," *Amer. Soc. Rev.*, Vol. 19 (1954): 678–87. J. M. Jackson and H. D. Saltzstein, "The Effect of Person-Group Relationships on Conformity Processes," *J. Abnorm. Soc. Psychol.*, Vol. 57 (1959): 17–24.

[32] G. E. Swanson, T. M. Newcomb, and E. L. Hartley, *Readings in Social Psychology* (New York: Henry Holt, 1952).

[33] K. W. Back, "Influence through Social Communication," *J. Abnorm. Soc. Psychol.*, Vol. 46 (1951): 9–23. Festinger, *op. cit.* L. Festinger *et al.*, "The Influence Process in the Presence of Extreme Deviates," *Hum. Relat.*, Vol. 5 (1952): 327–46. L. Festinger, S. Schachter, and K. Back, "The Operation of Group Standards," in *Group Dynamics: Research and Theory*, eds. D. Cartwright and A. Zander (Evanston, IL: Row, Peterson, 1953), pp. 204–23. H. B. Gerard, "The Anchorage of Opinions in Face-to-Face Groups," *Hum. Relat.*, Vol. 7 (1954): 313–25. Kelman, *op. cit.* Lippitt, *et al.*, *op. cit.*

[34] Lippitt *et al.*, *op. cit.*

[35] Festinger, "An Analysis . . ." *op. cit.* Kelman, *op. cit.*

[36] Festinger *et al.*, *op. cit.* H. T. Moore, "The Comparative Influence of Majority and Expert Opinion," *Amer. J. Psychol.*, Vol. 32 (1921): 16–20.

[37] M. Deutsch and H. B. Gerard, "A Study of Normative and Informational Influences upon Individual Judgment," *J. Abnorm. Soc. Psychol.*, Vol. 51 (1955): 629–36.

[38] C. I. Hovland, A. A. Lumsdaine, and F. D. Sheffield, *Experiments on Mass Communication* (Princeton, NJ: Princeton University Press, 1949). C. I. Hovland and W. Weiss, "The Influence of Source Credibility on Communication Effectiveness," *Public Opinion Quarterly*, Vol. 15 (1951): 635–50. Kelman, *op. cit.* H. Kelman and C. I. Hovland, "'Reinstatement' of the Communicator in Delayed Measurement of Opinion Change," *J. Abnorm. Soc. Psychol.*, Vol. 48 (1953): 327–35.

[39] Hovland and Weiss, *op. cit.* Kelman and Hovland, *op. cit.*

[40] Kelman and Hovland, *op. cit.*

33

Leadership Role-Making and Leader-Member Exchange

George Graen and James F. Cashman

Role making is a set of processes by which an actor and a functionally interdependent other: (1) work through how each will behave in certain situations (interlocking behavior by reciprocal reinforcement), and (2) agree upon the general nature of their relationship (constructing relationship norms) against the background of the formal organization (Graen, 1975). These processes thus produce dyadic (two-person) social structures (Weick, 1969).

A special case of role making, namely that involving the functional interdependence between a person in a leader position and one in a follower position, can be used to describe a vertical development process. If our focus is restricted to these vertical dyad linkages (VDL), role-making processes can be used to describe the development of both interlocked behavior and relationship norms between leaders and each of their members. Moreover, by appropriately investigating the development of these dyadic linkages during periods when role-making processes are active, we may discover not only the nature of dyadic structures and the processes of becoming, but also the leadership-associated outcomes.

Developmental Approach

A developmental approach focuses on early interactions among members of loosely knit dyads and searches for signs (early warning detectors) of the emerging dyadic social structures. These signs, once discovered are used to predict over time the nature of the fully developed social structure, even the outputs of that structure. By accepting this approach, we make two basic assumptions about the leadership situation in managerial units. First, we assume that some interlocked behaviors must be shaped (successive application of reinforcement) beginning early in the history of the VDL, e.g., critical tasks cannot be commanded of strangers or the consequences may harm the leader. Second, we assume that some relationships must be developed carefully over an extended period of time, e.g., mutual trust must be earned by both parties. Therefore, we expect that early interactions between a leader and a member will emit signs which can be used to predict the nature of the emergent leadership structure: the leader-member exchange.

A Natural Experiment

To examine the development of leader-member exchange within organizational units requires a setting where the parties to the vertical relationships are in the process of working through their respective roles (role making). By longitudinally studying a setting of this kind from several different points of view, the early indicators of leader-member exchange can be related to later behavioral outcomes.

Fortunately, a setting meeting these requirements was available for investigation. A large department of 60 managers was undergoing a complete reorganization. While 50 percent of the managers were in new positions and one-third were new to the organization, nearly 90 percent of the reporting relationships contained at least one new member. The development of leader-member exchanges was investigated over a nine-month period. Employing a wide array of instruments (incorporated into interview schedules), each of the 60 vertical dyad relationships was monitored from both the member's and the leader's points of view during four interview waves: (a) the second month after reorganization; (b) the fourth month; (c) the seventh month; and (d) the ninth month. (For further details on this natural experiment, see Dansereau, Graen, and Haga, 1975; Graen, 1975; Graen et al., 1975; and Haga, Graen, and Dansereau, 1974).

Our sign (early warning detector) of the emerging dyadic social structure and the naturally occurring treatment variable of this experiment was called "negotiating latitude between a member and his leader." The basic notion was that an early sign of the nature of the developing leader-member exchange is the member's evaluation of his relationship with his leader as a source of individualized assistance. A dyadic relationship characterized by a high degree of individualized assistance is more likely to produce negotiated exchanges between a member and a leader than one characterized by a low degree. In fact, a necessary condition for the development of members may be the early application of individualized assistance. Only after a member comes to view his leader as open to dyadic exchanges with him can he be expected to propose, much less engage in, such exchanges.

On the other hand, a leader may not be equally open to such exchanges with all of his members. Therefore, when a member indicates that his leader is open to his requests for individualized assistance, it is taken as a sign that dyadic negotiation is likely and that an in-group exchange is developing. In contrast, when a member indicates that his leader is relatively closed to such requests, it is taken as a sign that dyadic negotiation is unlikely and that an out-group exchange is developing.

Unit Composition

Consider the distribution of in-group and out-group exchanges within units (a unit consists of all members who report to the same leader). The traditional assumption of an average leadership style approach is that each leader will develop homogeneous exchanges with his members within a unit, all will be in-group exchanges or all will be out-group exchanges, but none will be mixed. The vertical dyad linkage approach, in contrast, assumes that many units will be mixed. Only 15 percent of the units showed all exchanges the same. The remaining 85 percent of the units showed mixtures. This result is more compatible with the assumption of heterogeneous vertical relationships within units.

Job Type

Job type was viewed as a validating dimension for our measures of role behavior and job problems. Managers in functionally different types of jobs can be expected to perform their roles using different involvement patterns and to confront different job problems (e.g., resistance to change, red-tape delays, and inadequate authority to do the job). Therefore, our measures of involvement in activities and job problems severity should demonstrate differences among job types. Gratifyingly, job type showed reliable differences on three of the four dimensions of job problems as reported by managers and as reported by superiors. Only the factor dealing with supervisory problems failed to differentiate among job types; however, as we shall see, this was the job problem dimension relevant to leadership. Finally, although job type demonstrated reliable differences on job attitudes, it failed to show such differences on leadership measures.

Leader-Member Exchange

Classification of leader-member exchanges based upon the extent of negotiating latitude during the second month after reorganization revealed two quite different developing situations. In terms of the positional resources of the leader and working relationship with the leader, those classified at two months as showing early in-group exchanges received consistently over time greater amounts of resources assessed and more supportive and sensitive treatment, than did those showing out-group exchanges. In-group members received greater latitude in developing their roles, more inside information, greater influence in decision making, stronger support for their actions, and more consideration for their feelings than did out-group members. On the members' side of the exchange, those members showing in-group exchanges indicated greater involvement in administering and communicating activities than did out-group members.

Output of Exchanges

In addition, leaders indicated that in-group members acted consistently according to the leader's expectations, while the out-group members acted progressively more deviant from the leader's expectations. Out-group-members thus deviated further and further from what the leader wanted. Other outcomes from these two types of exchanges were indicated by the job problems confronting the managers and by the work attitudes of the managers. Although job problems clustered into four separate factors, only one factor dealing with supervisory problems differentiated the in-group from the out-group. From both the members' and the leaders' reports, out-group members faced more severe problems with their superiors than did in-group members. On work attitudes, the in-group showed more positive attitudes toward the job situation in general, the work itself, technical supervision, interpersonal supervision, and job performance rewards.

In summary, the results formed a consistent network of reliable relationships. This network was quite consistent with the model: leaders do routinely differentiate their units by developing in-group exchanges with selected members and out-group exchanges with their remaining members. Furthermore, in addition to developing more effective relationships, members developing in-group exchanges with their leaders assume greater involvement in unit activities and receive greater positional resources from their leader than do their out-group colleagues.

Boss-Leader Exchange

Classification of boss-leader exchanges based upon the latitude of the leaders with their respective bosses during the second month showed predictable differences in the situations confronting both the leaders and their members. Those leaders showing early in-group exchanges with their bosses reported participation in decisions and were given greater job latitude. Their relationships demonstrated more support and greater consideration for their feelings than those reported by their out-group colleagues. In addition, these differences were mirrored in the work attitudes of the leaders, especially in attitudes toward supervision and job performance rewards.

Reports of members revealed that leaders who establish in-group exchanges with their bosses can influence events beyond the boundaries of their units and hence can facilitate the programs of their members to a greater extent than can those leaders who fail to develop such exchanges with their bosses. Consequently, members' reports of problems dealing with extra-unit issues were strongly related to their leader's exchange with his boss. This difference in the instrumental value of the leader for the members was reflected in the members' work attitudes. Leaders who established in-group exchanges with their own bosses were seen as more technically competent and as possessing greater reward potential than those failing to develop such exchanges.

Thus, a boss-leader exchange to which a member is not a party can influence the member's job situation for good or ill. If his leader develops an in-group exchange with his boss, a member may find that his own effectiveness is enhanced and his frustrations are reduced compared with his peer whose leader fails to develop such an exchange with his boss. Although a member may rejoice in his good fortune or curse his misfortune, he can do very little to change this parameter of his situation. In this sense, the exchange relationship of a leader with his boss is an important variable describing the structure of a member's situation. . . .

A Theoretical Interpretation of the Initial Study

Team Building

The model (shown in Table 1) which emerges from our role-making studies of managerial dyads within formal organizations is one of team building within units based upon different leader-member exchanges. Leaders of managerial units, when faced with the task of developing new working relationships with most of the members they lead, responded in manners which served to differentiate their units. Only with some of their subordinate managers did leaders attempt to develop special exchange relationships which transcended the formal employment contract. All subordinate managers so selected may or may not have accepted such a special exchange relationship.

But those who did consummate such an exchange promised to develop into members of the leader's trusted in-group. In contrast, those who either were not given the opportunity, or who declined the opportunity of the special exchange, became members of the leader's out-group. Thus, the units became differentiated over time into two distinct subgroups. Clearly, the key to this model is leader-member exchange.

Table 1   A Developmental Model of Role Making in Vertical Dyads

Model Components		
Input	**Process**	**Output**
Members' Characteristics	**Leader-Member Exchange**	**Job Performance** (rating)
Education, Job Experience, Age, Job Tenure, Sex	1. Interlocked Behavior (a) member behavior— tasks	*Satisfaction:* Overall, Work, Supervision, Interpersonal Relationships, Supervision-Technical Competence,
Leader's Characteristics Education, Job Experience, Job Tenure, Age, Sex, Early Dyadic Relationship, Negotiating Latitude	(b) leader behavior— resources 2. Working Relationship (a) support (b) sensitivity (c) trust	Performance Rewards *Job Problems:* Member Report and Superior Report

Leader-Member Exchange

A distinction made by Jacobs (1970) between "leadership" and "supervisor" exchanges aptly describes some of the differences between in-group and out-group leader-member exchanges. Using Jacobs' labels, leadership exchange involves influencing members without regard to authority, whereas supervisor exchange involves influence through the use of authority based on the employment contract. In developing a leadership exchange with his member, a leader does not rely on the use of position power. Rather, he seeks an alternative basis of influence—one anchored in the interpersonal exchange between leader and member. But what can the leader exchange with his member that is not covered by the employment contract?

Interlocking of Behavior between Leader and Member

A leader, by virtue of his superior position in a hierarchy, possesses certain resources which are not available to his members. If these so-called positional resources (Graen et al., 1973) are or can be made attractive outcomes for his members, a leader may exchange these resources on his own authority. A leader need not wait for formal approval from higher officials to exchange these resources as he must do with contractual outcomes, such as salary increases, promotions, and the like. Further, this immediacy of exchange probably enhances the attractiveness of these outcomes. What resources does a leader possess that can be transformed into outcomes having either intrinsic or instrumental value for members?

A leader of a managerial unit usually has considerable discretion in task assignments, especially with non-routine tasks. He may assign a member: (a) to a task that the member may find too difficult, hence he becomes frustrated and fails; or (b) to a task that the member may find too easy, hence he becomes bored; or (c) to a task that the member may find challenging, hence he grows. Moreover, a leader, through his own actions, can adjust the difficulty level of an assigned task. He can provide or withhold necessary information and support. He also can mediate the consequences of the member's actions by appropriate intervention. He may allow a member to participate in decision making regarding not only his own situation, but that of the entire unit. By virtue of his position on a higher rung of the ladder, a superior may mediate the visibility of his members with other superiors. In addition to the above, even the leader's interpersonal behavior as a person can become a positional resource by virtue of his position. His confidence in and consideration for a member may become attractive outcomes for that member.

A leader may share a portion of some or all of these positional resources with his members. If these resources are or can be made sufficiently attractive to members, they can serve as a leader's contribution to an exchange. If they cannot be made attractive enough to members, such an exchange is unlikely.

What can a member exchange in return for a share of the leader's positional resources? A member can reciprocate with greater than required expenditures of time and energy, the assumption of greater responsibility and risk, and concern for, if not commitment to, the success of the entire unit or organization. A member, in short, can enlarge the area of his vested interest to encompass that of his leader. If these outcomes are sufficiently attractive to a leader, a leader may attempt to establish such an exchange.

Benefits and Costs of an In-Group Exchange

For a leader, some of the costs of entering into such an in-group exchange are greater dependence upon that member and a reduction in control over him. Under such an exchange, a member gains greater capacity to make the leader appear effective or ineffective. Although a leader can delegate critical tasks to such a member, the leader maintains primary responsibility for the accomplishment of these tasks. If the member fails, the leader also fails. With this greater dependence on a member, a leader must relinquish some degree of control over him. A leader must allow this member more latitude and provide him with the confidence and support required to perform adequately. This may mean actually negotiating with the member on unit-wide issues.

Without resorting to authority, some actions cannot be commanded. They must be worked through—taking precious time to arrive at decisions. Resorting to authority on occasion may not be too damaging to a leadership exchange; however, indiscriminate use of formal authority to gain compliance from a member threatens to transform leadership into supervision. Of course, the benefits of more efficient and effective performance by in-group members may well be worth these potential costs.

Entering into a leadership exchange can also be costly for a member. Although under a supervision exchange a member receives only a minimal amount of his leader's various positional resources (those required to perform his duties adequately), he is required to perform only specified duties and to assume only specified responsibilities as conditions of employment. His compensation is equitable only under the terms of his contract. If a member assumes greater responsibility without changing the contract he is placing his trust in his leader. On the other hand, his payoffs should be worth this risk. He should receive higher performance ratings, experience less severe problems with supervision, and feel greater satisfaction with the job situation than his out-group colleague.

To summarize the model shown in Table 1, the inputs to team development are the characteristics of each member and those of their leader. These characteristics are harnessed to outputs, such as member performance, satisfaction, and job problems, through their interactions with leader-member exchanges. Based upon the compatibility of some combination of member's characteristics and some combination of leader's characteristics, a leader initiates either an in-group or an out-group exchange with his member early in the life of the dyadic relationship. Our early warning detector of the signs of these exchanges (negotiating latitude) focuses upon the relative openness of a leader to extend individualized assistance to his member and is an attempt to tap dyadic negotiation. Over a period of time, the leader-member exchanges develop into distinct social structures of very different kinds. In-group exchanges involve interlocking different task behaviors and forming different working relationships than do out-group exchanges. Specifically, in-group exchanges will involve first the interlocking of more responsible tasks accepted by members and higher levels of assistance provided by leaders; and second, working relationships will be characterized by greater support, sensitivity, and trust than occurs in out-group exchanges. Furthermore, the mechanism of this interlocking of member and leader behavior probably is reciprocal reinforcement (member task behavior reinforces leader resource allocation behavior; leader resource allocation behavior reinforces member task behavior—and the cycle repeats). These leader-member exchange *structures* are strongly and consistently related to the outputs of member performance, job satisfaction, and job problems. In addition, once these structures emerge, they demonstrate high stability over time. Thus, until the nature of the linkage becomes altered, both member and leader behavior can be both understood and predicted over time. . . .

Implications for Organizations

Should this model of leadership prove under further testing to provide valid descriptions of leadership processes, it may have implications for training leaders and members in team-building skills (Campbell et al., 1970). It seems reasonable to expect that the outcomes of team building may be enhanced by coaching both parties to the leader-member exchange both before and during the process. In addition, it may have implications for normative models of operating. For example, the decision-making model of Vroom and Yetton (1973) may need to be modified to include considerations of team structure. It may change the prescriptive decision of whether or not to let a member who holds needed information participate in a decision. Within this normative program, the leader-member exchange may become a crucial contingency factor.

Given that leaders of managerial units must be granted adequate latitude to build a team to deal with many non-routine contingencies, few positive programs exist to improve the processes or to correct mistakes in the process. Seldom are leaders trained adequately to assess, select, and develop talent for maximum efficiency. Without a positive program, few alternative opportunities may be made available to even the more talented out-group members. One promising development along these lines is the experimental program within American Telephone and Telegraph, which is part of a program to train managers to assess and select talent through management assessment center procedures (Bray, 1974). This special program allows potential out-group members to request to be more objectively assessed and, if found deserving, to be given an opportunity to prove themselves in a new position.

Our findings suggest the fruitfulness of our decision to forsake the traditional path to leadership (involving the assumption of homogeneous vertical dyads) for the relatively unexplored role-making path (allowing heterogeneous vertical dyads). We hope that the fruits of this role-making approach to leadership will convince others to view these processes as developmental phenomena and seek to understand them through longitudinal and "open systems" designs (Graen, 1975)

Once leadership is viewed as part of a larger developmental process it begins to lose much of its mystique. For example, the influence of a leader need not be attributed to some mysterious inner power called charisma. Rather, it can be viewed as developing within vertical dyads into leader-member exchanges which contain interlocking behavior and relationship norms. Of course, these processes may not be active at all times. More likely, they are activated by appropriate sets of events, complete their sequences, and become dormant until activated anew. Only by monitoring these processes when they are active can we hope to document their nature. Cross-sectional studies of the dormant period can only reveal residual traces of these events and foster further mystery.

It seems apparent that to enhance the positive outcomes of managerial team building we must achieve a better understanding of these developmental processes. We must discover the conditions which activate these processes and learn to guide them toward desired outcomes and away from undesired outcomes. At the present time we have a beginning—only a beginning.

Notes

Bray, D. W. 1974. "Maximizing Human Resource Utilization with Sophisticated Selection Techniques." Paper presented at the American Psychological Association Symposium, New Orleans, La.

Campbell, D. T., M.D. Dunnette, E. E. Lawler, and K. E. Weick. 1970. *Managerial Behaviors, Performance and Effectiveness.* New York: McGraw-Hill.

Dansereau, F., G. Graen, and W. J. Haga. 1975. "A Vertical Dyad Linkage Approach to Leadership within Formal Organizations." *Organizational Behavior and Human Performance,* 13:46–78.

Graen, G. 1975. "Role Making Processes within Complex Organizations." In M. D. Dunnette (ed.), *Handbook of Industrial and Organizational Psychology,* Chap. 28. Chicago: Rand McNally.

Graen, G., F. Dansereau, W. Haga, and J. Cashman. 1975. *The Invisible Organization.* Boston: Shenkman Publishing Company.

Graen, G., F. Dansereau, T. Minami, and J. Cashman. 1973. "Leadership Behaviors as Cues to Performance Evaluation." *Academy of Management Journal,* 16:611–23.

Haga, W. J., G. Graen, and F. Dansereau. 1974. "Professionalism and Role Making within Service Organization." *American Sociological Review,* 39:122–33.

Jacobs, T. O. 1970. *Leadership and Exchange in Formal Organizations.* Alexandria, Va.: Human Resources Research Organization.

Vroom, V. H., and P. W. Yetton. 1973. *Leadership and Decision Making.* Pittsburgh: Univ. of Pittsburgh Press.

Weick, K. E. 1969. *The Social Psychology of Organizing.* Reading, Mass.: Addison-Wesley Publishing Co.

34

Power Acquisition and Retention

Gerald R. Salancik and Jeffrey Pfeffer

Power is held by many people to be a dirty word or, as Warren Bennis has said, "It is the organization's last dirty secret."

This article will argue that traditional "political" power, far from being a dirty business, is, in its most naked form, one of the few mechanisms available for aligning an organization with its own reality. However, institutionalized forms of power—what we prefer to call the cleaner forms of power: authority, legitimization, centralized control, regulations, and the more modern management information systems—tend to buffer the organization from reality and obscure the demands of its environment. Most great states and institutions declined, not because they played politics, but because they failed to accommodate to the political realities they faced. Political processes, rather than being mechanisms for unfair and unjust allocations and appointments, tend toward the realistic resolution of conflicts among interests. And power, while it eludes definition, is easy enough to recognize by its consequences—the ability of those who possess power to bring about the outcomes they desire.

The model of power we advance is an elaboration of what has been called strategic-contingency theory, a view that sees power as something that accrues to organizational subunits (individuals, departments) that cope with critical organizational problems. Power is used by subunits, indeed, used by all who have it, to enhance their own survival through control of scarce critical resources, through the placement of allies in key positions, and through the definition of organizational problems and policies. Because of the processes by which power develops and is used, organizations become both

Excerpt reprinted with permission of Elsevier from *Organizational Dynamics,* Vol. 5, No. 3 (Winter 1977), pp. 3–21. Originally titled "Who Gets the Power and How They Hold on to It: A Strategic-Contingency Model of Power." Copyright © 1977 by Elsevier Science & Technology Journals.

more aligned and more misaligned with their environments. This contradiction is the most interesting aspect of organizational power, and one that makes administration one of the most precarious of occupations.

What Is Organizational Power?

Yon can walk into most organizations and ask without fear of being misunderstood, "Which are the powerful groups or people in this organization?" Although many organizational informants may be *unwilling* to tell you, it is unlikely they will be *unable* to tell you. Most people do not require explicit definitions to know what power is.

Power is simply the ability to get things done the way one wants them to be done. For a manager who wants an increased budget to launch a project that he thinks is important, his power is measured by his ability to get that budget. For an executive vice-president who wants to be chairman, his power is evidenced by his advancement toward his goal.

People in organizations not only know what you are talking about when you ask who is influential but they are likely to agree with one another to an amazing extent. Recently, we had a chance to observe this in a regional office of an insurance company. The office had 21 department managers; we asked ten of these managers to rank all 21 according to the influence each one had in the organization. Despite the fact that ranking 21 things is a difficult task, the managers sat down and began arranging the names of their colleagues and themselves in a column. Only one person bothered to ask, "What do you mean by influence?" When told "power," he responded, "Oh," and went on. We compared the rankings of all ten managers and found virtually no disagreement among them in the managers ranked among the top five or the bottom five. Differences in the rankings came from department heads claiming more influence for themselves than their colleagues attributed to them.

Such agreement on those who have influence, and those who do not, was not unique to this insurance company. So far we have studied over 20 very different organizations—universities, research firms, factories, banks, retailers, to name a few. In each one we found individuals able to rate themselves and their peers on a scale of influence or power. We have done this both for specific decisions and for general impact on organizational policies. Their agreement was unusually high, which suggests that distributions of influence exist well enough in everyone's mind to be referred to with ease, and we assume, with accuracy.

Where Does Organizational Power Come From?

Earlier we stated that power helps organizations become aligned with their realities. This hopeful prospect follows from what we have dubbed the strategic-contingencies theory of organizational power. Briefly, those subunits most able to cope with the organization's critical problems and uncertainties acquire power. In its simplest form, the strategic-contingencies theory implies that when an organization faces a number of lawsuits that threaten its existence, the legal department will gain power and influence over organizational decisions. Somehow other organizational interest groups will recognize its critical importance and confer upon it a status and power never before enjoyed. This influence may extend beyond handling legal matters and into decisions about product design, advertising production, and so on. Such extensions undoubtedly would be accompanied by appropriate, or acceptable, verbal justifications. In time, the head of the legal department may become the head of the corporation, just as in times past the vice-president for marketing had become the president when market shares were a worrisome problem and, before him, the chief engineer, who had made the production line run as smooth as silk.

Stated in this way, the strategic-contingencies theory of power paints an appealing picture of power. To the extent that power is determined by the critical uncertainties and problems facing the organization and, in turn, influences decisions in the organization, the organization is aligned with the realities it faces. In short, power facilitates the organization's adaptation to its environment or its problems.

We can cite many illustrations of how influence derives from a subunit's ability to deal with critical contingencies. Michael Crozier described a French cigarette factory in which the maintenance engineers had a considerable say in the plant-wide operation. After some probing he discovered that the group possessed the solution to one of the major problems faced by the company, that of troubleshooting the elaborate, expensive, and irascible automated machines that kept breaking down and dumbfounding everyone else. It was the one problem that the plant manager could in no way control.

The production workers, while troublesome from time to time, created no insurmountable problems; the manager could reasonably predict their absenteeism or replace them when necessary. Production scheduling was something he could deal with since, by watching inventories and sales, the demand for cigarettes was known long in advance. Changes in demand could be accommodated by slowing down or speeding up the line. Supplies of tobacco and paper were also easily dealt with through stockpiles and advance orders.

The one thing that management could neither control nor accommodate to, however, was the seemingly happenstance breakdowns. And the foremen couldn't instruct the workers what to do when emergencies developed since the maintenance department kept its records of problems and solutions locked up in a cabinet or in its members' heads. The breakdowns were, in truth, a critical source of uncertainty for the organization, and the maintenance engineers were the only ones who could cope with the problem.

The engineers' strategic role in coping with breakdowns afforded them a considerable say on plant decisions. Schedules and production quotas were set in consultation with them. And the plant manager, while formally their boss, accepted their decisions about personnel in their operation. His submission was to his credit, for without their cooperation he would have had an even more difficult time in running the plant. In this cigarette factory, sharing influence with the maintenance workers reflected the plant manager's awareness of the critical contingencies. However, when organizational members are not aware of the critical contingencies they face, and do not share influence accordingly, the failure to do so can create havoc. In one case, an insurance company's regional office was having problems with the performance of one of its departments, the coding department. From the outside, the department looked like a disaster area. The clerks who worked in it were somewhat dissatisfied; their supervisor paid little attention to them, and they resented the hard work. Several other departments were critical of this manager, claiming that she was inconsistent in meeting deadlines. The person most critical was the claims manager. He resented having to wait for work that was handled by her department, claiming that it held up his claims adjusters. Having heard the rumors about dissatisfaction among her subordinates, he attributed the situation to poor supervision. He was second in command in the office and therefore took up the issue with her immediate boss, the head of administrative services. They consulted with the personnel manager and the three of them concluded that the manager needed leadership training to improve her relations with her subordinates. The coding manager objected, saying it was a waste of time, but agreed to go along with the training and also agreed to give more priority to the claims department's work. Within a week after the training, the results showed that her workers were happier but that the performance of her department had decreased, save for the people serving the claims department.

About this time, we began, quite independently, a study of influence in this organization. We asked the administrative services director to draw up flow charts of how the work of one department moved to the next department. In the course of the interview, we noticed that the coding department began or interceded in the work flow of most of the other departments and casually mentioned to him, "The coding manager must be very influential." He said "No, not really. Why would you think so?" Before we could reply he recounted the story of her leadership training and the fact that things were worse. We then told him that it seemed obvious that the coding department would be influential from the fact that all the other departments depended on it. It was also clear why productivity had fallen. The coding manager took the training seriously and began spending more time raising her workers' spirits than she did worrying about the problems of all the departments that depended on her. Giving priority to the claims area only exaggerated the problem, for their work was getting done at the expense of the work of the other departments. Eventually the company hired a few more clerks to relieve the pressure in the coding department and performance returned to a more satisfactory level.

Originally we got involved with this insurance company to examine how the influence of each manager evolved from his or her department's handling of critical organizational contingencies. We reasoned that one of the most important contingencies faced by all profit-making organizations was that of generating income. Thus we expected managers would be influential to the extent to which they contributed to this function. Such was the case. The underwriting managers, who wrote the policies that committed the premiums, were the most influential; the claims managers, who kept a lid on the funds flowing out, were a close second. Least influential were the managers of functions unrelated to revenue, such as mailroom and payroll managers. And contrary to what the administrative services manager believed, the third most powerful department head (out of 21) was the woman in charge of the coding function, which consisted of rating, recording, and keeping track of the codes of all policy applications and contracts. Her peers attributed more influence to her than could have been inferred from her place on the organization chart. And it was not surprising, since they all depended on her department. The coding department's records, their accuracy and the speed with which they could be retrieved, affected virtually every other operating department in the insurance office. The underwriters depended on them in getting the contracts straight; the typing department depended on them in preparing the formal contract document; the claims department depended on them in adjusting claims; and accounting depended on them for billing. Unfortunately, the "bosses" were not aware of these dependencies, for unlike the cigarette factory, there were no massive breakdowns that made them obvious, while the coding manager, who was a hard-working but quiet person, did little to announce her importance.

The cases of this plant and office illustrate nicely a basic point about the source of power in organizations. The basis for power in an organization derives from the ability of a person or subunit to take or not take actions that are desired by others. The coding manager was seen as influential by those who depended on her department, but not by the people at the top. The engineers were influential because of their role in keeping the plant operating. The two cases differ in these respects: The coding supervisor's source of power was not as widely recognized as that of the maintenance engineers, and she did not use her source of power to influence decisions; the maintenance engineers did. Whether power is used to influence anything is a separate issue. We should not confuse this issue with the fact that power derives from a social situation in which one person has a capacity to do something and another person does not, but wants it done.

Power Sharing in Organizations

Power is shared in organizations; and it is shared out of necessity more than out of concern for principles of organizational development or participatory democracy. Power is shared because no one person controls all the desired activities in the organization. While the factory owner may hire people to operate his noisy machines, once hired they have some control over the use of the machinery. And thus they have power over him in the same way he has power over them. Who has more power over whom is a mooter point than that of recognizing the inherent nature of organizing as a sharing of power.

Let's expand on the concept that power derives from the activities desired in an organization. A major way of managing influence in organizations is through the designation of activities. In a bank we studied we saw this principle in action. This bank was planning to install a computer system for routine credit evaluation. The bank, rather progressive-minded, was concerned that the change would have adverse effects on employees and therefore surveyed their attitudes.

The principal opposition to the new system came, interestingly, not from the employees who performed the routine credit checks, some of whom would be relocated because of the change, but from the manager of the credit department. His reason was quite simple. The manager's primary function was to give official approval to the applications, catch any employee mistakes before giving approval, and arbitrate any difficulties the clerks had in deciding what to do. As a consequence of his role, others in the organization, including his superiors, subordinates, and colleagues, attributed considerable importance to him. He, in turn, for example, could point to the low proportion of credit approvals, compared with other financial institutions, that resulted in bad debts. Now, to his mind, a wretched machine threatened to transfer his role to a computer programmer, a man who knew nothing of finance and who, in addition, had ten years less seniority. The credit manager eventually quit for a position at a smaller firm with lower pay, but one in which he would have more influence than his redefined job would have left him with.

Because power derives from activities rather than individuals, an individual's or subgroup's power is never absolute and derives ultimately from the context of the situation. The amount of power an individual has at any one time depends, not only on the activities he or she controls, but also on the existence of other persons or means by which the activities can be achieved and on those who determine what ends are desired and, hence, on what activities are desired and critical for the organization. One's own power always depends on other people for these two reasons. Other people, or groups or organizations, can determine the definition of what is a critical contingency for the organization and can also undercut the uniqueness of the individual's personal contribution to the critical contingencies of the organization.

Perhaps one can best appreciate how situationally dependent power is by examining how it is distributed. In most societies, power organizes around scarce and critical resources. Rarely does power organize around abundant resources. In the United States, a person doesn't become powerful because he or she can drive a car. There are simply too many others who can drive with equal facility. In certain villages in Mexico, on the other hand, a person with a car is accredited with enormous social status and plays a key role in the community. In addition to scarcity, power is also limited by the need for one's capacities in a social system. While a racer's ability to drive a car around a 90-degree turn at 80 mph may be sparsely distributed in a society, it is not likely to lend the driver much power in the society. The ability simply does not play a central role in the activities of the society.

The fact that power revolves around scarce and critical activities, of course, makes the control and organization of those activities a major battleground in struggles for power. Even relatively abundant or trivial resources can become the bases for power if one can organize and control their allocation and the definition of what is critical. Many occupational and professional groups attempt to do just this in modern economies. Lawyers organize themselves into associations, regulate the entrance requirements for novitiates, and then get laws passed specifying situations that require the services of an attorney. Workers had little power in the conduct of industrial affairs until they organized themselves into closed and controlled systems. In recent years, women and blacks have tried to define themselves as important and critical to the social system, using law to reify their status.

In organizations there are obviously opportunities for defining certain activities as more critical than others. Indeed, the growth of managerial thinking to include defining organizational objectives and goals has done much to foster these opportunities. One sure way to liquidate the power of groups in the organization is to define the need for their services out of existence. David Halberstam presents a description of how just such a thing happened to the group of correspondents that evolved around Edward R. Murrow, the brilliant journalist, interviewer, and war correspondent of CBS News. A close friend of CBS chairman and controlling stockholder William S. Paley, Murrow, and the news department he directed, were endowed with freedom to do what they felt was right. He used it to create some of the best documentaries and commentaries ever seen on television. Unfortunately, television became too large, too powerful, and too suspect in the eyes of the federal government that licensed it. It thus became, or at least the top executives believed it had become, too dangerous to have in-depth, probing commentary on the news. Crisp, dry, uneditorializing headliners were considered safer. Murrow was out and Walter Cronkite was in.

The power to define what is critical in an organization is no small power. Moreover, it is the key to understanding why organizations are either aligned with their environments or misaligned. If an organization defines certain activities as critical when in fact they are not critical, given the flow of resources coming into the organization, it is not likely to survive, at least in its present form.

Most organizations manage to evolve a distribution of power and influence that is aligned with the critical realities they face in the environment. The environment, in turn, includes both the internal environment, the shifting situational contexts in which particular decisions get made, and the external environment that it can hope to influence but is unlikely to control.

The Critical Contingencies

The critical contingencies facing most organizations derive from the environmental context within which they operate. This determines the available needed resources and thus determines the problems to be dealt with. That power organizes around handling these problems suggests an important mechanism by which organizations keep in tune with their external environments. The strategic-contingencies model implies that subunits that contribute to the critical resources of the organization will gain influence in the organization. Their influence presumably is then used to bend the organization's activities to the contingencies that determine its resources. This idea may strike one as obvious. But its obviousness in no way diminishes its importance. Indeed, despite its obviousness, it escapes the notice of many organizational analysts and managers, who all too frequently think of the organization in terms of a descending pyramid, in which all the departments in one tier hold equal power and status. This presumption denies the reality that departments differ in the contributions they are believed to make to the overall organization's resources, as well as to the fact that some are more equal than others. . . .

The Impact of Organizational Power on Decision Making

Our study of the university led us to ask the following question: Does power lead to influence in the organization? To answer this question, we found it useful first to ask another one, namely: Why should department heads try to influence organizational decisions to favor their own departments to the exclusion of other departments? While this second question may seem a bit naive to anyone who has witnessed the political realities of organizations, we posed it in a context of research on organizations that sees power as an illegitimate threat to the greater rational authority of modern bureaucracies. In this context, decisions are not believed to be made because of the dirty business of politics but because of the overall goals and purposes of the organization. . . .

Will organizational decisions always reflect the distribution of power in the organization? Probably not. Using power for influence requires a certain expenditure of effort, time, and resources. Prudent and judicious persons are not likely to use their power needlessly or wastefully. And it is likely that power will be used to influence organizational decisions primarily under circumstances that both require and favor its use. We have examined three conditions that are likely to affect the use of power in organizations: scarcity, criticality, and uncertainty. The first suggests that subunits will try to exert influence when the resources of the organization are scarce. If there is an abundance of resources, then a particular department or a particular individual has little need to attempt influence. With little effort, he can get all he wants anyway.

The second condition, criticality, suggests that a subunit will attempt to influence decisions to obtain resources that are critical to its own survival and activities. Criticality implies that one would not waste effort, or risk being labeled obstinate, by fighting over trivial decisions affecting one's operations.

The third condition that we believe affects the use of power is uncertainty: When individuals do not agree about what the organization should do or how to do it, power and other social processes will affect decisions. The reason for this is simply that, if there are no clear-cut criteria available for resolving conflicts of interest, the only means for resolution is some form of social process, including power, status, social ties, or some arbitrary process like flipping a coin or drawing straws. Under conditions of uncertainty, the powerful manager can argue his case on any grounds and usually win it. Since there is no real consensus, other contestants are not likely to develop counter arguments or amass sufficient opposition. Moreover, because of his power and their need for access to the resources he controls, they are more likely to defer to his arguments. . . .

Changing Contingencies and Eroding Power Bases

The critical contingencies facing the organization may change. When they do, it is reasonable to expect that the power of individuals and subgroups will change in turn. At times the shift can be swift and shattering, as happened in New York City. A few years ago it was believed that David Rockefeller was one of the ten most powerful people in the city, as tallied by *New York* magazine, which annually sniffs out power for the delectation of its readers. But that was before it was revealed that the city was in financial trouble, before Rockefeller's Chase Manhattan Bank lost some of its own financial luster, and before brother Nelson lost some of his political influence in Washington. Obviously David Rockefeller was no longer as well positioned to help bail the city out. Another loser was an attorney with considerable personal connections to the political and religious leaders of the city. His talents were no longer in much demand. The persons with more influence were the bankers and union pension fund executers who fed money to the city; community leaders who represent blacks and Spanish-Americans, in contrast, witnessed the erosion of their power bases.

One implication of the idea that power shifts with changes in organizational environments is that the dominant coalition will tend to be that group that is most appropriate for the organization's environment, as will be the leaders of an organization. One can observe this historically in the top executives of industrial firms in the United States. Up until the early 1950s, many top corporations were headed by former production line managers or engineers who gained prominence because of their abilities to cope with the problems of production. Their success, however, only spelled their demise. As production became routinized and mechanized, the problem of most firms became one of selling all those goods they so efficiently produced. Marketing executives were more frequently found in corporate boardrooms. Success outdid itself again, for keeping markets and production steady and stable requires the kind of control that can only come from acquiring competitors and suppliers or the invention of more and more appealing products—adventures that typically require enormous amounts of capital. During the 1960s, financial executives assumed the seats of power. And they, too, will give way to others. Edging over the horizon are legal experts, as regulation and antitrust suits are becoming more and more frequent in the 1970s, suits that had their beginnings in the success of the expansion generated by prior executives. The more distant future, which is likely to be dominated by multinational corporations, may see former secretaries of state and their minions increasingly serving as corporate figureheads.

The Non-Adaptive Consequences of Adaptation

From what we have said thus far about power aligning the organization with its own realities, an intelligent person might react with a resounding ho-hum, for it all seems too obvious: Those with the ability to get the job done are given the job to do.

However, there are two aspects of power that make it more useful for understanding organizations and their effectiveness. First, the "job" to be done has a way of expanding itself until it becomes less and less clear what the job is. Napoleon began by doing a job for France in the war with Austria and ended up Emperor, convincing many that only he could keep the peace. Hitler began by promising an end to Germany's troubling postwar depression and ended up convincing more people than is comfortable to remember that he was destined to be the savior of the world. In short, power is a capacity for influence that extends far beyond the original bases that created it. Second, power tends to take on institutionalized forms that enable it to endure well beyond its usefulness to an organization.

There is an important contradiction in what we have observed about organizational power. On the one hand we have said that power derives from the contingencies facing an organization and that when those contingencies change so do the bases for power. On the other hand we have asserted that subunits will tend to use their power to influence organizational decisions in their own favor, particularly when their own survival is threatened by the scarcity of critical resources. The first statement implies that an organization will tend to be aligned with its environment since power will tend to bring to key positions those with capabilities relevant to the context. The second implies that those in power will not give up their positions so easily; they will pursue policies that guarantee their continued domination. In short, change and stability operate through the same mechanism, and, as a result, the organization will never be completely in phase with its environment or its needs. . . .

Mistaking Critical Contingencies

One thing that allows subunits to retain their power is their ability to name their functions as critical to the organization when they may not be.

For example, in the university study graduate education and scholarly research were deemed the most critical and this brought power to departments that brought in grants and contracts. But why not something else? The reason is that the more powerful departments argued for those criteria and won their case, partly because they were more powerful.

In other analyses we found that all departments advocate self-serving criteria for budget allocation. We further found that advocating such self-serving criteria actually benefited a department's budget allocations but, also, it paid off more for departments that were already powerful.

Organizational needs are consistent with a current distribution of power also because of a human tendency to categorize problems in familiar ways. This bias, while not intentionally self-serving, further concentrates power among those who already possess it, independent of changes in the organization's context.

Institutionalizing Power

A third reason for expecting organizational contingencies to be defined in familiar ways is that the current holders of power can structure the organization in ways that institutionalize themselves. By institutionalization we mean the establishment of relatively permanent structures and policies that favor the influence of a particular subunit. While in power, a dominant coalition has the ability to institute constitutions, rules, procedures, and information systems that limit the potential power of others while continuing their own.

The key to institutionalizing power always is to create a device that legitimates one's own authority and diminishes the legitimacy of others. When the "Divine Right of Kings" was envisioned centuries ago it was to provide an unquestionable foundation for the supremacy of royal authority. There is generally a need to root the exercise of authority in some higher power. Modern leaders are no less affected by this need. Richard Nixon, with the aid of John Dean, reified the concept of executive privilege, which meant in effect that what the president wished not to be discussed need not be discussed.

In its simpler form, institutionalization is achieved by designating positions or roles for organizational activities. The creation of a new post legitimizes a function and forces organization members to orient to it. By designating how this new post relates to older, more established posts, moreover, one can structure an organization to enhance the importance of the function in the organization. Equally, one can diminish the importance of traditional functions. This is what happened in the end with the insurance company we mentioned that was having trouble with its coding department. As the situation unfolded, the claims director continued to feel dissatisfied about the dependency of his functions on the coding manager. Thus he instituted a reorganization that resulted in two coding departments. In so doing, of course, he placed activities that affected his department under his direct control, presumably to make the operation more effective. Similarly, consumer-product firms enhance the power of marketing by setting up a coordinating role to interface production and marketing functions and then appoint a marketing manager to fill the role.

The structures created by dominant powers sooner or later become fixed and unquestioned features of the organization. Eventually, this can be devastating. It is said that the battle of Jena in 1806 was lost by Frederick the Great, who died in 1786. Though the great Prussian leader had no direct hand in the disaster, his imprint on the army was so thorough, so embedded in its skeletal underpinnings, that the organization was inappropriate for others to lead in different times.

Another important source of institutionalized power lies in the ability to structure information systems. Setting up committees to investigate particular organizational issues and having them report only to particular individuals or groups, facilitates the awareness of problems by members of those groups while limiting the awareness of problems by members of other groups. Obviously, those who have information are in a better position to interpret the problems of an organization, regardless of how realistically they may, in fact, do so.

Still another way to institutionalize power is to distribute rewards and resources. The dominant group may quiet competing interest groups with small favors and rewards. The credit for this artful form of co-optation belongs to Louis XIV. To avoid usurpation of his power by the nobles of France and the Fronde that had so troubled his father's reign, he built the palace at Versailles to occupy them with hunting and gossip. Awed, the courtiers basked in the reflected glories of the "Sun King" and the overwhelming setting he had created for his court.

At this point, we have not systematically studied the institutionalization of power. But we suspect it is an important condition that mediates between the environment of the organization and the capabilities of the organization for dealing with that environment. The more institutionalized power is within an organization, the more likely an organization will be out of phase with the realities it faces. President Richard Nixon's structuring of his White House is one of the better documented illustrations. If we go back to newspaper and magazine descriptions of how he organized his office from the beginning in 1968, most of what occurred subsequently follows almost as an afterthought. Decisions flowed through virtually only the small White House staff; rewards, small presidential favors of recognition, and perquisites were distributed by this staff to the loyal; and information from the outside world—the press, Congress, the people on the streets—was filtered by the staff and passed along only if initialed "bh." Thus it was not surprising that when Nixon met war protestors in the early dawn, the only thing he could think to talk about was the latest football game, so insulated had he become from their grief and anger.

One of the more interesting implications of institutionalized power is that executive turnover among the executives who have structured the organization is likely to be a rare event that occurs only under the most pressing crisis. If a dominant coalition is able to structure the organization and interpret the meaning of ambiguous events like declining sales and profits or lawsuits, then the "real" problems to emerge will easily be incorporated into traditional molds of thinking and acting. If opposition is designed out of the organization, the interpretations will go unquestioned. Conditions will remain stable until a crisis develops, so overwhelming and visible that even the most adroit rhetorician would be silenced.

Implications for the Management of Power in Organizations

While we could derive numerous implications from this discussion of power, our selection would have to depend largely on whether one wanted to increase one's power, decrease the power of others, or merely maintain one's position. More important, the real implications depend on the particulars of an organizational situation. To understand power in an organization one must begin by looking outside it—into the environment—for those groups that mediate the organization's outcomes but are not themselves within its control.

Instead of ending with homilies, we will end with a reversal of where we began. Power, rather than being the dirty business it is often made out to be, is probably one of the few mechanisms for reality testing in organizations. And the cleaner forms of power, the institutional forms, rather than having the virtues they are often credited with, can lead the organization to become out of touch. The real trick to managing power in organizations is to ensure somehow that leaders cannot be unaware of the realities of their environments and cannot avoid changing to deal with those realities. That, however, would be like designing the "self-liquidating organization," an unlikely event since anyone capable of designing such an instrument would be obviously in control of the liquidations.

Management would do well to devote more attention to determining the critical contingencies of their environments. For if you conclude, as we do, that the environment sets most of the structure influencing organizational outcomes and problems, and that power derives from the organization's activities that deal with those contingencies, then it is the environment that needs managing, not power. The first step is to construct an accurate model of the environment, a process that is quite difficult for most organizations. Most organizations have the requisite experts on hand but they are positioned so that they can be comfortably ignored.

One conclusion you can, and probably should, derive from our discussion is that power, because of the way it develops and the way it is used, will always result in the organization sub-optimizing its performance. However, to this grim absolute we add a comforting caveat: If any criteria other than power were the basis for determining an organization's decisions, the results would be even worse. A word of caution is required about our judgment of "appropriateness." When we argue some capabilities are more appropriate

for one context than another, we do so from the perspective of an outsider
and on the basis of reasonable assumptions as to the problems the organization will face and the capabilities they will need. The fact that we have been
able to predict the distribution of influence and the characteristics of leaders
suggests that our reasoning is not incorrect. However, we do not think that all
organizations follow the same pattern. The fact that we have not been able to
predict outcomes with 100 percent accuracy indicates they do not.

Selected Bibliography

The literature on power is at once both voluminous and frequently empty
of content. Some is philosophical musing about the concept of power, while
other writing contains popularized palliatives for acquiring and exercising
influence. Machiavelli's *The Prince,* if read carefully, remains the single best
prescriptive treatment of power and its use. Most social scientists have
approached power descriptively, attempting to understand how it is acquired,
how it is used, and what its effects are. Mayer Zald's edited collection *Power
in Organization* (Vanderbilt University Press, 1970) is one of the more useful
sets of thoughts about power from a sociological perspective, while James
Tedeschi's edited book, *The Social Influence Processes* (Aldine-Atherton, 1972)
represents the social psychological approach to understanding power and
influence. The strategic contingency's approach, with its emphasis on the
importance of uncertainty for understanding power in organizations, is
described by David Hickson and his colleagues in "A Strategic Contingencies
Theory of Intraorganizational Power" (*Administrative Science Quarterly,*
December 1971, pp. 216–229).

Unfortunately, while many have written about power theoretically, there
have been few empirical examinations of power and its use. Most of the work
has taken the form of case studies. Michel Crozier's *The Bureaucratic Phenomenon* (University of Chicago Press, 1964) is important because it describes a
group's source of power as control over critical activities and illustrates how
power is not strictly derived from hierarchical position. J. Victor Baldridge's
Power and Conflict in the University (John Wiley & Sons, 1971) and Andrew
Pettigrew's study of computer purchase decisions in one English firm *(Politics
of Organizational Decision-Making,* Tavistock, 1973) both present insights into
the acquisition and use of power in specific instances. Our work has been
more empirical and comparative, testing more explicitly the ideas presented
in this article. The study of university decision making is reported in articles
in the June 1974, pp. 135–151, and December 1974, pp. 453–473, issues of
the *Administrative Science Quarterly,* the insurance firm study in J. G. Hunt and
L. L. Larson's collection, *Leadership Frontiers* (Kent State University Press,
1975), and the study of hospital administrator succession in the *Academy of
Management Journal,* 1977.

35

Leadership
The Art of Empowering Others

Jay A. Conger

One ought to be both feared and loved, but as it is difficult for the two to go together, it is much safer to be feared than loved . . . for love is held by a chain of obligation which, men being selfish, is broken whenever it serves their purpose; but fear is maintained by a dread of punishment which never fails.

The Prince, Niccolo Machiavelli

In his handbook, *The Prince,* Machiavelli assures his readers—some being aspiring leaders, no doubt—that only by carefully amassing power and building a fearsome respect could one become a great leader. While the shadowy court life of 16th-century Italy demanded such treachery to ensure one's power, it seems hard to imagine Machiavelli's advice today as anything but a historical curiosity. Yet, interestingly, much of the management literature has focused on the strategies and tactics that managers can use to increase their own power and influence.[1] As such, a Machiavellian quality often pervades the literature, encouraging managers to ensure that their power base is strong and growing. At the same time a small but increasing number of management theorists have begun to explore the idea that organizational effectiveness also depends on the sharing of power—that the distribution of power is more important than the hoarding of power.[2]

While the idea of making others feel more powerful contradicts the stereotype of the all-powerful executive, research suggests that the traditional ways of explaining a leader's influence may not be entirely correct. For example, recent leadership studies argue that the practice of empowering—or instilling a sense of power—is at the root of organizational effectiveness, especially during times of transition and transformation.[3] In addition, studies

Reprinted with permission of the Academy of Management (NY) from *Academy of Management Executive,* Vol. 3, No. 1, pp. 17–24. Copyright © 1989 Academy of Management (NY).

of power and control within organizations indicate that the more productive forms of organizational power increase with superiors' sharing of power and responsibility with subordinates.[4] And while there is an increasing awareness of this need for more empowering leadership, we have only recently started to see documentation about the actual practices that leaders employ to effectively build a sense of power among organizational members as well as the contexts most suited for empowerment practices.[5]

In this article, I will explore these practices further by drawing upon a recent study of senior executives who proved themselves highly effective leaders. They were selected by a panel of professors at the Harvard Business School and management consultants who were well-acquainted with them and their companies. The study included eight chief executive officers and executive vice-presidents of *Fortune* 500 companies and successful entrepreneurial firms, representing industries as diverse as telecommunications, office automation, retail banking, beverages, packaged foods, and management consulting. In each case, these individuals were responsible for either the creation of highly successful companies or for performing what were described as remarkable turnarounds. During my study of these executives, I conducted extensive interviews, observed them on the job, read company and other documents, and talked with their colleagues and subordinates. While the study focused on the broader issue of leadership styles, intensive interviews with these executives and their subordinates revealed that many were characterized as empowering leaders. Their actions were perceived as building confidence and restoring a sense of personal power and self-efficacy during difficult organizational transitions. From this study, I identified certain organizational contexts of powerlessness and management practices derived to remedy them.

In this article I will also illustrate several of these practices through a series of vignettes. While the reader may recognize some of the basic ideas behind these practices (such as providing greater opportunities for initiative), it is often the creative manner in which the leader deploys the particular practice that distinguishes them. The reader will discover how they have been carefully tailored to fit the context at hand. I might add, however, that these practices represent just a few of the broad repertoire of actions that leaders can take to make an empowering difference in their organizations.

A Word about Empowerment

We can think of empowerment as the act of strengthening an individual's beliefs in his or her sense of effectiveness. In essence, then, empowerment is not simply a set of external actions; it is a process of changing the internal beliefs of people.[6] We know from psychology that individuals believe themselves powerful when they feel they can adequately cope with environmental demands—that is, situations, events, and people they confront. They feel powerless when they are unable to cope with these demands. Any management practice that increases an individual's sense of self-determination will tend to make that individual feel more powerful. The theory behind these ideas can be traced to the work of Alfred Bandura, who conceptualized the notion of self-efficacy beliefs and their role in an individual's sense of personal power in the world.[7]

From his research in psychology, Bandura identified four means of providing empowering information to others: (1) through positive emotional support during experiences associated with stress and anxiety, (2) through words of encouragement and positive persuasion, (3) by observing others' effectiveness—in other words, having models of success with whom people identified—and (4) by actually experiencing the mastering of a task with success (the most effective source). Each of these sources of empowerment was used by the study executives and will be identified in the practice examples, as will other sources identified by organizational researchers.

Several Empowering Management Practices

Before describing the actual practices, it is important to first draw attention to an underlying attitude of the study participants. These empowering leaders shared a strong underlying belief in their subordinates' abilities. It is essentially the Theory Y argument;[8] if you believe in people's abilities, they will come to believe in them. All the executives in the study believed that their subordinates were capable of managing their current situations. They did not employ wholesale firings as a means of transforming their organizations. Rather, they retained the majority of their staff and moved those who could not perform up to standard to positions where they could. The essential lesson is that an assessment of staff skills is imperative before embarking on a program of empowerment. This basic belief in employees' abilities underlies the following examples of management practices designed to empower. We will begin with the practice of providing positive emotional support.

1. The Squirt-gun Shootouts: Providing a Positive Emotional Atmosphere. An empowering practice that emerged from the study was that of providing positive emotional support, especially through play or drama. For example, every few months, several executives would stage dramatic "up sessions" to sustain the motivation and excitement of their staff. They would host an afternoon-long, or a one- or two-day event devoted solely to confidence building. The event would open with an uplifting speech about the future, followed by a special, inspirational speaker. At these events there would often be films meant to build excitement or confidence—for example, a film depicting a mountain climber ascending a difficult peak. The message being conveyed is that this person is finding satisfaction in the work he or she does at an extraordinary level of competence. There would also be rewards for exceptional achievements. These sessions acted as ceremonies to enhance the personal status and identity of employees and revive the common feelings that binded them together.[9]

An element of play appears to be especially liberating in situations of great stress and demoralization. In the study's examples, play allowed for the venting of frustrations and in turn permitted individuals to regain a sense of control by stepping back from their pressures for a moment. As Bandura suggests, the positive emotional support provided by something like play alleviates, to some extent, concerns about personal efficacy.[10]

For example, one of the subjects of the study, Bill Jackson, was appointed the head of a troubled division. Demand had outstripped the division's ability to maintain adequate inventories, and product quality had slipped. Jackson's predecessors were authoritarian managers, and subordinates were demoralized as well as paranoid about keeping their jobs. As one told me, "You never knew who would be shot next." Jackson felt that he had to break the tension in a way that would allow his staff to regain their sense of control and power. He wanted to remove the stiffness and paranoia and turn what subordinates perceived as an impossible task into something more fun and manageable.

So, I was told, at the end of his first staff meeting, Jackson quietly pulled out a squirt-gun and blasted one of his managers with water. At first, there was a moment of stunned silence, and then suddenly the room was flooded with laughter. He remarked with a smile, "You gotta have fun in this business. It's not worth having your stomach in ulcers." This began a month of squirt-gun fights between Jackson and his managers.

The end result? A senior manager's comment is representative: "He wanted people to feel comfortable, to feel in control. He used waterguns to do that. It was a game. It took the stiffness out of the business, allowed people to play in a safe environment—as the boss says, 'to have fun.'" This play restored rapport and morale. But Jackson also knew when to stop. A senior manager told me, "We haven't used waterguns in nine months. It has served its purpose. . . . The waterfights were like being accepted into a club. Once it achieved its purpose, it would have been overdone."

Interview after interview with subordinates confirmed the effectiveness of the squirt-gun incident. It had been experienced as an empowering ritual. In most contexts, this behavior would have been abusive. Why did it work? Because it is a management practice that fit the needs of subordinates at the appropriate time.

The executive's staff consisted largely of young men, "rough and ready" individuals who could be described as fun-loving and playful. They were accustomed to an informal atmosphere and operated in a very down-to-earth style. Jackson's predecessor, on the other hand, had been stiff and formal.

Jackson preferred to manage more informally. He wanted to convey, quickly and powerfully, his intentions of managing in a style distinct from his predecessor's. He was concerned, however, that his size—he is a very tall, energetic, barrel-chested man—as well as his extensive background in manufacturing would be perceived as intimidating by his young staff and increase their reluctance to assume initiative and control. Through the squirt-gun fights, however, he was able to (1) relieve a high level of tension and restore some sense of control, (2) emphasize the importance of having fun in an otherwise trying work environment, and (3) direct subordinates' concerns away from his skills and other qualities that intimidated them. It was an effective management practice because he understood the context. In another setting, it might have been counter-productive.

2. The "I Make a Difference" Club: Rewarding and Encouraging in Visible and Personal Ways. The majority of executives in the study rewarded the achievements of their staffs by expressing personal praise and rewarding in highly visible and confidence-building ways. They believed that people appreciated recognition of their hard work and success. Rewards of high incentive value were particularly important, especially those of personal recognition from the leader. As Rosabeth Kanter notes, a sense of power comes ". . . when one has relatively close contact with sponsors (higher level people who confer approval, prestige, or backing)."[11] Combined with words of praise and positive encouragement, such experiences become important sources of empowerment.

The executives in the study took several approaches to rewards. To reward exceptional performance, one executive established the "I Make a Difference Club." Each year, he selects two or three staff members to be recognized for their excellence on the job. It is a very exclusive club, and only the executive knows the eligibility rules, which are based on outstanding performance. Inductees are invited to dinner in New York City but are not told beforehand that they are about to join the "I Make a Difference Club." They arrive and meet with other staff members whom they believe are there for a staff dinner. During dinner, everyone is asked to speak about what is going on in his or her part of the company. The old-timers speak first, followed by the inductees (who are still unaware of their coming induction). Only after they have given their speeches are they informed that they have just joined the club. As one manager said, "It's one of the most wonderful moments in life."

This executive and others also make extensive use of personal letters to individuals thanking them for their efforts and projects. A typical letter might read, "Fred, I would personally like to thank you for your contribution to _____ and I want you to know that I appreciate it." Lunches and dinners are hosted for special task accomplishments.

Public recognition is also employed as a means of rewarding. As one subordinate commented about his boss,

> He will make sure that people know that so and so did an excellent job on something. He's superb on giving people credit. If the person has done an exceptional job on a task or project, he will be given the opportunity to present his or her findings all the way to the board. Six months later, you'll get a call from a friend and learn that he has dropped your name in a speech that you did well. It makes you want to do it again.

I found that the investment in rewards and recognition made by many of these executives is unusually high, consuming a significant portion of their otherwise busy day. Yet the payoff appeared high. In interviews, subordinates described these rewards as having an empowering impact on them.

To understand why some of these rewards proved to be so successful, one must understand their organizational contexts. In some cases, the organizations studied were quite large, if not enormous. The size of these organizations did little to develop in employees a sense of an "I"—let alone an "I" that makes a difference. It was easy for organization members to feel lost in the hierarchy and for their achievements to be invisible, for recognition not to be received for personal contributions. The study's executives countered this tendency by institutionalizing a reward system that provided visibility and recognition—for example, the "I Make a Difference Club," presentations to the Board, and names dropped in speeches. Suddenly, you as a member of a large organization stood out—you were special.

Outstanding performance from each of the executives' perspectives was also something of a necessity. All the executives had demanding goals to achieve. As such, they had to tend to subordinates' sense of importance and contribution. They had to structure reward systems that would keep people "pumped up"—that would ensure that their confidence and commitment would not be eroded by the pressures placed on them.

3. "Praising the Troops": Expressing Confidence.   The empowering leaders in the study spent significant amounts of time expressing their confidence in subordinates' abilities. Moreover, they expressed their confidence throughout each day—in speeches, in meetings, and casually in office hallways. Bandura comments that "people who are persuaded verbally that they possess the capabilities to master given tasks are likely to mobilize greater sustained effort than if they harbor self-doubts and dwell on personal deficiencies when difficulties arise."[12]

A quote from Irwin Federman, CEO of Monolithic Memories, a highly successful high-tech company, captures the essence and power of a management practice that builds on this process:

> If you think about it, we love others not for who they are, but for how they make us feel. In order to willingly accept the direction of another individual, it must make you feel good to do so. . . . If you believe what I'm saying, you cannot help but come to the conclusion that those you have followed passionately, gladly, zealously—have made you feel like somebody. . . . This business of making another person feel good in the unspectacular course of his daily comings and goings is, in my view, the very essence of leadership.[13]

This proactive attitude is exemplified by Bob Jensen. Bob assumed control of his bank's retail operations after a reorganization that transferred away the division's responsibility for large corporate clients. Demoralized by a perceived loss in status and responsibility, branch managers were soon asking, "Where's our recognition?" Bob, however, developed an inspiring strategic vision to transform the operation. He then spent much of his time championing his strategy and expressing his confidence in employees' ability to carry it out. Most impressive was his personal canvass of some 175 retail branches.

As he explained,

> I saw that the branch system was very down, morale was low. They felt like they'd lost a lot of their power. There were serious problems and a lot of staff were just hiding. What I saw was that we really wanted to create a small community for each branch where customers would feel known. To do that, I needed to create an attitude change. I saw that the attitudes of the branch staff were a reflection of the branch manager. The approach then was a manageable job—now I had to focus on only 250 people, the branch managers, rather than the 3,000 staff employees out there. I knew I had to change their mentality from being lost in a bureaucracy to feeling like the president of their own bank. I had to convince them they were special—that they had the power to transform the organization. . . . All I did was talk it up. I was up every night. In one morning, I hit 17 branches. My goal was to sell a new attitude. To encourage people to "pump iron." I'd say, "Hi, how's business?", encourage them. I'd arrange tours of the branches for the chairman on down. I just spent a lot of time talking to these people—explaining that they were the ones who could transform the organization.

It was an important tactic—one that made the branch managers feel special and important. It was also countercultural. As one executive told me, "Bob would go out into the field to visit the operations, which was very unusual for senior people in this industry." His visits heightened the specialness that branch managers felt. In addition, Bob modeled self-confidence and personal success—an important tactic to build a sense of personal effectiveness among subordinates.[14]

I also watched Jack Eaton, president of a regional telephone company, praise his employees in large corporate gatherings, in executive council meetings, and in casual encounters. He explained his philosophy:

> I have a fundamental belief and trust in the ability and conscientiousness of others. I have a lot of good people. You can turn them loose, let them feel good about their accomplishments. . . . You ought to recognize accomplishment as well as build confidence. I generally do it in small ways. If someone is doing well, it's important to express your confidence to that person—especially among his peers. I tend to do it personally. I try to be genuine. I don't throw around a lot of b.s.

This practice proved especially important during the transition of the regional phone companies away from the parent organization.

4. "President of My Own Bank": Fostering Initiative and Responsibility. Discretion is a critical power component of any job.[15] By simply fostering greater initiative and responsibility in subordinates' tasks, a leader can empower organizational members. Bob Jensen, the bank executive, is an excellent example of how one leader created opportunities for greater initiative despite the confines of his subordinates' positions. He transformed what had been a highly constricted branch manager's job into a branch "president" concept. The idea was simple—every manager was made to feel like the president of his own community bank, and not just in title. Goals, compensation, and responsibilities were all changed to foster this attitude. Existing measurement systems were completely restructured. The value-of-funds-generated had been the principal yardstick—something over which branch managers had only very limited control because of interest rate fluctuations. Managers were now evaluated on what they could control—that is, deposits. Before, branch managers had rotated every couple of years. Now they stayed put. "If I'm moving around, then I'm not the president of my own bank, so we didn't move them any more," Jensen explained. He also decentralized responsibilities that had resided higher in the hierarchy—allowing the branch manager to hire, give money to charities, and so on. In addition, a new ad agency was hired to mark the occasion, and TV ads were made showing the branch managers being in charge, rendering personal services themselves. The branch managers even thought up the ad lines.

What Jensen did so skillfully was recognize that his existing managers had the talent and energy to turn their operations around successfully, but that their sense of power was missing. He recognized their pride had been hurt and that he needed to restore a sense of ownership and self-importance. He had to convince his managers through increased authority that they were no longer "pawns" of the system—that they were indeed "presidents" of their own banks.

Another example—this one demonstrating a more informal delegation of initiative—was quite surprising. The setting was a highly successful and rapidly growing computer firm, and the study participant was the vice-president of manufacturing. The vice-president had recently been hired away from another firm and was in the process of revamping manufacturing. During the process, he discovered that his company's costs on its terminal video monitors were quite high. However, he wanted his staff to discover the problem for themselves and to "own" the solution. So one day, he placed behind his desk a black-and-white Sony TV with a placard on top saying $69.95. Next to it he placed a stripped-down version of the company's monitor with a placard of $125.95. Both placards reflected the actual costs of the two products. He never said a word. But during the day as staff and department managers entered their boss's office, they couldn't help but notice the two sets. They quickly got the message that their monitor was costing twice as much as a finished TV set. Within a month, the manufacturing team had lowered the monitor's costs by 40%.

My first impression on hearing this story was that, as a subordinate, I would be hard pressed not to get the point and, more important, I would wonder why the boss was not more direct. Ironically, the boss appears to be hitting subordinates over the head with the problem. Out of context, then, this example hardly seems to make others feel more competent and powerful. Yet staff described themselves as "turned on" and motivated by this behavior. Why, I wondered? A little history will illustrate the effectiveness of this action.

The vice-president's predecessor had been a highly dictatorial individual. He tightly controlled his staff's actions and stifled any sense of discretion. Implicitly, his behavior said to subordinates, "You have no ideas of your own." He fired freely, leaving staff to feel that they had little choice in whether to accept his orders or not. By his actions, he essentially transformed his managers into powerless order-takers. When the new vice-president arrived, he found a group of demoralized subordinates whom he felt were nonetheless quite talented. To restore initiative, he began to demonstrate the seriousness of his intentions in highly visible and symbolic ways. For example, rather than tell his subordinates what to do, he started by seeding ideas and suggestions in humorous and indirect ways. The TV monitor is only one of many examples. Through these actions, he was able eventually to restore a sense of initiative and personal competence to his staff. While these examples are illustrative of effective changes in job design, managers contemplating job enrichment would be well advised to consult the existing literature and research before undertaking major projects.[16]

5. Early Victories: Building on Success. Many of the executives in the study reported that they often introduced organizational change through pilot or otherwise small and manageable projects. They designed these projects to ensure early success for their organizations. For example, instead of introducing a new sales structure nationwide, they would institute the change in one region; a new technology would have a pilot introduction at a single plant rather than systemwide. Subordinates described these early success experiences as strongly reinforcing their sense of power and efficacy. As Mike Beer argues:

> In order for change to spread throughout an organization and become a permanent fixture, it appears that early successes are needed. . . . When individuals, groups, and whole organizations feel more competent than they did before the change, this increased sense of competence reinforces the new behavior and solidifies learning associated with change.[17]

An individual's sense of mastery through actual experience is the most effective means of increasing self-efficacy.[18] When subordinates are given more complex and difficult tasks, they are presented with opportunities to test their competence. Initial success experiences will make them feel more capable and, in turn, empowered. Structuring organizational changes to ensure initial successes builds on this principle.

Contexts of Powerlessness

The need to empower organizational members becomes more important in certain contexts. Thus, it is important to identify conditions within organizations that might foster a sense of powerlessness. Certain circumstances, for instance, appear to lower feelings of self-efficacy. In these cases, subordinates typically perceive themselves as lacking control over their immediate situation (e.g., a major reorganization threatens to displace responsibility and involves limited or no subordinate participation),[19] or lacking the required capability, resources, or discretion needed to accomplish a task (e.g., the development of new and difficult-to-learn skills for the introduction of a new technological process).[20] In either case, these experiences maximize feelings of inadequacy and lower self-confidence. They, in turn, appear to lessen motivation and effectiveness.

Exhibit 1 identifies the more common organizational factors that affect these self-efficacy or personal power beliefs and contribute to feelings of powerlessness. They include organizational factors, supervisory styles, reward systems, and job design.

Exhibit 1
Context Factors Leading to Potential State of Powerlessness

Organizational Factors:
Significant organizational changes/transitions
Start-up ventures
Excessive, competitive pressures
Impersonal bureaucratic climate
Poor communications and limited network-forming systems
Highly centralized organizational resources

Supervisory Style:
Authoritarian (high control)
Negativism (emphasis on failures)
Lack of reason for actions/consequences

Reward Systems:
Noncontingency (arbitrary reward allocations)
Low incentive value of rewards
Lack of competence-based rewards
Lack of innovation-based rewards

Job Design:
Lack of role clarity
Lack of training and technical support
Unrealistic goals
Lack of appropriate authority/discretion
Low task variety
Limited participation in programs, meetings, and decisions that have a direct
  impact on job performance
Lack of appropriate/necessary resources
Lack of networking-forming opportunities
Highly established work routines
Too many rules and guidelines
Low advancement opportunities
Lack of meaningful goals/tasks
Limited contact with senior management

Source: Adapted from J. A. Conger and R. N. Kanungo, "The Empowerment Process: Integrating Theory and Practice," *Academy of Management Review*, July 1988.

For example, during a major organizational change, goals may change—often dramatically—to respond to the organization's new direction. Rules may no longer be clearly defined as the firm seeks new guidelines for action. Responsibilities may be dramatically altered. Power alliances may shift, leaving parts of the organization with a perceived loss of power or increasing political activity. Certain functional areas, divisions, or acquired companies may experience disenfranchisement as their responsibilities are felt to be diminished or made subordinate to others. As a result, employees' sense of competence may be seriously challenged as they face having to accept and acquire new responsibilities, skills, and management practices as well as deal with the uncertainty of their future.

In new venture situations, uncertainty often appears around the ultimate success of the company's strategy. A major role for leaders is to build an inspiring picture of the firm's future and convince organizational members of their ability to achieve that future. Yet, market lead times are often long, and tangible results may be slow in coming. Long work hours with few immediate rewards can diminish confidence. Frustration can build, and questions about the organization's future can arise. In addition, the start-up's success and responses to growth can mean constant change in responsibility, pushing managers into responsibilities where they have had little prior experience; thus, failure may be experienced initially as new responsibilities are learned. Entrepreneurial executives may be reluctant to relinquish their control as expansion continues.

Bureaucratic environments are especially conducive to creating conditions of powerlessness. As Peter Block points out, bureaucracy encourages dependency and submission because of its top-down contract between the organization and employees.[21] Rules, routines, and traditions define what can and cannot be done, allowing little room for initiative and discretion to develop. Employees' behavior is often guided by rules over which they have no say and which may no longer be effective, given the present-day context.

From the standpoint of supervision, authoritarian management styles can strip away subordinates' discretion and, in turn, a sense of power. Under an authoritarian manager, subordinates inevitably come to believe that they have little control—that they and their careers are subject to the whims or demands of their boss. The problem becomes acute when capable subordinates begin to attribute their powerlessness to internal factors, such as their own personal competence, rather than to external factors, such as the nature of the boss's temperament.

Rewards are another critical area for empowerment. Organizations that do not provide valued rewards or simply do not reward employees for initiative, competence, and innovation are creating conditions of powerlessness. Finally, jobs with little meaningful challenge, or jobs where the task is unclear, conflicting, or excessively demanding can lower employees' sense of self-efficacy.

Implications for Managers

Managers can think of the empowerment process as involving several stages.[22] Managers might want to begin by identifying for themselves whether any of the organizational problems and characteristics described in this article are present in their own firms. In addition, managers assuming new responsibilities should conduct an organizational diagnosis that clearly identifies their current situation, and possible problems and their causes. Attention should be aimed at understanding the recent history of the organization. Important questions to ask would be: What was my predecessor's supervisory style? Has there been a recent organizational change that negatively affected my subordinates? How is my operation perceived by the rest of the corporation? Is there a sense of disenfranchisement? Am I planning to change significantly the outlook of this operation that would challenge traditional ways of doing things? How are people rewarded? Are jobs designed to be motivating?

Once conditions contributing to feelings of powerlessness are identified, the managerial practices identified in this article and in the management literature can be used to provide self-efficacy information to subordinates. This information in turn can result in an empowering experience for subordinates and may ultimately lead to greater initiative, motivation, and persistence.

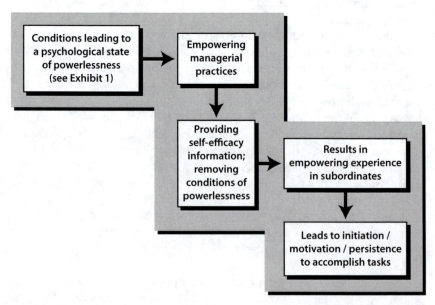

Source: Adapted from J. A. Conger and R. N. Kanungo, "The Empowerment Process: Integrating Theory and Practice," *Academy of Management Review,* July 1988.

Figure 1   Stages of the Empowerment Process

However, in applying these practices, it is imperative that managers tailor their actions to fit the context at hand. For example, in the case of an authoritarian predecessor, you are more likely to need praise and confidence-building measures and greater opportunities for job discretion. With demanding organizational goals and tasks, the practices of confidence building and active rewarding, an element of play, and a supportive environment are perhaps most appropriate. The specific character of each practice must necessarily vary somewhat to fit your particular situation. For instance, what makes many of the previous examples so important is that the executives responded with practices that organizational members could relate to or that fit their character—for instance, the television and squirt-gun examples. Unfortunately, much of today's popular management literature provides managers with tools to manage their subordinates, yet few highlight the importance of matching the practice to the appropriate context. Empowering is not a pill; it is not simply a technique, as many workshops and articles would lead us to believe. Rather, to be truly effective it requires an understanding of subordinates and one's organizational context.

Finally, although it is not as apparent in the examples themselves, each of the study executives set challenging and appealing goals for their organizations. This is a necessary component of effective and empowering leadership. If goals are not perceived as appealing, it is difficult to empower managers in a larger sense. As Warren Bennis and Burt Nanus argue:

> Great leaders often inspire their followers to high levels of achievement by showing them how their work contributes to worthwhile ends. It is an emotional appeal to some of the most fundamental needs—the need to be important, to make a difference, to feel useful, to be part of a successful and worthwhile enterprise.[23]

Such goals go hand in hand with empowering management practices. They were and are an integral part of the empowerment process I observed in the companies I studied.

A Word of Caution

In closing, it is important to add a note of caution. First of all, empowerment is not the complete or always the appropriate answer to building the confidence of managers. It can lead to overconfidence. A false sense of confidence in positive outcomes may lead employees and organizations to persist in what may, in actuality, prove to be tactical errors. Thus, a system of checks and balances is needed. Managers must constantly test reality and be alert to signs of "group think."

Some managers may be incapable of empowering others. Their own insecurities may prevent them from instilling a sense of power in subordinates. This is ironic, since often these are the individuals who need to develop such skills. Yet, as Kanter argues, "Only those leaders who feel secure about their own power outward . . . can see empowering subordinates as a gain rather than a loss."[24]

Certain situations may not warrant empowerment. For example, there are contexts where opportunities for greater initiative or responsibility simply do not exist and, in some cases, subordinates may be unwilling or unable to assume greater ownership or responsibility. As Lyman Porter, Edward Lawler, and Richard Hackman point out, research "strongly suggests that only workers with reasonably high strength of desire for higher-order need satisfaction . . . will respond positively and productively to the opportunities present in jobs which are high in meaning, autonomy, complexity, and feedback."[25] Others may not have the requisite experience or knowledge to succeed. And those given more than they are capable of handling may fail. The end result will be the opposite of what you are seeking—a sense of powerlessness. It is imperative that managers assess as accurately as possible their subordinates' capabilities before undertaking difficult goals and empowering them to achieve.

Second, certain of the empowerment practices described in this article are not appropriate for all situations. For example, managers of subordinates who require structure and direction are likely to find the example of the manager "seeding" ideas with the television set an ineffective practice. In the case of a pressing deadline or crisis, such seeding is inappropriate, given its longer time horizons.

When staging playful or unconventional events, the context must be considered quite carefully. What signals are you sending about yourself and your management philosophy? Like rewards, these events can be used to excess and lose their meaning. It is imperative to determine the appropriateness and receptivity of such practices. You may inadvertently mock or insult subordinates, peers, or superiors.

In terms of expressing confidence and rewarding, both must be done sincerely and not to excess. Praising for nonaccomplishments can make rewards meaningless. Subordinates may suspect that the boss is simply flattering them into working harder.

In general, however, empowerment practices are an important tool for leaders in setting and achieving higher goals and in moving an organization past difficult transitions.[26] But remember that they do demand time, confidence, an element of creativity, and a sensitivity to one's context to be effective.

Notes

[1] See, for example, J. P. Kotter, *Power in Management*, New York: AMACOM, 1979, and J. Pfeffer, *Power in Organizations*, Marshfield, MA: Pitman, 1981.

[2] See P. Block, *The Empowered Manager*, San Francisco: Jossey-Bass, 1987; W. W. Burke, "Leadership as Empowering Others," in S. Srivastva (Ed.), *Executive Power*, San Francisco: Jossey-Bass, 1986, pp. 51–77; and R. M. Kanter, *The Change Masters*, New York: Simon & Schuster, 1983.

[3] W. Bennis and B. Nanus, *Leaders*, New York: Harper & Row, 1985; and R. M. Kanter, "Power Failure in Management Circuits," *Harvard Business Review*, July-August 1979, pp. 65–75.

[4] See Kanter, Endnote 3; and A. S. Tannenbaum, *Control in Organizations*, New York: McGraw-Hill, 1968.

⁵ See J. A. Conger and R. N. Kanungo, "The Empowerment Process: Integrating Theory and Practice," *Academy of Management Review,* July 1988; and R. J. House, "Power and Personality in Complex Organizations," in L. L. Cummings and B. M. Staw (Eds.), *Research in Organizational Behavior: An Annual Review of Critical Essays and Reviews,* Vol. 10, Greenwich, CT: JAI Press, 1988. The author is grateful to Rabindra N. Kanungo for his insights and help in conceptualizing the empowerment process.

⁶ See Conger and Kanungo, Endnote 5.

⁷ A. Bandura, "Self-Efficiency: Toward a Unifying Theory of Behavioral Change," *Psychological Review,* 1977, 84(2), pp. 191–215.

⁸ D. McGregor, *The Human Side of Enterprise,* New York: McGraw-Hill, 1960.

⁹ See J. M. Beyer and H. M. Trice, "How an Organization's Rites Reveal Its Culture," *Organizational Dynamics,* Spring 1987, pp. 4–25.

¹⁰ A. Bandura, *Social Foundations of Thought and Action: A Social Cognitive View,* Englewood Cliffs, NJ: Prentice-Hall, 1986.

¹¹ See Kanter, Endnote 3, p. 66.

¹² See Bandura, Endnote 10, p. 400.

¹³ W. Bennis and B. Nanus, *Leaders,* New York: Harper & Row, 1985, pp. 64–65.

¹⁴ See Bandura, Endnote 10.

¹⁵ See Kanter, Endnote 3.

¹⁶ See J. R. Hackman, "The Design of Work in the 1980s," *Organizational Dynamics,* Summer 1978, pp. 3–17.

¹⁷ M. Beer, *Organizational Change and Development,* Santa Monica, CA: Goodyear, 1980, p. 64.

¹⁸ See Bandura, Endnote 10.

¹⁹ F. M. Rothbaum, J. R. Weisz, and S. S. Snyder, "Changing the World and Changing Self: A Two Process Model of Perceived Control," *Journal of Personality and Social Psychology,* 1982, 42, pp. 5-37; and L. Y. Abramson, J. Garber, and M. E. P. Seligman, "Learned Helplessness in Humans: An Attributional Analysis," in J. Garber and M. E. P. Seligman (Eds.), *Human Helplessness: Theory and Applications,* New York: Academic Press, 1980, pp. 3–34.

²⁰ See Kanter, Endnote 2.

²¹ See Block, Endnote 2.

²² See Conger and Kanungo, Endnote 5.

²³ Bennis and Nanus, Endnote 13, p. 93.

²⁴ See Kanter, Endnote 3, p. 73.

²⁵ L. W. Porter, E. E. Lawler, and J. R. Hackman, *Behavior in Organizations,* New York: McGraw-Hill, 1975, p. 306.

²⁶ See N. M. Tichy and M. A. Devanna, *The Transformational Leader,* New York: John Wiley, 1986.

36

Goodbye, Command and Control

Margaret Wheatley

Old ways die hard. Amid all the evidence that our world is radically changing, we cling to what has worked in the past. We still think of organizations in mechanistic terms, as collections of replaceable parts capable of being reengineered. We act as if even people were machines, redesigning their jobs as we would prepare an engineering diagram, expecting them to perform to specifications with machine-like obedience. Over the years, our ideas of leadership have supported this metaphoric myth. We sought prediction and control, and also charged leaders with providing everything that was absent from the machine: vision, inspiration, intelligence, and courage. They alone had to provide the energy and direction to move their rusting vehicles of organization into the future.

But in the late 1990s, we are surrounded by too many organizational failures to stay with this thinking. We know, for example, that in many recent surveys senior leaders report that more than two-thirds of their organizational change efforts fail. They and their employees report deep cynicism at the endless programs and fads; nearly everyone suffers from increased stress of the organizational lives we have created together. Survey after survey registers our loss of hope and increased uncertainty for every major institutional form in our society. Do we know how to organize anything anymore so that people want to engage in productive and contributing work?

But there is good news also. We have known for nearly half a century that self-managed teams are far more productive than any other form of organizing. There is a clear correlation between participation and productivity; in fact, productivity gains in truly self-managed work environments are at minimum 35 percent higher than in traditionally managed organizations. And in all forms of institutions, Americans are asking for more local autonomy, insisting that they, at their own level, can do it better than the huge structures of organizations now in place. There is both a desire to participate more and strong evidence that such participation leads to the effectiveness and productivity we crave.

With so much evidence supporting participation, why isn't everyone working in a self-managed environment right now? This is a very bothersome question because it points to the fact that over the years, leaders consistently have chosen control rather than productivity. Rather than rethinking our fundamental assumptions about organizational effectiveness, we have stayed preoccupied with charts and plans and designs. We have hoped they would yield the results we needed but when they have failed consistently, we still haven't stopped to question whether such charts and plans are the real route to productive work. We just continue to adjust and tweak the various control measures, still hoping to find the one plan or design that will give us what we need.

Organizations of all kinds are cluttered with control mechanisms that paralyze employees and leaders alike. Where have all these policies, procedures, protocols, laws, and regulations come from? And why is it so difficult to avoid creating more, even as we suffer from the terrible confines of over-control? These mechanisms seem to derive from our fear, our fear of one another, of a harsh competitive world, and of the natural processes of growth and change that confront us daily. Years of such fear have resulted in these byzantine systems. We never effectively control people with these systems, but we certainly stop a lot of good work from getting done.

In the midst of so much fear, it's important to remember something we all know: People organize together to accomplish more, not less. Behind every organizing impulse is a realization that by joining with others we can accomplish something important that we could not accomplish alone. And this impulse to organize so as to accomplish more is not only true of humans, but is found in all living systems. Every living thing seeks to create a world in which it can thrive. It does this by creating systems of relationships where all members of the system benefit from their connections. This movement toward organization, called self-organization in the sciences, is everywhere, from microbes to galaxies. Patterns of relationships form into effective systems of organization. Organization is a naturally occurring phenomenon. The world seeks organization, seeks its own effectiveness. And so do the people in our organizations.

As a living system self-organizes, it develops shared understanding of what's important, what's acceptable behavior, what actions are required, and how these actions will get done. It develops channels of communication, networks of workers, and complex physical structures. And as the system develops, new capacities emerge from living and working together. Looking at this list of what a self-organizing system creates leads to the realization that the system can do for itself most of what leaders have felt was necessary to do to the systems they control.

Whenever we look at organizations as machines and deny the great self-organizing capacity in our midst, we, as leaders, attempt to change these systems from the outside in. We hope to change our organization by tinkering with the incentives, reshuffling the pieces, changing a part, or retraining a colleague or group. But these efforts are doomed to fail, and nothing will make them work. What is required is a shift in how we think about organizing. Where does organization come from? Organization occurs from the inside out, as people see what needs to happen, apply their experience and perceptions to the issue, find those who can help them, and use their own creativity to invent solutions. This process is going on right now, all over our organizations, in spite of our efforts at control. People are exercising initiative from a deeper desire to contribute, displaying the creativity that is common to all living things. Can we recognize the self-organizing behaviors of those in our organizations? Can we learn to support them and forgo our fear-based approaches to leadership?

Belief in the System

To lead in a self-organizing system, we have to ask ourselves, "How much trust do I really have in the people who work here? Have they demonstrated any of these self-organizing behaviors already?" This question of trust leads to a moment of deep reflection for any leader. Those leaders who have embraced a more participative, self-organizing approach tell of their astonishment. They are overwhelmed by the capacity, energy, creativity, commitment, and even love that they receive from the people in their organization. In the past they had simply assumed that most people were there for the money, that they didn't care about the welfare of the whole enterprise, that they were self-serving and narrowly focused. No leader would voice these assumptions, but most leader behaviors reveal these beliefs. Does the leader believe that his or her vision is required to energize the whole company? Does the leadership team keep searching for new incentives to motivate employees as if they have no intrinsic motivation? Does the organization keep imposing new designs and plans on people and avoid real participation like the plague?

Every so often, we open ourselves to a moment of truth and realize the conflict between our behaviors and our deeper knowledge. As one manager of a *Fortune* 100 company said to me: "I know in my heart that when people are driving in to work that they're not thinking, 'How can I mess things up today? How can I give my boss a hard time?' No one is driving here with that intent, but we then act as if we believed that. We're afraid to give them any slack."

Most of us know that as people drive to work they're wondering how they can get something done for the organization despite the organization—despite the political craziness, the bureaucratic nightmares, the mindless procedures piled up in their way. Those leaders who have opened to participation and self-organization have witnessed the inherent desire that most people have to contribute to their organizations. The commitment and energy resident in their organizations takes leaders by surprise. But in honoring and trusting the people who work with them, they have unleashed startlingly high levels of productivity and creativity.

Strategies for Change

If we think of organizations as living systems capable of self-organizing, then how do we think about change in these systems? The strategy for change becomes simpler and more localized. We need to encourage the creativity that lives throughout the organization, but keep local solutions localized. Most change efforts fail when leaders take an innovation that has worked well in one area of the organization and attempt to roll it out to the entire organization. This desire to replicate success actually destroys local initiative. It denies the creativity of everyone except a small group. All living systems change all the time, in new and surprising ways, discovering greater effectiveness, better solutions. They are not acting from some master plan. They are tinkering in their local environments, based on their intimate experience with conditions there and their tinkering shows up as effective innovation. But only for them. Information about what has worked elsewhere can be very helpful. However, these solutions cannot be imposed; they have to remain local.

This highly localized change activity does not mean that the organization spins off wildly in all directions. If people are clear about the purpose and true values of their organization—if they understand what their organization stands for and who it shows itself to be through its actions—their individual tinkering will result in system-wide coherence. In organizations that know who they are and mean what they announce, people are free to create and contribute. A plurality of effective solutions emerges, each expressing a deeper coherence, an understanding of what this organization is trying to become.

Mort Meyerson, chairman of Perot Systems, said that the primary task of being a leader is to make sure that the organization knows itself. That is, we must realize that our task is to call people together often, so that everyone gains clarity about who we are, who we've just become, who we still want to be. This includes the interpretations available from our customers, our markets, our history, our mistakes. If the organization can stay in a continuous conversation about who it is and who it is becoming, then leaders don't have to undertake the impossible task of trying to hold it all together. Organizations that are clear at their core hold themselves together because of their deep congruence. People are then free to explore new avenues of activity, new ventures and customers in ways that make sense for the organization. It is a strange and promising paradox of living systems. Clarity about who we are as a group creates freedom for individual contributions. People exercise that freedom in the service of the organization, and their capacity to respond and change becomes a capability of the whole organization.

If we as leaders can ensure that our organization knows itself, that it's clear at its core, we must also tolerate unprecedented levels of "messiness" at the edges. This constant tinkering, this localized hunt for solutions does not look neat. There is no conformity possible unless we want to kill local initiative. Freedom and creativity create diverse responses. We have to be prepared to support such diversity, to welcome the surprises people will invent, and to stop wasting time trying to impose solutions developed elsewhere.

People always want to talk about what they do, what they see, how they can improve things, what they know about their customers. Supporting these conversations is an essential task of leaders. It's not about you, "the leader," developing the mission statement or employing experts to do a detailed analysis of your market strategy. These exercises, because they exclude more people than they include, never work as planned. Only when everyone in our organization understands who we are, and has contributed to this deep understanding, do we gain the levels of commitment and capacity we so desperately need. As a leader supports the processes that help the organization know itself, the organization flourishes.

It's also notable that when we engage in meaningful conversations as an organization, and when we engage our customers, suppliers, community, and regulators in these conversations, that everything changes. People develop new levels of trust for one another that show up as more cooperation and more forgiveness. People stop being so arbitrarily demanding when they are part of the process, when they no longer are looking in from the outside trying to get someone's attention.

Moving to Action

Leaders put a premium on action. Organizations that have learned how to think together and that know themselves are filled with action. People are constantly taking initiative and making changes, often without asking or telling. Their individual freedom and creativity becomes a critical resource to the organization. Their local responsiveness translates into a much faster and more adaptable organization overall.

But leaders need to know how to support these self-organizing responses. People do not need the intricate directions, time lines, plans, and organization charts that we thought we had to give them. These are not how people accomplish good work, they are what impede contributions. But people need a lot from their leaders. They need information, access to one another, resources, trust, and follow-through. Leaders are necessary to foster experimentation, to help create connections across the organization, to feed the system with rich information from multiple sources—all while helping everyone stay clear on what we agreed we wanted to accomplish and who we wanted to be.

Most of us were raised in a culture that told us that the way to manage for excellence was to tell people exactly what they had to do and then make sure they did it. We learned to play master designer, assuming we could engineer people into perfect performance. But you can't direct people into perfection; you can only engage them enough so that they want to do perfect work.

For example, in a few chemical plants that operate with near-perfect safety records for years at a time, they achieve these results because their workers are committed to safety. It becomes a personal mission. The regulations, the EPA, OSHA, are all necessary parts of their system, but they never can spell out the route to perfect safety. That comes from hundreds and thousands of workers who understand their role in safety, who understand the whys of safety, who understand that it's up to them.

For all the unscripted events—an irate customer, a leak, a winter storm—we depend on individual initiative. Ultimately, we have to rely not on the procedure manuals, but on peoples' brains and their commitment to doing the right thing. If they are acting by rote or regimen, they actually have lost the capacity for excellence. Imposed control breeds passivity. But people do have to know what "right" means. They have to know what safety really means. If they know what's right, then we have engaged their intelligence and heart on behalf of the organization.

No More Quick Fixes

Self-organization is a long-term exploration requiring enormous self-awareness and support. This is true partially because it represents such a fundamentally different way of thinking about organization, and partially because all changes in organization take much longer than we want to acknowledge. If we've learned anything in the past 20 years, it's that there are no quick fixes. For most organizations, meaningful change is at least a three to five-year process—although this seems impossibly long for many managers. Yet multiyear strategic change efforts are the hard reality we must face. These things take time. How long, for instance, has your organization been struggling with total quality? At Motorola, it's been more than a decade. How many years have you been working with the concept of teams? Jack Welch, for one, understood that it would take at least 10 years to develop the capacities of GE's people. In the crazed world of the late '80s, that was a radical insight and a shocking commitment.

Most CEOs aren't trying to simply squeeze their organizations for short-term profitability or shortsighted outcomes that don't endure. Most leaders would never say, "I just want this organization to perform well for a few quarters." More and more, leaders talk about their legacy. They talk about a deep desire for their work, which is to be a leader. Leaders are not immune to the terrible destruction we've seen in many organizations. "This has been a difficult time," a senior executive of a major industrial firm, speaking for many, said in a meeting. "I've just destroyed what I spent 20 years creating." Who among us wants to end a career with that realization?

But if we are to develop organizations of greater and enduring capacity, we have to turn to the people of our organization. We have to learn how to encourage the creativity and commitment that they wanted to express when they first joined the organization. We have to learn how to get past the distress and cynicism that's been created in the past several years, and use our best talents to figure out how to reengage people in the important work of organizing.

The Leader's Journey

Whenever we're trying to change a deeply structured belief system, everything in life is called into question—our relationships with loved ones, children, colleagues, our relationships with authority and major institutions. One group of senior leaders, reflecting on the changes they've gone through, commented that the higher you are in the organization, the more change is required of you personally. Those who have led their organizations into new ways of organizing often say that the most important change was what occurred in themselves. Nothing would have changed in their organizations if they hadn't changed.

All this seems true to me, but I think the story is more complex. Leaders managing difficult personal transitions are usually simultaneously opening new avenues for people in the organization. They are moving toward true team structures, opening to more and more participative processes, introducing new ways of thinking. They are setting a great many things in motion inside the organization. These ripple through the system; some work, some don't, but the climate for experimentation is evident. A change here elicits a response there, which calls for a new idea, which elicits yet another response. It's an intricate exchange and co-evolution, and it's nearly impossible to look back and name any one change as the cause of all the others. Organizational change is a dance, not a forced march.

Leaders experience their own personal change most intensely, and so I think they report on this as the key process. But what I observe is far more complex. In the end, you can't define a list of activities that were responsible for the organization shifting, and you certainly can't replicate anyone else's exact process for success. But you can encourage the experimentation and tinkering, the constant feedback and learning, and the wonderful sense of camaraderie that emerges as everyone gets engaged in making the organization work better than ever before, even in the most difficult of circumstances.

Sustainability, Not Employability

I believe there is one principle that should be embraced by all organizations as they move into the future, and that is sustainability. How can we endure over time? What about us is worth sustaining long-term? This focus flies in the face of current fashion. Our infatuation with fleeting "virtual" organizations misses an important truth: We cannot create an organization that means something to its people if that organization has no life beyond the next project or contract. We cannot promise people, for instance, only three years of employment with vague assurances of their future "employability"— and expect the kind of energy and commitment that I've described.

Employability in lieu of mutual commitment is a cop-out. We seem to focus on it as a response to the grave uncertainty we feel about the future. Since we can't predict markets, products, customers, governments, or anything, we decide not to promise anything to anyone. Too many leaders are saying, in effect, "We don't know what the future will be or how to manage this uncertainty, so let's think of our employees as negotiable commodities." What they've really said is "Let's buy flexibility by giving up loyalty."

Commitment and loyalty are essential in human relationships. So how can we pretend we don't need them at work? The real issue is that we don't know yet how to engage people's loyalty and yet maintain the flexibility we require. But leaders should be searching for creative answers to this dilemma, not ignoring it by settling on the non-solution of so-called employability. Employability is a far more destructive practice than we have imagined. The organizations that people love to be in are ones that have a sense of history and identity and purpose. These are things that people want to work for. The belief that a company has stood for something in the past is a reason to want to move it into the future.

The Real Criteria for Measuring Change

You know when you walk in the door of an organization whether people want to be there or not. The sense of belonging (or not) is palpable. Yet few change efforts take that into account and far too many end up killing the organization's capacity for more change. To measure whether a change effort has been successful, we need to ask, "Are people in the organization more committed to being here now than at the beginning of this effort?" In terms of sustainability, we need to ask if, at the end of this change effort, people feel more prepared for the next wave of change. Did we develop capacity or just stage an event? Do people feel that their creativity and expertise contributed to the changes?

If we're focused on these questions as indicators, we can create organizations that know how to respond continuously to shifts in markets and environments, organizations that have learned how to access the intelligence that lives everywhere in the system. We will have supported people's innate capacity to deal with changing conditions because we will have learned how to engage them. We will have honored their innate capacity for self-organization. And they will respond with the initiative and creativity that is found only in life, never in machines.

Questions and Learning Activities

Section V

Questions

1. Why are leaders who use expert and referent power often more success-ful in their attempt to influence than leaders who rely exclusively on the power of their position (authority) and reward power?

2. Do you think older generations might be more willing than younger ones to accept authority, power of position? Why?

3. "The easiest way to enhance personal power is to give it away." Do you agree or disagree with this statement? Why?

4. "No leader can empower his or her followers, they must empower them-selves." Do you agree or disagree with this statement? Why?

5. There are many people who do not have high need for power—they sim-ply do not have a need to influence others. Does this mean they could never be effective leaders?

6. Why do you think some use Machiavelli's teachings even though they do not fit with commonly held beliefs about effective leadership?

7. What are the practical implications of the Salancik and Pfeffer reading on power acquisition and retention? According to this article, what should leader/managers be alert to in order to retain and build their power?

8. How does power arise from leader-member exchange? To whom does power accrue in leader-member exchange? Provide examples to support your position.

9. Conger's article on empowerment provides several examples of empow-ering practices. Although the practices are quite different, they all share a commonality or essence. What is this?

10. What are four organizational conditions that cause people to feel powerless?

11. Margaret Wheatley believes that the command and control approach to organizations is not effective. What is the essence of her argument?

12. What major personal change will most leader/managers have to make if they are to exploit the advantages of self-organizing systems?

Activities

1. Briefly research the Milgram experiments and related writings. Write a paper entitled "The Dark Side of Power: Implications for Leader/Manag-ers and Followers."

2. There undoubtedly have been times in your life when leaders have attempted to influence you using different power bases. Describe your reactions to influence attempts based on each of the five leadership power bases.

3. Referring to the leader-member exchange reading, write a paper entitled "Role-Making and Exchange: My Experiences as a Follower."

4. As a current or future leader/manager, write a three-page paper about what you are going to take from the article by Conger.

5. Discuss with classmates/colleagues powerful leaders you have directly encountered or observed. What made them powerful?

6. Discuss with classmates/colleagues instances in which you were subjected to true empowerment. What made it seem real and what were your reactions?

7. Describe a situation with which you are familiar where a leader talked about empowerment but didn't really follow through. What did followers say? How did they react? Did perceptions of the leader change? If yes, how?

8. How "Machiavellian" are you? Complete the suggested power profile exercise on the editor's Web site (www.waveland.com/McMahon/) to gain some insight.

9. Is power important to you? The self-awareness suggestion on the Web site will provide some clarification.

SECTION VI

ENHANCING
LEADERSHIP EFFECTIVENESS

All of the readings in this book are directed toward understanding leadership and improving the effectiveness of current and aspiring leader/managers. With that said, this final section offers prescriptions for leader/managers across a wide variety of situations. The implications of these readings are generally not in conflict with foundational elements presented throughout the book. Some are aimed at a very specific issue, such as execution, while others offer insights that are general enough to be relevant for all leader/managers.

In the first reading we again encounter Douglas McGregor. In *Conditions for Effective Leadership*, he addresses the issue of the follower's dependence on the leader and what is needed for employees to feel secure enough to engage in work in an independent manner. At the heart of the matter are conditions that facilitate need satisfaction as well as growth and development of employees. McGregor's insights into the organizations of the 1940s are relevant today in spite of a very different organizational landscape.

All social groups, including organizations, have a culture that plays a powerful role. Culture permeates a myriad of dynamics—motivation, communications, conflict, goal setting, and the engagement and motivation of members, just to name a few. Culture also operates as an ever-present and invisible "control-system" vis-à-vis the behavior of individuals, teams, and the organization as a whole. All leader/managers need to understand how culture affects the organization and the role they play in determining and communicating culture. Edgar Schein, the preeminent authority on this topic for the last couple of decades, supplies valuable lessons in *How Leaders Embed and Transmit Culture*.

W. Edwards Deming is considered by many to be the father of total quality management. Though he is not often referred to in publications about leadership, he has some insightful observations on the topic. In *The Deming Leadership Method*, Nicholas Mauro outlines the four core values, four cornerstones, and fourteen points that comprise Deming's very specific model. Deming believes that all leader/managers need to understand not only the system in which they operate but also the causes of variation within the system. Deming's contributions to the leadership literature are unique and warrant serious consideration.

James M. Kouzes and Barry Z. Posner have been conducting research on leadership effectiveness for over two decades. Their findings are covered in detail in their popular book, *The Leadership Challenge*. The fourth reading in this section, *The Five Practices of Exemplary Leadership*, provides an overview of their work. These authors assert that leadership is not a position but rather a process available to many. Progress toward higher levels of organizational effectiveness is dependent upon recognizing, developing, and nurturing leadership throughout the organization.

Personal growth and development are common topics in today's leadership discussions. Two decades ago, however, such was not the case. One of the pioneers in this area is Peter Senge, well known for his book *The Fifth Discipline*. In *The Discipline of Personal Mastery*, an excerpt from this book, he describes and discusses personal mastery and why it is an aspect of leader/manager development of the highest order. His thoughtful discussion applies not only to leader/managers but to followers, coworkers, and, indeed, all who wish to be active participants in life.

It was noted in the preface that not applying what we know is common with respect to leadership. A refreshing rebuke to this condition is the case of Johnsonville Sausage and its CEO, Ralph Stayer. In *How I Learned to Let My Workers Lead,* Stayer chronicles a process of change at Johnsonville that embraced many elements of effective leadership, including employee empowerment and leader development throughout the organization. As Stayer so vividly describes, some of a leader's hardest work relates not to employees but to oneself.

Stephen R. Covey, author of *Seven Habits of Highly Successful People,* applies his thinking on effectiveness to leadership in *Principle-Centered Leadership*. Sections of this article relate well to many of the earlier readings. Furthermore, his practical, specific advice with regard to the daily life of leader/managers supplies useful guidance on how to enhance effectiveness.

There is much research on leader behaviors and their relationship to performance and satisfaction that never finds its way into the public arena. One exception is *First, Break all the Rules* by Marcus Buckingham and Curt Coffman. This book contains their research findings on specific leader behaviors significantly related to hard performance measures such as profitability, productivity, retention, and customer satisfaction. The excerpt here, titled *Leader Behaviors and Organizational Performance,* contains a brief summary of the significant findings. Their observation that the immediate manager is more important than pay, perks, or a charismatic CEO in building a strong workplace is an intriguing conclusion that further confirms the importance of leadership development throughout organizations.

Peter Drucker has authored a significant number of important books and articles in the areas of management and leadership. One that does not focus on business or organizational issues, fits with contemporary trends in leadership development, and contains specific and useful suggestions is *Managing Oneself*. The premise that each person is responsible for his or her growth and development is irrefutable in today's corporate environment. Drucker's case for self-knowledge, considered by many to be the bedrock of leadership development, is strengthened by the blueprint he offers for gaining insight into one's values, working style, and learning style.

Jim Collins's *Level 5 Leadership*, drawn from his book *Good to Great*, is considered a classic by many despite its relative youth. Collins sought to answer the question of whether good companies can transform themselves into great companies, and if so—how? The answer ran contrary to popular notions of charismatic, larger-than-life leaders and instead focused on personal humility and fierce resolve—the central attributes of the Level 5 leader.

It is too often the case that leader/managers develop a compelling vision, arouse enthusiasm and commitment among followers, and yet, fail to realize organizational dreams. A common reason for such failures is poor execution, the subject of *Leadership and Execution* by Larry Bossidy and Ram Charan. Drawn from their book, *Execution: The Discipline of Getting Things Done*, this selection clearly articulates what leader/managers must do to help ensure that visions are realized and the energies of participants are effectively directed.

In *Crucibles of Leadership*, Warren Bennis and Robert J. Thomas explore the role of adversity—in particular, how one reacts and copes with difficulties—in developing the critical skills for effective leadership. The authors believe that the skills required to overcome challenges and emerge stronger and smarter are those that define extraordinary leaders. This article will remind readers of Zaleznik's thoughts regarding encountering smooth or difficult times during maturation and the implications for leadership (see Section II).

Marshall Goldsmith, a well-known expert on executive coaching, describes an interesting process for enhancing leadership effectiveness in *Try Feedforward Instead of Feedback*. As he notes, feedback is past-oriented and often perceived as criticism, which causes defensiveness and an eventual decline in motivation. Furthermore, many leader/managers simply do not like to give feedback and lack the skills to do it well. Feedforward, on the other hand, is future-oriented, nonthreatening, and easy to implement. This process has excellent potential for helping leader/managers achieve maximum results from subordinates.

Leadership development is more than an ongoing process of acquiring knowledge and skills. It also involves self-development; that is, self-awareness, values clarification, and self-mastery. Bill George's *Authentic Leadership* is an enlightening and timely look at authenticity as a critical prerequisite for leadership. George believes that authenticity is absolutely required to build trust and advises leader/managers and those aspiring to such positions to do the "inner work" necessary to enhance their authenticity.

37

Conditions for Effective Leadership

Douglas McGregor

This discussion of relationships among people at work is written from the point of view of dynamic psychology which, because of its origin in the clinic, directs attention to the whole individual living and interacting within a world of other individuals. Life, from the point of view of dynamic psychology, is a continuous striving to satisfy ever-changing needs in the face of obstacles. The work life is but a segment—although a large one—of the whole.

The Setting

Within this framework we shall examine some of the important forces and events in the work situation which aid or hinder the individual as he strives to satisfy his needs. First of all, we must recognize a fundamental fact: The direct impact of almost all these forces upon the individual is through the behavior of other people. This is obvious when we speak of an order from the boss, or pressures exerted by fellow workers to get the individual to join a union. It is perhaps less obvious when we speak of the impact of the business cycle, or the consequences of a fundamental technological change. Nevertheless, the direct influence of these forces on the individual—whether he is a worker or a plant manager—occurs through the medium of the actions of other people. We must include not only the easily observed actions of others, but subtle, fleeting manifestations of attitude and emotion to which the individual reacts almost unconsciously.

For purposes of discussion we may arbitrarily divide the actions of other people which influence the individual in the work situation into three classes: actions of superiors, of subordinates, and of associates. We shall limit our

Reprinted from *Journal of Consulting Psychology,* Vol. 8, No. 2 (March–April 1944), pp. 55–63. Originally titled "Conditions of Effective Leadership in the Industrial Organization."

attention mainly to the actions of superiors as they affect the subordinate in his striving to satisfy his needs. This relationship is logically prior to the others, and it is in many ways the most important human relationship in industry.

The fundamental characteristics of the subordinate-superior relationship are identical whether one talks of the worker and the supervisor, the assistant superintendent and the superintendent, or the vice-president and the president. There are, to be sure, differences in the content of the relationship, and in the relative importance of its characteristics, at different levels of the industrial organization. The underlying aspects, however, are common to all levels.

The Dependence of the Subordinate

The outstanding characteristic of the relationship between the subordinate and his superiors is his dependence upon them for the satisfaction of his needs. Industry in our civilization is organized along authoritative lines. In a fundamental and pervasive sense, the subordinate is dependent upon his superiors for his job, for the continuity of his employment, for promotion with its accompanying satisfactions in the form of increased pay, responsibility, and prestige, and for a host of other personal and social satisfactions to be obtained in the work situation.

This dependence is not adequately recognized in our culture. For one thing, it is not consistent with some of our basic social values. The emphasis is usually placed upon the importance of the subordinate's own efforts in achieving the satisfaction of his needs. Nevertheless, the dependence is real, and subordinates are not unaware of it. Among workers, surveys of attitudes invariably place "fair treatment by superiors" toward the top of the list of factors influencing job satisfaction.[1,2] And the extent to which unions have attempted to place restrictions upon management's authority reflects not only a desire for power but a conscious attempt to reduce the dependence of workers upon their bosses.[3,4]

Psychologically, the dependence of the subordinate upon his superiors is a fact of extraordinary significance, in part because of its emotional similarity to the dependence characteristic of another earlier relationship: that between the child and his parents. The similarity is more than an analogy. The adult subordinate's dependence upon his superiors actually reawakens certain emotions and attitudes which were part of his childhood relationship with his parents, and which apparently have long since been outgrown. The adult is usually unaware of the similarity because most of this complex of childhood emotions has been repressed. Although the emotions influence his behavior, they are not accessible to consciousness under ordinary circumstances.

Superficially, it may seem absurd to compare these two relationships, but one cannot observe human behavior in industry without being struck by the fundamental similarity between them. Space limitations prevent elaboration of this point here, in spite of its great importance.[5]

There are certain inevitable consequences of the dependence of the subordinate upon his superiors. The success or failure of the relationship depends on the way in which these consequences are handled. An understanding of them provides a more useful basis than the usual "rules of thumb" for a consideration of problems of industrial relations. These consequences of the dependence of the subordinate will be discussed under two main headings: (1) the necessity for security in the work situation, and (2) the necessity for self-realization.

The Necessity for Security

Subordinates will struggle to protect themselves against real or imagined threats to the satisfaction of their needs in the work situation. Analysis of this protective behavior suggests that the actions of superiors are frequently perceived as the source of the threats.[6] Before subordinates can believe that it is possible to satisfy their wants in the work situation, they must acquire a convincing sense of security in their dependent relationship to their superiors.

Management has recognized the financial aspects of this need for security, and has attempted to provide for it by means of employee retirement plans, health and accident insurance, the encouragement of employee credit unions, and even guaranteed annual wages.[7] However, this recognition does not get at the heart of the problem: the personal dependence of the subordinate upon the judgments and decisions of his superior.

Labor unions have attacked the problem more directly in their attempts to obtain rules governing promotions and layoffs, grievance procedures, arbitration provisions, and protection against arbitrary changes in workloads and rates.[8,9] One important purpose of such "protective" features in union contracts is to restrict superiors in the making of decisions which, *from the worker's point of view,* are arbitrary and threatening. They help to provide the subordinate with a measure of security despite his dependence on his superiors.

The Conditions of Security: An Atmosphere of Approval

There are three major aspects of the subordinate-superior relationship—*at any level of the organization*—which affect the security of the subordinate. The most important of these is what we may term the "atmosphere" created by the superior.[10] This atmosphere is revealed not by what the superior does but by the manner in which he does it, and by his underlying attitude toward his subordinates. It is relatively independent of the strictness of the superior's discipline, or the standards of performance which he demands.

A foreman who had unwittingly created such an atmosphere attempted to establish a rule that union officials should obtain his permission when they left the job to meet with higher management, and report to him when they returned. This entirely reasonable action aroused intense resentment, although the same rule was readily accepted by union officials in another part of the plant. The specific actions were unimportant except in terms of the background against which the subordinates perceived them: an atmosphere of disapproval in the one case and of approval in the other.

Security for subordinates is possible only when they know they have the genuine approval of their superior. If the atmosphere is equivocal, or one of disapproval, they can have no assurance that their needs will be satisfied, *regardless of what they do*. In the absence of a genuine attitude of approval subordinates are threatened, fearful, insecure. Even neutral and innocuous actions of the superior are regarded with suspicion. Effective discipline is impossible, high standards of performance cannot be maintained, "sabotage" of the superior's efforts is almost inevitable. Resistance, antagonism, and ultimately open rebellion are the consequences.

The Conditions of Security: Knowledge

The second requirement for the subordinate's security is knowledge. *He must know what is expected of him.* Otherwise he may, through errors of commission or omission, interfere with the satisfaction of his own needs. There are several kinds of knowledge which the subordinate requires:

1. *Knowledge of overall company policy and management philosophy.* Security is impossible in a world of shifting foundations. This fact was convincingly demonstrated—to management in particular—during the first few months of the existence of the War Labor Board. The cry for a national labor policy was frequently heard. "Without it we don't know how to act." Likewise, subordinates in the individual company require a knowledge of the broad policy and philosophy of top management.[11]

2. *Knowledge of procedures, rules and regulations.* Without this knowledge, the subordinate can only learn by trial and error, and the threat of punishment because of innocent infractions hangs always over his head.[12]

3. *Knowledge of the requirements of the subordinate's own job; his duties, responsibilities, and place in the organization.* It is surprising how often subordinates (particularly within the management organization) are unable to obtain this essential knowledge. Lacking it, one can never be sure when to make a decision, or when to refer the matter to someone else; when to act or when to "pass the buck."[13] The potential dangers in this kind of insecurity are apparent upon the most casual consideration.

4. *Knowledge of the personal peculiarities of the subordinate's immediate superior.* The good salesman never approaches a new prospect without learning all he can about his interests, habits, prejudices, and opinions. The subordinate must sell *himself* to his superior, and consequently such knowledge is indispensable to him. Does the boss demand initiative and originality, or does he want to make all the decisions himself? What are the unpardonable sins, the things this superior never forgives or forgets? What are his soft spots, and what are his blind spots? There can be no security for the subordinate until he has discovered the answers to these questions.

5. *Knowledge by the subordinate of the superior's opinion of his performance.* Where do I stand? How am I doing? To know where you stand in the eyes of your superiors is to know what you must do in order to satisfy your needs.[14] Lacking this knowledge, the subordinate can have, at best, only a false sense of security.

6. *Advance knowledge of changes that* may *affect the subordinate.* Resistance to change is a common phenomenon among employees in industry.[15,16,17] One of the fundamental reasons is the effect of unpredictable changes upon security. If the subordinate knows that he will always be given adequate warning of changes, and an understanding of the reasons for them, he does not fear them half so much. Conversely, the normal inertia of human habits is tremendously reinforced when one must be forever prepared against unforeseen changes in policy, rules, methods of work, or even in the continuity of employment and wages.

It is not necessary to turn to industry for evidence in support of the principles outlined above. Everywhere in our world today we see the consequences of the insecurity caused by our inability to know what we need to know in order to insure even partially the satisfaction of our needs. Knowledge is power, primarily because it decreases dependence upon the unknown and unpredictable.

The Conditions of Security: Consistent Discipline

The third requirement for the subordinate's security in his relationship of dependence on his superiors is that of consistent discipline. It is a fact often unrecognized that discipline may take the form of positive support for "right" actions as well as criticism and punishment for "wrong" ones. The subordinate, in order to be secure, requires consistent discipline in both senses.[18]

He requires first of all the strong and willing backing of his superiors for those actions which are in accord with what is expected of him. There is much talk among some managements about superiors who fail to "back up" their subordinates. The insecurity that arises when a subordinate does not know under what conditions he will be backed up leads him to "keep his neck pulled in" at all times. Buck-passing and its consequent frictions and resentment are inevitable under such circumstances.

Given a clear knowledge of what is expected of him, the subordinate requires in addition the definite assurance that he will have the unqualified support of his superiors so long as his actions are consistent with those policies and are taken within the limits of his responsibility. Only then can he have the security and confidence that will enable him to do his job well.

At the same time the subordinate must know that failure to live up to his responsibilities, or to observe the rules which are established, will result in punishment. Every individual has many wants which conflict with the demands of his job. If he knows that breaking the rules to satisfy these wants will *almost inevitably* result in the frustration of his vital long-range needs, self-discipline will be less difficult. If, on the other hand, discipline is inconsistent and uncertain, he may be unnecessarily denying himself satisfaction by obeying the rules. The insecurity, born of uncertainty and of guilt, which is inevitably a consequence of lax discipline, is unpleasant and painful for the subordinate.

What frequently happens is this: The superior, in trying to be a "good fellow," fails to maintain discipline and to obtain the standards of performance which are necessary. His subordinates—human beings striving to satisfy their needs—"take advantage of the situation." The superior then begins to disapprove of his subordinates (in spite of the fact that he is to blame for their behavior). Perhaps he "cracks down" on them, perhaps he simply grows more and more critical and disapproving. In either event, because he has failed to establish consistent discipline *in an atmosphere of genuine approval,* they are threatened. The combination of guilt and insecurity on the part of the subordinates leads easily to antagonism, and therefore to further actions of which the superior disapproves. Thus a vicious circle of disapproval → antagonistic acts → more disapproval → more antagonistic acts is set up. In the end it becomes extremely difficult to remedy a situation of this kind because both superior and subordinates have a chip-on-the-shoulder attitude which must be abolished before the relationship can improve.

Every subordinate, then, requires the security of knowing that he can count on the firm support of his superiors for doing what is "right," and firm pressure (even punishment) to prevent his doing what is "wrong." *But this discipline must be established and maintained in an atmosphere of approval.* Otherwise, the subordinate's suspicion and resentment of his superiors will lead to the opposite reaction from the desired one. A mild degree of discipline is sufficient in an atmosphere of approval; even the most severe discipline will in the end be unsuccessful in an atmosphere of disapproval. The behavior of the people in the occupied countries of Europe today provides a convincing demonstration of this psychological principle.

The Necessity for Independence

When the subordinate has achieved a reasonable degree of genuine security in his relationship to his superiors, he will begin to seek ways of utilizing more fully his capacities and skills, of achieving through his own efforts a larger degree of satisfaction from his work. Given security, the subordinate seeks to develop himself. This *active* search for independence is constructive and healthy. It is collaborative and friendly, yet genuinely self-assertive.

If on the other hand, the subordinate feels that his dependence on his superiors is extreme, and if he lacks security,[19] he will fight blindly for freedom. This *reactive* struggle for independence is founded on fear and hatred. It leads to friction and strife, and it tends to perpetuate itself because it interferes with the development of an atmosphere of approval which is essential to security.

These two fundamentally opposite ways in which subordinates seek to acquire independence have entirely different consequences. Since we are concerned with the conditions of the successful subordinate–superior relationship, we shall emphasize the active rather than the reactive striving for independence.[20]

The Conditions of Active Independence: Participation

One of the most important conditions of the subordinate's growth and development centers around his opportunities to express his ideas and to contribute his suggestions before his superiors take action on matters which involve him.[21,22] Through participation of this kind he becomes more and more aware of his superiors' problems, and he obtains a genuine satisfaction in knowing that his opinions and ideas are given consideration in the search for solutions.[23]

Participation of this kind is fairly prevalent in the upper levels of industrial organizations. It is often entirely lacking further down the line. Some people insist that the proponents of participation at the lower levels of industry are unrealistic idealists. However, there are highly successful instances in existence of "consultative supervision,"[24] "multiple management,"[25] and "union-management cooperation."[26] The important point is that participation cannot be successful unless the conditions of security are adequately met. Many failures among the currently popular Labor-Management Production Drive Committees can be traced directly to this fundamental fact that active independence cannot be achieved in the absence of adequate security.[27,28]

There is a real challenge and a deep satisfaction for the subordinate who is given the opportunity to aid in the solution of the difficult but fascinating problems that arise daily in any industrial organization. The superior who, having provided security for his subordinates, encourages them to accept this challenge and to strive *with him* to obtain this satisfaction, is almost invariably surprised at the fruitfulness of the results. The president of one company remarked, after a few management conferences designed to encourage this kind of participation, that he had never before realized in considering his problems how many alternative possibilities were available, nor how inadequate had been the knowledge upon which he based his decisions. Contrary to the usual opinion, this discovery is as likely at the bottom of an organization as at the top, once the initial feelings of inadequacy and hesitancy among workers are overcome.[29]

The genuine collaboration among all the members of an industrial organization which is eulogized by "impractical idealists" is actually quite possible. But it can only begin to emerge when the mechanisms of genuine participation become an established part of the organization routines.

Conditions of Active Independence: Responsibility

A corollary of the desire for participation is a desire for responsibility. It is another manifestation of the active search for independence. Insecure or rebellious subordinates—seeking independence in the reactive sense—do not accept responsibility. They are seeking freedom, not the opportunity for self-realization and development.

The willingness to assume responsibility is a genuine maturational phenomenon. Just as children cannot grasp the meaning of the algebraic use of symbols until their intellectual development has reached a certain level, so subordinates cannot accept responsibility until they have achieved a certain degree of emotional security in their relationship to their superiors. Then they want it. They accept it with obvious pleasure and pride. And if it is given to them gradually, so that they are not suddenly made insecure again by too great a load of it, they will continue to accept more and more.

The process of granting responsibility to subordinates is a delicate one. There are vast individual differences in tolerance for the inevitable pressures and insecurities attendant upon the acceptance of responsibility. Some subordinates seem to be content to achieve a high degree of security without independence. Others thrive on the risks and the dangers of being "on their own." However, there are few subordinates whose capabilities in this direction are fully realized. It is unwise to attribute the absence of a desire for responsibility to the individual's personality alone until one has made certain that his relationship to his superiors is genuinely secure.

Many superiors are themselves so insecure that they cannot run the risk of being responsible for their subordinates' mistakes. Often they are unconsciously afraid to have capable and developing subordinates. The delegation of responsibility, as well as its acceptance, requires a confident and secure relationship with one's superiors.[30]

Conditions of Active Independence: The Right of Appeal

There are occasions when subordinates differ radically but sincerely with their superiors on important questions. Unless the superior follows an "appeasement" policy (which in the end will cost him his subordinates' respect), there exists in such disagreement the possibility of an exaggerated feeling of dependence and helplessness in the minds of the subordinates. They disagree for reasons which seem *to them* sound; yet they must defer to the judgment of one person whom they know to be fallible.

If these occasions are too frequent, the subordinates will be blocked in their search for independence, and they may readily revert to a reactive struggle. The way out of the dilemma is to provide the subordinate with a mechanism for appealing his superior's decisions to a higher level of the organization. The subordinate can then have at hand a check upon the correctness and fairness of his superior's actions. His feeling of independence is thereby increased.

This is one of the justifications for an adequate grievance procedure for workers.[31,32] All too often, however, there is no similar mechanism provided for members of management. To be sure, in the absence of a union it is difficult to safeguard the individual against retaliative measures by his immediate superior, but it is possible to guarantee a reasonable degree of protection.

If the relationship between subordinate and superior is a successful one, the right of appeal may rarely be exercised. Nevertheless, the awareness that it is there to be used when needed provides the subordinate with a feeling of independence which is not otherwise possible.

Summary

The subordinate in the industrial organization is dependent for the satisfaction of many of his vital needs upon the behavior and attitudes of his superiors. He requires, therefore, a feeling of confidence that he can satisfy his needs if he does what is expected of him. Given this security, he requires opportunities for self-realization and development.

Among the conditions influencing the subordinate's feelings of security are: (1) an "atmosphere" of approval, (2) knowledge of what is expected of him, and of how well he is measuring up to these expectations, (3) forewarning of changes that may affect him, and (4) consistent discipline both in the form of backing when he is "right" and in the form of punishment when he is "wrong."

The conditions under which the subordinate can realize his own potentialities include: (1) an adequate sense of security in relation to his superiors, (2) opportunities to participate in the solution of problems and in the discussion of actions which may affect him, (3) the opportunity to assume responsibility as he becomes ready for it, and (4) the right of appeal over the head of his immediate superior.

These conditions are minimal. Upon their fulfillment in some degree rests the success or failure of the subordinate-superior relationship at every level of the industrial organization from that of the vice-president to that of the worker.

Notes

[1] Harold B. Bergen. "Measuring Attitudes and Morale in Wartime." *The Conference Board Management Record,* April, 1942, Vol. 4, No. 4, pp. 101–104.

[2] Robert N. McMurry. "Management Mentalities and Worker Reactions," *Advanced Management,* October–December, 1942, Vol. 7, No. 4, pp. 165–172.

[3] Robert R. R. Brooks. *When Labor Organizes.* New Haven: Yale University Press, 1938.

[4] Twentieth Century Fund. *How Collective Bargaining Works: A* Survey *of Experience in Leading American Industries.* New York: The Fund, 1942.

[5] The relevant literature is vast. A fair introduction to it may be obtained through the following: Walter C. Langer, *Psychology and Human Living.* New York: D. Appleton-Century Co., 1943; A. H. Maslow and Bela Mittelmann, *Principles of Abnormal Psychology.* New York: Harper & Bros., 1941; John Dollard, Leonard W. Doob, et al., *Frustration and Aggression.* New Haven: Yale University Press, 1939; John Levy and Ruth Monroe, *The Happy Family.* New York: Alfred A. Knopf, 1941.

[6] *Cf.* for example, the detailed observation of the "bank-wiring" group at the Hawthorne Plant of Western Electric, reported in Chaps. XVII to XXIII of F. J. Roethlisberger and W. J. Dickson, *Management and the Worker.* Cambridge, Mass.: Harvard University Press, 1939. For evidence at another level of the industrial organization, see Conrad M. Arensberg and Douglas McGregor, "Determination of Morale in an Industrial Company," *Applied Anthropology,* January–March, 1942, Vol. 1, No. 2, pp. 12–34.

[7] Discussions of plans for financial security will be found in the research reports of the National Industrial Conference Board and the Personnel Division of the American Management Association, and in the publications of the Policyholders' Service Bureau of the Metropolitan Life Insurance Company.

⁸ *Cf.* United States Department of Labor, Bureau of Labor Statistics. *Union Agreement Provisions.* Washington, G.P.O., 1942. (Bulletin No. 686).

⁹ Sumner H. Slichter, *Union Policies and Industrial Management.* Washington: The Brookings Institution, 1941.

¹⁰ The vital importance of this attitude in familial superior-subordinate relationships is stressed everywhere in the literature of dynamic psychology. See, for example, J. McV. Hunt, *Personality and the Behavior Disorders.* New York: The Ronald Press, 1944, Vol. II.

¹¹ A few employee "handbooks" demonstrate an awareness of this point. See for example, *Employee Relations in General Foods.* New York: General Foods Corporation, Second Edition, May 19, 1941.

¹² This is the usually recognized reason for the publication of employee handbooks. *Cf.* Alexander R. Heron, *Sharing Information With Employees.* Stanford University, Cal.: Stanford University Press, 1942.

¹³ Donaldson Brown, "Industrial Management as a National Resource." *The Conference Board Management Record,* April, 1943, Vol. V, No. 4, pp. 142–148.

¹⁴ This, of course, is the reason for merit rating plans. *Cf.* National Industrial Conference Board, Inc. *Employee Rating. Methods of Appraising Ability, Efficiency and Potentialities.* (Studies in Personnel Policy No. 39) New York, N.I.C.B., 1941.

¹⁵ F. J. Roethlisberger and W. J. Dickson, *loc. cit.*

¹⁶ Douglas McGregor and Irving Knickerbocker, "Industrial Relations and National Defense: A Challenge to Management." *Personnel,* July, 1941, Vol. 18, No. 1, pp. 49–63.

¹⁷ Sumner H. Slichter, *loc. cit.* Chaps. VII–IX.

¹⁸ This, of course, is simply the well known principle underlying all theories of learning. We need not discuss here its many complicated features.

¹⁹ It is the *subordinate's own feelings* and not the "objective" facts which are vital in this connection.

²⁰ A. H. Maslow. "The Authoritarian Character Structure," *The Journal of Social Psychology,* 1943, 18: 401–411.

²¹ The work of Kurt Lewin and his students at the University of Iowa on group dynamics is relevant to this whole discussion, but it is especially pertinent to this matter of participation. *Cf.* K. Lewin, R. Lippitt, and S. K. Escalona, *Studies in Topological and Vector Psychology I,* University of Iowa Studies in Child Welfare, 1940, Vol. 16, No. 3.

²² Alex Bavelas, "Morale and the Training of Leaders," in Goodwin Watson, [Editor], *Civilian Morale,* Second Yearbook of the Society for the Psychological Study of Social Issues. New York: Houghton Mifflin Co., 1942.

²³ The fear is often expressed that subordinates, given the slightest opportunity, will seek to usurp their superiors' "prerogatives." Actually, such attempts are symptomatic of the *reactive* struggle for independence. These fears are groundless when subordinates are given adequate security.

²⁴ H. H. Carey. "Consultative Supervision and Management," *Personnel,* March 1942, Vol. 18, No. 5, pp. 286–295.

²⁵ Charles P. McCormick. *Multiple Management.* New York: Harper & Bros., 1938.

²⁶ Clinton S. Golden and Harold J. Ruttenberg. *The Dynamics of Industrial Democracy.* New York: Harper & Bros., 1942.

²⁷ Mill and Factory's Survey of the Labor-Management Production Drive." *Mill and Factory,* June, 1942, Vol. 30, No. 6, pp. 57–60.

²⁸ "Are War Production Drives Worth While?" *Factory Management and Maintenance,* October, 1942, Vol. 100, No. 10, pp. 74–80.

²⁹ Clinton S. Golden and Harold J. Ruttenberg, *loc. cit.* Chap. IX.

³⁰ Irving Knickerbocker and Douglas McGregor, "Union-Management Cooperation: A Psychological Analysis," *Personnel,* November, 1942, Vol. 19, No. 3, pp. 530–533.

³¹ Solomon Barkin, "Unions and Grievances," *Personnel Journal,* June, 1943, Vol. 22, No. 2, pp. 38–48.

³² United States Department of Labor, Division of Labor Standards. *Settling Plant Grievances,* (Bulletin No. 60) Washington: Government Publications Office, 1943.

38

How Leaders Embed
and Transmit Culture

Edgar H. Schein

The simplest explanation of how leaders get their message across is through charisma, in that one of the main elements of that mysterious quality undoubtedly is a leader's ability to communicate major assumptions and values in a vivid and clear manner (Bennis and Nanus, 1985; Conger, 1989; Leavitt, 1986). The problem with charismatic vision as an embedding mechanism is that leaders who have it are rare and their impact is hard to predict. Historians can look back and say that certain people had charisma or had a great vision. It is not always clear at the time, however, how they transmitted the vision. For clues to that process we must look to more mundane organizational phenomena.

Some of the mechanisms that leaders use to communicate their beliefs, values, and assumptions are conscious deliberations; others are unconscious and may even be unintended (Kunda, 1992). The leader may be conflicted and may be sending mutually contradictory messages (Kets de Vries and Miller, 1984, 1987). Subordinates will tolerate and accommodate contradictory messages because, in a sense, persons at higher levels are always granted the right to be inconsistent and, in any case, are too powerful to be confronted. The emerging culture will then reflect not only the leader's assumptions but the complex internal accommodations created by subordinates to run the organization in spite of or around the leader. The group, sometimes acting on the assumption that the leader is a creative genius who has idiosyncrasies, may develop compensatory mechanisms, such as buffering layers of managers, to protect the organization from the dysfunctional aspects of the leader's behavior. In those cases the culture may become a defense mechanism against the anxieties unleashed by inconsistent leader behavior. In other

Excerpt reprinted with permission of John Wiley & Sons, Inc. from *Organizational Culture and Leadership*, 2nd edition, by Edgar H. Schein. Copyright © 1985 John Wiley & Sons, Inc.

cases the organization's style of operating will reflect the very biases and unconscious conflicts that the leader experiences, thus causing some scholars to call such organizations neurotic (Kets de Vries and Miller, 1984). In the extreme, the subordinates or the board of directors may have to find ways to move the leader out altogether.

Because the initiative tends always to be with the leader, however, we will examine the process of cultural embedding from the point of view of how the power of the leader can be used to inculcate assumptions. The mechanisms, as shown in Exhibit 1, vary along several dimensions: (1) how widespread their effects are, (2) how implicit or explicit the messages conveyed are, and (3) how intentional they are.

Primary Embedding Mechanisms

Taken together, the six primary embedding mechanisms shown in Exhibit 1 create what would typically be called the "climate" of the organization (Schneider, 1990). At this stage, climate created by founder leaders precedes the existence of group culture. At a later stage, climate will be a reflection and manifestation of cultural assumptions, but early in the life of a group it reflects only the assumptions of leaders.

What Leaders Pay Attention to, Measure, and Control

One of the most powerful mechanisms that founders, leaders, managers, or even colleagues have available for communicating what they believe in or

---

Exhibit 1   Culture-Embedding Mechanisms

Primary Embedding Mechanisms	Secondary Articulation and Reinforcement Mechanisms
What leaders pay attention to, measure and control on a regular basis	Organization design and structure
How leaders react to critical incidents and organizational crises	Organizational systems and procedures
Observed criteria by which leaders allocate scarce resources	Design of physical space, facades, and buildings
Deliberate role modeling, teaching and coaching	Stories, legends and myths about people and events
Observed criteria by which leaders allocate rewards and status	Formal statements of organizational philosophy, values and creed
Observed criteria by which leaders recruit, select, promote, retire and excommunicate organizational members	

care about is what they systematically pay attention to. This can mean anything from what they notice and comment on to what they measure, control,
reward, and in other ways *systematically deal with*. Even casual remarks and
questions that are consistently geared to a certain area can be as potent as formal control mechanisms and measurements.

If leaders are aware of this process, then being systematic in paying attention to certain things becomes a powerful way of communicating a message,
especially if the leaders are totally consistent in their own behavior. On the
other hand, if leaders are not aware of the power of this process or they are
inconsistent in what they pay attention to, subordinates and colleagues will
spend inordinate time and energy trying to decipher what a leader's behavior
really reflects and even project motives where none may exist. As a consultant I have learned that my own consistency in what I ask questions about
sends clear signals to my audience about my priorities, values, and beliefs. It
is the consistency that is important, not the intensity of the attention. To illustrate, McGregor (1960) tells of a company that wanted him to install a management development program. The president hoped McGregor would
propose exactly what to do and how to do it. Instead, McGregor asked the
president whether he really cared about identifying and developing managers.
On being assured that he did, McGregor proposed that he should build his
concern into the reward system and set up a consistent way of monitoring
progress; in other words, start to pay attention to it.

The president agreed and announced that henceforth 50% of each senior
manager's annual bonus would be contingent on what he had done to develop
his own immediate subordinates during the past year. He added that he himself
had no specific program in mind, but that each quarter he would ask each senior
manager what he had done. The senior managers launched a whole series of different activities, many of them pulled together from work that was already going
on piecemeal in the organization. A coherent program was forged over a two-
year period and has continued to serve this company well. The president continued his quarterly questions and once a year evaluated how much each manager
had done for development. He never imposed any program, but by paying consistent attention to management development, he clearly signaled to the organization that he considered management development to be important.

Some of the most important signals of what leaders care about are sent
during meetings and in other activities devoted to planning and budgeting,
which is one reason why planning and budgeting are such important managerial processes. In questioning subordinates systematically on certain issues,
leaders can transmit their own view of how to look at problems. The ultimate
concern of the plan may not be as important as the learning that goes on during the planning process.

Attention is focused in part by the kinds of questions that leaders ask and
how they set the agendas for meetings. An even more powerful signal, however, is their emotional reactions, especially the emotional outbursts that
occur when leaders feel an important assumption is being violated. Such out-

bursts are not necessarily very overt because many managers believe that one should not allow one's emotions to become too involved in the decision process. On the other hand, some leaders allow themselves to get angry and upset and use those feelings as the messages. Even for those leaders who attempt to suppress their emotions, subordinates generally know they are upset.

Subordinates find emotional outbursts on the part of their bosses painful and try to avoid them. In the process they gradually come to adopt the assumptions of the leader.

Other powerful signals that subordinates interpret for evidence of the leader's assumptions are what leaders *do not react to*. For example, in one company, managers were frequently in actual trouble with cost overruns, delayed schedules, and imperfect products, but such trouble rarely caused comment if the manager had displayed that he or she was in control. Trouble could be expected and was assumed to be a normal condition of doing business; only failure to cope and regain control was unacceptable. In the product design departments one frequently found excess personnel, very high budgets, and lax management with regard to cost controls, none of which occasioned much comment. Subordinates correctly interpreted this to mean that it was far more important to come up with a good product than to control costs.

The combination of what leaders do and do not pay attention to can create problems in deciphering because they reveal the area where unconscious conflicts may exist. For example, at one company the clear concern for customers was signaled by outbursts if customers complained. But this attitude coexisted with an implicit arrogance toward certain classes of customers because the engineers often assumed that they knew what the customer would like in the way of product design.

In summary, what leaders consistently pay attention to communicates most clearly what their own priorities, goals, and assumptions are. If they pay attention to too many things or if their pattern of attention is inconsistent, subordinates will use other signals or their own experience to decide what is really important, leading to a much more diverse set of assumptions and many more subcultures.

Leader Reactions to Critical Incidents and Organizational Crises

When an organization faces a crisis, the manner in which leaders and others deal with it creates new norms, values, and working procedures and reveals important underlying assumptions. Crises are especially significant in culture creation and transmission because the heightened emotional involvement during such periods increases the intensity of learning. Crises heighten anxiety, and anxiety reduction is a powerful motivator of new learning. If people share intense emotional experiences and collectively learn how to reduce anxiety, they are more likely to remember what they have learned.

What is defined as a crisis is, of course, partly a matter of perception. There may or may not be actual dangers in the external environment, and what is considered to be dangerous in itself is often a reflection of the culture. For purposes of this analysis, a crisis is what is perceived to be a crisis and what is defined as a crisis by founders and leaders. Crises that arise around the major external survival issues are the most potent in revealing the deep assumptions of the leaders and therefore the most likely to be the occasions when those assumptions become the basis of shared learning and thus become embedded.

A story told about Tom Watson, Jr., in the context of IBM's concern for people and for management development has it that a young executive had made some bad decisions that cost the company several million dollars. He was summoned to Watson's office, fully expecting to be dismissed. As he entered the office, the young executive said, "I suppose after that set of mistakes you will be wanting to fire me." Watson was said to have replied, "Not at all, young man, we have just spent a couple of million dollars educating you."

Innumerable organizations have faced the crises of shrinking sales, excess inventories, technological obsolescence, and the subsequent necessity of laying off employees in order to cut costs. How leaders deal with such a crisis reveals some of their assumptions about the importance of people and their view of human nature. Ouchi (1981) cites several dramatic examples in which U.S. companies faced with layoffs decided instead to go to short work weeks or to have all employees and managers take cuts in pay to manage the cost reduction without people reduction. At one such company, Hewlett-Packard, which survived a financial crisis early in its history without laying off anyone, many organizational stories are told and retold to show what kinds of values were operating in their leaders at the time.

One company's assumption that "we are family who will take care of each other" came out most clearly during periods of crisis. When the company was doing well, the leader often had emotional outbursts reflecting his concern that people were getting complacent. When the company was in difficulty, however, he never punished anyone or displayed anger; instead, he became the strong and supportive father figure, pointing out to both the external world and the employees that things were not as bad as they seemed, that the company had great strengths that would ensure future success, and that people should not worry about layoffs because things would be controlled by slowing down hiring.

On the other hand, in a different company the leader displayed his lack of concern for his own young managers by being punitive under crisis conditions, sometimes impulsively firing people only to have to try to rehire them later because he realized how important they were to the operation of the company. This gradually created an organization built on distrust and low commitment, leading good people to leave when a better opportunity came along.

Crises around issues of internal integration can also reveal and embed leader assumptions. I have found that a good time to observe an organization very closely is when acts of insubordination take place. So much of an organization's culture is tied up with hierarchy, authority, power, and influence that the mechanisms of conflict resolution have to be constantly worked out and consensually validated. No better opportunity exists for leaders to send signals about their own assumptions about human nature and relationships.

Observed Criteria for Resource Allocation

How budgets are created in an organization is another process that reveals leader assumptions and beliefs. As Donaldson and Lorsch (1983) show in their study of top-management decision making, leader beliefs about the distinctive competence of their organization, acceptable levels of financial risks, and the degree to which the organization must be financially self-sufficient strongly influence their choices of goals, the means to accomplish them, and the management processes to be used. Such beliefs not only function as decision criteria, but are constraints on decision making in that they limit perception of alternatives.

One organization's budgeting and resource allocation processes clearly revealed the leader's belief in the entrepreneurial bottom-up system. He always resisted senior management's setting targets, formulating strategies, and setting goals, preferring instead to stimulate the managers below him to come up with business plans and budgets that he and other senior executives would approve if they made sense. He was convinced that people would only give their best ideas and maximum commitment to programs that they themselves had invented, sold, and were accountable for.

However, this system created problems as the company grew and found itself increasingly operating in a competitive environment where costs had to be controlled. In its early days the company could afford to invest in all kinds of projects whether they made sense or not. In today's environment one of the biggest and as yet unresolved issues is how to choose among projects that sound equally good when there are insufficient resources to fund them all. Strong pressures are building for a more centralized strategy and some broader criteria of what businesses the company wants to be in, but there is steadfast resistance to undermining in any way the entrepreneurial spirit that the leader believes to be the strength of the company.

Deliberate Role Modeling, Teaching, and Coaching

Founders and new leaders of organizations generally seem to know that their own visible behavior has great value for communicating assumptions and values to other members, especially newcomers. At one company, the leader and some other senior executives made videotapes that outline their explicit philosophy, and these tapes are shown to new members of the organization as part of their initial training. However, there is a difference between the messages delivered from staged settings, as when a leader gives a welcoming speech to newcomers, and the messages received when that leader is observed informally. The informal messages are the more powerful teaching/coaching mechanism.

One leader, for example, demonstrated his need to be involved in everything at a detailed level by his frequent visits to stores and minute inspections once he got there. When he went on vacation, he called the office every day at a set time and asked detailed questions about all aspects of the business. This behavior persisted into his semiretirement, when he would call every day from his retirement home thousands of miles away. Through his questions, his lectures, and his demonstration of personal concern for details, he hoped to show other managers what it meant to be highly visible and on top of one's job. Through his unwavering loyalty to family members, this leader also trained people how to think about family members and the rights of owners.

Another leader made an explicit attempt to downplay status and hierarchy because of his assumption that good ideas come from anyone. He communicated this assumption in many formal and informal ways. For example, he drove a small car, had an unpretentious office, dressed informally, and spent many hours wandering among the employees at all levels, getting to know them personally. Stories developed around this informality, and such stories institutionalized his behavior.

An example of more explicit coaching occurred in yet another company where the family owners brought back a former manager as the CEO after several other CEOs had failed. One of the first things he did as the new president was to display at a large meeting his own particular method of analyzing the performance of the company and planning its future. He said explicitly to the group: "Now that's an example of the kind of good planning and management I want in this organization." He then ordered his key executives to prepare a long-range planning process in the format in which he had just lectured and gave them a target time to be ready to present their plans in the new format. At the presentation meeting he coached their presentations, commented on each one, corrected the approach where he felt it had missed the point, and gave them new deadlines for accomplishing their goals as spelled out in the plans. Privately, he told an observer of this meeting the organization had done virtually no planning for decades and that he hoped to institute formal strategy planning as a way of reducing the massive deficits that the organization had been experiencing. From his point of view, he had to change the mentality of his subordinates, which he felt required him to instruct, model, correct, and coach.

Observed Criteria for Allocation of Rewards and Status

Members of any organization learn from their own experience with promotions, performance appraisals, and discussions with the boss what the organization values and what the organization punishes. Both the nature of the behavior rewarded and punished and the nature of the rewards and punishments themselves carry the messages. Leaders can quickly get across their own priorities, values, and assumptions by consistently linking rewards and punishments to the behavior they are concerned with.

What I am referring to here are actual practices, what really happens, not what is espoused, published, or preached. If leaders are trying to ensure that their values and assumptions will be learned, they must create a reward, promotion, and status system that is consistent with these assumptions. Whereas the message initially gets across in the daily practice of the leader, it is judged in the long run by whether the important rewards are allocated consistently with that daily behavior. If these levels of message transmission are inconsistent, one will find a highly conflicted organization without a clear culture or any culture at all at a total organization level.

Observed Criteria for Recruitment, Selection, Promotion, Retirement, and Excommunication

One of the most subtle yet most potent ways through which cultural assumptions get embedded and perpetuated is the process for selecting new members. If a leader assumes that the best way to build an organization is to hire very tough, independent people and then leave them alone and he is successful in continuing to hire tough and independent people, he will create the kind of culture that he assumes will work best. He may never realize that the success of the culture lies in the success of the recruitment effort and that his beliefs about how to organize might become disconfirmed if he could no longer hire the right kinds of people to fit his assumptions.

This cultural embedding mechanism is subtle because it operates unconsciously in most organizations. Leaders tend to find attractive those candidates who resemble present members in style, assumptions, values, and beliefs. They are perceived to be the best people to hire and are assigned characteristics that will justify their being hired. Unless someone outside the organization is explicitly involved in the hiring, there is no way of knowing how much the current implicit assumptions are dominating recruiters' perceptions of the candidates. (It would be interesting to study search firms from this perspective. Because they operate outside the cultural context of the employing organization, do they become implicitly culture reproducers or changers, and are they aware of their power in this regard? Do organizations that employ outside search firms do so in part to get away from their own biases in hiring?) In any case, it is clear that initial selection decisions for new members, followed by the criteria applied in the promotion system, are powerful mechanisms for embedding and perpetuating the culture, especially when combined with socialization tactics designed to teach cultural assumptions.

Basic assumptions are further reinforced through criteria of who does or does not get promoted, and who is in effect excommunicated by being actually fired or given a job that is clearly perceived to be less important, even if at a higher level (being kicked upstairs).

The foregoing mechanisms all interact and tend to reinforce each other if the leader's own beliefs, values, and assumptions are consistent. By separating these categories I am trying to show in how many different ways leaders can and do communicate their assumptions. Most newcomers to an organization have a wealth of data available to them to decipher what the leader's assumptions really are. Much of the socialization process is, therefore, embedded in the organization's normal working routines. It is not necessary for newcomers to attend special training or indoctrination sessions to learn important cultural assumptions. They become quite evident through the behavior of leaders.

Secondary Articulation and Reinforcement Mechanisms

In a young organization, design, structure, architecture, rituals, stories, and formal statements are cultural reinforcers, not culture creators. Once an organization has matured and stabilized, these same mechanisms come to be primary culture-creating mechanisms that will constrain future leaders. I have labeled these mechanisms secondary because they work only if they are consistent with the primary mechanisms discussed above. When they are consistent, they begin to build organizational ideologies and thus to formalize much of what is informally learned at the outset. If they are inconsistent, they either will be ignored or will be a source of internal conflict.

All the items in this list can be thought of at this stage as cultural artifacts that are highly visible but may be difficult to interpret without insider knowledge obtained from observing leaders' actual behaviors. When an organization is in its developmental phase, the driving and controlling assumptions will always be manifested first and most clearly in what the leaders demonstrate in their own behavior, not in what is written down or inferred from visible designs, procedures, rituals, stories, and published philosophies. These secondary mechanisms can become primary ones in perpetuating the assumptions even when new leaders in a mature organization would prefer to change them. Once again, the leader is reminded that here we are still talking of how cultures get built in a growing organization.

Organization Design and Structure

As I have observed executive groups in action, particularly first generation groups led by their founder, I have noticed that the design of the organization—how product lines, market area functional responsibilities, and so on are divided up—elicits high degrees of passion but not too much clear logic. The requirements of the primary task—how to organize in order to survive in the external environment—seem to get mixed up with powerful assumptions about internal relationships and with theories of how to get things done that derive more from the founder's background than from current analysis. If it is a family business, the structure must make room for key family member or trusted colleagues, cofounders, and friends. Even in the first-generation publicly held company, the organization's design is often built around the talents of the individual managers rather than the external task requirements.

Founders often have strong theories about how to organize for maximum effectiveness. Some assume that only they can ultimately determine what is correct; therefore, they build a tight hierarchy and highly centralized controls. Others assume that the strength of their organization is in their people and therefore build a highly decentralized organization that pushes authority down as low as possible. Still others believe that their strength is in negotiated solutions; therefore, they hire strong people but then create a structure that forces such people to negotiate their solutions with each other. Some leaders believe in minimizing interdependence in order to free each unit of the organization; others believe in creating checks and balances so that no one unit can ever function autonomously.

Beliefs also vary about how stable a given structure should be, with some leaders seeking a solution and sticking with it, while others are perpetually redesigning their organization in a search for solutions that better fit the perceived problems of the ever-changing external conditions. The initial design of the organization and the periodic reorganizations that companies go through thus provide ample opportunities for the founders and leaders to embed their deeply held assumptions about the task, the means to accomplish it, the nature of people, and the right kinds of relationships to foster among people. Some leaders are able to articulate why they have designed their organization the way they have; others appear to be rationalizing and are not really consciously aware of the assumptions they are making, even though such assumptions can sometimes be inferred from the results. In any case, the organization's structure and design can be used to reinforce leader assumptions but is rarely an accurate initial basis for embedding them because structure can usually be interpreted by the employees in a number of different ways.

Organizational Systems and Procedures

The most visible parts of life in any organization are the daily, monthly, quarterly, and annual cycles of routines, procedures, reports, forms, and other recurrent tasks that have to be performed. The origin of such routines is often not known to participants or sometimes even to senior management, but their existence lends structure and predictability to an otherwise vague and ambiguous organizational world. The system's procedures thus serve a function quite similar to the formal structure in that they make life predictable and thereby reduce ambiguity and anxiety. Though employees often complain of stifling bureaucracy, they need some recurrent processes to avoid the anxiety of an uncertain and unpredictable world.

Given that group members seek this kind of stability and anxiety reduction, founders and leaders have the opportunity to reinforce their assumptions by building systems and routines around them. Systems and procedures can formalize the process of "paying attention" and thus reinforce the message that the leader really cares about certain things. This is why the president who wanted management development programs helped his cause immensely by formalizing his quarterly reviews of what each subordinate had done. Formal budgeting or planning routines are often adhered to less to produce plans and budgets and more to provide a vehicle to remind subordinates of what the leader considers to be important matters to pay attention to.

If founders or leaders do not design systems and procedures as reinforcement mechanisms, they open the door to historically evolved inconsistencies in the culture or weaken their own message from the outset. Thus, a strong president who believes that line managers should be in full control of their own operation must ensure that the organization's financial control procedures are consistent with that belief. If he allows a strong centralized corporate financial organization to evolve and if he pays attention to the data generated by this organization, he is sending a signal inconsistent with the assumption that managers should control their own finances. Then a subculture may evolve in the line organization and a different subculture in the corporate finance organization. If those groups end up fighting each other, it will be the direct result of the initial inconsistency in design logic, not the result of the personalities or the competitive drives of the managers of those functions.

Rites and Rituals of the Organization

Some students of culture would view the special organization processes of rites and rituals as central to the deciphering as well as the communicating of cultural assumptions (Deal and Kennedy, 1982; Trice and Beyer, 1984, 1985). I suspect the centrality of rites in traditional anthropology has something to do with the difficulty of observing firsthand the primary embedding mechanisms described earlier. When the only salient data we have are the rites and rituals that have survived over a period of time, we must, of course, use them as best we can; as with structure and processes. However, if we have only these data, it is difficult to decipher just what assumptions leaders have held that have led to the creation of particular rites and rituals. On the other hand, from the point of view of the leader, if one can ritualize certain behaviors that one considers important, that becomes a powerful reinforcer.

At one company, for example, the monthly meetings devoted to important long-range strategic issues were always held off-site in highly informal surroundings that strongly encouraged informality, status equality, and dialogue. The meetings usually lasted two or more days and involved some physical activity such as a hike or a mountain climb. The leader strongly believed that people would learn to trust each other and be more open with each other if they did enjoyable things together in an informal setting. As the company grew, various functional areas adopted this style of meeting as well, to the point where periodic off-site meetings have become a corporate ritual with their own names, locales, and informal procedures.

At a different company the annual meeting always involved the surprise athletic event that no one was good at and would therefore equalize status. The participants would let their hair down, try their best, fail, and be laughed at in a good-humored fashion. It was as if the group was trying to say to itself, "We are serious scientists and businesspeople, but we also know how to play." And in the play, informal messages that would not be allowed in the formal work world could be conveyed, thus compensating somewhat for the strict hierarchy.

One can find examples of ritualized activities and formalized ritual events in most organizations, but they typically reveal only very small portions of the range of assumptions that make up the culture of an organization. Therein lies the danger of putting too much emphasis on the study of rituals. One can perhaps decipher one piece of the culture correctly, but one may have no basis for determining what else is going on and how important the ritualized activities are in the larger scheme of things.

Design of Physical Space, Facades, and Buildings

The physical design category is intended to encompass all the visible features of the organization that clients, customers, vendors, new employees, and visitors would encounter. The messages that can be inferred from the physical environment, as in the case of structure and procedures, potentially reinforce the leader's messages, but only if they are managed to do so (Steele, 1973). If they are not explicitly managed, they may reflect the assumptions of architects, the planning and facilities managers in the organization, local norms in the community, or other subcultural assumptions.

Leaders who have a clear philosophy and style often choose to embody that style in the visible manifestations of their organization. For example, a company with assumptions about truth through conflict and the importance of open communications chose an open office layout. This layout clearly articulates the emphasis on equality, ease of communication, and importance of relationships. What the visitor experiences visually in this organization is an accurate reflection of deeply held assumptions, and one indicator of this is that the effects are reproduced in the offices of this organization all over the world.

Another example is a company that strongly values individual expertise and autonomy. But because of its assumption that an occupant of a given job becomes the ultimate expert on the area covered by that job, it physically symbolizes turf by giving people privacy. Managers spend much more time thinking things out alone, having individual conferences with others who are centrally involved, and protecting the privacy of individuals so that they can get their work done. In both companies these are not incidental or accidental physical artifacts. They reflect the basic assumptions of how work gets done, how relationships should be managed, how one arrives at truth. One can learn a great deal from such artifacts if one knows how to interpret them, and leaders can communicate a great deal if they know how to structure and create such settings.

Stories about Important Events and People

As a group develops and accumulates a history, some of this history becomes embodied in stories about events and leadership behavior (Martin and Powers, 1983; Wilkins, 1983). Thus, the story—whether it is in the form of a parable, legend, or even myth—reinforces assumptions and teaches assumptions to newcomers. However, since the message to be found in the story is highly distilled or even ambiguous, this form of communication is somewhat unreliable. Leaders cannot always control what will be said about them in stories, though they can certainly reinforce stories that they feel good about and perhaps even launch stories that carry desired messages. Leaders make themselves highly visible to increase the likelihood stories will be told about them, but sometimes attempts to message in this manner backfire; that is, the story focuses more on the inconsistencies and conflicts that observers detect in the leader.

Efforts to decipher culture from collecting stories have the same problem as the deciphering of rituals. Unless one knows about the leaders, one cannot always infer correctly what the point of the story is. If one understands the culture, stories can be used to enhance that understanding and make it concrete, but it is dangerous to try to achieve that understanding in the first place from stories alone.

Formal Statements of Organizational Creeds and Charters

The final mechanism of articulation and reinforcement to be mentioned is the formal statement, the attempt by the leaders to state explicitly their values or assumptions. These statements typically highlight only a small portion of the assumption set that operates in the group and, most likely, will highlight only those aspects of the leader's philosophy or ideology that lend themselves to public articulation. Such public statements may have a value for the leader as a way of emphasizing special things to be attended to in the organization, as values around which to rally the troops, and as reminders of fundamental assumptions not to be forgotten. However, formal statements cannot be viewed as a way of defining the organization's culture. At best they cover a small, publicly relevant segment of the culture, those aspects that leaders find useful to publish as an ideology or focus for the organization.

Summary and Conclusions

The purpose of this effort is to examine how leaders embed the assumptions that they hold and thereby create cultures. How do they get others to gradually share those assumptions? Culture embedding in a young organization is essentially a socialization process, but one in which most of the socialization mechanisms are in the hands of the leaders. In more mature organizations, the socialization process takes on a different shape (for example, Schein, 1978; Van Maanen and Schein, 1979), but in young organizations one must focus primarily on leadership behavior to understand cultural growth.

Six of the mechanisms discussed are powerful primary means by which founders or leaders are able to embed their own assumptions in the ongoing daily life of their organizations. Through what they pay attention to and reward, through the ways they allocate resources, through role modeling, through the manner in which they deal with critical incidents, and through the criteria they use for recruitment, selection, promotion, and excommunication, leaders communicate both explicitly and implicitly the assumptions they really hold. If they are conflicted, the conflicts and inconsistencies are also communicated and become a part of the culture or become the basis for subcultures and countercultures.

Less powerful, more ambiguous, and more difficult to control are the messages embedded in the organization's structure, its procedures and routines, its rituals, its physical layout, its stories and legends, and its formal statements about itself. Yet these secondary mechanisms can provide powerful reinforcement of the primary messages if the leader is able to control them. The important point to grasp is that all these mechanisms do communicate culture content to newcomers. Leaders do not have a choice about whether or not to communicate. They only have a choice about how much to manage what they communicate.

What are secondary mechanisms at the growth stage will, of course, to a large degree become primary maintenance mechanisms as the organization matures and stabilizes, what we ultimately call bureaucratization. The more the structure, procedures, rituals, and espoused values work in making the organization successful, the more they become the filter or criteria for the selection of new leaders. As a result, the likelihood of new leaders becoming cultural change agents declines as the organization matures. The socialization process then begins to reflect what has worked in the past, not what may be the primary agenda of the management of today. The dynamics of the "midlife" organization are therefore quite different from those of the young and emerging organization.

Though the leadership examples presented here come primarily from founders, any manager can begin to focus on these mechanisms when attempting to teach subordinates some new ways of perceiving, thinking, and feeling. What the manager must recognize is that all of the primary mechanisms must be used, and all of them must be consistent with each other. Many change programs fail because the manager who wants the change fails to use the entire set of mechanisms described. To put it positively, when a manager decides to change the assumptions of a work group by using all of these mechanisms, that manager is becoming a leader.

References

Bennis, W. G. and B. Nanus. *Leaders: Strategies for Taking Charge.* New York: Harper-Collins, 1985.

Conger, Jay A. *The Charismatic Leader.* San Francisco: Jossey-Bass, 1989.

Deal, T. E. and A. A. Kennedy. *Corporate Cultures.* Reading, MA: Addison-Wesley, 1982.

Donaldson, G. and J. W. Lorsch. *Decision Making at the Top.* New York: Basic Books, 1983.

Kets de Vries, Manfred F. R. and Danny Miller. *Unstable at the Top.* New York: New American Library Penguin, 1987.

Kets de Vries, Manfred F. R. and Danny Miller. *The Neurotic Organization.* San Francisco: Jossey-Bass, 1984.

Kunda, G. *Engineering Culture.* Boston: MIT Press, 1992.

Leavitt, H. L. *Corporate Pathfinders.* New York: Dow Jones-Irwin, 1986.

Martin, J. and M. Powers. "Organization Stories: More Vivid and Persuasive than Quantitative Data." In Staw, Barry M. (ed.), *Psychological Foundations of Organizational Behavior.* Glenview, IL: Scott-Foresman, 1983.

McGregor, Douglas. *The Human Side of Enterprise.* New York: McGraw-Hill, 1960.

Ouchi, W. G. *Theory Z.* Reading, MA: Addison-Wesley, 1981.

Schein, E. H. *Career Dynamics.* Reading, MA: Addison-Wesley, 1978.

Schneider, B. *Organization Climate and Culture.* San Francisco: Jossey-Bass, 1990.

Steele, Fritz. *Physical Settings and Organization Development.* Reading, MA: Addison-Wesley, 1973.

Trice, H. M. and J. M. Beyer. "Studying Organizational Culture through Rites and Ceremonies." *Academy of Management Journal,* 9, 4, pp. 653–659.

Trice, H. M. and J. M. Beyer. *Gaining Control of the Corporate Culture.* San Francisco: Jossey-Bass, 1985.

Van Maanen, J. and E. H. Schein. "Fact or Fiction in Organization Ethnography." *Administrative Science Quarterly,* 24, 1979, pp. 520–527.

Wilkens, D. *Domain-Independent Planning.* Washington, DC: Storming Media, 1983.

39

The Deming
Leadership Method

Nicholas J. Mauro

Deming's Theory of Profound Knowledge helps us gain an understanding of certain interrelated and theory-driven truths which contain four core values, four cornerstones, and 14 points for management as shown in Exhibit 1.[1] "Profound" implies deep insight that is far beneath the surface and originates in the depth of one's being.[2] Profound knowledge supplies the foundation and essence of the Deming Leadership Method. . . .

The Core Values

1. *Appreciation for a system.* When Deming speaks of appreciation for a system, he means that a leader must be *conscious of how the world about him functions,* particularly in the world of work. . . .

2. *Some knowledge of statistical theory.* To have Profound Knowledge, a leader must possess some knowledge and understanding of the *theory of variation* and its relationship to statistical theory. No two things are identical, and when closely examined, even items of the finest craft contain variation. Therefore, to study and understand this variation and its relationship to the optimization of a system, a leader must understand statistical theory.[3] . . .

3. *A theory of knowledge.* Knowledge means to be acquainted with facts, principles and truths acquired through sight, experience or report. Knowledge also implies being in a state of knowing, with a clear perception of facts and truths.[4] For a leader to possess Profound Knowledge, Deming also requires a *theory of knowledge.* Although Deming is preoccupied with the need for all theory to touch the real world, he is emphatic that knowledge is the-

Excerpt reprinted with permission from *Cross Cultural Management: An International Journal,* Vol. 6, No. 3 (1999), pp. 13–24. Originally titled "The Deming Leadership Method and Profound Knowledge." Copyright © 1999 by Emerald Group Publishing Limited.

Exhibit 1	Dr. Deming's Theory of Profound Knowledge[5]	
The Core Values	**The Four Cornerstones**	**The Fourteen Points**
1. Appreciation for a system	1. The purpose of a business is to stay in business and to create jobs	1. Establish constancy of purpose 2. Adopt the new philosophy 3. Cease dependence on mass inspection 4. End the practice of awarding business on price tag alone 5. Constantly improve every system
2. Some knowledge of the theory of variation	2. To expand the market	6. Institute training 7. Institute leadership 8. Drive out fear
3. To possess a theory of knowledge	3. For business to continually improve	9. Break down barriers between staff areas 10. Abandon slogans 11. Eliminate numerical quotas 12. Remove barriers to pride of workmanship
4. To possess some knowledge of psychology	4. For business to grow intelligently	13. Promote education and self-improvement 14. Take action to accomplish the transformation

ory-driven: There can be no knowledge without theory, no learning. Any rational plan, however simple, requires prediction concerning conditions, behavior, comparison of each of two procedures or materials. One of Deming's favorite quotes about leaders is "A leader's job is to know!"[6] . . .

4. *Knowledge of psychology.* Finally, leaders need to possess knowledge of psychology so they may understand why people behave as they do, what makes them behave as they do, and that people learn at different speeds and in different ways. It is here that Deming also challenges the conventional role of the psychologists who are engaged in the practice of testing for management: people are different from one another, and their success is so entwined with the system that any attempt at prediction is nonsense. The role of the psychologist is not to provide management with tests that attempt to predict how well an individual is suited to or will achieve their objectives.[7]

Deming tells us that a leader need not be an expert in these four areas, but possessing a working knowledge of the Core Values will bring one to understand the meaning of Profound Knowledge and ultimately will transform supervisors and managers into leaders who understand and implement both the behavioral and technical aspects of the Deming Leadership Method.

Deming Leadership Method

The Behavioral Perspective

In his book *Out of the Crisis,*[8] Deming discusses in depth a leader's role and responsibility and deals with both the behavioral and technical aspects of leadership. In his view, a leader's primary job is to be aware of and to identify (a) the components of the system, and (b) what the system is delivering at any given moment in the process. Contrary to the views of many critics,[9] the Deming leadership paradigm, and thus his road to quality, is not complex but profoundly simple.[10] According to Deming, a leader has only two straightforward responsibilities: (1) to solve problems and (2) to help his people in every and any way possible. Deming further tells us that leaders should not become preoccupied with busy work, as many today so often are. Rather, Deming suggests that managers and supervisors at all levels must narrow their focus to concentrate on improving the system: The aim of leadership should be to improve the performance of man and machine, to improve quality.[11] . . .

In the journey toward quality the sequence must run as follows. The organization must first understand and act on Deming's Theory of Profound Knowledge in order to answer two questions:

1. What are the components of the system?

2. What is the system delivering?

Then leadership training follows, which allows managers and supervisors to understand better their role from the behavioral perspective. Finally, statistical tools (the technical perspective of leadership) are applied to improve the performance of the system and its people. . . .

The Technical Perspective

Prevailing wisdom might suggest that behavioral leadership and the technical aspects of quality are automatically in conflict with each other and cannot be reconciled, like oil and water. To the surprise of those who might be driven strictly by the numbers end of the business, Deming will have none of it. This technical side of leadership demands that the leader have knowledge of variation, a functional knowledge that results from statistical theory, and that he/she be able to apply the tools used to achieve total quality management. Thus it is from the technical side of leadership that new knowledge about the system is acquired, and through the application of these tools leaders come to know their people and become able to predict the system's capability, respectively. Here is where leaders need knowledge of variation to gain a better understanding of systems thinking, as it affects quality in both the service and production sectors of an economy. Therefore, variation in any activity will invite statistical analysis and will require statistical expertise. This is the technical side of the Deming Leadership Method, according to both Deming and Shewart, who both support the point of view that statistical theory and leadership are compatible.[12] . . .

The questions—what are the system's components and what is the system delivering—force a leader into the technical side of leadership. A manager or supervisor must always be mindful of the fact that Deming's leader is required to have or to seek knowledge pertaining to these two questions at all times. To be without such knowledge would be unacceptable to Deming and absent of Profound Knowledge.

Leadership, Deming's Toolbox, and the Application of Statistical Theory

The need for knowledge about the system generates the technical application of the seven statistical tools, which provide a leader with detailed information not only on the system but also on its people. As both people and the system, the latter with all its parts, are functioning in what can best be described as a symbiotic relationship, such information becomes critical to the system's success. Here is formed the triad of technical tools (the flowchart, the cause and effect diagram, the Pareto chart, the run-trend chart, the scatter diagram, the histogram, the Shewart/Deming control chart), distribution theory, and the human resource. It is through the use of these tools by every worker, coached by their leaders, that Kelso's view is realized, in which leadership encourages the whole team to contribute to solving problems. . . .

Motivation and Training

It is the leader's responsibility to motivate people and to retrain those who may be bored with their job. Deming claims that a leader should be ever conscious of worker boredom and its effects on quality. With this warning he links statistical quality control and motivation of workers. If a worker has brought his work to a state of statistical control, whether she was trained well or badly, the worker may be in a rut and become bored, having completed her learning of that particular job. It is not economical to try to provide further training of the same kind. Nevertheless, she may, with good *new* training, learn some other job very well.

It is a leader's job to know exactly at what point resources are being wasted or may need to be shifted so that these resources will be better engaged for the overall benefit of the organization and/or other people. He clarifies what a leader needs to know in order to make the most critical decisions in an organization, which may be of unknown magnitude: decisions that directly concern people and how they will perform while they create the quality that the system is expected to deliver. . . .

Conclusion

The approach that Deming provides those who wish to become leaders is one of *patience, process,* and *perseverance* through knowledge. The concepts and the ideas he ascribes to today's leaders are indeed different than those that have been put forward by many previous and contemporary management scholars. Thus, the core of Deming's Theory of Profound Knowledge and its relationship to both the behavioral and the technical aspects of leadership is the need to know as much about the system and its components as is humanly possible. That is to say, a leader's job is to (a) understand how the system functions; (b) know how the system's components—both people and resources—interact and may cause variation; and (c) see clearly what the system is delivering. . . .

Notes

[1] Mauro, N.J. *A Perspective of Dr. Deming's Theory of Profound Knowledge.* SPC Press: Knoxville, TN (1992). *Author's Note:* The Four Core Values and the Four Cornerstones appearing in Exhibit 1 and in the text represent a perspective of Dr. Deming's teachings as synthesized by the author, and are not thus stated by Dr. Deming himself.

[2] *The Random House Dictionary, College Edition.* Random House: New York (1968).

[3] Deming, W.E., *Osaka Paper.* This and several other concepts are taken from a paper presented by Dr. Deming at a meeting of the Institute of Management Services in Osaka, Japan, on July 24, 1989, and revised on September 1, 1990b. The revised paper is hereafter referred to as the Osaka Paper.

[4] *The Random House Dictionary, College Edition.* Random House: New York (1968).

[5] British Deming Association. *A System of Profound Knowledge.* SPC Press: Knoxville, TN (1992).

[6] Deming, 1990b.

[7] Osaka Paper, p.23.

[8] Deming, W.E. *Out of the Crisis.* Center for Advanced Engineering Study, Massachusetts Institute of Technology. Cambridge University Press: Cambridge, MA (1986).

[9] Neave, H.R. *Deming is Different.* Knoxville, TN: SPC Press (Summer 1991), 1-2.

[10] Aguayo, R. *Dr. Deming, The American Who Taught the Japanese about Quality.* Carol Publishing Group: New York (1990).

[11] Deming, 1986, 248.

[12] Shewart, W. *A Statistical View of Quality Control.* Dover Publications: Mineola, NY (1939).

40

The Five Practices
of Exemplary Leadership

James M. Kouzes and Barry Z. Posner

Since 1983 we've been conducting research on personal-best leadership experiences, and we've discovered that there are countless examples of how leaders mobilize others to get extraordinary things done in virtually every arena of organized activity. We've found them in profit-based firms and non-profits, manufacturing and services, government and business, health care, education and entertainment, and work and community service. Leaders reside in every city and every country, in every position and every place. They're employees and volunteers, young and old, women and men. Leadership knows no racial or religious bounds, no ethnic or cultural borders. We find exemplary leadership everywhere we look.

From our analysis of thousands of personal-best leadership experiences, we've discovered that ordinary people who guide others along pioneering journeys follow rather similar paths. Though each experience we examined was unique in expression, every case followed remarkably similar patterns of action. We've forged these common practices into a model of leadership, and we offer it as guidance for leaders as they attempt to keep their own bearings and steer others toward peak achievements.

As we looked deeper into the dynamic process of leadership, through case analyses and survey questionnaires, we uncovered five practices common to personal-best leadership experiences. When getting extraordinary things done in organizations, leaders engage in these Five Practices of Exemplary Leadership: (1) model the way, (2) inspire a shared vision, (3) challenge the process, (4) enable others to act, and (5) encourage the heart.

The Five Practices aren't the private property of the people we studied or of a few select shining stars. Leadership is not about personality; it's about behavior. The Five Practices are available to anyone who accepts the leadership challenge. And they're also not the accident of a unique moment in history. The Five Practices have stood the test of time, and our most recent research confirms that they're just as relevant today as they were when we first began our investigation more than twenty-five years ago.

Model the Way

Titles are granted, but it's your behavior that wins you respect. As Tom Brack, with Europe's SmartTeam AG, told us, "Leading means you have to be a good example, and live what you say." This sentiment was shared across all the cases that we collected. Exemplary leaders know that if they want to gain commitment and achieve the highest standards, they must be models of the behavior they expect of others. *Leaders model the way.*

To effectively model the behavior they expect of others, leaders must first be clear about guiding principles. They must *clarify values.* As Lindsay Levin, chairman for Whites Group in England, explained, "You have to open up your heart and let people know what you really think and believe. This means talking about your values." Leaders must find their own voice, and then they must clearly and distinctively give voice to their values. As the personal-best stories illustrate, leaders are supposed to stand up for their beliefs, so they'd better have some beliefs to stand up for. But it's not just the leader's values that are important. Leaders aren't just representing themselves. They speak and act on behalf of a larger organization. Leaders must forge agreement around common principles and common ideals.

Eloquent speeches about common values, however, aren't nearly enough. Leaders' deeds are far more important than their words when one wants to determine how serious leaders really are about what they say. Words and deeds must be consistent. Exemplary leaders go first. They go first by *setting the example* through daily actions that demonstrate they are deeply committed to their beliefs. As Prabha Seshan, principal engineer for SSA Global, told us, "One of the best ways to prove something is important is by doing it yourself and setting an example." She discovered that her actions spoke volumes about how the team needed to "take ownership of things they believed in and valued." There wasn't anything Prabha asked others to do that she wasn't willing to do herself, and as a result, "while I always trusted my team, my team in turn trusted me." For instance, she wasn't required to design or code features but by doing some of this work she demonstrated to others not only what she stood for but also how much she valued the work they were doing and what their end user expected from the product.

The personal-best projects we heard about in our research were all distinguished by relentless effort, steadfastness, competence, and attention to detail. We were also struck by how the actions leaders took to set an example were often simple things. Sure, leaders had operational and strategic plans. But the examples they gave were not about elaborate designs. They were about the power of spending time with someone, of working side by side with colleagues, of telling stories that made values come alive, of being highly visible during times of uncertainty, and of asking questions to get people to think about values and priorities. Modeling the way is about earning the right and the respect to lead through direct involvement and action. People follow first the person, then the plan.

Inspire a Shared Vision

When people described to us their personal-best leadership experiences, they told of times when they imagined an exciting, highly attractive future for their organization. They had visions and dreams of what *could be*. They had absolute and total personal belief in those dreams, and they were confident in their abilities to make extraordinary things happen. Every organization, every social movement, begins with a dream. The dream or vision is the force that invents the future. *Leaders inspire a shared vision.* As Mark D'Arcangelo, system memory product marketing manager at Hitachi Semiconductor, told us about his personal-best leadership experience, "What made the difference was the vision of how things could be and clearly painting this picture for all to see and comprehend."

Leaders gaze across the horizon of time, imagining the attractive opportunities that are in store when they and their constituents arrive at a distant destination. They *envision exciting and ennobling possibilities*. Leaders have a desire to make something happen, to change the way things are, to create something that no one else has ever created before. In some ways, leaders live their lives backward. They see pictures in their mind's eye of what the results will look like even before they've started their project, much as an architect draws a blueprint or an engineer builds a model. Their clear image of the future pulls them forward. Yet visions seen only by leaders are insufficient to create an organized movement or a significant change in a company. A person with no constituents is not a leader, and people will not follow until they accept a vision as their own. Leaders cannot command commitment, only inspire it.

Leaders have to *enlist others in a common vision*. To enlist people in a vision, leaders must know their constituents and speak their language. People must believe that leaders understand their needs and have their interests at heart. Leadership is a dialogue, not a monologue. To enlist support, leaders must have intimate knowledge of people's dreams, hopes, aspirations, visions, and values. Evelia Davis, merchandise manager for Mervyns, told us that while she was good at telling people where they were going together, she also needed to do a good job of explaining why they should follow her, how they could help reach the destination, and what this meant for them. As Evelia put it, "If you don't believe enough to share it, talk about it, and get others excited about it then it's not much of a vision!"

Leaders breathe life into the hopes and dreams of others and enable them to see the exciting possibilities that the future holds. Leaders forge a unity of purpose by showing constituents how the dream is for the common good. Leaders stir the fire of passion in others by expressing enthusiasm for the compelling vision of their group. Leaders communicate their passion through vivid language and an expressive style. Whatever the venue, and without exception, the people in our study reported that they were incredibly enthusiastic about their personal-best projects. Their own enthusiasm was catching; it spread from leader to constituents. Their belief in and enthusiasm for the vision were the sparks that ignited the flame of inspiration.

Challenge the Process

Every single personal-best leadership case we collected involved some kind of challenge. The challenge might have been an innovative new product, a cutting-edge service, a groundbreaking piece of legislation, an invigorating campaign to get adolescents to join an environmental program, a revolutionary turnaround of a bureaucratic military program, or the start-up of a new plant or business. Whatever the challenge, all the cases involved a change from the status quo. Not one person claimed to have achieved a personal best by keeping things the same. All leaders *challenge the process*.

Leaders venture out. None of the individuals in our study sat idly by waiting for fate to smile upon them. "Luck" or "being in the right place at the right time" may play a role in the specific opportunities leaders embrace, but those who lead others to greatness seek and accept challenge. Jennifer Cun, in her role as a budget analyst with Intel, noted how critical it is for leaders "to always be looking for ways to improve their team, taking interests outside of their job or organization, finding ways to stay current of what the competition is doing, networking, and taking initiative to try new things."

Leaders are pioneers. They are willing to step out into the unknown. They *search for opportunities to innovate, grow, and improve*. But leaders aren't the only creators or originators of new products, services, or processes. In fact, it's more likely that they're not; innovation comes more from listening than from telling. Product and service innovations tend to come from customers, clients, vendors, people in the labs, and people on the front lines; process innovations, from the people doing the work. Sometimes a dramatic external event thrusts an organization into a radically new condition. Leaders have to constantly be looking outside of themselves and their organizations for new and innovative products, processes, and services. "Mediocrity and status quo will never lead a company to success in the marketplace" is what Mike Pepe, product marketing manager at 03 Entertainment, told us. "Taking risks and believing that taking them is worthwhile" he went on to say, "are the only way companies can 'jump' rather than simply climb the improvement ladder."

When it comes to innovation, the leader's major contributions are in the creation of a climate for experimentation, the recognition of good ideas, the support of those ideas, and the willingness to challenge the system to get new products, processes, services, and systems adopted. It might be more accurate, then, to say that leaders aren't the inventors as much as they are the early patrons and adopters of innovation.

Leaders know well that innovation and change involve *experimenting and taking risks*. Despite the inevitability of mistakes and failures, leaders proceed anyway. One way of dealing with the potential risks and failures of experimentation is to approach change through incremental steps and small wins. Little victories, when piled on top of each other, build confidence that even the biggest challenges can be met. In so doing, they strengthen commitment to the long-term future. Not everyone is equally comfortable with risk and uncertainty. Leaders must pay attention to the capacity of their constituents to take control of challenging situations and become fully committed to change. You can't exhort people to take risks if they don't also feel safe.

It would be ridiculous to assert that those who fail over and over again eventually succeed as leaders. Success in any endeavor isn't a process of simply buying enough lottery tickets. The key that unlocks the door to opportunity is learning. Claude Meyer, with the Red Cross in Kenya, put it to us this way: "Leadership is learning by doing, adapting to actual conditions. Leaders are constantly learning from their errors and failures." Life is the leader's laboratory, and exemplary leaders use it to conduct as many experiments as possible. Try, fail, learn. Try, fail, learn. Try, fail, learn. That's the leader's mantra. Leaders are learners. They learn from their failures as well as their successes, and they make it possible for others to do the same.

Enable Others to Act

Grand dreams don't become significant realities through the actions of a single person. It requires a team effort. It requires solid trust and strong relationships. It requires deep competence and cool confidence. It requires group collaboration and individual accountability. To get extraordinary things done in organizations, leaders have to *enable others to act*.

After reviewing thousands of personal-best cases, we developed a simple test to detect whether someone is on the road to becoming a leader. That test is the frequency of the use of the word *we*. In our interviews, we found that people used *we* nearly three times more often than *I* in explaining their personal-best leadership experience. Hewlett-Packard's Angie Yim was the technical IT team leader on a project involving core team members from the United States, Singapore, Australia, and Hong Kong. In the past, Angie told us, she "had a bad habit of using the pronoun *I* instead of *we*," but she learned that people responded more eagerly and her team became more cohesive when people felt part of the *we*. "This is a magic word," Angie realized. "I would recommend that others use it more often."

Leaders *foster collaboration and build trust*. This sense of teamwork goes far beyond a few direct reports or close confidants. They engage all those who must make the project work and in some way, all who must live with the results. In today's virtual organizations, cooperation can't be restricted to a small group of loyalists; it must include peers, managers, customers and clients, suppliers, citizens—all those who have a stake in the vision.

Leaders make it possible for others to do good work. They know that those who are expected to produce the results must feel a sense of personal power and ownership. Leaders understand that the command-and-control techniques of traditional management no longer apply. Instead, leaders work to make people feel strong, capable, and committed. Leaders enable others to act not by hoarding the power they have but by giving it away. Exemplary leaders *strengthen everyone's capacity to deliver* on the promises they make. As Kathryn Winters learned working with the communications department at NVIDIA Corporation, "You have to make sure that no one is outside the loop or uninvolved in all the changes that occur." She continually ensures that each person has a sense of ownership for his or her projects. She seeks out the opinions of others and uses the ensuing discussion not only to build up their capabilities but also to educate and update her own information and perspective. "Inclusion (not exclusion)" she finds, "ensures that everyone feels and thinks that they are owners and leaders—this makes work much easier." Kathryn realized that when people are trusted and have more discretion, more authority, and more information, they're much more likely to use their energies to produce extraordinary results.

In the cases we analyzed, leaders proudly discussed teamwork, trust, and empowerment as essential elements of their efforts. A leader's ability to enable others to act is essential. Constituents neither perform at their best nor stick around for very long if their leader makes them feel weak, dependent, or alienated. But when a leader makes people feel strong and capable—as if they can do more than they ever thought possible—they'll give it their all and exceed their own expectations. Authentic leadership is founded on trust, and the more people trust their leader, and each other, the more they take risks, make changes, and keep organizations and movements alive. Through that relationship, leaders turn their constituents into leaders themselves.

Encourage the Heart

The climb to the top is arduous and long. People become exhausted, frustrated, and disenchanted. They're often tempted to give up. Leaders *encourage the heart* of their constituents to carry on. Genuine acts of caring uplift the spirits and draw people forward. In her personal-best leadership experience Ankush Joshi, the service line manager with Informix USA, learned that "writing a personal thank-you note, rather than sending an e-mail, can do wonders." Janel Ahrens of National Semiconductor echoed Ankush's observation. Janel would make notes about important events in other people's lives and then follow up with them directly after or simply wish them luck prior to an important event. Every person was "genuinely touched that I cared enough to ask them about how things are going." She told us that in her organization "work relationships have been stronger since this undertaking." Janel's and Ankush's experiences are testimony to the power of a "thank you."

Recognizing contributions can be one-to-one or with many people. It can come from dramatic gestures or simple actions. One of the first actions that Abraham Kuruvilla took upon becoming CEO of the Dredging Corporation of India (a government-owned private-sector company providing services to all ten major Indian ports) was to send out to every employee a monthly newsletter (*DCI News*) that was full of success stories. In addition, he introduced, for the first time, a public-recognition program through which awards and simple appreciation notices were given out to individuals and teams for doing great work. Abraham made sure that people were recognized for their contributions, because he wanted to provide a climate in which "people felt cared about and genuinely appreciated by their leaders."

It's part of the leader's job to show appreciation for people's contributions and to create a culture of *celebrating values and victories.* In the cases we collected, we saw thousands of examples of individual recognition and group celebration. We've heard and seen everything from handwritten thank-yous to marching bands and "This Is Your Life"-type ceremonies. Recognition and celebration aren't about fun and games, though there is a lot of fun and there are a lot of games when people encourage the hearts of their constituents. Neither are they about pretentious ceremonies designed to create some phony sense of camaraderie. When people see a charlatan making noisy affectations, they turn away in disgust. Encouragement is, curiously, serious business. It's how leaders visibly and behaviorally link rewards with performance. When striving to raise quality, recover from disaster, start up a new service, or make dramatic change of any kind, leaders make sure people see the benefit of behavior that's aligned with cherished values. Leaders also know that celebrations and rituals, when done with authenticity and from the heart, build a strong sense of collective identity and community spirit that can carry a group through extraordinarily tough times.

Leadership Is a Relationship

Our findings from the analysis of personal-best leadership experiences challenge the myth that leadership is something that you find only at the highest levels of organizations and society. We found it everywhere. These findings also challenge the belief that leadership is reserved for a few charismatic men and women. Leadership is not a gene and it's not an inheritance. Leadership is an identifiable set of skills and abilities that are available to all of us. The "great person"—woman or man—theory of leadership is just plain wrong. Or, we should say, the theory that there are only a few great men and women who can lead others to greatness is just plain wrong. Likewise, it is plain wrong that leaders only come from large, or great, or small, or new organizations, or from established economies, or from start-up companies. We consider the women and men in our research to be great, and so do those with whom they worked. They are the everyday heroes of our world. It's because there are so many—not so few—leaders that extraordinary things get done on a regular basis, especially in extraordinary times.

To us this is inspiring and should give everyone hope. Hope, because it means that no one needs to wait around to be saved by someone riding into town on a white horse. Hope, because there's a generation of leaders searching for the opportunities to make a difference. Hope, because right down the block or right down the hall there are people who will seize the opportunity to lead you to greatness. They're your neighbors, friends, and colleagues. And you are one of them, too.

There's still another crucial truth about leadership. It's something that we've known for a long time, but we've come to prize even more today. In talking to leaders and reading their cases, there was a very clear message that wove itself throughout every situation and every action. The message was: *leadership is a relationship.* Leadership is a relationship between those who aspire to lead and those who choose to follow. It's the quality of this relationship that matters most when we're engaged in getting extraordinary things done. A leader-constituent relationship that's characterized by fear and distrust will never, ever produce anything of lasting value. A relationship characterized by mutual respect and confidence will overcome the greatest adversities and leave a legacy of significance.

Evidence abounds for this point of view. For instance, in examining the critical variables for executive success in the top three jobs in large organizations, Jodi Taylor and Valerie Sessa at the Center for Creative Leadership found the number one success factor to be "relationships with subordinates." We were intrigued to find that even in this nanosecond world of e-everything, opinion is consistent with the facts. In an online survey, respondents were asked to indicate, among other things, which would be more essential to business success in five years—social skills or skills in using the Internet. Seventy-two percent selected social skills; 28 percent, Internet skills. Internet literati completing a poll online realize that it's not the web of technology that matters the most, it's the web of people.

Similar results were found in a study by Public Allies, an AmeriCorps organization dedicated to creating young leaders who can strengthen their communities. Public Allies sought the opinions of eighteen- to thirty-year-olds on the subject of leadership. Among the items was a question about the qualities that were important in a good leader. Topping the respondents' list is "Being able to see a situation from someone else's point of view." In second place is "Getting along well with other people."

Success in leadership, success in business, and success in life have been, are now, and will continue to be a function of how well people work and play together. Success in leading will be wholly dependent upon the capacity to build and sustain those human relationships that enable people to get extraordinary things done on a regular basis.

41

The Discipline of Personal Mastery

Peter M. Senge

The way to begin developing a sense of personal mastery is to approach it as a *discipline,* as a series of practices and principles that must be applied to be useful. Just as one becomes a master artist by continual practice, so the following principles and practices lay the groundwork for continually expanding personal mastery.

Personal Vision

Most adults have little sense of real vision. We have goals and objectives, but these are not visions. When asked what they want, many adults will say what they want to get rid of. They'd like a better job—that is, they'd like to get rid of the boring job they have. They'd like to live in a better neighborhood, or not have to worry about crime, or about putting their kids through school. They'd like it if their mother-in-law returned to her own house, or if their back stopped hurting. Such litanies of "negative visions" are sadly commonplace, even among very successful people. They are the by-product of a lifetime of fitting in, of coping, of problem solving. As a teenager in one of our programs once said, "We shouldn't call them 'grown ups' we should call them 'given ups.'"

A subtler form of diminished vision is "focusing on the means not the result." Many senior executives, for example, choose "high market share" as part of their vision. But why? "Because I want our company to be profitable." Now, you might think that a high profit is an intrinsic result in and of itself, and indeed it is for some. But for surprisingly many other leaders, profits too are a means toward a still more important result. Why choose high annual profits?

"Because I want us to remain an independent company, to keep from being taken over." Why do you want that? "Because I want to keep our integrity and our capacity to be true to our purpose in starting the organization." While all the goals mentioned are legitimate, the last—being true to our purpose—has the greatest intrinsic significance to this executive. All the rest are means to the end, means which might change in particular circumstances. *The ability to focus on ultimate intrinsic desires, not only on secondary goals, is a cornerstone of personal mastery.*

Real vision cannot be understood in isolation from the idea of purpose. By purpose, I mean an individual's sense of why he is alive. No one could prove or disprove the statement that human beings have purpose. It would be fruitless even to engage in the debate. But as a working premise, the idea has great power. One implication is that happiness may be most directly a result of living consistently with your purpose. George Bernard Shaw expressed the idea pointedly when he said:

> This is the true joy in life, the being used for a purpose recognized by yourself as a mighty one . . . the being a force of nature instead of a feverish, selfish little clod of ailments and grievances complaining that the world will not devote itself to making you happy.[1]

This same principle has been expressed in some organizations as "genuine caring." In places where people felt uncomfortable talking about personal purpose, they felt perfectly at ease talking about genuine caring. When people genuinely care, they are naturally committed. They are doing what they truly want to do. They are full of energy and enthusiasm. They persevere, even in the face of frustration and setbacks, because what they are doing is what they must do. It is *their work*.

Everyone has had experiences when work flows fluidly; when he feels in tune with a task and works with a true economy of means. Someone whose vision calls him to a foreign country, for example, may find himself learning a new language far more rapidly than he ever could before. You can often recognize your personal vision because it creates such moments; it is the goal pulling you forward that makes all the work worthwhile.

But vision is different from purpose. Purpose is similar to a direction, a general heading. Vision is a specific destination, a picture of a desired future. Purpose is abstract. Vision is concrete. Purpose is "advancing man's capability to explore the heavens." Vision is "a man on the moon by the end of the 1960s." Purpose is "being the best I can be," "excellence." Vision is breaking four minutes in the mile.

It can truly be said that nothing happens until there is vision. But it is equally true that a vision with no underlying sense of purpose, no calling, is just a good idea—all "sound and fury, signifying nothing." Conversely, purpose without vision has no sense of appropriate scale. As Bill O'Brien, former president of Hanover Insurance, says,

> You and I may be tennis fans and enjoy talking about ground strokes, our backhands, the thrill of chasing down a corner shot, of hitting a winner.

> We may have a great conversation, but then we find out that I am gearing up to play at my local country club and you are preparing for Wimbledon. We share the same enthusiasm and love of the game, but at totally different scales of proficiency. Until we establish the scales we have in mind, we might think we are communicating when we're not.[2]

Vision often gets confused with competition. You might say, "My vision is to beat the other team." And indeed, competition can be a useful way of calibrating a vision, of setting scale. To beat the number-ten player at the tennis club is different from beating the number one. But to be number one of a mediocre lot may not fulfill my sense of purpose. Moreover, what is my vision after I reach number one?

Ultimately, vision is intrinsic not relative. It's something you desire for its intrinsic value, not because of where it stands you relative to another. Relative visions may be appropriate in the interim, but they will rarely lead to greatness. Nor is there anything wrong with competition. Competition is one of the best structures yet invented by humankind to allow each of us to bring out the best in each other. But after the competition is over, after the vision has (or has not) been achieved, it is one's sense of purpose that draws you further, that compels you to set a new vision. *This, again, is why personal mastery must be a discipline. It is a process of continually focusing and refocusing on what one truly wants, on one's visions.*

Vision is multifaceted. There are material facets of our visions, such as where we want to live and how much money we want to have in the bank. There are personal facets, such as health, freedom, and being true to ourselves. There are service facets, such as helping others or contributing to the state of knowledge in a field. All are part of what we truly want. Modern society tends to direct our attention to the material aspects, and simultaneously foster guilt for our material desires. Society places some emphasis on our personal desires—for example, it is almost a fetish in some circles to look trim and fit—and relatively little on our desires to serve. In fact, it is easy to feel naive or foolish by expressing a desire to make a contribution. Be that as it may, it is clear from working with thousands of people that personal visions span all these dimensions and more. It is also clear that it takes courage to hold visions that are not in the social mainstream.

But it is exactly that courage to take a stand for one's vision that distinguishes people with high levels of personal mastery. Or, as the Japanese say of the master's stand, "When there is no break, not even the thickness of a hair comes between a man's vision and his action."[3]

In some ways, clarifying vision is one of the easier aspects of personal mastery. A more difficult challenge, for many, comes in facing current reality.

Holding Creative Tension

People often have great difficulty talking about their visions, even when the visions are clear. Why? Because we are acutely aware of the gaps between our vision and reality. "I would like to start my own company," but "I don't have the capital." Or, "I would like to pursue the profession that I really love," but "I've got to make a living." These gaps can make a vision seem unrealistic or fanciful. They can discourage us or make us feel hopeless. But the gap between vision and current reality is also a source of energy. If there was no gap, there would be no need for any action to move toward the vision. Indeed, the gap is *the* source of creative energy. We call this gap *creative tension.*

Imagine a rubber band, stretched between your vision and current reality. When stretched, the rubber band creates tension, representing the tension between vision and current reality. What does tension seek? Resolution or release. There are only two possible ways for the tension to resolve itself: pull reality toward the vision or pull the vision toward reality. Which occurs will depend on whether we hold steady to the vision.

The principle of creative tension is the central principle of personal mastery, integrating all elements of the discipline. Yet, it is widely misunderstood. For example, the very term "tension" suggests anxiety or stress. But creative tension doesn't feel any particular way. It is the force that comes into play at the moment when we acknowledge a vision that is at odds with current reality.

Still, creative tension often leads to feelings or emotions associated with anxiety, such as sadness, discouragement, hopelessness, or worry. This happens so often that people easily confuse these emotions with creative tension. People come to think that the creative process *is all about being in a state of anxiety.* But it is important to realize that these "negative" emotions that may arise when there is creative tension are not creative tension itself. These emotions are what we call *emotional tension.*

If we fail to distinguish emotional tension from creative tension, we predispose ourselves to lowering our vision. If we feel deeply discouraged about a vision that is not happening, we may have a strong urge to lighten the load of that discouragement. There is one immediate remedy: lower the vision! "Well, it wasn't really that important to shoot seventy-five. I'm having a great time shooting in the eighties."

Or, "I don't really care about being able to play in recital. I'll have to make money as a music teacher in any case; I'll just concentrate there." The dynamics of relieving emotional tension are insidious because they can operate unnoticed. Emotional tension can always be relieved by adjusting the one pole of the creative tension that is completely under our control at all times—the vision. The feelings that we dislike go away because the creative tension that was their source is reduced. Our goals are now much closer to our current reality. Escaping emotional tension is easy—the only price we pay is abandoning what we truly want, our vision.

The dynamics of emotional tension deeply resemble the dynamics of eroding goals that have so troubled many companies. The interaction of creative tension and emotional tension is a "shifting the burden" dynamic, similar to that of eroding goals that can be represented as follows:

When we hold a vision that differs from current reality, a gap exists (the creative tension) which can be resolved in two ways. The lower balancing process represents the "fundamental solution": taking actions to bring reality into line with the vision. But changing reality takes time. This is what leads to the frustration and emotional tension in the upper balancing process, the "symptomatic solution" of lowering the vision to bring it into line with current reality.

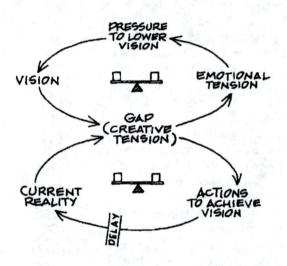

But a onetime reduction in the vision usually isn't the end of the story. Sooner or later new pressures pulling reality away from the (new, lowered) vision arise, leading to still more pressures to lower the vision. The classic "shifting the burden" dynamic ensues, a subtle reinforcing spiral of failure to meet goals, frustration, lowered vision, temporary relief, and pressure anew to lower the vision still further. Gradually, the "burden" is shifting increasingly to lowering the vision.

In organizations, goals erode because of low tolerance for emotional tension. Nobody wants to be the messenger with bad news. The easiest path is to just pretend there is no bad news, or better yet, "declare victory"—to redefine the bad news as not so bad by lowering the standard against which it is judged.

The dynamics of emotional tension exist at all levels of human activity. They are the dynamics of compromise, the path of mediocrity. As Somerset Maugham said, "Only mediocre people are always at their best."

We allow our goals to erode when we are unwilling to live with emotional tension. On the other hand, when we understand creative tension and allow it to operate by not lowering our vision, vision becomes an active force. Robert Fritz says, "It's not what the vision is, it's what the vision does. Truly creative people use the gap between vision and current reality to generate energy for change."[4]

Mastery of creative tension transforms the way one views "failure." Failure is, simply, a shortfall, evidence of the gap between vision and current reality. Failure is an opportunity for learning—about inaccurate pictures of current reality, about strategies that didn't work as expected, about the clarity of the vision. Failures are not about our unworthiness or powerlessness. Ed

Land, founder and president of Polaroid for decades and inventor of instant photography, had one plaque on his wall. It read: "A mistake is an event, the full benefit of which has not yet been turned to your advantage."

Mastery of creative tension brings out a capacity for perseverance and patience. More broadly, current reality itself is, for many of us, the enemy. We fight against what is. We are not so much drawn to what we want to create as we are repelled by what we have, from our current reality. By this logic, the deeper the fear, the more we abhor what is, the more "motivated" we are to change. "Things must get bad enough, or people will not change in any fundamental way."

This leads to the mistaken belief that fundamental change *requires* a threat to survival. This crisis theory of change is remarkably widespread. Yet, it is also a dangerous oversimplification.

Often in workshops or presentations, I will ask, "How many of you believe people and organizations only change, fundamentally, when there is a crisis?" Reliably, 75 to 90 percent of the hands go up. Then I ask people to consider a life where everything is exactly the way they would like—there are absolutely no problems of any sort in work, personally, professionally, in their relationships, or their community. Then I ask, "What is the first thing you would seek if you had a life of absolutely no problems?" The answer, overwhelmingly, is "change—to create something new." So human beings are more complex than we often assume. We both fear and seek change. Or, as one seasoned organization change consultant once put it, "People don't resist change. They resist being changed."

Mastery of creative tension leads to a fundamental shift in our whole posture toward reality. Current reality becomes the ally not the enemy. *An accurate, insightful view of current reality is as important as a clear vision.*

Both are equally vital to generating creative tension. Or, as Robert Fritz puts it, "The truly creative person knows that all creating is achieved through working with constraints. Without constraints there is no creating."

"Structural Conflict": The Power of Your Powerlessness

Many people, even highly successful people, harbor deep beliefs contrary to their personal mastery. Very often, these beliefs are below the level of conscious awareness. To see what I mean, try the following experiment. Say out loud the following sentence: "I can create my life exactly the way I want it, in all dimensions—work, family, relationships, community, and larger world." Notice your internal reaction to this assertion, the "little voice" in the back of your head. "Who's he kidding?" "He doesn't really believe that." "Personally and in work, sure—but not 'community' and 'the larger world.'" "What do I care about the 'larger world' anyhow?" All of these reactions are evidence of deep-seated beliefs.

Robert Fritz, who has worked with literally tens of thousands of people to develop their creative capacities, has concluded that practically all of us have a "dominant belief that we are not able to fulfill our desires." Where does this belief come from? Fritz argues that it is an almost inevitable by-product of growing up:

> As children we learn what our limitations are. Children are rightfully taught limitations essential to their survival. But too often this learning is generalized. We are constantly told we can't have or can't do certain things, and we may come to assume that we have an inability to have what we want.[5]

Most of us hold one of two contradictory beliefs that limit our ability to create what we really want. The more common is belief in our powerlessness—our inability to bring into being all the things we really care about. The other belief centers on unworthiness—that we do not deserve to have what we truly desire. Fritz claims that he has met only a handful of individuals who do not seem to have one or the other of these underlying beliefs. Such an assertion is difficult to prove rigorously because it is difficult to measure deep beliefs. But if we accept it as a working premise, it illuminates systemic forces that can work powerfully against creating what we really want.

Fritz uses a metaphor to describe how contradictory underlying beliefs work as a system, counter to achieving our goals. Imagine, as you move toward your goal, there is a rubber band, symbolizing creative tension, pulling you in the desired direction. But imagine also a second rubber band, anchored to the belief of powerlessness or unworthiness. Just as the first rubber band tries to pull you toward your goal, the second pulls you back toward the underlying belief that you can't (or don't deserve to) have your goal. Fritz calls the system . . . "structural conflict" because it is a structure of conflicting forces: pulling us simultaneously toward and away from what we want.

Thus, the closer we come to achieving our vision, the more the second rubber band pulls us away from our vision. This force can manifest itself in many ways. We might lose our energy. We might question whether we really wanted the vision. "Finishing the job" might become increasingly difficult. Unexpected obstacles develop in our path. People let us down. All this happens even though we are unaware of the structural conflict system, because it originates in deep beliefs of which we are largely unaware—in fact, our unawareness contributes to the power of structural conflict.

BELIEF IN
POWERLESSNESS
OR UNWORTHINESS   YOUR
                          CURRENT
                          REALITY   YOUR
                                            VISION

Given beliefs in our powerlessness or unworthiness, structural conflict implies that systemic forces come into play to keep us from succeeding *whenever* we seek a vision. Yet, we *do* succeed sometimes, and in fact many of us have become adept at identifying and achieving goals, at least in some areas of our lives. How do we overcome the forces of structural conflict?

Fritz has identified three generic "strategies" for coping with the forces of structural conflict, each of which has its limitations.[6] Letting our vision erode is one such coping strategy. The second is "conflict manipulation," in which we try to manipulate ourselves into greater effort toward what we want by creating artificial conflict, such as through focusing on avoiding what we don't want. Conflict manipulation is the favored strategy of people who incessantly worry about failure, managers who excel at "motivational chats" that point out the highly unpleasant consequences if the company's goals are *not* achieved, and of social movements that attempt to mobilize people through fear. In fact, sadly, most social movements operate through conflict manipulation or "negative vision," focusing on getting away from what we don't want, rather than on creating what we do want: anti-drugs, anti-nuclear arms, anti-nuclear power, anti-smoking, anti-abortion, or anti-government corruption.

But many ask, "What's wrong with a little worry or fear if it helps us achieve our goals?" The response of those who seek personal mastery is the simple question: "Do you really want to live your life in a state of fear of failure?" The tragedy is that many people who get hooked on conflict manipulation come to believe that *only* through being in a state of continual anxiety and fear can they be successful. These are the people who, rather than shunning emotional tension, actually come to glorify it. For them, there is little joy in life. Even when they achieve their goals, they immediately begin worrying about losing what they have gained.

Fritz's third generic strategy is the strategy of "willpower," where we simply "psych ourselves up" to overpower all forms of resistance to achieving our goals. Lying behind willpower strategies, he suggests, is the simple assumption that we "motivate ourselves through heightened volition." Willpower is so common among highly successful people that many see its characteristics as synonymous with success: a maniacal focus on goals, willingness to "pay the price," ability to defeat any opposition and surmount any obstacle.

The problems with "willpower" are many, but they may hardly be noticed by the person focused narrowly on "success." First, there is little economy of means; in systems thinking terms, we act without leverage. We attain our goals, but the effort is enormous and we may find ourselves exhausted and wondering if "it was worth it" when we have succeeded. Ironically, people hooked on willpower may actually look for obstacles to overcome, dragons to slay, and enemies to vanquish—to remind themselves and others of their own prowess. Second, there are often considerable unintended consequences. Despite great success at work, the master of "willpower" will often find that he or she has gone through two marriages and has terrible relationships with his or her children. Somehow, the same dogged determination and goal orientation that "works" at work doesn't quite turn the trick at home.

Worse still, just as with all of the coping strategies, "willpower" leaves the underlying system of structural conflict unaltered. In particular, the underlying belief in powerlessness has not really changed. Despite significant accomplishments, many "highly successful people" still feel a deep, usually unspoken, sense of powerlessness in critical areas of their lives—such as in their personal and family relationships, or in their ability to achieve a sense of peace and spiritual fulfillment.

These coping strategies are, to a certain extent, unavoidable. They are deeply habitual and cannot be changed overnight. We all tend to have a favorite strategy—mine has long been "willpower," as those close to me can attest.

Where then is the leverage in dealing with structural conflict? If structural conflict arises from deep underlying beliefs, then it can be changed only by changing the beliefs. But psychologists are virtually unanimous that fundamental beliefs such as powerlessness or unworthiness cannot be changed readily. They are developed early in life (remember all those "can'ts" and "don'ts" that started when you were two?). For most of us, beliefs change gradually as we accumulate new experiences—as we develop our personal mastery. But if mastery will not develop so long as we hold unempowering beliefs, and the beliefs will change only as we experience our mastery, how may we begin to alter the deeper structures of our lives?

Commitment to the Truth

We may begin with a disarmingly simple yet profound strategy for dealing with structural conflict: telling the truth.

Commitment to the truth often seems to people an inadequate strategy. "What do I need to do to change my behavior?" "How do I change my underlying belief?" People often want a formula, a technique, something tangible that they can apply to solve the problem of structural conflict. But, in fact, being committed to the truth is far more powerful than any technique.

Commitment to the truth does not mean seeking the "Truth," the absolute final word or ultimate cause. Rather, it means a relentless willingness to root out the ways we limit or deceive ourselves from seeing what is, and to continually challenge our theories of why things are the way they are. It means continually broadening our awareness, just as the great athlete with extraordinary peripheral vision keeps trying to "see more of the playing field." It also means continually deepening our understanding of the structures underlying current events. Specifically, people with high levels of personal mastery see more of the structural conflicts underlying their own behavior.

Thus, the first critical task in dealing with structural conflicts is to recognize them, *and their* resulting behavior, when they are operating. It can be very difficult to recognize these coping strategies while we are playing them out, especially because of tensions and pressures that often accompany them.

It helps to develop internal warning signals, such as when we find ourselves blaming something or somebody for our problems: "The reason I'm giving up is nobody appreciates me," or "The reason I'm so worried is that they'll fire me if I don't get the job done."

In my life, for example, I often felt that people let me down at critical junctures in major projects. When this happened, I would "bulldoze" through, overcoming the obstacle of their disloyalty or incompetence. It took many years before I recognized this as a recurring pattern, my own special form of the "willpower" strategy, rooted in a deep feeling of being powerless to change the way others let me down. Invariably, I ended up feeling as if "I've got to do it all myself."

Once I recognized this pattern, I began to act differently when a colleague let me down. I became angry less often. Rather, there was a twinge of recognition—"Oh, there goes my pattern." I looked more deeply at how my own actions were part of the outcome, either by creating tasks that were impossible to accomplish, or by undermining or demotivating the other person. Further, I worked to develop skills to discuss such situations with the people involved without producing defensiveness.

I would never have developed those skills or known how to put them into practice without a shift of mind. So long as I saw the problem in terms of events, I was convinced that my problems were externally caused—"*they* let me down." Once I saw the problem as structurally caused, I began to look at what I could do, rather than at what "they had done."

Structures of which we are unaware hold us prisoner. Once we can see them and name them, they no longer have the same hold on us. This is as much true for individuals as it is for organizations. In fact, an entire field is evolving, structural family therapy, based on the assumption that individual psychological difficulties can be understood and changed only by understanding the structures of interdependencies within families and close personal relationships. Once these structures are recognized, in the words of David Kantor, a pioneer in the field, "It becomes possible to begin to alter structures to free people from previously mysterious forces that dictated their behavior."[7]

Discovering structures at play is the stock and trade of people with high levels of personal mastery. Sometimes these structures can be readily changed. Sometimes, as with structural conflict, they change only gradually. Then the need is to work more creatively within them while acknowledging their origin, rather than fighting the structures. Either way, once an operating structure is recognized, the structure itself becomes part of "current reality." The more my commitment to the truth, the more creative tension comes into play because current reality is seen more for what it really is. In the context of creative tension, commitment to the truth becomes a generative force, just as vision becomes a generative force.

One of the classic illustrations of this process is Charles Dickens's *A Christmas Carol*. Through the visitations of the three ghosts on Christmas Eve, Scrooge sees more and more of the reality from which he has turned away.

He sees the reality of his past, how the choices he made steadily whittled away his compassion and increased his self-centeredness. He sees the reality of his present, especially those aspects of reality that he has avoided, such as Tiny Tim's illness. And he sees the reality of his likely future, the future that will occur if he continues in his present ways. But then he wakes up. He realizes that he is not the captive of these realities. He realizes that he has a choice. He chooses to change.

Significantly, Scrooge can't make the choice to change before he becomes more aware of his current reality. In effect, Dickens says that life always avails the option of seeing the truth, no matter how blind and prejudiced we may be. And if we have the courage to respond to that option, we have the power to change ourselves profoundly. Or, to put it in more classic religious terms, only through the truth do we come to grace.

The power of the truth, seeing reality more and more as it is, cleansing the lens of perception, awakening from self-imposed distortions of reality—different expressions of a common principle in almost all the world's great philosophic and religious systems. Buddhists strive to achieve the state of "pure observation," of seeing reality directly. Hindus speak of "witnessing," observing themselves and their lives with an attitude of spiritual detachment. The Koran ends with the phrase, "What a tragedy that man must die before he wakes up." The power of the truth was no less central to early Christian thinking, although it has lost its place in Christian practice over the last two thousand years. In fact, the Hebrew symbols used to form the word *Yeheshua*, "Jesus," include the symbols for Jehovah with an additional letter, *shin*, inserted in the middle. The symbols for Jehovah carry the meaning, "That which was, is, and will be." The inserted *shin* modifies the meaning to "that which was, is, and will be, *delivers*." This is the probable origin of the statement "The truth shall set you free."

Using the Subconscious, or, You Really Don't Need to Figure it all Out

One of the most fascinating aspects of people with high levels of personal mastery is their ability to accomplish extraordinarily complex tasks with grace and ease. We have all marveled at the breathtakingly beautiful artistry of the championship ice skater or the prima ballerina. We know that their skills have been developed through years of diligent training, yet the ability to execute their artistry with such ease and seeming effortlessness is *still* wondrous.

Implicit in the practice of personal mastery is another dimension of the mind, the subconscious. It is through the subconscious that *all of us* deal with complexity. What distinguishes people with high levels of personal mastery is they have developed a higher level of rapport between their normal awareness and their subconscious. What most of us take for granted and exploit haphazardly, they approach as a discipline.[8]

Is the subconscious relevant in management and organizations? Inamori of Kyocera says:

> When I am concentrating . . . I enter the subconscious mind. It is said that
> human beings possess both a conscious and subconscious mind, and that
> our subconscious mind has a capacity that is larger by a factor of ten . . .

When I talk about our "mind," I risk being called crazy. Nonetheless, I think therein may lie the hint to the secret that may determine our future. O'Brien of Hanover likewise sees tapping mental capabilities formerly ignored as central to building the new organization: "The greatest unexplored territory in the world is the space between our ears." Seriously, I am certain that learning organizations will find ways to nurture and focus the capabilities within us all that today we call "extraordinary."

But what is "extraordinary" is actually closely related to aspects of our lives that are so "ordinary" that we hardly notice them. Our lives are full of myriad complex tasks which we handle quite competently with almost no conscious thought. Try an experiment: touch the top of your head. Now, *how* did you do that? For most of us, the answer resembles, "Well, I just thought about my hand on my head—or, I formed a mental image of my hand on top of my head—and *voila,* it just was there." But at a neurophysiological level, raising your hand to the top of your head is an extraordinarily complex task, involving hundreds of thousands of neural firings as signals move from the brain to your arm and back again. This entire complex activity is coordinated without our conscious awareness. Likewise, if you had to think about every detail of walking, you'd be in big trouble. Walking, talking, eating, putting on your shoes, and riding a bicycle are all accomplished with almost no conscious attention— yet all are, in fact, enormously complex tasks.

These tasks are accomplished reliably because there is an aspect of our mind that is exceedingly capable of dealing with complexity. We call this dimension of mind the "subconscious," because it operates "below" or "behind" the level of conscious awareness. Others call it "unconscious" or "automatic mind."[5] Whatever it is called, without this dimension of mind it would be quite impossible to explain how human beings ever succeed in mastering any complex task. For one thing we can say confidently is that these tasks are not accomplished through our normal awareness and thinking alone.

Equally important, the subconscious is critical to how we learn. At one point in your life you were unable to carry out "mundane" tasks such as walking, talking and eating. Each had to be *learned.* The infant does not get the spoon in her mouth the first time out—it goes over the left shoulder, then the right shoulder, then the cheek. Only gradually does she learn to reliably reach her mouth. Initially, any new task requires a great deal of conscious attention and effort. As we "learn" the skills required of the task, the whole activity gradually shifts from conscious attention to subconscious control.

For example, when you first learned to drive a car, it took considerable conscious attention, especially if you were learning to drive on a standard transmission. In fact, you might have found it difficult to carry on a conversation with the person next to you. If that person had asked you to "slow down, downshift, and turn right" at the next corner, you might have given up then and there. Yet, within a few months or less, you executed the same task with little or no conscious attention. It had all become "automatic." Amazingly, before long you drove in heavy traffic while carrying on a conversation with the person sitting next to you—apparently giving almost no conscious attention to the literally hundreds of variables you had to monitor and respond to.

For example, when we first learn to play the piano or any musical instrument, we start by playing scales. Gradually, we move up to simple and then more complex compositions, leaving scales behind as a task that can be handled with little conscious attention. Even concert pianists, when sitting down to an unfamiliar piece, will play that piece at half speed in order to allow concentration on the mechanics of hand and pedal positions, rhythm and tempo. But when the concert comes, the same pianist places no conscious attention on the mechanics of playing the piece. This leaves his conscious attention to focus exclusively on the aesthetics of the performance.

We have all mastered a vast repertoire of skills through "training" the subconscious. Once learned, they become so taken for granted, so "subconscious," we don't even notice when we are executing them. But, for most of us, we have never given careful thought to *how* we mastered these skills and how we might continue to develop deeper and deeper *"rapport"* between our normal awareness and subconscious. Yet, these are matters of the greatest importance to the discipline of personal mastery.[9]

This is why, for instance, people committed to continually developing personal mastery practice some form of "meditation." Whether it is through contemplative prayer or other methods of simply "quieting" the conscious mind, regular meditative practice can be extremely helpful in working more productively with the subconscious mind. The subconscious appears to have no particular volition. It neither generates its own objectives nor determines its own focus. It is highly subject to direction and conditioning—what we pay attention to takes on special significance to the subconscious. In our normal highly active state of mind, the subconscious is deluged with a welter of contradictory thoughts and feelings. In a quieter state of mind, when we then focus on something of particular importance, some aspect of our vision, the subconscious is undistracted.

Moreover, there are particular ways that people with high levels of personal mastery direct their focus. As discussed earlier, they *focus on the desired result itself,* not the "process" or the means they assume necessary to achieve that result.

Focusing on the desired intrinsic result is a skill. For most of us it is not easy at first, and takes time and patience to develop. For most of us, as soon as we think of some important personal goal, almost immediately we think of all the reasons why it will be hard to achieve—the challenges we will face and the obstacles we will have to overcome. While this is very helpful for thinking through alternative strategies for achieving our goals, it is also a sign of lack of discipline when thoughts about "the process" of achieving our vision continually crowd out our focus on the outcomes we seek. We must work at learning how to separate what we truly want from what we think we need to do in order to achieve it.

A useful starting exercise for learning how to focus more clearly on desired results is to take any particular goal or aspect of your vision. First imagine that that goal is fully realized. Then ask yourself the question, "If I actually had this, what would it get me?" What people often discover is that the answer to that question reveals "deeper" desires lying behind the goal. In fact, the goal is actually an interim step they assume is necessary to reach a more important result. For example, a person has a goal of reaching a certain level in the organizational hierarchy. When she asks herself, "What would it get me to be a senior VP?" she discovers that the answer is "respect of my peers" or "being where the action is." Though she may still aspire to the position, she now sees that there is also a deeper result she desires—a result she can start to hold as part of her vision now, independent of where she is in the organizational hierarchy. (Moreover, if she doesn't clarify "the result" she truly seeks, she may reach her stated goal and find that the more senior position is somehow still dissatisfying.)

The reason this skill is so important is precisely because of the responsiveness of the subconscious to a clear focus. When we are unclear between interim goals and more intrinsic goals, the subconscious has no way of prioritizing and focusing.

Making clear choices is also important. Only after choice are the capabilities of the subconscious brought fully into play. In fact, making choices and focusing on the results that are really important to us may be one of the highest leverage uses of our normal awareness. As Inamori puts it:

> I often tell a researcher who is lacking in dedication . . . unless [he] is motivated with determination to succeed, he will not be able to go past the obstacles . . . When his passion, his desire, becomes so strong as to rise out of his body like steam, and when the condensation of that which evaporated occurs . . . and drops back like raindrops, he will find his problem solved.

Commitment to the truth is also important for developing subconscious rapport—for the same basic reasons that lie detectors work. Lie detectors work because when most human beings do not tell the truth they create some level of internal stress, which in turn generates measurable physiological effects—blood pressure, pulse rate, and respiration. So, not only does deceiving ourselves about current reality prevent the subconscious from having accurate information about where we are relative to our vision, but it also creates distracting input to the subconscious, just as our "chatter" about why we can't achieve our vision is distracting. The principle of creative tension recognizes that the subconscious operates most effectively when it is focused clearly on our vision and our current reality.

The art of working effectively with the subconscious incorporates many techniques. An effective way to focus the subconscious is through imagery and visualization. For example, world-class swimmers have found that by imagining their hands to be twice their actual size and their feet to be webbed, they actually swim faster. "Mental rehearsal" of complex feats has become routine psychological training for diverse professional performers.

But the real effectiveness of all of this still hinges on knowing what it is that is most important to you. In the absence of knowing what truly matters to you, the specific practices and methods of working with the subconscious run the risk of becoming mechanical techniques—simply a new way of manipulating yourself into being more productive. This is not an idle concern. Almost all spiritual traditions warn against adopting the techniques of increased mental powers without diligently continuing to refine one's sense of genuine aspiration.

Ultimately, what matters most in developing the subconscious rapport characteristic of masters is the genuine caring for a desired outcome, the deep feeling of it being the "right" goal toward which to aspire. The subconscious seems especially receptive to goals in line with our deeper aspirations and values. According to some spiritual disciplines, this is because these deeper aspirations input directly to, or are part of, the subconscious mind.

A wonderful example of what can be accomplished in the pursuit of something truly important to a person is the story of Gilbert Kaplan, a highly successful publisher and editor of a leading investment periodical. Kaplan first heard Mahler's Second Symphony in a rehearsal in 1965. He found himself unable to sleep—"I went back for the performance and walked out of the hall a different person. It was the beginning of a long love affair." Despite his having had *no* formal musical training, he committed time and energy and a considerable sum of his personal finances (he had to hire an orchestra) to the pursuit of learning how to conduct the piece. Today, his performances of the symphony have received the highest praise by critics throughout the world. The *New York Times* praised his 1988 recording of the symphony with the London Symphony Orchestra as one of the five finest classical recordings of the year and the president of the New York Mahler Society called it "the outstanding recorded performance." A strict reliance on only conscious learning could never have achieved this level of artistry, even with all the "willpower" in the world. It had to depend on a high level of subconscious rapport which Kaplan could bring to bear on his new "love affair." In many ways, the key to developing high levels of mastery in subconscious rapport comes back to the discipline of developing personal vision. This is why the concept of vision has always figured so strongly in the creative arts. Picasso once said:

> It would be very interesting to record photographically, not the stages of a painting, but its metamorphoses. One would see perhaps by what course a mind finds its way toward the crystallization of its dream. But what is really very serious is to see that the picture does not change basically, that the initial vision remains almost intact in spite of appearance.[10]

As individuals practice the discipline of personal mastery, several changes gradually take place within them. Many of these are quite subtle and often go unnoticed. In addition to clarifying the "structures" that characterize personal mastery as a discipline (such as creative tension, emotional tension, and structural conflict), the systems perspective also illuminates subtler aspects of personal mastery—especially: integrating reason and intuition; continually seeing more of our connectedness to the world; compassion; and commitment to the whole.

Integrating Reason and Intuition

According to an ancient Sufi story, a blind man wandering lost in a forest tripped and fell. As the blind man rummaged about the forest floor he discovered that he had fallen over a cripple. The blind man and the cripple struck up a conversation, commiserating on their fate. The blind man said, "I have been wandering in this forest for as long as I can remember, and I cannot see to find my way out." The cripple said, "I have been lying on the forest floor for as long as I can remember, and I cannot get up to walk out." As they sat there talking, suddenly the cripple cried out. "I've got it," he said. "You hoist me up onto your shoulders and I will tell you where to walk. Together we can find our way out of the forest." According to the ancient storyteller, the blind man symbolized rationality. The cripple symbolized intuition. We will not find our way out of the forest until we learn how to integrate the two.

Intuition in management has recently received increasing attention and acceptance, after many decades of being officially ignored. Now numerous studies show that experienced managers and leaders rely heavily on intuition—that they do not figure out complex problems entirely rationally. They rely on hunches, recognize patterns, and draw intuitive analogies and parallels to other seemingly disparate situations.[11] There are even courses in management schools on intuition and creative problem solving. But we have a very long way to go, in our organizations and in society, toward reintegrating intuition and rationality.

People with high levels of personal mastery do not set out to integrate reason and intuition. Rather, they achieve it naturally—as a by-product of their commitment to use all resources at their disposal. They cannot afford to choose between reason and intuition, or head and heart, any more than they would choose to walk on one leg or see with one eye.

Bilateralism is a design principle underlying the evolution of advanced organisms. Nature seems to have learned to design in pairs; it not only builds in redundancy but achieves capabilities not possible otherwise. Two legs are critical for rapid, flexible locomotion. Two arms and hands are vital for climbing, lifting, and manipulating objects. Two eyes give us stereoscopic vision, and along with two ears, depth perception. Is it not possible that, following the same design principle, reason and intuition are designed to work in harmony for us to achieve our potential intelligence?

Systems thinking may hold a key to integrating reason and intuition. Intuition eludes the grasp of linear thinking, with its exclusive emphasis on cause and effect that are close in time and space. The result is that most of our intuitions don't make "sense"—that is, they can't be explained in terms of linear logic.

Very often, experienced managers have rich intuitions about complex systems, which they cannot explain. Their intuitions tell them that cause and effect are not close in time and space, that obvious solutions will produce more harm than good, and that short-term fixes produce long-term problems. But they cannot explain their ideas in simple linear cause-effect language. They end up saying, "Just do it this way. It will work."

For example, many managers sense the dangers of eroding goals or standards but cannot fully explain how they create a reinforcing tendency to underinvest and a self-fulfilling prophecy of underrealized market growth. Or, managers may feel that they are focusing on tangible, easily measured indicators of performance and masking deeper problems, and even exacerbating these problems. But they cannot explain convincingly why these are the wrong performance indicators or how alternatives might produce improved results. Both of these intuitions can be explained when the underlying systemic structures are understood.

The conflict between intuition and linear, non-systemic thinking has planted the seed that *rationality* itself is opposed to intuition. This view is demonstrably false if we consider the synergy of reason and intuition that characterizes virtually all great thinkers. Einstein said, "I never discovered anything with my rational mind." He once described how he discovered the principle of relativity by imagining himself traveling on a light beam. Yet, he could take brilliant intuitions and convert them into succinct, rationally testable propositions.

As managers gain facility with systems thinking as an alternative language, they find that many of their intuitions become explicable. Eventually, reintegrating reason and intuition may prove to be one of the primary contributions of systems thinking.

Seeing Our Connectedness to the World

My six-week-old son Ian does not yet seem to know his hands and feet. I suspect that he is aware of them, but he is clearly not aware that they are *his* hands and feet, or that he controls their actions. The other day, he got caught in a terrible reinforcing feedback loop. He had taken hold of his ear with his left hand. It was clearly agitating him, as you could tell from his pained expression and increasing flagellations. But, as a result of being agitated, he pulled harder. This increased his discomfort, which led him to get more agitated and pull still harder. The poor little guy might still be pulling if I hadn't detached his hand and quieted him down.

Not knowing that his hand was actually within his control, he perceived the source of his discomfort as an external force. Sound familiar?

As I thought about Ian, I began to think that a neglected dimension of personal growth lies in "closing the loops"—in continually discovering how apparent external forces are actually interrelated with our own actions. Fairly soon, Ian will recognize his feet and hands and learn he can control their motions. Then he will discover that he can control his body position—if it is unpleasant on his back, he can roll over. Then will come internal states such as temperature, and the realization that they can be influenced by moving closer or further from a heat source such as Mommy or Daddy. Eventually comes Mommy and Daddy themselves, and the realization that their actions and emotions are subject to his influence. At each stage in this progression, there will be corresponding adjustments in his internal pictures of reality, which will steadily change to incorporate more of the feedback from his actions to the conditions in his life.

But for most of us, sometime early in life this process of closing the loops is arrested. As we get older, our rate of discovery slows down; we see fewer and fewer new links between our actions and external forces. We become locked into ways of looking at the world that are, fundamentally, no different from little Ian's.

The learning process of the young child provides a beautiful metaphor for the learning challenge faced by us all: to continually expand our awareness and understanding, to see more and more of the interdependencies between actions and our reality, to see more and more of our connectedness to the world around us. We will probably never perceive fully the multiple ways in which we influence our reality. But simply being open to the possibility is enough to free our thinking. Einstein expressed the learning challenge when he said:

> [the human being] experiences himself, his thoughts and feelings as something separated from the rest—a kind of optical delusion of our consciousness. This delusion is a kind of prison for us, restricting us to our personal desires and to affection for a few persons nearest to us. Our task must be to free ourselves from this prison by widening our circle of compassion to embrace all living creatures and the whole of nature in its beauty.

The experience of increasing connectedness which Einstein describes is one of the subtlest aspects of personal mastery, one that derives most directly from the systems perspective. His "widening . . . circle of compassion" is another.

Compassion

The discipline of seeing interrelationships gradually undermines older attitudes of blame and guilt. We begin to see that *all of us* are trapped in structures, structures embedded both in our ways of thinking and in the interpersonal and social milieus in which we live. Our knee-jerk tendencies to find fault with one another gradually fade, leaving a much deeper appreciation of the forces within which we all operate.

This does not imply that people are simply victims of systems that dictate their behavior. Often, the structures are of our own creation. But this has little meaning until those structures are seen. For most of us, the structures within which we operate are invisible. We are neither victims nor culprits but human beings controlled by forces we have not yet learned how to perceive.

We are used to thinking of compassion as an emotional state, based on our concern for one another. But it is also grounded in a level of awareness. In my experience, as people see more of the systems within which they operate, and as they understand more clearly the pressures influencing one another, they naturally develop more compassion and empathy.

Commitment to the Whole

"Genuine commitment," according to Bill O'Brien, "is always to something larger than ourselves." Inamori talks about "action of our heart," when we are guided by "sincere desire to serve the world." Such action, he says, "is a very important issue since it has great power."

The sense of connectedness and compassion characteristic of individuals with high levels of personal mastery naturally leads to a broader vision. Without it, all the subconscious visualizing in the world is deeply self-centered— simply a way to get what I want.

Individuals committed to a vision beyond their self-interest find they have energy not available when pursuing narrower goals, as will organizations that tap this level of commitment. "I do not believe there has been a single person who has made a worthwhile discovery or invention," Inamori states, "who has not experienced a spiritual power." He describes the will of a person committed to a larger purpose as "a cry from the soul which has been shaken and awakened."

Fostering Personal Mastery in an Organization

It must always be remembered that embarking on any path of personal growth is a matter of choice. No one can be forced to develop his or her personal mastery. It is guaranteed to backfire. Organizations can get into considerable difficulty if they become too aggressive in promoting personal mastery for their members.

Still many have attempted to do just that by creating compulsory internal personal growth training programs. However well intentioned, such programs are probably the most sure-fire way to impede the genuine spread of commitment to personal mastery in an organization. Compulsory training or "elective" programs that people feel expected to attend if they want to advance their careers, conflict directly with freedom of choice.

For example, there have been numerous instances in recent years of over-zealous managers requiring employees to participate in personal development training, which the employees regarded as contradictory to their own religious beliefs. Several of these have resulted in legal action against the organization.[12]

What then can leaders intent on fostering personal mastery do? They can work relentlessly to foster a climate in which the principles of personal mastery are practiced in daily life. That means building an organization where it is safe for people to create visions, where inquiry and commitment to the truth are the norm, and where challenging the status quo is expected—especially when the status quo includes obscuring aspects of current reality that people seek to avoid.

Such an organizational climate will strengthen personal mastery in two ways. First, it will continually reinforce the idea that personal growth is truly valued in the organization. Second, to the extent that individuals respond to what is offered, it will provide an "on the job training" that is vital to developing personal mastery. As with any discipline, developing personal mastery must become a continual, ongoing process. There is nothing more important to an individual committed to his or her own growth than a supportive environment. An organization committed to personal mastery can provide that environment by continually encouraging personal vision, commitment to the truth, and a willingness to face honestly the gaps between the two.

The core leadership strategy is simple: be a model. Commit yourself to your own personal mastery. Talking about personal mastery may open people's minds somewhat, but actions always speak louder than words. There's nothing more powerful you can do to encourage others in their quest for personal mastery than to be serious in your own quest.

Notes

1 George Bernard Shaw, *Man and Superman*. (New York: Penguin), 1950.
2 William O'Brien, *Character and the Corporation*. (Cambridge, MA: SoL), 2006.
3 K. Inamori, "The Perfect Company: Goal for Productivity." Speech given at Case Western Reserve University, June 5, 1985.
4 Robert Fritz, *The Path of Least Resistance*. (New York: Fawcett-Columbine), 1989.
5 Ibid.
6 Ibid.
7 David Kantor and William Lehr, *Inside the Family: Toward a Theory of Family Process* (San Francisco: Jossey-Bass), 1975.
8 The term "subconscious" has been used by many others, such as Freud and Jung, to represent phenomena somewhat different from those discussed here.
9 The following brief discussion borrows from many spiritual traditions from developmental Christianity to Zen, but owes a special debt to the work of Robert Fritz (see note 4). Useful readings from these different traditions include, *Finding Grace at the Center*, Thomas Keating et al., eds. (Still River, MA: St. Bede Publications), 1978; Shunryu Suzuki Roshi, *Zen Mind, Beginner's Mind* (New York and Tokyo: Weatherhill), 1975.
10 Quoted in Fritz, *The Path of Least Resistance*.
11 Weston Agor, *Intuitive Management: Integrating Left and Right Brain Management Skills* (Englewood Cliffs, NJ: Prentice-Hall), 1984; Henry Mintzberg, "Planning on the Left Side and Managing on the Right," *Harvard Business Review* (July/August 1976): 49-58; Daniel Isenberg, "How Top Managers Think," *Harvard Business Review* (July/August 1976): 49.
12 Karen Cook, "Scenario for a New Age: Can American Industry Find Renewal in Management Theories Born of Counterculture?" *New York Times Magazine*, Sept. 25, 1988; Robert Lindsey, "Gurus Hired to Motivate Workers are Raising Fears of a Mind Control," *New York Times*, April 17, 1987.

42

How I Learned to Let My Workers Lead

Ralph Stayer

In 1980, I was the head of a successful family business—Johnsonville Sausage—that was in great shape and required radical change.

Our profits were above the average for our industry, and our financial statements showed every sign of health. We were growing at a rate of about 20% annually, with sales that were strong in our home state of Wisconsin and steadily rising in Minnesota, Michigan, and Indiana. Our quality was high. We were respected in the community. I was making a lot of money.

And I had a knot in my stomach that wouldn't go away. For one thing, I was worried about competition. We were a small, regional producer with national competitors who could outpromote, outadvertise, and underprice us any time they chose.

In addition to our big national competitors, we had a host of local and regional producers small enough to provide superior service to customers who were virtually their neighbors. We were too big to have the small-town advantage and too small to have advantages of national scale. Our business was more vulnerable than it looked.

What worried me more than the competition, however, was the gap between potential and performance. Our people didn't seem to care. Every day I came to work and saw people so bored by their jobs that they made thoughtless, dumb mistakes. They mislabeled products or added the wrong seasonings or failed to mix them into the sausage properly. Someone drove the prongs of a forklift right through a newly built wall. Someone else ruined a big batch of fresh sausage by spraying it with water while cleaning the work area. These were accidents. No one was deliberately wasting money, time, and materials; it was just that people took no responsibility for their work.

They showed up in the morning, did halfheartedly what they were told to do, and then went home.

Now, I didn't expect them to be as deeply committed to the company as I was. I owned it, and they didn't. But how could we survive a serious competitive challenge with this low level of attentiveness and involvement?

Getting to Points B and A

In 1980, I began looking for a recipe for change. I started by searching for a book that would tell me how to get people to care about their jobs and their company. Not surprisingly, the search was fruitless. No one could tell me how to wake up my own work force; I would have to figure it out for myself.

And yet, I told myself, why not? I had made the company, so I could fix it. This was an insight filled with pitfalls but it *was* an insight: the fault was not someone else's, the fault was mine.

Of course, I hadn't really built the company all alone, but I had created the management style that kept people from assuming responsibility. Of course, it was counterproductive for me to own all the company's problems by myself, but in 1980 every problem did, in fact, rest squarely on my shoulders, weighing me down and—though I didn't appreciate it at the time—crippling my subordinates and strangling the company. If I was going to fix what I had made, I would have to start by fixing myself. In many ways that was my good luck, or, to put the same thought another way, thank God I was the problem so I could be the solution.

As I thought about what I should do, I first asked myself what I needed to do to achieve the company's goals. But what *were* the company's goals? What did I really want Johnsonville to be? I didn't know.

This realization led me to a second insight: nothing matters more than a goal. The most important question any manager can ask is, "In the best of all possible worlds, what would I really want to happen?"

I tried to picture what Johnsonville would have to be to sell the most expensive sausage in the industry and still have the biggest market share. What I saw in my mind's eye was definitely not an organization where I made all the decisions and owned all the problems. What I saw was an organization where people took responsibility for their own work, for the product, for the company as a whole. If that happened, our product and service quality would improve, our margins would rise, and we could reduce costs and successfully enter new markets. Johnsonville would be much less vulnerable to competition.

The image that best captured the organizational end state I had in mind for Johnsonville was a flock of geese on the wing. I didn't want an organizational chart with traditional lines and boxes, but a "V" of individuals who knew the common goal, took turns leading, and adjusted their structure to the task at hand. Geese fly in a wedge, for instance, but land in waves. Most important, each individual bird is responsible for its own performance.

With that end state in mind as Point B, the goal, I turned to the question of our starting point, Point A. Johnsonville was financially successful, but I was dissatisfied with employee attitudes. So I conducted an attitude survey to find out what people thought about their jobs and the company and to get an idea of how they perceived the company's attitude toward them. I knew there was less commitment than I wanted, but I was startled all the same to find that Johnsonville attitudes were only average—no better than employee attitudes at big, impersonal companies like General Motors.

At first I didn't want to believe the survey, and I looked for all kinds of excuses. The methodology was faulty. The questions were poorly worded. I didn't want to admit that we had an employee motivation problem because I didn't know how to deal with that. But however strong the temptation, the mistakes and poor performance were too glaring to ignore.

The survey told me that people saw nothing for themselves at Johnsonville. It was a job, a means to some end that lay outside the company. I wanted them to commit themselves to a company goal, but they saw little to commit to. And at that stage, I still couldn't see that the biggest obstacle to changing their point of view was me. Everything I had learned and experienced to that point had convinced me that anything I didn't do myself would not be done right. As I saw it, my job was to create the agenda and then motivate "them" to carry it out.

In fact, I expected my people to follow me the way buffalo follow their leader—blindly. Unfortunately, that kind of leadership model almost led to the buffalo's extinction. Buffalo hunters used to slaughter the herd by finding and killing the leader. Once the leader was dead, the rest of the herd stood around waiting for instructions that never came, and the hunters could (and did) exterminate them one by one.

I realized that I had been focused entirely on the financial side of the business—margins, market share, return on assets—and had seen people as dutiful tools to make the business grow. The business *had* grown nicely—and that very success was my biggest obstacle to change. I had made all the decisions about purchasing, scheduling, quality, pricing, marketing, sales, hiring, and all the rest of it. Now the very things that had brought me success—my centralized control, my aggressive behavior, my authoritarian business practices—were creating the environment that made me so unhappy. I had been Johnsonville Sausage, assisted by some hired hands who, to my annoyance, lacked commitment. But why should they make a commitment to Johnsonville? They had no stake in the company and no power to make decisions or control their own work. If I wanted to improve results, I had to increase their involvement in the business.

This was an insight that I immediately misused. Acting on instinct, I ordered a change. "From now on," I announced to my management team, "you're all responsible for making your own decisions." I went from authoritarian control to authoritarian abdication. No one had asked for more responsibility; I forced it down their throats. They were good soldiers, and

JOHNSONVILLE FOODS, INC.
COMPANY PERFORMANCE-SHARE EVALUATION FORM

Please check one: _____ Self _____ Coach

PERFORMANCE

A. Customer Satisfaction

How do I rate the quality of the work I do? Do I contribute my best to producing a product to be proud of—one that I would purchase or encourage someone else to purchase?

Score _____

B. Cost-Effectiveness

To what extent do I perform my job in a cost-effective manner? Do I strive to work smarter? To work more productively with fewer errors? To complete my job functions in a timely manner, eliminating overtime when possible? To reduce waste where possible in all departments?

Score _____

C. Attitude

To what extent do I have a positive attitude toward my personal, department, and company goals as expressed by my actions, feelings, and thoughts? Do I like to come to work? Am I thoughtful and considerate toward fellow members? Do I work to promote better attitudes? Do I demonstrate company loyalty?

Score _____

D. Responsibility

To what extent do I take responsibility for my own job? Do I accept a challenge? Do I willingly take on or look for additional responsibilities? Do I work independently of supervision?

Score _____

E. Ideas

To what extent have I offered ideas and suggestions for improvements? Do I suggest better ways of doing things instead of just complaining?

Score _____

F. Problem Solver/Preventer

To what extent have I contributed to solving or preventing problems? Do I anticipate problem situations and try to avoid them? Do I push-pull when necessary? Do I keep an open line of communication?

Score _____

G. Safety

To what extent do my actions show my concern for safety for myself and others? Do I alert coworkers to unsafe procedures? Do I alert my coach to unsafe conditions in my department?

Score _____

H. Quality Image

To what extent have I displayed a high-quality image in my appearance, language, personal hygiene, and working environment?

Score _____

(continued)

II. TEAMWORK

A. Contribution to Groups

How would I rate my contribution to my department's performance? Am I aware of department goals? Do I contribute to a team? Do I communicate with team members?

Score _____

B. Communication

To what extent do I keep others informed to prevent problems from occurring? Do I work to promote communication between plants and departments? Do I relay information to the next shift? Do I speak up at meetings and let my opinions and feelings be known?

Score _____

C. Willingness to Work Together

To what extent am I willing to share the responsibility of getting the work done? Do I voluntarily assist others to obtain results? Do I demonstrate a desire to accomplish department goals? Do I complete paperwork accurately and thoroughly and work toward a smooth flow of information throughout the company? Am I willing to share in any overtime?

Score _____

D. Attendance and Timeliness

Do I contribute to the team by being present and on time for work (including after breaks and lunch)? Do I realize the inconvenience and hardship caused by my absence or tardiness?

Score _____

III. PERSONAL DEVELOPMENT

A. To what extent am I actively involved in lifelong learning? Taking classes is not the only way to learn. Other ways include use of our resource center or libraries for reading books, articles, etc.

Score _____

B. Do I improve my job performance by applying what I have learned?

Score _____

C. Do I ask questions pertaining to my job and other jobs too?

Score _____

D. Do I try to better myself not only through work but in all aspects of my life?

Score _____

E. Do I seek information about our industry?

Score _____

TOTAL POINTS: _____

they did their best, but I had trained them to expect me to solve their problems. I had nurtured their inability by expecting them to be incapable; now they met my expectations with an inability to make decisions unless they knew which decisions I wanted them to make.

After more than two years of working with them, I finally had to replace all three top managers. Worst of all, I now see that in a way they were right. I didn't really *want* them to make independent decisions. I wanted them to make the decisions I would have made. Deep down, I was still in love with my own control; I was just making people guess what I wanted instead of telling them. And yet I had to replace those three managers. I needed people who didn't guess so well, people who couldn't read my mind, people strong enough to call my bluff and seize ownership of Johnsonville's problems whether I "really" wanted to give it up or not.

I spent those two years pursuing another mirage as well—detailed strategic and tactical plans that would realize my goal of Johnsonville as the world's greatest sausage maker. We tried to plan organizational structure two to three years before it would be needed—who would be responsible for what and who would report to whom, all carefully diagramed in boxes and lines on charts. Later I realized that these structural changes had to grow from day-to-day working realities; no one could dictate them from above, and certainly not in advance. But at the time, my business training told me this was the way to proceed. The discussions went on at an abstract level for months, the details overwhelmed us, and we got nowhere.

In short, the early 1980s were a disaster. After two years of stewing, it began to dawn on me that my first reactions to most situations were usually dead wrong. After all, my organizational instincts had brought us to Point A to begin with. Pursuing those instincts now would only bring us *back* to Point A. I needed to start thinking before I acted, and the thought I needed to think was, "Will this action help us achieve our new Point B?"

Point B also needed some revision. The early 1980s taught me that I couldn't give responsibility. People had to expect it, want it, even demand it. So my end state needed redefining. The goal was not so much a state of shared responsibility as an environment where people insist on being responsible.

To bring people to that new Point B, I had to learn to be a better coach. It took me additional years to learn the art of coaching, by which, in a nutshell, I mean communicating a vision and then getting people to see their own behavior, harness their own frustrations, and own their own problems.

Early in the change process, for example, I was told that workers in one plant disliked working weekends, which they often had to do to meet deliveries. Suspecting that the weekends weren't really necessary, I pressed plant managers to use the problem as an opportunity. I asked them if they had measured production efficiency, for instance, and if they had tried to get their workers to take responsibility for the overtime problem. The first thing everyone discovered was that machine downtime hovered between 30% and 40%. Then they started coming to terms with the fact that all that downtime had its causes—lateness, absences, sloppy maintenance, slow shift startups. Once the workers began to see that they themselves were the problem, they realized that they could do away with weekend work. In three weeks, they cut downtime to less than 10% and had Saturdays and Sundays off.

Managing the Context

The debacle of ordering change and watching it fail to occur showed me my limitations. I had come to realize that I didn't directly control the performance of the people at Johnsonville, that as a manager I didn't really manage people. They managed themselves. But I did manage the context. I provided and allocated the resources. I designed and implemented the systems. I drew up and executed the organizational structure. The power of any contextual factor lies in its ability to shape the way people think and what they expect. So I worked on two contextual areas: systems and structures.

Systems

I first attacked our quality control system. Quality was central to our business success, one of our key competitive advantages. But even though our quality was better than average, it wasn't yet good enough to be great.

We had the traditional quality control department with the traditional quality control responsibilities—catching errors before they got to the customer. Senior management was a part of the system. Several times a week we evaluated the product—that is to say, we *checked* it—for taste, flavor, color, and texture.

One day it struck me that by checking the product, top management had assumed responsibility for its quality. We were not encouraging people to be responsible for their own performance. We were not helping people commit themselves to making Johnsonville a great company.

This line of reasoning led me to another insight: the first strategic decision I needed to make was who should make decisions. On the theory that those who implement a decision and live with its consequences are the best people to make it, we changed our quality control system. Top management stopped tasting sausage, and the people who made sausage started. We informed line workers that from now on it would be their responsibility to make certain that only top-quality product left the plant. In the future, they would manage quality control.

It surprised me how readily people accepted this ownership. They formed teams of workers to resolve quality problems. For example, one team attacked the problem of leakers—vacuum-packed plastic packages of sausage that leaked air and shortened shelf life. The team gathered data, identified problems, worked with suppliers and with other line workers to develop and implement solutions, even visited retail stores to find out how retailers handled the product so we could make changes that would prevent their problems from occurring. The team took complete responsibility for measuring quality and then used those measurements to improve production processes. They owned and expected to own all the problems of producing top-quality sausage, and they wanted to do the best possible job. The results were amazing. Rejects fell from 5% to less than 0.5%.

Clearly this new quality control system was helping to create the end state we were after. Its success triggered changes in several other systems as well.

Teams of workers in other areas began to taste the product every morning and discuss possible improvements. They asked for information about costs and customer reactions, and we redesigned the information system to give it to them.

We began to forward customer letters directly to line workers. They responded to customer complaints and sent coupons for free Johnsonville sausage when they felt it was warranted. They came to own and expect responsibility for correcting the problems that customers raised in their letters.

People in each section on the shop floor began to collect data about labor costs, efficiency, and yield. They posted the data and discussed it at the daily tasting meeting. Increasingly, people asked for more responsibility, and the information system encouraged them to take it. We were progressing toward our end state, and as we made progress we uncovered deeper and more complex problems.

One of these arose when people on the shop floor began to complain about fellow workers whose performance was still slipshod or indifferent. In fact, they came to senior management and said, "You don't take your own advice. If you did, you wouldn't let these poor performers work here. It's your job to either fix them or fire them."

Our first reaction was to jump in and do something, but by now we had learned to think before acting. We asked ourselves if accepting responsibility for this problem would help us reach Point B. The answer was clearly no. More important, we asked ourselves who was in the best position to own the problem and came to the obvious conclusion that the people on the shop floor knew more about shop-floor performance than we did, so they were the best ones to make these decisions.

We offered to help them set performance standards and to coach them in confronting poor performers, but we insisted that since they were the production-performance experts, it was up to them to deal with the situation. I bit my tongue time and time again, but they took on the responsibility for dealing with performance problems and actually fired individuals who wouldn't perform up to the standards of their teams.

This led to a dramatic change in Johnsonville's human resource system. Convinced that inadequate selection and training of new workers caused performance problems, line workers asked to do the selection and training themselves. Managers helped them set up selection and training procedures, but production workers made them work. Eventually, line workers assumed most of the traditional personnel functions.

The compensation system was another early target for change. We had traditionally given across-the-board annual raises like most other businesses. What mattered was longevity, not performance. That system was also a stumbling block on our way to Point B, so we made two changes.

First, we eliminated the annual across-the-board raise and substituted a pay-for-responsibility system. As people took on new duties—budgeting, for instance, or training—they earned additional base income. Where the old system rewarded people for hanging around, regardless of what they contributed, the new one encouraged people to seek responsibility.

How Johnsonville Shares Profits on the Basis of Performance

Every six months, we evaluate the performance of everyone at Johnsonville to help us compute shares in our profit-sharing program. Except "we" is the wrong word. In practice, performance evaluations are done by the employees themselves. For example, 300 wage earners—salaried employees have a separate profit-sharing pool and a different evaluation system—fill out forms in which they rate themselves on a scale of 1 to 9 in 17 specific areas grouped into three categories: performance, teamwork, and personal development.

Scores of 3, 4, or 5—the average range—are simply entered on the proper line. Low scores of 1 or 2 and high scores of 6 to 9 require a sentence or two of explanation.

Each member's coach fills out an identical form, and later both people sit down together and discuss all 17 areas. In cases of disagreement, the rule is only that their overall point totals must agree within nine points, whereupon the two totals are averaged to reach a final score. If they cannot narrow the gap to nine points, an arbitration group is ready to step in and help, but so far mediation has never been needed.

All final scores, names deleted, are then passed to a profit-sharing team that carves out five categories of performance: a small group of superior performers (about 5% of the total), a larger group of better-than-average workers (roughly 20%), an average group amounting to about 50% of the total work force, a below-average group of 20%, and a small group of poor performers who are often in some danger of losing their jobs.

The total pool of profits to be shared is then divided by the number of workers to find an average share—for the purpose of illustration, let's say $1,000. Members of the top group get a check for 125% of that amount or $1,250. Members of the next group get 110% ($1,100), of the large middle group, 100% or $1,000, and so on down to $900 and $750.

Yes, people do complain from time to time, especially if they think they've missed a higher share by only a point or two. The usual way of dealing with such situations is to help the individual improve his or her performance in enough areas to ensure a higher score the next time. But overall satisfaction with the system is very high, partly because fellow workers invented it, administer it, and constantly revise it in an effort to make it more equitable. The person currently in charge of the Johnsonville profit-sharing team is an hourly worker from the shipping department.

Many forms have been used over the years—a new one is under consideration at this moment—but the questions most recently asked, in a slightly edited version, are reprinted in this article.

Second, we instituted what we called a "company performance share," a fixed percentage of pretax profits to be divided every six months among our employees. We based individual shares on a performance-appraisal system designed and administered by a volunteer team of line production workers from various departments. The system is explained in the insert "How Johnsonville Shares Profits on the Basis of Performance."

These system changes taught me two more valuable lessons. First, just start. Don't wait until you have all the answers. When I set out to make these changes, I had no clear picture of how these new systems would interact with one another or with other company systems and procedures, but if I had waited until I had all the answers, I'd still be waiting. A grand plan was impossible; there were too many variables. I wasn't certain which systems to change; I just knew I had to change something in order to alter expectations and begin moving toward my goal.

Second, start by changing the most visible system you directly control. You want your first effort to succeed. I knew I could control who tasted the product because I was doing the tasting. I also knew it was a highly visible action. Everyone waited to hear my taste-test results. By announcing that I wasn't going to taste the product anymore and that the people who made it were, everyone knew immediately that I was serious about spreading responsibility.

Structures

Along with the system changes, I introduced a number of changes in company structure. Teams gradually took over a number of the functions previously performed by individual managers in the chain of command, with the result that the number of hierarchical layers went from six to three.

Teams had already taken on responsibility for selecting, training, evaluating, and, when necessary, terminating fellow employees. Now they began to make all decisions about schedules, performance standards, assignments, budgets, quality measures, and capital improvements as well. In operations, teams assumed the supervisors' functions, and those jobs disappeared. Those former supervisors who needed authority in order to function left the company, but most went into other jobs at Johnsonville, some of them into technical positions.

The function of the quality control department was redefined. It stopped checking quality—now done by line workers—and began providing technical support to the production people in a cooperative effort to *improve* quality. The department developed systems for continuous on-line monitoring of fat, moisture, and protein content, for example, and it launched a program of outside taste testing among customers.

The traditional personnel department disappeared and was replaced by a learning and personal development team to help individual employees develop their own Points B and A—their destinations and starting points—and figure out how to use Johnsonville to reach their goals. We set up an educational allowance for each person, to be used however the individual saw fit. In the beginning, some took cooking or sewing classes; a few took flying lessons. Over time, however, more and more of the employees focused on job-related learning. Today more than 65% of all the people at Johnsonville are involved in some type of formal education.

The end state we all now envision for Johnsonville is a company that never stops learning. One part of learning is the acquisition of facts and knowledge—about accounting, machine maintenance, marketing, even about sky diving and Italian cooking. But the most important kind of learning teaches us to question our own actions and behavior in order to better understand the ways we perform, work, and live.

Helping human beings fulfill their potential is of course a moral responsibility, but it's also good business. Life is aspiration. Learning, striving people are happy people and good workers. They have initiative and imagination, and the companies they work for are rarely caught napping.

Learning is change, and I keep learning and relearning that change is and needs to be continuous. For example, our system and structural changes were reciprocal. The first led to the second, which then in turn led to new versions of the first.

Initially, I had hoped the journey would be as neat and orderly as it now appears on paper. Fortunately—since original mistakes are an important part of learning—it wasn't. There were lots of obstacles and challenges, much backsliding, and myriad false starts and wrong decisions.

For example, team leaders chosen by their team members were supposed to function as communication links, leaving the traditional management functions of planning and scheduling to the group itself. No sooner had the team leaders been appointed, however, than they began to function as supervisors. In other words, they immediately fell into the familiar roles they had always seen. We had neglected to give them and the plant managers adequate training in the new team model. The structure changed, but mind-sets didn't. It was harder to alter people's expectations than I had realized.

Influencing Expectations

I discovered that change occurs in fits and starts, and that while I could plan individual changes and events, I couldn't plan the whole process. I also learned that expectations have a way of becoming reality, so I tried to use every available means—semantic, symbolic, and behavioral—to send messages that would shape expectations to Johnsonville's advantage.

For example, we wanted to break down the traditional pictures in people's minds of what managers do and how subordinates and employees behave, so we changed the words we used. We dropped the words employee and subordinate. Instead we called everyone a "member" of the organization, and managers became "coordinators" or "coaches."

Our promotion system had always sent a powerful message: to move up the ladder you need to become a manager and solve problems for your people. But this was now the wrong message. I wanted coordinators who could build problem-solving capacities in others rather than solve their problems for them. I recast the job requirements for the people whose work I directly coordinated (formerly known as "my management team"), and they, in turn, did the same for the people whose work they coordinated. I took every opportunity to stress the need for coaching skills, and I continually de-emphasized technical experience. Whenever someone became a coordinator, I made sure word got around that the promotion was for demonstrated abilities as a teacher, coach, and facilitator.

This new promotion standard sent a new message: to get ahead at Johnsonville, you need a talent for cultivating and encouraging problem solvers and responsibility takers.

I discovered that people watched my every action to see if it supported or undermined our vision. They wanted to see if I practiced what I preached. From the outset I did simple things to demonstrate my sincerity. I made a sign for my desk that said THE QUESTION IS THE ANSWER, and when people came to me with questions, I asked myself if they were questions I should answer. Invariably, they weren't. Invariably, people were asking me to make decisions for them. Instead of giving answers, I turned the tables and asked the questions myself, trying to make them repossess their own problems. Owning problems was an important part of the end state I'd envisioned. I wasn't about to let people give theirs to me.

I also discovered that in meetings people waited to hear my opinion before offering their own. In the beginning, I insisted they say what they thought, unaware that I showed my own preferences in subtle ways—my tone of voice, the questions I asked—which, nevertheless, anyone could read and interpret expertly. When I realized what was happening, I began to stay silent to avoid giving any clue to where I stood. The result was that people flatly refused to commit themselves to any decision at all. Some of those meetings would have gone on for days if I hadn't forced people to speak out before they'd read my mind.

In the end, I began scheduling myself out of many meetings, forcing others to make their decisions without me. I also stopped collecting data about production problems. I learned that if I had information about daily shortages and yields, I began to ask questions that put me firmly back in possession of the problems.

Eventually, I came to understand that everything I did and said had a symbolic as well as a literal meaning. I had to anticipate the potential impact of every word and act, ask myself again and again if what I was about to do or say would reinforce the vision or undermine it, bring us closer to Point B or circle us back to Point A, encourage people to own their own problems or palm them off on me. My job, as I had come to see it, was to put myself out of a job.

Watershed

By mid-1985, we had all come a long way. Johnsonville members had started wanting and expecting responsibility for their own performance, and they usually did a good job. Return on assets was up significantly, as were margins and quality. But on the whole, the process of change had been a journey without any major mileposts or station stops.

Then Palmer Sausage (not its real name) came along and gave us our watershed—a golden opportunity and a significant threat to our existence.

Palmer is a much larger sausage company that had contracted with us for private-label products during a strike in the early 1980s. Our quality was so high that they kept us on as a supplier after the strike ended. Now Palmer had decided to consolidate several facilities and offered to let us take over part of the production of a plant they were closing. It represented a huge increase in their order, and the additional business was very tempting: it could be very profitable, and it would justify the cost of a new and more efficient plant of our own. The upside was extremely attractive—if we could handle it.

That was what worried me. To handle an expanded Palmer contract, we'd have to hire and train a large group of people quickly and teach our present people new skills, keep quality high on both the Palmer products and our own, work six and seven days a week for more than a year until our new plant was ready, and run the risk if Palmer cancelled—which it could do on 30-days' notice—of saddling ourselves with big layoffs and new capacity we no longer had a market for. Maybe it wasn't a bet-the-company decision, but it was as close as I'd like to come.

Before 1982, I would have met for days with my senior team to discuss all these issues, and we would probably have turned down the opportunity in the face of such an overwhelming downside. But by 1985, it was clear to me that the executive group was the wrong group to make this decision. The executives would not be responsible for successfully implementing such a move. The only way we could do Palmer successfully was if everyone at Johnsonville was committed to making it work, so everyone had to decide.

Until that moment, my senior team had always made the strategic decisions. We took advice from people in the operating departments, but the senior staff and I had dealt with the ultimate problems and responsibilities. We needed to move to a new level. This was a problem all of our people had to own.

My senior managers and I called a meeting of the entire plant, presented the problem, and posed three questions. What will it take to make it work? Is it possible to reduce the downside? Do we want to do it?

We asked the teams in each area to discuss these questions among themselves and develop a list of pros and cons. Since the group as a whole was too large to work together effectively, each team chose one member to report its findings to a plantwide representative body to develop a plantwide answer.

The small groups met almost immediately, and within days their representatives met. The discussion moved back and forth several times between the representative body and the smaller groups.

To make it work, the members decided we'd have to operate seven days a week, hire and train people to take new shifts, and increase efficiency to get more from current capacity. They also thought about the downside risk. The biggest danger was that we'd lose the added business after making all the investments and sacrifices needed to handle it. They figured the only way to

---

Ralph Stayer's Guide to Improving Performance

Getting better performance from any group or individual, yourself included, means a permanent change in the way you think and run your business. Change of this kind is not a single transaction but a journey, and the journey has a specific starting point and a clear destination.

The journey is based on six observations about human behavior that I didn't fully grasp when I started, though I'd have made faster progress and fewer mistakes if I had.

1. People want to be great. If they aren't, it's because management won't let them be.

2. Performance begins with each individual's expectations. Influence what people expect and you influence how people perform.

3. Expectations are driven partly by goals, vision, symbols, semantics, and partly by the context in which people work, that is, by such things as compensation systems, production practices, and decision-making structures.

4. The actions of managers shape expectations.

5. Learning is a process, not a goal. Each new insight creates a new layer of potential insights.

6. The organization's results reflect me and my performance. If I want to change the results, I have to change myself first. This is particularly true for me, the owner and CEO, but it is equally true for every employee.

So to make the changes that will lead to great performance, I recommend focusing on goals, expectations, contexts, actions, and learning. Lee Thayer, a humanities professor at the University of Wisconsin, has another way of saying pretty much the same thing. He argues that since performance is the key to organizational success, management's job is to establish the conditions under which superb performance serves both the company's and the individual's best interests.

CEOs need to focus first on changing themselves before they try to change the rest of the company. The process resembles an archaeological dig, or at least it did for me. As I uncovered and solved one problem, I almost invariably exposed another, deeper problem. As I gained one insight and mastered one situation, another situation arose that required new insight and more learning. As I approached one goal, a new, more important, but more distant goal always began to take shape.

reduce that downside potential was to achieve quality standards so high that we would actually improve the already first-rate Palmer product and, at the same time, maintain standards on our own products to make sure Johnsonville brands didn't fall by the wayside.

Two weeks later, the company decided almost unanimously to take the business. It was one of the proudest moments of my life. Left to our traditional executive decision making, we would have turned Palmer down. The Johnsonville people, believing in themselves, rose to the challenge. They really did want to be great.

The results surpassed our best projections. Learning took place faster than anticipated. Quality rose in our own product line as well as for Palmer. The new plant came on line in 1987. Palmer has come back to us several times since to increase the size of its orders even further.

Success—The Greatest Enemy

The pace of change increased after Palmer. Now that all of Johnsonville's people expected and wanted some degree of responsibility for strategic decisions, we had to redefine Point A, our current situation. The new level of involvement also led us to a more ambitious view of what we could ultimately achieve—Point B, our vision and destination.

We made additional changes in our career-tracking system. In our early enthusiasm, we had played down the technical aspects of our business, encouraging everyone to become a coordinator, even those who were far better suited to technical specialties. We also had some excellent salespeople who became coordinators because they saw it as the only path to advancement, though their talents and interests lay much more in selling than in coaching. When they became coordinators, we lost in three ways: we lost good salespeople, we created poor coordinators, and we lost sales from other good salespeople because they worked for these poor coordinators.

A career team recommended that Johnsonville set up dual career tracks—one for specialists and one for coordinators—that would enable both to earn recognition, status, and compensation on the basis of performance alone. The team, not the senior coordinators, agreed to own and fix the compensation problem.

Everyone at Johnsonville discovered they could do considerably better and earn considerably more than they had imagined. Since they had little trouble meeting the accelerated production goals that they themselves had set, members raised the minimum acceptable performance criteria and began routinely to expect more of themselves and others.

Right now, teams of Johnsonville members are meeting to discuss next year's capital budget, new product ideas, today's production schedule, and yesterday's quality, cost, and yield. More important, these same teams are redesigning their systems and structures to manage their continuing journey toward Point B, which, along with Point A, they are also continually redefining. Most important of all, their general level of commitment is now as high or higher than my own.

In fact, our greatest enemy now is our success. Our sales, margins, quality, and productivity far exceed anything we could have imagined in 1980. We've been studied and written about, and we've spent a lot of time answering questions and giving advice. We've basked in the limelight, telling other people how we did it. All the time we kept telling ourselves, "We can't let this go to our heads." But of course it had already gone to our heads. We had begun to talk and brag about the past instead of about what we wanted for the future. Once we saw what we were doing, we managed to stop and, in the process, learn a lesson about the hazards of self-congratulation.

When I began this process of change ten years ago, I looked forward to the time when it would all be over and I could get back to my real job. But I've learned that change is the real job of every effective business leader because change is about the present and the future, not about the past. There is no end to change. This story is only an interim report.

Yet another thing I've learned is that the cause of excitement at Johnsonville Sausage is not change itself but the process used in producing change. Learning and responsibility are invigorating, and aspirations make our hearts beat. For the last five years, my own aspiration has been to eliminate *my* job by creating such a crowd of self-starting, problem-solving, responsibility-grabbing, independent thinkers that Johnsonville would run itself.

Two years ago, I hired a new chief operating officer and told him he should lead the company and think of me as his paid consultant. Earlier this year, he invited me to a management retreat, and I enjoyed myself. Other people owned the problems that had once been mine. My whole job was to generate productive conversations about Johnsonville's goals and to communicate its vision.

On the second evening of the retreat, I was given a message from my COO. There was a special session the next morning, he wrote, and added, "I want you there at 8:15." Instinctively, it made me mad. Johnsonville was my company; I built it; I fixed it; he owed me his job. Who the hell did he think he was giving me orders like a hired consultant?

Then, of course, I laughed. It's not always easy giving up control, even when it's what you've worked toward for ten years. He wanted me there at 8:15? Well, good for him. I'd be there.

43

Principle-Centered Leadership

Stephen R. Covey

From study and observation and from my own strivings, I have isolated eight discernible characteristics of people who are principle-centered leaders. These traits not only characterize effective leaders, they also serve as signs of progress for all of us. I will briefly discuss each in turn.

They Are Continually Learning

Principle-centered people are constantly educated by their experiences. They read, they seek training, they take classes, they listen to others, they learn through both their ears and their eyes. They are curious, always asking questions. They continually expand their competence, their ability to do things. They develop new skills, new interests. They discover that the more they know, the more they realize they don't know; that as their circle of knowledge grows, so does its outside edge of ignorance. Most of this learning and growth energy is self-initiated and feeds upon itself.

You will develop your abilities faster by learning to make and keep promises or commitments. Start by making a small promise to yourself; continue fulfilling that promise until you have a sense that you have a little more control over yourself. Now take the next level of challenge. Make yourself a promise and keep it until you have established control at that level. Now move to the next level; make the promise, keep it. As you do this, your sense of personal worth will increase; your sense of self-mastery will grow, as will your confidence that you can master the next level.

Be serious and intent in the whole process, however, because if you make this commitment to yourself and then break it, your self-esteem will be weakened and your capacity to make and keep another promise will be decreased.

They Are Service-Oriented

Those striving to be principle-centered see life as a mission, not as a career. Their nurturing sources have armed and prepared them for service. In effect, every morning they "yoke up" and put on the harness of service, thinking of others.

See yourself each morning yoking up, putting on the harness of service in your various stewardships. See yourself taking the straps and connecting them around your shoulders as you prepare to do the work assigned to you that day. See yourself allowing someone else to adjust the yoke or harness. See yourself yoked up to another person at your side—a co-worker or spouse—and learning to pull together with that person.

I emphasize this principle of service or yoking up because I have come to believe that effort to become principle-centered without a load to carry simply will not succeed. We may attempt to do it as a kind of intellectual or moral exercise, but if we don't have a sense of responsibility, of service, of contribution, something we need to pull or push, it becomes a futile endeavor.

They Radiate Positive Energy

The countenances of principle-centered people are cheerful, pleasant, happy. Their attitude is optimistic, positive, upbeat. Their spirit is enthusiastic, hopeful, believing.

This positive energy is like an energy field or an aura that surrounds them and that similarly charges or changes weaker, negative energy fields around them. They also attract and magnify smaller positive energy fields. When they come into contact with strong, negative energy sources, they tend either to neutralize or to sidestep this negative energy. Sometimes they will simply leave it, walking away from its poisonous orbit. Wisdom gives them a sense of how strong it is and a sense of humor and of timing in dealing with it.

Be aware of the effect of your own energy and understand how you radiate and direct it. And in the middle of confusion or contention or negative energy, strive to be a peacemaker, a harmonizer, to undo or reverse destructive energy. You will discover what a self-fulfilling prophecy positive energy is when combined with the next characteristic.

They Believe in People

Principle-centered people don't overreact to negative behaviors, criticism, or human weaknesses. They don't feel built up when they discover the weaknesses of others. They are not naive; they are aware of weakness. But they realize that behavior and potential are two different things. They believe in the unseen potential of all people. They feel grateful for their blessings and feel naturally to compassionately forgive and forget the offenses of others. They don't carry grudges. They refuse to label other people, to stereotype, categorize, and prejudge. Rather, they see the oak tree in the acorn and understand the process of helping the acorn become a great oak.

Once my wife and I felt uneasy about the labels we and others had attached to one of our sons, even though these labels were justified by his behavior. By visualizing his potential, we gradually came to see him differently. When we believed in the unseen potential, the old labels vanished naturally, and we stopped trying to change him overnight. We simply knew that his talent and potential would come in its own time. And it did, to the astonishment, frankly, of others, including other family members. We were not surprised because we knew who he was.

Truly, believing is seeing. We must, therefore, seek to believe in the unseen potential. This creates a *climate for growth and opportunity*. Self-centered people believe that the key lies in them, in their techniques, in doing "their thing" to others. This works only temporarily. If you believe it's "in" them, not "in" you, you relax, accept, affirm, and let it happen. Either way it is a self-fulfilling prophecy.

They Lead Balanced Lives

They read the best literature and magazines and keep up with current affairs and events. They are active socially, having many friends and a few confidants. They are active intellectually, having many interests. They read, watch, observe, and learn. Within the limits of age and health, they are active physically. They have a lot of fun. They enjoy themselves. They have a healthy sense of humor, particularly laughing at themselves and not at others' expense. You can sense they have a healthy regard for and honesty about themselves.

They can feel their own worth, which is manifest by their courage and integrity and by the absence of a need to brag, to drop names, to borrow strength from possessions or credentials or titles or past achievements. They are open in their communication, simple, direct, non-manipulative. They also have a sense of what is appropriate, and they would sooner err on the side of understatement than on the side of exaggeration.

They are not extremists—they do not make everything all or nothing. They do not divide everything into two parts, seeing everything as good or bad, as either/or. They think in terms of continuums, priorities, hierarchies. They have the power to discriminate, to sense the similarities and differences in each situation. This does not mean they see everything in terms of situational ethics. They fully recognize absolutes and courageously condemn the bad and champion the good.

Their actions and attitudes are proportionate to the situation—balanced, temperate, moderate, wise. For instance, they're not workaholics, religious zealots, political fanatics, diet crashers, food bingers, pleasure addicts, or fasting martyrs. They're not slavishly chained to their plans and schedules. They don't condemn themselves for every foolish mistake or social blunder. They don't brood about yesterday or daydream about tomorrow. They live sensibly in the present, carefully plan the future, and flexibly adapt to changing circumstances. Their self-honesty is revealed by their sense of humor, their willingness to admit and then forget mistakes, and to cheerfully do the things ahead that lie within their power.

They have no need to manipulate through either intimidating anger or self-pitying martyrdom. They are genuinely happy for others' successes and do not feel in any sense that these take anything from them. They take both praise and blame proportionately without head trips or overreactions. They see success on the far side of failure. The only real failure for them is the experience not learned from.

They See Life as a Sense of Adventure

Principle-centered people savor life. Because their security comes from within instead of from without, they have no need to categorize and stereotype everything and everybody in life to give them a sense of certainty and predictability. They see old faces freshly, old scenes as if for the first time. They are like courageous explorers going on an expedition into uncharted territories; they are really not sure what is going to happen, but they are confident it will be exciting and growth producing and that they will discover new territory and make new contributions. Their security lies in their initiative, resourcefulness, creativity, willpower, courage, stamina, and native intelligence rather than in the safety, protection, and abundance of their home camps, of their comfort zones.

They rediscover people each time they meet them. They are interested in them. They ask questions and get involved. They are completely present when they listen. They learn from them. They don't label them from past successes or failures. They see no one bigger than life. They are not overawed by top government figures or celebrities. They resist becoming any person's disciple. They are basically unflappable and capable of adapting virtually to anything that comes along. One of their fixed principles is flexibility. They truly lead the abundant life.

They Are Synergistic

Synergy is the state in which the whole is more than the sum of the parts. Principle-centered people are synergistic. They are change catalysts. They improve almost any situation they get into. They work as smart as they work hard. They are amazingly productive, but in new and creative ways.

In team endeavors they build on their strengths and strive to complement their weaknesses with the strengths of others. Delegation for results is easy and natural to them, since they believe in others' strengths and capacities. And since they are not threatened by the fact that others are better in some ways, they feel no need to supervise them closely.

When principle-centered people negotiate and communicate with others in seemingly adversarial situations they learn to separate the people from the problem. They focus on the other person's interests and concerns rather than fight over positions. Gradually others discover their sincerity and become part of a creative problem-solving process. Together they arrive at synergistic solutions, which are usually much better than any of the original proposals, as opposed to compromise solutions wherein both parties give and take a little.

They Exercise for Self-Renewal

Finally, they regularly exercise the four dimensions of the human personality: physical, mental, emotional, and spiritual.

They participate in some kind of balanced, moderate, regular program of aerobic exercise, meaning cardiovascular exercise—using the large leg muscles and working the heart and lungs. This provides endurance—improving the capacity of the body and brain to use oxygen—along with many other physical and mental benefits. Also valuable are stretching exercises for flexibility and resistance exercises for strength and muscle tone.

They exercise their minds through reading, creative problem-solving, writing, and visualizing. Emotionally they make an effort to be patient, to listen to others with genuine empathy, to show unconditional love, and to accept responsibility for their own lives and decisions and reactions. Spiritually they focus on prayer, scripture study, meditation, and fasting.

I'm convinced that if a person will spend one hour a day on these basic exercises, he or she will improve the quality, productivity, and satisfaction of every other hour of the day, including the depth and restfulness of sleep.

No other single hour of your day will return as much as the hour you invest in sharpening the saw—that is, in exercising these four dimensions of the human personality. If you will do this daily, you will soon experience the impact for good on your life.

Some of these activities may be done in the normal course of the day; others will need to be scheduled into the day. They take some time, but in the long run they save us a great deal of time. We must never get too busy sawing to take time to sharpen the saw, never too busy driving to take time to get gas.

I find that if I do this hour of exercise early in the morning, it is like a private victory and just about guarantees public victories throughout the day. But if I take the course of least resistance and neglect all or part of this program, I forfeit that private victory and find myself uprooted by public pressures and stresses through the day.

These principles of "self-renewal" will gradually produce a strong and healthy character with a powerfully disciplined, service-focused will.

44

Leader Behaviors and Organizational Performance

Marcus Buckingham and Curt Coffman

Over the last twenty-five years the Gallup Organization has interviewed more than a million employees. We have asked each of them hundreds of different questions, on every conceivable aspect of the workplace. We had to sift through the data to identify those questions that were truly measuring the core of a strong workplace. . . .

We employed factor analysis, concurrent validity studies, and follow-up interviews. Our goal was to identify those special questions where the most engaged employees, those who were loyal *and* productive, answered positively and everyone else, including average and below average performers, answered neutrally or negatively. Questions that we thought were a shoo-in like those dealing with pay and benefits fell by the wayside. At the same time, innocuous little questions, such as those dealing with expectations, forced their way to the forefront.

When the dust finally settled, we made a discovery: measuring the strength of a workplace can be simplified to twelve questions. These twelve questions don't capture everything you may want to know about your workplace, but they do capture the *most* information and the most *important* information. They measure the core elements needed to attract, focus, and keep the most talented employees. These questions, which we labeled the "Q12 metric" deal with elements of the work environment, including the immediate manager. Many of the questions deal directly with leader behaviors noted in all important writing about leadership such as expectations, development, recognition, participation, caring, and providing opportunities. . . .

Excerpt reprinted with permission of the Gallup Organization from *First, Break all the Rules* by Marcus Buckingham and Curt Coffman, 1999, pp. 27–29; 32–34. New York: Simon and Schuster. Copyright © 1999 by the Gallup Organization.

521

It is important to note that no questions dealing with pay, benefits, senior management, or organizational structure found their way into the Q12 metric.* This doesn't mean they are unimportant. It simply means they are equally important to every employee, good, bad, and mediocre. Yes, if you are paying 20 percent below the market average, you may have difficulty attracting people. But bringing your pay and benefits package up to market levels, while a sensible first step, will not take you very far. These kinds of issues are like tickets to the ballpark—they can get you into the game, but they can't help you win.

Testing the Q12 Metric[†]

Throughout the spring and summer of 1998 Gallup launched a massive investigation where we asked twenty-four different companies, representing a cross section of twelve distinct industries, to provide us with scores measuring four different kinds of business outcomes: productivity, profitability, employee retention, and customer satisfaction. In the end, we secured performance data from 2500 business units.

We then interviewed the employees who worked in these branches, restaurants, hotels, factories, and departments, asking them to respond to each of the twelve questions on a scale of 1 to 5, "1" being strongly disagree, "5" being strongly agree. One hundred five thousand employees took part. . . .

First, we saw that those employees who responded more positively to the twelve questions worked in business units with higher levels of productivity, profit, employee retention, and customer satisfaction. This demonstrated the link between employee opinions and business unit performance, across many different companies.

Second, a meta-analysis revealed that employees rated the questions differently depending on which business unit they worked for rather than which company. This meant that, for the most part, these twelve opinions were being formed by the employees' immediate manager rather than by the policies or procedure of the overall company. We discovered that the manager, not pay, benefits, perks, or a charismatic corporate leader, was the critical element in building a strong workplace.

The Links between Employee Opinions and Unit Performance

- Every one of the twelve questions was linked to at least one of the four business outcomes: productivity, profitability, retention, and customer satisfaction.

---

* Editor's Note: Although restrictions prevent us from listing the Q12 metric, readers will not be surprised when they identify them. The important point here is that included in the 12 are common leadership behaviors and they are shown to be related to hard performance measures in a very large study. Interested readers may want to consult the 2005 edition of the book for updated findings.

† Readers should consult *First, Break All the Rules* for details on the research methodology and the Q12 scale items.

- The most consistent links (ten of the twelve questions) were to the "productivity" measure. People have always believed there is a direct link between employees' opinions and work group productivity.

- Eight of the twelve questions showed a link to the "profitability" measure.

- Strangely enough, only five of the twelve questions revealed a link to employee retention. Most people would instinctively agree with the generalization "engaged employees will stay longer." But our research suggests that the link between employee opinion and employee retention is subtler and more specific than this kind of generalization has allowed. Even more than the rest, these five questions are most directly influenced by the employee's immediate manager. What does this tell us? It tells us that people leave managers, not companies. So much money has been thrown at the challenge of keeping good people—in the form of better pay, better perks, and better training—when, in the end, turnover is mostly a manager issue.

- Of the twelve, the most powerful questions are six with a combination of the *strongest* links to the *most* business outcomes. In general, these questions deal with expectations, autonomy, and reinforcement. . . .

Managers Trump Companies

Once each year a study is published entitled "The Hundred Best Companies to Work For." The criteria for selection are such factors as does the company have an on-site day care facility? How much vacation does the company provide? Does the company offer any kind of profit sharing? Is the company committed to employee training? Companies are examined, and the list of the top one hundred is compiled.

Our research suggests that these criteria miss the mark. It's not that these employee-focused initiatives are unimportant. It's just that the immediate manager is *more* important. She defines and pervades your work environment. If she is clear in the area of expectations and treats you well, then you can forgive the company for its lack of a profit-sharing program. But if your relationship with your manager is fractured, then no amount of company perks will persuade you to stay and perform. It is better to work for a great manager in an old-fashioned company than for a terrible manager in a company offering an enlightened, employee-focused culture.

The message of this study is clear. The behavior of the immediate manager is significantly related to profitability, turnover, productivity, and customer satisfaction.

45

Managing Oneself

Peter F. Drucker

History's great achievers—a Napoleón, a da Vinci, a Mozart—have always managed themselves. That, in large measure, is what makes them great achievers. But they are rare exceptions, so unusual both in their talents and their accomplishments as to be considered outside the boundaries of ordinary human existence. Now, most of us, even those of us with modest endowments, will have to learn to manage ourselves. We will have to learn to develop ourselves. We will have to place ourselves where we can make the greatest contribution. And we will have to stay mentally alert and engaged during a 50-year working life, which means knowing how and when to change the work we do.

What Are My Strengths?

Most people think they know what they are good at. They are usually wrong. More often, people know what they are not good at and even then more people are wrong than right. And yet, a person can perform only from strength. One cannot build performance on weaknesses, let alone on something one cannot do at all.

Throughout history, people had little need to know their strengths. A person was born into a position and a line of work: The peasant's son would also be a peasant; the artisan's daughter, an artisan's wife; and so on. But now people have choices. We need to know our strengths in order to know where we belong.

The only way to discover your strengths is through feedback analysis. Whenever you make a key decision or take a key action, write down what you expect will happen. Nine or 12 months later, compare the actual results with your expectations. I have been practicing this method for 15 to 20 years now, and every time I do it, I am surprised. The feedback analysis showed me, for instance—and to my great surprise—that I have an intuitive understanding of technical people, whether they are engineers or accountants or market researchers. It also showed me that I don't really resonate with generalists.

Feedback analysis is by no means new. It was invented sometime in the fourteenth century by an otherwise totally obscure German theologian and picked up quite independently, some 150 years later, by John Calvin and Ignatius of Loyola, each of whom incorporated it into the practice of his followers. In fact, the steadfast focus on performance and results that this habit produces explains why the institutions these two men founded, the Calvinist church and the Jesuit order, came to dominate Europe within 30 years.

Practiced consistently, this simple method will show you within a fairly short period of time, maybe two or three years, where your strengths lie—and this is the most important thing to know. The method will show you what you are doing or failing to do that deprives you of the full benefits of your strengths. It will show you where you are not particularly competent. And finally, it will show you where you have no strengths and cannot perform.

Several implications for action follow from feedback analysis. First and foremost, concentrate on your strengths. Put yourself where your strengths can produce results.

Second, work on improving your strengths. Analysis will rapidly show where you need to improve skills or acquire new ones. It will also show the gaps in your knowledge—and those can usually be filled. Mathematicians are born, but everyone can learn trigonometry.

Third, discover where your intellectual arrogance is causing disabling ignorance and overcome it. Far too many people—especially people with great expertise in one area—are contemptuous of knowledge in other areas or believe that being bright is a substitute for knowledge. First-rate engineers, for instance, tend to take pride in not knowing anything about people. Human beings, they believe, are much too disorderly for the good engineering mind. Human resources professionals, by contrast, often pride themselves on their ignorance of elementary accounting or of quantitative methods altogether. But taking pride in such ignorance is self-defeating. Go to work on acquiring the skills and knowledge you need to fully realize your strengths.

It is equally essential to remedy your bad habits—the things you do or fail to do that inhibit your effectiveness and performance. Such habits will quickly show up in the feedback. For example, a planner may find that his beautiful plans fail because he does not follow through on them. Like so many brilliant people, he believes that ideas move mountains. But bulldozers move mountains; ideas show where the bulldozers should go to work. This planner will have to learn that the work does not stop when the plan is completed. He must find people to carry out the plan and explain it to them. He must adapt and change it as he puts it into action. And finally, he must decide when to stop pushing the plan.

At the same time, feedback will also reveal when the problem is a lack of manners. Manners are the lubricating oil of an organization. It is a law of nature that two moving bodies in contact with each other create friction. This is as true for human beings as it is for inanimate objects. Manners—simple things like saying "please" and "thank you" and knowing a person's name or asking after her family—enable two people to work together whether they like each other or not. Bright people, especially bright young people, often do not understand this. If analysis shows that someone's brilliant work fails again and again as soon as cooperation from others is required, it probably indicates a lack of courtesy—that is, a lack of manners.

Comparing your expectations with your results also indicates what not to do. We all have a vast number of areas in which we have no talent or skill and little chance of becoming even mediocre. In those areas a person—and especially a knowledge worker—should not take on work, jobs, and assignments. One should waste as little effort as possible on improving areas of low competence. It takes far more energy and work to improve from incompetence to mediocrity than it takes to improve from first-rate performance to excellence. And yet most people—especially most teachers and most organizations—concentrate on making incompetent performers into mediocre ones. Energy, resources, and time should go instead to making a competent person into a star performer.

How Do I Perform?

Amazingly few people know how they get things done. Indeed, most of us do not even know that different people work and perform differently. Too many people work in ways that are not their ways, and that almost guarantees nonperformance. For knowledge workers, How do I perform? may be an even more important question than What are my strengths?

Like one's strengths, how one performs is unique. It is a matter of personality. Whether personality be a matter of nature or nurture, it surely is formed long before a person goes to work. And *how a* person performs is a given, just as *what* a person is good at or not good at is a given. A person's way of performing can be slightly modified, but it is unlikely to be completely changed—and certainly not easily. Just as people achieve results by doing what they are good at, they also achieve results by working in ways that they best perform. A few common personality traits usually determine how a person performs.

Am I a Reader or a Listener?

The first thing to know is whether you are a reader or a listener. Far too few people even know that there are readers and listeners and that people are rarely both. Even fewer know which of the two they themselves are. But some examples will show how damaging such ignorance can be.

When Dwight Eisenhower was Supreme Commander of the Allied forces in Europe, he was the darling of the press. His press conferences were famous for their style—General Eisenhower showed total command of whatever question he was asked, and he was able to describe a situation and explain a policy in two or three beautifully polished and elegant sentences. Ten years later, the same journalists who had been his admirers held President Eisenhower in open contempt. He never addressed the questions, they complained, but rambled on endlessly about something else. And they constantly ridiculed him for butchering the King's English in incoherent and ungrammatical answers.

Eisenhower apparently did not know that he was a reader, not a listener. When he was Supreme Commander in Europe, his aides made sure that every question from the press was presented in writing at least half an hour before a conference was to begin. And then Eisenhower was in total command. When he became president, he succeeded two listeners, Franklin D. Roosevelt and Harry Truman. Both men knew themselves to be listeners and both enjoyed free-for-all press conferences. Eisenhower may have felt that he had to do what his two predecessors had done. As a result, he never even heard the questions journalists asked. And Eisenhower is not even an extreme case of a nonlistener.

A few years later, Lyndon Johnson destroyed his presidency, in large measure, by not knowing that he was a listener. His predecessor, John Kennedy, was a reader who had assembled a brilliant group of writers as his assistants, making sure that they wrote to him before discussing their memos in person. Johnson kept these people on his staff—and they kept on writing. He never, apparently, understood one word of what they wrote. Yet as a senator, Johnson had been superb; for parliamentarians have to be, above all, listeners.

Few listeners can be made, or can make themselves, into competent readers—and vice versa. The listener who tries to be a reader will, therefore, suffer the fate of Lyndon Johnson, whereas the reader who tries to be a listener will suffer the fate of Dwight Eisenhower. They will not perform or achieve.

How Do I Learn?

The second thing to know about how one performs is to know how one learns. Many first-class writers—Winston Churchill is but one example—do poorly in school. They tend to remember their schooling as pure torture. Yet few of their classmates remember it the same way. They may not have enjoyed the school very much, but the worst they suffered was boredom. The explanation is that writers do not, as a rule, learn by listening and reading. They learn by writing. Because schools do not allow them to learn this way, they get poor grades.

Schools everywhere are organized on the assumption that there is only one right way to learn and that it is the same way for everybody. But to be forced to learn the way a school teaches is sheer hell for students who learn differently. Indeed, there are probably half a dozen different ways to learn.

There are people, like Churchill, who learn by writing. Some people learn by taking copious notes. Beethoven, for example, left behind an enormous number of sketchbooks, yet he said he never actually looked at them when he composed. Asked why he kept them, he is reported to have replied, "If I don't write it down immediately, I forget it right away. If I put it into a sketchbook, I never forget it and I never have to look it up again." Some people learn by doing. Others learn by hearing themselves talk.

A chief executive I know who converted a small and mediocre family business into the leading company in its industry was one of those people who learn by talking. He was in the habit of calling his entire senior staff into his office once a week and then talking at them for two or three hours. He would raise policy issues and argue three different positions on each one. He rarely asked his associates for comments or questions; he simply needed an audience to hear himself talk. That's how he learned. And although he is a fairly extreme case, learning through talking is by no means an unusual method. Successful trial lawyers learn the same way, as do many medical diagnosticians (and so do I).

Of all the important pieces of self-knowledge, understanding how you learn is the easiest to acquire. When I ask people, "How do you learn?" most of them know the answer. But when I ask, "Do you act on this knowledge?" few answer yes. And yet, acting on this knowledge is the key to performance; or rather, *not* acting on this knowledge condemns one to nonperformance.

Am I a reader or a listener? and How do I learn? are the first questions to ask. But they are by no means the only ones. To manage yourself effectively, you also have to ask, Do I work well with people, or am I a loner? And if you do work well with people, you then must ask, In what relationship?

Some people work best as subordinates. General George Patton, the great American military hero of World War II, is a prime example. Patton was America's top troop commander. Yet when he was proposed for an independent command, General George Marshall, the U.S. chief of staff—and probably the most successful picker of men in U.S. history—said, "Patton is the best subordinate the American army has ever produced, but he would be the worst commander."

Some people work best as team members. Others work best alone. Some are exceptionally talented as coaches and mentors; others are simply incompetent as mentors.

Another crucial question is, Do I produce results as a decision maker or as an adviser? A great many people perform best as advisers but cannot take the burden and pressure of making the decision. A good many other people, by contrast, need an adviser to force themselves to think; then they can make decisions and act on them with speed, self-confidence, and courage.

This is a reason, by the way, that the number two person in an organization often fails when promoted to the number one position. The top spot requires a decision maker. Strong decision makers often put somebody they trust into the number two spot as their adviser—and in that position the person is outstanding. But in the number one spot, the same person fails. He or she knows what the decision should be but cannot accept the responsibility of actually making it.

Other important questions to ask include, Do I perform well under stress, or do I need a highly structured and predictable environment? Do I work best in a big organization or a small one? Few people work well in all kinds of environments. Again and again, I have seen people who were very successful in large organizations flounder miserably when they moved into smaller ones. And the reverse is equally true.

The conclusion bears repeating: Do not try to change yourself—you are unlikely to succeed. But work hard to improve the way you perform. And try not to take on work you cannot perform or will only perform poorly.

What Are My Values?

To be able to manage yourself, you finally have to ask, What are my values? This is not a question of ethics. With respect to ethics, the rules are the same for everybody, and the test is a simple one. I call it the "mirror test."

In the early years of this century, the most highly respected diplomat of all the great powers was the German ambassador in London. He was clearly destined for great things—to become his country's foreign minister, at least, if not its federal chancellor. Yet in 1906 he abruptly resigned rather than preside over a dinner given by the diplomatic corps for Edward VII. The king was a notorious womanizer and made it clear what kind of dinner he wanted. The ambassador is reported to have said, "I refuse to see a pimp in the mirror in the morning when I shave."

That is the mirror test. Ethics requires that you ask yourself, What kind of person do I want to see in the mirror in the morning? What is ethical behavior in one kind of organization or situation is ethical behavior in another. But ethics is only part of a value system—especially of an organization's value system.

To work in an organization whose value system is unacceptable or incompatible with one's own condemns a person both to frustration and to nonperformance.

Consider the experience of a highly successful human resources executive whose company was acquired by a bigger organization. After the acquisition, she was promoted to do the kind of work she did best, which included selecting people for important positions. The executive deeply believed that a company should hire people for such positions from the outside only after exhausting all the inside possibilities. But her new company believed in first looking outside "to bring in fresh blood." There is something to be said for both approaches—in my experience, the proper one is to do some of both. They are, however, fundamentally incompatible—not as policies but as values. They bespeak different views of the relationship between organizations and people; different views of the responsibility of an organization to its people and their development; and different views of a person's most important contribution to an enterprise. After several years of frustration, the executive quit—at considerable financial loss. Her values and the values of the organization simply were not compatible.

Similarly, whether a pharmaceutical company tries to obtain results by making constant, small improvements or by achieving occasional, highly expensive, and risky "breakthroughs" is not primarily an economic question.

The results of either strategy may be pretty much the same. At bottom, there is a conflict between a value system that sees the company's contribution in terms of helping physicians do better what they already do and a value system that is oriented toward making scientific discoveries.

Whether a business should be run for short-term results or with a focus on the long term is likewise a question of values. Financial analysts believe that businesses can be run for both simultaneously. Successful businesspeople know better. To be sure, every company has to produce short-term results. But in any conflict between short-term results and long-term growth, each company will determine its own priority. This is not primarily a disagreement about economics. It is fundamentally a value conflict regarding the function of a business and the responsibility of management.

Value conflicts are not limited to business organizations. One of the fastest-growing pastoral churches in the United States measures success by the number of new parishioners. Its leadership believes that what matters is how many newcomers join the congregation. The Good Lord will then minister to their spiritual needs or at least to the needs of a sufficient percentage. Another pastoral, evangelical church believes that what matters is people's spiritual growth. The church eases out newcomers who join but do not enter into its spiritual life.

Again, this is not a matter of numbers. At first glance, it appears that the second church grows more slowly. But it retains a far larger proportion of newcomers than the first one does. Its growth, in other words, is more solid. This is also not a theological problem, or only secondarily so. It is a problem about values. In a public debate, one pastor argued, "Unless you first come to church, you will never find the gate to the Kingdom of Heaven."

"No," answered the other. "Until you first look for the gate to the Kingdom of Heaven, you don't belong in church."

Organizations, like people, have values. To be effective in an organization, a person's values must be compatible with the organization's values. They do not need to be the same, but they must be close enough to coexist. Otherwise, the person will not only be frustrated but also will not produce results.

A person's strengths and the way that person performs rarely conflict; the two are complementary. But there is sometimes a conflict between a person's values and his or her strengths. What one does well—even very well and successfully—may not fit with one's value system. In that case, the work may not appear to be worth devoting one's life to (or even a substantial portion thereof).

If I may, allow me to interject a personal note. Many years ago, I too had to decide between my values and what I was doing successfully. I was doing very well as a young investment banker in London in the mid-1930s, and the work clearly fit my strengths. Yet I did not see myself making a contribution as an asset manager. People, I realized, were what I valued, and I saw no point in being the richest man in the cemetery. I had no money and no other job prospects. Despite the continuing Depression, I quit—and it was the right thing to do. Values, in other words, are and should be the ultimate test.

Where Do I Belong?

A small number of people know very early where they belong. Mathematicians, musicians, and cooks, for instance, are usually mathematicians, musicians, and cooks by the time they are four or five years old. Physicians usually decide on their careers in their teens, if not earlier. But most people, especially highly gifted people, do not really know where they belong until they are well past their mid-twenties. By that time, however, they should know the answers to the three questions: What are my strengths? How do I perform? and, What are my values? And then they can and should decide where they belong.

Or rather, they should be able to decide where they do *not* belong. The person who has learned that he or she does not perform well in a big organization should have learned to say no to a position in one. The person who has learned that he or she is not a decision maker should have learned to say no to a decision-making assignment. A General Patton (who probably never learned this himself) should have learned to say no to an independent command.

Equally important, knowing the answer to these questions enables a person to say to an opportunity, an offer, or an assignment, "Yes, I will do that. But this is the way I should be doing it. This is the way it should be structured. This is the way the relationships should be. These are the kind of results you should expect from me, and in this time frame, because this is who I am."

Successful careers are not planned. They develop when people are prepared for opportunities because they know their strengths, their method of work, and their values. Knowing where one belongs can transform an ordinary person—hardworking and competent but otherwise mediocre—into an outstanding performer.

What Should I Contribute?

Throughout history, the great majority of people never had to ask the question, What should I contribute? They were told what to contribute, and their tasks were dictated either by the work itself—as it was for the peasant or artisan—or by a master or a mistress—as it was for domestic servants. And until very recently, it was taken for granted that most people were subordinates who did as they were told. Even in the 1950s and 1960s, the new knowledge workers (the so-called organization men) looked to their company's personnel department to plan their careers.

Then in the late 1960s, no one wanted to be told what to do any longer. Young men and women began to ask, What do *I* want to do? And what they heard was that the way to contribute was to "do your own thing." But this solution was as wrong as the organization men's had been. Very few of the people who believed that doing one's own thing would lead to contribution, self-fulfillment, and success achieved any of the three.

But still, there is no return to the old answer of doing what you are told or assigned to do. Knowledge workers in particular have to learn to ask a question that has not been asked before: What *should* my contribution be? To answer it, they must address three distinct elements: What does the situation require? Given my strengths, my way of performing, and my values, how can I make the greatest contribution to what needs to be done? And finally, What results have to be achieved to make a difference?

Consider the experience of a newly appointed hospital administrator. The hospital was big and prestigious, but it had been coasting on its reputation for 30 years. The new administrator decided that his contribution should be to establish a standard of excellence in one important area within two years. He chose to focus on the emergency room, which was big, visible, and sloppy. He decided that every patient who came into the ER had to be seen by a qualified nurse within 60 seconds. Within 12 months, the hospital's emergency room had become a model for all hospitals in the United States, and within another two years, the whole hospital had been transformed.

As this example suggests, it is rarely possible—or even particularly fruitful—to look too far ahead. A plan can usually cover no more than 18 months and still be reasonably clear and specific. So the question in most cases should be, Where and how can I achieve results that will make a difference within the next year and a half? The answer must balance several things. First, the results should be hard to achieve—they should require "stretching," to use the current buzzword. But also, they should be within reach. To aim at results that cannot be achieved—or that can be only under the most unlikely circumstances—is not being ambitious; it is being foolish. Second, the results should be meaningful. They should make a difference. Finally, results should be visible and, if at all possible, measurable. From this will come a course of action: what to do, where and how to start, and what goals and deadlines to set.

Responsibility for Relationships

Very few people work by themselves and achieve results by themselves— a few great artists, a few great scientists, a few great athletes. Most people work with others and are effective with other people. That is true whether they are members of an organization or independently employed. Managing yourself requires taking responsibility for relationships. This has two parts.

The first is to accept the fact that other people are as much individuals as you yourself are. They perversely insist on behaving like human beings. This means that they too have their strengths; they too have their ways of getting things done; they too have their values. To be effective, therefore, you have to know the strengths, the performance modes, and the values of your coworkers.

That sounds obvious, but few people pay attention to it. Typical is the person who was trained to write reports in his or her first assignment because that boss was a reader. Even if the next boss is a listener, the person goes on writing reports that, invariably, produce no results. Invariably the boss will think the employee is stupid, incompetent, and lazy, and he or she will fail.

But that could have been avoided if the employee had only looked at the new boss and analyzed how *this* boss performs.

Bosses are neither a title on the organization chart nor a "function." They are individuals and are entitled to do their work in the way they do it best. It is incumbent on the people who work with them to observe them, to find out how they work, and to adapt themselves to what makes their bosses most effective. This, in fact, is the secret of "managing" the boss.

The same holds true for all your coworkers. Each works his or her way, not your way. And each is entitled to work in his or her way. What matters is whether they perform and what their values are. As for how they perform— each is likely to do it differently. The first secret of effectiveness is to understand the people you work with and depend on so that you can make use of their strengths, their ways of working, and their values. Working relationships are as much based on the people as they are on the work.

The second part of relationship responsibility is taking responsibility for communication. Whenever I, or any other consultant, start to work with an organization, the first thing I hear about are all the personality conflicts. Most of these arise from the fact that people do not know what other people are doing and how they do their work, or what contribution the other people are concentrating on and what results they expect. And the reason they do not know is that they have not asked and therefore have not been told.

This failure to ask reflects human stupidity less than it reflects human history. Until recently, it was unnecessary to tell any of these things to anybody. In the medieval city, everyone in a district plied the same trade. In the countryside, everyone in a valley planted the same crop as soon as the frost was out of the ground. Even those *few* people who did things that were not "common" worked alone, so they did not have to tell anyone what they were doing.

Today the great majority of people work with others who have different tasks and responsibilities. The marketing vice president may have come out of sales and know everything about sales, but she knows nothing about the things she has never done—pricing, advertising, packaging, and the like. So the people who do these things must make sure that the marketing vice president understands what they are trying to do, why they are trying to do it, how they are going to do it, and what results to expect.

If the marketing vice president does not understand what these high-grade knowledge specialists are doing, it is primarily their fault, not hers. They have not educated her. Conversely, it is the marketing vice president's responsibility to make sure that all of her coworkers understand how she looks at marketing: what her goals are, how she works, and what she expects of herself and of each one of them.

Even people who understand the importance of taking responsibility for relationships often do not communicate sufficiently with their associates. They are afraid of being thought presumptuous or inquisitive or stupid. They are wrong. Whenever someone goes to his or her associates and says, "This is what I am good at. This is how I work. These are my values. This is the contribution I plan to concentrate on and the results I should be expected to deliver," the response is always, "This is most helpful. But why didn't you tell me earlier?"

And one gets the same reaction—without exception, in my experience—if one continues by asking, "And what do I need to know about your strengths, how you perform, your values, and your proposed contribution?" In fact, knowledge workers should request this of everyone with whom they work, whether as subordinate, superior, colleague, or team member. And again, whenever this is done, the reaction is always, "Thanks for asking me. But why didn't you ask me earlier?"

Organizations are no longer built on force but on trust. The existence of trust between people does not necessarily mean that they like one another. It means that they understand one another. Taking responsibility for relationships is therefore an absolute necessity. It is a duty. Whether one is a member of the organization, a consultant to it, a supplier, or a distributor, one owes that responsibility to all one's coworkers: those whose work one depends on as well as those who depend on one's own work.

The Second Half of Your Life

When work for most people meant manual labor, there was no need to worry about the second half of your life. You simply kept on doing what you had always done. And if you were lucky enough to survive 40 years of hard work in the mill or on the railroad, you were quite happy to spend the rest of your life doing nothing. Today, however, most work is knowledge work, and knowledge workers are not "finished" after 40 years on the job, they are merely bored.

We hear a great deal of talk about the midlife crisis of the executive. It is mostly boredom. At 45, most executives have reached the peak of their business careers, and they know it. After 20 years of doing very much the same kind of work, they are very good at their jobs. But they are not learning or contributing or deriving challenge and satisfaction from the job. And yet they are still likely to face another 20 if not 25 years of work. That is why managing oneself increasingly leads one to begin a second career.

There are three ways to develop a second career. The first is actually to start one. Often this takes nothing more than moving from one kind of organization to another: the divisional controller in a large corporation, for instance, becomes the controller of a medium-sized hospital. But there are also growing numbers of people who move into different lines of work altogether: the business executive or government official who enters the ministry at 45, for instance; or the midlevel manager who leaves corporate life after 20 years to attend law school and become a small-town attorney.

We will see many more second careers undertaken by people who have achieved modest success in their first jobs. Such people have substantial skills, and they know how to work. They need a community—the house is empty with the children gone—and they need income as well. But above all, they need challenge.

The second way to prepare for the second half of your life is to develop a parallel career. Many people who are very successful in their first careers stay in the work they have been doing, either on a full-time or part-time or consulting basis. But in addition, they create a parallel job, usually in a nonprofit organization, that takes another ten hours of work a week. They might take over the administration of their church, for instance, or the presidency of the local Girl Scouts council. They might run the battered women's shelter, work as a children's librarian for the local public library, sit on the school board, and so on.

Finally, there are the social entrepreneurs. These are usually people who have been very successful in their first careers. They love their work, but it no longer challenges them. In many cases they keep on doing what they have been doing all along but spend less and less of their time on it. They also start another activity, usually a nonprofit. My friend Bob Buford, for example, built a very successful television company that he still runs. But he has also founded and built a successful nonprofit organization that works with Protestant churches, and he is building another to teach social entrepreneurs how to manage their own nonprofit ventures while still running their original businesses.

People who manage the second half of their lives may always be a minority. The majority may "retire on the job" and count the years until their actual retirement. But it is this minority, the men and women who see a long working-life expectancy as an opportunity both for themselves and for society, who will become leaders and models.

There is one prerequisite for managing the second half of your life: You must begin long before you enter it. When it first became clear 30 years ago that working-life expectancies were lengthening very fast, many observers (including myself) believed that retired people would increasingly become volunteers for nonprofit institutions. That has not happened. If one does not begin to volunteer before one is 40 or so, one will not volunteer once past 60.

Similarly, all the social entrepreneurs I know began to work in their chosen second enterprise long before they reached their peak in their original business. Consider the example of a successful lawyer, the legal counsel to a large corporation, who has started a venture to establish model schools in his state. He began to do volunteer legal work for the schools when he was around 35. He was elected to the school board at age 40. At age 50, when he had amassed a fortune, he started his own enterprise to build and to run model schools. He is, however, still working nearly full-time as the lead counsel in the company he helped found as a young lawyer.

There is another reason to develop a second major interest, and to develop it early. No one can expect to live very long without experiencing a serious setback in his or her life or work. There is the competent engineer who is passed over for promotion at age 45. There is the competent college professor who realizes at age 42 that she will never get a professorship at a big university, even though she may be fully qualified for it. There are tragedies in one's family life: the breakup of one's marriage or the loss of a child. At such times, a second major interest—not just a hobby—may make all the difference. The engineer, for example, now knows that he has not been very successful in his job. But in his outside activity—as church treasurer, for example—he is a success. One's family may break up, but in that outside activity there is still a community.

In a society in which success has become so terribly important, having options will become increasingly vital. Historically, there was no such thing as "success." The overwhelming majority of people did not expect anything but to stay in their "proper station," as an old English prayer has it. The only mobility was downward mobility.

In a knowledge society, however, we expect everyone to be a success. This is clearly an impossibility. For a great many people, there is at best an absence of failure. Wherever there is success, there has to be failure. And then it is vitally important for the individual, and equally for the individual's family, to have an area in which he or she can contribute, make a difference, and be *somebody*. That means finding a second area—whether in a second career, a parallel career, or a social venture—that offers an opportunity for being a leader, for being respected, for being a success.

The challenges of managing oneself may seem obvious, if not elementary. And the answers may seem self-evident to the point of appearing naive. But managing oneself requires new and unprecedented things from the individual, and especially from the knowledge worker. In effect, managing oneself demands that each knowledge worker think and behave like a chief executive officer. Further, the shift from manual workers who do as they are told to knowledge workers who have to manage themselves profoundly challenges social structure. Every existing society, even the most individualistic one, takes two things for granted, if only subconsciously—that organizations outlive workers, and that most people stay put.

But today the opposite is true. Knowledge workers outlive organizations, and they are mobile. The need to manage oneself is therefore creating a revolution in human affairs.

46

Level 5 Leadership
The Triumph of Humility and Fierce Resolve

Jim Collins

In 1971, a seemingly ordinary man named Darwin E. Smith was named chief executive of Kimberly-Clark, a stodgy old paper company whose stock had fallen 36% behind the general market during the previous 20 years. Smith, the company's mild-mannered in-house lawyer, wasn't so sure the board had made the right choice—a feeling that was reinforced when a Kimberly-Clark director pulled him aside and reminded him that he lacked some of the qualifications for the position. But CEO he was, and CEO he remained for 20 years.

What a 20 years it was. In that period, Smith created a stunning transformation at Kimberly-Clark, turning it into the leading consumer paper products company in the world. Under his stewardship, the company beat its rivals Scott Paper and Procter & Gamble. And in doing so, Kimberly-Clark generated cumulative stock returns that were 4.1 times greater than those of the general market, outperforming venerable companies such as Hewlett-Packard, 3M, Coca-Cola, and General Electric.

Smith's turnaround of Kimberly-Clark is one the best examples in the twentieth century of a leader taking a company from merely good to truly great. And yet few people—even ardent students of business history—have heard of Darwin Smith. He probably would have liked it that way. Smith is a classic example of a Level 5 leader—an individual who blends extreme personal humility with intense professional will. According to our five-year research study, executives who possess this paradoxical combination of traits are catalysts for the statistically rare event of transforming a good company into a great one. (The research is described in the sidebar "One Question, Five Years, 11 Companies.")

One Question, Five Years, 11 Companies

The Level 5 discovery derives from a research project that began in 1996, when my research teams and I set out to answer one question: Can a good company become a great company and, if so, how? Most great companies grew up with superb parents—people like George Merck, David Packard, and Walt Disney—who instilled greatness early on. But what about the vast majority of companies that wake up part-way through life and realize that they're good but not great?

To answer that question, we looked for companies that had shifted from good performance to great performance—and sustained it. We identified comparison companies that had failed to make that sustained shift. We then studied the contrast between the two groups to discover common variables that distinguished those who made and sustained a shift from those who could have but didn't.

More precisely, we searched for a specific pattern: cumulative stock returns at or below the general stock market for 15 years, punctuated by a transition point, then cumulative returns at least three times the market over the next 15 years. (See the accompanying exhibit.) We used data from the University of Chicago Center for Research in Security Prices and adjusted for stock splits and all dividends reinvested. The shift had to be distinct from the industry; if the whole industry showed the same shift, we'd drop the company. We began with 1,435 companies that appeared on the *Fortune* 500 from 1965 to 1995; we found 11 good-to-great examples. That's not a sample; that's the total number that jumped all our hurdles and passed into the study.

Those that made the cut averaged cumulative stock returns 6.9 times the general stock market for the 15 years after the point of transition. To put that in perspective, General Electric under Jack Welch outperformed the general stock market by 2.8:1 during his tenure from 1986 to 2000. One dollar invested in a mutual fund of the good-to-great companies in 1965 grew to $470 by 2000 compared with $56 in the general stock market. These are remarkable numbers, made all the more so by the fact that they came from previously unremarkable companies.

For each good-to-great example, we selected the best direct comparison, based on similarity of business, size, age, customers, and performance leading up to the transition. We also constructed a set of six "unsustained" comparisons (companies that showed a short-lived shift but then fell off) to address the question of sustainability. To be conservative, we consistently picked comparison companies that, if anything, were in better shape than the good-to-great companies were in the years just before the transition.

With 22 research associates working in groups of four to six at a time from 1996 to 2000, our study involved a wide range of both qualitative and quantitative analyses. On the qualitative front, we collected nearly 6,000 articles, conducted 87 interviews with key executives, analyzed companies' internal strategy documents, and culled through analysts' reports. On the quantitative front, we ran financial metrics, examined executive compensation, compared patterns of management turnover, quantified company layoffs and divestitures, restructurings, and calculated the effect of acquisitions and divesti-

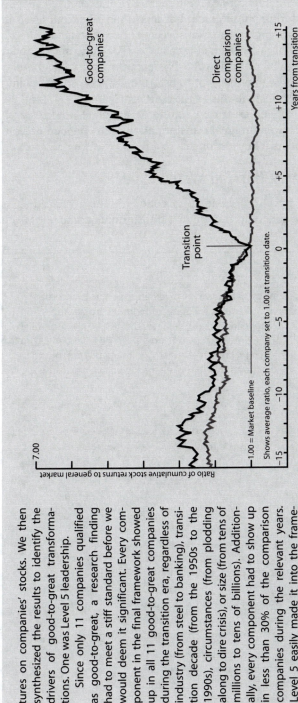

tures on companies' stocks. We then synthesized the results to identify the drivers of good-to-great transformations. One was Level 5 leadership.

Since only 11 companies qualified as good-to-great, a research finding had to meet a stiff standard before we would deem it significant. Every component in the final framework showed up in all 11 good-to-great companies during the transition era, regardless of industry (from steel to banking), transition decade (from the 1950s to the 1990s), circumstances (from plodding along to dire crisis), or size (from tens of millions to tens of billions). Additionally, every component had to show up in less than 30% of the comparison companies during the relevant years. Level 5 easily made it into the framework as one of the strongest, most consistent contrasts between the good-to-great and the comparison companies.

"Level 5" refers to the highest level in a hierarchy of executive capabilities that we identified during our research. Leaders at the other four levels in the hierarchy can produce high degrees of success but not enough to elevate companies from mediocrity to sustained excellence. (For more details about this concept, see the exhibit "The Level 5 Hierarchy.") And while Level 5 leadership is not the only requirement for transforming a good company into a great one—other factors include getting the right people on the bus (and the wrong people off the bus) and creating a culture of discipline—our research shows it to be essential. Good-to-great transformations don't happen without Level 5 leaders at the helm. They just don't.

Not What You Would Expect

Our discovery of Level 5 leadership is counterintuitive. Indeed, it is countercultural. People generally assume that transforming companies from

---

The Level 5 Hierarchy

The Level 5 leader sits on top of a hierarchy of capabilities and is, according to our research, a necessary requirement for transforming an organization from good to great. But what lies beneath? Four other layers, each one appropriate in its own right but none with the power of Level 5. Individuals do not need to proceed sequentially through each level of the hierarchy to reach the top, but to be a full-fledged Level 5 requires the capabilities of all the lower levels, plus the special characteristics of Level 5.

Level 5
Executive
Builds enduring greatness through a paradoxical
combination of personal humility plus professional will.

Level 4
Effective Leader
Catalyzes commitment to and vigorous pursuit of a clear and
compelling vision; stimulates the group to high performance standards.

Level 3
Competent Manager
Organizes people and resources toward the effective
and efficient pursuit of predetermined objectives.

Level 2
Contributing Team Member
Contributes to the achievement of group objectives;
works effectively with others in a group setting.

Level 1
Highly Capable Individual
Makes productive contributions through talent,
knowledge, skills, and good work habits.

good to great requires larger-than-life leaders—big personalities like Lee Iacocca, Al Dunlap, Jack Welch, and Stanley Gault, who make headlines and become celebrities.

Compared with those CEOs, Darwin Smith seems to have come from Mars. Shy, unpretentious, even awkward, Smith shunned attention. When a journalist asked him to describe his management style, Smith just stared back at the scribe from the other side of his thick black-rimmed glasses. He was dressed unfashionably, like a farm boy wearing his first J.C. Penney suit. Finally, after a long and uncomfortable silence, he said, "Eccentric." Needless to say, the *Wall Street Journal* did not publish a splashy feature on Darwin Smith.

But if you were to consider Smith soft or meek, you would be terribly mistaken. His lack of pretense was coupled with a fierce, even stoic, resolve toward life. Smith grew up on an Indiana farm and put himself through night school at Indiana University by working the day shift at International Harvester. One day, he lost a finger on the job. The story goes that he went to class that evening and returned to work the very next day. Eventually, this poor but determined Indiana farm boy earned admission to Harvard Law School.

He showed the same iron will when he was at the helm of Kimberly-Clark. Indeed, two months after Smith became CEO, doctors diagnosed him with nose and throat cancer and told him he had less than a year to live. He duly informed the board of his illness but said he had no plans to die anytime soon. Smith held to his demanding work schedule while commuting weekly from Wisconsin to Houston for radiation therapy. He lived 25 more years, 20 of them as CEO.

Smith's ferocious resolve was crucial to the rebuilding of Kimberly-Clark, especially when he made the most dramatic decision in the company's history: selling the mills.

To explain: Shortly after he took over, Smith and his team had concluded that the company's traditional core business—coated paper—was doomed to mediocrity. Its economics were bad and the competition weak. But, they reasoned, if Kimberly-Clark were thrust into the fire of the consumer paper products business, better economics and world-class competition like Procter & Gamble would force it to achieve greatness or perish.

And so, like the general who burned the boats upon landing on enemy soil, leaving his troops to succeed or die, Smith announced that Kimberly-Clark would sell its mills—even the namesake mill in Kimberly, Wisconsin. All proceeds would be thrown into the consumer business, with investments in brands like Huggies diapers and Kleenex tissues. The business media called the move stupid, and Wall Street analysts downgraded the stock. But Smith never wavered. Twenty-five years later, Kimberly-Clark owned Scott Paper and beat Procter & Gamble in six of eight product categories. In retirement, Smith reflected on his exceptional performance, saying simply, "I never stopped trying to become qualified for the job."

Not What We Expected, Either

We'll look in depth at Level 5 leadership, but first let's set an important *context* for our findings. We were not looking for Level 5 or anything like it. Our original question was, Can a good company become a great one and, if so, how? In fact, I gave the research teams explicit instructions to downplay the role of top executives in their analyses of this question so we wouldn't slip into the simplistic "credit the leader" or "blame the leader" thinking that is so common today.

But Level 5 found us. Over the course of the study, research teams kept saying, "We can't ignore the top executives even if we want to. There *is* something consistently unusual about them." I would push back, arguing, "The comparison companies also had leaders. So what's different here?" Back and forth the debate raged. Finally, as should always be the case, the data won. The executives at companies that went from good to great and sustained that performance for 15 years or more were all cut from the same cloth—one remarkably different from that which produced the executives at the comparison companies in our study. It didn't matter whether the company was in crisis or steady state, consumer or industrial, offering services or products. It didn't matter when the transition took place or how big the company. The successful organizations all had a Level 5 leader at the time of transition.

Furthermore, the absence of Level 5 leadership showed up consistently across the comparison companies. The point: Level 5 is an empirical finding, not an ideological one. And that's important to note, given how much the Level 5 finding contradicts not only conventional wisdom but much of management theory to date. (For more about our findings on good-to-great transformations, see the sidebar "Not by Level 5 Alone.")

Not by Level 5 Alone

Level 5 leadership is an essential factor for taking a company from good to great, but it's not the only one. Our research uncovered multiple factors that deliver companies to greatness. And it is the combined package—Level 5 plus these other drivers—that takes companies beyond unremarkable. There is a symbiotic relationship between Level 5 and the rest of our findings: Level 5 enables implementation of the other findings, and practicing the other findings may help you get to Level 5. We've already talked about who Level 5 leaders are; the rest of our findings describe what they do. Here is a brief look at some of the other key findings.

First Who

We expected that good-to-great leaders would start with the vision and strategy. Instead, they attended to people first, strategy second. They got the right people on the bus, moved the wrong people off, ushered the right people to the right seats—and then they figured out where to drive it.

Stockdale Paradox

This finding is named after Admiral James Stockdale, winner of the Medal of Honor, who survived seven years in a Vietcong POW camp by hanging on to two contradictory beliefs: His life couldn't be worse at the moment, and his life would someday be better than ever. Like Stockdale, people at the good-to-great companies in our research confronted the most brutal facts of their current reality, yet simultaneously maintained absolute faith that they would prevail in the end. And they held both disciplines—faith and facts—at the same time, all the time.

Buildup-Breakthrough Flywheel

Good-to-great transformations do not happen overnight or in one big leap. Rather, the process resembles relentlessly pushing a giant, heavy flywheel in one direction. At first, pushing it gets the flywheel to turn once. With consistent effort, it goes two turns, then five, then ten, building increasing momentum until—bang!—the wheel hits the breakthrough point, and the momentum really kicks in. Our comparison companies never sustained the kind of breakthrough momentum that the good-to-great companies did; instead, they lurched back and forth with radical change programs, reactionary moves, and restructurings.

The Hedgehog Concept

In a famous essay, philosopher and scholar Isaiah Berlin described two approaches to thought and life using a simple parable: The fox knows a little about many things, but the hedgehog knows only one big thing very well. The fox is complex; the hedgehog simple. And the hedgehog wins. Our research shows that breakthroughs require a simple, hedgehog-like understanding of three intersecting circles: what a company can be the best in the world at, how its economics work best, and what best ignites the passions of its people. Breakthroughs happen when you get the hedgehog concept and become systematic and consistent with it, eliminating virtually anything that does not fit in the three circles.

Technology Accelerators

The good-to-great companies had a paradoxical relationship with technology. On the one hand, they assiduously avoided jumping on new technology bandwagons. On the other, they were pioneers in the application of carefully selected technologies, making bold, farsighted investments in those that directly linked to their hedgehog concept. Like turbochargers, these technology accelerators create an explosion in flywheel momentum.

A Culture of Discipline

When you look across the good-to-great transformations, they consistently display three forms of discipline: disciplined people, disciplined thought, and disciplined action. When you have disciplined people, you don't need hierarchy. When you have disciplined thought, you don't need bureaucracy. When you have disciplined action, you don't need excessive controls. When you combine a culture of discipline with an ethic of entrepreneurship, you get the magical alchemy of great performance.

Humility + Will = Level 5

Level 5 leaders are a study in duality: modest and willful, shy and fearless. To grasp this concept, consider Abraham Lincoln, who never let his ego get in the way of his ambition to create an enduring great nation. Author Henry Adams called him "a quiet, peaceful, shy figure." But those who thought Lincoln's understated manner signaled weakness in the man found themselves terribly mistaken—to the scale of 250,000 Confederate and 360,000 Union lives, including Lincoln's own.

It might be a stretch to compare the 11 Level 5 CEOs in our research to Lincoln, but they did display the same kind of duality. Take Colman M. Mockler, CEO of Gillette from 1975 to 1991. Mockler, who faced down three takeover attempts, was a reserved, gracious man with a gentle, almost patrician manner. Despite epic battles with raiders—he took on Ronald Perelman twice and the former Coniston Partners once—he never lost his shy, courteous style. At the height of crisis, he maintained a calm business-as-usual demeanor, dispensing first with ongoing business before turning to the takeover.

And yet, those who mistook Mockler's outward modesty as a sign of inner weakness were beaten in the end. In one proxy battle, Mockler and other senior executives called thousands of investors, one by one, to win their votes. Mockler simply would not give in. He chose to fight for the future greatness of Gillette even though he could have pocketed millions by flipping his stock.

Consider the consequences had Mockler capitulated. If a share flipper had accepted the full 44% price premium offered by Perelman and then invested those shares in the general market for ten years, he still would have come out 64% behind a shareholder who stayed with Mockler and Gillette. If Mockler had given up the fight, it's likely that none of us would be shaving with Sensor, Lady Sensor, or the Mach III—and hundreds of millions of people would have a more painful battle with daily stubble.

Sadly, Mockler never had the chance to enjoy the full fruits of his efforts. In January 1991, Gillette received an advance copy of *Forbes*. The cover featured an artist's rendition of the publicity-shy Mockler standing on a mountaintop, holding a giant razor above his head in a triumphant pose. Walking back to his office just minutes after seeing this public acknowledgment of his 16 years of struggle, Mockler crumpled to the floor and died of a massive heart attack.

Even if Mockler had known he would die in office, he could not have changed his approach. His placid persona hid an inner intensity, a dedication to making anything he touched the best—not just because of what he would get but because he couldn't imagine doing it any other way. Mockler could not give up the company to those who would destroy it, any more than Lincoln would risk losing the chance to build an enduring great nation.

A Compelling Modesty

The Mockler story illustrates the modesty typical of Level 5 leaders. (For a summary of Level 5 traits, see the exhibit "The Yin and Yang of Level 5.") Indeed, throughout our interviews with such executives, we were struck by the way they talked about themselves—or rather, didn't talk about themselves. They'd go on and on about the company and the contributions of other executives, but they would instinctively deflect discussion about their own role. When pressed to talk about themselves, they'd say things like, "I hope I'm not sounding like a big shot," or "I don't think I can take much credit for what happened. *We* were blessed with marvelous people." One Level 5 leader even asserted, "There are a lot of people in this company who could do my job better than I do."

By contrast, consider the courtship of personal celebrity by the comparison CEOs. Scott Paper, the comparison company to Kimberly-Clark, hired Al Dunlap as CEO—a man who would tell anyone who would listen (and many who would have preferred not to) about his accomplishments. After 19 months atop Scott Paper, Dunlap said in *Business Week,* "The Scott story will go down in the annals of American business history as one of the most successful, quickest turnarounds ever. It makes other turnarounds pale by comparison." He personally accrued $100 million for 603 days of work at Scott Paper—about $165,000 per day—largely by slashing the workforce, halving the R&D budget, and putting the company on growth steroids in preparation for sale. After selling off the company and pocketing his quick millions, Dun-

---

The Yin and Yang of Level 5

Personal Humility

Demonstrates a compelling modesty, shunning public adulation; never boastful.

Acts with quiet, calm determination; relies principally on inspired standards, not inspiring charisma, to motivate.

Channels ambition into the company, not the self; sets up successors for even more greatness in the next generation.

Looks in the mirror, not out the window, to apportion responsibility for poor results, never blaming other people, external factors, or bad luck.

Professional Will

Creates superb results, a clear catalyst in the transition from good to great.

Demonstrates an unwavering resolve to do whatever must be done to produce the best long-term results, no matter how difficult.

Sets the standard of building an enduring great company; will settle for nothing less.

Looks out the window, not in the mirror, to apportion credit for the success of the company—to other people, external factors, and good luck.

lap wrote an autobiography in which he boastfully dubbed himself "Rambo in pinstripes." It's hard to imagine Darwin Smith thinking, "Hey, that Rambo character reminds me of me," let alone stating it publicly.

Granted, the Scott Paper story is one of the more dramatic in our study, but it's not an isolated case. In more than two-thirds of the comparison companies, we noted the presence of a gargantuan ego that contributed to the demise or continued mediocrity of the company. We found this pattern particularly strong in the unsustained comparison companies—the companies that would show a shift in performance under a talented yet egocentric Level 4 leader, only to decline in later years.

Lee Iacocca, for example, saved Chrysler from the brink of catastrophe, performing one of the most celebrated (and deservedly so) turnarounds in U.S. business history. The automaker's stock rose 2.9 times higher than the general market about halfway through his tenure. But then Iacocca diverted his attention to transforming himself. He appeared regularly on talk shows like the *Today Show* and *Larry King Live,* starred in more than 80 commercials, entertained the idea of running for president of the United States, and promoted his autobiography, which sold 7 million copies worldwide. Iacocca's personal stock soared, but Chrysler's stock fell 31% below the market in the second half of his tenure.

And once Iacocca had accumulated all the fame and perks, he found it difficult to leave center stage. He postponed his retirement so many times that Chrysler's insiders began to joke that Iacocca stood for "I Am Chairman of Chrysler Corporation Always." When he finally retired, he demanded that the board continue to provide a private jet and stock options. Later, he joined forces with noted takeover artist Kirk Kerkorian to launch a hostile bid for Chrysler. (It failed.) Iacocca did make one final brilliant decision: He picked a modest yet determined man—perhaps even a Level 5—as his successor. Bob Eaton rescued Chrysler from its second near-death crisis in a decade and set the foundation for a more enduring corporate transition.

An Unwavering Resolve

Besides extreme humility, Level 5 leaders also display tremendous professional will. When George Cain became CEO of Abbott Laboratories, it was a drowsy, family-controlled business sitting at the bottom quartile of the pharmaceutical industry, living off its cash cow, erythromycin. Cain was a typical Level 5 leader in his lack of pretense; he didn't have the kind of inspiring personality that would galvanize the company. But he had something much more powerful: inspired standards. He could not stand mediocrity in any form and was utterly intolerant of anyone who would accept the idea that good is good enough. For the next 14 years, he relentlessly imposed his will for greatness on Abbott Labs.

Among Cain's first tasks was to destroy one of the root causes of Abbott's middling performance: nepotism. By systematically rebuilding both the board and the executive team with the best people he could find, Cain made his statement. Family ties no longer mattered. If you couldn't become the best executive in the industry within your span of responsibility, you would lose your paycheck.

Such near-ruthless rebuilding might be expected from an outsider brought in to turn the company around, but Cain was an 18-year insider—and a part of the family, the son of a previous president. Holiday gatherings were probably tense for a few years in the Cain clan—"Sorry I had to fire you. Want another slice of turkey?"—but in the end, family members were pleased with the performance of their stock. Cain had set in motion a profitable growth machine. From its transition in 1974 to 2000, Abbott created shareholder returns that beat the market 4.5:1, outperforming industry superstars Merck and Pfizer by a factor of two.

Another good example of iron-willed Level 5 leadership comes from Charles R. "Cork" Walgreen III, who transformed dowdy Walgreen's into a company that outperformed the stock market 16:1 from its transition in 1975 to 2000. After years of dialogue and debate within his executive team about what to do with Walgreen's food-service operations, this CEO sensed the team had finally reached a watershed: The company's brightest future lay in convenient drugstores, not in food service. Dan Jorndt, who succeeded Walgreen in 1988, describes what happened next:

> Cork said at one of our planning committee meetings, "Okay, now I am going to draw the line in the sand. We are going to be out of the restaurant business completely in five years." At the time we had more than 500 restaurants. You could have heard a pin drop. He said, "I want to let everybody know the clock is ticking." Six months later we were at our next planning committee meeting and someone mentioned just in passing that we had only five years to be out of the restaurant business. Cork was not a real vociferous fellow. He sort of tapped on the table and said, "Listen, you now have four and a half years. I said you had five years six months ago. Now you've got four and a half years." Well, that next day things really clicked into gear for winding down our restaurant business. Cork never wavered. He never doubted. He never second-guessed.

Like Darwin Smith selling the mills at Kimberly-Clark, Cork Walgreen required stoic resolve to make his decisions. Food service was not the largest part of the business, although it did add substantial profits to the bottom line. The real problem was more emotional than financial. Walgreen's had, after all, invented the malted milk shake, and food service had been a long-standing family tradition dating back to Cork's grandfather. Not only that, some food-service outlets were even named after the CEO—for example, a restaurant chain named Corky's. But no matter; if Walgreen had to fly in the face of family tradition in order to refocus on the one arena in which Walgreen's could be the best in the world—convenient drugstores—and terminate everything else that would not produce great results, then Cork would do it. Quietly, doggedly, simply.

One final, yet compelling, note on our findings about Level 5: Because Level 5 leaders have ambition not for themselves but for their companies, they routinely select superb successors. Level 5 leaders want to see their companies become even more successful in the next generation and are comfortable with the idea that most people won't even know that the roots of that success trace back to them. As one Level 5 CEO said, "I want to look from my porch, see the company as one of the great companies in the world someday, and be able to say, 'I used to work there.'" By contrast, Level 4 leaders often fail to set up the company for enduring success. After all, what better testament to your own personal greatness than that the place falls apart after you leave?

In more than three-quarters of the comparison companies, we found executives who set up their successors for failure, chose weak successors, or both. Consider the case of Rubbermaid, which grew from obscurity to become one of *Fortune's* most admired companies—and then, just as quickly, disintegrated into such sorry shape that it had to be acquired by Newell.

The architect of this remarkable story was a charismatic and brilliant leader named Stanley C. Gault, whose name became synonymous in the late 1980s with Rubbermaid's success. Across the 312 articles collected by our research team about the company, Gault comes through as a hard-driving, egocentric executive. In one article, he responds to the accusation of being a tyrant with the statement, "Yes, but I'm a sincere tyrant." In another, drawn directly from his own comments on leading change, the word "I" appears 44 times, while the word "we" appears 16 times. Of course, Gault had every reason to be proud of his executive success: Rubbermaid generated 40 consecutive quarters of earnings growth under his leadership—an impressive performance, to be sure, and one that deserves respect.

But Gault did not leave behind a company that would be great without him. His chosen successor lasted a year on the job and the next in line faced a management team so shallow that he had to temporarily shoulder four jobs while scrambling to identify a new number-two executive. Gault's successors struggled not only with a management void but also with strategic voids that would eventually bring the company to its knees.

Of course, you might say—as one *Fortune* article did—that the fact that Rubbermaid fell apart after Gault left proves his greatness as a leader. Gault was a tremendous Level 4 leader, perhaps one of the best in the last 50 years. But he was not at Level 5, and that is one crucial reason why Rubbermaid went from good to great for a brief, shining moment and then just as quickly went from great to irrelevant.

The Window and the Mirror

As part of our research, we interviewed Alan L. Wurtzel, the Level 5 leader responsible for turning Circuit City from a ramshackle company on the edge of bankruptcy into one of America's most successful electronics retailers. In the 15 years after its transition date in 1982, Circuit City outperformed the market 18.5:1.

We asked Wurtzel to list the top five factors in his company's transformation, ranked by importance. His number one factor? Luck. "We were in a great industry, with the wind at our backs," he said. But wait a minute, we retorted, Silo—your comparison company—was in the same industry, with the same wind and bigger sails. The conversation went back and forth, with Wurtzel refusing to take much credit for the transition, preferring to attribute it largely to just being in the right place at the right time. Later, when we asked him to discuss the factors that would sustain a good-to-great transformation, he said, "The first thing that comes to mind is luck. I was lucky to find the right successor."

Luck. What an odd factor to talk about. Yet the Level 5 leaders we identified invoked it frequently. We asked an executive at steel company Nucor why it had such a remarkable track record for making good decisions. His response? "I guess we were just lucky." Joseph F. Cullman III, the Level 5 CEO of Philip Morris, flat out refused to take credit for his company's success, citing his good fortune to have great colleagues, successors, and predecessors. Even the book he wrote about his career—which he penned at the urging of his colleagues and which he never intended to distribute widely outside the company—had the unusual title *I'm a Lucky Guy*.

At first, we were puzzled by the Level 5 leaders' emphasis on good luck. After all, there is no evidence that the companies that had progressed from good to great were blessed with more good luck (or more bad luck, for that matter) than the comparison companies. But then we began to notice an interesting pattern in the executives at the comparison companies: They often blamed their situations on bad luck, bemoaning the difficulties of the environment they faced.

Compare Bethlehem Steel and Nucor, for example. Both steel companies operated with products that are hard to differentiate, and both faced a competitive challenge from cheap imported steel. Both companies paid significantly higher wages than most of their foreign competitors. And yet executives at the two companies held completely different views of the same environment.

Bethlehem Steel's CEO summed up the company's problems in 1983 by blaming the imports: "Our first, second, and third problems are imports." Meanwhile, Ken Iverson and his crew at Nucor saw the imports as a blessing: "Aren't we lucky; steel is heavy, and they have to ship it all the way across the ocean, giving us a huge advantage." Indeed, Iverson saw the first, second, and third problems facing the U.S. steel industry not in imports but in management. He even went so far as to speak out publicly against government protection against imports, telling a gathering of stunned steel executives in 1977 that the real problems facing the industry lay in the fact that management had failed to keep pace with technology.

The emphasis on luck turns out to be part of a broader pattern that we have come to call "the window and the mirror." Level 5 leaders, inherently humble, look out the window to apportion credit—even undue credit—to factors outside themselves. If they can't find a specific person or event to give credit to, they credit good luck. At the same time, they look in the mirror to assign responsibility, never citing bad luck or external factors when things go poorly. Conversely, the comparison executives frequently looked out the window for factors to blame but preened in the mirror to credit themselves when things went well.

The funny thing about the window-and-mirror concept is that it does not reflect reality. According to our research, the Level 5 leaders were responsible for their companies' transformations. But they would never admit that. We can't climb inside their heads and assess whether they deeply believed what they saw through the window and in the mirror. But it doesn't really matter, because they acted as if they believed it, and they acted with such consistency that it produced exceptional results.

Born or Bred?

Not long ago, I shared the Level 5 finding with a gathering of senior executives. A woman who had recently become chief executive of her company raised her hand. "I believe what you've told us about Level 5 leadership," she said, "but I'm disturbed because I know I'm not there yet, and maybe I never will be. Part of the reason I got this job is because of my strong ego. Are you telling me that I can't make my company great if I'm not Level 5?"

"Let me return to the data," I responded. "Of 1,435 companies that appeared on the *Fortune* 500 since 1965, only 11 made it into our study. In those 11, all of them had Level 5 leaders in key positions, including the CEO role, at the pivotal time of transition. Now, to reiterate, we're not saying that Level 5 is the only element required for the move from good to great, but it appears to be essential."

She sat there, quiet for a moment, and you could guess what many people in the room were thinking. Finally, she raised her hand again. "Can you learn to become Level 5?" I still do not know the answer to that question. Our research, frankly, did not delve into how Level 5 leaders come to be, nor did we attempt to explain or codify the nature of their emotional lives. We speculated on the unique psychology of Level 5 leaders. Were they "guilty" of displacement—shifting their own raw ambition onto something other than themselves? Were they sublimating their egos for dark and complex reasons rooted in childhood trauma? Who knows? And perhaps more important, do the psychological roots of Level 5 leadership matter any more than do the roots of charisma or intelligence? The question remains: Can Level 5 be developed?

My preliminary hypothesis is that there are two categories of people: those who don't have the Level 5 seed within them and those who do. The first category consists of people who could never in a million years bring themselves to subjugate their own needs to the greater ambition of something larger and more lasting than themselves. For those people, work will always be first and foremost about what they get—the fame, fortune, power, adulation, and so on. Work will never be about what they build, create, and contribute. The great irony is that the animus and personal ambition that often drives people to become a Level 4 leader stands at odds with the humility required to rise to Level 5.

When you combine that irony with the fact that boards of directors frequently operate under the false belief that a larger-than-life, egocentric leader is required to make a company great, you can quickly see why Level 5 leaders rarely appear at the top of our institutions. We keep putting people in positions of power who lack the seed to become a Level 5 leader, and that is one major reason why there are so few companies that make a sustained and verifiable shift from good to great.

The second category consists of people who could evolve to Level 5; the capability resides within them, perhaps buried or ignored or simply nascent. Under the right circumstances—with self-reflection, a mentor, loving parents, a significant life experience, or other factors—the seed can begin to develop. Some of the Level 5 leaders in our study had significant life experiences that might have sparked development of the seed. Darwin Smith fully blossomed as a Level 5 after his near-death experience with cancer. Joe Cullman was profoundly affected by his World War II experiences, particularly the last-minute change of orders that took him off a doomed ship on which he surely would have died; he considered the next 60-odd years a great gift. A strong religious belief or conversion might also nurture the seed. Colman Mockler, for example, converted to evangelical Christianity while getting his MBA at Harvard, and later, according to the book *Cutting Edge* by Gordon McKibben, he became a prime mover in a group of Boston business executives that met frequently over breakfast to discuss the carryover of religious values to corporate life.

We would love to be able to give you a list of steps for getting to Level 5 —other than contracting cancer, going through a religious conversion, or getting different parents—but we have no solid research data that would support a credible list. Our research exposed Level 5 as a key component inside the black box of what it takes to shift a company from good to great. Yet inside that black box is another—the inner development of a person to Level 5 leadership. We could speculate on what that inner box might hold, but it would mostly be just that: speculation.

In short, Level 5 is a very satisfying idea, a truthful idea, a powerful idea, and, to make the move from good to great, very likely an essential idea. But to provide "ten steps to Level 5 leadership" would trivialize the concept.

My best advice, based on the research, is to practice the other good-to-great disciplines that we discovered. Since we found a tight symbiotic relationship between each of the other findings and Level 5, we suspect that conscientiously trying to lead using the other disciplines can help you move in the right direction. There is no guarantee that doing so will turn executives into full-fledged Level 5 leaders, but it gives them a tangible place to begin, especially if they have the seed within.

We cannot say for sure what percentage of people have the seed within, nor how many of those can nurture it enough to become Level 5. Even those of us on the research team who identified Level 5 do not know whether we will succeed in evolving to its heights. And yet all of us who worked on the finding have been inspired by the idea of trying to move toward Level 5. Darwin Smith, Colman Mockler, Alan Wurtzel, and all the other Level 5 leaders we learned about have become role models for us. Whether or not we make it to Level 5, it is worth trying. For like all basic truths about what is best in human beings, when we catch a glimpse of that truth, we know that our own lives and all that we touch will be the better for making the effort to get there.

47

Leadership and Execution

Larry Bossidy and Ram Charan

What exactly does a leader who's in charge of execution do? How does he keep from being a micromanager, caught up in the details of running the business? There are seven essential behaviors that form the basis for the first building lock of execution: (1) know your people and your business, (2) insist on realism, (3) set clear goals and priorities, (4) follow through, (5) reward the doers, (6) expand people's capabilities, and (7) know yourself.

Know Your People and Your Business

Leaders have to *live* their businesses. In companies that don't execute, the leaders are usually out of touch with the day-to-day realities. They're getting lots of information delivered to them, but it's filtered—presented by direct reports with their own perceptions, limitations, and agendas, or gathered by staff people with their own perspectives. The leaders aren't where the action is. They aren't engaged with the business, so they don't know their organizations comprehensively, and their people don't really know them.

LARRY: Suppose a leader goes to a plant or business headquarters and speaks to the people there. He is sociable and courteous. He shows superficial interest in his subordinates' kids—how well they're doing in school, how they like the community, and so on. Or he chats about the World Series, the Super Bowl, or the local basketball team. He may ask some shallow questions about the business, such as "What's your level of revenue?" This leader is not engaged in his business.

When the visit is over, some of the managers may feel a sense of relief, because everything seemed to go so well and pleasantly. But the managers who are any good will be disappointed. They'll ask themselves, *What was the point?* They had prepared for tough questions—good people like to be quizzed, because they know more about the business than the leader. They'll feel frustrated and drained of energy. They didn't get a chance to make a good impression on the leader—and the leader certainly didn't make a good impression on them.

And of course, the leader hasn't learned anything. The next time he makes prognostications about the company, the press or the securities analysts may be awed, but the people in the business will know better. They'll ask each other, "How on earth could he say those things so confidently when he doesn't have a clue about what's happening down here." It's kind of like the American politicians who used to visit Vietnam, look around a bit, talk to the top brass in the military command, review some statistics, and then proclaim that the war was being won and they could see the light at the end of the tunnel. Right! . . .

Insist on Realism

Realism is the heart of execution, but many organizations are full of people who are trying to avoid or shade reality. Why? It makes life uncomfortable. People don't want to open Pandora's Box. They want to hide mistakes, or buy time to figure out a solution rather than admit they don't have an answer at the moment. They want to avoid confrontations. Nobody wants to be the messenger who gets shot or the troublemaker who challenges the authority of her superiors.

Sometimes the leaders are simply in denial. When we ask leaders to describe their organization's strengths and weaknesses, they generally state the strengths fairly well.

But they're not so good on identifying the weaknesses. And when we ask what they're going to *do* about the weaknesses, the answer is rarely clear or cohesive. They say, "We have to make our numbers." Well, of course you have to make your numbers; the question is *how* you are going to make your numbers.

Was it realistic for AT&T to acquire a bunch of cable businesses it didn't know how to run? The record shows it wasn't. Was it realistic for Richard Thomas to simultaneously launch two sweeping initiatives at Xerox without being able to install the critical leaders? Clearly not.

How do you make realism a priority? You start by being realistic yourself. Then you make sure realism is the goal of all dialogues in the organization. . . .

Set Clear Goals and Priorities

Leaders who execute focus on a very few clear priorities that everyone can grasp. Why just a few? First, anybody who thinks through the logic of a business will see that focusing on three or four priorities will produce the best results from the resources at hand. Second, people in contemporary organizations need a small number of clear priorities to execute well. In an old-fashioned hierarchical company, this wasn't so much of a problem—people generally knew what to do, because the orders came down through the chain of command. But when decision making is decentralized or highly fragmented, as in a matrix organization, people at many levels have to make end-less trade-offs. There's competition for resources, and ambiguity over decision rights and working relationships. Without carefully thought-out and clear pri-orities, people can get bogged down in warfare over who gets what and why.

A leader who says "I've got ten priorities" doesn't know what he's talk-ing about—he doesn't know himself what the most important things are. You've got to have these few, clearly realistic goals and priorities, which will influence the overall performance of the company. . . .

Follow Through

Clear, simple goals don't mean much if nobody takes them seriously. The failure to follow through is widespread in business, and a major cause of poor execution. How many meetings have you attended where people left without firm conclusions about who would do what and when? Everybody may have agreed the idea was good, but since nobody was named accountable for results, it doesn't get done. Other things come up that seem more important, or people decide it wasn't such a good idea after all. (Maybe they even felt that way during the meeting, but didn't speak up.)

For example, a high-tech company was hit hard by the recession of 2001, suffering a 20 percent decline in revenue. The CEO was reviewing the revised operating plan for one of his most important divisions. He congratulated the division president on how well he and his people had reduced its cost struc-ture, but noted that the business would still fall short of its target for return on investment. And he offered a possible solution. He'd recently learned about the importance of velocity, and suggested that the division could make real gains by working with its suppliers to increase inventory turnover. "What do you think you can do?" he asked the purchasing manager. The manager replied that with some engineering help, he thought he could make substan-tial improvements. "I'd need twenty engineers," the manager added.

The CEO turned to the engineering vice president and asked him if he would assign the engineers to the task. The vice president hemmed and hawed for half a minute. Then he said, in chilly tones, "Engineers don't want to work for purchasing." The CEO looked at the vice president for several moments. Finally he said: "I am *sure* you will transfer twenty engineers to purchasing on Monday." Then he walked toward the door, turned, and looked at the purchasing executive, and said: "I want you to set up a monthly videoconference with yourself, engineering, the CFO, and me and the manu-facturing manager to review the progress of this important effort."

What did the CEO do here? First he surfaced a conflict that stood in the way of achieving results. Second, by creating a follow-through mechanism, he ensured that everyone would indeed do what they were supposed to. This included the division president, who had sat passively on the sidelines until the CEO delivered his ultimatum. And the CEO's action sent a signal through the rest of the company that others, too, could expect follow-through actions.

Reward the Doers

If you want people to produce specific results, you reward them accordingly. This fact seems so obvious that it shouldn't need saying. Yet many corporations do such a poor job of linking rewards to performance that there's little correlation at all. They don't distinguish between those who achieve results and those who don't, either in base pay or in bonuses and stock options.

LARRY: When I see companies that don't execute, the chances are that they don't measure, don't reward, and don't promote people who know how to get things done. Salary increases in terms of percentage are too close between the top performers and those who are not. There's not enough differentiation in bonus, or in stock options, or in stock grants. Leaders need the confidence to explain to a direct report why he got a lower than expected reward.

A good leader ensures that the organization makes these distinctions and that they become a way of life, down throughout the organization. Otherwise people think they're involved in socialism. That isn't what you want when you strive for a culture of execution. You have to make it clear to everybody that rewards and respect are based on performance. . . .

Expand People's Capabilities through Coaching

As a leader, you've acquired a lot of knowledge and experience, even wisdom, along the way. One of the most important parts of your job is passing it on to the next generation of leaders. This is how you expand the capabilities of everyone else in your organization, individually and collectively. It's how you will get results today and leave a legacy that you can take pride in when you move on.

Coaching is the single most important part of expanding others' capabilities. You've surely heard the saying, "Give a man a fish, and you'll feed him for a day; teach a man how to fish, and you'll feed him for a lifetime." That's coaching. It's the difference between giving orders and teaching people how to get things done. Good leaders regard every encounter as an opportunity to coach.

RAM: The most effective way to coach is to observe a person in action and then provide specific useful feedback. The feedback should point out examples of behavior and performance that are good or that need to be changed.

When the leader discusses business and organizational issues in a group setting, everybody learns. Wrestling with challenging issues collectively, exploring pros and cons and alternatives, and deciding which ones make sense increases people's capabilities both individually and collectively—if it's done with honesty and trust. . . .

Know Yourself

Everyone pays lip service to the idea that leading an organization requires strength of character. In execution it's absolutely critical. Without what we call emotional fortitude, you can't be honest with yourself, deal honestly with business and organizational realities, or give people forthright assessments. You can't tolerate the diversity of viewpoints, mental architectures, and personal backgrounds that organizations need in their members in order to avoid becoming ingrown. If you can't do these things, you can't execute.

It takes emotional fortitude to be open to whatever information you need, whether it's what you like to hear or not. Emotional fortitude gives you the courage to accept points of view that are the opposite of yours and deal with conflict, and the confidence to encourage and accept challenges in group settings. It enables you to accept and deal with your own weaknesses, be firm with people who aren't performing, and to handle the ambiguity inherent in a fast-moving, complex organization. . . .

Emotional fortitude comes from self-discovery and self-mastery. It is the foundation of people skills. Good leaders learn their specific personal strengths and weaknesses, especially in dealing with other people, then build on the strengths and correct the weaknesses. They earn their leadership when the followers see their inner strength, inner confidence, and ability to help team members deliver results, while at the same time expanding their own capabilities. . . .

In our years of working and observing in organizations, we have pinpointed four core qualities that make up emotional fortitude:

Authenticity

A psychological term, *authenticity* means pretty much what you might guess: you're real, not a fake. Your outer person is the same as your inner person, not a mask you put on. Who you are is the same as what you do and say. Only authenticity builds trust, because sooner or later people spot the fakers.

Whatever leadership ethics you may preach, people will watch what you do. If you're cutting corners, the best will lose faith in you. The worst will follow in your footsteps. The rest will do what they must to survive in a muddy ethical environment. This becomes a pervasive barrier to getting things done.

Self-Awareness

Know thyself—it's advice as old as the hills, and it's the core of authenticity. When you know yourself, you are comfortable with your strengths and not crippled by your shortcomings. You know your behavioral blind sides and emotional blockages, and you have a modus operandi for dealing with them—you draw on the people around you. Self-awareness gives you the capacity to learn from your mistakes as well as your successes. It enables you to keep growing.

Nowhere is self-awareness more important than in an execution culture, which taps every part of the brain and emotional makeup. Few leaders have the intellectual fire-power to be good judges of people, good strategists, and good operating leaders, and at the same time talk to customers and do all the other things the job demands. But if you know where you're short, at least you can reinforce those areas and get some help for your business or unit. You put mechanisms in place to help you get it done. The person who doesn't even recognize where she is lacking never gets it done.

Self-Mastery

When you know yourself, you can master yourself. You can keep your ego in check, take responsibility for your behavior, adapt to change, embrace new ideas, and adhere to your standards of integrity and honesty under all conditions.

Self-mastery is the key to true self-confidence. We're talking about the kind that's authentic and positive, as opposed to the kinds that mask weakness or insecurity—the studied demeanor of confidence, or outright arrogance.

Self-confident people contribute the most to dialogues. Their inner security gives them a methodology for dealing with the unknown and for linking it to the actions that need to be taken. They know they don't know everything; they are actively curious, and encourage debate to bring up opposite views and set up the social ambience of learning from others. They can take risks, and relish hiring people who are smarter than themselves. So when they encounter a problem, they don't have to whine, cast blame, or feel like victims. They know they'll be able to fix it.

Humility

The more you can contain your ego, the more realistic you are about your problems. You learn how to listen and admit that you don't know all the answers. You exhibit the attitude that you can learn from anyone at any time. Your pride doesn't get in the way of gathering the information you need to achieve the best results. It doesn't keep you from sharing the credit that needs to be shared. Humility allows you to acknowledge your mistakes. Making mistakes is inevitable, but good leaders both admit and learn from them and over time create a decision-making process based on experience. . . .

How do you develop these qualities in yourself? There are, of course, books on the subject, some of them useful. Many companies, including GE and Citicorp, include self-assessment tools in their leadership development programs.

But the ultimate learning comes from paying attention to experience. As people reflect on their experiences, or as they get coached, blockages crumble and emotional strengths develop. Sometimes the ahas also come from watching others' behaviors; your observational capabilities make you realize that you too have a blockage that you need to correct. Either way, as you gain experience in self-assessment, your insights get converted into improvements that expand your personal capacity.

Such learning is not an intellectual exercise. It requires tenacity, persistence, and daily engagement. It requires reflection and modifying personal behavior. But my experience is that once an individual gets on this track, his or her capacity for growth is almost unlimited.

The behavior of a business's leaders is, ultimately, the behavior of the organization. As such, it's the foundation of the culture.

48

Crucibles of Leadership

Warren G. Bennis and Robert J. Thomas

As lifelong students of leadership, we are fascinated with the notion of what makes a leader. Why is it that certain people seem to naturally inspire confidence, loyalty, and hard work, while others (who may have just as much vision and smarts) stumble, again and again? It's a timeless question, and there's no simple answer. But we have come to believe it has something to do with the different ways that people deal with adversity. Indeed, our recent research has led us to conclude that one of the most reliable indicators and predictors of true leadership is an individual's ability to find meaning in negative events and to learn from even the most trying circumstances. Put another way, the skills required to conquer adversity and emerge stronger and more committed than ever are the same ones that make for extraordinary leaders.

Take Sidney Harman. Thirty-four years ago, the then-48-year-old businessman was holding down two executive positions. He was the chief executive of Harman Kardon (now Harman International), the audio components company he had cofounded, and he was serving as president of Friends World College, now Friends World Program, an experimental Quaker school on Long Island whose essential philosophy is that students, not their teachers, are responsible for their education. Juggling the two jobs, Harman was living what he calls a "bifurcated life," changing clothes in his car and eating lunch as he drove between Harman Kardon offices and plants and the Friends World campus. One day while at the college, he was told his company's factory in Bolivar, Tennessee, was having a crisis.

He immediately rushed to the Bolivar factory, a facility that was, as Harman now recalls, "raw, ugly, and, in many ways, demeaning." The problem, he found, had erupted in the polish and buff department, where a crew of a dozen workers, mostly African Americans, did the dull, hard work of polishing mirrors and other parts, often under unhealthy conditions. The men on the night shift were supposed to get a coffee break at 10 PM. When the buzzer that announced the workers' break went on the fritz, management arbitrarily decided to postpone the break for ten minutes, when another buzzer was scheduled to sound. But one worker, "an old black man with an almost biblical name, Noah B. Cross," had "an epiphany," as Harman describes it. "He said, literally, to his fellow workers, 'I don't work for no buzzer. The buzzer works for me. It's my job to tell me when it's ten o'clock. I got me a watch. I'm not waiting another ten minutes. I'm going on my coffee break.' And all 12 guys took their coffee break, and, of course, all hell broke loose."

The worker's principled rebellion—his refusal to be cowed by management's senseless rule—was, in turn, a revelation to Harman: "The technology is there to serve the men, not the reverse," he remembers realizing. "I suddenly had this awakening that everything I was doing at the college had appropriate applications in business." In the ensuing years, Harman revamped the factory and its workings, turning it into a kind of campus—offering classes on the premises, including piano lessons, and encouraging the workers to take most of the responsibility for running their workplace. Further, he created an environment where dissent was not only tolerated but also encouraged. The plant's lively independent newspaper, the *Bolivar Mirror,* gave workers a creative and emotional outlet—and they enthusiastically skewered Harman in its pages.

Harman had, unexpectedly, become a pioneer of participative management, a movement that continues to influence the shape of workplaces around the world. The concept wasn't a grand idea conceived in the CEO's office and imposed on the plant, Harman says. It grew organically out of his going down to Bolivar to, in his words, "put out this fire." Harman's transformation was, above all, a creative one. He had connected two seemingly unrelated ideas and created a radically different approach to management that recognized both the economic and humane benefits of a more collegial workplace. Harman went on to accomplish far more during his career. In addition to founding Harman International, he served as the deputy secretary of commerce under Jimmy Carter. But he always looked back on the incident in Bolivar as the formative event in his professional life, the moment he came into his own as a leader.

The details of Harman's story are unique, but their significance is not. In interviewing more than 40 top leaders in business and the public sector over the past three years, we were surprised to find that all of them—young and old—were able to point to intense, often traumatic, always unplanned experiences that had transformed them and had become the sources of their distinctive leadership abilities.

We came to call the experiences that shape leaders "crucibles," after the vessels medieval alchemists used in their attempts to turn base metals into gold. For the leaders we interviewed, the crucible experience was a trial and a test, a point of deep self-reflection that forced them to question who they were and what mattered to them. It required them to examine their values, question their assumptions, hone their judgment. And, invariably, they emerged from the crucible stronger and more sure of themselves and their purpose—changed in some fundamental way.

Leadership crucibles can take many forms. Some are violent, life-threatening events. Others are more prosaic episodes of self-doubt. But whatever the crucible's nature, the people we spoke with were able, like Harman, to create a narrative around it, a story of how they were challenged, met the challenge, and became better leaders. As we studied these stories, we found that they not only told us how individual leaders are shaped but also pointed to some characteristics that seem common to all leaders—characteristics that were formed, or at least exposed, in the crucible.

Learning from Difference

A crucible is, by definition, a transformative experience through which an individual comes to a new or an altered sense of identity. It is perhaps not surprising then that one of the most common types of crucibles we documented involves the experience of prejudice. Being a victim of prejudice is particularly traumatic because it forces an individual to confront a distorted picture of him- or herself, and it often unleashes profound feelings of anger, bewilderment, and even withdrawal. For all its trauma, however, the experience of prejudice is for some a clarifying event. Through it, they gain a clearer vision of who they are, the role they play, and their place in the world.

Consider, for example, Liz Altman, now a Motorola vice president, who was transformed by the year she spent at a Sony camcorder factory in rural Japan, where she faced both estrangement and sexism. It was, says Altman, "by far, the hardest thing I've ever done." The foreign culture—particularly its emphasis on groups over individuals—was both a shock and a challenge to a young American woman. It wasn't just that she felt lonely in an alien world. She had to face the daunting prospect of carving out a place for herself as the only woman engineer in a plant, and nation, where women usually serve as low-level assistants and clerks known as "office ladies."

Another woman who had come to Japan under similar circumstances had warned Altman that the only way to win the men's respect was to avoid becoming allied with the office ladies. But on her very first morning, when the bell rang for a coffee break, the men headed in one direction and the women in another—and the women saved her a place at their table, while the men ignored her. Instinct told Altman to ignore the warning rather than insult the women by rebuffing their invitation.

Over the next few days, she continued to join the women during breaks, a choice that gave her a comfortable haven from which to observe the unfamiliar office culture. But it didn't take her long to notice that some of the men spent the break at their desks reading magazines, and Altman determined that she could do the same on occasion. Finally, after paying close attention to the conversations around her, she learned that several of the men were interested in mountain biking. Because Altman wanted to buy a mountain bike, she approached them for advice. Thus, over time, she established herself as something of a free agent, sometimes sitting with the women and other times engaging with the men.

And as it happened, one of the women she'd sat with on her very first day, the department secretary, was married to one of the engineers. The secretary took it upon herself to include Altman in social gatherings, a turn of events that probably wouldn't have occurred if Altman had alienated her female coworkers on that first day. "Had I just gone to try to break in with [the men] and not had her as an ally, it would never have happened," she says.

Looking back, Altman believes the experience greatly helped her gain a clearer sense of her personal strengths and capabilities, preparing her for other difficult situations. Her tenure in Japan taught her to observe closely and to avoid jumping to conclusions based on cultural assumptions—invaluable skills in her current position at Motorola, where she leads efforts to smooth alliances with other corporate cultures, including those of Motorola's different regional operations.

Altman has come to believe that she wouldn't have been as able to do the Motorola job if she hadn't lived in a foreign country and experienced the dissonance of cultures: ". . . even if you're sitting in the same room, ostensibly agreeing . . . unless you understand the frame of reference, you're probably missing a bunch of what's going on." Altman also credits her crucible with building her confidence—she feels that she can cope with just about anything that comes her way.

People can feel the stigma of cultural differences much closer to home, as well. Muriel ("Mickie") Siebert, the first woman to own a seat on the New York Stock Exchange, found her crucible on the Wall Street of the 1950s and 1960s, an arena so sexist that she couldn't get a job as a stockbroker until she took her first name off her résumé and substituted a genderless initial. Other than the secretaries and the occasional analyst, women were few and far between. That she was Jewish was another strike against her at a time, she points out, when most of big business was "not nice" to either women or Jews. But Siebert wasn't broken or defeated. Instead, she emerged stronger, more focused, and more determined to change the status quo that excluded her.

When we interviewed Siebert, she described her way of addressing anti-Semitism—a technique that quieted the offensive comments of her peers without destroying the relationships she needed to do her job effectively. According to Siebert, at the time it was part of doing business to have a few drinks at lunch. She remembers, "Give somebody a couple of drinks, and they would talk about the Jews." She had a greeting card she used for those occasions that went like this:

> Roses are reddish,
> Violets are bluish,
> In case you don't know,
> I am Jewish.

Siebert would have the card hand-delivered to the person who had made the anti-Semitic remarks, and on the card she had written, "Enjoyed lunch." As she recounts, "They got that card in the afternoon, and I never had to take any of that nonsense again. And I never embarrassed anyone, either." It was because she was unable to get credit for the business she was bringing in at any of the large Wall Street firms that she bought a seat on the New York Stock Exchange and started working for herself.

In subsequent years, she went on to found Muriel Siebert & Company (now Siebert Financial Corporation) and has dedicated herself to helping other people avoid some of the difficulties she faced as a young professional. A prominent advocate for women in business and a leader in developing financial products directed at women, she's also devoted to educating children about financial opportunities and responsibility.

We didn't interview lawyer and presidential adviser Vernon Jordan for this article, but he, too, offers a powerful reminder of how prejudice can prove transformational rather than debilitating. In *Vernon Can Read! A Memoir* (Public Affairs, 2001), Jordan describes the vicious baiting he was subjected to as a young man. The man who treated him in this offensive way was his employer, Robert F. Maddox. Jordan served the racist former mayor of Atlanta at dinner, in a white jacket, with a napkin over his arm. He also functioned as Maddox's chauffeur. Whenever Maddox could, he would derisively announce, "Vernon can read!" as if the literacy of a young African American were a source of wonderment.

Geeks and Geezers

We didn't set out to learn about crucibles. Our research for this article and for our new book, *Geeks and Geezers,* was actually designed to uncover the ways that *era* influences a leader's motivation and aspirations. We interviewed 43 of today's top leaders in business and the public sector, limiting our subjects to people born in or before 1925, or in or after 1970. To our delight, we learned a lot about how age and era affect leadership style.

Our geeks and geezers (the affectionate shorthand we eventually used to describe the two groups) had very different ideas about paying your dues, work-life balance, the role of heroes, and more. But they also shared some striking similarities—among them a love of learning and strong sense of values. Most intriguing, though, both our geeks and our geezers told us again and again how certain experiences inspired them, shaped them, and, indeed, taught them to lead. And so, as the best research often does, our work turned out to be even more interesting than we thought it would be. We continued to explore the influences of era—our findings are described in our book—but at the same time we probed for stories of these crucible experiences. These are the stories we share with you here.

Subjected to this type of abuse, a lesser man might have allowed Maddox to destroy him. But in his memoir, Jordan gives his own interpretation of Maddox's sadistic heckling, a tale that empowered Jordan instead of embittering him. When he looked at Maddox through the rearview mirror, Jordan did not see a powerful member of Georgia's ruling class. He saw a desperate anachronism, a person who lashed out because he knew his time was up. As Jordan writes about Maddox,

> His half-mocking, half-serious comments about my education were the death rattle of his culture. When he saw that I was . . . crafting a life for myself that would make me a man in . . . ways he thought of as being a man, he was deeply unnerved.

Maddox's cruelty was the crucible that, consciously or not, Jordan imbued with redemptive meaning. Instead of lashing out or being paralyzed with hatred, Jordan saw the fall of the Old South and imagined his own future freed of the historical shackles of racism. His ability to organize meaning around a potential crisis turned it into the crucible around which his leadership was forged.

Prevailing over Darkness

Some crucible experiences illuminate a hidden and suppressed area of the soul. These are often among the harshest of crucibles, involving, for instance, episodes of illness or violence. In the case of Sidney Rittenberg, now 79, the crucible took the form of 16 years of unjust imprisonment, in solitary confinement, in Communist China. In 1949 Rittenberg was initially jailed, without explanation, by former friends in Chairman Mao Zedong's government and spent his first year in total darkness when he wasn't being interrogated. (Rittenberg later learned that his arrest came at the behest of Communist Party officials in Moscow, who had wrongly identified him as a CIA agent.) Thrown into jail, confined to a tiny, pitch-dark cell, Rittenberg did not rail or panic. Instead, within minutes, he remembered a stanza of verse, four lines recited to him when he was a small child:

> They drew a circle that shut me out,
> Heretic, rebel, a thing to flout.
> But love and I had the wit to win,
> We drew a circle that took them in!

That bit of verse (adapted from "Outwitted," a poem by Edwin Markham) was the key to Rittenberg's survival. "My God," he thought, "there's my strategy." He drew the prison guards into his circle, developing relationships that would help him adapt to his confinement. Fluent in Chinese, he persuaded the guards to deliver him books and, eventually, provide a candle so that he could read. He also decided, after his first year, to devote himself to improving his mind—making it more scientific, more pure, and more dedicated to socialism. He believed that if he raised his consciousness, his captors would understand him better. And when, over time, the years in the dark began to take an intellectual toll on him and he found his reason faltering, he could still summon fairy tales and childhood stories such as *The Little Engine That Could* and take comfort from their simple messages.

By contrast, many of Rittenberg's fellow prisoners either lashed out in anger or withdrew. "They tended to go up the wall. . . . They couldn't make it. And I think the reason was that they didn't understand . . . that happiness . . . is not a function of your circumstances; it's a function of your outlook on life."

Rittenberg's commitment to his ideals continued upon his release. His cell door opened suddenly in 1955, after his first six-year term in prison. He recounts, "Here was a representative of the central government telling me that I had been wronged, that the government was making a formal apology to me . . . and that they would do everything possible to make restitution." When his captors offered him money to start a new life in the United States or to travel in Europe, Rittenberg declined, choosing instead to stay in China and continue his work for the Communist Party.

And even after a second arrest, which put him into solitary confinement for ten years as retaliation for his support of open democracy during the Cultural Revolution, Rittenberg did not allow his spirit to be broken. Instead, he used his time in prison as an opportunity to question his belief system—in particular, his commitment to Marxism and Chairman Mao. "In that sense, prison emancipated me," he says.

Rittenberg studied, read, wrote, and thought, and he learned something about himself in the process: "I realized I had this great fear of being a turncoat, which . . . was so powerful that it prevented me from even looking at [my assumptions]. . . . Even to question was an act of betrayal. After I got out . . . the scales fell away from my eyes and I understood that . . . the basic doctrine of arriving at democracy through dictatorship was wrong."

What's more, Rittenberg emerged from prison certain that absolutely nothing in his professional life could break him and went on to start a company with his wife. Rittenberg Associates is a consulting firm dedicated to developing business ties between the United States and China. Today, Rittenberg is as committed to his ideals—if not to his view of the best way to get there—as he was 50 years ago, when he was so severely tested.

Meeting Great Expectations

Fortunately, not all crucible experiences are traumatic. In fact, they can involve a positive, if deeply challenging, experience such as having a demanding boss or mentor. Judge Nathaniel R. Jones of the U.S. Court of Appeals for the Sixth Circuit, for instance, attributes much of his success to his interaction with a splendid mentor. That mentor was J. Maynard Dickerson, a successful attorney—the first black city prosecutor in the United States—and editor of a local African-American newspaper.

Dickerson influenced Jones at many levels. For instance, the older man brought Jones behind the scenes to witness firsthand the great civil rights struggle of the 1950s, inviting him to sit in on conversations with activists like Thurgood Marshall, Walter White, Roy Wilkins, and Robert C. Weaver. Says Jones, "I was struck by their resolve, their humor . . . and their determination not to let the system define them. Rather than just feel beaten down, they turned it around." The experience no doubt influenced the many important opinions Judge Jones has written in regard to civil rights.

Dickerson was both model and coach. His lessons covered every aspect of Jones's intellectual growth and presentation of self, including schooling in what we now call "emotional intelligence." Dickerson set the highest standards for Jones, especially in the area of communication skills—a facility we've found essential to leadership. Dickerson edited Jones's early attempts at writing a sports column with respectful ruthlessness, in red ink, as Jones remembers to this day—marking up the copy so that it looked, as Jones says, "like something chickens had a fight over." But Dickerson also took the time to explain every single mistake and why it mattered.

His mentor also expected the teenage Jones to speak correctly at all times and would hiss discreetly in his direction if he stumbled. Great expectations are evidence of great respect, and as Jones learned all the complex, often subtle lessons of how to succeed, he was motivated in no small measure by his desire not to disappoint the man he still calls "Mr. Dickerson." Dickerson gave Jones the kind of intensive mentoring that was tantamount to grooming him for a kind of professional and moral succession—and Jones has indeed become an instrument for the profound societal change for which Dickerson fought so courageously as well. Jones found life-changing meaning in the attention Dickerson paid to him—attention fueled by a conviction that he, too, though only a teenager, had a vital role to play in society and an important destiny.

Another story of a powerful mentor came to us from Michael Klein, a young man who made millions in Southern California real estate while still in his teens, only to lose it by the time he turned 20 and then go on to start several other businesses. His mentor was his grandfather Max S. Klein, who created the paint-by-numbers fad that swept the United States in the 1950s and 1960s. Klein was only four or five years old when his grandfather approached him and offered to share his business expertise. Over the years, Michael Klein's grandfather taught him to learn from and to cope with change, and the two spoke by phone for an hour every day until shortly before Max Klein's death.

The Essentials of Leadership

In our interviews, we heard many other stories of crucible experiences. Take Jack Coleman, 78-year-old former president of Haverford College in Pennsylvania. He told us of one day, during the Vietnam War, when he heard that a group of students was planning to pull down the American flag and burn it—and that former members of the school's football team were going to make sure the students didn't succeed. Seemingly out of nowhere, Coleman had the idea to preempt the violence by suggesting that the protesting students take down the flag, wash it, and then put it back up—a crucible moment that even now elicits tremendous emotion in Coleman as he describes that day.

There's also Common Cause founder John W. Gardner, who died earlier this year at 89. He identified his arduous training as a Marine during World War II as the crucible in which his leadership abilities emerged. Architect Frank Gehry spoke of the biases he experienced as a Jew in college. Jeff Wilke, a general manager at a major manufacturer, told us of the day he learned that an employee had been killed in his plant—an experience that taught him that leadership was about much more than making quarterly numbers.

So, what allowed these people to not only cope with these difficult situations but also learn from them? We believe that great leaders possess four essential skills, and, we were surprised to learn, these happen to be the same skills that allow a person to find meaning in what could be a debilitating experience. First is the ability to engage others in shared meaning. Consider Sidney Harman, who dived into a chaotic work environment to mobilize employees around an entirely new approach to management. Second is a distinctive and compelling voice. Look at Jack Coleman's ability to defuse a potentially violent situation with only his words. Third is a sense of integrity (including a strong set of values). Here, we point again to Coleman, whose values prevailed even during the emotionally charged clash between peace demonstrators and the angry (and strong) former football team members.

But by far the most critical skill of the four is what we call "adaptive capacity." This is, in essence, applied creativity—an almost magical ability to transcend adversity, with all its attendant stresses, and to emerge stronger than before. It's composed of two primary qualities: the ability to grasp context, and hardiness. The ability to grasp context implies an ability to weigh a welter of factors, ranging from how very different groups of people will interpret a gesture to being able to put a situation in perspective. Without this, leaders are utterly lost, because they cannot connect with their constituents. M. Douglas Ivester, who succeeded Roberto Goizueta at Coca-Cola, exhibited a woeful inability to grasp context, lasting just 28 months on the job. For example, he demoted his highest-ranked African-American employee even as the company was losing a $200 million class-action suit brought by black employees—and this in Atlanta, a city with a powerful African-American majority. Contrast Ivester with Vernon Jordan. Jordan realized his boss's time was up—not just his time in power, but the era that formed him. And so Jordan was able to see past the insults and recognize his boss's bitterness for what it was—desperate lashing out.

Hardiness is just what it sounds like—the perseverance and toughness that enable people to emerge from devastating circumstances without losing hope. Look at Michael Klein, who experienced failure but didn't let it defeat him. He found himself with a single asset—a tiny software company he'd acquired. Klein built it into Transoft Networks, which Hewlett-Packard acquired in 1999. Consider, too, Mickie Siebert, who used her sense of humor to curtail offensive conversations. Or Sidney Rittenberg's strength during his imprisonment. He drew on his personal memories and inner strength to emerge from his lengthy prison term without bitterness.

It is the combination of hardiness and ability to grasp context that, above all, allows a person to not only survive an ordeal, but to learn from it, and to emerge stronger, more engaged, and more committed than ever. These attributes allow leaders to grow from their crucibles, instead of being destroyed by them—to find opportunity where others might find only despair. This is the stuff of true leadership.

49

Try Feedforward Instead of Feedback

Marshall Goldsmith

Providing feedback has long been considered to be an essential skill for leaders. As they strive to achieve the goals of the organization, employees need to know how they are doing. They need to know if their performance is in line with what their leaders expect. They need to learn what they have done well and what they need to change. Traditionally, this information has been communicated in the form of "downward feedback" from leaders to their employees. Just as employees need feedback from leaders, leaders can benefit from feedback from their employees. Employees can provide useful input on the effectiveness of procedures and processes as well as input to managers on their leadership effectiveness. This "upward feedback" has become increasingly common with the advent of 360° multi-rater assessments.

But there is a fundamental problem with all types of feedback: it focuses on *the past*, on what has already occurred, not on the infinite variety of opportunities that can happen in the future. As such, feedback can be limited and static, as opposed to expansive and dynamic.

Over the past several years, I have observed more than ten thousand leaders as they participated in a fascinating experiential exercise. In the exercise, participants are each asked to play two roles. In one role, they are asked to provide *feedforward**—that is, to give someone else suggestions for the future and *help as much as they can*. In the second role, they are asked to accept *feedforward*—that is, to listen to the suggestions for the future and *learn as much as they can*. The exercise typically lasts for 10–15 minutes, and the average participant has 6–7 dialogue sessions. In the exercise participants are asked to:

---

* The term "feedforward" was coined in a discussion that I had with Jon Katzenbach, author of *The Wisdom of Teams, Real Change Leaders*, and *Peak Performance*.

- Pick one behavior that they would like to change. *Change in this behavior should make a significant, positive difference in their lives.*
- Describe this behavior to randomly selected fellow participants.
- This is done in one-on-one dialogues. It can be done quite simply, such as, "I want to be a better listener."
- Ask for *feedforward* for two suggestions for the future that might help them achieve a positive change in their selected behavior. *If participants have worked together in the past, they are not allowed to give ANY feedback about the past. They are only allowed to give ideas for the future.*
- Listen attentively to the suggestions and take notes. *Participants are not allowed to comment on the suggestions in any way. They are not allowed to critique the suggestions or even to make positive judgmental statements, such as, "That's a good idea."*
- Thank the other participants for their suggestions.
- Provide *feedforward*—two suggestions aimed at helping the other person change.
- Say, "You are welcome," when thanked for the suggestions. *The entire process of both giving and receiving feedforward usually takes about two minutes.*

Find another participant and keep repeating the process until the exercise is stopped.

When the exercise is finished, I ask participants to provide one word that best describes their reaction to this experience. I ask them to complete the sentence, "This exercise was . . . ." The words provided are almost always extremely positive, such as "great," "energizing," "useful" or "helpful." The most common word mentioned is "fun!"

What is the *last* word that most of us think about when we receive feedback, coaching, and developmental ideas? Fun!

Participants are then asked why this exercise is seen as fun and helpful as opposed to painful, embarrassing, or uncomfortable. Their answers provide a great explanation of why feedforward can often be more useful than feedback as a developmental tool.

Eleven Reasons to Try Feedforward

1. *We can change the future. We can't change the past.* Feedforward helps people envision and focus on a positive future, not a failed past. Athletes are often trained using feedforward. Racecar drivers are taught to "look at the road ahead, not at the wall." Basketball players are taught to envision the ball going in the hoop and to imagine the perfect shot. By giving people ideas on how they can be even more successful, we can increase their chances of achieving this success in the future.

2. *It can be more productive to help people be "right," than prove they were "wrong."* Negative feedback often becomes an exercise in "let me prove you

were wrong." This tends to produce defensiveness on the part of the receiver and discomfort on the part of the sender. Even constructively delivered feedback is often seen as negative as it necessarily involves a discussion of mistakes, shortfalls, and problems. Feedforward, on the other hand, is almost always seen as positive because it focuses on solutions—not problems.

3. *Feedforward is especially suited to successful people.* Successful people like getting ideas that are aimed at helping them achieve their goals. They tend to resist negative judgment. We all tend to accept feedback that is consistent with the way we see ourselves. We also tend to reject or deny feedback that is inconsistent with the way we see ourselves. Successful people tend to have a very positive self-image. I have observed many successful executives respond to (and even enjoy) feedforward. I am not sure that these same people would have had such a positive reaction to feedback.

4. *Feedforward can come from anyone who knows about the task. It does not require personal experience with the individual.* One very common positive reaction to the previously described exercise is that participants are amazed by how much they can learn from people that they don't know! For example, if you want to be a better listener, almost any fellow leader can give you ideas on how you can improve. They don't have to know you. Feedback requires knowing about the person. Feedforward just requires having good ideas for achieving the task.

5. *People do not take feedforward as personally as feedback.* In theory, constructive feedback is supposed to "focus on the performance, not the person." In practice, almost all feedback is taken personally (no matter how it is delivered). Successful people's sense of identity is highly connected with their work. The more successful people are, the more this tends to be true. It is hard to give a dedicated professional feedback that is not taken personally. Feedforward cannot involve a personal critique, since it is discussing something that has not yet happened! Positive suggestions tend to be seen as objective advice—personal critiques are often viewed as personal attacks.

6. *Feedback can reinforce personal stereotyping and negative self-fulfilling prophecies.* Feedforward can reinforce the possibility of change. Feedback can reinforce the feeling of failure. How many of us have been "helped" by a spouse, significant other or friend, who seems to have a near-photographic memory of our previous "sins" that they share with us in order to point out the history of our shortcomings. Negative feedback can be used to reinforce the message, "this is just the way you are." Feedforward is based on the assumption that the receiver of suggestions can make positive changes in the future.

7. *Face it! Most of us hate getting negative feedback, and we don't like to give it.* I have reviewed summary 360° feedback reports for over 50 companies. The items, "provides developmental feedback in a timely manner" and "encourages and accepts constructive criticism" almost always score near the bottom on co-worker satisfaction with leaders. Traditional training does not seem to make a great deal of difference. If leaders got better at providing feedback every time the performance appraisal forms were "improved," most should

be perfect by now! Leaders are not very good at giving or receiving negative feedback. It is unlikely that this will change in the near future.

8. *Feedforward can cover almost all of the same "material" as feedback.* Imagine that you have just made a terrible presentation in front of the executive committee. Your manager is in the room. Rather than make you "relive" this humiliating experience, your manager might help you prepare for future presentations by giving you suggestions for the future. These suggestions can be very specific and still be delivered in a positive way. In this way your manager can "cover the same points" without feeling embarrassed and without making you feel even more humiliated.

9. *Feedforward tends to be much faster and more efficient than feedback.* An excellent technique for giving ideas to successful people is to say, "Here are four ideas for the future. Please accept these in the positive spirit that they are given. If you can only use two of the ideas, you are still two ahead. Just ignore what doesn't make sense for you." With this approach almost no time gets wasted on judging the quality of the ideas or "proving that the ideas are wrong." This "debate" time is usually negative; it can take up a lot of time, and it is often not very productive. By eliminating judgment of the ideas, the process becomes much more positive for the sender, as well as the receiver. Successful people tend to have a high need for self-determination and will tend to accept ideas that they "buy" while rejecting ideas that feel "forced" upon them.

10. *Feedforward can be a useful tool to apply with managers, peers, and team members.* Rightly or wrongly, feedback is associated with judgment. This can lead to very negative—or even career-limiting—unintended consequences when applied to managers or peers. Feedforward does not imply superiority or judgment. It is more focused on being a helpful "fellow traveler" than an "expert." As such it can be easier to hear from a person who is not in a position of power or authority. An excellent team-building exercise is to have each team member ask, "How can I better help our team in the future?" and listen to feedforward from fellow team members (in one-on-one dialogues).

11. *People tend to listen more attentively to feedforward than feedback.* One participant in the feedforward exercise noted, "I think that I listened more effectively in this exercise than I ever do at work!" When asked why, he responded, "Normally, when others are speaking, I am so busy *composing* a reply that will make sure that I sound smart—that I am not fully *listening* to what the other person is saying. In feedforward the only reply that I am allowed to make is 'thank you.' Since I don't have to worry about composing a clever reply, I can focus all of my energy on listening to the other person!"

In summary, the intent of this article is not to imply that leaders should never give feedback or that performance appraisals should be abandoned. The intent is to show how feedforward can often be preferable to feedback in day-to-day interactions. Aside from its effectiveness and efficiency, feedforward can make life a lot more enjoyable. When managers are asked, "How did you feel the last time you received feedback?" their most common responses are very negative. When managers are asked how they felt after receiving feedforward, they reply that feedforward was not only useful, it was also fun!

Quality communication—between and among people at all levels and every department and division—is the glue that holds organizations together. By using feedforward, and by encouraging others to use it, leaders can dramatically improve the quality of communication in their organizations, ensuring that the right message is conveyed, and that those who receive it are receptive to its content. The result is a much more dynamic, much more open organization—one whose employees focus on the promise of the future rather than dwelling on the mistakes of the past.

50

Authentic Leadership

Bill George

Not long ago I was meeting with a group of high-talent young executives at Medtronic. We were discussing career development when the leader of the group asked me to list the most important characteristics one has to have to be a leader in Medtronic. I said, "I can summarize it in a single word: authenticity."

After years of studying leaders and their traits, I believe that leadership begins and ends with authenticity. It's being yourself; being the person you were created to be. This is not what most of the literature on leadership says, nor is it what the experts in corporate America teach. Instead, they develop lists of leadership characteristics one is supposed to emulate. They describe the styles of leaders and suggest that you adopt them.

This is the opposite of authenticity. It is about developing the image or *persona* of a leader. Unfortunately, the media, the business press, and even the movies glorify leaders with high-ego personalities. They focus on the style of leaders, not their character. In large measure, making heroes out of celebrity CEOs is at the heart of the crisis in corporate leadership.

The Authentic Leader

Authentic leaders genuinely desire to serve others through their leadership. They are more interested in empowering the people they lead to make a difference than they are in power, money, or prestige for themselves. They are as guided by qualities of the heart, by passion and compassion, as much as they are by qualities of the mind.

Authentic leaders are not born that way. Many people have natural leadership gifts, but they have to develop them fully to become outstanding leaders. Authentic leaders use their natural abilities but they also recognize their shortcomings and work hard to overcome them. They lead with purpose, meaning, and values. They build enduring relationships with people. Others follow them because they know where they stand. They are consistent and self-disciplined. When their principles are tested, they refuse to compromise. Authentic leaders are dedicated to developing themselves because they know that becoming a leader takes a lifetime of personal growth.

Being Your Own Person

Leaders are all very different people. Any prospective leader who buys into the necessity of attempting to emulate all the characteristics of a leader is doomed. I know because I tried it early in my career. It simply doesn't work.

The one essential quality a leader must have is to be your own person, authentic in every regard. The best leaders are autonomous and highly independent. Those who are too responsive to the desires of others are likely to be whipsawed by competing interests, too quick to deviate from their course or unwilling to make difficult decisions for fear of offending. My advice to the people I mentor is simply to be themselves.

Being your own person is most challenging when it feels like everyone is pressuring you to take one course and you are standing alone. In the first semester of business school we watched *The Loneliness of the Long Distance Runner.* In many ways I did not relate to the film's message, as I had always surrounded myself with people to avoid being lonely. Learning to cope with the loneliness at the top is crucial so that you are not swayed by the pressure. Being able to stand alone against the majority is essential to being your own person.

Shortly after I joined Medtronic as president, I walked into a meeting where it quickly became evident that a group of my new colleagues had pre-arranged a strategy to settle a major patent dispute against Siemens on the basis of a royalty-free cross-license as a show of good faith.

Intuitively, I knew the strategy was doomed to fail, so I stood alone against the entire group, refusing to go along. My position may not have made me popular with my new teammates, but it was the right thing to do. We later negotiated a settlement with Siemens for more than $400 million, at the time the second-largest patent settlement ever.

Developing Your Unique Leadership Style

To become authentic, each of us has to develop our own leadership style, consistent with our personality and character. Unfortunately, the pressures of an organization push us to adhere to a normative style. But if we conform to a style that is not consistent with who we are, we will never become authentic leaders.

Contrary to what much of the literature says, your type of leadership style is not what matters. Great world leaders—George Washington, Abraham Lincoln, Winston Churchill, Franklin Roosevelt, Margaret Thatcher, Martin Luther King, Mother Theresa, John F. Kennedy—all had very different styles.

Yet each of them was an entirely authentic human being. There is no way you could ever attempt to emulate any of them without looking foolish.

The same is true for business leaders. Compare the last three CEOs of General Electric; the statesmanship of Reginald Jones, the dynamism of Jack Welch, and the empowering style of Jeff Immelt. All of them are highly successful leaders with entirely different leadership styles. Yet the GE organization has rallied around each of them, adapted to their styles, and flourished as a result. What counts is the authenticity of the leader, not the style.

Having said that, it is important that you develop a leadership style that works well for you and is consistent with your character and your personality. Over time you will have to hone your style to be effective in leading different types of people and to work in different types of environments; this is integral to your development as a leader.

To be effective in today's fast-moving, highly competitive environment, leaders also have to adapt their style to fit the immediate situation. There are times to be inspiring and motivating, and times to be tough about people decisions or financial decisions. There are times to delegate and times to be deeply immersed in the details. There are times to communicate public messages and times to have private conversations. The use of adaptive styles is not inauthentic and is very different from playing a succession of roles rather than being yourself. Good leaders are able to nuance their styles to the demands of the situation and to know when and how to deploy different styles.

Let me share a personal example to illustrate this point. When I first joined Medtronic I spent a lot of time learning the business and listening to customers. I also focused on inspiring employees to fulfill the Medtronic mission of restoring people to full health. At the same time, I saw many ways in which we needed to be more disciplined about decisions and spending, so I was very challenging in budget sessions and put strict controls on headcount additions. At first some people found this confusing. Eventually, they understood my reasons for adapting myself to the situation, and that I had to do so to be effective as their leader.

Being Aware of Your Weaknesses

Being true to the person you were created to be means accepting your faults as well as using your strengths. Accepting your shadow side is an essential part of being authentic. The problem comes when people are so eager to win the approval of others that they try to cover their shortcomings and sacrifice their authenticity to gain the respect and admiration of their associates.

I too have struggled in getting comfortable with my weaknesses—my tendency to intimidate others with an overly challenging style, my impatience, and my occasional lack of tact. Only recently have I realized that my strengths and weaknesses are two sides of the same coin. By challenging others in business meetings, I am able to get quickly to the heart of the issues, but my approach unnerves and intimidates less confident people. My desire to get things done fast leads to superior results, but it exposes my impatience with people who move more slowly. Being direct with others gets the message across clearly but often lacks tact. Over time I have moderated my style and adapted my approach to make sure that people are engaged and empowered and that their voices are fully heard.

I have always been open to critical feedback, but also quite sensitive to it. For years I felt I had to be perfect, or at least appear that I was on top of everything. I tried to hide my weaknesses from others, fearing they would reject me if they knew who I really was. Eventually, I realized that they could see my weaknesses more clearly than I could. In attempting to cover things up I was only fooling myself.

The poem "Love after Love," by Nobel Prize-winning poet Derek Walcott speaks to the benefits of being in touch with your disowned aspects and welcoming them into your life. As I have been able to do so in recent years, I have become more comfortable with myself and more authentic in my interactions with others.

> *The time will come*
> *when, with elation,*
> *you will greet yourself arriving*
> *at your own door, in your own mirror,*
> *and each will smile at the other's welcome,*
>
> *and say, sit here. Eat.*
> *You will love again the stranger who was yourself.*
> *Give wine. Give bread. Give back your heart to itself,*
> *To the stranger who has loved you all your life*
> *whom you ignored for another, who knows you by heart.*
> *Take down the love letters from the bookshelf, the photographs, the desperate notes*
> *Sit. Feast on your life.*

The Temptations of Leadership

Congressman Amory Houghton, one of the most thoughtful members of the U.S. Congress, tells the story of his predecessor's advice as he was taking over as CEO of Corning Glass. "Think of your decisions being based on two concentric circles. In the outer circle are all the laws, regulations, and ethical standards with which the company must comply. In the inner circle are your core values. Just be damn sure that your decisions as CEO stay within your inner circle."

We are all painfully aware of corporate leaders that pushed beyond the outer circle and got caught, either by the law or by the financial failure of their companies. More worrisome are the leaders of companies who moved outside their inner circles and engaged in marginal practices, albeit legal ones. Examples include cutting back on long-term investments just to make the short-term numbers, bending compensation rules to pay executives in spite of marginal performance, using accounting tricks to meet the quarterly expectations of security analysts, shipping products of marginal quality, compromising security analysts by giving them a cut on investment banking deals, and booking revenues before the products are shipped in an effort to pump up revenue growth. The list goes on and on.

All of us who sit in the leader's chair feel the pressure to perform. As CEO, I felt it every day as problems mounted or sales lagged. I knew that the livelihood of tens of thousands of employees, the health of millions of patients, and the financial fortunes of millions of investors rested on my shoulders and those of our executive team. At the same time I was well aware of the penalties for not performing, even for a single quarter. No CEO wants to appear on CNBC to explain why his company missed the earnings projections—even by a penny.

Little by little, step by step, the pressures to succeed can pull us away from our core values, just as we are reinforced by our "success" in the market. Some people refer to this as "CEO-itis." The irony is that the more successful we are, the more tempted we are to take shortcuts to keep it going. And the rewards—compensation increases, stock option gains, the myriad of executive perquisites, positive stories in the media, admiring comments from our peers—all reinforce our actions and drive us to keep it going.

In a recent interview with *Fortune* magazine, Novartis CEO Daniel Vasella talked about these pressures:

> Once you get under the domination of making the quarter—even unwittingly—you start to compromise in the gray areas of your business that cut across the wide swath of terrain between the top and the bottom. Perhaps you'll begin to sacrifice things that are important and may be vital for your company over the long term . . . The culprit that drives this cycle isn't the fear of failure so much as it is the craving for success. For the tyranny of quarterly earnings is a tyranny that is imposed from within. For many of us the idea of being a successful manager is an intoxicating one. It is a pattern of celebration leading to belief leading to distortion. When you achieve good results, you are typically celebrated, and you begin to believe that the figure at the center of all that champagne toasting is yourself. You are idealized by the outside world, and there is a natural tendency to believe that what is written is true.

Like Vasella, who is one of the finest and most authentic leaders I know, all leaders have to resist these pressures while continuing to perform, especially when things aren't going well. The test I used with our team at Medtronic is whether we would feel comfortable having the entire story appear on the front page of the *New York Times*. If we didn't we went back to the drawing boards and reexamined our decision.

Dimensions of Authentic Leaders

Let's examine the essential dimensions of all authentic leaders, the qualities that true leaders must develop. I have determined through many experiences in leading others that authentic leaders demonstrate these five qualities:

- Understanding their purpose
- Practicing solid values
- Leading with heart
- Establishing connected relationships
- Demonstrating self-discipline

Acquiring the five dimensions of an authentic leader is not a sequential process; rather, leaders are developing them continuously throughout their lives.

Understanding Your Purpose

In Wonderland, Alice comes to a fork in the road where she sees a cat in a tree. Alice asks the cat, "Which road should I take?" "Do you know where you want to go?" inquires the cat. "No," says Alice. To which the cat replies, "Then any road will get you there."

To become a leader it is essential that you first answer the question: "Leadership for what purpose?" If you lack purpose and direction in leading, why would anyone want to follow you?

Many people want to become leaders without giving much thought to their purpose. They are attracted to the power and prestige of leading an organization and the financial rewards that go with it. But without a real sense of purpose, leaders are at the mercy of their egos and are vulnerable to narcissistic impulses. There is no way you can adopt someone else's purpose and still be an authentic leader. You can study the purposes others pursue and you can work with them in common purposes, but in the end the purpose for your leadership must be uniquely yours.

To find your purpose, you must first understand yourself, your passions, and your underlying motivations. Then you must seek an environment that offers a fit between the organization's purpose and your own. Your search may take experiences in several organizations before you can find the one that is right for you.

The late Robert Greenleaf, a former AT&T executive, is well known for his concept of leaders as servants of the people. In *Servant Leadership* he advocates service to others as the leader's primary purpose. If people feel you are genuinely interested in serving others then they will be prepared not just to follow you but to dedicate themselves to the common cause.

One of the best examples of a leader with purpose was the late David Packard, cofounder of Hewlett-Packard. I met him in early 1969 when he was the new Deputy Secretary of Defense and I was the special assistant to the Secretary of Navy. Packard had taken a leave from H-P to serve his country. A big, powerful, if modest man he immediately impressed me with his openness, his sincerity, and his commitment to make a difference through his work.

He returned to H-P a few years later to build it into one of the great companies of its time through his dedication to the company's mission, known as "The H-P Way," and to excellence in R&D and customer service. He inspired

H-P's employees to incredible levels of commitment. At his death he was one of the wealthiest people in the world, yet no one would ever have known it by his personal spending. Most of his money went into funding philanthropic projects. Dave Packard was a truly authentic leader, a role model for me and for many in my generation.

Then there's John Bogle, who for fifty years has been a man with a mission to transform the management of investors' funds. Bogle created the first no-load mutual fund in 1974 and founded Vanguard, the nation's leading purveyor of index funds. Bogle has not only been a pioneer in financial services, he has been the leading advocate of financial funds as stewards of their investors' money. His values and his integrity stand in stark relief with those in the financial community who seek to use investment funds for their personal gain.

Practicing Solid Values

Leaders are defined by their values and their character. The values of the authentic leader are shaped by personal beliefs, developed through study, introspection, and consultation with others—and a lifetime of experience. These values define their holder's moral compass. Such leaders know the "true north" of their compass, the deep sense of the right thing to do. Without a moral compass, any leader can wind up like the executives who are facing possible prison sentences today because they lacked a sense of right and wrong.

While the development of fundamental values is crucial, integrity is the one value that is required in every authentic leader. Integrity is not just the absence of lying, but telling the whole truth, as painful as it may be. If you don't exercise complete integrity in your interactions, no one can trust you. If they cannot trust you, why would they ever follow you?

I once had a colleague who would never lie to me, but often he shared only positive parts of the story, sheltering me from the ugly side. Finally, I told him that real integrity meant giving me the whole story so that together we could make sound decisions. Rather than thinking less of him if he did so, I assured him I would have a higher opinion of his courage and integrity.

Most business schools and academic institutions do not teach values as part of leadership development. Some offer ethics courses, often in a theoretical context, but shy away from discussing values. Others assume erroneously their students already have well-solidified values. What they fail to realize is the importance of solidifying your values through study and dialogue and the impact that your environment has in shaping your values.

As Enron was collapsing in the fall of 2001, the *Boston Globe* published an article by a Harvard classmate of Enron CEO Jeff Skilling. The author described how Skilling would argue in class that the role of the business leader was to take advantage of loopholes in regulations and push beyond the laws wherever he could to make money. As Skilling saw the world, it was the job of the regulators to try and catch him. Sound familiar? Twenty-five years later, Skilling's philosophy caught up with him, as he led his company into bankruptcy.

One of my role models of value-centered leadership is Max DePree, the former CEO of furniture maker Herman Miller. DePree is a modest man guided by a deep concern for serving others; he is true to his values in every aspect of his life. His humanity and values can be seen through the exemplary way in which his company conducts itself. DePree describes his philosophy of values-centered leadership in his classic book, *Leadership Is an Art.* DePree also subscribes to Greenleaf's ideas on servant leadership, and expands them by offering his own advice, "The leader's first job is to define reality. The last is to say thank you. In between the leader must become a servant and a debtor."

DePree believes that a corporation should be "a community of people," all of whom have value and share in the fruits of their collective labor. DePree practices what he preaches. While he was CEO, his salary was capped at twenty times that of an hourly worker. In his view tying the CEO's salary to that of the workers helps cement trust in leadership. Compare that with today's CEOs, who are earning—on average—five hundred times their hourly workers' wage. As DePree said recently, "When leaders indulge themselves with lavish perks and the trappings of power they are damaging their standing as leaders."

Leading with Heart

Over the last several decades, businesses have evolved from maximizing the physical output of their workers to engaging the minds of their employees. To excel in the twenty-first century, great companies will go one step further by engaging the hearts of their employees through a sense of purpose. When employees believe their work has a deeper purpose, their results will vastly exceed those who use only their minds and their bodies. This will become the company's competitive advantage.

Sometimes we refer to people as being bighearted. What we really mean is that they are open and willing to share themselves fully with us, and are genuinely interested in us. Leaders who do that, like Sam Walton, founder of Wal-Mart, and Earl Bakken, founder of Medtronic, have the ability to ignite the souls of their employees to achieve greatness far beyond what anyone imagined possible.

One of the most bighearted leaders I know is Marilyn Nelson, chair and CEO of the Carlson Companies, the privately held hospitality and travel services giant. When she became CEO several years ago, she inherited a hard-nosed organization that was driven for growth but not known for empathy for its employees. Shortly after joining the company, Nelson had what she refers to as her "epiphany." She was meeting with the group of MBA students that had been studying the company's culture. When she asked the students for feedback, Nelson got a stony silence from the group. Finally, a young woman raised her hand and said, "We hear from employees that Carlson is a sweatshop that doesn't care."

That incident sent Nelson into high gear. She created a motivational program called "Carlson Cares." As the company was preparing for its launch,
Nelson's staff told her they needed more time to change the culture before introducing the program. Nelson decided that she could not wait and decided to
become the company's role model for caring and empathy. She immediately set
out to change the environment using her passion, motivational skills, and sincere interest in her employees and her customers. She took the lead on customer sales calls and interacted every day with employees in Carlson
operations. Her positive energy has transformed the company's culture, built its
customer relationships, accelerated its growth, and strengthened its bottom line.

Establishing Enduring Relationships

As Krishnamurti says, "Relationship is the mirror in which we see ourselves as we are." The capacity to develop close and enduring relationships is
one mark of a leader. Unfortunately, many leaders of major companies
believe their job is to create the strategy, organization structure, and organizational processes. Then they just delegate the work to be done, remaining
aloof from the people doing the work.

The detached style of leadership will not be successful in the twenty-first
century. Today's employees demand more personal relationships with their
leaders before they will give themselves fully to their jobs. They insist on having access to their leaders, knowing that it is in the openness and the depth of
the relationship with the leader that trust and commitment are built. Bill
Gates, Michael Dell, and Jack Welch are so successful because they connect
directly with their employees and realize from them a deeper commitment to
their work and greater loyalty to the company. Welch, in particular, is an
interesting case because he was so challenging and hard on people. Yet it was
those very challenges that let people know that he was interested in their success and concerned about their careers.

In *Eyewitness to Power,* David Gergen writes, "At the heart of leadership is
the leader's relationship with followers. People will entrust their hopes and
dreams to another person only if they think the other is a reliable vessel."
Authentic leaders establish trusting relationships with people throughout the
organization as well as in their personal lives. The rewards of these relationships, both tangible and intangible, are long lasting.

I always tried to establish close relationships with my colleagues, looking
to them as a closely knit team whose collective knowledge and wisdom about
the business vastly exceeds my own. Many corporate leaders fear these kinds
of relationships. As another CEO said to me, "Bill, I don't want to get too
close to my subordinates because someday I may have to terminate them."
Actually the real reason goes much deeper than that. Many leaders—men in
particular—fear having their weaknesses and vulnerabilities exposed. So they
create distance from employees and a sense of aloofness. Instead of being
authentic, they are creating a persona for themselves.

Demonstrating Self-Discipline

Self-discipline is an essential quality of an authentic leader. Without it, you cannot gain the respect of your followers. It is easy to say that someone has good values but lacks the discipline to convert those values into consistent actions. This is a hollow excuse. None of us is perfect, of course, but authentic leaders must have the self-discipline to do everything they can to demonstrate their values through their actions. When we fall short, it is equally important to admit our mistakes.

Leaders are highly competitive people. They are driven to succeed in whatever they take on. Authentic leaders know that competing requires a consistently high level of self-discipline to be successful. Being very competitive is not a bad thing; in fact, it is an essential quality of successful leaders, but it needs to be channeled through purpose and discipline. Sometimes we mistake competitive people who generate near-term results by improving operational effectiveness for genuine leaders. Achieving operational effectiveness is an essential result for any leader, but it alone does not ensure authenticity or long-term success.

The most consistent leader I know is Art Collins, my successor as CEO of Medtronic. His self-discipline is evident every day and in every interaction. His subordinates never have to worry about what kind of mood Art is in, or where he stands on an important issue. Nor does he deviate in his behavior or vacillate in his decisions. He never lets his ego or his emotions get in the way of taking the appropriate action. These qualities make working with Art easy and predictable, enabling Medtronic employees to do their jobs effectively.

Mother Theresa is a compelling example of an authentic leader. Many think of her as simply a nun who reached out to the poor, yet by 1990 she had created an organization of four thousand missionaries operating in a hundred countries. Her organization, Missionaries of Charity, began in Calcutta and spread to 450 centers around the world. Its mission was "to reach out to the destitute on the streets, offering wholehearted service to the poorest of the poor." Not only did she have a purpose, clear values, and a heart filled with compassion, she also created intimate relationships with people and exercised self-discipline, all the dimensions of an authentic leader. I doubt that any of us will ever be like Mother Theresa, but her life is indeed an inspiration.

Questions and Learning Activities

Section VI

Questions

1. McGregor outlines the conditions that ensure security, a necessary prerequisite for effective leadership. Do these same conditions apply today or have they changed since he wrote the article some 60-plus years ago?

2. Why does McGregor believe in the importance of active independence of subordinates? What conditions must be met for this to happen? Does his position differ substantially from today's writings on empowerment?

3. What are three things leaders can do to transmit and embed culture?

4. Schein makes the point that the budgeting process is important vis-à-vis transmitting and embedding culture. How is this so?

5. Is there anything in Kouzes and Posner's five practices of exemplary leadership that contradicts the Hersey/Blanchard contingency approach in Section IV? Justify your answer.

6. Are there elements of Kouzes and Posner's approach to exemplary leadership that could be in conflict with Hofstede's (Section IV) concept of power distance?

7. Deming strongly suggests that all leaders need to have relevant technical knowledge. Do you generally agree? Are there any situations where this may not be true?

8. How does Deming reconcile the apparent conflict between the technical aspects of quality control and the behavioral aspects of leadership?

9. Senge discusses the problem of focusing on means rather than ends. What is the major issue here? How can leader/managers avoid the consequences of focusing on means or activities?

10. According to Senge, what is the difference between purpose and vision? Why is it important to have both?

11. Why does Senge believe that it is important to distinguish between creative tension and emotional tension as they relate to vision?

12. How does Senge's concept of structural conflict keep one from reaching his or her goal?

13. What are two of the most important messages for leaders from Stayer's experience at Johnsonville Foods?

14. The employees at Johnsonville were neither highly educated nor involved in technical work. Does this make this success story more impressive or less impressive? Why?

584

15. What is the relationship between Covey's principle-centered leadership and Goleman's article (Section II) on emotional intelligence?

16. Buckingham and Coffman believe that "leadership trumps companies." What do they mean by this? Do you agree?

17. Drucker states that a useful way to get in touch with our strengths is by practicing feedback analysis. What would one do to implement this process?

18. Drucker believes that an important element of self-awareness is knowing how we learn. Why is this important and what actions can be taken based upon this awareness?

19. What is the essence of the Level 5 leader?

20. Collins believes that companies cannot become great by Level 5 leadership alone. What else is required and are these "leadership" or "management" activities?

21. Bossidy and Charan discuss the importance of realism. Does their concept of realism differ from Senge's concept of "truth"? If yes, in what ways?

22. How is Bossidy and Charan's idea of emotional fortitude related to Senge's concept of holding creative tension?

23. What skills are necessary for leaders to cope with and learn from leadership crucibles?

24. What are the similarities and differences between Bennis and Thomas's reading and Zaleznik's (Section II) conceptualization of first-born and second-born personalities?

25. Goldsmith discusses why traditional forms of feedback may not be effective in developing leaders. What is his rationale? Do you agree?

26. How does Goldsmith's idea of feedforward overcome the difficulties associated with feedback?

27. Is it possible for a leader to change style from time to time and still be "authentic" as described by George?

28. According to George, is authenticity an inherited or acquired trait?

29. Do the Drucker and Senge readings in this section reinforce or contradict the George reading? How?

Activities

1. Discuss with classmates/colleagues your experiences or observations that illustrate how leaders transmit culture.

2. For an example of exemplary leadership in action, view *Remember the Titans*.

3. Covey talks about the importance of radiating positive energy. Based upon readings in this book and library research, write a paper titled: "Attention All Leaders—Emotions are Contagious."

4. Based on Senge's reading and some library research, construct a plan to develop your intuition. The plan should include the steps and actions you will take as well as ways to assess your progress.

5. Self-awareness suggestion—learning styles inventory. How do you learn? See the editor's Web site (www.waveland.com/McMahon/) for a learning styles inventory.

6. Based on readings in this book, write a five-page paper entitled "Why Enhancing Leadership Effectiveness Is Impossible without Personal Growth."

7. Discuss with classmates/colleagues experiences and observations of excellent and poor execution.

8. Assess the effectiveness of your goal setting. See the Web site for this activity.

9. Read the following two articles in *Academy of Management Perspectives* (Vol. 22, No. 4, November 2008):

   From Good to Great to . . . (pp. 6–12)

   Good to Great, or Just Good? . . . (pp. 13–20)

   Write a paper noting the impact these two articles had on your confidence in the research findings of the Level 5 Leadership reading.

10. Write a paper describing what you have learned about yourself from selected readings, exercises, and self-awareness suggestions, and how this relates to your leadership potential.

11. Conduct Goldsmith's feedforward exercise with at least two classmates or colleagues. Describe your reactions as well as theirs to this exercise.

12. Based upon this book's readings, exercises, and suggestions for self-awareness, develop an action plan to enhance your leadership skills now and in the future. Your plan should specify what you will do, and why, and how you intend to monitor your progress.